VN $1175

AF859769

Accounting I

A programmed text

Accounting I

A programmed text

JAMES DON EDWARDS Ph.D., C.P.A.
Professor of Accounting
The University of Georgia

ROGER H. HERMANSON Ph.D., C.P.A.
Professor of Accounting
Georgia State University

R. F. SALMONSON Ph.D., C.P.A.
Professor of Accounting
Michigan State University

1974 • Third Edition

RICHARD D. IRWIN, INC. *Homewood, Illinois 60430*
Irwin-Dorsey International *London, England WC2H 9NJ*
Irwin-Dorsey Limited *Georgetown, Ontario L7G 4B3*

© RICHARD D. IRWIN, INC. 1967, 1970, and 1974

All rights reserved. No part of this publication may be reproduced, stored in a retrieval system, or transmitted, in any form or by any means, electronic, mechanical, photocopying, recording, or otherwise, without the prior written permission of the publisher.

Earlier editions of this book were published under the title *Accounting: A Programmed Text*

Third Edition

First Printing, February 1974

ISBN 0-256-01517-1

Printed in the United States of America

Preface

In this third edition of *Accounting I: A Programmed Text,* the authors have continued the use of a programmed learning technique in a *complete financial accounting text.* This book and *Accounting II: A Programmed Text,* which deals with managerial accounting, constitute a two-volume series that covers fundamental financial and managerial accounting concepts and standards and external and internal use of accounting information. Our objective has been to include the materials most useful to the undergraduate student in business administration and accounting.

We have employed a new simplified programming technique to facilitate the use of the text materials and to make it easier for the student to review. We urge each user of the text to read the section entitled *Using the Programmed Text,* which follows this preface.

In our experience the primary objectives, indeed, the advantages, of a programmed text such as this are threefold: (1) to require a more active and therefore more alert participation by the student to heighten his interest in the subject matter; (2) to provide immediate reinforcement of correct understanding and immediate correction of misinterpretations during the reading process; and (3) to enable the student to come to class with a higher level of comprehension so that the instructor can concentrate his attention upon clarification of difficult points, reinforcement through illustration and expansion, and demonstration of the practical, real-world utility of the knowledge acquired. The first is accomplished by requiring the student to respond to the question(s) posed at the end of each frame of text material. The type of question is varied to most effectively test that segment of material. Each answer frame provides explanations of the proper answers. If the student's responses indicate a lack of understanding, he is instructed to restudy the frame; otherwise, he proceeds to the next frame.

Thus, at the same time that the first objective is being realized, the second is also attained. The student's understanding of the material is immediately tested and reinforced or corrected. It is not necessary for him to wait until he receives the results of an examination to evaluate his understanding of the material at hand.

The third advantage stems from the fact that the programmed text communicates with the student in the same way the instructor does—on a first person level. The scope of the material covered may be expanded and the instructor may utilize the classroom time in a more creative fashion to show the relevance of the material covered to the student.

In this volume we have incorporated a number of special features that we have found assist in the learning process.

We believe the following elements increase the effectiveness of each chapter in this book: (1) a clear statement of *learning objectives,* (2) the *text* of the programmed chapter, (3) a *summary* of chapter contents, (4) a *glossary,* (5) a *student review quiz,* (6) *questions,* (7) *exercises,* and (8) two series of *problems. Solutions* for the student review quiz, with an explanation of why each solution is correct, are given at the back of the book.

Learning objectives. Each chapter has a set of clearly stated learning objectives. These are intended to assist the student by expressly stating the major learning objectives to be achieved by study of each chapter.

Student review quiz. A set of questions, exercises, and problems, constituting a self-administered quiz, has been included at the end of each chapter. The student should use these to test his knowledge and understanding of the material in the chapter he has just studied. This provides an opportunity for the student to judge his level of understanding prior to working the problems that may be assigned by the instructor. The solutions to the student review quiz for each chapter are included at the end of each volume. The authors have given additional reinforcement to this phase of the learning process by providing rather complete statements as to why the answer given for each question is correct.

Questions, exercises, and problems. At the end of each chapter are separate series of questions, exercises, and two sets of problems (Series A and Series B). Any of these may be assigned as homework or may be discussed in class. The questions provide a vehicle to discuss the specific points in theory introduced in the chapter, whereas the exercises can be used to apply the theory to specific issues. Each set of problems is of approximately equal difficulty and contains roughly similar or parallel problems. The 6 to 12 problems in each series provide the instructor a wide range of choices for possible assignments.

Study guide and review manual. A study guide and review manual designed to accompany the text is available as a separate volume. It contains a detailed outline of the material in each chapter and a series of questions, exercises, and short problems to be answered by the student. Answers to the questions, exercises, and short problems are provided. The study guide and review manual provides additional reinforcement of the knowledge obtained from the text and should be helpful to the student in his first contacts with the material of each chaper and in review for examinations.

Check list of key figures in answers. As was true for the prior editions, a check list of the key figures in the answers to both Series A and Series B problems is available to instructors in quantity for distribution to students. The purpose of the list is to provide the students with a key figure in each problem against which they can compare their own solutions, and, if necessary, make corrections.

Work Papers. The work papers are specially designed accounting forms for use with specific problems in either Series A or Series B of the homework problems in each chapter. In some instances, they are partially filled in to save the student time in completing his homework. Also available within the work papers volume are answer sheets to serve as a permanent record of the student's (1) responses to the questions in each frame, (2) answer sheets for the student review quizzes, and (3) work papers used in solving the homework problems.

Acknowledgments

We are indebted to many persons for the comments and constructive criticism they have made on this and earlier editions. Included among them are the following:

James P. Bedingfield	University of Maryland
R. Glen Berryman	University of Minnesota
Kenneth L. Block	Macomb County Community College, South Campus
Richard E. Czarnecki	University of Michigan (Dearborn)
Paul E. Dascher	Drexell University
Frederick G. Davis	Ohio University
Daniel J. Davitt	University of Virginia
Ray D. Dillon	Georgia State University
Geraldine R. Dominiak	Texas Christian University
Dwane Dowell	Texas Tech University
Shirley Glass	Macomb County Community College, South Campus
Carl Grame	de Anza College
Raymond Green	Texas Tech University
Douglas R. Haines	Rutgers University
William C. Hockett	University of Nebraska (Omaha)
V. Bruce Irvine	University of Saskatchewan
Patrick Kelley	University of Georgia
Robert Kelley	Corning Community College
Richard Kelsey	University of Washington
Jack Kiger	University of Georgia
Stephen E. Loeb	University of Maryland
Leonard E. Plachta	Central Michigan University
Charles R. Purdy	University of Minnesota
Larry E. Rittenberg	University of Minnesota
John W. Ruswinckel	Michigan State University
Harold M. Sollenberger	Michigan State University
Robert H. Strawser	Texas A & M University
Edward E. Stumpf	Fullerton Junior College

Richard G. Walter	The Sao Paulo School of Business Administration of the Getulio Vargas Foundation
John Waters	University of Georgia
Doyle Williams	Texas Tech University
Jan Williams	University of Georgia
Lee C. Wilson	Mesa Community College
Mrs. Betty Taylor (typist)	University of Maryland

The authors wish to thank all of the above and reserve to themselves the responsibility for any shortcomings of this text.

February 1974

JAMES DON EDWARDS
ROGER H. HERMANSON
R. F. SALMONSON

Using the programmed text

The method of programming used in this text is simple to use. You begin by reading Frame 1^1 in Chapter 1. At the end of that frame, you will find questions to be answered. You may use the answer form provided for that chapter in the *Work Papers,* or a separate sheet of paper. To determine the correctness of your responses, you merely turn the next page and examine the answers given in Answer Frame 1^1. You are told why each answer is right or wrong. You should use your performance on the questions given as a measure of your understanding of the material in Frame 1^1. If you miss any of the questions asked, you are encouraged to restudy Frame 1^1 before continuing on to Frame 1^2. This same procedure should be used throughout the book. Specific instructions are given throughout as to where to turn next to continue working the program.

When you have completed working through a chapter, you will find a glossary of new terms introduced in the chapter. After completing study of the glossary you should continue on to the student review quiz which follows and use it as an immediate self-administered test of your understanding of the content of the chapter. Special answer sheets are provided in the *Work Papers* for use in answering these questions and the answers are printed at the back of the text. Forms for use in solving the Series A or Series B problems are also provided in the *Work Papers.*

If you need to study the text a second time (as, for example, in reviewing for an examination), the programming questions and answers may be omitted. Since the frames are arranged sequentially on successive pages, the contents of a Chapter may be read in the same manner as a nonprogrammed text. Or, you may desire to further test your understanding of the chapters by answering all the programming questions once again and rereading only those frames in which your comprehension is unsatisfactory. Another alternative would be to read again only those frames where you missed any questions your first time through the material. (If you use and retain the answer sheets in the *Work Papers* you will be able to do this.)

Contents

The nature and uses of accounting information

Learning objectives

Study of the material in this chapter is designed to achieve a number of learning objectives. These include an introductory level comprehension of:

1. The possible value to every person in society of some knowledge of accounting.
2. The nature of accounting and its various subfunctions.
3. Accountancy as a professional career field comprising public, private, and governmental accounting, and the areas of specialization lying within each.
4. The need for and use of accounting information in decision making both within and outside a business firm.
5. Basic financial statements prepared for a business firm and the underlying process that yields these statements, including the crucial importance of proper transaction analysis.
6. Some basic concepts—entity, duality, transaction, continuity, cost basis of valuation, money measurement, and periodicity.

When undertaking initial study of any discipline, new terms are usually encountered. To assist in the process of becoming familiar with the language of accounting, a glossary of the terms introduced in each chapter is presented at the end of the chapter.

Frame 1[1]

Repeatedly, in their daily lives, individuals make decisions that consist basically of choosing between alternatives that have different expected outcomes. These decisions may be of an intimately personal, social, or economic nature. Some doubt usually exists as to the preferred course of action in achieving a known objective. This doubt, this uncertainty, can be reduced through the use of relevant information with the result that a rational, informed decision is made.

Accounting, because it is the primary source of information on economic activity, seeks to reduce doubt in the minds of those charged with conducting such activity. Because it includes the production, exchange, and consumption of scarce goods, economic activity is found everywhere in our society. Accounting is nearly as extensive. Wherever economic resources are employed, an accounting is likely to be required to show what was accomplished, at what cost or sacrifice. And this follows whether the resources are employed by individuals; employers; churches; some unit of local, state, or national government; or some other organization in which individuals are interested, such as the local hospital.

Thus it follows that the welfare of nearly every individual in our society is affected, directly or indirectly, by accounting information. This is sufficient reason for maintaining that some knowledge of accounting is essential to every person who seeks to function intelligently and efficiently in our society.

Accounting defined

Accounting is a systematic process of measuring and reporting to various users relevant financial information for decision making regarding the economic activity of an organization or unit. While not ignoring other kinds of information completely, it is financial information—that is, information capable of being expressed in money terms—with which accounting is primarily concerned.

Although described as a measuring and reporting process, the entire accounting process consists of a number of more or less distinct functions. Before measurement can take place, a decision must be made as to what is to be measured. Since they are to report upon economic activity, it follows logically that accountants must *observe* the economic scene and *select* (or identify) those happenings, events, or transactions that may be considered evidence of economic activity. (The purchase and sale of goods and services are examples.) Accountants then, through the use of natural numbers, a monetary scale, and certain other rules and procedures, seek to *measure* the selected events. Their next task is to *record* these measurements in order to provide a permanent, historical record of the financial activities of the organization. Together, all of the above functions may be referred to as the collection or accumulation process of accounting.

As was true for measuring, before reporting can take place a decision must be made as to what to *report,* that is, what is truly relevant. Since it would be meaningless to present an almost endless diary-like narrative of recorded events, accountants seek to classify them into meaningful groups through use of a logical framework, as will be illustrated and discussed later. The next step is to further classify and *summarize* the recorded data in financial statements and other accounting reports. Frequently, accountants are asked to *interpret* these statements and reports. Interpretation may involve explanation of the uses, meaning, and limitations of accounting information as well as the drawing of attention to significant items through percentage and ratio analysis. The functions of classifying, summarizing, reporting, and interpreting collectively comprise the communication function of accounting.

Accounting distinguished from bookkeeping. Many uninformed persons fail to perceive the difference between accounting and bookkeeping. Even though persons referred to as bookkeepers do prepare financial statements, bookkeeping is concerned largely with procedural matters and the development and maintenance of accounting records. Accounting, on the other hand, is more conceptual in nature, dealing with matters such as why a given measurement is preferable in certain circumstances and what uses are made of accounting information and why. In addition to financial statement preparation, accounting also is concerned with income tax returns, budgets, audits, managerial cost studies, and the design of accounting systems.

On the answer form provided in the *Work Papers* or on a separate sheet of paper, indicate whether each of the following statements is true or false.

1. The welfare of a prisoner in a state penitentiary is quite likely to be affected by decisions made that are based in part on accounting information.
2. Accounting is primarily concerned with providing financial information on the economic activities of an organization.
3. Accounting could be briefly defined as a measurement and communication process.
4. Accounting information is useful in correcting past decisions regarding the use of economic resources.

To check the correctness of your answers, turn to Answer Frame 1[1] on page 4.

Frame 2[1]

Accountancy as a profession

In our society accountants typically are employed in (1) public accounting, (2) private industry, or (3) the not-for-profit sector. Within

Answer frame 1[1]

1. True. The amount of money given to prison authorities for food and medical care of prisoners will undoubtedly be determined, in part at least, by information in accounting reports on the amount of money available to the state for a variety of purposes.
2. True. Briefly stated, this is the function of accounting.
3. True. It has been defined in this manner in this text.
4. False. Past decisions are water over the dam and cannot be changed. But one can, of course, learn not to repeat a past mistake.

If you missed any of the above, you should read Frame 1[1] again before going to Frame 2[1] on page 3.

2[1] *continued*

each of these areas, specialization is possible; an accountant may, for example, be considered an expert in auditing, systems development, budgeting, or cost or tax accounting.

Public accounting

An accountant may offer his or her services, individually or as a member of a firm, to the general public for a fee in much the same manner as does a doctor or an attorney. Although the business enterprise is the primary client, individuals and not-for-profit organizations are included. If an accountant has passed a rigorous examination prepared and graded by the American Institute of Certified Public Accountants (AICPA)—the accounting equivalent of the American Bar Association or the American Medical Association—and has met certain other requirements, such as having a certain number of years of experience, he or she may be licensed by the state to practice as a certified public accountant (CPA). As an independent, professional person, a CPA may offer clients auditing, management advisory, and tax services.

Auditing. When a business seeks a loan or seeks to have its securities traded on a stock exchange, it is usually required to provide financial statements containing information on its financial affairs. Users of these statements may accept them much more readily and rely upon them more freely when they are accompanied by an *auditor's report.* This auditor's report contains the professional opinion of the CPA regarding the fairness of the statements.[1] In order to have the knowledge necessary for an informed opinion, the CPA conducts an audit of the underlying accounting and related records and seeks supporting evidence from external sources.

Management advisory services. As a result of knowledge gained in an audit, CPAs typically offer suggestions to their clients on how to improve their operations. From these as well as other direct contacts, CPAs may be engaged to provide a wide range of what are called management

[1] For an example of an actual auditor's report, see the appendix to Chapter 14, page 690. Included in that appendix is a complete set of financial statements of the type often presented to external users.

advisory services. Although such services may include, for example, executive recruiting and production scheduling, they are more likely to involve services related to the accounting process—the design and installation of an accounting system, electronic processing of accounting data, inventory control, budgeting, or financial planning.

Tax services. CPAs often are called upon for expert advice regarding the preparation and filing of federal, state, and local tax returns. The objective here is to use legal means to minimize the amount of taxes paid. But of equal importance, because of high tax rates and complex tax laws, is the area known as tax planning. Proper tax planning requires that the tax effects, if any, of every business decision be known fully and understood before the decision is made, as there may be little opportunity to alter its tax effects after it has been made.

Private or industrial accounting

Accountants employed by a single business organization are often referred to as private or industrial accountants, and may be the employer's only accountant, or one of several hundred or more. They may or may not be CPAs. If they have passed a rigorous examination prepared and administered by the National Association of Accountants—an organization composed primarily of accountants employed in private industry—they will possess a Certificate in Management Accounting (CMA). As in public accounting, they may be recognized as specialists in providing certain types of services.

They may, for example, be primarily concerned with the recording of events and transactions involving outsiders and in the preparation of financial statements that are, for the most part, issued to external parties. Or they may be engaged primarily in accumulating and controlling the costs of producing goods manufactured by their employer. They may be specialists in budgeting—that is, in the development of plans relating to future operations. Many private accountants (as well as public accountants) become specialists in the design and installation of systems for the accumulation and processing of accounting data. Others are called internal auditors because they are employed by a firm to see that its policies and procedures are being adhered to in its various departments and divisions.

Accounting in the not-for-profit sector

Many accountants, including CPAs, are employed by not-for-profit organizations, including governmental agencies at the federal, state, and local levels. Here again specialization is possible as, for example, in budgeting or systems design, although the governmental accountant is likely to be concerned with the accounting for and control of tax revenues and their appropriation and expenditure. Accountants are also employed by governmental agencies whose main function is the regulation of business activity—for example, the regulation by a state public service commission of public utilities.

It should also be noted that many accountants (including CPAs) are employed in the academic arm of the profession. Here attention is directed toward the teaching of accounting and to research into the uses, limitations, and improvement of accounting information and of the theories and procedures under which it is accumulated and communicated.

On the answer form provided in the *Work Papers* or on a separate sheet of paper, indicate whether each of the following statements is correct or incorrect.

1. An accountant may be an expert auditor and not be a CPA.
2. To become a CPA, an accountant must be expert in providing management advisory services.
3. A CPA may practice as an independent professional person, or may be employed as an accountant by a manufacturing company.
4. A CPA employed by a mining company would be permitted to express a professional opinion on the fairness of that company's financial statements.

Check your answers in Answer Frame 2[1] on page 8.

Frame 3[1]

The need for accounting information

The usefulness of accounting information in making decisions regarding economic resources has been repeatedly noted. But little has been said about the decision-making process, to which attention is now directed.

The decision-making process

Basically, as shown in the diagram in Illustration 1.1, any decision-making process involves (1) recognition of the existence of and the

Illustration 1.1, *A Model of the Decision-Making Process*

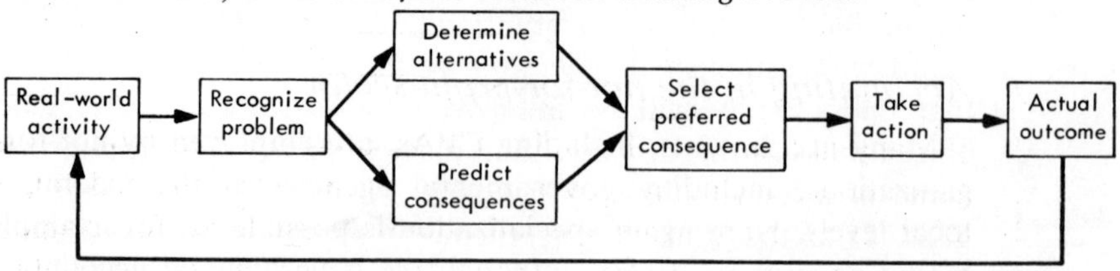

formulation of a problem, (2) determination of the alternative courses of action or approaches considered to be solutions to the problem, (3) prediction of the possible consequence or outcome of each of the alternatives considered, (4) selection of the preferred consequence as determined by reference to the decision maker's personal preferences or previously established goals or objectives, which automatically indicates the alternative chosen, and (5) taking action to see that the alternative chosen is implemented.

The problem is caused, at least in part, by events or happenings in the real world of human activity and scarce resources. Its existence must be recognized or there will be no decision. Consider how frequently decisions are not made because of a failure to perceive that a problem exists. The nature and scope of the problem must be properly formulated in order that the proper alternatives to be considered as solutions to the problem can be determined.

Only those alternatives considered presently feasible should be studied, since nothing is to be gained by choosing a course of action that cannot be implemented as a possible solution to a problem. The list of alternatives should be complete, or the best solution may be overlooked. And the suggested actions should be competing, since one need not choose between two approaches if one can have both.

The consequences or outcomes of the alternatives must be predicted, since they represent expected future happenings and therefore cannot be known presently. Since individual decision makers are unique, they are likely to have different personal preferences. Consequently, different decision makers may make different decisions even though they predict the same set of consequences from the same alternatives.

Note in the illustration that the implementation of a decision causes events and happenings in the real world which, in turn, cause problems to arise; these in turn bring about a recycling of the whole process.

To place the decision-making process in a practical setting, assume that a bank faces a problem: (1) it has received requests for loans from Company X and Company Y and cannot, because of a shortage of loanable money, honor both requests; (2) it is in doubt as to which loan will meet its objectives relative to risk, interest earnings, use of the money, date of repayment, and similar matters; and (3) a loan to X is a different commitment than a loan to Y.

To solve the problem the bank *gathers information* on such matters as the rate of interest it can charge, the credit-worthiness of each company, how the money is to be used, and when it will be repaid. It predicts the probable outcomes of granting each loan. These outcomes are compared with established objectives of the bank, and a decision is reached that undoubtedly will be influenced by the personal preferences of the officer making the decision. She may, for example, predict that the outcome of a loan to X does not differ significantly from that of a loan to Y as far as the bank is concerned. But she may have a strong preference for loaning money to X because it intends to acquire pollution abatement equipment, while Y intends to acquire new smelting equipment.

In any event, a decision is made; and whether the loan is granted or not, or whether or not repaid if granted, the bank's relationship with its environment is now changed. This causes new problems requiring new information and further decisions.

Answer frame 2[1]

1. Correct. Many expert auditors employed by large companies as internal auditors are not CPAs and have little reason to seek the CPA certificate.
2. Incorrect. It is demonstrated ability in fulfilling the attest function, not in providing management services, that is required before an accountant can become a CPA.
3. Correct. When properly licensed by the state, CPAs may practice as independent professional persons. But if they believe their personal prospects for success (however defined) are greater, they may be employed as accountants by a manufacturing company.
4. Incorrect. An accountant, even though a CPA, is not practicing as a CPA when in the employ of a mining company. He or she would not be considered an independent professional accountant and, consequently, would not be permitted to express an opinion on the fairness of the employer's financial statements. In order to express such an opinion, the CPA must, in addition to being licensed to practice as a CPA, be *independent*.

If you answered incorrectly, read Frame 2[1] again before beginning Frame 3[1] on page 6.

3[1] *continued*

Undoubtedly, part of the information gathered by the bank would be accounting information about each company. In this example, the bank would be considered an external user of accounting information. But the same decision process would be employed, with accounting again supplying part of the information, in reaching a decision on an internal matter (such as a business manager deciding whether to begin offering a new line of merchandise). Internal decisions requiring accounting information are now examined more closely.

Internal decisions

In all but the smallest of companies, internal decisions are made at various levels of management and will require accounting information. The types of decisions made can be classified roughly into four major categories. These categories and examples of the types of decisions made in each are:

1. Financing decisions—deciding what amounts of capital are needed and whether it is to be secured from owners or creditors; and, if it is to come from owners, whether it is to be obtained by new investment or by plowing back profits.

2. Resource allocation decisions—deciding how the total capital of the business is to be invested in productive resources such as plant and equipment.

3. Production decisions—determining what products are to be produced, by what means, and when; deciding whether new product lines are to be added or old ones discontinued.

4. Marketing decisions—establishing selling prices and advertising

budgets; determining markets and choosing appropriate channels of distribution for the products sold.

Managerial accounting. That part of the accounting discipline asked to provide accounting information for such internal decisions is called managerial (or management) accounting. Managerial accounting information varies from the very broad (long-range planning budgets) to the quite detailed (determining the reasons why individual costs varied from their planned or budgeted amounts). Typically, the information must meet two tests. It must be useful and must not cost more to accumulate than it is worth. The information generally relates to a part of an enterprise—a certain plant, division, or department—because these are the levels at which decisions are made. Management accounting information often is used to measure the success of managers and to motivate them to help a firm achieve its goals. It is forward-looking, often involving short-range and long-range planning.

Indicate whether each of the following statements is true or false.

1. The decision-making process will vary from firm to firm and according to the type of problem requiring a solution (decision).
2. Management accounting information generally relates to some part rather than the whole of an enterprise.
3. In any situation requiring a decision, the decision maker may forgo securing information if it will not be worth its cost.
4. In general, the purpose of information is to reduce doubt.

Check your responses in Answer Frame 3[1] on page 10.

Frame 4[1]

External users and their decisions

The many external users of accounting information relative to business enterprises can be classified broadly into six major categories. These categories and examples of the questions for which accounting information is used are:

1. Owners and prospective owners (stockholders in the case of a corporation) and their advisers—financial analysts and investment counselors. Should an ownership interest be acquired in this particular business? Or, if one is now held, should it be increased, decreased, disposed of entirely, or simply retained at its present level? Has the management of the firm earned a satisfactory level of profits in the past year?

2. Creditors and lenders. Should the business firm be permitted to buy on a credit rather than a cash-only basis? Should a long-term loan be granted the firm? Will the firm be able to pay its debts as they come due?

3. Employees and the unions representing them. Does the business

Answer frame 3[1]

1. False. The decision-making process will not change. It will consist of the recognition and formulation of the problem, determination of the alternative possible courses of action, prediction of the outcomes for each possible alternative, selection of the preferred outcome or consequence (the actual decision), and implementation of the decision. This generalized pattern will hold regardless of the type of firm involved or the nature of the decision to be made.
2. True. Management accounting information is most widely used by internal management personnel who are responsible for a part rather than the whole of an organization.
3. True. As is true in any situation involving a purchasable commodity, the cost of information may exceed its value to some user.
4. True. In brief, this is the purpose of all information.

If you missed any of the above answers, you should read Frame 3[1] again before proceeding to Frame 4[1] on page 9.

4[1] *continued*

firm have the ability to pay increased wages? Without raising prices? Does the firm appear to be financially able to provide permanent employment?

4. Customers and consumers. Will the company remain in operation so that its product warranties will be honored, if necessary? Can the business install costly pollution control equipment and still remain profitable? Is it financially able to install such equipment? Are its profit margins reasonable?

5. Governmental units and agencies. Is this business, a public utility, earning a fair profit on its capital investment? How much federal or state income tax does the firm owe? Should the Department of Justice file suit to block a proposed merger between two business firms? In the aggregate, is total business activity at the desired level for sound growth without inflation?

6. The general public. What might be the possible effects of raising the legal minimum wage? Are profits too high? Do they represent an increasing or decreasing proportion of national income? Are the firms in this industry contributing to inflation? To what extent do tax laws favor the firms in a certain industry?

Although some governmental agencies have the power to prescribe in detail the information to be provided to them, the information needs of the above users typically are met by providing a single set of general purpose financial statements. These statements are the end products of a process known as financial accounting.

Financial accounting. In general, in a business setting, financial accounting provides reports or statements on a firm's financial condition, the changes in its financial condition, and on the results of its operations, that is, its profitability. These statements usually are published in a document containing roughly 30 to 40 pages known as the *annual report*. The annual report also contains the CPA's auditor's report or opinion as to the fairness of the financial statements, as well as considerable other information about the reporting company's activities, plans or expectations.

Financial accounting information generally relates to the company as a whole, since outsiders typically do not participate in internal decisions and can make decisions only on matters pertaining to the enterprise in its entirety, such as a decision to extend credit. Such information is usually historical in nature, being a report upon what has happened. Because it is used externally and often compared between companies, the information supplied must conform to certain standards or principles.

But it would be a mistake to assume that a clear-cut distinction can be drawn between financial accounting information and managerial accounting information. Key management officials often are keenly aware of the fact that their jobs may depend upon how the figures come out in the annual report. Also, much of what is called managerial accounting information is first accumulated in an accounting system designed with financial reporting in mind.

Recycling. Whether financial or managerial accounting information is involved, the role of the accountant and of accounting information in a recycling process should be noted. The accountant observes economic activity, selects certain aspects for measurement, records these measurements, and then classifies, summarizes, and reports these measurements in financial statements or reports. The recipients of these reports use this information as well as information obtained from other sources in making further decisions. These decisions cause new economic activity for the accountant to observe, measure, record, and report upon. Thus, accounting information plays an important role in the continuous chain of events that constitutes economic activity.

Indicate whether each of the following statements is true or false.

1. The annual report of a company contains a statement showing the financial condition of the reporting company.
2. Financial accounting information is often called general purpose information because it is believed that the information needs of different external parties can be satisfied by the same information.
3. As part of the management advisory services rendered, the CPA will express a professional opinion on the fairness of the bulk of the managerial accounting information accumulated by a company.
4. Basically, and in very broad general terms, managerial accounting information is used internally while financial accounting information is used by external parties.

Check your responses in Answer Frame 4[1] on page 12.

Frame 5[1]

Although accounting information is absolutely essential in the successful management of a not-for-profit organization, primary attention in this

Answer frame 4[1]

1. True. One of the important statements included in the annual report is the one showing financial position.
2. True. Many classes of external users are provided with the same general financial information about a company.
3. False. The purpose of securing the professional opinion of a CPA as to the fairness of the information contained in financial statements is to increase its reliability to *outsiders*. The management of a firm might wish to color the information it reports externally to make management appear more efficient and effective to outsiders. But management would only be deceiving itself if it sought to manipulate or distort managerial accounting information. Hence, there is little if any need for a CPA to attest to managerial accounting information.
4. True. As a broad generalization, the statement is true, although some of the information released to outsiders may very well be used at the top levels of management within a company.

If you answered incorrectly, restudy Frame 4[1] before going to Frame 5[1] on page 11.

5[1] *continued*

text is devoted to business firms. And because, as already noted, much of the management accounting information needed is developed from data accumulated for financial reporting, the discussion in this volume will focus upon financial accounting.

Financial statements of business enterprises

Current literature discusses at length the fact that a modern business firm may have a number of objectives or goals. Among those mentioned are earning a satisfactory profit, providing good-paying jobs and comfortable working conditions for employees, being a good citizen, controlling pollution, providing equal employment opportunities for minority groups, and maintaining a sound financial position. But the two primary objectives of every business firm are *profitability* and *solvency*. Unless a firm can earn a reasonable profit and pay its debts as they become due, the other objectives it may have will never be realized simply because the firm will not survive.

Whether a business is reaching these objectives can be determined, in part, from its financial statements. The statement of financial position can be used in appraising a firm's ability to pay its maturing debts, while its earnings statement is clearly intended to provide information on profitability. The discussion of financial accounting which follows begins with financial statements, even though these statements are the end products of the process. Knowledge of what is sought by engaging in the process may aid considerably in understanding the process itself.

The statement of financial position

The statement of financial position (often called a balance sheet) presents measures of the assets, liabilities, and owners' equity in a business firm as of a specific moment in time. Assets are things of value; they constitute the *resources* of the firm. They have value to the firm because of the uses to which they can be put or the things that can be acquired by exchanging them. In Illustration 1.2, the assets of the Bond

Illustration 1.2, *A Statement of Financial Position*

BOND COMPANY
Statement of Financial Position
July 31, 1976

ASSETS			LIABILITIES AND STOCKHOLDERS' EQUITY		
Current Assets:			Current Liabilities:		
Cash..................	$13,470		Accounts payable.......	$ 1,600	
Accounts receivable.....	700	$14,170	Notes payable..........	3,000	$ 4,600
Property, Plant, and Equipment:			Stockholders' Equity:		
Delivery equipment.....	$20,000		Capital stock...........	$30,000	
Office equipment.......	2,500	22,500	Retained earnings.......	2,070	32,070
Total Assets..........		$36,670	Total Liabilities and Stockholders' Equity............		$36,670

Company amount to $36,670 and consist of current assets of cash and accounts receivable (amounts due from customers) and property, plant, and equipment consisting of delivery equipment and office equipment. Current assets consist of cash and other short-lived assets that are reasonably expected to be converted into cash or to be consumed or used up in the operations of the business within a short period, usually one year.[2] Property, plant, and equipment refers to relatively long-lived assets that are to be used in the production or sale of other assets or services rather than being sold.

Liabilities are the debts owed by a firm. Typically, they must be paid at certain known moments in time. The liabilities of the Bond Company are both relatively short-lived current liabilities, consisting of accounts payable (amounts owed to suppliers) and notes payable (a written promise to pay) totaling $4,600.

The Bond Company is a corporation and it is customary to refer to the owners' interest in a corporation as stockholders' equity. Bond Company's stockholders' equity consists of $30,000 paid in for shares of capital stock and retained earnings (earnings not paid out to stockholders) of $2,070. All of these items will be discussed further below. At this point, simply note that the statement of financial position heading includes the name of the organization, the title of the statement, and the

[2] Technically speaking, the time period is one operating cycle or one year, whichever is longer. An operating cycle is the length of time that it takes cash spent for merchandise to be sold to come back to the selling company in the form of collections from its customers. Thus, in some industries (distilling, for example) the operating cycle extends for a number of years.

date of the statement. Also, note that the claims upon or interests in assets equal the assets—an equality explained later in this chapter.

The earnings statement

The purpose of the earnings statement (often called an income statement) is to report upon the profitability of a business organization for a stated period of time. In accounting, profitability is measured by comparing the revenues generated in a period with the expenses incurred to produce those revenues. Revenue is defined as the product of the business organization—the products it delivers or the services it renders. Revenues are usually measured by the assets customers are willing to surrender for the products or services. Expense is defined as the sacrifice made or the cost incurred to produce revenue. It is measured by the assets surrendered or consumed in serving customers. If revenues exceed expenses, net earnings result. If the reverse is true, the business is said to be operating at a loss. Illustration 1.3 contains the earnings statement of the Bond Company for the month of July 1976. It shows that revenues were generated by serving customers in the amount of $4,700. Expenses for the month amounted to $2,630 resulting in net earnings for the month of $2,070.

Illustration 1.3, *An Earnings Statement*

Bond Company
Earnings Statement
For the Month of July 1976

Service revenues		$4,700
Expenses:		
Wages	$1,600	
Gas and oil	400	
Rent	300	
Advertising	200	
Utilities	100	
Interest	30	2,630
Net Earnings		$2,070

Note that the heading of an earnings statement always specifies the time period covered by the statement. Failure to specify the time period covered would render an earnings statement useless, or nearly so.

Indicate whether each of the following statements is true or false.

1. The basic elements of accounting are assets, liabilities, owners' equity, revenues, and expenses.
2. A statement of financial position reports upon the financial position of an organization as of a given moment in time.
3. The solvency of a business organization can be appraised through study of its earnings statement.

4. Broadly speaking, revenue represents accomplishment and expense represents sacrifice.

Check your responses in Answer Frame 5[1] on page 16.

Frame 6[1]

The financial accounting process

Having briefly introduced the two principal financial statements, attention is now directed to the process underlying such statements.

The accounting equation

It has already been noted that in the statement of financial position presented in Illustration 1.2 the total assets of the Bond Company are equal to its liabilities and stockholders' equity. This equality follows inevitably from the basic assumption in accounting that the assets of a business are equal to the equities in those assets; that is, Assets = Equities. Assets have already been defined simply as things of value. In a more sophisticated sense, the accountant designates and records as assets all those economic resources owned by a business which he can measure. And all desired things, except those available in unlimited quantity without cost or effort, are economic resources.

Equities are interests in or claims upon assets. If, for example, you purchased a new automobile for $4,000 by withdrawing $400 from your savings account and borrowing $3,600 from your credit union, your equity in the automobile is $400 and that of your credit union is $3,600. The $3,600 can be further described as a liability, while your $400 equity is often described as the owner's equity or the residual equity or interest in the asset. Since, in the case of a corporation, the owners are the stockholders, the basic equation becomes:

ASSETS = LIABILITIES + STOCKHOLDERS' EQUITY

This equation must always be in balance because the sum of the interests in assets must always be equal to the assets themselves. It is intuitively logical to hold that everything of value belongs to someone or to some organization.

The right side of the above equation is also looked upon in yet another manner—namely, it shows the sources of the existing stock of assets. Thus, liabilities are not only claims to assets but they also are sources of assets. And, in a corporation, all of the assets are provided by either creditors (liability holders) or owners (stockholders).

As a business engages in economic activity, the dollar amounts and the composition of its assets, liabilities, and stockholders' equity change. But the equality of the basic equation always holds.

Answer frame 5[1]

1. True. Accounting is indeed concerned with these elements, as well as the difference between revenues and expenses—the net earnings or net loss of the business for a period.
2. True. This is the function of the statement of financial position.
3. False. A business could be profitable and yet be unable to pay its maturing debts due to a lack of cash.
4. True. This is a broad generalization well worth remembering.

If you responded incorrectly to any of the above questions, read Frame 5[1] again before proceeding to Frame 6[1] on page 15.

Transaction analysis

6[1] *continued*

Our society is characterized by exchange. That is, the bulk of the goods and services produced are exchanged rather than consumed by their producers. From this it follows that much of the economic activity of our society can be observed from the exchanges that take place. In accounting, these exchanges (as well as other changes) are called *transactions* and provide much of the raw data entered in the accounting system. There are several reasons why this is so. First, an exchange is a readily observable event providing good evidence that activity has occurred. Second, an exchange usually takes place at an agreed-upon price and this price provides a highly objective measure of the economic activity that has transpired. Thus, the analysis of transactions is a most important part of the financial accounting process.

To illustrate the analysis of transactions and their effect upon the basic accounting equation, the activities of the Bond Company that led to the statements in Illustrations 1.2 and 1.3 are presented and discussed below. Assume that the Bond Company was organized as a corporation on July 1, 1976 and that in its first transaction it issued shares of capital stock to Lee Bond, his wife, and their son. Analyzed, the transaction increased the assets (cash) of the Bond Company by $30,000 and increased its equities (the capital stock element of stockholders' equity) by $30,000. Consequently, the transaction yields a basic accounting equation containing the following:

Assets	= Liabilities	+ Stockholders' Equity
(Cash, $30,000)	($0)	(Capital Stock, $30,000)

As its next transaction, the company borrowed $6,000 from Mrs. Bond's father, giving its written promise to repay the amount in one year.

Which of the following properly describes the effects of this transaction upon the accounting equation?

1. Assets would increase by $6,000 and stockholders' equity would decrease by $6,000.
2. Assets would increase by $6,000 and liabilities would increase by $6,000.

3. Both assets and stockholders' equity would increase by $6,000.
4. Both assets and liabilities would decrease by $6,000.

Check your response in Answer Frame 6[1] on page 18.

Frame 7[1]

The basic equation depicting the financial status of the Bond Company now is:

ASSETS	=	LIABILITIES	+	STOCKHOLDERS' EQUITY
(Cash, $36,000)		(Notes Payable, $6,000)		(Capital Stock, $30,000)

As its third transaction, the Bond Company spent $20,000 for three delivery trucks and $1,500 for some office equipment. In this transaction the Bond Company received delivery equipment priced at $20,000 and office equipment priced at $1,500. It gave up cash of $21,500. This transaction thus does not change the totals in the basic equation, it merely changes the composition of the assets. The equation is as follows:

ASSETS		=	LIABILITIES		+	STOCKHOLDER'S EQUITY	
Cash..............	$14,500						
Delivery equipment.......	20,000		Notes payable.....	$6,000		Capital stock....	$30,000
Office equipment...	1,500						
	$36,000	=		$6,000	+		$30,000

Assume that as transaction four in the month of July, the Bond Company purchased an additional $1,000 of office equipment, agreeing to pay for it within 10 days after it receives a bill for it from the supplier. This transaction increases assets in the form of office equipment by $1,000. It also increases liabilities in the form of accounts payable (which are amounts owed to creditors for items purchased from them) by $1,000. The items making up the totals in the accounting equation now appear as follows:

ASSETS		=	LIABILITIES		+	STOCKHOLDERS' EQUITY	
Cash..............	$14,500						
Delivery equipment.......	20,000		Notes payable.....	$6,000		Capital stock....	$30,000
Office equipment...	2,500		Accounts payable..	1,000			
	$37,000	=		$7,000	+		$30,000

Revenue and expense transactions

Thus far the transactions presented have consisted of the acquisition of assets either by borrowing or by stockholder investment. But a business is not formed merely to acquire assets. Rather, it seeks to use the assets

Answer frame 6[1]

Statement 2 is the only correct response. The company received an additional $6,000 and gave in exchange a written promise to pay this sum at a later date. This written promise to pay is a note payable and is one type of liability. Thus, when this transaction is properly analyzed and recorded, the equation would remain in balance because both sides would be increased by $6,000.

If you missed this question, be sure that you understand why only the second statement is correct before going on to Frame 7[1] on page 17.

7[1] *continued*

entrusted to it as a means of securing still greater amounts of assets. This is accomplished by providing customers with goods or services, with the expectation that the value of the assets received from customers will exceed the cost of the assets consumed or surrendered in serving them. This total flow of services rendered or goods delivered (as measured by assets received from customers) has already been defined as *revenue*. Thus, revenue is a source of assets. The cost of serving customers is called *expense* and is measured by the cost of the assets surrendered or consumed. If revenues exceed expenses, net earnings exist. If not, a loss has been suffered.

Assume that as its fifth transaction in July the Bond Company renders delivery services for some of its customers for $3,800 cash. It is evident that cash has increased by $3,800. But what other change has occurred which, if properly recorded, would reflect the appropriate analysis of this transaction?

1. Liabilities would increase by $3,800.
2. Stockholders' equity would increase by $3,800.
3. Other assets would decrease by $3,800.

Check your response in Answer Frame 7[1] on page 20.

Frame 8[1]

Incorporating the effects of the revenue transaction upon the financial status of the Bond Company yields the following basic equation:

Assets			Liabilities			Stockholders' Equity	
Cash..........	$18,300		Notes payable....	$6,000		Capital stock.......	$30,000
Delivery equipment.........	20,000		Accounts payable....	1,000		Retained earnings....	3,800 (Service revenue)
Office equipment.........	2,500						
	$40,800	=		$7,000	+		$33,800

Note that the increase in stockholders' equity brought about by the revenue transaction is recorded as a separate item, "Retained earnings." It cannot be recorded as capital stock, since no additional shares of stock were issued. The expectation is that revenue transactions will yield net earnings. If net earnings are not distributed to stockholders, they are in fact retained, and the title "retained earnings" is quite descriptive. Subsequent chapters will show that because of complexities in handling large numbers of transactions, revenues will be shown as affecting retained earnings only at the end of an accounting period. The procedure presented above is a shortcut used to explain why the accounting equation remains in balance.

Assume that as its sixth transaction in July the Bond Company performs services for customers who agree to pay $900 at a later date. The transaction consists of an exchange of services for a promise by the customer to pay later. It is similar to the preceding transaction in that stockholders' equity is increased because revenues have been earned. It differs because cash has not been received. But a thing of value, an asset, has been received, and this is the claim upon the customer, the right to collect from him at the later date. Technically, such claims are called *accounts receivable,* but the important point is that accounting does recognize them as assets and does record them. The accounting equation, including this item, is as follows:

Assets		=	Liabilities		+	Stockholders' Equity		
Cash..........	$18,300		Notes payable....	$6,000		Capital stock......	$30,000	
Accounts receivable....	900		Accounts payable....	1,000		Retained earnings....	4,700	(Service revenue)
Delivery equipment........	20,000							
Office equipment........	2,500							
	$41,700	=		$7,000	+		$34,700	

To illustrate one more step in regards to accounts receivable, assume that $200 is collected from customers "on account," to use business terminology. The transaction consists of the giving up of claims upon customers in exchange for cash. The effect of the transaction is to increase cash to $18,500 and to decrease accounts receivable to $700. Note that this transaction consists solely of a change in the composition of the assets, not of an increase in assets resulting from the generation of revenue.

Attention may now be directed toward expenses, which are the sacrifices made, the assets surrendered or consumed, in serving customers. Suppose (transaction eight) that the Bond Company paid its employees $1,600 for services received in conducting business operations during the month of July. The transaction consists of an exchange of cash for employee services. But what is its effect upon the accounting equation?

1. There would be no effect upon the totals of the two sides of the equation.
2. Assets would decrease and liabilities would decrease.
3. Assets would decrease and stockholders' equity would decrease.

Check your response in Answer Frame 8[1] on page 20.

Answer frame 7^1

The second response is correct. Stockholders' equity would increase by \$3,800. The correctness of this answer can be observed by noting that no corresponding increase in liabilities was brought about by rendering services to customers. Furthermore, no specific assets were parted with. Thus, by a process of elimination, the conclusion is reached that rendering services to customers in exchange for assets increases stockholders' equity. In fact, this is the basic objective of a business corporation.

If you answered incorrectly, you should study the first part of Frame 7^1 again before proceeding to Frame 8^1 on page 18.

Answer frame 8^1

Statement 3 is the correct choice. Accountants typically, as is explained further in Frame 9^1, treat transactions such as these as expense transactions. Expenses indirectly reduce stockholders' equity in that their incurrence prevents stockholders' equity from increasing by the full amount of the revenue earned.

Even if you missed this question, continue on with Frame 9^1 below for additional explanation of expense transactions.

Frame 9^1

As already noted, the payment of wages consists of an exchange of cash for employee services and a proper analysis of such a transaction would appear to indicate an exchange of one form of asset for another. This seems especially true when one recognizes that business corporations generally will surrender assets only for other things of value, for other assets. But, because the value of the services typically has expired by the time payment is made, the accountant engages in a shortcut and treats the transaction as a decrease in an asset and in stockholders' equity. From a purely theoretical point of view, the transaction should be regarded as involving an increase in one asset (labor services) and a decrease in another (cash), and then a decrease in an asset (labor services) and a decrease in stockholders' equity because of the recognition of an expense—wages.

Let us further assume (as transactions 9 and 10) that the Bond Company paid cash of \$300 as rent for truck storage space and office space and that it paid its utilities bill for July in the amount of \$100. These transactions will be treated by the accountant as having the same effect upon the financial position of the company, namely, a decrease in the asset cash of \$400 and a decrease in stockholders' equity of \$400 because of the incurrence of rent expense of \$300 and utilities expense of \$100. Incorporating these two items and the wages of \$1,600 cumulatively into our accounting equation, it now reads:

Assets		=	Liabilities		+	Stockholders' Equity			
Cash	\$16,500		Notes payable	\$6,000		Capital stock	\$30,000		
Accounts receivable	700		Accounts payable	1,000		Retained earnings	2,700	Service revenue	\$4,700
Delivery equipment	20,000							Less expenses:	
Office equipment	2,500							Wages	1,600
								Rent	300
								Utilities	100
	\$39,700	=		\$7,000	+		\$32,700		

Because of their similar effects, transactions 11 and 12 of the Bond Company may be treated simultaneously. Assume that the company received a bill for gasoline, oil, and other delivery equipment supplies consumed during the month in the amount of $400 and a bill for $200 for advertising in July. Both transactions would be treated by the accountant as involving an increase in a liability, accounts payable, and a decrease in stockholders' equity because of the incurrence of an expense. Here again, in each instance, an asset was actually acquired. But, because it has been consumed in producing revenue during the month, the accountant treats it as an expense—a reduction in stockholders' equity, more specifically in the retained earnings item. The accounting equation depicting the financial position of the Bond Company now reads:

Assets		=	Liabilities		+	Stockholders' Equity			
Cash	$16,500		Notes payable	$6,000					
Accounts receivable	700		Accounts payable	1,600		Capital stock	$30,000		
						Retained earnings	2,100	Service revenue	$4,700
Delivery equipment	20,000							Les expenses:	
Office equipment	2,500							Wages	1,600
	$39,700	=		$7,600	+		$32,100	Rent	300
								Utilities	100
								Gas and oil	400
								Advertising	200

In reviewing his needs for cash at the end of the month of July, Mr. Bond decided that he would not need as much cash as he now holds. Consequently, he paid $3,000 on the note owed to his father-in-law, plus interest for the month of $30. The recording of this transaction would have what effect upon the accounting equation?

1. Assets and liabilities would both decrease by $3,030.
2. Assets and stockholders' equity would both decrease by $3,030.
3. Assets would decrease by $3,030, liabilities would decrease by $3,000, and stockholders' equity would decrease by $30.

Check your response in Answer Frame 9[1] on page 22.

Frame 10[1]

Summary of transactions

The effects of all of the transactions entered into by the Bond Company in the first month of its existence upon its assets, liabilities, and stockholders' equity are summarized in Illustration 1.4.

The ending balances in each of the columns are the dollar amounts reported in the statement of financial position in Illustration 1.2. The itemized data in the retained earnings column are the revenue and expense items reported in the earnings statement in Illustration 1.3. This summary shows how the basic equation of Assets = Equities is subdivided into the five major elements of financial accounting: assets, liabilities, owners' equity, revenues, and expenses.

Answer frame 9[1]

Statement 3 is the correct choice. The transaction decreased cash by the total amount paid out, $3,030. Of this amount, $3,000 was applied to reduce the principal amount owed on notes payable and the remaining $30 consisted of the payment of interest expense—an element that reduces retained earnings. This transaction serves to illustrate that any given transaction may affect assets, liabilities, and stockholders' equity simultaneously.

If you missed this question, restudy Frame 9[1] before going on to Frame 10[1] on page 21.

The statement of retained earnings

10[1]
continued

The financial reporting of a business corporation may include the presentation of a statement summarizing the changes in stockholders' equity if numerous changes have occurred in the items comprising stockholders' equity. More typically, only a statement of retained earnings is presented because changes in other stockholders' equity items are relatively few in number. The purpose of the statement of retained earnings is to explain the changes in retained earnings that occurred between two statement of financial position dates. Usually, these changes consist of the addition of net earnings (or deduction of net loss) and the deduction of dividends. Dividends are the means by which a corporation rewards its stockholders for providing it with capital.

The effects of a cash dividend transaction are to reduce cash and retained earnings by the amount paid out. In effect, the earnings are no longer retained but have been passed on to the stockholders. And this, of course, is one of the primary reasons why stockholders organize corporations.

The statement of retained earnings for the Bond Company for the month of July, 1976, would be quite simple. Since the company was organized on July 1, there would be no beginning retained earnings balance. Net earnings of $2,070 would be added and, since no dividends were paid, this would also be the ending balance.

To provide a more effective illustration, assume that the Bond Company's net earnings for August were $1,500 (revenues of $5,600 less expenses of $4,100) and that it declared and paid dividends of $1,000. Its statement of retained earnings for August is shown in Illustration 1.5.

Indicate whether each of the following statements is true or false.

1. Because dividends and expenses both reduce retained earnings, they are of the same basic nature.
2. Dividends usually consist of a cash distribution to stockholders.
3. Dividends should be deducted from revenues in calculating net earnings.
4. Generally, in order to pay dividends, a corporation should have retained earnings.

Check your responses in Answer Frame 10[1] on page 26.

Illustration 1.4, *Summary of Transactions*

BOND COMPANY
Summary of Transactions
Month of July 1976

		ASSETS				=	LIABILITIES		+	STOCKHOLDERS' EQUITY		
Trans-action	*Explanation*	*Cash*	+ *Accounts Receivable*	+ *Delivery Equipment*	+ *Office Equipment*		*Notes Payable*	+ *Accounts Payable*		*Capital Stock*	+ *Retained Earnings*	
	Beginning balances	$ 0	$ 0	$ 0	$ 0		$ 0	$ 0		$ 0	$ 0	
(1)	Issued stock for cash	+30,000								+30,000		
(2)	Borrowed money on note	+ 6,000					+ 6,000					
(3)	Purchased equipment for cash	−21,500		+20,000	+ 1,500							
(4)	Purchased equipment on account				+ 1,000			+ 1,000				
(5)	Service revenue for cash	+ 3,800									+ 3,800	(Service revenue)
(6)	Service revenue on account		+ 900								+ 900	(Service revenue)
(7)	Collection on account	+ 200	− 200									
(8)	Paid wages	− 1,600									− 1,600	(Wages expense)
(9)	Paid rent	− 300									− 300	(Rent expense)
(10)	Paid utilities bill	− 100									− 100	(Utilities expense)
(11)	Bill for gas and oil used							+ 400			− 400	(Gas and oil expense)
(12)	Bill for July advertising							+ 200			− 200	(Advertising expense)
(13)	Payment on note and interest	− 3,030					− 3,000				− 30	(Interest expense)
	Ending balances	$13,470 +	$ 700 +	$20,000 +	$ 2,500	=	$ 3,000 +	$ 1,600	+	$ 30,000 +	$ 2,070	
		$36,670				=	$4,600		+	$32,070		

Illustration 1.5, *A Statement of Retained Earnings*

BOND COMPANY	
Statement of Retained Earnings	
For the Month Ended August 31, 1976	
Retained earnings, July 31	$2,070
Add: Net earnings for August	1,500
	$3,570
Less: Dividends	1,000
Retained Earnings, August 31	$2,570

Frame 11[11]

Some basic concepts

The accountant, in seeking to provide useful information on economic activity, relies upon some basic concepts or assumptions. Those covered, explicitly or implicitly, thus far are summarized below.

Entity

The information gathered in an accounting information system relates to a specific business unit or entity. This entity is deemed to have an existence separate and apart from its owners, creditors, employees, or other interested parties.

Transaction

Those events or happenings that affect the assets, liabilities, owners' equity, revenues, or expenses of an entity are called transactions and are recorded in the accounting system. For the most part, transactions consist of exchanges.

Duality

Every transaction has a two-sided or dual effect upon each of the parties engaging in it. Consequently, if information is to be complete, both sides or both effects of every transaction must be included in the accounting system.

Money measurement

Economic activity is recorded and reported in terms of a common unit of measurement—the dollar. If not expressed in a common unit of measurement, accounting reports would be much less useful, if not unintelligible. Changes in the value of the dollar are usually ignored.

Cost

Most of the numbers entered in an accounting system are the bargained prices of exchange transactions. The result is that most assets (excluding cash and receivables) are recorded and reported at their cost of acquisition. Changes in the value of the asset are (with certain exceptions) usually ignored. This practice is usually defended on the grounds of objectivity and the absence of evidence that the acquiring firm would have been willing to pay more.

Periodicity

To be useful, information must be (among other things) timely and current. To provide such information, the accountant assumes that he can subdivide the life of an entity into periods and report upon its activities for those periods. The requirement of periodic reporting will require the use of estimates, thus making every accounting report somewhat tentative in nature.

Continuity

Unless strong evidence exists to the contrary, the accountant assumes that the entity will continue operations into the indefinite future. Consequently, assets that will be used up or consumed in future operations need not be reported at their current liquidation values.

All of these concepts or notions (as well as others) will be discussed in considerably greater detail in Chapter 14.

Indicate whether each of the following statements is true or false.

1. All events or happenings that affect an entity are recorded in its accounting system.
2. Assets are usually reported at their acquisition cost even though they may have a substantially higher current value.
3. Even though the value of a dollar may change as general price levels change, the accountant uses the dollar as if it were a constant unit of measure.
4. Because of his basic assumption that assets equal equities, the accountant is forced to assume that every transaction has two sides.

Check your responses in Answer Frame 11[1] on page 26.

Summary *chapter* 1

Accounting is a systematic or organized means of gathering and reporting information on economic activity. The information provided is used

Answer frame 10[1]

1. False. Although both reduce retained earnings (directly or indirectly), dividends and expenses are not of the same nature. Expenses are costs incurred to generate revenues in the expectation that revenues will exceed expenses—that is, that net earnings will result. Dividends are distributions of these net earnings, not costs incurred to generate revenues.
2. True. The common type of dividend usually involves a cash distribution to stockholders.
3. False. As explained in answer 1 above, dividends are distributions of net earnings, not expenses, and so should not be deducted from revenues in the determination of net earnings.
4. True. While covered only implicitly, it is true that, under certain circumstances, a corporation would be barred by law from paying dividends if it did not have retained earnings.

If you missed any of the above, you should read Frame 10[1] again before going on to Frame 11[1] on page 24.

Answer frame 11[1]

1. False. Many events or happenings occur that affect the well-being of a business. Some of these, such as a strike by the employees of a major competitor, are not recorded in an entity's accounting system simply because their effects cannot be measured. Unless the happening or event has a relatively direct bearing upon the assets and equities of an entity, its effects will not be entered in the entity's accounting system.
2. True. Most assets are recorded and reported at their acquisition cost as reflected in the exchange transaction in which they were acquired.
3. True. No direct reflection of the changing value of the dollar is recognized in accounting systems employed in current practice.
4. True. The notion that a transaction has a dual nature, or has two sides, is directly related to the basic assumption that assets equal equities.

If you answered incorrectly, you should read Frame 11[1] again before continuing with the chapter summary on page 25.

---

by many external and internal parties, together with other information, for a wide range of decisions.

An accountant may be employed in public, private, or governmental accounting and may be a specialist in one of many fields of expertise such as auditing, budgeting, systems development, taxation, or financial reporting.

Internally, accounting information is used by various levels of management personnel. External users include actual and potential stockholders and creditors and their professional advisers; employees and their unions; customers; suppliers; governmental agencies; and the public at large.

The basic end products of the financial accounting process are the statement of financial position, the earnings statement, and the statement of retained earnings. (A fourth major financial statement—the statement of changes in financial positions—will be introduced later.)

All transactions can be analyzed and their effects upon assets and equities determined. Liabilities are a form of equity; revenues and expenses are subdivisions of the equity, retained earnings. Thus, the basic elements of accounting are assets, liabilities, owners' equity, revenues, and expenses.

Fundamental to accounting are the concepts or assumptions of entity, transaction, duality, money measurement, cost basis of valuation, periodicity, and continuity.

You have completed the programmed portion of Chapter 1. As the first part of your review, read the glossary which follows and study the definitions of the new terms introduced in this chapter. Then go on to the Student Review Quiz for a self-administered test of your comprehension of the material in the chapter (see page 28).

Glossary *chapter* 1

Accounting—a systematic process of measuring and reporting to various users relevant financial information for decision making regarding the economic activity of an organization or unit. *Financial accounting* relates to the process of supplying financial information to parties external to the reporting entity. *Managerial accounting* relates to the process of supplying financial information for internal management use. As a field of employment, accounting is usually divided into *public accounting,* where accounting and related services are offered to the general public for a fee; *private* (*or industrial*) *accounting,* where the accountant performs services for one business employer; and *governmental accounting,* where the accountant is employed by and renders services for a governmental agency.

Accounting equation—basically, Assets = Equities; in slightly expanded form for a corporation, Assets = Liabilities + Stockholders' Equity.

Accounts payable—amounts owed to creditors for items or services purchased from them.

Accounts receivable—amounts owed to a concern by its customers.

American Institute of Certified Public Accountants—a professional organization of certified public accountants, most of whom are in public accounting practice.

Annual report—a pamphlet or document of varying length containing financial and other information about and distributed annually by a company to its stockholders.

Assets—roughly equatable to things of value or economic resources; things possessing service potential or utility to their owner that can be measured and expressed in money terms.

Auditing—that branch of the accounting profession that is concerned with checking, reviewing, testing, and verifying the accounting work of others, generally with the objective of expressing a formal opinion on the fairness of the resulting information.

Auditor's opinion or report—the formal written statement by a public accountant (usually a CPA) attesting to the fairness of the information contained in a set of financial statements; for an example, see page 690.

Capital stock—the title given to an equity account showing the investment in a business corporation by its stockholders.

Certified public accountant—an accountant who has been awarded a certificate and granted the right to refer to himself as a certified public accountant as a result of having passed a special examination and having met other requirements regarding such things as experience and education. In some states, the CPA certificate is a license to practice as a CPA; in others, an additional license must be obtained.

Continuity (going concern)—the assumption by the accountant that, unless specific evidence exists to the contrary, a business firm will continue to operate into the indefinite future.

Corporation—a legal form of organization often adopted by businesses; a business which is owned by many stockholders and frequently directed by hired managers.

Cost—the sacrifice made or the resources given up to acquire some desired thing; the basis of valuation of the bulk of the assets of a business.

Dividends—the means by which stockholders share in the earnings of a corporation.

Duality—the assumption by the accountant that every transaction has a dual or two-sided effect upon the party or parties engaging in it.

Earnings statement—a formal array or summary of the revenues and expenses of an organization for a specified period of time.

Entity—a unit that is deemed to have an existence separate and apart from its owners, creditors, employees, and other interested parties and for which an accounting is undertaken.

Equities—broadly speaking, all claims to or interests in assets.

Expenses—the sacrifice made, usually measured in terms of the cost of the assets surrendered or consumed, to generate revenues.

Liabilities—debts or obligations that usually possess a known or determinable amount, maturity date, and party to whom payment is to be made.

Money measurement—expression of a property of an object in terms of a number of units of a standard monetary medium, such as the dollar.

Net earnings—the amount by which the revenues of a period exceed the expenses of the same period.

Net loss—the amount by which the expenses of a period exceed the revenues of the same period.

Notes payable—a written promise to pay to another party a definite sum of money at a certain or determinable date, usually with interest at a specified rate.

Periodicity—the assumption that the life of an entity can be divided into periods of time and that useful information can be provided as to the activities of the entity for those periods.

Retained earnings—accumulated net earnings less dividend distributions to stockholders.

Revenues—the flow of goods or services from an enterprise to its customers, usually measured by the flow of assets received.

Statement of financial position—a formal statement or array of the assets, liabilities, and owners' equity of an entity as of a specific date; often called a balance sheet.

Statement of retained earnings—a formal statement showing the items causing changes in retained earnings during a stated period of time.

Transaction—recordable happenings or events (usually exchanges) that affect the assets, liabilities, owners' equity, revenues, or expenses of an entity.

Student review quiz *chapter* 1

To develop a permanent record of your responses, you may write them on the answer sheet provided in the *Work Papers* or on a separate sheet of paper.

1 If a company has stockholders' equity of $8,900—

a) A total of $8,900 in capital stock was issued by the company.
b) The business has total assets of $8,900.
c) Net earnings for the year were $8,900.
d) Revenue less expenses equals $8,900.
e) Total business assets less total liabilities equal $8,900.

2 Company Z has assets of $35,000, no liabilities, and stockholders' equity of $35,000. It buys delivery equipment on credit for $4,000. What effect would this transaction have on these amounts?

a) Both assets and stockholders' equity decrease $4,000.
b) Assets stay the same and stockholders' equity increases $4,000.
c) Both assets and liabilities increase $4,000.
d) Stockholders' equity decreases $4,000 and liabilities increase $4,000.
e) Both assets and stockholders' equity increase $4,000.

3 Revenue is:

a) The flow of products or services provided to customers.
b) Cash received from customers.
c) The difference between the selling price of a product or service and the cost of providing such product or service.
d) A decrease in stockholders' equity.
e) The same as net earnings.

4 The Acme Furniture Company recorded on the last day of the month the $400 of advertising which appeared in the local paper during the month. This advertising was contracted for on an annual basis, with payment required for each month's advertising by the 10th of the following month. Which statement describes the effect of this entry?
a) Both assets and liabilities increased by $400.
b) Liabilities increased by $400 and stockholders' equity decreased by $400.
c) Liabilities decreased by $400 and stockholders' equity increased by $400.
d) Liabilities decreased by $400 and assets increased by $400.
e) None of the above.

5 Company J collected $800 of its $1,000 of accounts receivable. How is the statement of financial position affected?
a) Total assets are decreased but liabilities and stockholders' equity remain the same.
b) Cash increases $800 and stockholders' equity increases $800 because revenue was received.
c) There is no change in total assets, liabilities, or stockholders' equity.
d) Accounts receivable are decreased $800, and stockholders' equity is decreased $800.
e) There is no change in any of the statement of financial position items.

6 Which of the following statements is *incorrect?*
a) The earnings statement summarizes revenue and expense transactions for a period of operation between two statement of financial position dates.
b) The heading of the earnings statement should clearly indicate the period of operation which the statement covers.
c) The earnings statement shows as a final item the net earnings or net loss for the period.
d) An earnings statement shows how much of the net earnings or net loss was derived from operations and how much was derived from other sources.
e) The earnings statement shows the changes in assets and liabilities which occurred during the period of operation covered by the statement.

7 Given two statements of financial position of the A Company dated December 31, 1975, and December 31, 1976, the retained earnings on the statement dated December 31, 1976—
a) Shows the amount of 1976 net earnings less dividends declared.
b) Includes the net earnings or net loss for 1976.
c) Is equal to the net earnings for 1976.
d) Shows the change in total assets in 1976.
e) Does none of the above.

8 Which of the following appear on more than one of the three financial statements (statement of financial position, earnings statement, and statement of retained earnings)?
a) Cash.
b) Net earnings.
c) Notes payable.
d) Retained earnings.
e) All of the above.
f) Only **(b)** and **(d)**.

9 With which of the following is accounting not likely to be concerned?
a) Long-range financial planning.
b) Cost studies of managerial effectiveness.
c) Executive recruitment.
d) Design of management information systems.
e) Income tax planning.

10 Which of the following is generally the sole province of the CPA?
a) Preparation of income tax returns.
b) Providing management advisory services.
c) Attesting to the fairness of published financial information.
d) Auditing.
e) Preparation of budgets.

11 Generally, the decision-making process involves all of the following except—
a) Determination of alternative courses of action.
b) Prediction of the consequence of each alternative course of action.
c) Selection of preferred consequence.

d) Reporting on actual outcome of the decision.
e) Recognition or formulation of the problem.

12 Assets are (choose the best answer)—
a) Things of value owned.
b) Economic resources owned.
c) Desired because of the future benefits they are expected to yield.
d) Generally recorded and reported at cost.
e) All of the above.

13 As contrasted with financial accounting information, management accounting information is—
a) Accumulated only if it is believed to be worth more than it costs.
b) Forward-looking rather than historical in nature.
c) Used internally rather than released to outsiders.
d) Likely to be related to a part rather than the whole of an entity.
e) All of the above.

14 Financial accounting information is likely to be used for all of the following types of decisions except—
a) Deciding whether to add a new product line.
b) Deciding whether dividends should be increased.
c) Deciding whether an entity should be allowed to purchase goods on a credit basis.
d) Appraising the ability of an entity to pay its debts when they mature.
e) Determining whether the net earnings for the last year were satisfactory.

Now compare your answers with the correct answers and explanations on page 705.

Questions *chapter* 1

1 What is accounting? What are the functions carried out in accounting?
2 What are some of the goals or objectives sought by a business? Is it possible that some of these goals are conflicting? Explain.
3 What is information? Can you distinguish information from facts?
4 What is the accounting equation? Can it take on several forms? If so, which form is most meaningful to you?
5 Define an asset. Would the payment of rent for the month of April on March 31 give rise to an asset or expense? Explain.
6 Assets are initially recorded and subsequently reported in the statement of financial position at their acquisition cost. Would not reporting them at their *current* worth or value provide more useful information?
7 What information is reported in an earnings statement?
8 What information is reported in a statement of financial position? Is this a more important statement than the earnings statement? Explain.
9 Contrast financial accounting with managerial accounting.
10 What is a CPA? What services is he likely to offer?
11 How might it be argued that the statement of financial position is deficient in reporting the actual financial position of an entity?
12 Contrast decisions that might be made internally by a firm with those that might be made externally.
13 Distinguish between the Capital Stock account and the Retained Earnings account. Is there any reason why these two accounts should not be combined?
14 What is meant by the duality assumption or concept in accounting? What are some other basic assumptions in accounting and what does each mean?
15 Although primary attention was paid to business enterprises in this chapter, would you expect the major financial statements of a not-for-profit entity, such as a city, to differ sharply from those of a business enterprise? Explain.

Exercises *chapter* 1

1 If retained earnings increased by $12,000 from December 31, 1975, to December 31, 1976; expenses amounted to $4,500; and $1,000 of dividends were declared and paid: determine the amount of revenue and net earnings for 1976.
2 On December 31, 1975, Company X had assets of $180,000, liabilities of $130,000, and capital stock of $40,000.

During 1976 it earned revenues of $60,000 and incurred expenses of $45,000. Dividends of $4,000 were declared and paid. Prepare the statement of retained earnings for the year 1976.

3 Determine which statement or statements (choose **I, II,** or **III** below) would contain each of the following:

a) Cash.
b) Retained earnings (beginning of period).
c) Retained earnings (end of period).
d) Rent expense.
e) Next month's rent, which has already been paid.
f) Revenue from delivery service.
g) Net earnings.

I Earnings statement.
II Statement of retained earnings.
III Statement of financial position.

4 From the list of happenings presented below, determine whether each is a recordable transaction. Then present an analysis of the transaction showing clearly its two sides or dual nature.

a) Owners of the corporation invested $20,000 of cash.
b) Purchased a truck for $5,000, payment to be made by the 10th of next month.
c) Employed Bill Jones as a salesman at $1,000 per month. He is to start work next week.
d) Paid $100 cash for utility services already consumed.
e) Paid for the truck in **(b)** above.

5 At the beginning of a year a company had liabilities of $18,000 and capital stock of $50,000. At the end of the year retained earnings amounted to $50,000. Net earnings for the year were $15,000, and $5,000 of dividends were declared and paid. How much were retained earnings and total assets at the beginning of the year?

6 Which of the following items would be reported as assets? For each asset reported, indicate the dollar amount that would be attached to it.

a) A tract of land purchased 30 years ago for $10,000 for which the company has received an offer of $50,000.
b) A building recently erected at an agreed-upon contract price of $100,000. The contractor's bill will be paid next month.
c) An agreement signed with a local bank in which the bank agrees that it will loan the company up to $200,000 any time within the next year.

7 Which of the following transactions would be viewed by the accountant as requiring the recording of an expense?

a) Cash paid to employees for services received during the month.
b) Cash paid to a supplier in settlement of a previously given promise to pay when some advertising supplies were purchased.
c) Cash paid to acquire a new truck to be used in a delivery service business.
d) Cash paid for some supplies received and already consumed or used up.

Problems, Series A *chapter* 1

1–1–A

Harwell, Inc., completes the following transactions.

Required: Show the effect of each transaction on the accounting equation of Assets = Liabilities + Stockholders' Equity. Prepare columns as shown below and enter the transactions in the proper columns.

Transactions:

July	1	The company is organized and receives its initial cash of $40,000 from issuing capital stock to the owners.
	5	The company borrows $20,000 from its bank, giving a note.
	7	The company buys $6,000 of delivery equipment from Madsen Motors on open account and agrees to pay for it within two weeks.
	11	The company pays $6,000 cash to Madsen Motors on the debt of July 7.
	17	The company receives $2,400 cash for services it performed to date.
	24	The company pays $1,600 for employee services used in making deliveries to date.

Form for answer:

	ASSETS	=	LIABILITIES	+	STOCKHOLDERS' EQUITY
July 1	$40,000	=			$40,000
5	20,000	=	$20,000		

1–2–A

Required: Show the effect of each of the following transactions on the accounting equation of the Devillo Company. Enter each transaction in the proper columns and show the balance of the equation after each transaction. Use the same form as in Problem 1–1–A above but set up columns for each of the following:

Date	Equipment
Explanation	Notes payable
Cash	Capital stock
Accounts receivable	Retained earnings

Transactions:

May	1	The owners organize the corporation with initial cash of $80,000 received from the issuance of capital stock.
	2	The company borrows $8,000 cash from the bank on a note.
	7	The company buys $45,600 of equipment for cash.
	11	Cash received for services performed to date is $3,800.
	14	Services performed for customers who agree to pay within a month are $2,500.
	15	Employee services received in operating the business to date are paid in cash, $3,300.
	19	The company pays $3,500 on the note to the bank.
	31	Interest paid to the bank for May is $35.
	31	Customers of May 14 pay $800 of the amount they owe the company.

31 An order is received from a customer for services to be rendered next week which will be billed at $2,000.

1–3–A

The Thorsten Company completes the following transactions. Show the effect of each transaction on the accounting equation. In a form similar to that used in Problem 1–1–A, set up columns with the following headings:

Date	Equipment
Explanation	Accounts payable
Cash	Capital stock
Accounts receivable	Retained earnings

Required: (1) Enter each transaction in the proper columns and show the balance of the equation after each transaction. (2) Prepare a statement of financial position as of April 30 of the current year.

Transactions:

Apr. 1 The company is organized and receives $20,000 cash from the owners in exchange for capital stock issued.
4 The company buys equipment for cash, $10,600.
9 The company buys additional equipment which costs $950 and agrees to pay for it in 30 days.
15 Cash received for services performed to date is $400.
16 Amounts due from customers for services performed total $550.
30 Of the receivables (see April 16), $320 are collected in cash.
30 Various costs of operating the business during the month of $650 are paid in cash.
30 An order is placed for equipment advertised at $3,000.

1–4–A

The Crestview Drive-In operates an outdoor movie theatre.

Required: Prepare an earnings statement for the month of August, 1976.

Transactions:

Aug. 2 Paid current month's rent for premises, $4,000.
7 Cash received for admissions during the week, $2,400.
14 Cash received for admissions during the week, $2,800.
15 Paid semimonthly payroll, $3,200.
21 Received cash of $1,600 for admissions during week.
23 Sundry expenses paid in cash are $700.
27 Advertising for month is $1,900.
31 Paid semimonthly payroll, $3,400.
31 Paid film rental, $5,000.
31 Received $6,200 cash revenue from operators of popcorn and other concessions for right to operate during August.
31 Cash received for admissions from August 22–31 inclusive, $4,200.
31 Paid a cash deposit of $750 to guarantee receipt of a special film to be shown in September.

1–5–A

Analysis of the transactions of the Maulin Drive-In Theatre for the month of June 1976, discloses the following:

Ticket revenue	$24,600
Rent of premises and equipment	5,000
Film rental paid	8,900
Receipts from concessionaires (percentage basis)	5,000
Advertising expense	3,100
Wages and salaries	7,800
Utilities expense	1,350

Statement of financial position figures at June 30 include the following:

Cash	$40,000
Franchise to show movies in area	8,000
Accounts payable	10,400
Capital stock	19,000
Retained earnings, June 1, 1976	15,150

Required:

a) Prepare an earnings statement for the month of June, 1976.
b) Prepare a statement of retained earnings for the month of June, 1976.
c) Prepare a statement of financial position at June 30, 1976.

1–6–A

MASTER SERVICE COMPANY
Statement of Financial Position
April 30, 1976

ASSETS			LIABILITIES AND STOCKHOLDERS' EQUITY		
Current Assets:			Current Liabilities:		
Cash	$12,000		Accounts payable		$ 14,000
Accounts receivable	20,000	$ 32,000	Stockholders' Equity:		
Land		150,000	Capital stock	$100,000	
			Retained earnings	68,000	168,000
Total Assets		$182,000	Total Liabilities and Stockholders' Equity		$182,000

Summarize, the activities for the month of May, 1976 are as follows:

a) Issued additional capital stock for cash, $30,000.
b) Collected $20,000 on accounts receivable.
c) Paid $14,000 on accounts payable.
d) Sold land costing $50,000 for $75,000.
e) Services rendered to customers: for cash, $40,000; on account, $30,000.
f) Employee services and other operating costs incurred: for cash, $15,000; on account, $40,000.
g) Paid dividends of $4,000.
h) Paid building rent for year beginning on June 1, 1976, $24,000.
i) Placed an order for new equipment expected to cost $80,000.

Required:

a) Prepare an earnings statement for the month of May, 1976.
b) Prepare a statement of retained earnings for the month of May, 1976.
c) Prepare a statement of financial position as of May 31, 1976.

(Hint: You may find it desirable to prepare, at least in rough form, a table such as that suggested in Problem 1–2–A.)

1–7–A

Given below are the statements of financial position and the earnings statement of the Heston Company:

HESTON COMPANY
Statement of Financial Position

	April 30, 1976	*May 31, 1976*
Assets:		
Current Assets:		
Cash	$ 8,000	$ 7,000
Accounts receivable	12,000	15,000
Prepaid rent	3,000	2,000
Total Assets	$23,000	$24,000
Liabilities and Stockholders' Equity:		
Liabilities	$ 6,000	$ 3,000
Capital stock	15,000	15,000
Retained earnings	2,000	6,000
Total Liabilities and Stockholders' Equity	$23,000	$24,000

HESTON COMPANY
Earnings Statement
For the Month Ended May 31, 1976

Revenues from services rendered		$15,000
Expenses:		
Salaries and wages	$10,000	
Rent	1,000	11,000
Net Earnings for May		$ 4,000

Required: Assume that all revenues earned are on account and state the probable causes of the changes in each of the statement of financial position accounts from April 30, 1976, to May 31, 1976.

Problems, Series B *chapter* 1

1–1–B

Sanitation Engineers, Inc., is organized and completes the following transactions in its first month of operations. Set up one column each for assets, liabilities, and stockholders' equity, as illustrated in Problem 1–1–A.

Required: Compute the balance of the items in the equation after each transaction.

Transactions:

a) The company issues 6,000 shares of its capital stock for $60,000 cash.
b) An additional 1,000 shares of capital stock are issued for a truck valued at $10,000.
c) The company borrows $18,000 from a local bank on a note.
d) Equipment is purchased for $30,000. Payment is to be made later.
e) Employee services and other operating costs for the month of $7,400 are paid.
f) Cash of $10,400 is received from customers for services rendered.
g) Cash of $20,000 is paid on the equipment purchase debt.

1–2–B

The Jackson Company completes the following transactions.

Required: Show the effect of each transaction on the accounting equation using the following column headings:

Date	Equipment
Explanation	Accounts payable
Cash	Capital stock
Accounts receivable	Retained earnings

Enter each transaction in the proper columns and show the balance of the equation after each transaction.

Transactions:

Sept. 1 The company is organized and receives $30,000 cash from the issuance of capital stock.
5 The company buys equipment for cash at a cost of $5,400.
7 The company performs services for customers who agree to pay $2,000 in one week.
14 The company receives the $2,000 from the transaction of September 7.
20 Equipment which costs $800 is acquired today; payment is postponed until September 28.
28 $600 is paid on the liability incurred on September 20.
30 Employee services for the month, $700, are paid.
30 Placed an order for new equipment advertised at $5,000.

1–3–B

The Canton Company completes the following transactions.

Transactions:

June 1 The company is organized and receives $70,000 cash from the issuance of capital stock.
4 The company pays $32,000 cash for equipment.
7 The company borrows $6,000 cash from its bank on a note.
9 Cash received for services performed to date is $3,000.
12 Costs of operating the business so far this month are paid in cash, $2,100.
18 Services performed for customers who agree to pay within a month amount to $3,600.
25 The company repays $2,700 of its loan from the bank.

30 Costs of operating the business from June 13 to date are $2,550 and are paid in cash.
30 An order is received from a customer for services to be performed tomorrow, which will be billed at $2,000.

Required:

a) Show the effect of each transaction on the accounting equation. Set up columns for the items using the following headings:

Date	Equipment
Explanation	Notes payable
Cash	Capital stock
Accounts receivable	Retained earnings

Enter each transaction in the proper columns and show the balance of the equation after each transaction.

b) Prepare a statement of financial position as of June 30 of the current year.

1–4–B

Required: From the following transactions for Baker, Inc., prepare an earnings statement for the month of May, 1976.

Transactions:

May 1 Paid current month's rent for premises, $5,000.
8 Cash received for eight days' parking service, $2,420.
15 Cash received for week's parking service, $3,020.
16 Paid wages for two weeks, $1,200.
19 Paid advertising expenses of $400.
22 Cash received for week's parking service, $3,960.
31 Cash received for nine days' parking service, $3,520.
31 Paid wages for last half of May, $1,500.
31 Purchased a mechanized sweeper for $3,000 cash.
31 Purchased supplies for cash, $400.

1–5–B

Required: From the following data for the Arnold Corporation, prepare an earnings statement for the year ended June 30, 1976.

Rent revenue from building owned	$300,000
Interest revenue from bonds owned	36,000
Dividend revenue from stocks owned	28,000
Interest revenue from bank savings accounts	1,800
Building repairs	8,200
Building cleaning, labor cost	9,100
Property taxes on the building	10,300
Insurance on the building	3,500
Commissions paid to rental agent	15,000
Legal fees (for preparation of tenant leases)	3,600
Heating	8,400
Electricity	15,100
Cleaning supplies on hand	3,000

1–6–B

The following data relate to the Auto Home Corporation. At October 1, 1976, the statement of financial position of the company is as follows:

Cash	$58,000	Accounts payable	$ 8,000
Accounts receivable	6,000	Capital stock	44,000
		Retained earnings	12,000
	$64,000		$64,000

Transactions:

Oct. 3 The company pays the accounts payable in the statement of financial position, $8,000.

7 The company receives cash of $1,400 for parking by daily customers during the week.

10 The company collects $4,800 of the accounts receivable in the statement of financial position at October 1.

14 Cash receipts for the week from daily customers are $2,200.

15 The company sets up a receivable of $1,000 as the amount due from Boyer Company for the right to park its fleet of cars during the remainder of October. The receivable is due November 10.

16 The company pays wages of $800 for the period October 1–15.

19 The company pays advertising expenses of $400 for October.

21 Cash receipts for the week from daily customers are $2,400.

24 The company incurred sundry expenses of $280 which will be due November 10.

31 Cash receipts for the last 10 days of the month from daily customers are $2,800.

31 The company pays wages of $1,000 for the period October 16–31.

31 Billings to monthly customers total $7,200 for October, exclusive of the Boyer Company.

31 The company pays rent for the premises for October, $6,400.

Required:

a) Show the effect of each transaction on the accounting equation, using the same format as in Problem 1–1–A except that the accounts to be used are those in the statement of financial position above (for October 1).

b) Prepare an earnings statement for the month of October, 1976.

c) Prepare a statement of retained earnings for the month ended October 31, 1976.

d) Prepare a statement of financial position at October 31, 1976.

1–7–B

Given below are the statements of financial position and the earnings statement of the Dollar Company:

DOLLAR COMPANY
Statement of Financial Position

	May 31, 1976	*June 30, 1976*
Assets:		
Current Assets:		
Cash	$5,000	$6,000
Accounts receivable	—0—	2,000
Supplies	3,000	1,000
Total Assets	$8,000	$9,000
Liabilities and Stockholders' Equity:		
Liabilities	$2,000	$1,000
Capital stock	5,000	5,000
Retained earnings	1,000	3,000
Total Liabilities and Stockholders' Equity	$8,000	$9,000

DOLLAR COMPANY
Earnings Statement
For the Month Ended June 30, 1976

Revenue from services rendered		$8,000
Expenses:		
Salaries	$4,000	
Supplies used	2,000	6,000
Net Earnings for June		$2,000

Required: From the information given, state the probable causes of the changes in each of the statement of financial position accounts from May 31 to June 30, 1976.

The recording process

Learning objectives

To achieve a working knowledge of the basic design of an accounting system and of the steps taken in accumulating accounting information, this chapter introduces:

1. The account as the basic classificational category and storage unit for information in the accounting system.
2. The technical accounting terms of debit and credit and how the effects of business transactions must first be expressed in these terms before they can be entered into the accounting system.
3. The journal as the original record in which the effects of a business transaction are recorded in the accounting system.
4. The process of journalizing a transaction and then posting the journal entries to the accounts in the accounting system.
5. The use of a trial balance as a partial means of testing the accuracy of the operation of the accounting system.
6. The adjustments required to bring the accounts up to date prior to the preparation of financial statements.

Frame 1[2]

In Chapter 1 the effects of business transactions were depicted as increases or decreases in the elements in the basic accounting equation. This approach was adopted solely as a means of affording easy understanding of some basic relationships. It is far too cumbersome to be used in actual practice, since even a small business enters into a huge number of transactions every week, month, or year.

The purpose of this chapter is to introduce the basic components of the accounting system—the ledger (book) of accounts and the journal—and to illustrate their use in the information-gathering process. Here again the expectation is that knowledge of the underlying process will yield greater understanding of the end products—the financial statements.

The accounting system

The account

Because, as already noted, a relatively small business may engage in thousands of transactions, the data in these transactions must be classified and summarized before they constitute useful information. Making the accountant's task somewhat easier is the fact that most business transactions are somewhat repetitive in nature and can accordingly be classified into groups possessing common characteristics. For example, there may be thousands of transactions involving receipts or payments of cash. As a result, a part of every transaction affecting cash will be recorded and summarized in a device called an account. An account will be established whenever the data to be recorded in it are believed to constitute useful information to some party having a valid interest in the activities of the business. Thus, every business will have a cash account in its accounting system simply because knowledge of the amount of cash owned is likely to be useful information.

An account may take on a variety of forms, from a printed format in which entries are written by hand to an invisible encoding on a piece of magnetic tape. Although exact form is not important, several types will be illustrated later. What is required is that an account readily accept money measurements representing increases or decreases in the item for which it was established while at the same time allowing the difference between the increases and decreases—the balance of the account, as it is called—to be readily determined.

The number of accounts in a given accounting system will depend largely upon the information needs of those interested in the business. The primary requirement is that the account provide useful information. Thus, one account may be established for cash—the company's immediate spending power—rather than separate accounts for cash in the form of coins, cash in the form of currency, and cash in the form of deposits in banks, simply because the amount of cash is useful information while the form of cash is not.

A definite trend exists, especially in computer-based accounting systems, toward establishing ever larger numbers of accounts. The primary reason for this is that it is far easier to sum the balances in a number of accounts into a useful total than it is to subdivide (or disaggregate) a large balance, once it has been recorded, into smaller bits of useful information. In fact, it may be impossible to disaggregate a balance without analyzing again every item affecting it.

Indicate whether each of the following statements is true or false. (You may wish to respond on the answer sheet provided in the *Work Papers* or on a separate sheet of paper so that you will have a permanent record of your responses.)

1. An account is a means of classifying the effects of transactions upon an entity.
2. The number of accounts established in the accounting systems of different entities is likely to differ.
3. In constructing an accounting system the guiding principle should be: the fewer the accounts, the better.
4. In a large corporation, the accounting system is likely to contain more accounts than are reported in its financial statements.

Check your response in Answer Frame 1^2 on page 44.

Frame 2^2

The T account

The way an account functions is demonstrated by use of a T account. It is used in this text for illustrative purposes only (it is not a replica of a form of account actually used) and derives its name from its resemblance to the letter T. The name of the item accounted for (such as cash) is written across the top of the T, and increases are recorded on one side and decreases on the other side of the vertical line of the T.

Recording changes in assets and equities. By convention, increases in assets are recorded on the left side of the account, decreases on the right side. For reasons to be explained later, the process is reversed for equity in the form of capital stock which is recorded on the right side. Thus, a corporation would record the receipt of $10,000 for shares of its capital stock as follows (the figure in parentheses is used to tie the two sides of the transaction together):

Cash				*Capital Stock*	
(1)	10,000			(1)	10,000

The transaction involves an increase in the asset cash which is recorded on the left side of the Cash account, and an increase in stockholders'

Answer frame 1²

1. True. An account is a classificational category and a place for storing the classified effects of transactions upon an entity.
2. True. The accounting system for a giant manufacturing corporation is certain to contain a different number of accounts from the accounting system of the corner drug store, because they differ not only in size but also in the nature of their activities.
3. False. The guiding principle should be to include as many accounts as are necessary to provide users with relevant information about the activities of the entity. This does not mean that an accounting system might not be overloaded with useless accounts and become too costly to operate considering the information obtained.
4. True. Although not covered specifically, it is possible that the reader has seen an earnings statement of a corporation with worldwide activities that contains only 8 or 10 items.

If you missed any of the above questions, read Frame 1² again before proceeding to Frame 2² on page 43.

2² *continued* equity in the form of capital stock which is recorded on the right side of the Capital Stock account.

Because liabilities are a subset of equities, changes in them are recorded in the same manner as for equities—increases on the right side, decreases on the left. Note the consistency between the placement of amounts for assets and equities in the accounts and their presentation in the statement of financial position. Asset amounts are shown on the left side of the account and the left side of the statement of financial position; equity (liabilities and stockholders' equity) amounts are shown on the right side of the account and the right side of the statement of financial position. But for easy recollection of these rules, all that one need remember is that increases in assets are recorded on the left side of the account. Increases in equities are recorded in the opposite manner as for assets and, for any account, decreases are the opposite of increases.

Indicate whether each of the following is a correct or incorrect recording of the transaction described.

1. The purchase of equipment for cash would involve an entry on the left side of the Equipment account and on the right side of the Cash account.
2. The payment of a liability established to record the purchase of a new truck would involve an entry on the right side of the Cash account and the left side of the Automotive Equipment account.
3. The borrowing of money by giving a note would involve an entry on the left side of the Cash account and the right side of the Notes Payable account.
4. The payment of an amount owed a vendor would involve an entry on the right side of the Cash account and on the left side of the Accounts Payable account.

Check your responses in Answer Frame 2² on page 46.

Frame 3[2]

Recording changes in expenses and revenues. To understand the logic behind the recording of changes in expense and revenue accounts it is necessary first to recall that all expenses and revenues could be recorded directly in Retained Earnings. Thus, the recording of (2) the receipt of $1,000 of cash from customers for services rendered and (3) the payment of $600 of cash to employees as wages could be recorded as follows:

Cash			
(2)	1,000	(3)	600

Retained Earnings			
(3)	600	(2)	1,000

But since their dollar amounts are likely to be significant information, separate accounts are maintained for the various types of revenues and expenses. The recording rules for these are:

1. Since revenues increase stockholders' equity (and increases in stockholders' equity are recorded on the right side), it follows that increases in revenues should be recorded on the right side, decreases on the left.
2. Similarly, since expenses decrease stockholders' equity (and decreases in stockholders' equity are recorded on the left side), it follows that increases in expenses are recorded on the left, decreases on the right.

Following these rules, the service revenue and the wages mentioned above would be recorded in the following manner:

Cash			
(2)	1,000	(3)	600

Service Revenue			
		(2)	1,000

Wages Expense			
(3)	600		

Debits and credits. Before presenting a graphic summarization of the recording rules discussed above, the technical accounting terms of debit and credit must be introduced. The accountant uses the term debit in lieu of saying "place an entry on the left side of an account" and credit for "place an entry on the right side of an account." While the terms debit (abbreviated Dr.) and credit (abbreviated Cr.) did have special meanings in their Latin origins, these have long been lost and no special significance should be attached to the terms. Debit means simply left side; credit, right side.

Note that since assets and expenses are increased by debits, these accounts normally have debit (or left side) balances. Conversely, liability, stockholders' equity, and revenue accounts are increased by credits and normally have credit (or right side) balances.

Answer frame 2^2

1. Correct. The equipment is an asset and increases in assets are recorded on the left side of an asset account. Cash was given up and decreases in the asset cash are recorded on the right side of the Cash account.
2. Incorrect. The entry on the right side of the Cash account is correct, but an entry must be made in the left side of the liability account Accounts Payable to record the reduction in the liability brought about by the cash payment. This liability was previously increased when the purchase of the truck on a credit basis was entered.
3. Correct. This is the way such a transaction would be recorded.
4. Correct. This is the way such a transaction would be recorded and is the way the transaction described in 2 above should be recorded.

If you missed any of the above questions, you should read Frame 2^2 again before continuing in Frame 3^2 on page 45.

3^2 here
continued

The balance of any account is obtained by summing the debits to the account, summing the credits to the account, and subtracting the smaller sum from the larger. If the sum of the debits exceeds the sum of the credits, the account has a debit balance. For example, the Cash account has a debit balance of $4,000, computed as total debits of $14,000 less total credits of $10,000, in the following T account:

Cash

(1)	5,000	(2)	2,000
(3)	9,000	(4)	8,000

Similarly, the Accounts Payable account has a credit balance of $3,000:

Accounts Payable

(7)	10,000	(5)	7,000
		(6)	6,000

For the most part, the amounts entered into the various accounts are found in the transactions entered into by the business. Business transactions are first analyzed to determine the effects (increase or decrease) that they have upon the assets, liabilities, stockholders' equity, revenues, or expenses of the business. Then these increases or decreases are encoded into the special accounting terminology of debit and credit. For example, an increase in an asset is recorded as a debit in the proper asset account. When an asset account is debited, depending upon the transaction, there may be any of five credits:

1. Another asset account may be credited, that is, decreased.
2. A liability account may be credited, that is, increased.

3. A stockholders' equity account may be credited, that is, increased.
4. A revenue account may be credited, that is, increased.
5. An expense account may be credited, that is, decreased.

This double-entry procedure maintains the accounting equation in balance. The possibilities in every transaction can be analyzed similarly into debits and credits.

The rules of debit and credit may be presented in account form as follows:

Debits	*Credits*
1. Increase assets.	1. Decrease assets.
2. Decrease liabilities.	2. Increase liabilities.
3. Decrease stockholders' equity.	3. Increase stockholders' equity.
4. Decrease revenues.	4. Increase revenues.
5. Increase expenses.	5. Decrease expenses.

These rules may also be summarized graphically as shown below. Note especially the treatment of expense accounts as if they were merely subsets of the debit side of the Retained Earnings account. And remember that increases in expenses do tend to reduce what would otherwise be a larger growth in Retained Earnings; and if expenses are reduced, Retained Earnings will increase. The exact reverse holds true for revenues.

ASSETS = LIABILITIES + STOCKHOLDERS' EQUITY

An Asset Account

Debit	Credit
+ Increases	− Decreases

A Liability Account

Debit	Credit
− Decreases	+ Increases

A Stockholders' Equity Account

Debit	Credit
− Decreases	+ Increases

Expense Accounts

Debit	Credit
+ Increases	− Decreases

Revenue Accounts

Debit	Credit
− Decreases	+ Increases

Indicate whether each of the following could be a correct or incorrect analysis of a transaction.

1. Plus asset, plus expense.
2. Minus asset, minus liability.
3. Plus expense, plus liability.
4. Plus asset, minus asset.

Check your response in Answer Frame 3^2 on page 48.

Answer frame 3²

1. Incorrect. When analyzed in terms of debit and credit, this statement yields debit asset, debit expense, which is obviously incorrect since there is no credit in the analysis.
2. Correct. A transaction of this type would be the cash payment of a debt, which in debit-credit terminology would be debit liability, credit asset.
3. Correct. A transaction of this would be the receipt of a bill or invoice for advertising services already received. This would call for a debit (increase) in an expense account and a credit (increase) in a liability account.
4. Correct. Any of a wide variety of cash purchases of assets would yield this type of analysis. Such transactions would call for a debit (increase) in one asset account and a credit (decrease) in another—cash.

If you missed any of the above questions, you should read Frame 3² again before proceeding to Frame 4² below.

Frame 4²

The ledger

The accounts in an accounting system customarily are classified into two general groups: (1) the statement of financial position accounts (assets, liabilities, and stockholders' equity) and (2) the earnings statement accounts (revenues and expenses). Whether maintained in a bound volume, handwritten in loose-leaf form, or magnetically encoded on plastic tape and visible only as a computer printout, the accounts in an accounting system are collectively referred to as the ledger.

The list of the names of the accounts in an accounting system is known as the *chart of accounts*. Each account typically has an identification number as well as a name. For example, assets might be numbered from 100-199, liabilities from 200-299, stockholders' equity from 300-399, revenues from 400-499, and expenses from 500-599. The accounts would then, of course, be arranged in numerical sequence in the ledger. The use of numbers and a numerical arrangement of the accounts helps to identify and locate accounts when undertaking the recording process.

Having completed this generalized introduction to accounts and the recording process, attention is now directed to the journal and to journal entries, as the means whereby data are formally entered into an accounting system.

The journal

Every business transaction, under double-entry accounting, is analyzed as having a dual effect upon the entities engaging in it. And with the rare exception of transactions such as an exchange of land for land, almost every recorded business transaction will affect at least two ledger accounts. Since each ledger account shows only the increases and decreases in the item for which it was established, the entire effects of a single business transaction normally will not appear in any one account. For example, the Cash account contains only information with respect to changes in cash and does not show the exact accounts credited for sources of cash or the exact accounts debited for cash disbursements.

Therefore, if transactions are recorded directly in the accounts, it is quite difficult to ascertain the entire effects of any transaction upon an entity by looking at the accounts. To remedy this deficiency, the accountant employs a book or a record known as a journal. A journal contains a chronological record of the transactions of a business. Because each transaction is initially recorded in a journal, a journal is often called a book of *original entry*. Here every business transaction is analyzed for its effects upon the entity and these effects are expressed in terms of debit and credit—the inputs of the accounting system.

Illustration 2.1

GENERAL JOURNAL — *Page 1*

Date		Accounts and Explanation	L.F.	Debit	Credit
1976					
Jan.	1	Cash..................	100	5,000	
		Capital Stock......	300		5,000
		Capital stock issued for cash.			
	5	Office Equipment.......	110	1,200	
		Accounts Payable..	201		1,200
		Equipment purchased for the office on account.			

The general journal. The simplest form of journal, the general journal, is illustrated and discussed in this chapter, while other forms or types of journals are discussed in Chapter 5. As shown in Illustration 2.1, a general journal contains columns for:

1. The date.
2. The name of the account to be debited and the name of the account to be credited, shown on the following line and indented to the right. (Any necessary explanation of a transaction appears below the transaction, indented halfway between the debit and credit entry.)
3. The ledger folio (L.F.) column; this will be explained in the section below headed "Cross-indexing."
4. The debit column, in which the money amount of the debit is placed on the same line as the name of the account debited.
5. The credit column, in which the money amount of the credit is placed on the same line as the name of the account credited.

A blank line should appear between transactions for purposes of easy identification.

Indicate whether each of the following statements is correct or incorrect.

1. Each entry in the journal gives the names of the accounts to be debited and credited, their dollar amounts, and an explanation of the transaction.
2. Since each transaction normally affects at least two accounts, one cannot generally perceive the effects of a transaction by looking only at one account.
3. The account to be credited is the first account named in a journal entry.
4. Because it contains a transaction-by-transaction record of the activities of an entity, a journal is very similar to a diary.

Check your response in Answer Frame 4[2] on page 52.

Frame 5[2]

Journalizing

Journalizing is the act of entering a transaction in a journal. Information on the transactions to be journalized originates on a variety of source materials or documents such as invoices, cash register tapes, timecards, and checks issued. The activity recorded on these documents must be carefully analyzed to determine whether a recordable transaction has occurred. If so, the specific accounts affected, the dollar amounts of the changes, and their direction (whether increases or decreases) must also be determined. Then all of these changes must be translated into terms of debit and credit. As previously noted, the importance of proper analysis of business transactions cannot be overemphasized.

Posting

In a sense, a journal entry is a set of instructions. It tells the accountant to enter a certain dollar amount as a debit in a specific account. It also tells him to enter a certain dollar amount as a credit in a specific account. The carrying out of these instructions is a process known as posting. In Illustration 2.2, the first entry directs that $10,000 be posted as a debit to the Cash account and as a credit to the Capital Stock account. The three-column balance type of accounts shown in that illustration for Cash and Capital Stock show that these instructions have been carried out. In other words, the entry has been posted.

Postings to the ledger accounts may be made (1) at the time the transaction is journalized; (2) at the end of the day, week, or month; or (3) as each journal page is filled.

Illustration 2.2

GENERAL JOURNAL *Page 1*

Date		Accounts and Explanation	L.F.	Debit	Credit
1976 May	1	Cash..................	100	10,000	
		Capital Stock......	300		10,000
		Cash invested in the business.			
	2	Rent Expense..........	410	500	
		Cash..............	100		500
		Rent for May 1976.			
	3	Equipment............	110	2,200	
		Accounts Payable..	201		2,200
		Tables and chairs, Diller Company.			

GENERAL LEDGER

Cash *Account No. 100*

Date		Explanation	Folio	Debit	Credit	Balance
1976 May	1		J 1	10,000		10,000
	2		J 1		500	9,500

Equipment *Account No. 110*

1976 May	3		J 1	2,200		2,200

Accounts Payable *Account No. 201*

1976 May	3	Diller Company	J 1		2,200	2,200

Capital Stock *Account No. 300*

1976 May	1		J 1		10,000	10,000

Rent Expense *Account No. 410*

1976 May	2		J 1	500		500

Answer frame 4²

1. Correct. Each entry does consist of the names of the accounts to be debited and credited, their dollar amounts, and an explanation of the transaction.
2. Correct. The entire effects of a single transaction are seldom observable in one account.
3. Incorrect. All accounts to be debited are listed first, followed by the accounts to be credited.
4. Correct. A journal and a diary are indeed quite similar.

If you missed any of the above, you should study Frame 4² again before continuing with Frame 5² on page 50.

Cross-indexing

5² *continued* The number of the ledger account to which the posting was made is placed in the ledger folio (L. F.) column of the journal. The number of the journal page *from* which the entry was posted is placed in the folio column of the ledger account. Posting is always from the journal to the ledger account. Cross-indexing is the placing of the account number in the journal and the placing of the journal page number in the account, as shown in Illustration 2.2.

Cross-indexing aids the tracing of any recorded transaction, either from the journal to the ledger or from the ledger to the journal. Cross-reference numbers usually are not placed in the L. F. column of the journal until the entry is posted; thereafter, the cross-reference numbers indicate that the entry has been posted.

By tracing the entries in the journal to the entries in the ledger, the reader will understand the posting and cross-indexing process. The ledger accounts need not contain explanations of all the entries, since they can be obtained from the journal. In spite of this, some accountants favor placing explanations in the ledger accounts. No harm results and the practice may be helpful, particularly if the transaction is one of a non-routine nature.

When a necessary explanation is placed in the journal, it should be complete enough to fully describe the transaction and informative enough to prove or disprove the entry's accuracy and validity, and at the same time be concise and pointed. If a journal entry is self-explanatory, the explanation may be omitted.

Compound journal entries

The analysis of a business transaction often shows that more than two accounts are directly affected. In such cases the journal entry involves more than one debit or more than one credit or both. A journal entry with more than one debit or credit is a compound journal entry. An entry with one debit and one credit is a simple journal entry.

As an illustration of a compound journal entry:

J. T. Stine purchases $8,000 of machinery from the Myers Company, paying $2,000 cash with the balance due on open account. The journal entry for Stine is as follows:

Machinery	8,000	
Cash		2,000
Accounts Payable, Myers Company		6,000
Machinery purchased from Myers Company, Invoice No. 42.		

On a separate piece of paper, write out the compound entry to journalize the following transaction: David Henton owes $5,000 on a note payable. He pays the note, together with interest of $150. Check your response in Answer Frame 5[2] on page 54.

Frame 6[2]

The functions and other advantages of using a journal are summarized below. The journal:

1. Sets forth the transactions of each day.
2. Records the transactions in chronological order.
3. Shows the analysis of each transaction in terms of debit and credit.
4. Supplies an explanation of each transaction when an explanation is necessary.
5. Serves as a source for future reference to accounting transactions.
6. Removes lengthy explanations from the accounts.
7. Makes possible posting to the ledger at convenient times.
8. Assists in maintaining the ledger in balance.
9. Aids in the tracing of errors.
10. Promotes the division of labor (for example, one person may enter the journal entries and another may post them).

Indicate whether each of the following statements is true or false.

1. All input into an accounting system must first pass through a journal.
2. The analysis of a transaction in terms of debit and credit is an extremely important step in the journalizing process.
3. It is conceivable that a journal entry to record a complex transaction could contain several debits and several credits.
4. The accounts used in journalizing transactions determine the accounts to be included in an accounting system.

Check your responses in Answer Frame 6[2] on page 54.

Frame 7[2]

The accounting system in operation

Presented below is a formal illustration of the type of accounting system that might be employed by a small merchandising company, the Paxton

Answer frame 5^2

The required entry is:

Notes Payable	5,000	
Interest Expense	150	
Cash		5,150
Paid note and interest.		

If you answered incorrectly, study Frame 5^2 again before continuing with Frame 6^2 on page 53.

Answer frame 6^2

1. True. All journals are books of original entry and all transactions must pass through a journal.
2. True. If the analysis is improper, the data in the accounts can hardly be correct. If the data in the accounts are not correct, it is quite unlikely that reliable financial statements can be prepared. Thus, proper financial reporting depends upon proper analysis of business transactions.
3. True. Not all business transactions can be properly and completely analyzed into a simple entry consisting of one debit and one credit.
4. False. Generally speaking, the informational needs of interested parties and users will determine the accounts to be included in an accounting system. On occasion a transaction may be encountered that cannot be properly recorded using only previously established accounts, and a new account may be opened. But the primary reason for opening the new account will be to provide useful information to users of the financial statements.

If you missed any of the above, study Frame 6^2 again before going on to Frame 7^2 on page 53.

7^2 *continued*

Company. The company's statement of financial position at December 31, 1975, is as follows:

PAXTON COMPANY
Statement of Financial Position
December 31, 1975

ASSETS		LIABILITIES AND STOCKHOLDERS' EQUITY	
Current Assets:		Current Liabilities:	
Cash	$10,000	Accounts payable	$ 2,000
Accounts receivable	4,500	Stockholders' Equity:	
Merchandise inventory	5,000	Capital stock	30,000
Total Current Assets	$19,500	Retained earnings	3,500
Property, Plant, and Equipment:		Total Stockholders' Equity	$33,500
Furniture and equipment	$ 6,000		
Salesroom fixtures	10,000		
Total Property, Plant, and Equipment	$16,000		
Total Assets	$35,500	Total Liabilities and Stockholders' Equity	$35,500

The statement of financial position reflects ledger account balances as of the close of business on December 31, 1975. These are, of course, the opening balances on January 1, 1976, and are shown as such in the illustrated ledger accounts.

The Paxton Company's chart of accounts is as follows:

Acct. No.	*Account Title*	*Acct. No.*	*Account Title*
1	Cash	30	Cost of Goods Sold
2	Accounts Receivable	32	Advertising Expenese
3	Commissions Receivable	33	Depreciation—Salesroom Fixtures
4	Merchandise Inventory	34	Sales Salaries
6	Furniture and Equipment	35	Salesroom Rent Expense
8	Salesroom Fixtures	36	Other Selling Expense
11	Accounts Payable	37	Office Rent Expense
15	Capital Stock	38	Administrative Salaries
16	Retained Earnings	39	Office Supplies Expense
20	Sales	40	Other Administrative Expense
21	Commissions Earned	41	Depreciation—Furniture and Equipment

Now assume that the following is a complete list (somewhat condensed) of the transactions entered into by the Paxton Company in January 1976:

Jan. 2 Paid January rent: office, $400; salesroom, $600.
3 Purchased additional office furniture for cash, $1,500.
4 Received an invoice from the Burk Agency, $200, for planning January's advertising.
4 Collected $3,000 on account.
6 Paid $2,000 on account.
6 Sales on account for the week, $3,200. Cost of the products delivered to customers, $2,400. (Paxton earns some of its revenue—Sales—by selling and delivering products to its customers. During the week it delivered to its customers products that cost $2,400 in exchange for its customers' promises to pay of $3,200.) Sales would normally be recorded daily, but, for obvious reasons, the illustration must be shortened.
8 Paid the advertising bill received on January 4.
9 Purchased merchandise on account, $6,000. (This transaction consists of the receipt of an asset, merchandise inventory, in exchange for a promise to pay for the goods at a later date.)
9 Received and paid an invoice for $120 for office supplies received and used.
10 Collections on account, $1,500.
13 Sales on account for the week, $4,400. Cost of the products sold, $3,300.
15 Paid sales salaries of $1,800 and administrative salaries of $2,100 for the first half of the month. (Payroll taxes and deductions are to be dealt with later.)
16 Paid other administrative expenses, $150.
17 Paid other selling expenses, $600.
20 Sales on account for the week, $1,400. Cost of products sold, $1,100.
23 Received an invoice from the *New York News* for advertising in the first half of January, $300.

31 Sales on account for the rest of the month, $1,600. Cost of the products sold, $1,200.
31 Paid invoice for $80 for additional office supplies received and used.
31 Paid salaries for last half of January (same as on January 15).
31 Paid sundry other administrative expenses, $250.

The general journal of the Paxton Company for January 1976 is presented below. Some of the above transactions have been completely journalized, others only partially. To test your understanding of the process of analyzing and journalizing transactions, you are to write out on a separate sheet of paper the information that should be inserted in the blank spaces below. Use the chart of accounts presented above for your account titles and numbers. To present the general journal as it would appear when completed, account numbers have been inserted in the L.F. (or reference) column. As already noted, these numbers typically would be inserted only after the posting of the item to the proper ledger account.

GENERAL JOURNAL *Page 1*

Date		Accounts and Explanation	L.F.	Debit	Credit
1976					
Jan.	2	Salesroom Rent Expense	35	600	
		Office Rent Expense	37	400	
		Cash	1		1,000
		Rent for January, 1976.			
	3	Furniture and Equipment	6	1,500	
		Cash	1		1,500
		Purchased additional furniture.			
	4	Advertising Expense	32	200	
		Accounts Payable	11		200
		Advertising expense on account.			
	4	Cash	1	3,000	
		Accounts Receivable	2		3,000
		Collections on account.			
	6	Acct. Pay. ________	?	2,000	
		CASH ________	?		2,000
		Payments on account.			
	6	Accounts Receivable	2	3,200	
		Sales	20		3,200
		Sales for the week ended January 6.			
	6	Cost of Goods Sold	30	2,400	
		Merchandise Inventory	4		2,400
		Cost of goods sold.			
	8	A/c Pay. ________	?	200	
		Cash ________	?		200
		Paid invoice of January 4.			

GENERAL JOURNAL continued *Page 2*

Date		Accounts and Explanation	L.F.	Debit	Credit
1976 Jan.	9	Merch. Inv.	?	6,000	
		Acct. Pay.	?		6,000
		Purchased merchandise on account.			
	9	Off. Sup. Exp.	?	120	
		Cash	?		120
		Office supplies purchased and used.			
	10	Cash	?	1,500	
		Accts. Rec.	?		1,500
		Collections on account.			
	13	Acct. Rec.	?	4,400	
		Sales	?		4,400
		Sales for the week ended January 13.			
	13	Cost of Goods Sold	?	3,300	
		Merch. Inv.	?		3,300
		Cost of goods sold.			
	15	Sales Sal. Exp	?	1,800	
		Admin. Sal. Exp	?	2,100	
		Cash	?		3,900
		Paid salaries for first half of January.			
	16	Adm. Exp	?	150	
		Cash	?		150
		Paid other administrative expenses.			
	17	Selling Exp	?	600	
		Cash	?		600
		Paid other selling expenses.			
	20	Acct. Rec.	?	1,400	
		Sales	?		1,400
		Sales for week ended January 20.			
	20	Cost of Goods Sold	?	1,100	
		Merch. Inv.	?		1,100
		Cost of goods sold.			
	23	Adv. Exp.	?	300	
		Acct. Pay	?		300
		Advertising expense on account.			
	31	Accounts Receivable	2	1,600	
		Sales	20		1,600
		Sales in rest of January.			

Date		Accounts and Explanation	L.F.	Debit	Credit
1976					
Jan.	31	Cost of Goods Sold	30	1,200	
		Merchandise Inventory	4		1,200
		Cost of goods sold.			
	31	______ ?	?	80	
		______ ?	?		80
		Supplies purchased and used.			
	31	Sales Salaries	34	1,800	
		Administrative Salaries	38	2,100	
		Cash	1		3,900
		Paid salaries for last half of January.			
	31	______ ?	?	250	
		______ ?	?		250
		Paid other administrative expenses.			

After you have supplied the missing account titles and account numbers for the blank spaces, check your responses in Answer Frame 7[2] on page 60.

Frame 8[2]

Presented below are the general ledger accounts of the Paxton Company. The accounts are nearly completely posted. You are to write out on a separate sheet of paper the missing items which are indicated by a blank space and a question mark.

GENERAL LEDGER

Cash *Account No. 1*

Date		Explanation	Folio	Debit	Credit	Balance
1976						
Jan.	1	Balance				10,000
	2		J 1		1,000	9,000
	3		J 1		1,500	7,500
	4		J 1	3,000		10,500
	6		J 1		2,000	8,500
	8		J 1		200	8,300
	9		J 2		120	8,180
	10		J 2	1,500		9,680
	15		J 2		3,900	5,780
	16		J 2		150	5,630
	17		J 2		600	5,030
	31		J 3		80	4,950
	31		J3		3,900	1,050
	31		J 3		250	800

GENERAL LEDGER *continued*

Accounts Receivable — *Account No. 2*

Date		Explanation	Folio	Debit	Credit	Balance
1976						
Jan.	1	Balance				4,500
	4		J 1		3,000	1,500
	6		J 1	3,200		4,700
	10		J 2		1,500	3,200
	13		J 2	4,400		7,600
	20		J 2	1,400		9,000
	31		J 2	1,600		10,600

Merchandise Inventory — *Account No. 4*

Date		Explanation	Folio	Debit	Credit	Balance
1976						
Jan.	1	Balance				5,000
	6		J 1		2,400	2,600
	9		J 2	6,000		8,600
	13		J 2		3,300	5,300
	20		J 2		1,100	4,200
	31		J 3		1,200	3,000

Furniture and Equipment — *Account No. 6*

Date		Explanation	Folio	Debit	Credit	Balance
1976						
Jan.	1	Balance				6,000
	3		J 1	1,500		7,500

Salesroom Fixtures — *Account No. 8*

Date		Explanation	Folio	Debit	Credit	Balance
1976						
Jan.	1	Balance				10,000

Accounts Payable — *Account No. 11*

Date		Explanation	Folio	Debit	Credit	Balance
1976						
Jan.	1	Balance				2,000
	4		J 1		200	2,200
	6		J 1	2,000		200
	8		J 1	200		—0—
	9		J 2		6,000	6,000
	23		J 2		300	6,300

Capital Stock — *Account No. 15*

Date		Explanation	Folio	Debit	Credit	Balance
1976						
Jan.	1	Balance				30,000

Retained Earnings — *Account No. 16*

Date		Explanation	Folio	Debit	Credit	Balance
1976						
Jan.	1	Balance				3,500

Answer frame 7^2

The missing account numbers and titles in the Paxton Company general journal for January 1976 are:

Jan.	*Account Titles*	*L.F.*
6	Accounts Payable	11
	Cash	1
8	Accounts Payable	11
	Cash	1
9	Merchandise Inventory	4
	Accounts Payable	11
9	Office Supplies Expense	39
	Cash	1
10	Cash	1
	Accounts Receivable	2
13	Accounts Receivable	2
	Sales	20
13	Cost of Goods Sold	30
	Merchandise Inventory	4
15	Sales Salaries	34
	Administrative Salaries	38
	Cash	1
16	Other Administrative Expense	40
	Cash	1
17	Other Selling Expense	36
	Cash	1
20	Accounts Receivable	2
	Sales	20
20	Cost of Goods Sold	30
	Merchandise Inventory	4
23	Advertising Expense	32
	Accounts Payable	11
31	Office Supplies Expense	39
	Cash	1
31	Other Administrative Expense	40
	Cash	1

If you missed any of the above answers, you may want to restudy the example in Frame 7^2 before continuing with Frame 8^2 on page 58. The above information is used in the continuing illustration.

8^2
continued

GENERAL LEDGER continued

Sales — *Account No. 20*

Date		Explanation	Folio	Debit	Credit	Balance
1976						
Jan.	6		J 1		3,200	3,200
	13		J 1		4,400	7,600
	20		J 2		1,400	9,000
	31		J 2		?	?
					1600	10,600

GENERAL LEDGER concluded

Cost of Goods Sold — Account No. 30

Date		Explanation	Folio	Debit	Credit	Balance
1976						
Jan.	6		J 1	2,400		2,400
	13		J 1	3,300		5,700
	20		J 2	1,100		6,800
	31		J 3	1,200		8,000

Advertising Expense — Account No. 32

Date		Explanation	Folio	Debit	Credit	Balance
1976						
Jan.	4		J 1	200		200
	23		J 2	300		500

Sales Salaries — Account No. 34

Date		Explanation	Folio	Debit	Credit	Balance
1976						
Jan.	15		J 2	1,800		1,800
	31		J 3	1,800		3,600

Salesroom Rent Expense — Account No. 35

Date		Explanation	Folio	Debit	Credit	Balance
1976						
Jan.	2		J 1	600		600

Other Selling Expense — Account No. 36

Date		Explanation	Folio	Debit	Credit	Balance
1976						
Jan.	17		J 2	600		600

Office Rent Expense — Account No. 37

Date		Explanation	Folio	Debit	Credit	Balance
1976						
Jan.	2		J 1	400		400

Administrative Salaries — Account No. 38

Date		Explanation	Folio	Debit	Credit	Balance
1976						
Jan.	15		J 2	2,100		2,100
	31		J 3	2,100		4,200

Office Supplies Expense — Account No. 39

Date		Explanation	Folio	Debit	Credit	Balance
1976						
Jan.	9		J 2	120		120
	31		J 3	80		200

Other Administrative Expense — Account No. 40

Date		Explanation	Folio	Debit	Credit	Balance
1976						
Jan.	16		J 2	150		150
	31		J 3	250		400

Check your responses to the missing items in the above set of ledger accounts in Answer Frame 8[2] on page 62.

Answer frame 8²

The missing items in the ledger accounts are:

Cash account: January 31, Folio J 3.
Accounts Receivable account: January 10, Balance $3,200.
Sales account: January 31, Credit $1,600, Balance $10,600.

After you have determined the nature and cause of your errors, if any, continue in Frame 9² below.

Frame 9²

Control of the recording process

In Frame 2² an explanation was promised later as to why the accountant records increases in assets (and expenses) as debits and increases in equities (and revenues) as credits. It would be quite possible to devise a recording scheme whereby all accounts were increased by entries on the debit side. At the end of any given period, then, all accounts would have positive debit balances. But, under such a scheme, how would the accountant know whether his basic equation of Assets = Equities was true? Furthermore, a valuable automatic check for arithmetic errors would be missing. If he wished to check upon the arithmetic accuracy of his work, he would have to repeat virtually every step in the initial recording process. Fortunately, there is an easier way.

When increases in assets (and expenses) are recorded as debits and increases in equities (and revenues) as credits, two sets of accounts are developed—those with debit balances and those with credit balances. If the totals of these two groups of accounts agree, the accountant has some assurance that he has carried out the arithmetic part of the recording process properly. The double-entry system of accounting requires, and the above illustration demonstrates, that the debits must equal the credits in the entry made to record every transaction. This equality of debits and credits for each transaction will always hold, because both sides of every transaction are recorded. Note that this does not mean that the increases must equal the decreases. A perfectly valid transaction could involve an increase in both an asset and an equity account or a decrease in both an asset and an equity account, as well as an increase in one account and a decrease in another. It is this equality of debits and credits, not of increases and decreases, that provides the important control device. If every transaction is recorded in terms of equal debits and credits, it follows that the total of the accounts with debit balances must equal the total of the accounts with credit balances.

The trial balance

The proof of the arithmetic accuracy of the recording process is generally accomplished by preparing a listing of the accounts and their debit or credit balances. Such a listing (called a trial balance) for the Paxton Company is shown in Illustration 2.3. Note the listing of the account titles on the left (account numbers could be included, if desired), the column for debit balances, the column for credit balances, and the equality of the two totals.

Illustration 2.3, *A Trial Balance*

PAXTON COMPANY
Trial Balance
January 31, 1976

	Debits	*Credits*
Cash	$ 800	
Accounts receivable	10,600	
Merchandise inventory	3,000	
Furniture and equipment	7,500	
Salesroom fixtures	10,000	
Accounts payable		$ 6,300
Capital stock		30,000
Retained earnings		3,500
Sales		10,600
Cost of goods sold	8,000	
Advertising expense	500	
Sales salaries	3,600	
Salesroom rent expense	600	
Other selling expense	600	
Office rent expense	400	
Administrative salaries	4,200	
Office supplies expense	200	
Other administrative expense	400	
	$50,400	$50,400

While the inequality of the totals of the debits and credits columns would automatically signal the presence of an error, the equality of the two totals does not mean that the accounting undertaken has been error-free. Indeed, serious errors may have been made, such as the complete omission of an important transaction or the recording of an entry in the wrong account (for example, the recording of an asset as an expense, or vice versa).

A trial balance may be prepared at any time—at the end of a day, a week, a month, a quarter, or a year. Typically, one is prepared whenever financial statements are to be prepared. Thus, the trial balance provides a listing of the accounts for statement preparation. A trial balance that is out of balance will also indicate the period in which an error was made.

Indicate whether each of the following statements is true or false.

1. An out-of-balance trial balance always signals the presence of an error.
2. A trial balance is one of the financial statements usually published by a business firm.
3. A trial balance may balance even though serious accounting errors have been made.
4. An in-balance trial balance shows only that equal amounts of debits and credits have been entered and that account balances have been correctly drawn.
5. A trial balance will reveal an error in selecting an account title in journalizing a transaction.

Check your response in Answer Frame 9[2] on page 66.

Frame 10[2]

Adjusting entries

Continuing the Paxton Company illustration, assume that its management is especially concerned with the profitability of the company for the month. Its directive that financial statements be prepared for January poses the problem for the accountant of ensuring that the accounts properly reflect operations for the month and the financial status at the end of the month. Because economic activity can take place without a discernible transaction occurring, the accounts must be analyzed to determine whether any updating adjustments are required. The entries to record these updating adjustments are called adjusting entries and are discussed in depth in Chapter 4.

But, to illustrate briefly here, a study of the Paxton Company's accounts would quickly reveal that no expense is shown for the use of the salesroom fixtures and the furniture and equipment which, let it be assumed, were acquired on December 31, 1975. Assets such as these will not continue to provide benefits or services indefinitely. Wear and tear resulting from their use will eventually cause them to be disposed of as worthless. Since the assets were used in January, it seems logical and reasonable to assign some part of the cost of such assets as an expense of the month of January. This expense is called *depreciation*. Assume that by spreading the recorded costs of $10,000 for the salesroom fixtures and $7,500 for the furniture and equipment over their estimated useful lives, the monthly depreciation expense is $100 and $125. The required journal entry to record these expenses is:

Depreciation—Salesroom Fixtures	100	
Depreciation—Furniture and Equipment	125	
Allowance for Depreciation—Salesroom Fixtures		100
Allowance for Depreciation—Furniture and Equipment		125
Depreciation for the month of January.		

Note that the depreciation expense recorded is not credited directly to the assets being depreciated but rather to separate Allowance for Depreciation accounts. As is explained more fully in Chapter 4, these allowance accounts are special subdivisions of the credit side of the asset accounts established for depreciable assets and are used primarily because of the estimated, tentative nature of the depreciation expense recorded. Illustration 2.6 below shows how these allowances are reported in the statement of financial position.

Assume that another adjustment is needed to record commissions earned by the Paxton Company, but not yet collected, in the amount of $6,000. Paxton earned these commissions in January by acting as a selling agent for the Brown Wholesale Company, which delivered the merchandise sold by Paxton directly to the customers. The required entry is:

Commissions Receivable	6,000	
Commissions Earned		6,000
Commissions earned in the month of January.		

Commissions Earned is, of course, a revenue account and will appear in the earnings statement, while Commissions Receivable is a current asset that will appear in the statement of financial position.

These two adjusting entries are posted in the same manner that every journal entry is posted. The debits would be posted as debits to the named accounts, the credits as credits, and the proper balances brought forward.

Indicate whether each of the following statements is true or false.

1. Commissions Receivable is a current asset primarily because it will be converted into cash in the very near future and because it results from normal operations.
2. After the above adjusting entries are posted, the Commissions Receivable account has a debit balance of $6,000.
3. The Depreciation—Salesroom Fixtures account is an expense account that will appear in the earnings statement.
4. Adjusting entries are usually required before financial statements are prepared.

Check your responses in Answer Frame 10[2] on page 66.

Frame 11[2]

Financial statements

The financial statements desired by the management of the Paxton Company are presented in Illustrations 2.4, 2.5, and 2.6. As shown by the earnings statement in Illustration 2.4, the management of the com-

Answer frame 9^2

1. True. If a trial balance does not balance, there must be an error of some kind.
2. False. A trial balance is a statement that is used internally only by the accountant as a means of checking upon the arithmetic accuracy of his work.
3. True. An error consisting of treating an expenditure as an asset when it should be accounted for as an expense is an example of a potentially serious error that would not be disclosed by the taking of a trial balance.
4. True. A trial balance that balances shows only that the procedural aspects of the information-gathering process have been undertaken without error.
5. False. If an error is made in choosing an account to be debited or credited, the trial balance will still balance, so it is not likely that the trial balance will reveal the error.

If you answered any of the above questions incorrectly, study Frame 9^2 again before continuing in Frame 10^2 on page 64.

Answer frame 10^2

1. True. Commissions Receivable is a current asset for the reasons stated.
2. True. Since there is no Commissions Receivable account in the trial balance, the debit to the account from the adjusting entry is the only entry into the account. It must, therefore, have a debit balance of $6,000.
3. True. See Illustration 2.4 for its inclusion as an expense in an earnings statement.
4. True. Some adjustments are usually needed simply because not all economic activity takes place in readily observable business transactions.

If you answered any of the above incorrectly, study Frame 10^2 again before proceeding to Frame 11^2 on page 65.

11^2
continued

Illustration 2.4, *An Earnings Statement*

PAXTON COMPANY
Earnings Statement
For the Month Ended January 31, 1976

Revenues:		
Sales	$10,600	
Commissions earned	6,000	$16,600
Expenses:		
Cost of goods sold	$ 8,000	
Advertising	500	
Depreciation—salesroom fixtures	100	
Sales salaries	3,600	
Salesroom rent	600	
Other selling expense	600	
Office rent	400	
Administrative salaries	4,200	
Office supplies	200	
Other administrative expense	400	
Depreciation—furniture and equipment	125	18,725
Net Loss		$ 2,125

Illustration 2.5, A Statement of Retained Earnings

PAXTON COMPANY Statement of Retained Earnings For the Month Ended January 31, 1976	
Retained earnings, December 31, 1975	$3,500
Net loss for January	2,125
Retained Earnings, January 31, 1976	$1,375

Illustration 2.6, A Statement of Financial Position

PAXTON COMPANY
Statement of Financial Position
January 31, 1976

ASSETS			
Current Assets:			
Cash		$ 800	
Accounts receivable		10,600	
Commissions receivable		6,000	
Merchandise inventory		3,000	
Total Current Assets			$20,400
Property, Plant, and Equipment:			
Salesroom fixtures	$10,000		
Allowance for depreciation	100	$ 9,900	
Furniture and equipment	$ 7,500		
Allowance for depreciation	125	7,375	
Total Property, Plant, and Equipment			17,275
Total Assets			$37,675
LIABILITIES AND STOCKHOLDERS' EQUITY			
Current Liabilities:			
Accounts payable			$ 6,300
Stockholders' Equity:			
Capital stock		$30,000	
Retained earnings		1,375	
Total Stockholders' Equity			31,375
Total Liabilities and Stockholders' Equity			$37,675

pany has good reason to be concerned about profitability, since the company reports a loss for the month.

The financial accounting process once again is back to its end products, the financial statements. (The fourth major financial statement, the statement of changes in financial position, is discussed in Chapter 11 of *Accounting II*.) Thus far the entire process has been shown to consist of (1) analyzing economic activity, (2) journalizing transactions, (3) posting to ledger accounts, (4) preparation of a trial balance, (5) adjusting the accounts, and (6) preparing financial statements.

Indicate whether each of the following statements is true or false.

1. Some of the input into the accounting system comes from checks and invoices.
2. The statement of retained earnings ties the earnings statement and the statement of financial position together.
3. The earnings of a company can be determined from its trial balance.
4. Apparently, over its entire life, the Paxton Company has operated profitably.

Check your response in Answer Frame 11[2] on page 70.

Summary *chapter* 2

This chapter introduced the basic components of an accounting system and the manner in which data are entered in the system.

An account is a means employed to summarize changes in the various types of asset, liability, stockholders' equity, revenue, and expense accounts. It may be further defined as a classificational category. By convention, asset and expense accounts are increased by entries on the left side of the account (called the debit side) and decreased by entries on the right (credit) side. Liability, stockholders' (owners') equity, and revenue accounts are increased by entries on the credit side and decreased by entries on the debit side. As a result, assets and expenses are usually debit balances and the others credit balances.

Recording increases and decreases in accounts in a manner which provides two groups of accounts—those with debit balances and those with credit balances—provides an automatic check upon the arithmetic accuracy of the accounting process.

Collectively, the accounts in an accounting system are referred to as the ledger. The chart of accounts is a list of the names and numbers of the accounts in an accounting system.

All data are entered in an accounting system by means of a journal, which is a chronological record of business transactions analyzed in terms of debit and credit. Business activity is analyzed and certain transactions recorded in the journal in a process known as journalizing. The amounts journalized are then posted to the accounts. A trial balance is a listing of all of the accounts in the ledger together with their debit or credit balances which, in total, must be equal. After adjusting entries have been prepared and posted, financial statements can be prepared.

Most accounting information is communicated to a wide variety of possible users in financial statements, which are the end products of the financial accounting process. The users find the information communicated useful and relevant in making decisions, which is the basic reason for acquiring any kind of information.

You have completed the programmed portion of Chapter 2. As the first part of your review, read the glossary which follows and study the definitions of the new terms introduced in this chapter. Then go on to the Student Review Quiz for a self-administered test of your comprehension of the material in the chapter.

Glossary *chapter* 2

Account—a device, means, classification category, or storage unit used to classify and summarize money measurements of business activity in an accounting system.

Adjusting entries—journal entries recorded to update the accounts in an accounting system for economic activity that has taken place but has not been reflected in readily discernible transactions.

Chart of accounts—the complete listing of the names (and possibly the account numbers) of all of the accounts in the ledger (or accounting system); somewhat comparable to a table of contents.

Credit—the right side of any account; when used as a verb, to enter a dollar amount on the right side of an account.

Credit balance—the balance in an account when the sum of the credits to the account exceeds the sum of the debits to that account.

Credit entry—an entry on the right side of an account; credits increase liability, stockholders' equity, and revenue accounts and decrease asset and expense accounts.

Cross-indexing—the act of placing in the journal the number of the ledger account to which an entry was posted and placing in the ledger account the page number of the journal on which the entry can be found.

Debit—the left side of any account; when used as a verb, to enter a dollar amount on the left side of an account.

Debit balance—the balance in an account when the sum of the debits to the account exceeds the sum of the credits to that account.

Debit entry—an entry on the left side of an account; debits increase asset and expense accounts and decrease liability, stockholders' equity, and revenue accounts.

Depreciation—that portion of the cost of a long-lived tangible asset used in a business that is allocated to each period of the asset's life. (For further discussion, see Chapter 9).

Journal—a chronological record of business transactions showing the changes to be recorded as a result of each transaction; the simplest form of journal is the two-column general journal.

Journal entry—a complete analysis of the effects of a business transaction as expressed in terms of debit and credit and recorded in a journal. A compound journal entry is a journal entry with more than one debit or credit.

Journalizing—a step in the accounting recording process that consists of entering a transaction in a journal.

Ledger—the complete collection of all of the accounts of an entity; often referred to as the general ledger.

Posting—the transfer of entries from a journal to a ledger.

Rule of double entry—the accounting requirement that every transaction be recorded in an entry that has equal debits and credits.

Trial balance—a list of all of the accounts in a ledger (excluding those with zero balances) at a given point in time, with debit balances listed in one column and credit balances listed in a second column to the right of the first column.

Student review quiz *chapter* 2

To develop a permanent record of your responses, you may write them on the answer sheet provided in the *Work Papers* or on a separate sheet of paper. For each of the following questions, select the one best answer.

1 Debits—

a) Increase assets and decrease expenses, liabilities, revenue, and stockholders' equity.

Answer frame 11²

1. True. The written evidence supporting many of the transactions journalized and entered in the accounting system is found in checks and invoices.
2. True. Because the statement of retained earnings includes the earnings of the period just completed and ends with the retained earnings of that same period, also reported in the statement of financial position, it does, in effect, tie the two statements together.
3. False. As the previous discussion pointed out, adjusting entries are made after the trial balance has been prepared and these entries adjust both revenue and expense accounts. Consequently, any attempt to measure net earnings using the data in the trial balance would yield an incomplete measure.
4. True. Although the company suffered a loss for the month of January, it still has positive retained earnings, which suggests that to date it has an overall record of profitability.

If you answered incorrectly, restudy Frame 11² before proceeding to the chapter summary on page 68.

---

b) Increase assets and expenses and decrease liabilities, revenue, and stockholders' equity.
c) Increase assets and stockholders' equity and decrease liabilities, expenses, and revenue.
d) Decrease assets and expenses and increase liabilities, revenue, and stockholders' equity.
e) Decrease assets and revenue and increase expenses, liabilities, and stockholders' equity.

2 Expense accounts—
a) Eventually increase the balance in the Retained Earnings account.
b) Usually have debit balances.
c) Show the costs associated with producing revenue during an accounting period.
d) Do all of the above.
e) Do only **(b)** and **(c)** above.

3 Steno Service, Inc., performed services for customers during the month totaling $1,400, for which it billed the customers. What entry should be made?
a) Debit Cash $1,400, credit Service Revenue $1,400.
b) Debit Accounts Receivable $1,400, credit Service Revenue $1,400.
c) Debit Notes Receivable $1,400, credit Service Revenue $1,400.
d) Debit Service Revenue $1,400, credit Accounts Receivable $1,400.
e) Debit Service Revenue $1,400, creddit Accounts Payable $1,400.

4 Received a bill for newspaper advertising services received, $25. The bill will be paid in 15 days. What entry is required?
a) Debit Advertising Expense $25, credit Accounts Payable $25.
b) Debit Accounts Receivable $25, credit Advertising Revenue $25.
c) Debit Cash $25, credit Advertising Revenue $25.
d) Debit Accounts Payable $25, credit Cash $25.
e) Debit Advertising Expense $25, credit Cash $25.

5 Received $825 from customers in payment of the bills sent to them. What entry is required?
a) Debit Cash $825, credit Accounts Payable $825.
b) Debit Cash $825, credit Notes Receivable $825.
c) Debit Cash $825, credit Accounts Receivable $825.
d) Debit Accounts Receivable $825, credit Cash $825.
e) Debit Accounts Payable $825, credit Cash $825.

6 Steno Service, Inc., purchased an electric calculator for $400 and new typists' chairs which cost $120. All items were purchased from the Office Equipment Supply Company on open account. The required entry is which of the following?
a) Debit Office Machines $400, credit Accounts Payable $400.
b) Debit Office Machines $520, credit Notes Payable $520.
c) Debit Office Machines $400 and

Office Furniture and Fixtures $120, credit Cash $520.

d) Debit Office Machines $400 and Office Furniture and Fixtures $120, credit Accounts Payable $520.

e) Debit Accounts Receivable $520, credit Office Machines $400 and Office Furniture and Fixtures $120.

7 Steno Service, Inc., performed a rush manuscript typing job for S. N. Stowell and received payment in cash of $18.50. The required entry is:

a) Debit Accounts Receivable $18.50, credit Office Supplies $18.50.

b) Debit Cash $18.50, credit Service Revenue $18.50.

c) Debit Cash $18.50, credit Accounts Receivable $18.50.

d) Debit Accounts Receivable $18.50, credit Service Revenue $18.50.

e) Debit Cash $18.50, credit Office Supplies $18.50.

8 Steno Service, Inc. paid weekly salaries of $275 in cash. The entry is:

a) Debit Salary Expense $275, credit Salaries Payable $275.

b) Debit Accounts Payable $275, credit Cash $275.

c) Debit Salary Expense $275, credit Accounts Payable $275.

d) Debit Cash $275, credit Salary Expense $275.

e) Debit Salary Expense $275, credit Cash $275.

9 Which of the following statements regarding a trial balance is *incorrect?*

a) A trial balance is a test of the equality of the debit and credit balances in the ledger.

b) A trial balance is a list of all of the open accounts in the ledger with their balances as of a given date.

c) A trial balance proves that no errors of any kind have been made in the accounts during the accounting period.

d) A trial balance helps to localize errors within an identifiable time period.

e) A trial balance is useful in preparing the statement of financial position and earnings statement.

10 A ledger is defined as—

a) A collection of transactions.

b) A collection of all statement of financial position accounts.

c) A collection of all earnings statement accounts.

d) A listing of all account titles and their balances.

e) None of the above.

11 Which of the following statements is *incorrect?*

a) The general journal is a record of transactions in chronological sequence.

b) Each general journal entry includes the date of the transaction, the title of the account debited, the title of the account credited, the amount of the debit, and the amount of the credit.

c) The general journal is the source of postings to the ledger accounts.

d) When making entries in the general journal, the accountant need not concern himself with equality of debits and credits.

12 Cross-indexing—

a) Provides a link between the journal and the ledger accounts.

b) Facilitates the finding of errors.

c) Reduces the likelihood of double-posting or forgetting to post an item.

d) Accomplishes all of the above.

e) Accomplishes only two of the above.

13 Posting is the act of—

a) Recording entries in the journal.

b) Transferring the balances in the ledger to the trial balance.

c) Entering amounts in the accounts in the ledger as indicated in the journal.

d) Tracing amounts from the journal to the ledger in an attempt to find errors.

e) Transferring amounts from the ledger to the journal so that balances may be determined for each account.

14 Which of the following statements is *incorrect?*

a) The journal shows all transactions chronologically while the ledger shows only those transactions affecting a given account in chronological sequence.

b) Every account title mentioned in the journal over a period of time also appears in the ledger, but accounts appearing in the ledger may not appear in the journal over a period of time.

c) The totals of all the debits and all the credits in the journal will equal the totals of the debit and credit balances in the ledger accounts if all entries have been posted.

d) The ledger represents a grouping of the amounts for the various accounts mentioned in the journal.

Now compare your answers with the correct answers and explanation on page 706.

Questions *chapter* 2

1 How can it be reasonable to state in Chapter 1 that A = L + SE, and then in Chapter 2 to state that A + E = L + SE + R when it is known that expenses and revenues are usually not equal?

2 Define debit and credit. Name the types of accounts which are:

a) Increased by debits.
b) Decreased by debits.
c) Increased by credits.
d) Decreased by credits.

Do you think this system makes sense? Can you conceive of other possible methods for recording changes in accounts?

3 Describe a ledger and a chart of accounts. How do these two compare with a book and its table of contents?

4 Why are expense and revenue accounts used when all revenues and expenses could be shown directly in the Retained Earnings account?

5 What types of accounts appear in the trial blance? What are the purposes of the trial balance?

6 You have found that the total of the debit column of the trial balance of the Burns Company is $100,000 while the total of the credit column is $90,000. What are some of the possible causes of this difference?

7 Store equipment was purchased for $1,500. Instead of debiting the asset Store Equipment, the debit was made to Delivery Equipment. Of what help will the trial balance be in locating this error? Why?

8 Differentiate between trial balance, chart of accounts, statement of financial position, and earnings statement.

9 A student remembered that the side toward the window in his classroom was the debit side of an account. He took his examination in a room where the windows were on the other side of the room. He became confused and consistently reversed his debits and credits. Would his trial balance have equal debit and credit totals? If there were no existing balances in any of the accounts to begin with, would his error prevent him from preparing correct financial statements? Why?

10 Are the following possibilities conceivable in an entry involving only one debit and one credit? Why?

a) Increase a liability and increase an expense.
b) Increase an asset and decrease a liability.
c) Increase a revenue and decrease an expense.
d) Decrease an asset and increase another asset.
e) Decrease an asset and increase a liability.
f) Decrease a revenue and decrease an asset.
g) Decrease a liability and increase a revenue.

11 Describe the nature and purposes of the general journal. What does "journalizing" mean? Give an example of a compound entry in the general journal.

12 Describe the act of posting. What difficulties could arise if no cross-indexing existed between the general journal and the ledger accounts?

13 Which of the following cash payments would involve the recording of an expense? Why?

a) Paid vendors for office supplies previously purchased on account.
b) Paid an automobile dealer for a new auto for a salesman.
c) Paid the current month's rent.
d) Paid salaries for the last half of the current month.
e) Paid cash and received merchandise that will be sold next month.

Exercises *chapter* 2

1 What debit and credit would be required for each of the following transactions?

a) Cash was received for services performed for customers, $800.
b) Services were performed for customers on open account, $800.

c) Services were performed for customers. The customers were required to sign written promises to pay $800 on a certain date in the future.

2 Give the debit and credit required for each of the following transactions:

a) Capital stock was issued for $30,000 cash.

b) A loan was arranged with a bank. The bank increased the customer's checking account balance by $10,000 after he signed a written promise to return the $10,000, plus interest at 6 percent, six months from the date of the loan.

3 Explain each of the sets of debits and credits existing in the accounts below. There are 10 transactions to be explained. Each set is designated by the small letters to the left of the amount. For example, the first transaction is the issuance of capital stock for cash and is denoted by the letter (*a*).

Cash

(*a*)	100,000	(*e*)	50,000
(*d*)	600	(*f*)	200
		(*g*)	1,200
		(*i*)	10,000

Accounts Payable

(*e*)	50,000	(*b*)	50,000
		(*h*)	400

Rent Expense

(*f*)	200		

Accounts Receivable

(*c*)	600	(*d*)	600
(*j*)	4,700		

Capital Stock

		(*a*)	100,000

Delivery Expense

(*h*)	400		

Delivery Equipment

(*b*)	50,000		
(*i*)	10,000		

Delivery Fee Revenue

		(*c*)	600
		(*j*)	4,700

Salaries Expense

(*g*)	1,200		

4 Assume that the ledger accounts given in Exercise 3 are those of the L. T. Kane Company as they appear at December 31, 1975. Prepare the trial balance as of that date.

5 Assume that the depreciation on the delivery equipment for the year ended December 31, 1975, is $4,000. Prepare the earnings statement for 1975 and the statement of financial position as of the end of 1975, assuming that the data given in Exercise 3 are for the L. T. Kane Company.

6 Give an example of a transaction which would involve the following combinations of types of accounts:

a) An asset and a liability.

b) An expense and an asset.

c) A liability and an expense.

d) A stockholders' equity and an asset.

e) Two asset accounts.

f) An asset and a revenue.

Problems, Series A *chapter* 2

2–1–A

Required:

a) Open T accounts for the Lucci Company and enter therein transactions given below for the month of August, 1975. Place the date of each transaction in the accounts.

b) Prepare a trial balance as of August 31, 1975.

Transactions:

Aug. 1 Issued capital stock for cash, $25,000.
3 Borrowed $10,000 from the bank on a note.
4 Purchased a truck for $3,300 cash.
6 Services are performed for customers who promise to pay later, $3,600.
7 Employee services received but not paid for, $700.
10 Collections are made for the services performed on August 6, $800.
11 The liability for employee services for the week ending August 7 is paid.
14 Supplies are purchased for use in future months, $300. They will be paid for next month.
17 A bill for $100 is received for gas and oil used to date.
25 Services are performed for customers who pay immediately, $4,500.
31 Employee services received but not paid for, $1,500.

2–2–A

Required:

a) Open proper T accounts for the Sayers Service Company and enter therein the transactions given below for the month of July, 1975. For identification, place the date of each transaction in the accounts.

b) Prepare a trial balance as of July 31, 1975.

Transactions:

July 2 Cash of $6,000 was received for capital stock issued to the owners.
3 The company paid rent for July, $250.
5 Office furniture was purchased for $3,000 cash.
9 A bill for $500 for advertising for July was received and paid.
14 Cash of $700 was received for fees for services to customers.
15 Wages of $200 for the first half of July were paid in cash.
20 The company sold services on open account to the Betz Company, $300. The account is to be paid August 10.
22 Office furniture was acquired on account from the Martin Metal Company; the price was $400.
30 Cash of $2,250 was received for fees for services to customers.
31 Wages of $250 for the second half of July were paid in cash.

2–3–A

Presented below are the transactions of the Lawton Company (partially summarized for the sake of brevity) for the month of March, 1975.

a) The company was organized and issued capital stock for cash of $70,000.
b) Paid $1,800 as the rent for March on a completely furnished store building.
c) Purchased merchandise by giving a promise to pay for it later, $50,000.
d) Paid $750 as the rent for March on two delivery trucks.
e) Paid $300 for delivery supplies received and used in March.
f) Sold merchandise costing $30,000 to customers who promised to pay $42,000 for it at a later date.
g) Paid suppliers for merchandise purchased on account (see **c** above), $38,000.
h) Collected cash of $31,000 from customers on account (see **f** above).
i) Received a bill for $300 for advertising in the local newspaper in March.
j) Paid cash for gas and oil consumed in March, $86.
k) Paid $1,400 to employees for services provided in March.
l) Unpaid wages for services received in March amount to $1,500 at the end of March.
m) Received an order for merchandise having a sale price of $10,000 and a cost of $6,000. The merchandise will be delivered in April.

Required: Prepare the general journal entries that would be required to record the above transactions in the records of the Lawton Company.

2–4–A

The trial balance prepared as of the end of the Halstead Company's calendar year accounting period is as follows:

HALSTEAD COMPANY
Trial Balance
December 31, 1975

	Debits	*Credits*
Cash	$ 4,000	
Accounts receivable	11,500	
Merchandise inventory	12,000	
Delivery equipment	26,000	
Allowance for depreciation on delivery equipment		$ 6,000
Office equipment	8,500	
Allowance for depreciation on office equipment		800
Accounts payable		8,000
Notes payable		10,000
Capital stock		25,000
Retained earnings		100
Sales		62,000
Cost of goods sold	29,000	
Rent expense	1,200	
Supplies expense	700	
Advertising expense	1,000	
Wages and salaries expense	18,000	
	$111,900	$111,900

The unrecorded depreciation expense for the year 1975 is $4,000 on the delivery equipment and $800 on the office equipment.

Required:

a) Prepare the general journal entries needed to record the depreciation expense for the year.
b) Prepare an earnings statement for the year ended December 31, 1975.

c) Prepare the statement of retained earnings for the year ended December 31, 1975.
d) Prepare the statement of financial position as of December 31, 1975.

2–5–A

Miller Cleaning Service, Inc., was organized July 1, 1975. The following account numbers and titles constitute the chart of accounts for the company:

Account No.	*Account Name*	*Account No.*	*Account Name*
101	Cash	332	Retained Earnings
102	Accounts Receivable	441	Cleaning Service Sales
111	Office Equipment	551	Salaries Expense
112	Cleaning Equipment	552	Insurance Expense
113	Service Truck	553	Service Truck Expense
221	Accounts Payable	554	Rent Expense
222	Notes Payable	555	Utilities Expense
331	Capital Stock	556	Cleaning Supplies Expense

Required:

a) Prepare ledger accounts for all of the above accounts except Retained Earnings.
b) Journalize the transactions given below for July, 1975.
c) Post the journal entries to the ledger accounts.
d) Prepare a trial balance.

Transactions:

July 1 The company issued $60,000 of capital stock for cash.
5 Office space was rented for July, and $600 cash was paid for the rental.
8 Desks and chairs were purchased for the office, on account, $3,000.
10 Cleaning equipment was purchased for $4,200; a note was given, to be paid in 30 days.
15 Purchased a service truck for $18,000, paying $12,000 cash and giving a 60-day note to the dealer for $6,000.
18 Paid for cleaning supplies received and already used, $300.
23 Cash cleaning service sales, $1,800.
27 Insurance expense for July was paid, $450 cash.
30 Paid for gasoline and oil used by the service truck in July, $60.
31 Billed customers for cleaning services rendered, $4,200.
31 Paid salaries for July, $5,400.
31 Paid utilities bills for July, $450.

2–6–A

York Company is a wholesaler of groceries and a canned food broker. Thus, it earns its revenue from sales of groceries and from commissions earned by acting as an agent for a seller who delivers the food sold by York directly to the customer. York Company's trial balance at the end of the first 11 months of its fiscal year is presented below:

YORK COMPANY
Trial Balance
June 30, 1975

Account No.	*Account Name*	*Debits*	*Credits*
1	Cash	$ 48,160	
2	Accounts receivable	52,400	
6	Merchandise inventory	54,100	
11	Office equipment	35,600	
11A	Allowance for depreciation—office equipment		$ 4,000
12	Automobiles	38,600	
12A	Allowance for depreciation—automobiles		14,000
21	Accounts payable		22,400
31	Capital stock		50,000
32	Retained earnings		54,000
40	Sales		261,000
41	Commissions earned		128,000
50	Cost of goods sold	160,400	
51	Office salaries expense	43,900	
52	Salesmen's commissions expense	49,600	
53	Advertising expense	12,200	
54	Automobile operating expense	14,600	
55	Office rent expense	11,000	
56	Office supplies expense	800	
57	Telephone and utilities	1,540	
58	Customer entertainment	1,700	
59	Depreciation—office equipment	2,800	
60	Depreciation—automobiles	6,000	
		$533,400	$533,400

Required:

a) Open three-column ledger accounts for each of the accounts in the trial balance under the date of July 1, 1975. Place the word "Balance" in the explanation space of each account.

b) Prepare general journal entries for the transactions given below for July, 1975.

c) Post the journal entries to the general ledger accounts.

d) Prepare a trial balance as of July 31, 1975.

e) Prepare adjusting journal entries to record the depreciation for July: autos, $1,000; office equipment, $300. Post these entries to the appropriate ledger accounts.

f) Prepare an earnings statement for the year ended July 31, 1975. Be sure to include the effects of the adjustments in **(e)**.

g) Prepare a statement of retained earnings for the year ended July 31, 1975.

h) Prepare the statement of financial position as of July 31, 1975.

Transactions:

July	2	Paid office rent for July, $1,000.
	5	Paid the accounts payable of $22,400.
	8	Paid advertising for the month of July, $800.
	10	Purchased a new office desk on account, $700.
	13	Purchased $140 of office supplies on account.
	15	Collected cash from customers on account, $47,200.
	20	Paid for customer entertainment, $50.
	22	The office supplies purchased on July 13 were incorrectly entered; the correct cost was $160.
	25	Collected an additional $4,000 from customers on account.
	26	Paid for gasoline used in the automobiles in July, $180.

28 Billed customers for commissions earned, $33,000.
30 Paid July commissions to salesmen, $13,200.
31 Paid July office salaries, $10,200.
31 Summarized, the sales for the month (all on account) were $27,000; the cost of goods sold was $15,000.

Problems, Series B *chapter* 2

2–1–B

The transactions listed below are those of the Sanders Company for the month of April, 1975.

Required:

a) Mentally analyze each transaction in terms of debit and credit and then enter them directly in suitable T accounts. To identify each part of each transaction also enter the date of the transaction in the accounts.
b) Prepare a trial balance as of April 30, 1975.

Transactions:

Apr. 1 Cash of $20,000 was received for capital stock issued to the owners.
3 Rent was paid for April, $150.
6 A delivery truck was purchased for $3,500, cash.
7 Office equipment was purchased on account from the Bollert Company for $5,800.
14 Wages were paid, $700.
15 $2,900 was received for services performed.
18 An invoice was received from Hugh's Gas Station for $25 for gas and oil used.
23 A loan was arranged with the bank for $5,000. The cash was received and a note was signed promising to return the $5,000 on May 30, 1976.
29 Purchased a delivery truck for $4,600 on account from the L & S Auto Agency.
30 Unpaid wages for services received amount to $900 and will be paid on May 1, 1975.

2–2–B

Set up the following T accounts for the Bascomb Company: Cash; Accounts Receivable, Purdue Company; Land; Office Building; Office Equipment; Accounts Payable, Mason Company; Notes Payable, Bank; Capital Stock; Service Sales; Salaries Expense; Office Expense.

Required:

a) Enter the transactions given below in the accounts. Date each transaction entry as indicated.
b) Prepare a trial balance after entering the last transaction.

Transactions:

Apr. 1 The Bascomb Company was organized and $50,000 of capital stock was issued for cash.

1 The company borrowed $25,000 from its bank and issued its note payable to the bank.
2 Paid $15,000 cash for land.
2 Paid $47,500 cash for an office building located on the land, above.
3 Purchased $6,000 of office equipment, on account, from the Mason Company.
4 Paid cash of $500 for office supplies to be consumed in April.
5 Sales of service, on account, to the Purdue Company were $250.
6 Sales of service, for cash, for the first week, were $1,000.
6 Paid salaries for the first week, $600.

2–3–B

The Darwin Corporation entered into the following transactions in August, 1975:

Aug. 2 Received cash for capital stock issued to owners, $50,000.
3 Paid rent for August on a building rented, $800.
4 Paid rent for August on a delivery truck, $400.
4 Purchased merchandise on account, $20,000.
6 Sold merchandise costing $2,000 for $3,000 cash.
8 Secured an order from a customer for merchandise with a selling price of $5,000 and a cost of $3,500. The merchandise is to be delivered next month.
13 Sold merchandise costing $4,000 for $6,000 on account to various customers.
15 Received and paid a bill for $73 for gasoline and oil used in delivering goods to customers.
21 Paid cash to suppliers on account, $7,000.
23 Cash collected from customers on account, $3,500.
31 Paid $1,700 to employees for services performed in August.
31 Received the electric and gas bill for the month of August, $55.

Required: Prepare general journal entries for the above transactions.

2–4–B

Given below is the trial balance of Waters Company, a computer programming and processing company:

WATERS COMPANY
Trial Balance
June 30, 1975

	Debits	*Credits*
Cash	$ 16,500	
Accounts receivable	17,000	
Office equipment	50,000	
Allowance for depreciation		$ 10,000
Accounts payable		5,400
Notes payable		10,000
Capital stock		20,000
Retained earnings (July 1, 1974)		12,700
Service revenue		50,000
Office rent expense	6,000	
Advertising expense	2,200	
Salaries expense	15,740	
Supplies expense	540	
Miscellaneous expense	120	
	$108,100	$108,100

The unrecorded depreciation for the year ended June 30, 1975, on the office equipment is $10,000.

Required:

a) Prepare the adjusting journal entry to record the depreciation for the year.
b) Prepare the earnings statement for the year ended June 30, 1975.
c) Prepare the statement of retained earnings for the year ended June 30, 1975.
d) Prepare the statement of financial position as of June 30, 1975.

2–5–B

Speedy Delivery, Inc., was organized January 1, 1975. Its chart of accounts is as follows:

Account No.	*Account Name*	*Account No.*	*Account Name*
101	Cash	331	Capital Stock
102	Accounts Receivable	332	Retained Earnings
106	Unexpired Insurance	441	Delivery Service Sales
107	Prepaid Taxes and Licenses	551	Garage Rent Expense
111	Delivery Trucks	552	Gasoline and Oil Used
112	Garage Equipment	553	Repairs to Delivery Trucks
113	Office Equipment	554	Salaries Expense
221	Accounts Payable	556	General Office Expense
222	Notes Payable		

Required:

a) Prepare ledger accounts for all the above accounts except Retained Earnings.
b) Journalize the transactions given below for January, 1975.
c) Post the journal entries to the ledger accounts.
d) Prepare a trial balance as of January 31, 1975.

Transactions:

Jan. 1 The company received $40,000 cash and $10,000 worth of garage equipment in exchange for $50,000 worth of capital stock.
2 Paid garage rent for the month of January, $500.
4 Purchased office equipment, on account, $1,200.
6 Purchased three delivery trucks at $7,500 each; payment was made by giving cash of $12,500 and a 30-day note for the remainder.
8 A corrected invoice for the office equipment purchased January 4 showed that the correct total was $1,100, not $1,200.
10 Paid $150 cash for annual licenses for the delivery trucks and $15 for title registration fees.
12 Purchased insurance for one year on the delivery trucks. The cost of the policy of $900 was paid in cash.
15 Received and paid January telephone and electric service bills, $80.
15 Paid salaries for first half of January, $300.
17 Cash sales of delivery service to date amounted to $150.
20 Received bill for gasoline purchased and used in January, $15.
23 Purchased one delivery truck for cash, $9,000. Paid $50 cash for the annual license and $5 for title registration fees.
25 Cash sales of delivery services were $240.

27 Purchased an adding machine on account, $300.
31 Paid salaries for last half of January, $400.
31 Open account sales of delivery service amounted to $950.
31 Paid for repairs to a delivery truck, $10 cash.

2–6–B

The trial balance of the Hoxey Company at the end of the first 11 months of its fiscal year is given below.

HOXEY COMPANY
Trial Balance
May 31, 1975

Account No.	*Account Name*	*Debits*	*Credits*
100	Cash	$ 24,120	
102	Accounts receivable	26,400	
106	Merchandise inventory	48,100	
121	Equipment	40,000	
121A	Allowance for depreciation		$ 10,000
210	Accounts payable		12,500
220	Notes payable		10,000
310	Capital stock		40,000
320	Retained earnings (July 1, 1974)		31,200
400	Sales		305,000
500	Cost of goods sold	181,000	
510	Sales salaries expense	33,000	
520	Advertising expense	14,000	
530	Selling supplies expense	1,500	
540	Equipment repairs	700	
550	Office salaries expense	28,500	
560	Building rent expense	4,800	
570	Telephone and utilities expense	1,400	
580	Entertainment expense	580	
590	Depreciation expense	4,400	
600	Interest expense	200	
		$408,700	$408,700

Required:

a) Open three-column ledger accounts for each of the accounts in the trial balance. Place the word "Balance" in the explanation space and enter the date June 1, 1975, on this same line.
b) Prepare general journal entries for the transactions given below for June, 1975.
c) Post the journal entries to the general ledger accounts.
d) Prepare a trial balance as of June 30, 1975.
e) Prepare the adjusting journal entry to record the depreciation on the equipment for June, $400, and post this entry to the ledger accounts.
f) Prepare an earnings statement for the year ended June 30, 1975.
g) Prepare a statement of retained earnings for the year ended June 30, 1975.
h) Prepare the statement of financial position as of June 30, 1975.

Transactions:

June 1 Paid building rent for June, $400.
2 Paid vendors on account, $12,000.

5 Purchased a new cash register on account, $500.
7 Sold merchandise on account, $18,000; cost, $12,000.
10 Paid the note payable of $10,000 plus interest of $100.
13 Cash collections from customers on account, $24,000.
15 Purchased merchandise on account, $26,500.
19 Received a bill for equipment repairs, $150.
24 Paid the June telephone bill, $55, and the June gas and electric bill, $65.
28 Received a bill for June advertising, $1,100.
29 Paid the equipment repair bill received on the 19th, $150.
30 Sold merchandise for cash, $3,000; cost, $2,000.
30 Paid office salaries, $2,500, and sales salaries, $3,000.
30 Sales on account since June 7, $12,000; cost, $8,000.
30 Reimbursed salesmen for costs incurred in entertaining customers in June, $70.

Sales, cost of goods sold, and merchandise inventories

Learning objectives

Study of the material in this chapter is designed to provide knowledge of:

1. What constitutes a sale and a purchase; the time that each is recorded and why; the nature and reasons for, as well as the accounting for and reporting of, sales (purchase) returns and allowances and sales (purchase) discounts.
2. The operating characteristics and advantages and disadvantages of perpetual and periodic inventory procedures as alternative approaches or means of accounting for merchandise inventories and the cost of merchandise sold; the adjusting entries needed to establish the expense account Cost of Goods Sold under the periodic procedure.
3. Common terms under which merchandise is sold, including freight terms; alternative approaches to accounting for purchase discounts; cash discounts distinguished from trade discounts.
4. The earnings statement usually prepared for a merchandising firm, with its basic classifications of operating and nonoperating revenues, operating and nonoperating expenses; criteria for distinguishing between these classifications and examples of each; the computation and significance attached to gross margin.
5. What goods should be included and excluded from inventory and why; the nature of inventory losses; some basic business documents employed in operating a merchandising business.

Frame 1[3]

Previous chapters have dealt with accounting for the activities of companies that earned their revenues by rendering services to customers for fees or commissions. Net earnings were determined by subtracting the various operating expenses incurred from these revenues. The fact that a company may earn its revenues and net earnings by buying and selling merchandise was introduced briefly, but discussion of the accounting for such activity was limited and centered primarily on three accounts—Sales, Cost of Goods Sold, and Merchandise Inventory. This chapter expands upon that initial discussion.

Sales revenue

The sales revenue (or net sales, as it is sometimes called) of a merchandising company, whether a retailer or a wholesaler, is an important measure of economic activity. It indicates the extent to which a company is satisfying its customers' needs and gives an approximate measure of the flow of assets from customers into the business. Sales revenue generally consists of sales (sometimes referred to as gross sales) less sales returns, sales allowances, and sales discounts.

Sales

The principal gross revenue of a merchandising company is derived from sales of merchandise. Basically, a sale consists of the transfer of legal ownership of goods (called passage of title) from one party to another and is usually accompanied by physical delivery of the goods. Each time a sale is made, a revenue account called Sales is increased (credited) by the amount of the selling price of the goods sold. The accompanying debit is to Cash if the terms of sale are cash or to Accounts Receivable if the goods are sold on account. For example, a $5,000 sale on account would be recorded as follows:

Accounts Receivable	5,000	
Sales		5,000
To record the sale of merchandise on account.		

Typically, the above entry will be based upon a business document called a *sales invoice,* such as is shown in Illustration 3.1. Since the sales invoice is prepared only after notification from the shipping department of the shipment of the goods to the customer, the accountant is, indeed, recording a completed sale. Furthermore, he has reason to believe it is a valid sale because the sales invoice has been compared with the customer's written *purchase order* for agreement on matters such as description of the goods, quantities, and prices.

Illustration 3.1, *Sales Invoice*

DIXON WHOLESALE CO.
476 Mason Street, Detroit, Michigan

Invoice No. 1258
Date Dec. 19, 1976

Customer's Order No. 218
Sold To Hanley Company
Address 2255 Hannon Street, Big Rapids, Michigan
Terms Net 30

Date Shipped Dec. 19, 1976
Shipped by York Trucking Co.

Description	*Quantity*	*Price per Unit*	*Amount*
True-tone AM/FM radios Model No. 5868–24393	100	$50	$5,000
	Total		$5,000

Indicate whether each of the following statements is true or false.

1. A sale of goods involves passage of legal title to the goods.
2. Usually, physical delivery of goods accompanies their sale.
3. Sales are credited to a revenue account because they tend to increase stockholders' equity and a revenue account is a subdivision of the stockholders' equity account Retained Earnings.
4. Net sales is an approximate measure of the assets flowing into a firm from its customers.

Now check your responses in Answer Frame 1[3] on page 86.

Frame 2[3]

Why record revenue at time of sale? In a merchandising firm, many activities are undertaken both before and after a sale that can be called revenue-producing activities. For example, goods may be purchased and stored before a selling season commences, advertising costs may be incurred, salesmen may call upon customers, orders may be received, and costs may be incurred to make good on guarantees. Yet recording revenue at the time of sale can be justified on the following grounds: (1) legal title to the goods has passed and the goods are now the responsibility and property of the buyer; (2) the amount of revenue can be measured—the selling price of the goods has been verified by obtaining assets of that amount from the customer; (3) the revenue has been earned, that is, the seller has completed his part of the contract; (4) the seller has realized revenue in that the goods have been exchanged for other valid assets; and (5) because the seller has completed his part of the contract, his costs presumably can be determined, with the result that net earnings can be calculated.

On the other hand, the selling price of the goods may not be a complete

Answer frame 1³

1. True. There can be no sale without legal passage of title to goods.
2. True. Although a sale can be made without physical delivery, the two normally go together.
3. True. The sale would be credited to a revenue account and would ultimately increase Retained Earnings, a part of stockholders' equity.
4. True. The amount of assets flowing into a firm from its customers is measured approximately by net sales.

If you missed any of the above, read Frame 1³ again before proceeding to Frame 2³ on page 85.

2³ *continued* measure of the revenue generated because of sales returns, sales allowances, and sales discounts.

Sales returns

Goods delivered to a customer in the belief that a sale had been made may be returned to the seller for a variety of reasons, such as wrong color, wrong size, wrong style, wrong amounts, or inferior quality. In fact, in some firms such as retail furniture stores, goods may be returned simply because the customer did not like them. The seller's policy may be "satisfaction guaranteed." In any event, a sales return is a cancellation of a sale and conceivably could be recorded as a debit in the Sales account. But costs are incurred in handling sales returns and, in a sense, sales returns may be a sign of inefficiency in the merchandising process. Thus, because the amount of sales returns may constitute significant information to management, owners, and other interested parties, they are recorded in a separate account entitled Sales Returns and Allowances. For example, if $150 worth of goods sold on account and $75 worth of goods sold for cash are returned by the customers, the required entry would be:

Sales Returns and Allowances	225	
Accounts Receivable		150
Cash		75
To record sales returns from customers.		

Sales allowances

Sales allowances are deductions from original invoiced sales prices. They may be granted to a customer for any of a number of reasons, including inferior quality or damage or deterioration in transit. As was true for sales returns, sales allowances could be recorded directly as debits in the Sales account because they do cancel a part of the recorded selling price. But, because their amounts may constitute significant information, they are either recorded in a separate Sales Allowances account or recorded in a combined Sales Returns and Allowances account. In either case, the account is a contra account (a reduction account) to Sales; or it can be viewed as a negative revenue account. It is not an expense account even though it has a debit balance.

To illustrate the recording of a sales allowance, assume that a $200 allowance is granted a customer for damage resulting from improperly packed merchandise shipped to him. If the customer has not yet paid his account, the required entry would read:

Sales Returns and Allowances	200	
Accounts Receivable		200
To record sales allowance granted for damaged merchandise.		

Indicate whether each of the following statements is true or false.

1. A sales allowance may be granted by a seller for goods sold that possess minor flaws that detract from their salability by the customer.
2. The Sales Returns account is an expense account.
3. If a customer has paid his account, a sales allowance may involve a cash refund to the customer.
4. The accountant justifies recording revenue at the time of sale by arguing that the revenue has been realized.

Check your responses in Answer Frame 2[3] on page 88.

Frame 3[3]

Sales discounts

Whenever goods are sold on account, the terms of payment are clearly specified on the sales invoice to avoid confusion and misunderstanding and are, in fact, a part of the sales contract. For example, in the invoice in Illustration 3.1, the terms are stated as "net 30" (which is sometimes written simply as "n/30"). This means that the $5,000 amount of the invoice must be paid on or before 30 days after December 19, 1976, or on or before January 18, 1977. If the terms read "n/10 E.O.M.," the invoice would be due on the 10th day of the month following the month of sale—January 10th in the case of the invoice in Illustration 3.1. Credit terms vary considerably from industry to industry according to trade practices.

In many instances, when credit periods are long, sellers will grant cash discounts in an attempt to induce early payment of an account. If obtained, such early payment reduces the amount of capital invested in accounts receivable and may also reduce losses resulting from uncollectible accounts. Theoretically, cash discounts represent adjustments to gross invoice price to arrive at the actual cost—the cash price—of the merchandise. These discounts, usually ranging from 1 to 3 percent of the gross invoice price of the merchandise, may or may not be taken by the buyer.

Answer frame 2^3

1. True. This is perhaps the most common reason for granting a sales allowance.
2. False. Even though the account has a debit balance, it is not an expense account. Sales returns are not costs incurred in generating revenue, but rather reductions in the amount of revenue originally recorded because a part of the revenue was canceled when the goods were returned.
3. True. The customer may request, and the seller may grant, a cash refund if a sales allowance is granted subsequent to the time that the customer paid his account balance.
4. True. The act of making a sale to a customer from whom payment is fully expected is often referred to in accounting jargon as an act of realizing revenue.

If you answered any of the above incorrectly, study Frame 2^3 again before going on to Frame 3^3 on page 87.

3^3 *continued*

To the purchaser, they are purchase discounts; to the seller, they are sales discounts.

Cash discount terms are often stated as follows:

2/10, n/30—which is read as "two ten, net thirty." Unfortunately, the statement is misleading. The terms actually offered are a 2 percent discount (2 percent of the gross invoice price of the merchandise) if payment is rendered within 10 days following the invoice date. No discount is allowed after 10 days, and the gross invoice price is due 30 days from the invoice date. The "n" in the terms should be interpreted as "no discount" rather than as "net" since the residual obtained when the discount is subtracted from the invoice price is properly described as "net."

2/E.O.M., n/60—which is read as "two E.O.M., net sixty." The terms actually mean a 2 percent discount may be deducted if the invoice is paid by the end of the month, no discount may be taken after the end of the month, and the invoice is due 60 days from the date of the invoice.

2/10/E.O.M., n/60—which is usually read as "two ten E.O.M., net sixty." The actual terms offered are a 2 percent discount if the invoice is paid by the 10th of the following month, no discount after this date, and the gross invoice amount is due 60 days from the date of the invoice.

Recording sales discounts. The granting of sales discounts, then, is another factor that tends to reduce the amount of cash actually collected from the sale of goods. But even when cash discount terms are offered, it is customary for a seller to record an invoice at gross invoice price. There are two reasons for this: (1) it is not known whether the customer will take the discount, and (2) the seller wants the buyer's account stated at gross invoice price so that the buyer will not be inadvertently billed for the net invoice price (gross invoice price less cash discount) when the discount privilege period has expired. To illustrate the conventional manner of recording sales discounts, assume that a sale on account of $1,000 was made on August 12, terms 2/10, n/30; a check in payment of the account was received on August 21 in the amount of $980. The required entries are:

Aug. 12	Accounts Receivable	1,000	
	Sales		1,000
	To record sale on account.		
Aug. 21	Cash	980	
	Sales Discounts	20	
	Accounts Receivable		1,000
	To record collection on account, less discount.		

While infrequently appearing among the operating expenses in the earnings statement, the Sales Discounts account is a contra account to Sales and should be shown as a deduction from gross sales in the earnings statement. It is not an expense incurred in generating revenue; rather its purpose is to reduce recorded revenue to the amount actually realized from the sale—the net invoice price.

Illustration 3.2 contains a partial earnings statement showing how sales, sales returns and allowances, and sales discounts might be reported. In highly condensed earnings statements, the information in the illustration might be reported as follows:

Illustration 3.2, *Partial Earnings Statement*

HARDISON COMPANY
Partial Earnings Statement
For the Year Ended June 30, 1976

Revenues:		
Gross sales		$282,345
Less: Sales discounts	$ 5,548	
Sales returns and allowances	15,436	20,984
Net sales		$261,361

Net sales (less sales discounts, $5,548, and sales returns and allowances, $15,436)	$261,361

Indicate whether each of the following statements is correct or incorrect.

1. The data in Illustration 3.2 suggest that the Hardison Company expects to collect roughly $260,000 of cash from sales made in the year ended June 30, 1976.
2. Theoretically, cash discounts are best viewed as adjustments of recorded amounts of sales (or purchases).
3. A sale on account in the amount of $1,500 made on June 15, terms 3/10, n/30, on which a sales allowance of $300 was granted, could be settled on June 25 for $1,155.
4. Cash discounts are called purchase discounts by a buyer and sales discounts by a seller.

Now check your responses in Answer Frame 3[3] on page 90.

Answer frame 3[3]

1. Correct. Some of the sales discounts and sales returns and allowances recorded might relate to sales of the prior year and a few discounts and returns and allowances might yet be taken on accounts receivable arising from sales of the current year that are still uncollected at year-end. Also, some of the accounts receivable might prove uncollectible.
2. Correct. Any rational buyer in deciding between two or more possible suppliers of goods will take cash discount terms into consideration in making his decision. That is, he will view them as reductions of quoted prices.
3. Incorrect. The account would be settled by payment of $1,164, computed as $1,500 – $300 – (0.03 × $1,200). The seller would not allow a discount on a return or an allowance.
4. Correct. Cash discounts are usually described from the viewpoint of the parties to a transaction involving a cash discount.

If you answered incorrectly, review Frame 3[3] before proceeding to Frame 4[3] below.

Frame 4[3]

Interest rate implied in cash discounts. Although the decision is likely to be influenced by the amount of cash on hand and a company's ability to borrow money, a simple analysis will readily show whether money should be borrowed to take advantage of proffered discounts. For example, $5,130 must be paid within 30 days or $5,027.40 must be paid within 10 days to settle an invoice in the amount of $5,130, terms 2/10, n/30. In other words, by advancing payment 20 days from the final due date, a discount of $102.60 is secured. The interest expense incurred on borrowing $5,027.40 at 6 percent per year for 20 days is $16.76. In this case, management would save $85.84 ($102.60 — $16.76) by borrowing the money and paying the invoice within the discount privilege period. In terms of an annual rate of interest, the 2 percent rate of discount for 20 days is equivalent to a 36 percent annual rate: (360 ÷ 20) × 2 percent. All cash discount terms can be converted into their approximate annual interest rate equivalents by the same process. Thus, a firm could afford to pay up to 18 percent on borrowed funds to take advantage of discount terms of 1/10, n/30; up to 7.2 percent for terms of 1/10, n/60; and, as already indicated, up to 36 percent for terms of 2/10, n/30. Thus, unless cash discount terms drop to fractions of 1 percent (as they in fact have in some instances), a firm is likely to benefit by borrowing to take advantage of discounts offered.

Determining cost of goods sold

Basically, there are two methods of determining what is for most merchandising firms the largest single element of expense incurred, namely, the cost of the goods sold. One method, called the *perpetual inventory procedure,* is usually employed by companies selling merchandise that has a high individual unit value, such as automobiles, furniture, and appliances. Here it is a relatively easy task to maintain records of the cost of each unit of merchandise and in this way determine the cost of each unit sold. The inventory records are designed and maintained in such a manner as to provide close control over the actual goods on hand by showing exactly what goods should be on hand.

The perpetual inventory procedure will be dealt with in greater depth in Chapter 7. Suffice it to note here that the entries required to record the purchase of three identical refrigerators (except for serial number tags) at a cost of $205 each and the subsequent sale of one unit on account for $300 are:

Merchandise Inventory	615	
Accounts Payable		615
To record purchase of three refrigerators on account.		
Accounts Receivable	300	
Sales		300
To record sale on account.		
Cost of Goods Sold	205	
Merchandise Inventory		205
To record cost of refrigerator sold.		

The alternative approach to determining cost of goods sold, called the periodic inventory procedure, is described, discussed, and illustrated in the remainder of this chapter.

Cost of goods sold, periodic procedure

Companies dealing in merchandise that has a low value per unit, such as nuts and bolts, nails, Christmas cards, pencils, and many similar items, often find that the extra costs of record keeping under the perpetual procedure more than outweigh the benefits derived. Close control of such items is not necessary nor is it economically wise. For these firms, the periodic inventory procedure is used. Under this procedure the Merchandise Inventory account is not adjusted after each purchase or sale; adjustment is made only at the end of the accounting period. Quantity records usually are not maintained, although it is conceivable that they might be. The record keeping is reduced considerably, but so is the control over inventory items. At the end of the period, when the physical inventory is taken, there is no account balance against which the physical count can be checked. The Merchandise Inventory account does not show the cost of the goods that should be on hand.

Also under the periodic procedure, no attempt is made to determine the cost of the goods sold for each sale at the time of the sale. Instead, the cost of all of the goods sold for all of the sales made in a period is determined at the end of the period. To do so requires knowledge of three items: (1) the cost of the goods on hand at the beginning of the period, (2) the cost of the goods purchased during the period, and (3) the cost of the unsold goods on hand at the end of the period. This information would then be arrayed in the following manner:

Cost of goods on hand at the beginning of the period	$12,000
Cost of goods purchased during the period	$70,000
Cost of goods available for sale during the period	$82,000
Cost of unsold goods on hand at the end of the period	10,000
Cost of goods sold during the period	$72,000

This schedule shows that the firm started the period with $12,000 of merchandise on hand and purchased an additional $70,000, making a total of $82,000 of goods that could have been sold during the period. But $10,000 remained unsold at the end of the period, which implies that $72,000 was the cost of goods sold during the period.

Indicate whether each of the following statements is true or false.

1. The approximate annual interest rate implied in cash discount terms of 3/15, n/60 is 24 percent.
2. The periodic inventory procedure provides tight internal control over inventories by showing at all times the units of merchandise that should be on hand.
3. Under the perpetual inventory procedure, the cost of the goods sold for each sale is determined at the time of sale.
4. Under the periodic procedure, the cost of the goods sold is determined by subtracting the cost of the goods unsold at the end of the period from the cost of the goods available for sale during the period.

Check your responses in Answer Frame 4[3] on page 94.

Frame 5[3]

Purchases

When merchandise is purchased, an asset is acquired. Purchases of merchandise which is to be offered for sale to customers are recorded by debits to a Purchases account instead of debits to the Merchandise Inventory account. The Purchases account is increased by debits because it is really a subdivision of the debit side of the asset account Merchandise Inventory. But it is usually listed with the earnings statement accounts in the chart of accounts because the balance in the account is transferred to other accounts at the end of every accounting period. By recording purchases in a separate account, management has knowledge of the cost of the merchandise purchased during the accounting period. This is the only information provided by the account, as it tells nothing about whether the goods have been sold.

To illustrate, assume that Top Quality Wholesale Stores purchased

$15,000 of merchandise from Wholesaler A on account and $10,000 for cash. The required entries are:

Purchases	15,000	
Accounts Payable		15,000
To record purchase of merchandise on account.		
Purchases	10,000	
Cash		10,000
To record purchase of merchandise for cash.		

All purchases of merchandise are posted to the Purchases account, which appears—with a debit balance—in both the ledger and the trial balance.

Transportation costs

Whenever goods are purchased, costs will be incurred to deliver them to the buyer. Whether these costs are given separate recognition in the accounts of the buyer depends upon the terms under which the goods were sold.

The term *f.o.b. shipping point* means free on board at the shipping point; that is, the buyer incurs all transportation costs after the merchandise is loaded on cars or trucks at the point of shipment.

The term *f.o.b. destination* means that the seller is responsible for transportation charges to the destination of the shipment. In general, title to the goods passes from the seller to the buyer at the point at which the buyer becomes responsible for the transportation charges. When the seller pays the freight before the goods arrive at their destination, the term "prepaid freight" is used. When the buyer is to pay the freight upon the arrival of the goods, the term "freight collect" is used.

Four situations for the payment of transportation costs may normally exist. They are illustrated below. In each case assume that a purchase of $1,000 of merchandise on account was properly recorded by the buyer as a debit to Purchases and a credit to Accounts Payable and by the seller as a debit to Accounts Receivable and a credit to Sales.

Case A. If the goods were shipped f.o.b. shipping point, freight collect, the buyer would pay the freight bill and would be responsible for the freight costs, which he would record as follows (assuming a $50 delivery charge):

Transportation-In	50	
Cash		50
To record payment of freight bill on goods purchased.		

The $50 is actually a part of the cost of the merchandise acquired and could be debited to the Purchases account. But a more complete record of the costs incurred is obtained through use of a separate Transportation-In account.

Answer frame 4^3

1. True. Since 45 is one eighth of 360, 3 percent for 45 days is the equivalent of 24 percent for 360 days. It costs 3 percent of the invoice price of the goods to extend the time of payment 45 days.
2. False. The perpetual procedure does this by adjusting inventory records after each purchase or sale.
3. True. Inventory records could not be kept up to date if this was not done.
4. True. As the schedule presented shows, the cost of the goods available for sale is the sum of two items: (1) cost of the goods on hand at the beginning of the period, and (2) cost of the goods purchased during the period.

If you answered incorrectly, review Frame 4^3 before going on to Frame 5^3 on page 92.

5^3 *continued*

The only entry required on the seller's books is to record the $1,000 sale on account.

Case B. If the goods were shipped f.o.b. shipping point, freight prepaid, the seller prepaid the freight for the buyer and would charge it to the buyer. The entry on the seller's books (in addition to the entry for the sale) would be:

Accounts Receivable	50	
Cash		50
To charge buyer for freight on goods shipped f.o.b. shipping point, freight prepaid.		

The buyer, in turn, would reimburse the seller when he paid the invoice. In this case, the proper entry for the freight on the buyer's books would be:

Transportation-In	50	
Accounts Payable		50
To record obligation for freight charges prepaid by seller.		

Case C. If the goods were shipped f.o.b. destination, freight prepaid, the seller paid the freight bill and bears the responsibility for them. No separate transportation cost is billed to the buyer, and no entry is required by the buyer except to record the $1,000 purchase. The transportation cost undoubtedly was taken into consideration by the seller in establishing his selling prices. But, since he paid the freight, the following entry would be required:

Transportation-Out	50	
Cash		50
To record freight cost on goods sold.		

The Transportation-Out account is an expense account, showing one of the expenses incurred in making the sale to the customer.

Case D. If the goods were shipped f.o.b. destination, freight collect, the buyer would pay the freight bill as a convenience to the seller. He would charge it against the balance in the seller's account payable as follows:

Accounts Payable	50	
Cash		50
To record payment of freight bill for seller.		

Assuming that the seller knew the amount of the freight cost at the time of shipment, he would make an entry to reduce the buyer's account balance as follows:

Transportation-Out	50	
Accounts Receivable		50
To record reduction in buyer's account for freight costs paid on goods shipped f.o.b. destination.		

The buyer would remit $950 to settle his account with the seller.

Purchase returns and allowances

For any of a number of reasons, such as wrong size or color, a buyer may return merchandise to a seller, giving rise to what is known as a purchase return. Similarly, a seller may grant an allowance or reduction in the price of goods shipped to the buyer because of defects, damage, or blemishes—a concession referred to by the buyer as a purchase allowance. Both returns and allowances serve to reduce the buyer's obligation to the seller and to reduce the cost of the goods purchased. But more importantly, management may be quite interested in knowing the dollar amount of returns and allowances as the first step in controlling the costs incurred in returning unsatisfactory merchandise or negotiating purchase allowances. For this reason, purchase returns and allowances are recorded in a separate account as follows:

Accounts Payable	175	
Purchase Returns and Allowances		175
To record return of damaged merchandise.		

Indicate whether each of the following statements is true or false.

1. A purchase return increases the cost of the merchandise purchased.
2. A purchase allowance reduces the buyer's obligation to the seller.
3. Although he may not pay the freight company directly, the seller is responsible for, and ultimately bears the burden of, any transportation costs incurred for goods shipped f.o.b. destination.
4. Under certain circumstances, a freight bill paid by a buyer on goods purchased will not be debited to the buyer's Transportation-In account.

Now check your responses in Answer Frame 5[3] on page 96.

Answer frame 5[3]

1. False. A purchase return, because it in effect cancels a purchase, reduces rather than increases the cost of goods purchased.
2. True. By granting an allowance, the seller has agreed to settle an invoice for less than the originally billed amount.
3. True. The term f.o.b. destination means that the seller promises to have the goods delivered to the buyer's location without charge to the buyer. But it is also quite true that the seller, in such circumstances, would take transportation charges into consideration in establishing selling prices. Thus, the buyer is likely to pay the transportation charges as part of a higher selling price.
4. True. When goods are shipped f.o.b. destination, freight collect, the buyer will have to pay the freight bill in order to get his hands on the goods. But he will charge the seller for whatever amount he paid by reducing the amount shown in the Accounts Payable account he maintains for the seller. And the buyer will, of course, deduct the transportation charges paid when making remittance to the seller.

If you answered any of the above incorrectly, restudy Frame 5[3] before proceeding to Frame 6[3] below.

Frame 6[3]

Purchase discounts

Merchandise is often purchased under credit terms that permit the buyer to deduct a stated discount if the invoice is paid within a specified period of time. Traditionally, such transactions are accounted for as in the following illustration:

Apr.	4	Purchases	1,000	
		Accounts Payable		1,000
		To record purchase on account; terms 2/10, n/30.		
	14	Accounts Payable	1,000	
		Cash		980
		Purchase Discounts		20
		To record payment on account within discount period.		

Note that the purchase invoice is recorded at gross invoice price and the purchase discount recorded only when the invoice is paid within the discount period and the discount taken. The Purchase Discounts account is looked upon as a contra account to Purchases having as its purpose the reduction of the recorded gross invoice cost of the purchase to the price actually paid. It is reported in the earnings statement as a deduction from purchases.

But, on occasion, the Purchase Discounts account is reported in the earnings statement as an element of miscellaneous revenue. Such a treatment can be accepted only as a practical expedient, since revenue is not generated by the buying of merchandise.

Net price procedure. A theoretically preferable, although not widely used, method of accounting for purchase discounts involves specific recognition in the accounts only of discounts *not* taken. To illustrate, assume that goods with a gross invoice price of $1,000 are purchased under terms 2/10, n/30. The purchase would be recorded at net invoice price, as follows:

May 4	Purchases	980	
	Accounts Payable		980
	To record $1,000 purchase; terms 2/10, n/30.		

This entry is considerably preferable theoretically because it states the cost of the goods at the amount of cash for which they could be acquired and because it states the liability accounts payable at the amount of cash for which it could be settled.

If the discount is taken, the entry is a debit to Accounts Payable and a credit to Cash for $980. Note that under this procedure discounts taken do not appear in the accounts.

If the invoice is paid after the discount period has passed, the entry required is:

May 31	Discounts Lost	20	
	Accounts Payable	980	
	Cash		1,000
	To record payment of an account and the discount lost.		

With discount rates around 2 percent, effective management of cash would call for establishing procedures so that all invoices are paid within their discount privilege period. The failure to take a discount should be highlighted and immediately brought out as a deviation from management policy. Note that the above procedure does exactly this; it calls management's attention to discounts not taken by recording them in a Discounts Lost account. The Discounts Lost account then actually contains losses from inefficiency, even though it is reported in the earnings statement among "other expenses."

Indicate whether each of the following statements is correct or incorrect.

1. For many firms, the recording of purchase discounts not taken is more significant information than that of purchase discounts taken.
2. If recorded, purchase discounts taken should be treated as adjustments of the recorded cost of purchases.
3. Under the net price procedure, purchases are recorded at net invoice price regardless of whether the discount is actually taken or not.
4. It can be argued that the net price procedure permits overstatement of purchases and accounts payable at the time of the initial recording of an invoice.

Now check your responses in Answer Frame 6[3] on page 98.

Answer frame 6[3]

1. Correct. In well-managed firms, taking discounts may be so much a matter of routine that missing a discount is the exception.
2. Correct. When discounts are taken, the actual cost of the purchases is less than the recorded gross invoice price of the goods.
3. Correct. The cash paid out when a discount is missed is treated as a loss rather than as a part of the cost of the goods purchased.
4. Incorrect. Theoretically, it can be maintained that the traditional gross price procedure yields overstated purchases and accounts payable.

If you answered incorrectly, review Frame 6[3] before going on to Frame 7[3] below.

Frame 7[3]

Purchase discounts and transportation charges. Purchase discounts are based on the invoice price of the goods and are not affected by transportation charges, regardless of whether the buyer or the seller is responsible for them. For example, assume that goods with an invoice price of $1,000 are purchased under terms of 2/10, n/30, f.o.b. shipping point, with freight charges of $50 prepaid. The seller's invoice would show the $1,000 invoice price of the goods, to which would be added the $50 of freight charges prepaid, for a total of $1,050. If the invoice is paid within the discount period, the discount allowed would be $20 (0.02 × $1,000), not $21 (0.02 × $1,050), and a net remittance of $1,030 would be required to pay the invoice.

Merchandise inventories

To determine the cost of the goods sold in any accounting period, information is needed as to the cost of the goods on hand at the start of the period (beginning inventory) as well as the cost of the goods on hand at the close of the period (ending inventory). But the task really consists only of determining the cost of the ending inventory, since, because one accounting period follows another, the ending inventory of one period is the beginning inventory of the following period.

Under the periodic procedure, the cost of the ending inventory is determined by (1) actually counting the physical units of merchandise on hand, on display, and in the storeroom; (2) multiplying the number of units of each kind of merchandise by unit cost; and (3) summing the costs of the various kinds of merchandise to obtain the cost of the total inventory.

Once obtained, the cost of the ending inventory is (1) reported in the earnings statement as a deduction from the cost of the goods available for sale to arrive at the cost of the goods sold, (2) entered in the Merchandise Inventory account in the ledger by way of an adjusting entry, and (3) reported as an asset in the statement of financial position prepared at the end of the accounting period. The first two of these uses are illustrated below.

Cost of goods sold. When information is available on the cost of the beginning and ending inventories and on the various elements making up the net cost of purchases, the cost of the goods sold in a period can be determined and reported as shown in Illustration 3.3.

Illustration 3.3, *Determination of Cost of Goods Sold*

Cost of goods sold:			
Merchandise inventory, July 1, 1975			$ 24,433
Purchases		$167,688	
Less: Purchase returns and allowances	$8,101		
Purchase discounts	3,351	11,452	
Net purchases		$156,236	
Add: Transportation-in		10,453	
Net cost of purchases			166,689
Cost of goods available for sale			$191,122
Merchandise inventory, June 30, 1976			31,010
Cost of Goods Sold			$160,112

Indicate whether each of the following statements concerning Illustration 3.3 is true or false.

1. The ending inventory on June 30, 1975, had a cost of $24,433.
2. The total cost of the goods that could have been sold in the year ended June 30, 1976, was $191,122.
3. It would appear that purchases made by the company were subject to an average cash discount in excess of 2 percent.
4. The net expense for the merchandise sold during the year was $160,112.

Check your responses in Answer Frame 7[3] on page 100.

Frame 8[3]

Adjusting entries for cost of goods sold. To yield the information contained in Illustration 3.3, the underlying ledger accounts and their balances would have to be:

Merchandise Inventory	$ 24,433 Dr.
Purchases	167,688 Dr.
Purchase Returns and Allowances	8,101 Cr.
Purchase Discounts	3,351 Cr.
Transportation-In	10,453 Dr.

Additionally, the cost of the ending inventory, $31,010, must be known. But until further entries are made the accounts actually contain raw, unadjusted data. They do not clearly differentiate between that portion of the above items that should be considered an expense for the

Answer frame 7[3]

1. True. The ending inventory for the year ended June 30, 1975, is the beginning inventory for the year ended June 30, 1976, and this is given as $24,433.
2. True. In Illustration 3.3, this amount is "cost of goods available for sale."
3. True. Purchase discounts of $3,351 amount to slightly more than 2 percent of $159,587 (purchases of $167,688 less purchase returns and allowances of $8,101).
4. True. The accounting term for this expense is "cost of goods sold," and this is stated to be $160,112 in Illustration 3.3.

If you missed any of the above, you should restudy Frame 7[3] before proceeding to Frame 8[3] on page 99.

8[3]
continued

period and that portion that should be reported as an asset in the statement of financial position prepared at the end of the period. The required additional entries could be prepared in several different ways, one of which is:

June 30	Cost of Goods Sold	191,122	
	Purchase Returns and Allowances	8,101	
	Purchase Discounts	3,351	
	Merchandise Inventory		24,433
	Purchases		167,688
	Transportation-In		10,453
	To transfer the beginning inventory and the accounts comprising net purchases to the Cost of Goods Sold expense account.		
30	Merchandise Inventory	31,010	
	Cost of Goods Sold		31,010
	To set up ending inventory and reduce Cost of Goods Sold by the cost of goods not sold.		

(As an alternative, the above two entries could be combined with all items remaining the same except that the debit to Cost of Goods Sold would be $160,112 and there would be a net debit to Merchandise Inventory of $6,577.)

The accounts are shown below (with posting references and account numbers omitted) as they would appear after the above adjusting entries were posted. Note that the balance in the Merchandise Inventory account of $24,433 is dated June 30, 1975, which shows clearly that the ending inventory of the prior year is the beginning inventory of the current year. Observe also that this balance remains unchanged throughout the year, a distinguishing feature of the periodic inventory procedure.

The balances shown in the Purchases, Purchase Returns and Allowances, Purchase Discounts, and Transportation-In accounts are the amounts of each of these items accumulated for the entire year and could result from the posting of dozens of entries to each of these accounts.

Now observe how the first of the adjusting entries given above transfers

Merchandise Inventory

Date		Explanation	L.F.	Debit	Credit	Balance
1975 June	30					24,433
1976 June	30	Transfer to Cost of Goods Sold			24,433	—0—
	30	Set up ending inventory		31,010		31,010

Purchases

Date		Explanation	L.F.	Debit	Credit	Balance
1975 July	1 to					
1976 June	30					167,688
	30	Transfer to Cost of Goods Sold			167,688	—0—

Purchase Returns and Allowances

Date		Explanation	L.F.	Debit	Credit	Balance
1975 July	1 to					
1976 June	30					8,101
	30	Transfer to Cost of Goods Sold		8,101		—0—

Purchase Discounts

Date		Explanation	L.F.	Debit	Credit	Balance
1975 July	1 to					
1976 June	30					3,351
	30	Transfer to Cost of Goods Sold		3,351		—0—

Transportation-In

Date		Explanation	L.F.	Debit	Credit	Balance
1975 July	1 to					
1976 June	30					10,453
	30	Transfer to Cost of Goods Sold			10,453	—0—

Cost of Goods Sold

Date		Explanation	L.F.	Debit	Credit	Balance
1976 June	30	Goods available for sale		191,122		191,122
	30	Set up ending inventory			31,010	160,112

into the Cost of Goods Sold account the net cost of all of the goods available for sale during the year. The second adjusting entry then removes from the Cost of Goods Sold account the cost of the goods unsold at year-end and establishes this amount as the ending inventory. This entry leaves in the Cost of Goods Sold account the amount of expense incurred during the year for the units of merchandise delivered to customers. The Cost of Goods Sold account is now ready to be closed, as illustrated and discussed in Chapter 4.

Indicate whether each of the following statements is true or false. When properly prepared, the adjusting entries to enter the cost of the goods sold into the accounts will include:

1. A credit to Transportation-In to reduce this account to a zero balance.
2. A credit to Merchandise Inventory to set up the ending inventory.
3. A debit to Purchase Discounts to reduce this account to a zero balance.
4. A credit to Purchases to reduce this account to a zero balance.

Now check your responses in Answer Frame 8[3] on page 104.

Frame 9[3]

Earnings statement for a merchandising company

The previously presented information on sales and cost of goods sold, together with additional assumed data on operating expenses and other expense and revenue, is arrayed to yield the earnings statement contained in Illustration 3.4. Note that the statement contains four sections, namely, sections for: (1) operating revenues, (2) cost of goods sold, (3) operating expenses, and (4) nonoperating revenues and expenses.

The term *operating revenues* refers to the revenues generated by the major activities of the business, usually the sale of products or services or both. All other revenues are nonoperating revenues and usually are of an incidental nature, such as those illustrated—gain on sale of equipment and interest revenue.

Operating expenses are those incurred in the normal buying, selling, and administrative functions of a business. In reality, cost of goods sold is an operating expense, and, indeed, the major one in mercantile firms. But it is customary to highlight the relationship between cost of goods sold and sales revenue by reporting as a specific amount called *gross margin* the amount by which sales revenues exceed the cost of the goods sold. Gross margin is often referred to as a percentage rate and is computed by dividing gross margin by net sales. In Illustration 3.4, it is approximately 38.7 percent. This rate is closely watched by management, since a small fluctuation can cause a substantial change in net earnings.

Illustration 3.4, *Earnings Statement for a Merchandising Company*

HARDISON COMPANY
Earnings Statement
For the Year Ended June 30, 1976

Revenues:				
Gross sales				$282,345
Less: Sales discounts			$ 5,548	
Sales returns and allowances			15,436	20,984
Net sales				$261,361
Cost of goods sold:				
Merchandise inventory, July 1, 1975			$ 24,433	
Purchases		$167,688		
Less: Purchase returns and allowances	$8,101			
Purchase discounts	3,351	11,452		
Net purchases		$156,236		
Add: Transportation-in		10,453		
Net cost of purchases			166,689	
Goods available for sale			$191,122	
Merchandise inventory, June 30, 1976			31,010	
Cost of goods sold				160,112
Gross margin				$101,249
Operating expenses:				
Selling expenses:				
Sales salaries and commissions		$ 26,245		
Salesmen's travel expense		2,821		
Transportation-out		2,729		
Advertising		3,475		
Rent		2,400		
Supplies used		1,048		
Utilities		1,641		
Depreciation—store equipment		750		
Other selling expense		412	$ 41,521	
Administrative expenses:				
Salaries, office		$ 29,350		
Rent		1,600		
Insurance		1,548		
Supplies used		722		
Contributions		500		
Depreciation—office equipment		600		
Other administrative expense		347	34,667	
Total operating expenses				76,188
Net earnings from operations				$ 25,061
Other revenue:				
Interest revenue			$ 256	
Gain on sale of equipment			1,175	1,431
				$26,492
Other expense:				
Interest expense				721
Net Earnings				$ 25,771

Answer frame 8³

1. True. The balance in this account is absorbed in determining the proper balance for the Cost of Goods Sold account.
2. False. Merchandise Inventory is debited to set up the ending inventory.
3. True. The balance in this account is absorbed in determining the proper balance for the Cost of Goods Sold account.
4. True. The balance in this account is absorbed in determining the proper balance for the Cost of Goods Sold account.

If you answered any of the above incorrectly, review Frame 8³ before proceeding to Frame 9³ on page 102.

9³
continued

Operating expenses can be classified in a number of different ways which are presented and discussed in Chapter 8 of *Acounting II*, the companion text in this series. But, as a minimum, they are usually divided into *selling* and *administrative* expenses. Selling expenses are those incurred that relate directly to the sale and delivery of a product or a service. Administrative expenses are those incurred in the overall management of a business. Examples of both types are given in Illustration 3.4. A careful classification of operating expenses will inevitably require allocation of certain expenses between the selling and administrative functions. For example, it would appear that the rent expense of the Hardison Company was allocated between selling expense and administrative expense. How this is done, and some of the pitfalls to be avoided, are discussed in Chapter 8 of *Accounting II*.

Note should also be made of the difference between transportation-in and transportation-out. The latter is an expense incurred to help sell a product, while transportation-in is a part of the cost of the merchandise acquired during the period.

The more important relationships in the earnings statement of a merchandising firm can be summarized in equation form:

1. NET SALES = GROSS SALES − SALES RETURNS AND ALLOWANCES − SALES DISCOUNTS
2. COST OF GOODS SOLD = INVENTORY AT BEGINNING OF PERIOD + (PURCHASES + TRANSPORTATION-IN − PURCHASE RETURNS AND ALLOWANCES − PURCHASE DISCOUNTS) − INVENTORY AT END OF PERIOD.
3. GROSS MARGIN = NET SALES − COST OF GOODS SOLD.
4. NET EARNINGS FROM OPERATIONS = GROSS MARGIN − OPERATING (SELLING AND ADMINISTRATIVE) EXPENSES.
5. NET EARNINGS = NET EARNINGS FROM OPERATIONS + OTHER REVENUE − OTHER EXPENSES.

It is, of course, entirely possible that the expenses incurred (operating and nonoperating) will exceed the revenues earned (operating and nonoperating), so that the final result for the period is a net loss rather than net earnings.

The multiple-step earnings statement of Illustration 3.4, with its many intermediate additions and subtractions, is more likely to be used for internal reporting and should be contrasted with the single-step earnings statement shown in Illustration 2.4 on page 66, which is more commonly used for external reporting.

Indicate whether each of the following statements is true or false.

1. Although not specifically referred to as such in the earnings statement, the cost of the goods sold is, in reality, an operating expense.
2. It would be quite unlikely that a business would have a negative gross margin.
3. The rent earned from leasing out a part of the building owned would be classified as an operating revenue by a merchandising company.
4. The balance in a Discounts Lost account probably would be reported as an administrative operating expense in the earnings statement.

Check your responses in Answer Frame 9[3] on page 106.

Frame 10[3]

The fundamental aspects of accounting for and reporting upon the merchandising activities of certain types of businesses have now been presented and discussed. Left for discussion at this time were certain related matters of sufficient importance to merit individual attention, namely, trade discounts, items of merchandise that should and that should not be included in inventory, inventory losses, and debit and credit memoranda.

Nature and computation of trade discounts

A trade discount is a deduction from the list or catalog price of an article. It is a means employed to determine the actual selling price of an item purchased. The amount of the trade discount probably will be shown on the seller's invoice but not recorded in his records, nor is it to be recorded on the books of the purchaser. Assume an invoice as follows:

List price, 200 swimsuits at $3	$600
Less: Trade discount, 30 percent	180
Gross invoice price	$420

The vendor would record the sale at $420, and the purchaser would record the cost of the merchandise at $420.

A policy of quoting trade discounts is followed for several reasons, such as:

1. To reduce the cost of catalog publication. If separate discount lists are given the salesmen whenever prices change, catalogs may be used for a long period of time. Prices may be changed by simply changing the trade discounts without reprinting the entire catalog.

Answer frame 9[3]

1. True. If expenses are classified broadly as operating or nonoperating, the cost of the goods sold can hardly be a nonoperating expense.
2. True. While certain goods may be closed out at selling prices less than cost, only in a firm that is going out of business is it likely that the cost of the goods sold will exceed sales revenue for a period of time.
3. False. It is likely to be incidental to the merchandising operations and classifiable as nonoperating revenue.
4. False. It would be better classified as a nonoperating expense, since it is more in the nature of a loss that did not have to be incurred.

If you answered incorrectly, review Frame 9[3] before going on to Frame 10[3] on page 105.

10[3]
continued

2. To grant quantity discounts. If discounts are increased, customers may be induced to buy in larger quantities. For example, a customer may be allowed a 20 percent discount if he buys up to 100 units and an additional 5 percent discount if he buys up to 300 units.
3. To be able to quote different prices to different types of customers, such as to retailers and wholesalers.

Trade discounts are computed as indicated below. Assume that the list price of an article is $50 subject to trade discounts as indicated:

On total purchases up to 50 units, 20 percent.
On total purchases of from 51 to 100 units, 20 and 10 percent.
On total purchases of from 101 to 150 units, 20, 10, and 5 percent.

The price for 150 units would be quoted as $50 less 20 percent, 10 percent, and 5 percent on each and every unit; this is known as a series of trade discounts, or as a chain discount.

The computation of the gross invoice price of the 150 units is as follows:

List price—150 @ $50	$7,500
Less: 20 percent of $7,500	1,500
Remainder	$6,000
Less: 10 percent of $6,000	600
Remainder	$5,400
Less: 5 percent of $5,400	270
Gross invoice price	$5,130

The same results can be obtained by multiplying the list price by the complements of the discounts allowed. For example, $7,500 × .80 × .90 × .95 = $5,130. The gross invoice price to be recorded in the accounting records of the seller and the buyer is $5,130. Price-determining trade discounts are not reflected in recorded sales or purchases. But an invoice for the above 150 units could quote terms of 2/10, n/30. And if the invoice is recorded at gross price by the buyer and paid within the discount period, a purchase discount of $10.26 (0.02 × $5,130) would be recorded.

Indicate whether each of the following statements is true or false.

1. Trade discounts may be granted to induce customers to buy in larger quantities.
2. Trade discounts are used by a seller to quote different prices to different types of customers, such as wholesalers and retailers.
3. A seller's invoice appears as follows (terms 2/10, n/30):

List price, 100 pairs of men's socks @ $0.50	$50.00
Less: Trade discount, 25%	12.50
Gross invoice price	$37.50

   The purchaser should record a $50 purchase in his records if he employs the gross price procedure.
4. In the invoice in statement 3 above, a purchase of $36.75 could be recorded if the buyer employs the net price procedure.

Now check your responses in Answer Frame 10[3] on page 108.

Frame 11[3]

Inventory exclusions and inclusions

In taking a physical inventory, care must be exercised to ensure that all goods owned, regardless of where they are located, are counted and included in the inventory. Thus, goods shipped to a potential customer "on approval" should not be recorded as sold and should be included in inventory if the customer has not indicated his intention to keep the goods by the date of the inventory taking. Similarly, goods delivered on a consignment basis should not be recorded as sold. Here the intent is that the goods remain the property of the shipper (consignor) until sold by the consignee. Such goods must be included in the shipper's inventory.

Merchandise in transit at the end of an accounting period must be recorded as a purchase by the buyer and included in his inventory if title to the goods has passed to him. Generally, whether title has passed can be determined from the freight terms under which the goods were shipped. Goods in the hands of the delivering agent (airfreight line, railroad, or trucking or steamship company) are (1) the property of the seller if shipped f.o.b. destination, or (2) the property of the buyer if shipped f.o.b. shipping point. Briefly stated, the goods belong to the party who must bear the transportation charges.

On occasion, goods may remain in the possession of the seller after they have been sold. Usually, such goods have been segregated from other items in stock, packaged, and placed in a convenient place awaiting pickup by the buyer. If title has actually passed, the goods must be excluded from the seller's inventory.

Goods rendered unsalable by damage, deterioration, or obsolescence

Answer frame 10³

1. True. This is a valid use of trade discounts.
2. True. This is also a valid and common use of trade discounts.
3. False. He should record the purchase at $37.50 if he is using the gross price procedure. List prices are not recorded in the accounts, since they do not represent actual exchange prices.
4. True. If the net price procedure is employed, a purchase in the amount of $36.75 would be recorded: $37.50 – (0.02 × $37.50).

If you answered incorrectly, review Frame 10³ before proceeding to Frame 11³ on page 107.

11³ *continued*

should not be included in inventory. If salable only at a reduced price, the dollar amount attached to the goods must be reduced. As a general rule this amount should not exceed the selling price of the goods less any expected disposition and selling costs. This procedure charges the amount of the write-down of the goods to the accounting period in which the loss occurred.

Inventory losses

Under the periodic inventory procedure, the general presumption is that the difference between goods available for sale and the ending inventory is the cost of the goods sold. In other words, it is assumed that, of all of the goods available for sale, those not on hand at the end of the acounting period were sold. But it is not necessarily true that all of the missing goods were sold. Some goods are subject to shrinkage or spoilage, and losses from shoplifting are estimated at billions of dollars annually in the United States. Such losses are, under the periodic inventory procedure, automatically buried in the cost of goods sold.

To illustrate, assume that the cost of certain goods available for sale was $100,000 and the actual ending inventory is $30,000. This suggests that the cost of the goods sold to customers was $70,000. But assume further that it is known that $1,000 of goods were shoplifted. If such goods had not been stolen, the ending inventory would have been $31,000 and the cost of goods sold only $69,000. Thus, the cost of goods sold of $70,000 includes the cost of the merchandise delivered to customers and the cost of merchandise stolen. Because the amount of goods lost to shoplifters may be significant information, a method of estimating inventory losses is presented in Chapter 8 in *Accounting II*.

Indicate whether each of the following statements is true or false.

1. Goods in transit sold under terms of f.o.b. destination are the property of the seller until they reach their destination.
2. Under certain rather rare circumstances, a seller may have goods in his possession that are legally the property of a buyer.
3. Goods shipped on consignment are the property of the shipper until sold by the consignee.

4. A disadvantage of the periodic inventory procedure is that it does not readily permit the determination of losses resulting from damaged, deteriorated, or obsolete goods.

Now check your responses in Answer Frame 11^3 on page 110.

Frame 12^3

Debit and credit memoranda

In view of the volume of business done, it is inevitable that the amounts billed for merchandise sold will, on occasion, require adjustment to correct errors or for returns permitted or allowances granted. The amount of an adjustment for an error, return, or allowance is usually entered on a business document called a debit or credit memorandum. Which type of memorandum will be employed depends upon the nature of the adjustment and whether the originating party is the buyer or the seller.

A buyer may, for example, discover that the items on an invoice were added incorrectly, with the result that the total price was overstated. He would then issue a debit memorandum as a means of informing the seller that the balance in the seller's Accounts Payable account on the buyer's books was being debited (decreased) because of the error. The buyer would record this debit memorandum as a debit to Accounts Payable and a credit to Purchases. The seller would debit Sales and credit Accounts Receivable. If the error were in the opposite direction, or if extra goods were shipped and the buyer found that he could use them, he would issue a credit memorandum notifying the seller that his Accounts Payable account was being credited (increased). The buyer would debit

Illustration 3.5, *Debit Memorandum*

Debit Memorandum No. 94
Date 7/18/76

CHANEY COMPANY
1001 Good Luck Road
Riverdale, Md. 21905

To: Top Quality Wholesale Stores
Address: 1542 Jolly Road
Port Erie, Mich. 48221

We Debit Your Account As Follows:

Error on your invoice #443321; price charged for 10 tables, model no. 5567, was $540; correct total price is $450. Difference $90.00

Chaney Company

by S. Brown

Answer frame 11^3

1. True. Generally, such goods are the legal property of the seller.
2. True. This is likely to be the case where the seller is to package the goods and set them aside and the buyer is to pick them up.
3. True. When sold by the consignee, they of course become the property of the buyer.
4. False. The periodic inventory procedure does not readily permit isolation of losses resulting from shinkage, spoilage, or shoplifting. But, since damaged, deteriorated, or obsolete goods are not likely to be sold, they remain on hand and should be written down when inventoried.

If you missed any of the above, review Frame 11^3 before proceeding to Frame 12^3 on page 109.

12^3 *continued*

Purchases and credit Accounts Payable, while the seller would debit Accounts Receivable and credit Sales.

A seller may issue a debit memorandum as a means of notifying a buyer that his Accounts Receivable account on the seller's books is being debited (increased) and the reason for the debit, which is likely to be a correction of an error. But a more likely event is for a seller to issue a credit memorandum, usually after negotiation with the buyer and after granting him an allowance or permission to return goods. Such a credit memorandum would be recorded by the seller by debiting Sales Returns and Allowances and crediting Accounts Receivable, while the buyer would debit Accounts Payable and credit Purchase Returns and Allowances.

An example of a debit memorandum is presented in Illustration 3.5, while Illustration 3.6 contains an example of a credit memorandum.

Illustration 3.6, *Credit Memorandum*

Credit Memorandum No. 145
Date 7/21/76

CHANEY COMPANY
1001 Good Luck Road
Riverdale, Md. 21905

To: Brice Stores, Inc.
1456 Mason Road
Lansing, Mich. 48824

We Credit Your Account As Follows:

Allowance granted, as per our telephone conversation, for blemishes and scratches on furniture shipped and billed on our invoice no. 516.................................. $400

Chaney Company

by Hal White

With regard to the debit memorandum in Illustration 3.5 or the credit memorandum in Illustration 3.6, indicate whether each of the following statements is true or false.

1. The debit memorandum was originated by the Chaney Company.
2. Chaney Company would record the debit memorandum as a debit to Accounts Receivable and a credit to Sales.
3. Top Quality Wholesale Stores would record the debit memorandum by a debit to Accounts Payable and a credit to Purchase Returns and Allowances.
4. Brice Stores, Inc. would record the credit memorandum by debiting Accounts Payable and crediting Purchase Returns and Allowances.
5. Chaney Company would record the credit memorandum by debiting Sales Returns and Allowances and crediting Accounts Receivable.

Now check your responses in Answer Frame 12[3] on page 112.

Summary *chapter* 3

Sales revenue (net sales, or gross sales less sales discounts and sales returns and allowances) is generally recognized when a sale has been completed. A completed sale involves legal transfer of title to goods and is usually accompanied by physical delivery of the goods. Recognition of revenue at the time of sale is usually justified on the grounds that the revenue has been earned and realized.

Three common adjustments of the gross invoice prices entered in the Sales account are for sales returns, sales allowances, and sales discounts, all of which are recorded in contra accounts to Sales. Net sales shows the approximate amount of assets expected to flow into a firm from its customers.

Theoretically, cash discounts are adjustments of the selling price of goods, although they are often viewed as rewards for prompt payment. A cash discount is a sales discount to the seller and a purchase discount to the buyer. Cash discount terms can be readily converted into equivalent annual interest rates as an aid in determining whether money should be borrowed to take cash discounts.

The cost of the goods sold can be determined under the perpetual procedure, in which the cost of each sale is determined at the time of sale, or under the periodic procedure, in which the cost of all sales made during a period is determined only at the end of the period. The periodic procedure involves less record keeping but fails to show the amount of goods that should be on hand at any one time. Under the periodic procedure, cost of goods sold is determined as being equal to beginning inventory plus net purchases less ending inventory. Net purchases is equal to purchases plus transportation-in less purchase returns and allowances and purchase discounts. Transportation charges are the responsibility of the

Answer frame 12³

1. True. The debit memorandum carries the Chaney Company name in its heading and is signed by an employee of the company.
2. False. Chaney Company would enter a debit to Accounts Payable and a credit to Purchases.
3. False. The correct entry would contain a debit to Sales and a credit to Accounts Receivable for $90 since an actual error, not a return or allowance is involved.
4. True. Brice Stores, Inc. has been granted a purchase allowance which reduces the cost of its purchases and its liability on open account to the Chaney Company.
5. True. From the Chaney Company point of view, it has granted a sales allowance and this reduces the debt owed to it by Brice Stories, Inc.

If you answered incorrectly, you should study Frame 12² again carefully and then proceed to the chapter summary on page 111.

---

seller for goods shipped f.o.b. destination, of the buyer for goods shipped f.o.b. shipping point.

Purchases may be recorded at gross invoice prices and (1) discounts taken recorded in a Purchase Discounts account, or recorded at net invoice prices, and (2) purchase discounts not taken recorded in a Discounts Lost account.

Under the periodic procedure, an adjusting entry is required at the end of an accounting period in order to record the proper balance in the Cost of Goods Sold expense account.

The earnings statement of a merchandising company is likely to have four sections, one each for operating revenues, cost of goods sold, operating expenses, and nonoperating revenues and expenses.

Trade discounts are deductions from list or catalog prices to determine actual selling prices. They are not formally recorded by either the buyer or the seller.

The ending inventory should include all goods owned, regardless of where located. It should exclude all goods not legally owned, as well as all unsalable goods. Goods salable only at reduced prices should normally be written down for inventory purposes.

Cost of goods sold, under the periodic procedure, includes the cost of goods missing because of shrinkage, spoilage, and shoplifting—a distinct disadvantage of the procedure.

Debit and credit memoranda are the business documents used to correct or adjust the invoiced selling prices of goods sold for reasons of error, return, or the granting of an allowance.

You have completed the programmed portion of Chapter 3. As the first part of your review, read the glossary which follows and study the definitions of the new terms introduced in this chapter. Then go on to the Student Review Quiz for a self-administered test of your comprehension of the material in the chapter.

Glossary *chapter* 3

Administrative expenses—operating expenses incurred in the overall management of a business.

Cash discount—to the seller, a sales discount; to the buyer, a purchase discount; a deduction allowed from the gross invoice price that can be taken only if the invoice is paid within a specified period of time; typically, cash discounts vary from less than 1 percent to 3 percent.

Consignment—goods shipped by one party (the consignor) to another (the consignee) who is to pay for the goods only if he is able to sell them to a third party.

Cost of goods sold—an expense incurred consisting of the cost to the seller of goods sold to customers; computed as Beginning Inventory + (Purchases + Transportation-In − Purchase Returns and Allowances − Purchase Discounts) − Ending Inventory.

Credit memorandum—a business document used by a seller to inform a customer that his Accounts Receivable account on the seller's books is being credited (reduced) for reasons such as errors, returns, or allowances granted; when prepared by the buyer it informs seller that his Accounts Payable account on the buyer's books is being credited (increased), usually in order to correct an error.

Debit memorandum—a business document used by a seller to inform a customer that his Accounts Receivable account on the seller's books is being debited (increased) for some reason, usually correction of an error; when prepared by a buyer it informs the seller that his Accounts Payable account on the buyer's books is being debited (reduced) for some reason, such as damaged merchandise.

Discounts Lost account—an account used to show discounts not taken when purchased merchandise is recorded at net invoice price.

F.o.b. destination—freight terms that mean goods are shipped to their destination without charge to the buyer; in other words, the seller bears the transportation charges.

F.o.b. shipping point—freight terms that mean goods are placed in the hands of the transporting company without charge to the buyer; the buyer is responsible for all transportation costs that follow.

Freight collect—terms that require the buyer to pay the freight bill when the goods are delivered; if the terms are f.o.b. destination, he will deduct the amount of freight when he remits to seller.

Freight prepaid—terms that indicate the seller has paid the freight bill at the time of shipment; if the terms are f.o.b. shipping point, he will bill the buyer for the amount paid.

Gross margin—Net Sales − Cost of Goods Sold.

Merchandise in transit—goods in the hands of a transport company on an inventory-taking date.

Merchandise inventory—the quantity of goods on hand and available for sale at any given time.

Net earnings—Net Earnings from Operations + Other Revenue − Other Expense.

Net earnings from operations—Gross Margin − Operating Expenses.

Net sales—Gross Sales − Sales Returns and Allowances − Sales Discounts.

Nonoperating expenses—expenses incurred that are not directly related to the acquisition and sale of the commodities or services regularly offered for sale; for example, interest expense.

Nonoperating revenues—revenues not directly related to the sale of products or services regularly offered for sale; for example, interest revenue.

Operating expenses—expenses incurred in the normal buying, selling, and administrative functions of a business.

Operating revenues—revenues resulting from the sale of products or services regularly offered for sale.

Passage of title—a legal term used to indicate transfer of legal ownership of goods.

Periodic inventory procedure—a system of accounting for merchandise acquired for sale to customers wherein the cost of such merchandise sold and the amount of such merchandise on hand are determined only through the taking of a physical inventory.

Perpetual inventory procedure—a system of accounting for merchandise acquired for sale to customers wherein the cost of such merchandise sold and the amount of such merchandise on hand can be determined at any time by reference to the Cost of Goods Sold and Merchandise Inventory accounts.

Purchase Discounts account—an account used under the periodic inventory procedure to record the amount of discounts taken when payment is made within a specified period of time; properly viewed as a reduction in the recorded cost of purchases.

Purchase invoice—a document prepared by the seller of merchandise and sent to the buyer that contains the details of a sale, such as the number of units, unit price, total price billed, terms of sale, and manner of shipment; a purchase invoice from the seller's point of view is a sales invoice.

Purchase order—a form prepared by a potential buyer ordering merchandise from a prospective seller.

Purchase Returns and Allowances account—an account used under the periodic inventory procedure to record the cost of merchandise returned to a seller and to record reductions in selling prices granted by a seller because merchandise was not satisfactory to buyer; viewed as a reduction in the recorded cost of purchases.

Purchases account—an account used under the periodic inventory procedure to record the cost of merchandise purchased during the current accounting period.

Sales allowances—deductions from the originally agreed-upon sales price for merchandise granted by the seller to the buyer because the merchandise sold was not fully satisfactory to the buyer; to the buyer, a purchase allowance.

Sales discounts—a reduction of the amount due from a buyer granted by the seller for prompt payment; theoretically, an adjustment of recorded sales price; to the buyer, a purchase discount.

Sales Discounts account—an account used to record sales discounts taken by customers; a contra account to Sales.

Sales invoice—see purchase invoice.

Sales returns—from the seller's point of view, merchandise returned by a buyer for any of a variety of reasons; to the buyer, a purchase return.

Sales Returns and Allowances account—a contra account to Sales used to record the selling price of merchandise returned by buyers or reductions in selling prices granted.

Selling expenses—operating expenses directly incurred in the sale and delivery of merchandise or in the rendering of services to customers.

Trade discounts—deductions from the list or catalog prices of merchandise to arrive at the gross invoice selling price; granted for quantity purchases or to particular categories of customers (e.g., retailers and wholesalers).

Transportation-In account—an account used under the periodic inventory procedure to record transportation costs incurred in the acquisition of merchandise; an addition to the cost of the merchandise purchased.

Student review quiz *chapter* 3

To develop a permanent record of your responses, you may write them on the answer sheet provided in the *Work Papers* or on a separate sheet of paper. Unless instructed otherwise, select the one best answer for each question.

1 Recording revenue at the time a sale is made is generally considered appropriate because—

a) The revenue has been earned—the seller has completed his part of the agreement.
b) The revenue has been realized—that is, valid assets have been received in an exchange.
c) The revenue is measurable with a fairly high degree of precision.
d) Legal title to the goods has passed to the buyer.
e) All of the above.

2 Choose the one incorrect statement regarding sales discounts.

a) They generally range in size from less than 1 percent to 3 percent of the gross invoice price of the goods sold.
b) They are usually granted to induce prompt payment of an account.
c) Theoretically, they are best viewed

as reductions in recorded selling prices.

d) They are usually credited to a Sales Discounts account when taken.

e) They are deducted from Sales to determine or arrive at Net Sales.

3 Given a list or catalog price of $1,000, trade discounts of 25, 20, and 10 percent, and cash discount terms of 2/10, n/30, the gross invoice price of this merchandise when sold would be:

a) $540.
b) $529.20.
c) $980.
d) $550.
e) $490.

4 Assuming that $540 is the correct answer in 3 above, prepare the entry that should be made on the buyer's books at the time of payment, assuming payment within the discount period.

5 A firm received an invoice in the amount of $5,000, terms 3/10, n/30. It can borrow funds at an 8 percent rate of interest. Compute the equivalent annual rate of interest paid if the invoice is paid on the 30th day. Also compute the dollar amount saved if funds are borrowed on the 10th day to pay the invoice and the loan is repaid 20 days later.

6 All of the following are contra (or reduction) accounts except—

a) Sales Discounts.
b) Purchase Discounts.
c) Transportation-In.
d) Sales Returns and Allowances.
e) Purchase Returns and Allowances.

7 As between the perpetual and the periodic inventory procedures of accounting for merchandise, the periodic procedure (choose the incorrect statement)—

a) Is less costly to apply, since it accumulates less detail.

b) Provides better control over inventory.

c) Buries losses from shrinkage and shoplifting in cost of goods sold.

d) Is more appropriate, economically, for merchandise having a low individual unit value.

8 On June 21 the Dorest Company purchased merchandise f.o.b. destination, freight collect. Having paid the freight bill on delivery of the goods, the company should, in order to record the payment properly, credit Cash and debit (assume the periodic inventory procedure)—

a) Transportation-In.
b) Accounts Receivable.
c) Merchandise Inventory.
d) Purchases.
e) Accounts Payable.

9 For which of the following purposes are trade discounts typically *not* used?

a) To encourage prompt payment of an invoice.

b) To facilitate charging different prices to different types of customers.

c) To induce purchasers to acquire larger amounts of merchandise.

d) To permit the changing of prices without reprinting an expensive catalog.

10 Which of the following should be excluded from inventory?

a) Goods salable only at reduced prices.

b) Goods out on consignment in the hands of a dealer in a nearby city.

c) Incoming goods in transit shipped f.o.b. shipping point.

d) Goods delivered to a customer on approval.

e) Goods on hand title to which has passed to a customer.

11 Given the following information:

Beginning inventory........	$ 5,000
Sales......................	15,900
Ending inventory..........	3,000
Purchases.................	9,000
Sales returns and allowances.	600
Transportation-in..........	700
Sales discounts............	300
Purchase discounts.........	200
Purchase returns and allowances.................	400

Which of the following statements are correct?

a) Net sales are $15,000.

b) Net cost of purchases is $9,100.

c) Cost of goods available for sale is $14,100.

d) Cost of goods sold is $11,100.

e) Gross margin is $3,900.

12 On June 1, the following entry was made to record an invoice received on that date:

Purchases...........	1,000	
Accounts Payable.		1,000
To record purchase on which the terms were 2/10, n/30.		

What entry would be correct if the invoice were paid on June 10?

a)

Accounts Payable...	1,000	
Cash...........		1,000

b)

Accounts Payable...	980	
Purchase Discounts..	20	
Cash..........		1,000

c)

Accounts Payable...	980	
Cash...........		980

d)

Accounts Payable...	1,000	
Cash...........		980
Purchase Discounts.......		20

13 Rae's Dress Shop received from Lorraine, Inc. merchandise having an invoice price of $4,000, terms 1/15, n/60, f.o.b. shipping point; and also paid $20 shipping charges to Speedy Delivery Company. If payment of the Lorraine, Inc. invoice is made within the discount period, the amount of the check should be:

a) $4,000 – ($4,000 × 0.01) = $3,960.
b) $4,000 – $20 – ($4,000 × 0.01) = $3,940.
c) $4,000 – $20 – ($3,980 × 0.01) = $3,940.20.
d) $4,000 – ($3,980 × 0.01) = $3,960.20.
e) $4,000 + $20 – ($4,020 × 0.01) = $3,979.80.

14 If the ending inventory is overstated—

a) Cost of goods sold is understated and net earnings for the period are overstated.
b) Cost of goods sold is understated and net earnings for the period are understated.
c) Cost of goods sold is overstated and net earnings are overstated.
d) Cost of goods sold is overstated and net earnings are understated.
e) Cost of goods sold is understated and gross margin is understated.

15 Which of the following correctly describes the makeup of the cost of goods sold section of the earnings statement under the periodic inventory procedure?

a) Beginning Inventory + Purchases – Transportation-In – Purchase Returns and Allowances – Purchase Discounts – Ending Inventory.
b) Beginning Inventory + Purchases – Transportation-In – Purchase Returns and Allowances – Purchase Discounts + Ending Inventory.
c) Beginning Inventory + Purchases + Transportation-In + Purchase Returns and Allowances – Purchase Discounts – Ending Inventory.
d) Beginning Inventory + Purchases + Transportation-In – Purchase Returns and Allowances – Purchase Discounts – Ending Inventory.

Now compare your answers with the correct answers and explanations on page 707.

Questions *chapter* 3

1 What account titles are likely to appear in the accounting system of a merchandising company that do not appear in the system employed by a service enterprise?

2 Explain the difference between trade discounts and cash discounts. What are chain discounts and purchase discounts?

3 A financial manager is engaged in explaining his policy to you and states, "Our firm is in a tight financial position. No one will lend us money to take advantage of our discounts. But even though we can't pay within the discount period, I do the next best thing. I pay each bill as soon as I can thereafter." Do you agree that this is the next best approach? Why?

4 Explain the meaning of the terms f.o.b. destination, freight collect, and f.o.b. shipping point, freight prepaid.

5 Determine the effect on net earnings of each of the following:

a) Ending inventory is overstated.
b) Purchases are understated.
c) Purchase discounts are overstated.
d) Transportation-in is overstated.
e) Beginning inventory is understated.

6 You find yourself in conversation with a businessman who employs the perpetual (rather than the periodic) inventory procedure. He says, "Sure, it's cumbersome to keep perpetual inventory records, but it's much easier than having to physically count your inventory at the end of every year as you have to under the periodic procedure." What would be your response?

7 Is it possible that a firm may use the perpetual procedure for some of the products it sells and the periodic procedure for others?

8 The perpetual inventory procedure is said to afford control over inventory. Explain exactly what this control consists of and how it is provided.

9 What kind of an account is the Purchases account? What useful purpose does it serve?

10 How can it be argued that the net price procedure of accounting for merchandise acquisitions permits application of the management by exception principle?

11 What are some of the problems encountered in taking a physical inventory? How does the accountant solve them?

12 What is a contra account? Why is it employed? What are some examples?

13 What is a debit memorandum? A credit memo?

14 What is gross margin? Why might management be interested in the percentage rate of gross margin?

15 What is a multiple-step earnings statement, and what is its alternative? What are the major sections in a multiple-step earnings statement and what is the nature of the items included in each?

Exercises *chapter* 3

1 Prepare a table with the following columnar headings: (*a*) name of account, (*b*) increased by (debit or credit), (*c*) decreased by (debit or credit), and (*d*) normal balance (debit or credit). Complete this table for the following accounts: Sales, Sales Returns and Allowances, Sales Discounts, Accounts Receivable, Purchases, Purchase Returns and Allowances, Purchase Discounts Lost, Cost of Goods Sold, Accounts Payable, and Transportation-In.

2 (*a*) The Warren Company purchased merchandise from the Mitchell Company on account, and before paying its account returned damaged merchandise with an invoice price of $525. Assuming use of the periodic inventory procedure, prepare entries on both firms' books to record the return. (*b*) Prepare the required entries assuming that the Mitchell Company granted an allowance of $175 on the damaged goods instead of accepting the return.

3 What is the last payment date on which the cash discount can be taken on goods sold on March 5 for $16,000, terms 3/10 E.O.M., n/60? Assume that the bill is paid on this date and prepare the correct entry on both the seller's and the buyer's books to record the payment.

4 You have purchased merchandise with a list price of $2,000. Because you are a wholesaler you are granted trade discounts of 30, 20, and 10 percent. The cash discount terms are 2/E.O.M., n/60. How much will you pay if you pay by the end of the month of purchase? How much will you pay if you do not pay until the following month?

5 Merchandise with a gross invoice price of $5,000 was purchased by you under terms of 3/10, n/60, on January 2, 1976. You believe that by March 2, 1976, you could pay a loan taken out to take advantage of the discount. What is the highest annual rate of interest you could afford to pay on the loan and be exactly as well off as if you had taken the discount? (Note: 1976 is a leap year.)

6 What is the total difference between the amount to be paid to the seller by the purchaser of goods if the terms are f.o.b. shipping point and the freight of $28 is paid by the seller and if the terms are f.o.b. destination and the freight of $28 is paid by the buyer?

7 The Z Company uses the periodic inventory procedure. Determine the cost of goods sold for the company assuming purchases during the period were $4,000, transportation-in was $30, purchase returns and allowances were $100, beginning inventory was $2,500, purchase discounts were $200, ending inventory was $1,300, and sales returns and allowances were $500.

8 The Dorchester Company purchased goods for $2,300 on June 14 under the following terms: 3/10, n/30; f.o.b. destination, freight collect. The bill for the freight amounted to $75. Assume that the invoice was paid within the discount period and prepare all entries required on Dorchester's books.

9 Refer to the data in 8 above and assume that the invoice was paid on July 11. Prepare the entry to record the payment made on that date.

Problems, Series A *chapter* 3

3–1–A

Compute the annual rate of interest implicit in each of the following terms under the assumption that the discount is not taken and the invoice is paid when due:

a) 3/10, n/60.
b) 1/10, n/30.
c) 2/10/E.O.M., n/90, goods purchased on May 1.
d) 2/E.O.M., n/60, goods purchased on October 15.

In view of your computations comment on the desirability of borrowing to take advantage of discounts.

3–2–A

The Brooker Company purchased merchandise with a list price of $5,000, f.o.b. destination, freight prepaid, from Arlington, Inc. on September 15, 1976. Trade discounts of 20 and 10 percent were allowed, and credit terms were 2/10, n/30. On September 17 Brooker Company requested a purchase allowance of $235 because some of the merchandise had been damaged in transit. On September 20 it received a credit memorandum from Arlington, Inc. granting the allowance.

Required: Record all the entries required on the books of both the buyer and the seller assuming that both firms use the periodic inventory procedure. Also assume that payment is made on the last day of the discount period.

3–3–A

Required:

a) Journalize the following transactions for Company R.
b) Journalize the following transactions for Company L. Both companies follow the periodic procedure of recording inventories.

Transactions:

May 12 Company R purchased merchandise from Company L, $13,500; terms, 2/10 E.O.M.
20 Company R returned $4,500 of the merchandise to Company L.
June 7 Company L received proper payment in full from Company R.
16 Company R had requested and on this date received a credit memorandum granting a gross allowance of $800 from Company L, due to improper quality of merchandise purchased on May 12.

3–4–A

The purchasing department of the Hanson Corporation asked for and received the following price quotations on 1,400 units of a given product that it wished to buy:

Castle, Inc.—List price $3.80, less 15 percent. Terms: 2/10, n/30, f.o.b. shipping point. (Transportation charges are determined to be $180.)

Dorner Corp.—List price: $3.40 each. Terms: n/30, f.o.b. destination. (Transportation charges are determined to be $175.)
Martini Corp.—List price: $5.50, less 20, 15, and 10 percent quantity discount. Terms: 3/10, n/45, f.o.b. destination. (Transportation charges are determined to be $265.)
Reston Co.—List price: $4.35, less 15 and 10 percent. Terms: n/30, f.o.b. shipping point. (Transportation charges are determined to be $250.)

Required: State which bid should be accepted and support your conclusion with a schedule showing the net cost of each bid.

3–5–A

Goods costing $4,000 were purchased on January 15, 1976, with terms of 2/10, n/30. Freight charges of $216 were paid on January 15.

Required: For each of the following cases give the entries that would be made on the books of both the buyer and the seller, assuming both use the periodic inventory procedure.

Case A—Terms: f.o.b. shipping point, freight prepaid. The invoice was paid on January 20.
Case B—Terms: f.o.b. destination, freight collect. The invoice was paid on February 10.
Case C—Terms: f.o.b. destination, freight prepaid. The invoice was paid on January 25.
Case D—Terms: f.o.b. shipping point, freight collect. The invoice was paid on February 14.

3–6–A

An examination of the records of the Orton Company on December 31, 1976, disclosed the following with regard to merchandise inventory for 1976 and prior years:

1. December 31, 1973: Inventory understated $40,000.
2. December 31, 1974: Inventory of $28,000 was included twice.
3. December 31, 1975: Inventory of $25,000 was omitted.
4. December 31, 1976: Inventory is correct.

The reported net earnings for each year were as follows:

1973...........	$235,000
1974...........	284,000
1975...........	307,000
1976...........	281,000

Required:

a) What are the correct net earnings for 1973, 1974, 1975, and 1976?
b) What is the error in each December 31 statement of financial position?

3–7–A

On August 1, 1976, the Benson Company sold merchandse to the Mandell Company, $6,000 list price, f.o.b. shipping point. (The seller prepaid the freight of $80 on August 1, 1976.) Other terms were trade discounts of 30 and 10 percent and cash discount of 2/10 E.O.M., n/60. On August 8, 1976, the Mandell Company returned

$1,000 (at list price) of the merchandise. The balance due was paid on September 9, 1976.

Required: Journalize all entries required on the books of both the buyer and the seller, assuming that both use the periodic inventory procedure.

3–8–A

Required: From the data given below for the Goldsmith Company (which uses the periodic inventory procedure):

a) Prepare journal entries for the summarized transactions (omit explanations).
b) Post the journal entries to the proper ledger accounts (after entering the balances as of December 31, 1975).
c) Prepare and post entries to record cost of goods sold.
d) Prepare an earnings statement for the year ended December 31, 1976.
e) Prepare a statement of financial position as of December 31, 1976.

GOLDSMITH COMPANY
Statement of Financial Position
December 31, 1975

ASSETS		LIABILITIES AND STOCKHOLDERS' EQUITY	
Cash	$19,000	Accounts payable	$21,000
Accounts receivable	33,000	Capital stock	25,000
Merchandise inventory	28,000	Retained earnings	34,000
Total Assets	$80,000	Total Liabilities and Stockholders' Equity	$80,000

Summarized Transactions for 1976

Sales for cash	$ 67,000
Sales on account (gross)	148,000
Purchases on account (gross)	160,000
Sales discounts	2,000
Sales returns (charge sales)	4,500
Purchase returns	2,200
Purchase discounts	2,400
Cash collected on accounts receivable	137,000
Cash payments on accounts payable	129,000
Land and building purchased (gave one half in cash and a mortgage note for one half)	62,000
Selling expenses incurred and paid for	19,600
Administrative expenses incurred and paid for	18,200
Interest expense on mortgage note on land and building incurred and paid for	1,200

Additional data:

Merchandise inventory at December 31, 1976, per physical listing is $34,400.

3–9–A

Required: From the following information:

a) Journalize the transactions on the records of the Menewell Company.
b) Post the entries to the proper ledger accounts and prepare a trial balance.

c) Journalize the adjusting entries, assuming the May 31 inventory is $14,000.
d) Post the adjusting entries to the proper accounts.
e) Prepare a trial balance as of May 31.
f) Prepare a partial earnings statement for May, through the gross margin figure.

The company was organized on May 1 and uses the periodic inventory procedure.

Transactions:

May	1	Issued 2,000 shares of common stock for $200,000 cash.
	1	Purchased merchandise on account from the Hande Company, $13,000; terms net/10 E.O.M., f.o.b. shipping point.
	3	Sold merchandise for cash, $8,000.
	6	Paid transportation charges on May 1 purchase, $200 cash.
	7	Returned $1,000 of merchandise to the Hande Company due to improper size.
	10	Requested and was granted an allowance of $500 by the Hande Company for improper quality of certain items.
	14	Sale on account to Crestal Company, $5,000; terms 2/20, n/30.
	16	Cash refund on returns of sales made on May 3, $50.
	18	Purchase on account from Westone Company invoiced at $8,100, including $100 of transportaition charges prepaid by Westone; terms 2/15, n/30, f.o.b. shipping point.
	19	Crestal Company returned $100 of merchandise purchased on May 14.
	24	Returned $800 of defective merchandise to Westone Company and requested and was granted a transportation allowance of $10 on the original purchase.
	28	Crestal Company remitted balance due on sale of May 14.
	31	Paid Westone Company for the purchase of May 18 after adjusting for transactions of May 24.

3–10–A

Sampson Company does not maintain a complete accounting system, but you believe the following account balances are accurate representations of the company's assets and liabilities at the stated dates:

	December 31	
	1975	*1976*
Cash	$ 4,125	$ 8,250
Accounts receivable	14,250	10,500
Merchandise inventory	24,000	30,250
Land	5,750	5,750
Accounts payable	16,250	19,750

An analysis of the company's checkbook for 1976 shows the following:

a) Total cash received from customers (the only cash receipts), $102,500.
b) Payments to vendors for merchandise purchased, $65,250; the balance of the cash disbursements was for 1976 expenses, all of which were paid in cash in 1976.

Required: Determine the amount of the 1976 sales, cost of goods sold, total expenses, purchases, gross margin, and net earnings, and the stockholders' equity (in total) as of December 31, 1975 and 1976.

Problems, Series B *chapter* 3

3–1–B

Compute the annual rate of interest implicit in each of the following terms if the discount is not taken and the invoice is paid when due:

a) 2/10, n/30.
b) 1/10, n/45.
c) 3/E.O.M., n/90, goods purchased on May 16.
d) 2/10/E.O.M., n/45, goods purchased on August 2.

3–2–B

On July 2, 1975, the Jacklin Corporation purchased merchandise with a list price of $4,600 from the January Company. The terms were 3/10/E.O.M., n/60; f.o.b. destination, freight collect. Trade discounts of 15, 10, and 5 percent were granted by the January Company. The Jacklin Corporation paid the freight bill of $120 on July 5. On July 6 it was discovered that merchandise with a list price of $400 had been damaged seriously in transit; these items were returned for full credit.

Required: Assume that the Jacklin Corporation makes payment on the last day of the discount period and prepare all the necessary entries. Assume the periodic inventory procedure is used.

3–3–B

The following are events and transactions of the Wheat Company during 1975:

June 1 The planning department requested the purchasing department to order 1,000 units of a given material.

3 The purchasing department sent out requests for quotations to companies E, M, and W.

7 Quotations received are as follows:

E—List price: $4.20 each, less 30 and 20 percent. On all orders for more than 500 units, an additional 10 percent discount is allowed on the total order. Terms: 3/10, n/30, f.o.b. destination.

M—List price: $4.80 each, less 35 and 30 percent. Terms: 2/10, n/30, f.o.b. shipping point.

W—List price: $2.10 each. Terms: n/30, f.o.b. destination.

(The shipping cost under each bid is determined to be $50, $20, and $30, respectively.)

8 Placed order with lowest bidder.

15 Invoice received covering above merchandise; freight was prepaid.

16 Receiving department report stated that merchandise is as ordered. Invoice is checked and found to be correct.

24 Invoice is paid.

Required: Prepare dated journal entries for the above, where appropriate, including computations showing the actual cost in each bid, assuming that Wheat Company uses the periodic inventory procedure.

3–4–B

Required: (Assume that both companies use the periodic inventory procedure.)

a) Journalize the following transactions for Company D.
b) Journalize the following transactions for Company E.

Transactions:

April	18	Company D sold to Company E merchandise with a sales price of $27,000; terms, 2/10 E.O.M.
	29	Company E returned $3,000 of the merchandise to Company D.
May	3	Company E requested a gross allowance of $2,000 from Company D due to defective merchandise. Company D issued a credit memo granting the allowance.
	7	Company E paid the net amount due.

3–5–B

The Bragg Company purchased merchandise on March 1, 1976, from the Ray Company at a list price of $5,000, f.o.b. destination. Trade discounts of 30, 25, and 5 percent were granted. Cash discount terms were 2/E.O.M., n/60. The buyer paid the freight of $124 on March 4, 1976. The buyer notified the seller that a $600 credit should be granted against the amount due because of damaged merchandise. The seller agreed and sent the buyer a credit memorandum on March 25, 1976.

Required: Record all entries, assuming payment on March 26, on the books of both the buyer and seller, assuming that both use the periodic inventory procedure.

3–6–B

As of December 31, 1976, the financial records of the Nichols Company were examined for the years ended December 31, 1973, 1974, 1975, and 1976. With regard to merchandise inventory, the examination disclosed the following:

1. December 31, 1973: Inventory of $20,000 was included twice.
2. December 31, 1974: Inventory overstated $10,000.
3. December 31, 1975: Inventory of $22,000 was omitted.
4. December 31, 1976: Inventory is correct.

The reported net earnings for each year were as follows:

1973	$38,400
1974	52,400
1975	67,000
1976	84,600

Required:

a) What are the correct net earnings for 1973, 1974, 1975, and 1976?
b) What is the error in each December 31 statement of financial position?
c) Comment on the implications of your corrected net earnings as contrasted with reported net earnings.

3–7–B

Required: From the following information:

a) Prepare an earnings statement for the year ended December 31, 1976.
b) Prepare a statement of financial position as of December 31, 1976.
c) Prepare the adjusting journal entries.

THE CAHILL COMPANY
Trial Balance
December 31, 1976

	Debits	*Credits*
Cash in bank	$ 10,550	
Accounts receivable	28,500	
Notes receivable, trade	4,000	
Merchandise inventory, January 1, 1975	22,350	
Unexpired insurance	900	
Store supplies inventory	350	
Land	5,000	
Store building	25,250	
Accounts payable		$ 7,000
Notes payable		13,500
Interest payable		550
Common stock		37,500
Retained earnings		25,000
Sales		205,000
Purchases	113,000	
Sales returns	2,850	
Purchase returns		1,200
Sales discounts	3,650	
Purchase discounts		2,050
Sales salaries	32,000	
General selling expenses	1,600	
General administrative expenses	3,950	
Office and officers' salaries	20,250	
Taxes, administrative	4,350	
Taxes, selling	6,100	
Interest revenue		200
Interest expense	1,150	
Delivery expense	4,300	
Heat and light for sales purposes	1,200	
Telephone, office	700	
	$292,000	$292,000

The merchandise inventory on hand December 31, 1976, had a cost of $23,100.

3–8–B

Required: From the data given below for the Lemon Company (which uses the periodic inventory procedure):

a) Prepare journal entries for the transactions.
b) Post the journal entries to the proper ledger accounts.
c) Journalize and post the adjusting entries.
d) Prepare an earnings statement for the month ended May 31, 1976.
e) Prepare a statement of financial position as of May 31, 1976.

Transactions:

1976

May 1 The Lemon Company is organized as a corporation. It issues $170,000 of common capital stock in exchange for $105,000 cash, $40,000 worth of merchandise, and $25,000 worth of store fixtures.

5 The company purchases and pays cash for merchandise having a gross cost of $45,000, from which a 2 percent cash discount was granted.

8 Cash of $1,050 is paid to a trucking company for delivery of the merchandise purchased May 5. The goods were sold f.o.b. shipping point.

14 The company sells merchandise on open account, $75,000; terms, 2/10, n/30.

16 Of the merchandise sold May 14, $3,300 worth is returned for credit.

19 Salaries for services received are paid as follows: to office employees, $3,300; to salesmen, $8,700.

23 The company collects the amount due on $30,000 of the accounts receivable arising from the sales of May 14.

25 The company purchases and pays cash for merchandise costing $36,000 gross; a 2 percent cash discount is allowed. Terms: f.o.b. shipping point.

27 Of the merchandise purchased May 25, $6,000 gross is returned to the vendor, who gives the Lemon Company a check for the proper amount.

28 A trucking company is paid $750 for delivery to the Lemon Company of the goods purchased May 25.

29 The company sells merchandise on open account, $3,600; terms, 2/10, n/30.

30 Cash sales are $18,000 gross, less a 2 percent discount.

30 Cash of $24,000 is received from the sales of May 14.

31 Paid store rent for May, $4,500.

Additional data:

The inventory on hand at the close of business May 31 is $69,700 at cost.

3–9–B

Required: From the following information for the Lubcke Company, prepare:

a) Journal entries for the summarized transactions for 1976.
b) An earnings statement for the year ended December 31, 1976.
c) A statement of financial position as December 31, 1976.

A suggestion: you may want to set up rough T accounts and enter the December 31, 1975, balances given below and post your journal entries to arrive at ending balances.

LUBCKE COMPANY
Account Balances
December 31, 1975

	Debits	*Credits*
Cash on hand and in banks	$ 47,500	
Accounts receivable	82,500	
Merchandise inventory	70,000	
Accounts payable		$ 52,500
Capital stock		62,500
Retained earnings		85,000
	$200,000	$200,000

Summarized Transactions for 1976

Cash sales	$177,500
Sales on account at gross invoice prices	370,000
Purchases on account at gross invoice prices	400,000
Accounts receivable collected (net of cash discounts of $30,000)	343,750
Sales returns (from open account sales)	11,250
Purchase returns (from open account purchases)	5,500
Accounts payable paid (net of cash discounts of $6,000)	322,500
Selling expenses incurred and paid	49,000
Store equipment purchased for cash	10,000
Administrative expenses incurred and paid	45,500
Land purchased for cash	20,000
Building purchased (half for cash and half on a mortgage note)	105,000
Interest expense incurred and paid	3,000

Additional data:

The merchandise inventory at December 31, 1976, was $86,000.

3–10–B

The owner of Bill's Supply House has asked you for help in preparing financial statements for the year 1976. He does not maintain a ledger of accounts but rather keeps a detailed list of the amounts due from customers, the amounts owed vendors, and all cash received and paid out and the reasons therefor. With this help you are able to develop the following account balances:

	December 31	
	1975	*1976*
Cash	$ 4,000	$ 8,000
Accounts receivable	14,000	10,000
Merchandise on hand	22,000	30,000
Land, at cost	6,000	6,000
Accounts payable	16,000	19,000

Your summary of cash receipts and disbursements for 1976 is as follows:

a) Total cash receipts, solely from customers, $110,000.

b) Payments to vendors for merchandise purchased, $60,000; all other cash payments were for 1976 expenses. There were no unpaid expenses at December 31, 1976.

Required: Compute the following amounts for 1976: sales, purchases, total expenses, cost of goods sold, gross margin, and net earnings; also, determine the amount of owner's equity at December 31, 1975, and 1976.

The financial accounting process completed

Learning objectives

Study of the material in this chapter is designed to bring about fulfillment of the following learning objectives:

1. An understanding of the nature of adjusting entries, their four major classes, the reasons why they must be entered into an accounting system, and the possible consequences of a failure to so enter them.
2. Knowledge of basic characteristics of the accrual and the cash bases of accounting and indication of the circumstances in which the cash basis is found acceptable; also recognition of what accounting measurements are likely to differ when the cash rather than the accrual basis is employed.
3. A working knowledge of the closing process and the reason why it must be undertaken.
4. Knowledge of the complete accounting cycle and the sequence in which accounting functions are performed as raw data are entered, processed, and transformed into output of the accounting system.
5. A brief introduction to the work sheet and ways in which it facilitates completion of the accounting process as described and discussed in an appendix to this chapter.

Frame 1[4]

The basic purpose of this chapter is to complete the discussion of the financial accounting process. Previous chapters have discussed and demonstrated how and why the accountant relies upon transactions as his basic source of input data, and how these transactions are analyzed, journalized, and summarized in accounts. Discussed only briefly was the need to adjust the accounts prior to the preparation of financial statements.

This chapter discusses more fully the need for adjusting entries by analyzing various adjusting entries and classifying them into four major categories. Closing entries and the closing of the nominal accounts are presented as necessary parts of the activities undertaken by the accountant at the end of the accounting period. Finally, in an appendix, the work sheet is introduced as a means of making somewhat easier the tasks of completing the financial accounting process and preparing financial statements.

The need for adjusting entries

Broadly speaking, adjusting entries are needed in order to provide useful information. For example, if the earnings statement of an entity for a certain period is believed to contain information needed in order to make an informed decision, it follows that it must report all of the entity's revenues for the period and all of the expenses incurred to generate those revenues. If it does not, it is certainly incomplete and inaccurate and is quite likely to be misleading, if the omissions are substantial. Similarly, a statement of financial position that does not report all of an entity's assets, liabilities, and stockholders' equities may be misleading.

But the very approach of the accountant in collecting information makes it quite unlikely that the accounts will automatically contain all of the information needed for proper financial statements. The accountant records the effects of business transactions, but not all economic activity is readily discernible in business transactions. Recording only activity evidenced by transactions and certain other discernible events would be appropriate if only one statement (an earnings statement) were to be issued covering an entity's entire life since all activity would be reflected in completed transactions. In fact, such a measurement of net earnings would be the only completely accurate measurement possible. But because interested parties need timely information, periodic financial statements must be prepared. In order to prepare such statements, the accountant must arbitrarily divide an entity's life into time periods and attempt to assign economic activity to specific periods. This requires the preparation of adjusting entries—that is, entries to record economic activity that has taken place but which has not yet culminated in a transaction or other recordable event. As a consequence of the absence of a transaction, adjusting entries are based in part upon estimates which subsequent events may prove to be in error—a price that must be paid if timely information is to be secured.

Thus, adjusting entries are an integral part of the financial accounting process under the accrual basis of accounting and are even required (to a much lesser extent) under cash basis accounting.

Cash versus accrual basis accounting. Some relatively small business firms, especially those engaged in rendering services for customers or clients, may account for their revenues and expenses on a cash basis. This means that (except for depreciation expense) expenses and revenues usually are not recorded until cash is received or paid out. Thus, for example, services rendered to clients in, say, 1974 for which cash was collected in 1975 would be treated as 1975 revenues and recorded in 1975. They would not be included in the revenues reported in the earnings statement for 1974 and the statement of financial position for December 31, 1974, would not include as an asset (as accounts receivable) the claims upon the clients for services rendered.

Similarly, expenses could be incurred in 1974 but not recorded until 1975, when cash was paid out, at which time they would be treated as 1975 expenses. Because of these improper assignments of revenues and expenses, the cash basis of accounting is generally considered unacceptable, except in those circumstances where its use yields results approximating those that would have been obtained under the accrual basis of accounting.

As already illustrated, the accrual basis of accounting seeks to bring about recognition in the accounts of the growth or expiration of an asset or a liability, as well as the related incurrence of an expense or generation of a revenue, in the period in which it occurs. Thus, revenues are recognized when sales are made even though cash is not received concurrently and expenses are recognized as incurred regardless of whether or not cash is paid out. But even under the accrual basis transactions are the source of input into the accounting system. Consequently, adjusting entries are required to bring the accounts up to date for financial reporting purposes. The crucial task of measuring net earnings through a proper assignment of expenses and revenues to periods cannot be fulfilled without the preparation of adjusting entries.

Indicate whether each of the following statements is true or false.

1. Under the cash basis, the cash purchase of a building would be recorded as an expense.
2. Under the cash basis, most expenses and revenues are recorded when cash is received or paid out.
3. When the accrual basis of accounting is properly applied, adjusting entries are not necessary.
4. The demand for periodic financial statements is the basic reason why adjusting entries are made.

Check your responses in Answer Frame 1[4] on page 130.

Answer frame 1[4]

1. False. The building would be recorded as an asset and depreciation expense subsequently recorded on it.
2. True. The major expense that would not be recorded when cash is paid out is depreciation.
3. False. Transactions constitute the basic source of information under the accrual basis of accounting. Thus, adjusting entries are needed to record the economic activity transpiring in a period that is not evidenced by a transaction.
4. True. If the information contained in the accounts is not to be reported to anyone, there would be no reason to make sure that it was complete or up to date.

If you missed any of the above, you should study Frame 1[4] again before proceeding to Frame 2[4] below.

Frame 2[4]

Time of preparation of adjusting entries

Adjusting entries must be prepared whenever financial statements are to be prepared. Thus, if monthly financial statements are prepared, monthly adjusting entries are required. By custom, and in some instances by law, business firms report to their stockholders at least annually. Consequently, adjusting entries will be required at least annually. In manual accounting systems, adjusting entries may be formally recorded in the accounts only at the end of the annual accounting period. If interim financial reports are to be prepared, the entries may be prepared and entered only on a work sheet—a procedure illustrated in the appendix to this chapter. On the other hand, in accounting systems employing electromechanical or electronic processing equipment, adjusting entries often are prepared and recorded in the accounts monthly.

Classes of adjusting entries

The adjusting entries illustrated and explained in this chapter can be grouped first into two broad classes. One class consists of those entries that relate to data previously recorded in the accounts. These entries involve the transfer of data from asset and liability accounts to expense and revenue accounts. The second class consists of entries relating to activity on which nothing has been previously recorded in the accounts. These entries involve the first recording of assets and liabilities and the related expenses or revenues. Since each class involves both expenses and revenues, there are four major types of adjusting entries, namely, those involving: (1) asset/expense adjustments, (2) asset/revenue adjustments, (3) liability/expense adjustments, and (4) liability/revenue adjustments.

Indicate whether each of the following statements is true or false.

1. As a minimum, adjusting entries will be entered in every accounting system once a year.
2. In some accounting systems (for example, those employing electronic processing equipment) adjusting entries may be recorded at the end of every month.
3. The preparation of adjusting entries may make accounting information less objective or verifiable and thus more tentative in nature.
4. Although adjusting entries will affect statement of financial position accounts, they are of prime concern because of their effects upon net earnings.

Check your responses in Answer Frame 2[4] on page 132.

Frame 3[4]

Asset/expense adjustments

One of the four major classes of adjusting entries involves the complete or partial expiration of the ability of an asset to render services (thus making it less valuable to its owner) as a result of its use in generating revenues. Because of its relative importance, five examples of this type of adjusting entry are presented below, specifically, for (1) insurance, (2) prepaid rent, (3) depreciation, (4) supplies, and (5) bad debts.

Insurance

When the premium on an insurance policy is paid in advance of the period covered by the policy, an asset is created that expires and becomes an expense with the passage of time. To illustrate, the advance payment of the premium on a one-year insurance policy that runs from August 1, 1976, to July 31, 1977, creates an asset called unexpired, or prepaid, insurance on August 1, 1976, because benefits—insurance protection—will be secured in the future. The journal entry to record this transaction is:

1976			
Aug. 1	Unexpired Insurance	3,600	
	Cash		3,600
	To record payment in advance of annual premium.		

Assume that the company has a calendar-year accounting period and that it records adjusting entries only at the end of its accounting year. By December 31, a part of the period covered by the policy has expired and, correspondingly, a part of the asset has expired. It now provides less benefit than when acquired. This diminution of the ability of the asset

Answer frame 2[4]

1. True. Every business firm has a fiscal year (accounting year) for which it presents financial statements. Thus, adjusting entries will be entered in every accounting system at least once a year.
2. True. Because of the speed and efficiency of electronic processing equipment in accepting and processing input data and the automatic printout of financial statements, adjusting entries are usually entered monthly in such systems.
3. True. Some adjusting entries, as will be illustrated later, are based upon estimates and not upon the dollar amounts in actual transactions. The result is the entry of less objective or verifiable data into the accounting system. And because the estimates may be in error, the accounting information is rendered somewhat tentative in nature—that is, subject to correction for error.
4. True. Although not covered specifically in exactly these words, the determination of net earnings has been called the crucial task of the accountant.

If you missed any of the above, read Frames 1[4] and 2[4] of this chapter again before proceeding to Frame 3[4] on page 131.

3[4] *continued*

to provide services must be recognized, and the cost of the services received from the asset treated as an expense. Since the policy provides the same services for every month of its one-year life, it seems intuitively logical to assign an equal amount of cost to each month. Thus, with 5 of the 12 months of coverage provided by payment of the premium having elapsed, $5/12$ of the annual premium is charged to expense on December 31. The journal entry and the accounts after posting appear as follows:

1976			
Dec. 31	Insurance Expense................................	1,500	
	Unexpired Insurance..........................		1,500
	To record expense for five months, August 1 to December 31, 1976.		

Unexpired Insurance — *Account No. 104*

Date		Explanation	Folio	Debit	Credit	Balance
1976						
Aug.	1	Cash paid	J 7*	3,600		3,600
Dec.	31	Adjustment	J 12		1,500	2,100

* Note: In this and all future illustrations, the folio references are assumed.

Insurance Expense — *Account No. 408*

Date		Explanation	Folio	Debit	Credit	Balance
1976						
Dec.	31	Adjustment	J 12	1,500		1,500

The insurance expense of $1,500 is reported in the company's earnings statement for the year ended December 31, 1976, as one of the expenses incurred in generating that year's revenues (in a highly condensed earnings statement the amount might be reported as part of a total described as "selling and administrative expenses"). The remaining amount of the annual premium, $2,100, is reported as a current asset, either presented as an individual item or combined with other similar items and reported as "prepaid expenses" in the statement of financial position for December 31, 1976. The $2,100 is a measure of the cost of the asset, unexpired insurance, and unexpired insurance is an asset because it provides future benefits.

The $2,100 is classified as a current asset because it represents a measure of an asset that will be consumed and converted into cash in the course of normal operations in the next operating cycle of the business or one year, whichever is longer. Although the insurance coverage is not literally sold and converted into cash in a single sales transaction, it is, in a sense, sold when customers pay the firm amounts of cash which are expected to be sufficient to cover all of the firm's expenses.

Indicate whether each of the following statements about the above example is true or false.

1. The monthly insurance expense is $300.
2. The $2,100 of unexpired insurance will become an expense in 1977.
3. If a proper adjusting entry had not been made, the company's assets at December 31, 1976, would have been overstated by $2,100.
4. The $2,100 of unexpired insurance is treated as an asset primarily because the policy could be surrendered and a cash refund of that amount received from the insurance company.

Check your responses in Answer Frame 3[4] on page 134.

Frame 4[4]

Prepaid rent

Prepaid rent is another example of the continuous incurrence of an expense and the corresponding expiration of a previously recorded asset. When rent is paid in advance for any substantial period of time, the prepayment is debited to the Prepaid Rent account (an asset account) at the date it is paid. Because the benefits resulting from the expenditure are yet to be received, the expenditure creates an asset. Services from the facilities being rented are received continuously through time, and the expense is literally incurred continuously as time elapses, since rental contracts are usually stated in terms of time periods. An entry could be made frequently, even daily, to record the expense incurred. But typically

Answer frame 3[4]

1. True. With an annual premium of $3,600, the monthly insurance cost is usually considered to be $300.
2. True. Since 7 of the 12 months of coverage fall in 1977, 7/12 of $3,600 will be treated as an expense in 1977. Or, since the period of insurance protection covered expires in 1977, the amount treated as unexpired at the end of 1976 is the amount of the expense recognized in 1977.
3. False. The assets would have been overstated by $1,500, the amount that should have been treated as an expense.
4. False. The $2,100 is treated as an asset primarily because it represents a measure of the cost of the benefits expected. In fact, if the policy is surrendered, the amount received as a refund would generally be somewhat less than $2,100 under typical insurance company practices.

If you missed any of the above questions, you should restudy Frame 3[4] carefully before proceeding to Frame 4[4] on page 133.

4[4]
continued

the entry is not made until financial statements are to be prepared. At that time an entry is made transferring from the asset account to an expense account the cost of that portion of the asset that has expired.

The measurement of rent expense usually presents no problems. Generally, the rental contract specifies the amount of rent per unit of time. If the contract states an annual rental, 1/12 of this annual rental is charged to each month. This is true even though there are varying numbers of days in some months. The variations are not considered significant enough to be taken into consideration.

To illustrate, assume that rent was paid in advance in the amount of $600 on September 1, 1976, for one year beginning on that date. The entry made at that time was:

1976			
Sept. 1	Prepaid Rent	600	
	Cash		600
	To record advance payment of one year's rent.		

Assume that adjusting entries are to be prepared and recorded in the accounts as of December 31, 1976. On a separate sheet of paper, prepare the required adjusting entry for the above rent. Then check your response in Answer Frame 4[4] on page 136.

Frame 5[4]

Rent expense is, of course, one of the operating expenses of the business and appears in its earnings statement either individually or, in a condensed statement, as part of a total summarizing several expenses. The balance of the prepaid rent in the example, \$400, would be reported as a current asset in the company's statement of financial position for December 31, 1976. It might be reported separately, although in condensed statements it undoubtedly would appear as part of a larger total summarizing several similar items described as "prepaid expenses."

Depreciation

The concept of depreciation was introduced briefly in Chapter 2 and is another example of the continuous incurrence of an expense which results from the gradual use and expiration of a previously recorded asset. The overall period of time involved in using up a depreciable asset, a building for example, is considerably less definite than in the case of an insurance premium or prepaid rent. In the case of a depreciable asset, its life must be estimated in advance and individuals are not able to peer 10 to 50 years into the future with any real degree of accuracy. Nevertheless, the pattern of incurring an expense because of the expiration of an asset is basically the same. The cost of the asset (less estimated salvage value) is divided by the estimated number of years in the life of the asset to find the amount of asset cost to be charged as an expense to each time period. This process is called depreciation accounting, and the cost allocated to each time period is called depreciation or depreciation expense. The method discussed and illustrated here is known as the *straight-line method.* (Other methods are presented and discussed in Chapter 9.) The three factors involved in the computation of depreciation are:

1. The cost of the asset.
2. The estimated useful life of the asset.
3. The estimated salvage or scrap value of the asset.

Expressed in equation form, the computation of straight-line depreciation is as follows:

$$\text{Annual Depreciation} = \frac{\text{Cost} - \text{Estimated Salvage Value}}{\text{Number of Years of Useful Life}}$$

In some cases, salvage value is estimated at zero; then the equation becomes simply cost divided by estimated number of years of useful life. The difference between the cost of an asset and its estimated salvage value is sometimes referred as an asset's *depreciable amount.* And it is this difference between the price paid upon acquisition and price received upon disposition of an asset that constitutes the net cost of using the asset during its useful life. This difference must be allocated to the various periods in an asset's life.

Depreciation is sometimes expressed as an annual percentage rate determined by dividing the annual amount of depreciation by the acquisition cost of the asset.

Answer frame 4[4]

The required adjusting entry would read:

1976			
Dec. 31	Rent Expense	200	
	Prepaid Rent		200
	To record rent expense for four months.		

Since one third of the period covered by the prepaid rent (4 of 12 months) has expired, one third of the $600 of prepaid rent is charged to expense.

Unless your mistake was arithmetic in nature, you should restudy Frame 4[4] if you missed the above entry. Then proceed to Frame 5[4] on page 134.

5[4] *continued*

Indicate whether each of the following statements is true or false with regard to a building purchased at a cost of $100,000 and expected to be sold for $25,000 at the end of 25 years, even though the building will last 50 years.

1. The building's depreciable amount is $75,000.
2. The annual depreciation on the building is $3,000.
3. The annual depreciation rate is 3 percent on acquisition cost.
4. The estimated salvage value is $25,000.

Check your responses in Answer Frame 5[4] on page 138.

Frame 6[4]

The allowance for depreciation account. As introduced in Chapter 2, depreciation is another example of expense as the consumption or using up of an asset. But the depreciation expense for a period is not credited directly to the asset account, but to a contra (reduction) account called Allowance for Depreciation (or Accumulated Depreciation). This account is merely a special subdivision of the credit side of the related plant asset account. The debit balance in the plant asset account minus the credit balance in the related Allowance for Depreciation contra account equals the cost of the benefits yet to be received from the asset.

Crediting depreciation to an allowance for depreciation account rather than directly to the asset account is justified largely on the grounds that recorded amounts of depreciation are quite tentative due to the use of estimates. In any event, depreciable asset accounts are maintained at their original acquisition cost. The balance in the related allowance for depreciation increases each year by the amount of depreciation recorded until it finally reaches an amount equal to the cost of the asset (less estimated salvage value), unless the asset is prematurely disposed of. Recording of depreciation on an asset ceases when the balance in the allowance equals the cost of the asset.

Depreciation accounting illustrated. To illustrate the accounting for depreciation assume that a trial balance at December 31, 1976, includes an account with one delivery truck that cost $2,100. The truck was purchased on January 1, 1976. It is expected to have a useful life of five years; scrap value is estimated at $100. Therefore, the depreciation expense for one year equals ($2,100 — $100) ÷ 5, or $400. This is the amount of depreciation expense allocable to the production of revenue for the year 1976.

Depreciation for 1976 is recorded by the following entry:

1976			
Dec. 31	Depreciation Expense, Delivery Equipment..............	400	
	Allowance for Depreciation of Delivery Equipment....		400
	To record the depreciation expense for the year.		

The ledger accounts will appear as follows:

Delivery Equipment *Account No. 130*

Date		Explanation	Folio	Debit	Credit	Balance
1976 Jan.	1	One truck	J 8	2,100		2,100

Allowance for Depreciation of Delivery Equipment *Account No. 131*

Date		Explanation	Folio	Debit	Credit	Balance
1976 Dec.	31	Adjustment	J 14		400	400

Depreciation Expense, Delivery Equipment *Account No. 418*

Date		Explanation	Folio	Debit	Credit	Balance
1976 Dec.	31	Adjustment	J 14	400		400

At December 31, 1976, after the adjustment, $1,600 of the cost of the truck remains to be converted into expense while the truck is used during future years.

Allowance for depreciation in the statement of financial position. In the statement of financial position at December 31, 1976, the asset accounts include the following:

Delivery equipment..	$2,100
Less: Allowance for depreciation of delivery equipment.........	400
	$1,700

The portion of the cost of the asset not yet charged to expense at the end of the first year is $1,700, although, since expected scrap value is

Answer frame 5[4]

1. True. \$100,000 – \$25,000 = \$75,000.
2. True. \$75,000 ÷ 25 = \$3,000.
3. True. \$3,000 ÷ \$100,000 = .03, or 3 percent.
4. True. As a general approximation, the expected selling price of an asset at the end of its useful life is its estimated salvage value.

Restudy Frame 5[4] if you missed any of the above before proceeding to Frame 6[4] on page 136.

6[4] *continued*

\$100, only \$1,600 is expected to be charged to expense in future years. Since another \$400 of depreciation would be recorded at the end of 1977, the statement of financial position at the end of that year would show:

Delivery equipment	\$2,100
Less: Allowance for depreciation of delivery equipment	800
	\$1,300

At the end of the fifth year, \$2,000 of depreciation will have been recorded and, if the estimates were correct, the asset will be retired from service and sold for \$100. If this occurs, the required entry would read:

Cash	100	
Allowance for Depreciation of Delivery Equipment	2,000	
Delivery Equipment		2,100
To record retirement and sale of one delivery truck.		

Depreciation expense is an operating expense and is reported in the earning's statement. In highly condensed published earnings statements, all of the periodic depreciation amounts are often added together and reported simply as "depreciation." In more detailed statements, the amounts of depreciation expense for the period on each major class of depreciable assets may be reported separately. In these instances, depreciation may be classified functionally as either selling expense or administrative expense.

The accounting for depreciable plant assets is discussed in greater depth in Chapter 9.

Indicate whether each of the following statements is true or false.

1. The recording of the expiration of prepaid rent as an expense and the recording of depreciation do not differ conceptually.
2. The depreciation on office equipment could be classified functionally as an administrative expense.
3. The objective of depreciation accounting is to spread the depreciable amount of an asset over its useful life.
4. The account showing the accumulated depreciation on an asset is reported as an operating expense in the earnings statement.

Now turn to Answer Frame 6[4] on page 140 to check your responses.

Frame 7[4]

Supplies

Every business consumes assets referred to as supplies in its operations. Such supplies may be classified as office supplies (paper, stationery, carbon paper, pencils) or selling supplies (gummed tape, string, paper bags or cartons, wrapping paper) or, possibly, as cleaning supplies (soap, disinfectants). They are frequently acquired in bulk and consumed or used gradually through time.

To illustrate, assume that office supplies were purchased at various times throughout the year and recorded by debiting an asset account, Office Supplies, and crediting Cash. At the end of the year, the Office Supplies account shows a debit balance of $700. An actual physical inventory shows that only $200 worth of supplies are on hand. Thus, an adjusting entry is required to bring the accounts up to date, that is, to recognize the diminution in the asset and the incurrence of an expense through the using up of office supplies. From the information given, the asset balance can readily be seen to be $200 and the expense incurred, $500. By making the following entry, the accounts will be adjusted to those balances:

1976			
Dec. 31	Office Supplies Expense	500	
	Office Supplies		500
	To record supplies used during the year.		

While the entry to record the usage of supplies could be made when the supplies are issued from the storeroom, it is usually not economically sound practice to account so carefully for so nominal an item.

The Office Supplies Expense account would appear as an operating expense in the earnings statement, while Office Supplies would be reported as a current asset in the statement of financial position, often lumped with similar items and entitled Prepaid Expenses.

Bad debts

No matter how carefully a company screens applications for credit from its customers, if it sells merchandise or renders services on a credit basis it will encounter the problem of bad debts—uncollectible accounts receivable. Currently, actual bad debts range from a fraction of 1 percent of sales to an amount considerably larger, depending, at least in part, upon economic conditions.

To illustrate the problems encountered in accounting for bad debts, assume that the December 31, 1976, trial balance of a company in its first year of operations shows accounts receivable of $25,000 and sales of $400,000. Assume further that the manager of the company, using trade association data, estimates that 1 percent, or $4,000, of the sales

Answer frame 6[4]

1. True. Both involve the recognition of an expense resulting from the consumption or using up of an asset in the operations of the business.
2. True. Depreciation on office equipment is an expense of operating the office of the business and this is where the administrative function is usually performed.
3. True. This is indeed the objective of depreciation accounting.
4. False. Depreciation is the operating expense that would be shown in the earning statement. The account showing the total accumulated depreciation is a contra account to the account containing the cost of the asset being depreciated and would be shown as such in the statement of financial position.

If you missed any of the above, read Frame 6[4] again before proceeding to Frame 7[4] on page 139.

7[4] *continued*

made during the year will never be collected. This information would require the following adjusting entry:

1976			
Dec. 31	Bad Debts Expense	4,000	
	Allowance for Doubtful Accounts		4,000
	To record estimated bad debts for the year as 1 percent of sales of $400,000.		

This entry accomplishes two things: (1) it brings about a proper matching of bad debts expense with revenue, since the uncollectible accounts arising from 1976 sales are recognized as an expense in 1976; and (2) the accounts receivable as of December 31, 1976, are properly valued at their net realizable value, the amount of cash expected to be collected.

The bad debts expense of $4,000 is shown as an operating expense in the earnings statement and looked upon as the cost of granting credit to customers. Theoretically, it can be argued that it should be deducted from sales to show the actual amount of revenue generated during the period. But in either event, the $4,000 serves to reduce net earnings (before income taxes) by that amount.

Since the estimated accounts expected to prove uncollectible cannot be specifically identified as being those of certain customers, an Allowance for Doubtful Accounts is credited rather than crediting Accounts Receivable directly. The allowance is a contra account and can be considered a special subdivision of the credit side of the Accounts Receivable account. The receivables and the related allowance may be reported in the current asset section of the statement of financial position as follows:

Accounts receivable	$25,000
Less: Allowance for doubtful accounts	4,000
	$21,000

In highly condensed statements, the reporting may be as follows:

Accounts receivable (net of estimated uncollectibles of $4,000).......... $21,000

In either case, it can be readily seen that the accounts receivables have a net realizable value of $21,000.

Assume that the trial balance of a certain company at the end of its accounting year shows:

	Debits	*Credits*
Office supplies..............	$ 4,000	
Accounts receivable.........	55,000	
Sales......................		$280,000

An inventory shows that $500 of supplies are on hand at year-end. Also, bad debts are estimated at one half of 1 percent of sales. On a separate sheet of paper, prepare the necessary adjusting entries. Turn to Answer Frame 7[4] on page 142 to check your responses.

Frame 8[4]

Writing off uncollectible accounts. Assume, to continue the example of Frame 7[4], that in April, 1977 the account of the Hurst Company in the amount of $75 is identified as definitely uncollectible. Since the account arose from a sale made in 1976, the expense arising from such an uncollectible account was recognized by an adjusting entry for bad debts at the end of that year. Consequently, in April, 1977 no expense need be recognized. The entry to record the write-off of the Hurst Company account is:

Allowance for Doubtful Accounts..............................	75	
Accounts Receivable..		75
To write off the account of Hurst Company as uncollectible.		

The debit to the Allowance for Doubtful Accounts indicates that $75 of the total allowance has been used to eliminate a specific account receivable. If Bad Debts Expense was debited when the Hurst Company account was written off, a double charge to expense would result, because the allowance for doubtful accounts was created by a charge to expense in 1976. Note that the entry for the write-off of the Hurst account, by reducing Accounts Receivable and the Allowance for Doubtful Accounts by the same amount, leaves the net realizable value of the receivables unchanged.

The Allowance for Doubtful Accounts account is credited periodically when adjusting entries are recorded; it is debited at irregular intervals when specific accounts receivable are identified as uncollectible. It may

Answer frame 7[4]

The two required adjusting entries are:

Dec. 31	Office Supplies Expense	3,500	
	Office Supplies		3,500
	To record supplies used as shown by inventory.		
Dec. 31	Bad Debts Expense	1,400	
	Allowance for Doubtful Accounts		1,400
	To record estimated bad debts of $1,400 (0.005 × $280,000).		

If you missed either of these entries, study Frame 7[4] again before proceeding to Frame 8[4] on page 141.

8[4] *continued* be that before the end-of-year adjustment is entered, some receivables from the current year's sales are identified as uncollectible and debited to the allowance. If this happens, it is possible for the Allowance for Doubtful Accounts to have a debit balance before the periodic adjusting entry for bad debts is entered. When adjustments are recorded at shorter intervals, such as monthly, the allowance usually has a credit balance. After adjustment, the allowance always has a credit balance.

Indicate whether each of the following statements is true or false.

1. One reason for making an adjusting entry for possible uncollectible accounts is to reduce the accounts receivable to their net realizable value.
2. If properly adjusted, the Allowance for Doubtful Accounts always has a credit balance.
3. Writing off an uncollectible account reduces net earnings in the period of write-off.
4. Writing off an uncollectible account reduces the net realizable value of the accounts receivable.

Now turn to Answer Frame 8[4] on page 144 to check your responses.

Frame 9[4]

Asset/revenue adjustments

In some instances, agreements are entered into which establish a right to collect an increasing amount of assets through time. Periodically, collection is effected. This growth in the right to collect is an asset arising from rendering services to others—the generation of revenue. Examples of this type of adjustment include the accruals made for commissions earned (discussed in Chapter 2), interest revenue, and rent revenue.

Interest revenue

The interest paid periodically on investments such as bonds and savings accounts is literally earned by the lender or investor moment by moment through time as the funds invested are used by the borrower. Except in the rare instance of payment of the interest on the last day of the accounting period, the accounting records will not show the amount of interest revenue earned nor the total assets owned by the investor unless an adjusting entry is made. An entry at the end of the accounting period is needed which debits a receivable account (an asset) and credits a revenue account to record the asset owned and the interest earned.

For example, assume that a company invests some funds in an interest-paying security. The interest is paid twice a year on May 1 and November 1 in the amount of $900 on each date. If the investment was purchased on May 2, 1976, Interest Revenue is credited with the $900 of cash received on November 1. At December 31, 1976, an additional two months' interest of the six months' interest to be received on May 1, 1977, has been earned. An entry must be made to show the amount of interest earned and the asset, the right to receive this interest, at December 31, 1976. The entry, which is said to be an entry to record the accrual of revenue, is:

Accrued Interest Receivable..................................	300	
Interest Revenue..................................		300
To record two months' interest revenue.		

The ledger accounts appear as follows:

Accrued Interest Receivable — *Account No. 107*

Date		Explanation	Folio	Debit	Credit	Balance
1976						
Dec.	31	Adjustment	J 14	300		300

Interest Revenue — *Account No. 506*

Date		Explanation	Folio	Debit	Credit	Balance
1976						
Nov.	1	Cash received	J 13		900	900
Dec.	31	Adjustment	J 14		300	1,200

The $300 debit balance in Accrued Interest Receivable is reported as a current asset in the December 31, 1976, statement of financial position. The $1,200 credit balance in Interest Revenue is the interest earned during the year and, under accrual basis accounting, it is irrelevant whether cash was collected during the year or not. The interest revenue earned is reported in the earnings statement for the year.

Entry in next period. If the same procedures are followed as shown

Answer frame 8[4]

1. True. Proper valuation of the receivables is one reason for making the adjusting entry.
2. True. A moment's reflection should reveal that it is impossible to have negative bad debts—that is, that more will be collected from customers than they were billed. This is what would be implied by a properly adjusted Allowance for Doubtful Accounts with a debit balance.
3. False. The adjusting entry causes a reduction in net earnings. The write-off entry does not involve an expense account.
4. False. If, prior to the write-off of an account, accounts receivable stand at \$21,000 and the allowance at \$1,000, the net realizable value of the receivables is \$20,000 (\$21,000 – \$1,000). If a \$500 account is now written off, the net realizable value of the receivables is still \$20,000 consisting of \$20,500 less an allowance of \$500.

A review of Frame 8[4] may be in order if you missed any of the above. Then proceed to Frame 9[4] on page 142.

9[4]
continued

above, the collection of \$900 of cash on May 1, 1977, is recorded as the collection of the accrued interest receivable established in the adjusting entry and as a cash collection of interest revenue. The required entry is:

1977			
May 1	Cash	900	
	Accrued Interest Receivable		300
	Interest Revenue		600
	Collected interest for six months ending May 1.		

Note how the preparation of the adjusting entry properly assigns the revenue earned to the proper accounting period. The \$900 collected represents interest earned in the six months ending May 1, 1977. But two of these months fell in calendar year 1976; therefore, one third of \$900 should be treated as 1976 revenue, the balance as 1977 revenue. The entries prepared yield exactly these results.

Indicate whether each of the following statements about the above example is true or false.

1. If no adjusting entry had been made, the interest earned in the last two months of 1976 would probably be recorded as 1977 revenue when collected on May 1, 1977.
2. The debit balance in the Accrued Interest Receivable account represents the amount of interest earned but not collected through December 31, 1976.
3. The adjusting entry is made so that the interest earned in November and December of 1976 is recorded as revenue of that year.
4. The credit balance (after adjustment) in the Interest Revenue account shows the amount of interest earned and collected in cash during the year.

Now turn to Answer Frame 9[4] on page 146 to check your responses.

Frame 10[4]

Rent revenue

Rental agreements typically require rent to be paid at the beginning of the rental period. But occasionally a situation may be encountered that requires the accrual of rent revenue and the recognition of an asset.

To illustrate, assume that a company rents the second floor of a building it owns to another party for a monthly rental of $1,200, with the first rental payment due on January 16, 1977. Occupancy is granted on December 16, 1976. Assuming that the company's accounting period ends on December 31, the adjusting entry required on December 31, 1976, is:

Accrued Rent Receivable	600	
Rent Revenue		600
To record accrual of one half of a month's rent revenue.		

The accrued rent receivable of $600 would be reported as a current asset in the statement of financial position, while the rent revenue would be reported in the earnings statement.

Entry in the next period. When the first monthly rental payment of $1,200 is received on January 16, 1977, the cash received would be accounted for as a $600 collection of the balance in the Accrued Rent Receivable account and $600 as a cash collection of January rent revenue. Thus, the adjusting entry provides for the assignment of the first $1,200 of rent earned to the proper periods, as well as correctly stating assets on December 31, 1976.

Liability/expense adjustments

In order to report on net earnings and financial position properly, adjustments involving liability and expense accounts are often required. Illustrated and discussed below are the adjustments relating to salaries and federal income taxes, although similar adjustments may be required for other forms of taxes, interest, and pension obligations.

Salaries

Employee services are assets when acquired. If they are not of value to the employer, why is he willing to pay cash for them? But the accountant seldom records employee services as assets for two reasons: (1) they are typically recorded when they are paid, and (2) by the time they are recorded the asset has expired because the benefits have been received. Consequently, the recording of employee services usually involves a debit to an expense account and a credit to cash (payroll withholdings and payroll taxes are ignored here). But if the receipt of employee services is recognized only when paid, an adjusting entry may be required

Answer frame 9[4]

1. True. The entry would be likely to consist of a debit to Cash and a credit to Interest Revenue for $900.
2. True. The interest for these two months is, by agreement, not payable until May 1; hence, the interest is earned but not collected.
3. True. One of the two reasons for making the entry is to secure a proper assignment to periods of the revenue earned.
4. False. Only $900 of cash was received; the remaining $300 was accrued.

Restudy Frame 9[4] carefully if you missed any of the above. Then proceed to Frame 10[4] on page 145.

10[4] *continued*

at the end of an accounting period to record those services received for which payment has not been made.

To illustrate, assume that the Office Salaries Expense account shows a debit balance at the end of January, 1976, of $4,400. This consists of four weekly payrolls (Monday through Saturday) of $1,100 each (paid on Saturday). But, assuming the last day of January falls on a Wednesday, the expense account does not show salaries earned by employees for the last three days of the month. Nor do the accounts show the employer's obligation to pay these salaries. If financial statements are to be prepared for January, the following adjusting entry is needed:

Office Salaries Expense..........	550	
Accrued Office Salaries Payable..........		550
To accrue one half of a week's office salaries.		

The two accounts involved now appear as follows:

Office Salaries Expense — *Account No. 422*

Date		Explanation	Folio	Debit	Credit	Balance
1976						
Jan.	6	1st week cash	J 3	1,100		1,100
	13	2d week cash	J 4	1,100		2,200
	20	3d week cash	J 4	1,100		3,300
	27	4th week cash	J 5	1,100		4,400
	31	Adjustment	J 5	550		4,950

Accrued Office Salaries Payable — *Account No. 309*

Date		Explanation	Folio	Debit	Credit	Balance
1976						
Jan.	31	Adjustment	J 5		550	550

The adjusting journal entry brings the month's salaries expense up to its correct amount for earnings statement purposes. The credit records the liability to employees for services for statement of financial position purposes.

Assume that the weekly office payroll is paid on February 3 in the amount of $1,100. On a separate sheet of paper, write out the entry to record this payment. Then check your answer in Answer Frame 10[4] on page 148.

Frame 11[4]

Federal income taxes

Profitable corporations are usually subject to federal income taxes. But the tax return will not be filed and the income taxes will not be paid until some time after the end of the accounting year. Consequently, an adjusting entry must be made if expenses and liabilities are to be correctly stated. Assuming that the estimated amount of federal income taxes for the year is $4,200, the required adjusting entry is:

Federal Income Taxes Expense	4,200	
Federal Income Taxes Payable		4,200
To record estimated federal income taxes for the year.		

Failure to make such an entry would cause net earnings to be overstated and current liabilities to be understated by $4,200 each.

Liability/revenue adjustments

This class of adjustments covers those circumstances in which the usual procedure of the seller extending credit to the customer is reversed. That is, the customer pays assets (usually cash) into the selling company prior to the receipt of merchandise or services and, in this way, extends credit to the seller. Such receipts are usually credited to an account entitled Prepaid Revenues, Revenues Received in Advance, or Unearned Revenue. Better terminology would be Advances by Customers to show clearly the liability nature of the account. The seller is obligated either to deliver the goods, provide the services, or return the customer's money. The liability is canceled and revenue generated by providing the agreed-upon goods or services.

Advance payments could be received for items such as tickets, rent, and magazine or newspaper subscriptions. Because of their similarity, only the advance receipt of subscriptions will be illustrated and discussed.

Subscription revenue

Assume that during 1976 a company received a total of $24,000 at various times as payment in advance for a number of one-year subscrip-

Answer frame 10[4]

The required entry is:

Accrued Office Salaries Payable	550	
Office Salaries Expense	550	
Cash		1,100
Paid office payroll for week ending February 3.		

Here again an adjusting entry has been used to obtain a proper assignment of expense to accounting periods for earnings statement purposes. The entry also brings about a reporting of the liability to employees for salaries earned but not paid.

If you missed the above entry, you may find review of the last part of Frame 9[4] and Frame 10[4] helpful. Then proceed to Frame 11[4] on page 147.

11[4] *continued* tions to a monthly magazine it sells. The entry, debit Cash and credit Subscriptions Received in Advance, was made to record each amount of cash collected. The liability established when the cash was received is gradually converted into revenue as the magazines contracted for are delivered. Thus, an adjusting entry to update the accounts is usually required before financial statements are prepared. Assuming that 40 percent of the magazines paid for in advance have been delivered by year-end, the required adjusting entry is:

1976			
Dec. 31	Subscriptions Received in Advance	9,600	
	Subscription Revenue		9,600
	To record subscription revenue earned in 1976.		

The Subscription Revenue of $9,600 is, of course, reported in the earnings statement for 1976, while the $14,400 ($24,000 − $9,600) balance in the Subscriptions Received in Advance account is reported as a current liability in the statement of financial position. The $14,400 will be earned in 1977 and transferred to a revenue account in that year.

Assume that on August 1, 1976, a theater company sold out all of the tickets for a series of 10 plays for $5,000 cash. The cash received was credited to an account entitled Admissions Received in Advance. One play was presented each month, with the first play given in August. Assuming that cash refunds are not paid for unused tickets, on a separate sheet of paper write out the required adjusting entry for December 31, 1976. Then check your response in Answer Frame 11[4] on page 150.

Frame 12[4]

Since the process of preparing financial statements after adjusting entries have been journalized and posted was illustrated in Chapter 2, it need not be dealt with here. Rather, attention will be directed toward the next steps in the financial accounting process.

Closing entries

After adjusting entries have been journalized and posted, up-to-date information of two major types is found in the accounts in an accounting system: (1) information relating to the activities occurring during the period just ended, and (2) information on the financial condition of the entity at the end of the period.

The first type of information is found largely in the expense and revenue accounts, although dividend accounts may also be used. These accounts have already been discussed as temporarily established subdivisions of the Retained Earnings account. The expense and revenue accounts help the accountant fulfill one of his most important tasks—the determination of periodic net earnings. After the financial statements for the period have been prepared, these temporary accounts have served their purpose and must now be brought to a zero balance in order that information pertaining to the next accounting period can be accumulated in them.

The balance in each expense and revenue account is transferred by journal entry to an account entitled Expense and Revenue Summary. This is a *clearing* account used only at the end of the accounting period to summarize the expenses and revenues for the period, with the difference between these two classes of items being the net earnings or loss for the period. Since revenue accounts have credit balances, they are debited and Expense and Revenue Summary is credited; conversely, expense accounts have debit balances, so they are credited and Expense and Revenue Summary is debited. The Expense and Revenue Summary account now contains either a debit (net loss) or credit (net earnings) balance. It is then debited or credited as required to bring it to a zero balance, with Retained Earnings credited or debited in order to keep the entry in balance. This closing process is often referred to as "closing the books."

Closing entries illustrated

To illustrate the preparation of closing entries, assume that the ledger of a company contains the following earnings statement accounts:

Sales....................	$100,000	Salaries Expense............	$20,000
Sales Discounts...........	2,000	Other Expenses.............	8,000
Cost of Goods Sold.......	60,000	Federal Income Taxes.......	2,500

Answer frame 11[4]

The required adjusting entry is:

1976			
Dec. 31	Admissions Received in Advance	2,500	
	Admissions Revenue		2,500
	To record admissions revenue earned in 1976.		

By presenting 5 of the 10 plays in the series, the theater company has provided one half of the required services. Hence, half of the liability has been satisfied and half of the revenue for which cash was received in advance has been earned.

Review Frame 11[4], if you missed this question, before proceeding to Frame 12[4] on page 149.

12[4] *continued*

The required closing entries, assuming a December 31, 1976, closing, are as follows:

1976			
Dec. 31	Sales	100,000	
	Sales Discounts		2,000
	Expense and Revenue Summary		98,000
	To close revenue accounts.		
Dec. 31	Expense and Revenue Summary	90,500	
	Cost of Goods Sold		60,000
	Salaries Expense		20,000
	Other Expenses		8,000
	Federal Income Taxes		2,500
	To close expense accounts.		
Dec. 31	Expense and Revenue Summary	7,500	
	Retained Earnings		7,500
	To close Expense and Revenue Summary account to Retained Earnings.		

If it can be further assumed that a Dividends account shows a debit balance of $2,500, a further closing entry is needed:

1976			
Dec. 31	Retained Earnings	2,500	
	Dividends		2,500
	To close dividends.		

The above entries are posted in the normal manner and, if properly prepared and posted, will reduce all of the revenue and expense accounts to a zero balance so that they can be used to accumulate data needed to determine the next period's net earnings. The Dividends account is also brought to a zero balance, ready to accept entries for dividends in the coming year. Although not an expense account, the Dividends account has the same effect on Retained Earnings.

Indicate whether each of the following statements is true or false.

1. An Interest Revenue account containing a balance of $500 is closed by an entry debiting Interest Revenue and crediting Expense and Revenue Summary for $500.
2. The net earnings for a period cannot be properly determined if closing entries are not made.
3. If the Expense and Revenue Summary account has a debit balance, the company has net earnings for the period.
4. Because annual reporting is the predominant practice, closing entries are usually prepared only once a year.

Check your responses in Answer Frame 12[4] on page 152.

Frame 13[4]

The Expense and Revenue Summary and Retained Earnings accounts as they appear after the above closing entries are posted are presented below. The beginning balance of $65,000 in the Retained Earnings account is assumed, as are the account numbers and the posting cross reference (folio J 15). Note that the Expense and Revenue Summary account shows clearly the net earnings for the period—the final amount transferred, or closed, to Retained Earnings. The balance in the Retained Earnings account of $70,000 is the amount of retained earnings shown in the statement of financial position for December 31, 1976.

While commonplace in manually operated accounting systems, the intermediate step of closing all expense and all revenue accounts to the Expense and Revenue Summary account is often omitted in automated systems. In such systems, the computer may be instructed simply to close all expense and all revenue accounts and to carry the difference to the Retained Earnings account—as a debit if expenses are larger, or as a credit if revenues are larger.

Expense and Revenue Summary — *Account No. 600*

Date		Explanation	Folio	Debit	Credit	Balance
1976						
Dec.	31	Net revenues	J 15		98,000	98,000
	31	Expenses	J 15	90,500		7,500
	31	To close	J 15	7,500		—0—

Retained Earnings — *Account No. 317*

Date		Explanation	Folio	Debit	Credit	Balance
1976						
Jan.	1	Balance				65,000
Dec.	31	Net earnings	J 15		7,500	72,500
	31	Dividends	J 15	2,500		70,000

Answer frame 12[4]

1. True. Since the Interest Revenue account normally has a credit balance, the entry given would close it, that is, reduce it to a zero balance.
2. False. The earnings statement is drawn before closing entries are made. Consequently, these entries do not affect the determination of net earnings. Even if the closing entries were not prepared for last year, net earnings could be determined by getting the changes in the various expense and revenue accounts that took place during the current year.
3. False. If a debit balance exists, the expenses debited to the account exceed the revenues credited there; and when expenses exceed revenues, a net loss has been incurred.
4. True. Even though financial statements may be issued for interim periods, the standard accounting period is the year and the books are formally closed only once a year.

If you missed any of the above, review Frame 12[4] before proceeding to Frame 13[4] on page 151.

Post-closing trial balance

13[4] *continued* After the closing process has been completed, the only open accounts in the ledger are the statement of financial position accounts. Since these accounts contain the opening balances for the coming accounting year, they must, of course, be in balance. The preparation of a post-closing trial balance thus serves as a means of checking upon the accuracy of the closing process (the preparation and posting of closing entries and the bringing forward of account balances) while at the same time ensuring that the books are in balance at the start of the new accounting period.

As in the case of a trial balance, a post-closing trial balance is simply a listing of all of the open accounts in a system or ledger. The total of the accounts with debit balances must be equal to the total of the accounts with credit balances, or an error has been made.

The accounting cycle summarized

In Chapter 1 the financial accounting process was depicted as consisting of a number of functions commencing with observation of economic activity and ending with interpretation of reports and statements upon such activity. In this process are a number of steps that relate to the formal accounting system and its use in accumulating, processing, and reporting useful financial information. These steps, which have been illustrated and discussed in this and previous chapters, are referred to collectively as the accounting cycle and, for a manually operated system, are summarized as consisting of the following:

1. Journalizing transactions (and other events) in the journal.
2. Posting journal entries to the accounts.
3. Taking a trial balance of the accounts.
4. Journalizing the adjusting entries.

5. Posting the adjusting entries to the accounts.
6. Preparing financial statements.
7. Journalizing the closing entries.
8. Posting the closing entries to the accounts.
9. Taking a post-closing trial balance.

Note that these steps relate to the operation of the accounting system and comprise a subset of the steps in the financial accounting process. Recall from the discussion in Chapter 1 that the functions of observation, selection, measurement, and analysis must take place before a transaction can be journalized.

As is set forth in the appendix to this chapter (Frame 14[4]), completion of many of the steps that fall at the end of an accounting period may be made somewhat easier through use of a work sheet.

Indicate whether each of the following statements is true or false.

1. After closing entries have been posted, balances will appear only in the statement of financial position accounts.
2. In automated systems, the Expense and Revenue Summary account is often omitted.
3. A post-closing trial balance contains only statement of financial position accounts.
4. The accounting cycle consists of the specific steps taken in the operation of an accounting system to accumulate, process, and report useful information.

Check your responses in Answer Frame 13[4] on page 154.

Summary *chapter* 4

Adjusting entries usually are made to include in the accounts, from which financial statements are prepared, information on economic activity that has transpired but is not evidenced by a specific transaction.

Adjusting entries fall into four major classes, namely, those involving adjustments of (1) asset and expense accounts, (2) asset and revenue accounts, (3) liability and expense accounts, and (4) liability and revenue accounts. In (1) the adjustment involves recognition of an expense as a result of the expiration of a previously recorded asset; examples include depreciation, supplies, insurance, bad debts, and rent. In (2) the adjustment involves recognition of the growth of an asset as a result of the rendering of services to customers; examples include commissions and interest. In (3) the adjustment involves recognition of an expense and the corresponding obligation to pay as a result of the receipt of services or the levying of taxes; examples include interest, salaries, and federal income taxes. In (4) the adjustment involves recognition of the earning of revenue and the cancellation of a liability by providing services for

Answer frame 13[4]

All of the statements in Frame 13[4] are true. Together, they cover most of the more important points made in Frame 13[4]. If you missed any of the above questions, you may wish to review Frame 13[4] before proceeding to the chapter summary on page 153.

which customers pay in advance; examples include subscriptions, tickets, and rent.

In all cases, adjusting entries involve changing account balances from what they presently contain to what they should contain for proper financial reporting.

After the balances in the expense and revenue accounts have been used to prepare the earnings statement (and the Dividends account, if any, reported in the statement of retained earnings), these accounts are brought to a zero balance. They have served their purpose of accumulating useful information for an accounting period and now must be closed in order that information relating to the next accounting period may be entered in them. The closing of these accounts is accomplished through the preparation and posting of closing entries. The balances in all of the expense and revenue accounts are transferred to an Expense and Revenue Summary account, whose balance in turn (representing net earnings or net loss) is transferred to Retained Earnings. The Dividends account is closed to Retained Earnings. A post-closing trial balance may be prepared to check upon the equality of the debit and credit account balances in the ledger after the closing process has been completed.

The steps undertaken to operate an accounting system are collectively referred to as the accounting cycle and are enumerated in Frame 13[4] on pages 152–53.

The appendix which follows (Frame 14[4]) discusses the use of the work sheet in the accounting process. The Glossary and Student Review Quiz for this chapter begin on pages 159 and 161.

Frame 14[4] (Appendix)

The work sheet

In manually operated accounting systems containing large numbers of accounts, the accounting activities to be completed at the end of a financial reporting period may be organized and handled more efficiently through use of a work sheet. A work sheet is simply a sheet of paper containing a number of columns and lines for recording account titles, item descriptions, and dollar amounts. Since it is used internally only, it can take on a variety of forms. But to be of any real value, it will, as a minimum, contain columns for a trial balance, adjusting entries, an earnings statement, and a statement of financial position. An expanded version of a work sheet is presented in Illustration 4.1 and is discussed below.

The trial balance columns

Instead of preparing a separate trial balance, the open accounts in the ledger are entered in the first pair of columns entitled Trial Balance in the work sheet prepared for the Falconer Company for the month ended June 30, 1976. The columns are summed and the equality of the debits and credits in the ledger demonstrated by entering the totals ($34,600) immediately after the last item in the trial balance.

The adjustments columns

In the next pair of columns, all of the adjustments required to bring the accounts up to date prior to the preparation of financial statements are entered. The assumed adjustments for the Falconer Company are as follows.

Entry A records $40 of insurance premium paid in advance which relates to coverage for the month of June; the debit and credit keyed with the letter A comprise the entry made to recognize the asset expiration and the related expense.

Entry B records the fact that supplies costing $600 were used during the month, as determined by a physical inventory.

Entry C records estimated uncollectible accounts for June at 1 percent of sales of $16,000 for June.

Entry D records depreciation expense for the month, determined by dividing the cost of the furniture and fixtures ($2,400) by their estimated useful lives of 10 years and dividing the result by 12.

Entry E records the expense and the liability resulting from the fact that there were unpaid office salaries of $120 at the end of the month.

Entry F indicates that at the time it advanced money to an employee to travel on company business, Falconer Company debited the amount advanced to Other Selling Expense (and credited Cash). But, since the travel will take place in July, the $130 advanced is not an expense of June. It is an asset, a prepaid expense, and must be removed from the expense account and set up as an asset. The debit and credit keyed with the letter F accomplish this.

Entry G transfers the beginning merchandise inventory of $7,200 and the net purchases for the month, $12,000 (purchases of $12,200 less purchase returns of $200), to Cost of Goods Sold. Note carefully the four items keyed G.

Entry H removes from the expense account Cost of Goods Sold the cost of the merchandise on hand, $11,000, as determined by a physical inventory, and establishes it as an asset, Merchandise Inventory. Note how Entry G enters in Cost of Goods Sold the cost of the goods available

Illustration 4.1

FALCONER COMPANY
Work Sheet
For the Month Ended June 30, 1976

Line No.	Acct. No.	Account Titles	Trial Balance Debit	Trial Balance Credit	Adjustments Debit	Adjustments Credit
1	101	Cash	4,020			
2	102	Accounts receivable	3,100			
3	102-A	Allow. for doubtful accts.		100		C 160
4	108	Merchandise inventory	7,200		H 11,000	G 7,200
5	112	Store supplies	720			B 600
6	114	Unexpired insurance	480			A 40
7	120	Furniture and fixtures	2,400			
8	120-A	Allowance for depreciation		200		D 20
9	201	Accounts payable		5,100		
10	301	Capital stock		10,000		
11	310	Retained earnings		3,000		
12	311	Dividends	250			
13	401	Sales		16,000		
14	512	Purchases	12,200			G 12,200
15	513	Purchase returns		200	G 200	
16	514	Sales salaries expense	1,800			
17	515	Advertising expense	700			
18	517	Other selling expense	430			F 130
19	521	Office salaries expense	800		E 120	
20	525	Other administrative expense	500			
			34,600	34,600		
23	519	Insurance expense			A 40	
24	516	Store supplies expense			B 600	
25	520	Bad debts expense			C 160	
26	518	Depreciation expense			D 20	
27	202	Accrued salaries payable				E 120
28	113	Travel advances			F 130	
29	510	Cost of goods sold			G 19,200	H 11,000
					31,470	31,470
31		Net earnings				
33		Retained earnings				

for sale, while Entry H removes from that account the cost of the goods not sold, leaving in the account the cost of the goods that were actually sold during the month.

One advantage of a work sheet is that it assembles all of the accounts in one place, where they may be easily studied to determine the need for possible adjustment. As a result, entries are not likely to be overlooked.

After all of the adjusting entries are entered in the Adjustments columns, the two columns are totaled and their equality noted as a partial check of the arithmetic accuracy of the work completed thus far.

Adjusted Trial Balance		Earnings Statement		Statement of Retained Earnings		Statement of Financial Position	
Debit	Credit	Debit	Credit	Debit	Credit	Debit	Credit
4,020						4,020	
3,100						3,100	
	260						260
11,000						11,000	
120						120	
440						440	
2,400						2,400	
	220						220
	5,100						5,100
	10,000						10,000
	3,000				3,000		
250				250			
	16,000		16,000				
1,800		1,800					
700		700					
300		300					
920		920					
500		500					
40		40					
600		600					
160		160					
20		20					
	120						120
130						130	
8,200		8,200					
34,700	34,700	13,240	16,000				
		2,760			2,760		
		16,000	16,000	250	5,760		
				5,510			5,510
				5,760	5,760	21,210	21,210

The adjusted trial balance columns

After the adjustments have been entered, the adjusted balance of each account is determined and entered in the adjusted trial balance columns. For example, the Allowance for Doubtful Accounts has a balance of $100, unadjusted, to which was added $160 in adjusting entry C, leaving a credit balance of $260. This $260 is shown in the credit column of the pair of columns headed Adjusted Trial Balance.

All accounts having balances are extended to the Adjusted Trial Balance columns. Note carefully how the rules of debit and credit apply as to whether an entry increases or decreases the balance in the account. For example, Merchandise Inventory has a debit balance of $7,200 which is increased by a debit of $11,000 to a total of $18,200 and this, in turn, is decreased by a credit of $7,200, leaving a balance of $11,000—the correct balance for financial reporting purposes.

The balances in the Adjusted Trial Balance columns are summed and the equality of the accounts with debit balances and those with credit balances noted as a check upon the arithmetic accuracy of the work completed.

The earnings statement columns

All of the accounts in the Adjusted Trial Balance columns that will appear in the earnings statement (the expense and revenue accounts) are now extended into the Earnings Statement columns—revenues as credits, expenses as debits. Each column is subtotaled, revealing expenses (debits) of $13,240 and revenues (credits) of $16,000. This means that the net earnings for the period amounted to $2,760, and this amount is entered in the debit column to bring the two column totals into agreement. Note the similarity of the debit here to the debit in the Expense and Revenue Summary account to close or transfer net earnings to the Retained Earnings account. A net loss would, of course, be recorded in the opposite manner—that is, as a credit.

The statement of retained earnings columns

These columns contain the items that appear in the statement of retained earnings, namely: the beginning balance of retained earnings, the net earnings for the period, dividends (if any), and the ending balance of retained earnings. Note that the illustrated columns contain the first three of these items, along with the entry as a credit of the net earnings for the period of $2,760. The columns are subtotaled and the difference between the two subtotals, the ending balance of retained earnings, $5,510 is entered in order to bring the two column totals into balance.

The statement of financial position columns

All of the asset, liability, and the stockholders' equity accounts are extended into the statement of financial position columns—assets as debits and the others as credits. Note that the ending rather than the beginning balance in Retained Earnings is carried into these columns. Once again, to check the arithmetic accuracy of the work completed, the columns are totaled and their agreement noted.

The completed work sheet

Some accountants, in completing a work sheet, enter brief explanations keyed to the adjusting entries in the lower left-hand corner of the work sheet. Such a practice is commendable for complicated adjustments, but not necessary for the relatively routine adjustments illustrated here.

When the work sheet is completed, all of the information needed to prepare the financial statements is readily available. It need only be recast into a more formal format.

Note, also, that it would be a relatively routine matter to journalize the adjusting and closing entries in the journal and then post them to the accounts. The adjusting entries can be readily prepared from information in the Adjustments columns, closing entries from the items in the Earnings Statement columns and the dividends item in the Statement of Retained Earnings columns. But, since financial statements can be prepared from the work sheet, such entries are not likely to be entered formally in the journal and posted to the accounts at any time other than at the formal annual closing of the books. Thus, one of the real advantages of using a work sheet is that interim financial statements can be prepared without going through the work of journalizing and posting adjusting and closing entries.

To summarize the discussion on work sheets, indicate whether each of the following statements is correct or incorrect.

1. Because it is an internal working tool rather than a published financial statement, the work sheet can vary in format.
2. A work sheet is likely, as an absolute minimum, to contain at least four pairs of debit and credit columns.
3. When a work sheet is used, the period-end adjustments need not be journalized.
4. The work sheet will indicate automatically which accounts are in need of adjustment.
5. If a work sheet does not contain a pair of columns headed Statement of Retained Earnings, the beginning balance of retained earnings and the net earnings for the period would be carried to the Statement of Financial Position columns as credits, while dividends would be entered in the same pair of columns as a debit.

Turn to Answer Frame 14[4] on page 160 to check your responses.

Glossary *chapter* 4

Accrual basis of accounting—a method of earnings determination under which revenues are recorded when goods are delivered or services are rendered, and expenses are recorded in the same period as the revenues which they helped to create are recognized.

Accrued (assets and liabilities)—those assets and liabilities which exist at the end of an accounting period but which have not been recorded up to the time at which adjusting entries are to be prepared. They represent rights to receive, or obligations to make, payments which are not legally due at the statement of financial position date. Examples are accrued interest receivable, accrued rent receivable, ac-

Answer frame 14[4]

1. Correct. Because he is likely to be the only one who uses it, the accountant can construct whatever form of work sheet he believes will serve his purposes most efficiently.
2. Correct. To be of any value, a work sheet probably must contain debit and credit columns for trial balance, adjustments, earnings statement, and statement of financial position. If the accounts and adjustments are few in number, there may be no need for the intermediate check upon the accuracy of the adjustment work that is afforded by the use of the Adjusted Trial Balance columns.
3. Incorrect. The adjustments need not be journalized for interim financial statements, but they would have to be formally journalized and posted to accounts at least at the end of the accounting year.
4. Incorrect. Which accounts need adjustment can be determined only from an analysis of the accounts, and the construction of a work sheet does not automatically entail analysis of any account. But a properly completed work sheet will show which accounts are in need of adjustment.
5. Correct. In relatively routine circumstances, the work sheet may not include a pair of columns headed Statement of Retained Earnings. In such cases, the data that would be shown in these columns must be carried to the Statement of Financial Position Columns in the manner indicated. Retained Earnings is a statement of financial position, not an earnings statement, account.

If you missed any of the above, you should review Frame 14[4]. Then turn to the Glossary of terms on page 159 and familiarize yourself with them before going on to the Student Review Quiz for a self-administered test of your comprehension of the material presented in this chaper.

---

crued salaries (or wages) payable, and accrued interest payable.

Accumulated Depreciation account—synonymous with Allowance for Depreciation account below.

Adjusting entries—journal entries made to record the accrued effects of economic activity. They are made at the end of the accounting period to bring the accounts to their proper balances before financial statements are prepared.

Allowance for Depreciation account—a contra asset account (defined as an account shown as a deduction from the asset to which it relates in the statement of financial position); an account which shows the sum of all amounts taken as depreciation on the asset up to the statement of financial position date.

Allowance for Doubtful Accounts account—an account showing the estimated amount of outstanding accounts receivable not expected to be collected; a contra asset account shown as a deduction from accounts receivable in the statement of financial position.

Cash basis of accounting—a procedure under which revenue is recorded when cash is received and expenses recorded when cash is paid.

Charge—synonymous with the term "debit."

Closing—the act of transferring the balances in the expense and revenue accounts to the Expense and Revenue Summary account and then to the Retained Earnings account. The balance in the dividend account, if one is used, is transferred to Retained Earnings.

Deferred costs—one interpretation or definition of assets in which they are viewed as charges awaiting assignment to expense in the determination of net earnings.

Depreciation accounting—the process of allocating and charging to expense the cost of a limited-life, long-term asset (such as a building) over its useful life.

Depreciation expense—the portion of the cost of a depreciable asset charged to expense in a given accounting period.

Depreciation formula—the procedure employed in calculating periodic depreciation, generally cost less estimated salvage value divided by the number of years of expected useful life, which is the procedure employed to determine the annual depreciation charge under the straight-line method.

Expense and Revenue account—a clearing account used to summarize all revenue and expense account balances at the end of an accounting period.

Post-closing trial balance—a trial balance taken after the expense and revenue (and dividend) accounts have been closed.

Prepaid expense—an asset which is awaiting assignment to expense. An example is unexpired insurance.

Revenue received in advance—a flow of assets received from customers in advance of the rendering of services for or the delivery of goods to them; since the revenue has not been earned, it is a liability; often called *prepaid revenue* or *unearned revenue,* although preferred terminology would be *advances by customers.*

Service potential—the benefits embodied in assets. The future services that assets can render are what makes assets "things of value" to a business.

Work sheet—an informal accounting statement used to summarize the trial balance and information needed to prepare the financial statements and the adjusting and closing entries.

Student review quiz *chapter* 4

To develop a permanent record of your responses, you may write them on the answer sheet provided in the *Work Papers* or on a separate sheet of paper.

1 Which of the following changes in the accounts is handled through an adjusting entry?

a) Gradual conversion of an asset into an expense.

b) Equal and gradual growth of an expense and a liability over the accounting period.

c) Earning of revenue received in advance.

d) Equal and gradual growth of an asset and a revenue over the accounting period.

e) All of the above.

2 If total net sales for the period are $18,000 ($17,000 credit sales, $1,000 cash sales), the accounts receivable balance is $10,000, and uncollectible accounts are estimated to be 1 percent of net credit sales, the correct entry to adjust the accounts at the end of the accounting period is:

a)	Allowance for Doubtful Accounts	180	
	Bad Debts Expense		180
b)	Bad Debts Expense	170	
	Allowance for Doubtful Accounts		170
c)	Allowance for Doubtful Accounts	100	
	Bad Debts Expense		100
d)	Bad Debts Expense	180	
	Allowance for Doubtful Accounts		180
e)	Bad Debts Expense	100	
	Allowance for Doubtful Accounts		100

3 A company's annual accounting period closes on December 31. On January 15, the account of P. L. Forrest (which arose as the result of a sale on December 20) in the amount of $75 is found to be definitely uncollectible. The company estimates and records its bad debts at the end of each year. What is the proper entry?

a)	Bad Debts Expense	75	
	Accounts Receivable—P. L. Forrest		75
b)	Allowance for Doubtful Accounts	75	
	Accounts Receivable—P. L. Forrest		75
c)	Bad Debts Expense	75	
	Allowance for Doubtful Accounts		75
d)	Allowance for Doubtful Accounts	75	
	Bad Debts Expense		75
e)	None of the above.		

4 On November 30, the close of an annual accounting period, interest in the amount of $500 has been earned but not received. The correct entry is:

a) No entry.
b) Cash.................. 500
Interest Revenue.... 500
c) Accrued Interest
Receivable........... 500
Interest Revenue... 500
d) Accounts Receivable.... 500
Interest Revenue.... 500
e) Interest Revenue....... 500
Accrued Interest
Receivable....... 500

5 The Unexpired Insurance account shows a balance of $900, representing the payment on July 1 of a three-year insurance premium of $900. The correct adjusting entry on December 31, the close of the annual accounting period in which the policy was purchased, is:

a) Insurance Expense...... 150
Unexpired Insurance. 150
b) Insurance Expense...... 300
Unexpired Insurance. 300
c) Unexpired Insurance.... 150
Insurance Expense.. 150
d) Unexpired Insurance.... 25
Insurance Expense.. 25
e) None of the above.

6 On June 30, the close of the monthly accounting period, employees of the Stamp Company have earned salaries totaling $921 payable on the payday of July 3. The entry required on June 30 is:

a) Salary Expense......... 921
Accrued Salaries
Payable.......... 921
b) Accrued Salaries Payable. 921
Salary Expense..... 921
c) Salary Expense 921
Cash.............. 921
d) Salary Expense......... 921
Accounts Payable... 921
e) None of the above.

7 Office furniture is purchased on October 1 at a cost of $3,400. Estimated salvage value is $200, and estimated useful life is four years. The entry to record the depreciation on December 31 is (assume this is the close of the annual accounting period):

a) Depreciation Expense—
Office Furniture....... 850
Allowance for Depreciation—Office
Furniture........ 850
b) Depreciation Expense—
Office Furniture....... 800
Allowance for Depreciation—Office
Furniture........ 800
c) Allowance for Depreciation—Office Furniture. 800
Depreciation Expense
—Office Furniture. 800
d) Depreciation Expense—
Office Furniture....... 200
Allowance for Depreciation—Office
Furniture........ 200
e) Allowance for Depreciation—Office Furniture. 200
Depreciation Expense—Office
Furniture........ 200

8 Company X pays its employees on the 15th day of each month. The accounting period ends on December 31. If the adjusting entry on December 31, 1975, were neglected, which of the following would be the effect at that date?

a) The assets of the company would be understated.
b) The stockholders' equity of the company would be understated.
c) Net earnings for the period ended would be understated.
d) The liabilities of the company would be understated.
e) Net earnings for the period ended would be unaffected.

9 Which of the following items is *not* important in the matching of expenses and revenues under the accrual basis of accounting?

a) Amortization of patent costs.
b) Depreciation of plant assets.
c) Estimated allowance for uncollectible accounts.
d) Beginning and ending inventory accounts.
e) Cash receipts.

10 Which type of entry is made necessary because of the employment of the accrual basis of accounting?

a) Recording collections of accounts receivable when received.
b) Establishing an allowance for uncollectible accounts.
c) Recording payments on accounts payable when made.
d) Recording the payment of dividends to stockholders when made.
e) Recording the interest expense which

has been incurred on bonds which the company has issued in the past if not paid at year-end.

11 Which of the following accounts is closed by an entry which includes a debit to Expense and Revenue Summary?

a) Service Revenue.
b) Accounts Receivable.
c) Rent Expense.
d) Accrued Salaries Payable.
e) Retained Earnings.

12 After the accounts have been closed—

a) All of the accounts have zero balances.
b) The asset, liability, and stockholders' equity accounts have zero balances.
c) The revenue, expense, Expense and Revenue Summary, and Retained Earnings accounts have zero balances.
d) The revenue, expense, and Expense and Revenue Summary accounts have zero balances.
e) None of the above is true.

The following questions relate to the material on the worksheet contained in the Appendix (Frame 14[4]).

13 Which of the following statements is true concerning the work sheet?

a) It is a formal accounting statement which is distributed to stockholders and creditors.
b) The accounting process could not possibly be completed without preparing a work sheet.
c) The work sheet must contain either 8 or 12 columns.
d) An explanation of each adjustment must appear toward the bottom of the work sheet.
e) Since the work sheet is an informal tool, the accountant can use any format he wants to use or choose not to prepare a work sheet at all.

14 The Trial Balance column of the work sheet shows store fixtures of $4,000. Estimated depreciation for the period is $400. The store fixtures amount in the Statement of Financial Position columns of the work sheet will be a:

a) $3,600 debit.
b) $3,600 credit.
c) $4,400 debit.
d) $4,000 debit.
e) $4,000 credit.

15 Supplies on hand are shown at $315 in the Trial Balance columns of the work sheet. The Adjustments columns show that $290 of these supplies were used during the month. The amount shown as supplies on hand in the Statement of Financial Position columns is a:

a) $25 debit.
b) $315 debit.
c) $290 debit.
d) $25 credit.
e) $290 credit.

16 The Williams Company follows the periodic inventory procedure in accounting for the cost of the merchandise it sells. For a particular period, its beginning inventory was $1,200 and its ending inventory $2,000. In a work sheet, which of the following responses *correctly* describe the treatment to be accorded both the beginning and ending inventories?

The beginning inventory appears in the—

a) Adjustments debit column.
b) Adjustments debit column and Statement of Financial Position debit column.
c) Adjustments credit column and Statement of Financial Position debit column.
d) Adjustments credit column.
e) None of the above.

The ending inventory appears in the—

f) Statement of Financial Position debit column and Adjustments debit column.
g) Statement of Financial Position credit column.
h) Statement of Financial Position debit column.
i) Statement of Financial Position debit column and Adjustments credit column.

Now compare your answers with the correct answers and explanations on page 708.

Questions *chapter* 4

1 In what important way do the pre-closing trial balance and the post-closing trial balance differ? Why is the post-closing trial balance prepared?

2 Assuming that the closing process has been accomplished properly, which of the following statements is true? Why?

a) After closing, expense and revenue accounts never have a balance other than zero.
b) After closing, statement of financial position accounts always have a balance other than zero.

3 Your uncle knows you are taking a course in accounting in college and he asks you to come over and help him. It seems his new bookkeeper has journalized all of the business transactions for the month and has posted the journal entries to the ledger accounts. She now admits that she does not know how to proceed in completing the accounting process for the month. He asks you to tell her what should now be done to complete the process.

4 Why are adjusting entries necessary? Why not treat every cash disbursement as an expense and every cash receipt as revenue when the cash changes hands?

5 Give an example of each of the following:
a) Equal growth of an expense and a liability.
b) Earning of revenue received in advance.
c) Equal growth of an asset and revenue.
d) Equal growth of an expense and decrease in an asset.

6 "Adjusting entries would not be necessary if the *pure* cash basis of accounting were followed (assuming no mistakes were made in recording cash transactions as they occurred). Under the pure cash basis, all receipts which are of a revenue nature are considered revenue when received and all expenditures (even for a building) which are of an expense nature are considered expenses when paid. It is the use of the accrual basis of accounting, where an effort is made to match expenses (incurred but not necessarily paid for in the same period) against the revenues (earned but not necessarily received in the same period) they create that makes adjusting entries necessary." Do you agree with this statement? Why?

7 Why don't accountants keep all the accounts at their proper balances continuously throughout the period so that adjusting entries would not have to be made before financial statements are prepared?

8 A fellow student makes the following statement: "It is easy to tell whether a company is using the cash or accrual basis of accounting. When an amount is paid for future rent or insurance services, a firm that is using the cash basis will debit an expense account while a firm that is using the accrual basis will debit an asset account." Correct his misconception.

9 You notice that the Supplies on Hand account has a debit balance of $2,700 at the end of the accounting period. How would you determine the extent to which this account needs adjustment?

10 It may be said that some assets are converted into expenses as they expire and that some liabilities become revenues as they are earned. Give examples of asset and liability accounts for which the statement is true. Give examples of asset and liability accounts to which the statement does not apply.

11 The accountant often speaks of expired costs. Do costs literally expire?

12 What does the word "accrued" mean? Is there a conceptual difference between interest payable and accrued interest payable?

13 It is more difficult to match expenses incurred with revenues earned than it would be to match expenses paid with revenues received. Do you think that the effort is worthwhile? Why are financial statements prepared?

14 Describe the purposes for which the work sheet is prepared.

15 You have taken over a set of accounting books for a small corporation as a part-time job. At the end of the first accounting period you have partially completed the work sheet by entering the proper ledger accounts and balances in the Trial Balance columns. You turn to the manager and ask, "Where is the list of additional information I can use in entering the adjusting entries?" The manager indicates there is no such list. (In all the textbook problems you have done you have always been given this information.) How would you obtain the information for this real-life situation? What are the consequences of not making all of the adjustments required at the end of the accounting period?

Exercises *chapter 4*

1 a) If a one-year insurance policy is purchased on July 1 for $1,200 and the following entry is made at that time:

Unexpired Insurance..........	1,200	
Cash.......		1,200

what adjusting entry is necessary at December 31?

b) Give the adjusting entry which would be necessary if the entry to record the purchase of the policy on July 1 had been:

Insurance Expense.........	1,200	
Cash.......		1,200

c) Show by the use of T accounts that the end result is the same under either **(a)** or **(b)**.

2 At December 31, 1975, an adjusting entry was made as follows:

Prepaid Rent........	250	
Rent Expense...		250

You know that the gross amount of rent paid was $600 and it was to cover a one-year period. Determine:

a) The opening date of the year to which the $600 of rent applies.

b) The entry that was made on the date the rent was paid.

3 A building is being depreciated by an amount of $14,000 per year. You know it had an original cost of $155,000 and was expected to last 10 years. How must the $14,000 have been determined? Give the entry for the sale of the building at the end of the 10-year period assuming the building was sold for its expected salvage value.

4 Office supplies were purchased for cash on May 2, 1975, for $800. Show two ways in which this entry could be recorded and then show the adjusting entry that would be necessary for each, assuming that $200 of the supplies remained at the end of the year.

5 Give entries for the following transactions. (A zero balance exists in the Allowance for Doubtful Accounts account before these entries are made.)

a) Company M estimates and records bad debts at $1,000 on December 31, 1975.

b) On February 10, 1976, the company finds that Joseph Barnett is unable to pay $600 which he owed on account as of December 31, 1975.

c) On June 8, 1976, Joseph Barnett pays the $600 that had previously been written off.

d) On August 5 an account receivable (Dick Cave) of $1,200 arising from a 1975 sale is identified as uncollectible.

6 The cash balance at the beginning of the year was $17,000. During the year $80,000 was paid out for assets and expenses and $20,000 was received from the issuance of capital stock. The cash balance at the end of the year was $28,000. The balance in accounts receivable decreased by $6,000 during the year. How much service revenue was earned during the year? There were no receipts or disbursements except those specifically mentioned or implied above.

7 Gross sales of the ABC Corporation amounted to $247,000 in 1975. Sales returns and allowances amounted to $2,000. If it is estimated that 1 percent of net sales will be uncollectible, make the adjusting entry which would be required at the end of the year.

8 A firm borrows $10,000 on November 1 for 120 days with interest payable at the maturity of the loan at the rate of 6 percent. Prepare the adjusting entry required on December 31. (It should be noted that by December 31, one half of the term of the loan has expired.)

9 A firm buys bonds as an investment. If the semiannual interest amounts to $600 and is paid on March 1 and September 1, what is the adjusting entry required on December 31 to record the interest revenue earned?

10 State the effect that each of the following would have on the amount of net earnings reported for 1974 and 1975. The company's accounting period ends on December 31.

a) No adjustment is made for accrued salaries of $800 as of December 31, 1974.

b) Ending inventory for 1974 is understated by $500. The company uses the periodic inventory procedure.

c) The collection of $600 for services yet unperformed as of December 31, 1974, is credited to a revenue account. The services are performed in 1975.

11 The three major column headings on a work sheet are: Trial Balance, Earnings Statement, Statement of Financial

Position. For each of the following items determine under which major column heading it would appear and whether it would be a debit or credit. (For instance, cash would appear under the debit side of the Trial Balance and Statement of Financial Position columns.)

a) Accounts receivable.
b) Accounts payable.
c) Retained earnings.
d) Advertising expense.
e) Capital stock.
f) Fees earned.
g) Net earnings for the month.

12 If a set of columns was included in a work sheet for the Statement of Retained Earnings, illustrate how it would be used. Assume a beginning balance in retained earnings of $14,000 and net earnings for the year of $6,000.

13 In Exercise 12, if there was a deficit of $9,000 as of the beginning of the year and a net loss of $8,000 for the year, show how these would be treated in these columns.

14 After adjustment, selected account balances of the Randall Corporation are:

Sales	$100,000
Sales returns	2,000
Cost of goods sold	58,000
Sales commissions	21,000
Advertising expense	4,000
Office expense	13,000

In journal form, give the entries required to close the books for the period.

Problems, Series A *chapter* 4

4–1–A

Required: For each of the following cases:

a) Prepare the adjusting journal entry, dating it December 31, 1975.
b) Set up ledger accounts in skeleton form, enter balances as given, if any, and post the adjusting entries made in part **(a)**.
c) Prepare and post closing entries. You will need a separate Expense and Revenue Summary account for each case.
d) State the correct figures for the statement of financial position. Show related accounts in each case as they should appear on that statement.
e) State the correct figures for the earnings statement.

	Account Name	*Trial Balance*	*Information for Adjustments*
Case 1:	Equipment	$ 40,000	Depreciation is computed at the rate of 15 percent per period.
	Allowance for depreciation—equipment	6,000	
Case 2:	Interest expense	1,500	Unpaid interest incurred on borrowed money amounts to $200.
Case 3:	Sales	300,000	One half of 1 percent of the sales is estimated as the bad debts expense.
	Allowance for doubtful accounts (credit)	1,200	
	Accounts receivable	70,000	
Case 4:	Unexpired insurance	8,400	Of the unexpired insurance in the trial balance, only $2,200 is for additional protection after December 31.

4–2–A

The trial balance of the Hall Company at December 31 of the current year includes, among other items, the following account balances:

	Debits	*Credits*
Unexpired insurance	$ 3,648	
Buildings	79,000	
Allowance for depreciation of buildings		$15,800
Salaries expense	55,000	
Prepaid rent	12,000	

Additional information:

a) The debit balance in the Unexpired Insurance account is the advance premium for one year from September 1 of the current year.
b) The buildings are being depreciated at the rate of 4 percent a year, with no salvage value expected.
c) Salaries accrued and payable at December 31 amount to $3,200.
d) The debit balance in Prepaid Rent is for a one-year period that started March 1 of the current year.

Required: Prepare the adjusting journal entries at December 31.

4–3–A

Among the account balances shown in the trial balance of the Hanson Company at December 31 of the current year are the following:

	Debits	*Credits*
Office supplies inventory	$ 1,740	
Unexpired insurance	2,400	
Accounts receivable	74,000	
Allowance for doubtful accounts		$ 800
Buildings	42,000	
Allowance for depreciation of buildings		9,750

Additional information:

a) The inventory of supplies on hand at December 31 amounts to $300.
b) The balance in the Unexpired Insurance account is for a two-year policy taken out June 1 of the current year.
c) It is estimated that $1,400 should be added to the Allowance for Doubtful Accounts.
d) The annual rate of depreciation for the buildings is based on the cost shown in the Buildings account, less scrap value estimated at $4,500. When acquired, the lives of the buildings were estimated at 50 years each.

Required:

a) Prepare the adjusting journal entries at December 31.
b) Open skeleton ledger accounts for each of the accounts involved, enter the balances as shown in the trial balance, post the adjusting entries, and bring down balances.

4–4–A

Required:

a) Set up the following three ledger accounts: Accounts Receivable, Bad Debts Expense, and Allowance for Doubtful Accounts.
b) Journalize the following transactions and post to the accounts (do not post to accounts not given):

May	1–31	Sales on account amounted to $66,000.
	1–31	Cash collected on account amounted to $16,000.
	31	One percent of accounts receivable on May 31 was estimated to be uncollectible.
June	1–30	Sales on account amounted to $72,000.
	1–30	Cash collected on account amounted to $30,000.
	30	Increased the balance in the Allowance for Doubtful Accounts to 1 percent of the balance in the Accounts Receivable account.
July	21	An account receivable of $186 proved to be uncollectible.

4–5–A

The Blanch Company occupies rented quarters on the main street of the city. In order to get this location it was necessary for the company to rent a store larger than needed, so a portion of the area is subleased (rented) to Leone's Restaurant.

Required: Present the period-end entries required by the statements of fact presented below. Show your calculations of the amounts as explanations of your entries.

The following partial trial balance was taken from the company's ledger as of the close of business December 31, 1975. All of the original entries applicable to the statements of fact were posted to one or more of these accounts.

BLANCH COMPANY
Partial Trial Balance
December 31, 1975

	Debits	*Credits*
Cash	$20,000	
Accounts receivable	25,000	
Allowance for doubtful accounts		$ 500
Unexpired insurance	2,850	
Store equipment	22,000	
Allowance for depreciation on store equipment		2,400
Notes payable		5,000
Sales		150,000
Supplies expense	2,700	
Rent expense	3,600	
Store salaries expense	24,500	
Rent revenue		1,100

Data to be considered:

a) The wages of the store clerks amount to $90 per day and were last paid through Friday, December 27. December 31 is a Tuesday. The store is closed Sundays.

b) Over the years the store's bad debt losses have averaged 2 percent of sales.

c) An analysis of the Store Equipment account disclosed:

Balance January 1, 1975	$16,000
Addition July 1, 1975	6,000
Balance December 31, 1975, per trial balance	$22,000

The company estimates that this equipment will last 20 years from the date it was acquired and that the salvage value will be nil.

d) The store carries one combined insurance policy which is taken out once a year effective August 1. The premium on the policy now in force amounts to $1,800 per year.

e) Unused store supplies on hand at December 31, 1975, have a cost of $180.

f) December's rent from Leone's Restaurant has not yet been received, $100.

g) The note payable is for 10 months, has an interest rate of 5 percent, and is dated July 1, 1975.

4–6–A

On June 1, 1975, Bill Roberts opened a swimming pool cleaning and maintenance service business. He vaguely recalled the process of making journal entries and establishing ledger accounts from a high school bookkeeping course he had taken some years ago. At the end of June, he prepared an earnings statement for the month of June, but he had the feeling that he had not proceeded correctly. He contacted his brother, Joe, a recent college graduate majoring in accounting, for assistance.

Joe immediately noted that his brother had, in effect, kept his records on a cash basis and set about to bring the books to a full accrual basis.

Required:

a) Prepare the entries for the following transactions as Bill must have recorded them under the cash basis of accounting.

b) Prepare the necessary adjusting entries as Joe must have prepared them to bring the books to a full accrual basis of accounting.

c) Calculate the change in the net earnings for June brought about by changing from the cash to the accrual basis of accounting.

Transactions:

June 1 Received cash of $9,000 from various customers in exchange for service agreements to clean and maintain their pools for the months of June, July, August, and September.

5 Paid rent for automotive and cleaning equipment to be used during the period June through September, $2,000. The payment covered the entire period.

8 Purchased a two-year liability insurance policy effective June 1 for $2,640 cash.

10 Received an advance of $2,500 from a Florida building contractor in exchange for an agreement to help service pools in his housing development during the months of October through May.

16 Paid wages for the first half of June, $2,800.

17 Paid $120 for advertising to be run in a local newspaper for two weeks in June and four weeks in July.

19 Paid the rent of $4,000 under a four-month lease on a building rented and occupied on June 1.

20 Borrowed $6,000 from the bank on a 90-day, 6 percent note.

26 Purchased $1,800 of supplies for cash. (Only $300 of these supplies were used in June.)

29 Billed various customers for services rendered, $4,200.

30 Unpaid employee services received in the last half of June amounted to $2,600.

30 Received a bill for $200 for gas and oil used in June.

4–7–A

Required: From the following trial balance and supplementary information, prepare

a) A 12-column work sheet for the year ended December 31, 1975. (See appendix, Frame 14[4], for illustration of form.)

b) The required closing entries.

Supplementary data:

a) The building is to be depreciated at the rate of 2 percent per year.

b) Depreciate the store fixtures 10 percent per year.

c) The allowance for doubtful accounts is to be increased by one half of 1 percent of net sales. (Round amount up to nearest full dollar.)

d) Accrued interest on notes receivable is $150.

e) Accrued interest on the mortgage note is $250.

f) Accrued salesmen's salaries are $700.

g) Unexpired insurance is $200.

h) Prepaid advertising is $500.

i) Included in the cash on hand is a check for $25 which was cashed for an ex-employee in 1975 and which is worthless.

j) Cost of merchandise inventory on hand December 31, 1975, $27,750.

PETERSON COMPANY
Trial Balance
December 31, 1975

	Debits	*Credits*
Cash on hand and in bank	$ 8,600	
Accounts receivable	41,250	
Allowance for doubtful accounts		$ 850
Notes receivable	3,750	
Merchandise inventory, January 1, 1975	20,800	
Land	30,000	
Building	55,000	
Allowance for depreciation of building		16,500
Store fixtures	27,800	
Allowance for depreciation of store fixtures		5,560
Accounts payable		18,950
Mortgage note payable		25,000
Capital stock		50,000
Retained earnings		35,090
Sales		275,750
Sales returns and allowances	1,000	
Sales discounts	1,850	
Purchases	156,450	
Purchase returns and allowances		700
Purchase discounts		1,300
Transportation-in	3,650	
Salesmen's salaries	32,000	
Advertising expense	6,000	
Transportation-out	2,300	
Officers' salaries	37,000	
Insurance expense	1,450	
Interest revenue		200
Interest expense	1,000	
	$429,900	$429,900

Problems, Series B *chapter* 4

4–1–B

Required: For each of the following cases:

a) Prepare the adjusting journal entry, dating it December 31, 1975.

b) Set up ledger accounts in skeleton form, enter balances as given, if any, and post the adjusting entries made in part **(a)**.

c) Prepare and post closing entries. You will need a separate Expense and Revenue Summary account for each case.

d) State the correct figures for the statement of financial position. Show related accounts in each case as they should appear on that statement.

e) State the correct figures for the earnings statement.

	Account Name	*Trial Balance*	*Information for Adjustments*
Case 1:	Office building	$420,000	Depreciation is computed each period at the rate of 2 percent of cost less salvage value. Salvage is estimated at $20,000.
	Allowance for depreciation—office building	80,000	
Case 2:	Wages expense	49,000	Wages earned by employees since last payday are $780.

Case 3:	Sales	650,000	One percent of the sales is estimated as the bad debts expense.
	Allowance for doubtful accounts (credit)	2,000	
	Accounts receivable	170,000	
Case 4:	Office supplies inventory	2,500	Of the office supplies purchased, only $900 worth remains at the end of the period.

4–2–B

The trial balance of the King Company at December 31 of the current year includes, among other items, the following account balances:

	Debits	*Credits*
Unexpired insurance	$24,000	
Prepaid rent	28,800	
Accounts receivable	82,000	
Allowance for doubtful accounts		$1,400
Office supplies inventory	5,600	

Examination of the records shows that adjustments should be made for the following items:

a) Of the unexpired insurance in the trial balance, $10,000 is for coverage during the months after December 31 of the current year.
b) The balance in the Prepaid Rent account is for a 12-month period that started October 1 of the current year.
c) It is estimated that $3,000 should be added to the Allowance for Doubtful Accounts.
d) Office supplies used during the year amount to $3,600.

Required: Prepare the adjusting journal entries at December 31.

4–3–B

Bavasi, Inc., has the following account balances, among others, in its trial balance at December 31 of the current year:

	Debits	*Credits*
Office supplies inventory	$ 1,240	
Prepaid rent	2,400	
Accounts receivable	25,000	
Allowance for doubtful accounts		$ 600
Sales		87,000
Salaries expense	41,000	

Additional information:

a) The inventory of supplies on hand at December 31 amounts to $90.
b) The balance in the Prepaid Rent account is for a one-year period starting October 1 of the current year.
c) It is estimated that 1 percent of the year's sales will be uncollectible.
d) Since the last payday, the employees of the company have earned additional salaries in the amount of $1,810.

Required:

a) Prepare the adjusting journal entries at December 31.

b) Open skeleton ledger accounts for each of the accounts involved, enter the balances as shown in the trial balance, and post the adjusting journal entries.

4–4–B

Required: Given the following information for the Nixon Company, calculate the correct net earnings for 1974 and 1975. The reported net earnings for 1974 and 1975 were $60,000 and $82,000, respectively. No adjusting entries were made at year-end for any of the transactions given below:

a) A fire insurance policy to cover a three-year period from the date of payment was purchased on March 1, 1974, for $3,600. The Insurance Expense account was debited at the date of purchase.

b) Subscriptions for magazines in the amount of $72,000 to cover an 18-month period from May 1, 1974, were received on April 15, 1974. The Subscriptions Revenue account was credited when the payments were received.

c) A building costing $150,000 and having an estimated useful life of 60 years and a scrap value of $30,000 was purchased and put into service on July 1, 1974.

d) $10,000 was borrowed from the bank on September 1, 1974, to be repaid on September 1, 1976, with 6 percent annual interest.

e) A $3,000 loan was made to a customer on November 1, 1974, to be repaid in three months with 5 percent annual interest.

f) On January 12, 1975, wages of $9,600 were paid to employees. The account debited was Wages Expense. One third of the amount paid was earned by employees in December of 1974.

4–5–B

The Henge Company adjusts and closes its books each December 31. It is to be assumed that the accounts for all prior years have been properly adjusted and closed. Given below are a number of the company's account balances prior to adjustment on December 31, 1975:

	Debits	*Credits*
Accounts receivable	$66,000	
Allowance for doubtful accounts		$ 170
Unexpired insurance	2,625	
Office supplies inventory	2,150	
Building	85,000	
Allowance for depreciation—building		32,000
Unearned rent revenue		900
Salaries expense	23,000	
Sales		92,500

Additional data (letter your entries to match these items):

a) For the past several years the company has experienced bad debt losses equal to about 1 percent of sales.

b) The Unexpired Insurance account balance represents the remaining cost of a four-year insurance policy dated June 30, 1973, having a total premium of $4,200.

c) The physical inventory of the office supply stock room indicates that the supplies on hand had a cost of $675.

d) The building was originally acquired on January 1, 1959, at which time it was estimated that it would last 40 years and have a scrap value of $5,000.

e) Salaries earned since the last payday but unpaid at December 31 amount to $875.

f) Interest earned but not collected on bonds during the year amounts to $75. This interest is not due to be paid to the company until March 1, 1976.

g) The Unearned Rent Revenue account arose through the prepayment of rent by a tenant in the building for 12 months beginning October 1, 1975.

Required: Prepare the adjusting entries indicated by the additional data. While explanations may be omitted, computations should be included.

4–6–B

The Hugh Publishing Company began operations on December 1, 1975. The company's bookkeeper intended to use the cash basis of accounting. Consequently, he recorded all cash receipts and disbursements for items relating to operations in revenue and expense accounts. He did not make any adjusting entries prior to preparing the financial statements for December. You are called in at the end of December to show the bookkeeper how he can adjust his accounts to the accrual basis.

Required:

a) Prepare journal entries for the following transactions as the bookkeeper prepared them.

b) Prepare the adjusting entries necessary at the end of the month to place the books on an accrual basis.

c) Compute the increase or decrease in net earnings which results from using the accrual basis of accounting rather than the cash basis.

Transactions:

Dec. 1 Issued capital stock for $10,000 cash.

3 Received $12,000 for magazine subscriptions to run for two years from this date. The magazine is published monthly on the 23d.

4 Paid for advertising to be run in a national periodical for each of six months (starting this month). The cost was $4,500.

7 Purchased an insurance policy to cover a two-year period beginning December 15, $3,600.

11 Borrowed $6,000 from the bank on a 60-day, 6 percent note dated today.

12 Paid the annual lease on the building, $6,000, effective through November 30, 1976.

15 Received $18,000 cash for two-year subscriptions starting with the December issue.

15 Salaries for the period December 1–15 amounted to $4,000. Salaries are paid on the 5th and 20th of each month for the preceding half of the month.

20 Salaries for the period December 1–15 paid.

23 Supplies purchased for cash, $1,800. (Only $150 of these were subsequently used in 1975.)

27 Printing costs applicable equally to the next six issues beginning with the December issue were paid in cash, $12,000.

31 Cash sales of the December issue, $7,000.

31 Unpaid salaries for the period December 16–31 amounted to $4,400.

31 Sales on account of December issue, $3,000.

4–7–B

Required: From the trial balance and additional data given below, prepare:

a) A 12-column work sheet for the year ended December 31, 1975. (See appendix, Frame 14[4], for an illustration.)

b) The December 31, 1975, closing entries, in general journal form.

KANTON COMPANY
Trial Balance
December 31, 1975

	Debits	*Credits*
Cash on hand and in bank	$ 35,320	
Accounts receivable	72,520	
Allowance for doubtful accounts		$ 2,760
Notes receivable	10,000	
Merchandise inventory, January 1, 1975	42,600	
Sales store supplies inventory	1,200	
Store equipment	44,000	
Allowance for depreciation of store equipment		8,800
Accounts payable		39,400
Notes payable		12,000
Capital stock		150,000
Retained earnings		60,820
Sales		461,180
Sales returns	2,580	
Interest revenue		500
Interest expense	300	
Purchases	250,420	
Purchase returns		2,020
Transportation-in	3,920	
Salesmen's salaries	69,200	
Advertising	39,000	
Sales store supplies expense	1,480	
General office expense	4,940	
Fire insurance expense	2,400	
Office salaries	40,400	
Officers' salaries	80,000	
Legal and auditing expenses	5,000	
Telephone and telegraph	2,400	
Rent expense	28,800	
Dividends	1,000	
	$737,480	$737,480

The company consistently followed the policy of initially debiting all prepaid items to expense accounts.

Additional data as of December 31, 1975:

a) Fire insurance unexpired, $700.
b) Sales store supplies on hand, $850.
c) Prepaid rent expense (store only), $3,500.
d) Depreciation rate on store equipment, 10 percent per year.
e) Increase in allowance for doubtful accounts, $4,586.
f) Accrued salesmen's salaries, $2,000.
g) Accrued office salaries, $1,500.
h) Merchandise inventory, $75,000.

Accumulation and control of data

Learning objectives

Study of the material in this chapter is designed to achieve several learning objectives. Among these are an understanding of:

1. The basic elements and advantages of a manual accounting system which utilizes various special journals in addition to a general journal.
2. How to use subsidiary ledgers to show detailed information not shown in the controlling account.
3. The specific design features of special journals for sales, purchases, cash receipts, cash disbursements, and payroll, and how these journals are maintained and posted.
4. The circumstances in which a voucher system may be utilized to good advantage and how such a system works.
5. Specifically how the voucher register and check register are designed, maintained, and posted.
6. Miscellaneous matters such as interim reports, posting directly from documents, using documentary ledgers, and recording in journals and ledgers simultaneously.

Frame 1[5]

The orderly and efficient processing of raw financial data is virtually an absolute prerequisite to the successful conduct of business. The masses of raw data generated by even a small business are largely unintelligible until processed—that is, recorded, analyzed, classified, summarized, and reported. Such processing facilitates the introduction of management control over operations and must be undertaken if financial reports are to be prepared.

More specifically, the following purposes are accomplished by the orderly and efficient processing of accounting data:

1. The results of operations and the financial position of the firm can be determined and reported on a timely basis in annual financial statements and interim financial reports.
2. Bills can be paid when due.
3. Shipments of merchandise can be made in the proper quantities and descriptions.
4. The conduct of other business also can be orderly and purposive rather than disorganized.
5. Reports required by governmental units can be prepared.

Accounting data may be recorded initially in a number of different ways, including pens or pencils, typewriters, adding machines, cash registers, bookkeeping machines, and computers. There should be a systematic flow of accounting data from the source activity to the ledger accounts. The method of initially recording and summarizing business data is influenced by the nature of the activity, the materiality of the amounts, the means available for processing, and the reports desired.

The initial evidence of activity is on source documents such as sales slips, cash register tapes, and invoices. The functions of the source documents are to communicate information, to serve as a record of completed transactions, and to serve as a source of data for reports to management.

Internal accounting control

Internal accounting control is the organization plan and all the procedures undertaken to check the accuracy of accounting data, safeguard assets against theft, promote efficiency of operations, and ensure that management's policies are being followed.

The way in which internal control is implemented in any given company depends on its lines of authority and communication and the nature of its activities.

Ideally the system of internal control operates by checking all transactions in such a way that the work of each person is automatically verified by another person without duplication of the work, each working independently of the other and each arriving at the same end result. The system of internal accounting control should be revised periodically as new and better ways of processing the data are developed and as the organization structure changes. A formal organization chart shows at least some of the internal control system by designating superior-subordinate relationships.

Source documents that are specifically designed for the needs of an individual business are essential to effective internal accounting control. The basic function of the documents is to communicate data. Thus, the flow of the documents through the organization must be planned carefully so that communication is prompt, effective, and efficient.

The next portion of this chapter is concerned with presenting and discussing specific noncomputerized means of journalizing transactions in such a way that efficiency will result and closer control will be possible. Computerized systems for accomplishing these tasks are dealt with in Chapter 13 of *Accounting II,* the companion text in this series.

Basic elements of a manual accounting system

Because of the number of transactions involved, an accounting system which includes only one book of original entry—the general journal—will be inadequate for even a relatively small business. The first step toward more efficient processing of data usually consists of the development of several special journals. These will allow for a division of labor and also for a reduction in posting time because of the grouping of similar types of transactions. Many different formats or types of journals could be used. The ones presented here are illustrative only. The special journals illustrated are the sales, purchases, cash receipts, cash disbursements, and payroll journals. A voucher system utilizing a voucher register and check register is also introduced. Those journals actually used by a particular company are functions of the nature of the transactions encountered by the company and of the imagination of the person designing them.

Special journals are also used to facilitate control. For instance, one of the primary reasons for using specialized journals for sales and purchases is to facilitate the accounting for receivables and payables so that debit-credit information and balances are available for each creditor and each customer. The cash receipts and cash disbursements journals (and the voucher system) provide handy information regarding receipts and disbursements so that control may exist over these cash flows. A payroll journal provides detailed employee payment information in one place for management's use in controlling related matters.

Before discussing these further, it is necessary to review a topic closely related to the posting of amounts from the special journals to the ledger accounts.

Controlling accounts and subsidiary accounts

A controlling account is an account in the general ledger that is supported by a detailed classification of accounting information in a subsidiary record. For example, an up-to-date record must be maintained with each customer to show the business done with him and the amount owed by him; therefore, outside the general ledger, an account is maintained with each individual customer, showing the debits and credits to his account and the balance due. The sum of the balances due from all customers equals the balance of the Accounts Receivable controlling account in the general ledger.

The individual account with each customer is known as a subsidiary account; all of the individual customers' accounts constitute the *subsidiary accounts receivable ledger,* or customers' ledger. A subsidiary ledger, then, is a group of related accounts showing the details of the balance of a controlling account in the general ledger. Subsidiary ledgers are separated from the general ledger in order (*a*) to relieve the general ledger of a mass of detail and thereby shorten the general ledger trial balance, (*b*) to promote the division of labor in the task of maintaining the ledgers, and (*c*) to strengthen the system of internal control. A subsidiary ledger may be used whether or not special journals are used.

When a transaction occurs that affects a controlling account and a subsidiary account, it is journalized in such fashion that it will be posted (*a*) to the general ledger and (*b*) to a subsidiary account. The usual way is to enter the transaction in a special column in a journal.

The key to effective operation and control of a subsidiary ledger is found in the posting procedure. The use of special columns in the journals makes it possible to post each transaction to an individual account in a subsidiary ledger during the period. Since the column totals are posted to the controlling accounts at the end of the period (usually a month), a comparison of the controlling account balance with the sum of the individual subsidiary account balances aids in determining that all amounts have been posted to the subsidiary accounts.

A few examples of frequently maintained subsidiary ledgers and the names of the related general ledger controlling accounts are:

Subsidiary Ledger	*General Ledger Controlling Account*
Accounts receivable ledger (account with each customer)	Accounts Receivable
Accounts payable ledger (account with each creditor)	Accounts Payable
Equipment ledger (account for each item of equipment)	Office Equipment Delivery Equipment Store Fixtures, etc.

The number of subsidiary ledgers maintained will vary according to the information requirements of each company. Control accounts and subsidiary ledgers generally will be maintained for control purposes where there is a high volume of transactions affecting a given account and where information as to the details of these transactions is needed on a continuing basis.

Indicate whether each of the following statements is correct or incorrect.

1. The balance in the controlling account in the general ledger and the total of all the subsidiary accounts showing the details of the controlling account must be in agreement after all postings have been made for an accounting period.
2. Reduction in posting time is one reason for using special journals.
3. Two firms, each with a knowledgeable management, may have different sets of subsidiary ledgers.
4. A primary purpose of both the general ledger and the general journal is to effect a division of labor.

Now turn to Answer Frame 1[5] on page 182 to check your answers.

Frame 2[5]

Grouping of similar transactions in journals

Special journals are designed to systematize the original recording of the major recurring transactions. One journal is set up to record the journal entries for purchases of merchandise on account. Another journal is set up to record the journal entries for sales on account. A cash receipts journal is provided for entry of cash receipts transactions, and a cash disbursements journal is provided for entry of cash disbursements. A payroll journal is set up to record the data on payroll transactions. The general journal remains for all transactions that cannot be entered readily in one of the special journals. All six are records of original entry containing data which will be posted to ledger accounts (with the possible exception of the payroll journal). In the folio column of the accounts, abbreviations are used to identify the source of the posting, for example, PJ for the purchases journal, and CDJ for the cash disbursements journal as shown:

	Abbreviation
Sales journal	SJ
Purchases journal	PJ
Cash receipts journal	CRJ
Cash disbursements journal	CDJ
Payroll journal	PRJ
General journal	GJ

The sales journal

Normally, sales are for cash or on open account. The sales journal in Illustration 5.1 should be used only for sales of merchandise on account. Cash sales should be recorded in the cash receipts journal. Sales of other assets should be recorded in the cash receipts journal (if cash is received at the time of sale) or in the general journal.

Answer frame 1⁵

1. Correct. The subsidiary ledger is merely a breakdown of the amounts in the controlling account. The balances, therefore, must be in agreement.
2. Correct. Column totals are posted in many instances rather than individual items.
3. Correct. The firms may have different types of transactions. For instance, one firm may receive many notes receivable and the other may receive few, if any.
4. Incorrect. Any firm that has a double-entry set of books presumably has at least a general journal and a general ledger. These are necessities rather than devices to promote the division of labor. The use of special journals rather than merely one general journal is considered a means to effect a division of labor.

If you missed any of the above, reread Frame 1⁵ before beginning Frame 2⁵ on page 181.

2⁵ *continued*

The simplest form of sales journal has only one money column, entitled Accounts Receivable Dr. and Sales Cr. Variations in the sales journal can be made. Special columns could be inserted for items such as state sales taxes, federal excise taxes, and sales returns and allowances. And a departmental breakdown can be obtained by providing a Sales Cr. column for each department in a company.

Posting sales. The posting of sales from the sales journal in Illustration 5.1 involves entering the total of the money column headed Accounts Receivable Dr. and Sales Cr. as a credit to the general ledger Sales account. The folio reference of SJ-1 (sales journal, p. 1) is also entered in the Sales account and the number (301) is written in the sales journal under the total of the money column to show that the $250 was posted as a credit to Sales. Since there generally is no subsidiary sales ledger, the individual items comprising sales are not posted.

Posting accounts receivable. To post accounts receivable from the sales journal in Illustration 5.1, the total of the money column ($250) is posted as a debit to the Accounts Receivable control account in the general ledger with a folio reference of SJ-1. The number (111) is entered under the total of the money column in the sales journal to show that the amount has been posted. The individual amounts in the money column are posted to each individual customer's account in the subsidiary ledger so that the account will show the amount currently due from him. As each individual amount is posted, a check mark (√) is placed in the column headed √ opposite the amount to show that it has been posted. When the posting of the accounts receivable has been completed, the Accounts Receivable control account will show a balance of $250, which is equal to the sum of the balances in the Accounts Receivable subsidiary ledger accounts, assuming no previous balances in the control account or the subsidiary accounts.

Subsidiary ledger accounts usually are not numbered but are kept in alphabetical order, since their composition is constantly changing.

Illustration 5.1

SALES JOURNAL — Page 1

Date		Description	Invoice Number	Accounts Receivable Dr. 111 Sales Cr. 301 Amount	✓
1975					
Apr.	3	Arthur Benson	100	30.00	✓
	4	Peter Cote	101	25.00	✓
	12	Kenneth Johnson	102	130.00	✓
	19	Peter Cote	103	10.00	✓
	30	Anthony Demambro	104	55.00	✓
				250.00	
				(111) (301)	

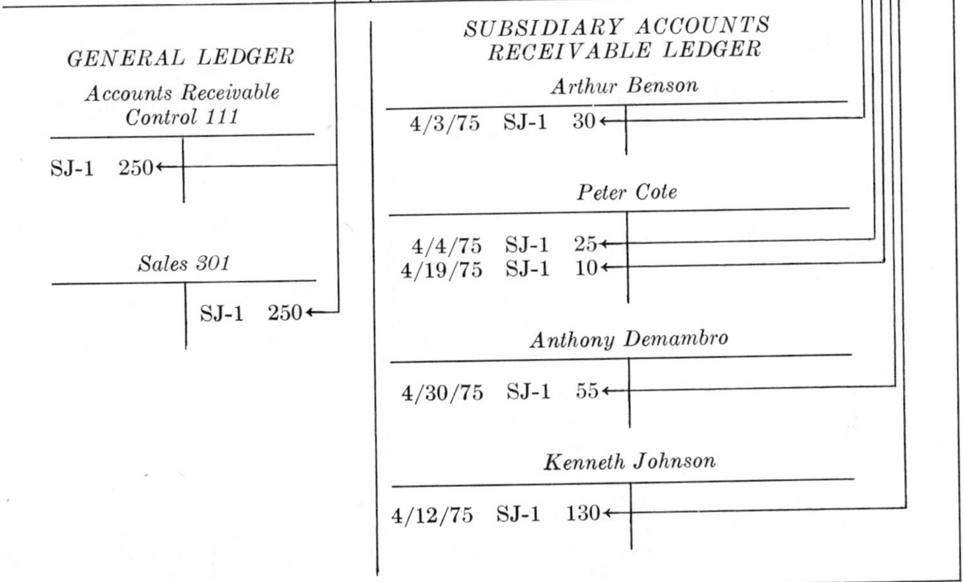

Is each of the following statements true or false?

1. The sales journal should be used only for sales of merchandise on account.
2. The total of the balances in the subsidiary accounts receivable accounts should be equal to the balance in the Accounts Receivable control account.
3. It is inconceivable that a sales journal would have more than one column.
4. The general journal is the only record of original entry, since all the other journals are special journals.

Now check your answers by turning to Answer Frame 2[5] on page 184.

Answer frame 2^5

1. True. Cash sales are entered in the cash receipts journal.
2. True. This is because the subsidiary ledger accounts are merely the control account broken down into individual cutomers' accounts.
3. False. If there are departments and a departmental breakdown of sales is desired, there will be two or more Sales Cr. columns. Also, there could be columns for sales taxes, federal excise taxes, and sales returns and allowances. Sundry columns also could be inserted.
4. False. The special journals are also books of original entry.

If you missed any of the above, reread Frame 2^5 before beginning Frame 3^5 below.

Frame 3^5

The cash receipts journal

The cash receipts journal, which might be used in combination with the sales journal, is shown in Illustration 5.2. Any number of different

Illustration 5.2

CASH RECEIPTS JOURNAL — Page 5

101 Cash Dr.	726 Sales Discounts Dr.	Date		Description	301 Sales Cr.	111 Accounts Receivable Cr. Amount	✓	Sundry Accounts Cr. Acct. No.	Sundry Accounts Cr. Amount	✓
		1975								
10,700.00		Apr.	1	Cash sales	10,700.00					
29.40	.60		6	Arthur Benson—Invoice No. 100		30.00	✓			
10,775.00			7	Cash sales	10,775.00					
6,000.00			10	Sold investments at cost to Wells Corporation				138*	6,000.00	✓
10,600.00			14	Cash sales	10,600.00					
25.00			19	Peter Cote—Invoice No. 101		25.00	✓			
127.40	2.60		20	Kenneth Johnson—Invoice No. 102		130.00	✓			
11,045.00			25	Cash sales	11,045.00					
200.00			26	Dividends received on Krantz Company common stock				303*	200.00	✓
49,501.80	3.20				43,120.00	185.00			6,200.00	
(101)	(726)				(301)	(111)				

* 138 Investments.
* 303 Dividend Revenue.

designs may be used for this journal also. For instance, if some of the items appearing in the Sundry (which means miscellaneous) Accounts Cr. column are frequently credited, it would be advisable to set up a separate column for each of these items.

Since the amounts appearing in the Sundry Accounts Cr. column usually pertain to different accounts, the column total is not posted and a check mark (✓) is placed immediately below the amount. The individual items are posted to the accounts indicated (Accounts 138 and 303 in Illustration 5.2).

The cash receipts journal shown in Illustration 5.2 has not been posted, since no posting marks are shown.

Assume that the general ledger and accounts receivable subsidiary ledger shown below are as they appear after the sales journal (Illustration 5.1, Frame 2, page 183, has been posted. On a separate sheet of paper, determine the missing information that would result from the posting of the cash receipts journal. Also indicate the proper posting marks that would be made in the cash receipts journal. Then turn to Answer Frame 3[5] on page 188 and check your responses.

PARTIAL GENERAL LEDGER

Cash — *Account No. 101*

Date		Explanation	Folio	Debit	Credit	Balance
1975 Apr.	1	Beginning balance (assumed)				10,000.00
	?		?	?		?

Accounts Receivable — *Account No. 111*

Date		Explanation	Folio	Debit	Credit	Balance
1975 Apr.	30		SJ-1	250.00		250.00
	?				?	?

Investments — *Account No. 138*

Date		Explanation	Folio	Debit	Credit	Balance
1975 Apr.	1	Beginning balance (assumed)				18,000.00
	?		?		?	?

Common Stock — *Account No. 250*

Date		Explanation	Folio	Debit	Credit	Balance
1975 Apr.	1	Beginning balance (assumed)				20,000.00

Retained Earnings — *Account No. 251*

Date		Explanation	Folio	Debit	Credit	Balance
1975 Apr.	1	Beginning balance (assumed)				8,000.00

Sales — *Account No. 301*

Date		Explanation	Folio	Debit	Credit	Balance
1975 Apr.	30		SJ-1		250.00	250.00
	?		?		?	?

Dividend Revenue — *Account No. 303*

Date		Explanation	Folio	Debit	Credit	Balance
?	?		?		?	?

Sales Discounts — *Account No. 726*

Date		Explanation	Folio	Debit	Credit	Balance
? ?	?		?	?		?

SUBSIDIARY ACCOUNTS RECEIVABLE LEDGER

Arthur Benson

Date		Explanation	Folio	Debit	Credit	Balance
1975 Apr.	3		SJ-1	30.00		30.00
	?		?		?	?

Peter Cote

Date		Explanation	Folio	Debit	Credit	Balance
1975 Apr.	4		SJ-1	25.00		25.00
	19		SJ-1	10.00		35.00
	?		?		?	?

Anthony Demambro

Date		Explanation	Folio	Debit	Credit	Balance
1975 Apr.	30		SJ-1	55.00		55.00

Kenneth Johnson

Date		Explanation	Folio	Debit	Credit	Balance
1975 Apr.	12 ?		SJ-1 ?	130.00		130.00 ?

Frame 4[5]

A combined sales and cash receipts journal

It is possible to combine the sales and cash receipts journals illustrated earlier. Illustration 5.3 (page 189) shows the two journals combined. This allows total sales to be posted as one amount rather than two.

But posting and journalizing convenience is not the only consideration. Remember that one of the reasons for creating special journals is so that several persons can work with them at the same time. Having separate sales and cash receipts journals does allow more persons to work with the data in the journals at the same time. A decision in any particular case has to be made so as to maximize the overall efficiency of working with the journals.

Is each of the following statements true or false?

1. Every company should use a combined sales and cash receipts journal rather than separate journals.
2. The greater the number of specialized journals a company has, in general, the more persons can work on them at the same time.
3. In Illustration 5.3 the subsidiary accounts receivable accounts would be both debited and credited during the posting process.
4. All of the items in the Cash Dr. column in Illustration 5.3 resulted from cash sales.

Now turn to Answer Frame 4[5] on page 188 to check your answers.

Frame 5[5]

The purchases journal

The total in the money column of the purchases journal in Illustration 5.4, page 190, (where periodic procedure is assumed) is posted to the Purchases account as a debit and to the Accounts Payable account as a credit at the end of the month. The individual amounts in the column are posted to the accounts in the accounts payable subsidiary ledger.

Most business firms are aware that in order to have an acceptable level of control over cash disbursements they must pay all bills by check. As-

Answer frame 3[5]

Answers for the blanks indicating missing information are:

Account	*Date*	*Folio*	*Debit*	*Credit*	*Balance*
Cash	30	CRJ-5	49,501.80		59,501.80
Accounts Receivable	30	CRJ-5		185.00	65.00
Investments	10	CRJ-5		6,000.00	12,000.00
Sales	30	CRJ-5		43,120.00	43,370.00
Dividend Revenue	1975 Apr. 26	CRJ-5		200.00	200.00
Sales Discounts	1975 Apr. 20	CRJ-5	3.20		3.20
Arthur Benson	6	CRJ-5		30.00	—0—
Peter Cote	19	CRJ-5		25.00	10.00
Kenneth Johnson	20	CRJ-5		130.00	—0—

You should have indicated that in the cash receipts journal you would place the account numbers under the totals in the Cash Dr. (101), Sales Discounts Dr. (726), Sales Cr. (301), and Accounts Receivable Cr. (111) columns. This indicates that the amounts have been posted. Under the $6,200 in the Sundry Accounts Cr. column you would place a check (✓) indicating that the total amount is not to be posted. Beside each of the amounts in the Accounts Receivable Cr. and Sundry Accounts Cr. columns you would place a check (✓) to indicate that each amount was posted.

A list of accounts receivable would contain the $10 due from Peter Cote and the $55 due from Anthony Demambro, which is, of course, in agreement with the balance of $65 in the Accounts Receivable controlling account.

If you missed any of the above, restudy Frame 3[5] before begining Frame 4[5] on page 187.

Answer frame 4[5]

1. False. While it may be advantageous for some firms to use a combined sales and cash receipts journal, other firms would find it disadvantageous to do so. The decision hinges on how many different persons need to work with the information in the journals at any one time.
2. True. This is one reason why some companies choose to use separate sales and cash receipts journals.
3. True. Notice that the journal has both an Accounts Receivable Dr. column and an Accounts Receivable Cr. column, with entries in both.
4. False. Only four of the items resulted from cash sales. The others were from payments on account, the sale of investments, and dividends received.

If you missed any of the above, reread Frame 4[5] before beginning Frame 5[5] on page 187.

5[5] *continued*

suming this to be the case here, all purchases are made on account and are therefore included in the purchases journal (even if the length of delay in payment is only long enough to write the check). The payment is then shown in the cash disbursements journal.

There are, of course, a number of designs which could be used. If there are separate departments, a separate purchases column could be provided for each department.

A column could be inserted for purchase returns and allowances if they

Illustration 5.3

COMBINED SALES AND CASH RECEIPTS JOURNAL

Page 11

101 Cash Dr.	726 Sales Discounts Dr.	111 Accounts Receivable Dr.		Date		Description	Invoice No.	301 Sales Cr.	111 Accounts Receivable Cr.		Sundry Accounts Cr.		
		Amount	✓						Amount	✓	Acct. No.	Amount	✓
				1975									
10,700.00				Apr.	1	Cash sales		10,700.00					
		30.00	✓		3	Arthur Benson	100	30.00					
		25.00	✓		4	Peter Cote	101	25.00					
29.40	.60				6	Arthur Benson	100		30.00	✓			
10,775.00					7	Cash sales		10,775.00					
6,000.00					10	Sold investments at cost					138*	6,000.00	✓
		130.00	✓		12	Kenneth Johnson	102	130.00					
10,600.00					14	Cash sales		10,600.00					
		10.00	✓		19	Peter Cote	103	10.00					
25.00					19	Peter Cote	101		25.00	✓			
127.40	2.60				20	Kenneth Johnson	102		130.00	✓			
11,045.00					25	Cash sales		11,045.00					
200.00					26	Dividends received					303*	200.00	✓
		55.00	✓		30	Anthony Demambro	104	55.00					
49,501.80	3.20	250.00						43,370.00	185.00			6,200.00	
(101)	(726)	(111)						(301)	(111)			(✓)	

* 138 Investments.
* 303 Dividend Revenue.

Illustration 5.4

			PURCHASES JOURNAL		Page 10	
Date		Terms	Invoice Number	Creditor	Purchases Dr. 801 Accounts payable Cr. 201 Amount	✓
1975						
Apr.	1	2/10, n/30	862	Smith Corporation	196.00	✓
	7	1/15, n/60	121	Lasky Company	99.00	✓
	12	2/20, n/60	561	Booth Corporation	4,900.00	✓
	15	2/10, n/30	1042	Gooch Corporation	2,940.00	✓
	21	3/15, n/60	633	Wyngarden Company	9,700.00	✓
	26	2/10, n/30	734	Mertz Company	98.00	✓
	30	2/10, n/30	287	Nelson Company	3,920.00	✓
	30	2/20, n/60	568	Booth Corporation	1,470.00	✓
					23,323.00	
					(801)(201)	

are frequently encountered. And since a Purchase Returns and Allowances account normally has a credit balance, an Accounts Payable debit column would have to be included also.

All amounts of purchases have been entered net of discount in the illustration. This procedure is described briefly in Chapter 3. Any discounts missed should be considered penalties due to inefficiency and recorded in a Discounts Lost account.

Determine whether each of the following statements about Illustration 5.4 is right or wrong.

1. Ten amounts have been posted from the purchases journal.
2. Four postings were made to the general ledger.
3. Eight amounts would be posted to the subsidiary ledger whether a purchases journal was used or not.
4. If only a general journal had been used, a total of 16 postings would have been made.

Now turn to Answer Frame 5[5] on page 192 to check your answers.

Frame 6[5]

The cash disbursements journal

Since it is assumed that all cash disbursements are made by check, the cash disbursements journal in Illustration 5.5 contains a column in which to record the number of each check written. Payments on accounts payable and salaries payable constitute the majority of items paid in the illustration.

Illustration 5.5

CASH DISBURSEMENTS JOURNAL

201 Accounts Payable Dr. Amount	✓	219 Salaries Payable Dr.	821 Discounts Lost Dr.	822 Supplies Expense Dr.	Sundry Accounts Dr. Acct. No.	Sundry Accounts Dr. Amount	✓	Date		Description	Check No.	101 Cash Cr.
								1975				
				42.00				Apr.	2	Brooklyn Square Paint Company	524	42.00
					123*	1,200.00	✓		3	Insurance policy to cover May 1975—April 30, 1976	525	1,200.00
					140*	500.00	✓		4	Furniture—office	526	500.00
					823*	200.00	✓			Rent for April 1975	527	200.00
196.00	✓								8	Smith Corporation—Invoice No. 862	528	196.00
				10.00					14	Allan Park Stationery Company	529	10.00
99.00	✓								18	Lasky Company—Invoice No. 121	530	99.00
4,900.00	✓								21	Booth Company—Invoice No. 561	531	4,900.00
9,700.00	✓								27	Wyngarden Company—Invoice No. 633	532	9,700.00
2,940.00	✓		60.00						28	Gooch Corporation—Invoice No. 1042	533	3,000.00
		1,553.60							30	Clarke Frankson	534	1,553.60
		1,172.90								Mead Stacy	535	1,172.90
		803.10								Jason Evans	536	803.10
		720.20								Marshall Watson	537	720.20
		403.00								Cleveland Avoy	538	403.00
		341.02								James Jackson	539	341.02
		366.60								Stuary Bently	540	366.60
		377.14								Robert Aleo	541	377.14
17,835.00		5,737.56	60.00	52.00		1,900.00						25,584.56
(201)		(219)	(821)	(822)		(✓)						(101)

* 123—Unexpired Insurance.
* 140—Furniture and Equipment.
* 823—Rent Expense.

Answer frame 5^5

1. Right. Eight individual amounts were posted, together with the column total which was posted twice.
2. Wrong. The column total was posted twice to the general ledger. The other eight items were posted to the accounts payable subsidiary ledger.
3. Right. In this particular instance the number of postings to the subsidiary ledger would not be affected.
4. Wrong. A total of 24 amounts would have been posted. Eight items would have been posted to the Purchases account, eight to the Accounts Payable controlling account, and another eight to the individual accounts in the accounts payable subsidiary ledger.

If you missed any of the above, reread Frame 5^5 before beginning Frame 6^5 on page 190.

6^5
continued

In companies with many employees, a separate payroll bank checking account probably would be established. Then the cash disbursements journal would show only one amount for payroll, the total amount of salaries payable. The entry would debit Payroll Cash and credit Cash (general). A separate payroll check register might then be maintained to record the payment of salaries out of the payroll checking account.

The payroll journal

Sometimes a formal payroll journal is maintained to record data for payroll accounting. (Payroll accounting is explained in detail in Chapter 8.) A payroll journal contains a debit column for each category of salary (e.g., administrative, salesmen's, officers', clerical, and warehouse). Credit columns are included for such accounts as Federal Income Tax Withheld, State Income Tax Withheld, FICA Taxes Withheld, Union Dues Withheld, and Salaries Payable, which are all liabilities, representing amounts that must be paid out either to employees or to others on the employees' behalf. Illustration 5.6 shows such a journal.

Some companies maintain a payroll journal only as a memorandum record, which means no postings are made from it. In these firms the entry for payroll would have to be made in some other journal, such as the general journal. The entry would be made for the totals of the columns shown in Illustration 5.6.

Is each of the following statements correct or incorrect?

1. The cash disbursements journal in Illustration 5.5 has not been completely posted.
2. A total of 14 postings was made from the cash disbursements journal illustrated.
3. Not all of the invoices in the cash disbursements journal illustrated were paid within the discount period allowed.
4. The column totals of the payroll journal are always posted.

Now turn to Answer Frame 6^5 on page 194 to check your answers.

Illustration 5.6

PAYROLL JOURNAL

Page 2

810 Adminis-trative Salaries Expense Dr.	811 Sales-men's Salaries Expense Dr.	812 Office Clerical Salaries Expense Dr.	813 Ware-house Salaries Expense Dr.	Date		Employee	215 Federal Income Tax Withheld Cr.	216 State Income Tax Withheld Cr.	217 F.I.C.A. Taxes Withheld Cr.	218 Union Dues Withheld Cr.	219 Salaries Payable Cr.
				1975							
2,000.00				Apr.	30	Clarke Frankson	355.40	64.60	117.00		1,463.00
1,500.00						Mead Stacy	220.70	40.40	87.75		1,151.15
	1,000.00					Jason Evans	124.70	28.20	58.50		788.60
	900.00					Marshall Watson	112.60	27.60	52.65		707.15
		500.00				Cleveland Avoy	56.20	16.80	29.25	2.00	395.75
		420.00				James Jackson	43.70	14.80	24.57	2.00	334.93
			450.00			Stuart Bently	46.70	15.40	26.33	1.50	360.07
			465.00			Robert Aleo	49.70	16.20	27.20	1.50	370.40
3,500.00	1,900.00	920.00	915.00				1,009.70	224.00	423.25	7.00	5,571.05
(810)	(811)	(812)	(813)				(215)	(216)	(217)	(218)	(219)

Answer frame 6[5]

1. Incorrect. It has been completely posted. Notice the posting marks in the journal.
2. Incorrect. Only 13 postings were made. The check mark under the Sundry Accounts Dr. column indicates that this amount should not be posted.
3. Correct. The payment to the Gooch Corporation, Invoice No. 1042, on April 28 was made after the discount period had expired. As a result, the total payment was $3,000 instead of $2,940.
4. Incorrect. Sometimes the payroll journal is maintained only as a memorandum record, which means that no postings are made from it.

If you missed any of the above, reread Frame 6[5] before starting Frame 7[5] below.

Frame 7[5]

The general journal and other journals

Every transaction that will not fit conveniently into the special journals is entered in the general journal. The general journal would be necessary to record the adjusting and closing entries even if all other entries fit the format of the special journals used.

Various other special journals are conceivable (e.g., purchase returns and allowances journal and sales returns and allowances journal). The proper combination for a particular company depends on the volume of transactions, the types of transactions, management's information needs, and the number of persons having to work with the data at any one time.

Summary of the advantages of using special journals

To summarize, the following advantages are obtained from the use of special journals.

a) *Time is saved in journalizing.* Only one line is used for each transaction; a full description is not necessary. The amount of writing is reduced because it is not necessary to repeat the account names printed at the top of the special column or columns.

b) *Time is saved in posting.* Many data are posted as totals of columns.

c) *Detail is eliminated from the general ledger.* Column totals are posted to the general ledger, and the detail is left in the journals.

d) *Division of labor is promoted.* Several persons can work simultaneously on the accounting records. This specialization and division of labor pinpoints responsibility and eases the location of errors.

e) *Use of accounting machines is facilitated.* The mass of routine transactions recorded in special journals frequently makes the use of accounting machines economical.

f) *Management analysis is aided.* The journals themselves can be useful to management in analyzing classes of transactions (such as credit sales).

Is each of the following statements true or false regarding the advantages to be obtained from the use of special journals?

1. General ledger accounts become less detailed.
2. Journalizing and posting time is reduced.
3. Accounting machines and special journals may be used in combination.
4. Only one person can work on recording transactions.

Now turn to Answer Frame 7[5] on page 196.

Frame 8[5]

Voucher system

In very small companies where the owner has an intimate knowledge of all transactions and where he personally signs all checks, there need be no great concern over the proper handling of cash disbursements. In larger companies where the owners or top management people have no direct part in the payment process, close control over this function should be provided via a formalized system of internal control. While the owner who has an intimate knowledge of all transactions might use special journals to reduce journalizing and posting time, he would not have need for the formalized system of internal control over disbursements (called a voucher system) presented here. The voucher system utilizes two special journals which have not yet been described.

With a voucher system, internal control over cash disbursements is achieved in the following way: each transaction that will involve the payment of cash is entered on a voucher and recorded in a voucher register some time before payment is made. A voucher is a form with spaces provided for data concerning the liability being set up (such as invoice number, invoice date, creditor's name and address, description of the goods or services, terms of payment, and amount due). It also has spaces for signatures of those approving the obligation for payment. The voucher usually forms a "jacket" for the invoice and other supporting documents. Each voucher goes through a rigorous process of examination and eventual approval or disapproval. By the time a voucher is approved for payment, one can be quite certain that the liability for payment is legitimate, since various persons have attested to the propriety and accuracy of the claim.

The voucher system eliminates entirely the formal subsidiary accounts payable ledger. The file of unpaid vouchers serves as the subsidiary accounts payable ledger.

When the voucher system is used, the term "vouchers payable" is usually substituted for the term "accounts payable" in the accounts. When financial statements are prepared, however, the more conventional term accounts payable is preferable.

Answer frame 7⁵

1. True. Since only special column totals are posted to the general ledger, much detail is removed from the accounts in the general ledger.
2. True. Time is saved in journalizing and posting.
3. True. The use of accounting machines in conjunction with special journals is feasible.
4. False. One of the most important advantages of special journals is that they promote the division of labor and thus facilitate the initial recording of transactions.

If you missed any of the above, review Frame 7⁵ before turning to Frame 8⁵ on page 195.

8⁵
continued

The system of internal control is enhanced by a separation of duties. For instance, the person or persons who authorize the incurrence of liabilities should not also prepare and distribute checks. The receipt of assets or services resulting from a liability incurrence must be acknowledged and approved by (*a*) the receiving department, or (*b*) others who do not have authority to prepare and distribute checks. The persons who have authority to sign checks should do so only when approved vouchers authorizing each check are presented. The possibilities of errors and of recording unauthorized liabilities or cash disbursements are therefore minimized.

Determine whether each of the following statements is correct or incorrect.

1. Under a voucher system each transaction that will involve the payment of cash will eventually be entered on a voucher and in the voucher register.
2. The voucher system provides a uniform method for the recording of liabilities that will result in cash disbursements.
3. An account called Vouchers Payable will normally appear in the chart of accounts of a company using a voucher system.
4. The voucher system provides internal control over cash disbursements by centralizing in one person the functions of authorizing the incurrence of liabilities and preparing and distributing checks.

Now turn to Answer Frame 8⁵ on page 198 to check your answers.

Frame 9⁵

Types of vouchers

The voucher system of recording liabilities that will result in cash disbursements is so named because every transaction involving the acquisition of productive factors needed to operate a business will result in the preparation of a voucher. Vouchers usually are numbered consecutively.

In a broad sense a voucher is any written document that serves as a receipt or as evidence of authority to act. In a narrow sense—as applied to the voucher system—a voucher is a form that substantiates a liability and thus serves as the basis for an accounting entry.

One form of voucher is presented in Illustration 5.7. Invoices and receiving tickets are the basis for preparing vouchers. It is assumed in Illustration 5.7 that a separate voucher is prepared for each invoice received from each creditor.

Illustration 5.7, *A Voucher*

ATWELL SUPPLY COMPANY
Atwell Plaza
Atwell, Texas 78712

VOUCHER

VOUCHER NO. 141
OUR P.O. NO. 2514
VENDOR'S INVOICE 416
PAID BY CHECK NO. 587
DATE PAID 7/18/75

Payable To: Gregory Corporation
48 Cadillac Square
Detroit, Michigan 48226

DATE		ACCT. NO.	DESCRIPTION	QUANTITY	UNIT PRICE	TOTAL
July	14	126	X-16 Transistors	100	$2.00	$200.00
			TOTAL			$200.00
			DISCOUNT	2%		4.00
			NET PAYABLE			$196.00

TERMS 2/10, n/30
EXPLANATIONS:

AUDITED AS TO CORRECTNESS	APPROVED FOR PAYMENT	ENTERED IN VOUCHER REGISTER	DATE ENTERED
a.T.	L.J.W.	R.E.L.	7/14/75

The procedures followed in this basic form of voucher system show clearly that a voucher system is a method of internal control over the *payment* of liabilities. Emphasis is placed on the time of payment rather than on the identity of the creditor. In the administration and control of cash, the primary matters are the time and the amount of the disbursement.

In some lines of business the terms of discount and of payment run from the date of the invoice. When this is the case a voucher should be prepared for each invoice, as in Illustration 5.7, and should be filed according to the date on which the discount period terminates or payment is due. Such a file is called a tickler file.

Answer frame 8⁵

1. Correct. All transactions that will involve the payment of cash will be entered on a voucher and recorded in a voucher register. For most short-term liabilities this is done at the time of the transaction creating the liability.
2. Correct. The uniformity is achieved by requiring that each transaction involving the payment of cash be entered on a voucher and in a voucher register.
3. Correct. The account Vouchers Payable will usually be substituted for the Accounts Payable account when a voucher system is used.
4. Incorrect. The internal control over cash disbursements is achieved by splitting up the functions mentioned, not combining them. The person who has the authority to approve the incurrence of a liability should not also prepare and distribute checks. Otherwise it would not be very difficult for him to commit fraud.

If you missed any of the above, reread Frame 8⁵ before turning to Frame 9⁵ on page 196.

9⁵ *continued*

When discount and payment terms are computed from the end of the month, it is possible to modify the voucher and reduce the number of vouchers prepared and, therefore, the number of entries made in the voucher register. All invoices received from each creditor may be accumulated and listed on one voucher at the month-end, since all will probably be paid by one check. The detail of the various invoices may be summarized on one voucher.

Is each of the following statements true or false?

1. The system of preparing one voucher for each creditor each month is most feasible when discount and payment terms are computed from the date of the invoice.
2. The system of preparing a voucher for each invoice is preferable when terms run from the end of the month and many purchases are made from the same creditors each month.
3. The preparation of one voucher for each creditor each month eliminates many entries from the voucher register.

Now check your answers by turning to Answer Frame 9⁵ on page 200.

Frame 10⁵

Special journals used

Voucher register. A voucher register is a multicolumn journal containing special debit columns for the accounts most frequently debited when a liability is incurred. Stated in a different manner, a voucher register contains a chronological and serial record of all vouchers prepared. It includes a brief description of the transactions and indicates the accounts involved. One line is allotted to each voucher.

A special Vouchers Payable Cr. column in the voucher register summarizes all vouchers approved. The total of the Vouchers Payable column in the voucher register is posted to the liability controlling account Vouchers Payable at the end of each month.

Illustration 5.8 on pages 200–201 is presented to show the entry of vouchers in the special journal for vouchers payable in cases where one voucher is prepared for each invoice. As each voucher is prepared and entered in the voucher register (Illustration 5.8), the voucher is placed in the unpaid voucher file. As each is paid, the voucher (or a duplicate copy of it) is transferred to the paid voucher file. A notation of the payment is made in the Date Paid and Check Number columns of the voucher register as illustrated.

Check register. A check register (or check record) is a special journal containing a chronological and serial record of all checks issued. One line is allotted to each check. An efficient system of internal control over cash requires that all disbursements be made by check. No check may be issued unless it is authorized by an approved voucher; therefore, the interrelationship of the voucher register and the check record is established. Rigorous compliance enhances the close control over cash disbursements.

A special debit column in the check register summarizes all vouchers paid. After the total of this column is posted as a debit to the Vouchers Payable controlling account in the general ledger, the balance of the account should equal the total of the vouchers in the unpaid vouchers file. The voucher register and the check register are the two primary journals in a voucher system from which postings are made to the Vouchers Payable controlling account. And when a voucher system is employed, these two registers replace the more traditional purchases and cash disbursements journals.

The check register, Illustration 5.9 (page 202) sets forth the entry and procedure when a check is issued in payment of each voucher. A check register usually has only one money column. The total of this column is posted as a debit to Vouchers Payable and a credit to Cash. If invoices are entered gross (before discount deductions) in the voucher register, a Purchase Discounts Cr. column should also be provided in the check register. In this latter instance, separate columns would be necessary for the debit to Vouchers Payable and credit to Cash, since the dollar amounts posted to these two accounts would be different by the amount of the discount taken.

When vouchers are prepared for the net amount of an invoice and the invoice is paid after the discount privilege period has expired, another voucher should be prepared for the amount of the discount (see line 13 in Illustration 5.8).

Answer frame 9^5

1. False. Since under this system all the invoices from a creditor during a month are listed on one voucher, it would not be a practical system to use if discount and payment terms run from the invoice dates rather than from the end of the month.
2. False. This system is preferable when terms run from the invoice date. If they run from the end of the month, several invoices may be recorded on one voucher (one voucher per creditor per month).
3. True. Since a number of invoices may be summarized on one voucher, this system reduces the number of entries to be made in the voucher register as opposed to the system which uses one voucher for each invoice.

If you missed any of the above, restudy Frame 9^5 before starting Frame 10^5 on page 198.

Illustration 5.8

VOUCHER REGISTER

Line No.	Voucher Date 1975		Voucher No.	Payee	Explanation	Terms	Date Paid		Check No.	Vouchers Payable Cr. 101	General Ledger Account Name
1	May	2	223	Hanley Company	Ring binders	2/10, n/30	May	12	1350	980.00	
2		4	224	Moore Transport	Transportation, binders	2/10, n/10		5	1347	13.00	
3		6	225	White Stationery Company	Office supplies	2/10, n/30		12	1351	102.00	
4		8	226	Specialty Advertisers	Advertising			8	1348	1,200.00	
5		10	227	Blanch Company	Note and interest			10	1349	1,010.00	
6		12	228	Internal Revenue Service	Income tax withheld, April 1975			12	1352	2,200.00	
7		14	229	Swanson Company	Filler paper	2/10, n/30		26	1356	3,920.00	
8		16	230	Rizzo Company	Office desk	n/30		25	1355	640.00	
9		18	231	Warren Company	Spiral binders	2/10, n/30		28	1357	4,900.00	
10		20	232	First National Bank	Interest on mortgage note			20	1353	154.00	
11		22	233	Falcone Company	Books	n/30				10,000.00	
12		24	234	Petty cash	Reimbursement			24	1354	132.00	
13		26	235	Swanson Company	Discount lost (No. 229).			26	1356	80.00	
14		28	236	Celoron Company	Drawing sets	2/20, n/30				9,800.00	
15		31	237	Payroll account	Salaries and wages			31	1358	21,600.00	FICA Tax Liability
16											Federal Income Tax Withheld
										56,731.00	

Decide whether each of the following statements is true or false.

1. The check register shown in Illustration 5.9 contains a chronological and sequential listing of the vouchers prepared by the company.
2. The voucher register shown in Illustration 5.8 has been completely posted.
3. The voucher register shown in Illustration 5.8 contains a chronological and sequential record of all the vouchers prepared by the company.
4. Each item in the column headed Vouchers Payable Cr. in Illustration 5.8 will be posted to the subsidiary accounts payable ledger.
5. The totals of the columns headed General Ledger Accounts Cr. and General Ledger Accounts Dr. in Illustration 5.8 will not be posted to any general ledger accounts.

Now check your responses with the correct answers in Answer Frame 10[5] on page 204.

Page No. *15*
Month *May 1975*

Accounts Cr. Acct. No.	Accounts Cr. Amount Cr.	✓	Discounts Lost Dr. 122	Merchandise Purchases Dr. 131	Transportation In Dr. 144	Salaries and Wages Dr. 158	Office Expense Dr. 175	Advertising Expense Dr. 262	Interest Expense Dr. 306	General Ledger Accounts Dr. Account Name	Acct. No.	Amount Dr.	✓
				980.00									
					13.00								
							102.00						
								1,200.00					
									10.00	Notes Payable	103	1,000.00	
										Federal Income Tax Withheld	108	2,200.00	
				3,920.00									
										Office Equipment	42	640.00	
				4,860.00	40.00								
									154.00				
				10,000.00									
					31.88		60.12	40.00					
			80.00										
				9,800.00									
107	400.00					24,000.00							
108	2,000.00												
	2,400.00		80.00	29,560.00	84.88	24,000.00	162.12	1,240.00	164.00			3,840.00	

Illustration 5.9

CHECK REGISTER Page No. *24* Month *May, 1975*

Line No.	Date 1975		Payee	Voucher No.	Check No.	Vouchers Payable Dr., Cash Cr.
1	May	5	Moore Transport	244	1347	13.00
2		8	Specialty Advertisers	226	1348	1,200.00
3		10	Blanch Company	227	1349	1,010.00
4		12	Hanley Company	223	1350	980.00
5		12	White Stationery Company	225	1351	102.00
6		12	Internal Revenue Service	228	1352	2,200.00
7		20	First National Bank	232	1353	154.00
8		24	Petty Cash	234	1354	132.00
9		25	Rizzo Company	230	1355	640.00
10		26	Swanson Company	235 229	1356	4,000.00
11		28	Warren Company	231	1357	4,900.00
12		31	Payroll account	237	1358	21,600.00
						36,931.00

Frame 11[5]

Files maintained in a voucher system

Unpaid and paid voucher files. Two files are always maintained when a voucher system is used: the unpaid voucher file, referred to earlier as the tickler file, and the paid voucher file.

The unpaid voucher file contains all vouchers that have been prepared and approved as proper liabilities but which have not yet been paid. When credit terms run from the invoice date, they are filed according to their due dates. When credit terms run from the end of the month, the invoices of each creditor are grouped and included in one voucher. The vouchers are then arranged by due date. It is important that they are carefully filed, since if one gets out of order an allowable discount may be missed.

The paid voucher file contains all vouchers which have been paid. They are filed by their voucher numbers in numerical order. Filed in this manner, they constitute a permanent and convenient reference for anyone desiring to check the details of previous cash disbursements.

When a voucher system is in use, the unpaid voucher file serves as (or takes the place of) the subsidiary accounts payable ledger. But when credit terms run from the invoice date, so that invoices are not grouped by creditor, it does not provide the information on total amounts owed to particular creditors quickly and conveniently. This information may be obtained by regrouping the vouchers by creditor, but this can often be cumbersome. Sometimes, therefore, it is useful to keep duplicate copies of the invoices filed alphabetically.

Procedure for preparing a voucher

Since the voucher system is a method of recording liabilities that will result in cash disbursements, the preparation of a voucher begins with the receipt of an invoice from a creditor, or with approved evidence that a liability has been incurred and cash will be disbursed. The procedure followed from that point is typically as follows. Basic data such as the invoice number, invoice date, creditor's name and address, description of the goods or services, terms of payment, and amount due are entered on the voucher from the invoice. The invoice, voucher, and receiving report are sent to the persons responsible for verifying the correctness of the description of the goods as to quantity and quality, the extensions and footings, and other details. Each of these persons initials the voucher when he is satisfied as to its correctness. When the voucher and accompanying documents are received by the accounting department, a notation is made on the voucher as to the proper accounts to be debited and credited. After a final review by an authorized person, the proper entry is made in the voucher register and the voucher is filed in the unpaid voucher file.

Under the voucher system an invoice or other business document is *not* the basis for making a journal entry; rather, it is the basis for preparing a voucher. The voucher is the basis for making the journal entry in the voucher register. All vouchers are entered serially in the voucher register.

Determine whether each of the following statements is correct or incorrect.

1. Before a voucher is recorded in the voucher register, its accuracy and validity should be verified.
2. The basis for making a journal entry in the voucher register is an invoice.
3. An invoice or other document is the basis for the preparation of a voucher.
4. The receipt of an invoice is the basis for making an entry in the voucher register.

Now check your answers by turning to Answer Frame 11[5] on page 204.

Answer frame 10^5

1. False. It contains a chronological and sequential listing of the checks prepared by the company.
2. False. As explained in the posting method used in the previous discussion, when the column totals are posted the account number is listed in parentheses under the column, and when individual amounts are posted from the general ledger columns check marks (✓) are entered beside the amount. This has not been done in the voucher register shown.
3. True. It does contain such a record.
4. False. There is no subsidiary accounts payable ledger when the voucher system is used. The unpaid voucher file serves this purpose.
5. True. Items in these columns need to be posted individually, since they are to different accounts.

If you missed any of the above, reread Frame 10^5 before turning to Frame 11^5 on page 202.

Answer frame 11^5

1. Correct. It is important that the validity and accuracy of the voucher be established before it is recorded in the voucher register.
2. Incorrect. Under a voucher system, vouchers, not source documents, provide the basis for making journal entries in a voucher register.
3. Correct. A source document is the basis for the preparation of a voucher. The voucher, in turn, is the basis for making a journal entry in the voucher register.
4. Incorrect. Under a voucher system, the invoice is only the basis for preparing a voucher. The voucher is then used as the basis for making an entry in the voucher register.

If you missed any of the above, restudy Frame 11^5 before turning to Frame 12^5 below.

Frame 12^5

Procedure for paying a voucher

When the voucher comes due for payment, it is removed from the unpaid voucher file. A check is prepared for the amount payable. The check, voucher, and supporting documents are then typically sent to the treasurer. The treasurer (or his representative) examines all of the documents. If he finds them in order, he initials the voucher (to show that final approval has been given) and signs the check. He then mails the check, and usually a remittance advice showing the details of payment, to the creditor. He returns the voucher to the accounting department.

On receipt of the voucher the accounting department makes an entry in the check register showing the date paid, check number, voucher number, and amount paid. The date paid and check number are also inserted in the voucher register and on the voucher itself. The voucher is then filed in the paid voucher file.

Review of voucher system

The basic features of the voucher system may be summarized as follows:

1. Vouchers are prepared for all transactions that will result in a general cash disbursement, whether payment is to be made immediately or at a later date.
2. All vouchers are entered in the voucher register at the time a transaction takes place by debits to the proper accounts and credits to Vouchers Payable.
3. All checks are entered in the check register as debits to Vouchers Payable and credits to Cash at the time of payment.
4. The subsidiary accounts payable ledger is replaced by a file of unpaid vouchers.

Determine whether each of the following statements is true or false.

1. A voucher is the basis for an entry in the voucher register.
2. No check may be issued unless it is authorized by an approved voucher.
3. A file of unpaid vouchers constitutes the subsidiary accounts payable ledger.
4. The voucher system provides an effective means of control over all cash flows.

Now turn to Answer Frame 12[5] on page 206 to check your answers.

Frame 13[5]

Miscellaneous matters

Interim reports

Special journals are useful in preparing accurate year-end financial statements which are prepared primarily for external users. These formal financial statements are discussed throughout the text. But special journals are also useful in preparing monthly or quarterly financial reports (called interim reports) which are primarily for the use of management in planning and controlling operations. Interim reports are usually more detailed than those released to stockholders and the public, and separate statements may be prepared for different departments, branches, or divisions of the company in order to identify managerial responsibility. This may necessitate some modifications in the special journals (such as breaking down sales by departments) so that the necessary detailed information will be available.

Interim earnings reports often include comparative figures. Common comparisons are of the amounts for a period of the current year with

Answer frame 12^5

1. True. A voucher rather than a source document is the basis for an entry in the voucher register.
2. True. This is one of the major means of control over cash disbursements resulting from the use of a voucher system.
3. True. Under a voucher system the file of unpaid vouchers does constitute the subsidiary accounts payable ledger.
4. False. The voucher system provides only an effective means of control over cash disbursements, not all cash flows.

If you missed any of the above, reread Frame 12^5 before going on to Frame 13^5 on page 205.

13^5 *continued*

the amounts for the same period of a preceding year. Amounts also may be included for the year to date for this year and last. Internally other comparisons may be made with the budgeted amounts of the current period and the year to date. Comparisons are also made between different units in the company, such as sales branches in different localities. The reports may include forecasts for the ensuing period.

In the internal interpretation of interim comparative reports, emphasis falls on the exceptional variations of actual revenue and expense items from the bases of comparison. Prompt interpretation of the variations permits responsible managers to make timely decisions which will rectify unfavorable operating conditions and control excessive expenses as soon as they are disclosed. The use of the electronic computer has enabled management to have a greater volume and variety of information for decision-making purposes on a more timely basis.

Interim reports:

1. Point out exceptions.
2. Should be prepared for comparable time periods.
3. Provide timely information.
4. Should not be too numerous or complex.

The amount of detail contained in an interim report (or in any financial report) depends primarily upon the nature of the user of the report. Generally, reporting throughout an organization should be such that individual departmental or functional managers will have specific, detailed information and top management and stockholders will have general information. Such reports are discussed in more detail in Chapter 7 of *Accounting II,* the companion text in this series.

Posting directly from documents

In order to maintain an efficient flow of paper work through an office, entries may be posted to the subsidiary accounts directly from the primary evidences of transactions. For example, credits to the individual subsidiary

Accounts Payable accounts may be made from the approved purchase invoices before they are entered in the purchases journal. Since the purchases journal is posted at the month-end, there is no day-to-day need for immediate entry in the purchases journal. This permits the personnel to schedule their time and work loads more effectively.

The use of documentary ledgers

In many cases of processing financial data, subsidiary ledgers are maintained in principle even though accounts are not used. The source documents or copies thereof take the place of the subsidiary accounts. To illustrate, as soon as invoices are recorded in the purchases journal, they are placed in an unpaid file according to the date when they should be paid. Placing an invoice in the file is the equivalent of a credit to a subsidiary ledger account payable. When the invoice is paid and an entry made in the cash disbursements journal, it is removed from the unpaid file and transferred to another file for paid invoices filed alphabetically by name of the vendor. Removal of the invoice from the unpaid file is the equivalent of a debit to a subsidiary account payable. At the end of the month, after the general ledger accounts are posted, the balance in the Accounts Payable controlling account should equal the sum of all invoices in the unpaid file.

The principle is equally applicable when the data are processed electronically. Through the medium of cards or paper tape, the individual receivables may be "debited" to a file of magnetic tape which can be read by a tape drive attached to an electronic computer. Also, through the use of cards or paper tape, the collections may be "credited" to the file of magnetic tape by the process of electronic collation of the data. Concurrently, the electronic computer can cause a tape to be prepared which contains a schedule of the outstanding receivables in the subsidiary file. A printed report can then be prepared from the tape.

Journals and ledgers recorded simultaneously

Traditionally, entry in the journal precedes the transcribing or posting of data to ledger accounts. But machines have been developed by which data can be recorded on two or more documents concurrently. Thus, data can be entered in a journal and posted to a ledger account simultaneously. For example, with suitably designed accounting machines and forms it is feasible to enter transactions for credit sales in the subsidiary accounts receivable ledger and in a sales journal concurrently. The need to transcribe the data from the journal to the accounts is eliminated. Thus, the sorting function of the journal no longer exists.

The accounting functions performed with a computer system are not unlike those found in pen-and-ink and machine accounting systems. But use of the computer will change the form of accounting records. Journals and ledgers appearing in the form illustrated in this chapter will no longer be used as recording or accumulation devices, although the computer printout may be in a form similar to the special journals illustrated.

Indicate whether each of the following statements is right or wrong.

1. Interim reports are normally prepared only once a year.
2. Postings to subsidiary accounts need not necessarily be made from a journal.
3. Source documents can serve effectively as subsidiary accounts.
4. Entry in the journal must precede entry of the same data in ledger accounts.

Now check your answers by turning to Answer Frame 13[5] on page 210.

Summary *chapter* 5

Because of the large volume of transactions, most companies use several special journals rather than one general journal in order to secure a more efficient and accurate accounting for business data.

The special journals illustrated are only representative of ones that may be used and include the sales, purchases, cash receipts, cash disbursements, and payroll journals.

The sales journal (Illustration 5.1) p. 183 should be used only for sales of merchandise on account. Of course, any number of variations could be made in the format of the sales journal, as is true for the other special journals.

The cash receipts journal (Illustration 5.2) p. 184 is used to record all receipts of cash from whatever source.

It is possible to combine the sales and cash receipts journals (Illustration 5.3) p. 189. The combined journal saves some effort as far as posting is concerned. But having separate sales and cash receipts journals does allow more persons to work with the data in the journals at the same time.

The purchases journal (Illustration 5.4) p. 190 is used to record all purchases (on credit) of merchandise for resale. And most firms record purchases as if made on a credit basis even if the length of delay in payment is only the time necessary to write a check. Control is facilitated by paying all bills by check. The payment is recorded in the cash disbursements journal (Illustration 5.5, page 191).

It would be possible to combine the purchases and cash disbursements journals. But this limits the number of persons who can work with the data in the journals at any one time.

A payroll journal may be used to summarize data pertaining to payroll accounting. Postings may be made from it or it may only serve as a memorandum record.

Every transaction that will not conveniently fit into the special journals is entered in the general journal.

The proper combination of journals in a particular company is a function of the volume of transactions, the types of transactions, management's information needs, and the number of persons having to work with the data at the same time. The advantages of using special journals are the following: time is saved in journalizing and posting, detail is eliminated from the general ledger, division of labor is promoted, and the use of accounting machines is facilitated.

The voucher system provides an effective means of control over cash disbursements, provides for an orderly processing of bills for payment, does away with the subsidiary accounts payable ledger, and results in a paid voucher file which serves as a permanent and convenient reference for checking the details of a transaction.

When a voucher system is used, the voucher register and check register are used in place of the purchases journal and cash disbursements journal.

Interim reports (monthly or quarterly) are often prepared to facilitate management control over operations. These reports are often more detailed than the annual statements and may show comparative figures for subunits of the organization, comparisons with budgeted figures, and forecasts of future performance.

Properly filed source documents are sometimes used in lieu of subsidiary ledgers made up of accounts. When electronic computers are used, the traditional journals and ledgers are not even used. The data are stored on punched cards or tape, or on magnetic tape or drums. The use of this type of accounting system is expanding rapidly.

The basic objectives of all accounting systems are the same. These are the timely provision of useful information to interested parties and the retention of necessary records.

To complete your review of this chapter, study the terms in the glossary which follows and familiarize yourself with them. Then go on to the Student Review Quiz for a self-administered test of your comprehension of the material in this chapter (page 211).

Glossary *chapter* 5

Accounts payable invoice file—an unpaid bill file in which invoices are filed according to due date. As invoices are paid they are removed from the file and are usually placed in alphabetical order in a paid invoice file. The accounts payable invoice file often serves as a subsidiary ledger.

Accounts receivable file—copies of sales invoices filed alphabetically (or in some other logical manner) in lieu of maintaining a subsidiary accounts receivable ledger. As payment is received the sales invoices are removed from the file and retained in alphabetical order in a permanent file.

Budget—a document containing planned or expected levels of financial performance. The actual results obtained are usually compared with the budgeted amounts.

Cash disbursements journal—a special journal in which all outflows of cash are recorded.

Cash receipts journal—a special journal in which all inflows of cash are recorded.

Check register—a special journal in which all checks written are recorded in numerical sequence; generally has

Answer frame 13[5]

1. Wrong. They are prepared as they are needed by management for planning and control purposes. They may be prepared quarterly, monthly, or even more frequently.
2. Right. For instance, credits to individual subsidiary Accounts Payable accounts may be made from approved purchase invoices before they are entered in the purchases journal.
3. Right. For instance, unpaid invoices can serve as a subsidiary accounts payable ledger.
4. Wrong. Machines have been developed by which data can be entered in a journal and posted to a ledger simultaneously. In a computerized system, journals and ledgers as described in this chapter are not even used.

If you missed any of the above, reread Frame 13[5] before turning to the chapter summary, page 208.

---

one column entitled Vouchers Payable Dr. and Cash Cr. See Illustration 5.9.

Controlling account—an account in the general ledger that is supported by a detailed classification of accounting information in a subsidiary record.

Direct posting—a procedure under which postings are made to the accounts directly from the primary source documents.

Documentary ledgers—the filing of source documents, or copies thereof, to take the place of subsidiary accounts.

Interim reports—financial statements prepared at intervals shorter than one year. They are prepared for management's use in controlling operations, although information may also be released to the public in the case of publicly held companies.

Notes receivable file—notes receivable which have been recorded in the journals and have then been filed by due date or by the makers' names. The basic documents often serve as the subsidiary ledger.

Paid voucher file—a permanent file where vouchers which have been paid are filed in numerical sequence.

Payroll journal—a special journal used to record data concerning payroll accounting.

Purchases journal—a special journal in which all purchases on account of merchandise for resale are recorded.

Sales journal—a special journal in which all sales of merchandise on account are recorded.

Source documents—documents such as invoices, sales tickets, and cash register tapes which serve as the basis for recording financial transactions in the journal.

Subsidiary ledger—a group of related accounts showing the details of the balance of a controlling account in the general ledger.

Sundry accounts—miscellaneous accounts.

Tickler file—another name for an unpaid voucher file when the vouchers are arranged by the date upon which the discount period terminates or payment is due.

Unpaid voucher file—serves as a subsidiary accounts payable ledger under a voucher system, unpaid vouchers are filed according to their due dates.

Voucher—a form with spaces provided for data concerning the liability being recorded (such as invoice number, invoice date, creditor's name and address, terms, description of the goods or services, and amount due); also has spaces for approval signatures, the date of the check used for payment, and the check number.

Vouchers Payable—an account title often substituted for Accounts Payable in the ledger when a voucher system is in use.

Voucher per creditor per month—the voucher system used when the terms of discount run from the end of the month; all invoices from a given creditor are grouped and entered on one voucher, since one check paying all of the invoices for that month will be written.

Voucher register—a special journal in which prenumbered vouchers are recorded in numerical sequence. In addition to a credit column for Vouchers Payable, it normally has various columns for debits such as Merchandise Purchases, Salaries, and Transportation-In. See Illustration 5.8.

Voucher system—a procedure used to ensure tight internal control over all cash disbursements.

Student review quiz *chapter* 5

To develop a permanent record of your responses, you may write them on the answer sheet provided in the *Work Papers* or on a separate sheet of paper.

1 Information relative to certain aspects of a business is processed through an accounting system so that—

a) The results of operations can be determined.
b) A degree of control can be exercised over operations.
c) The financial position of the firm can be determined.
d) All of the above may take place.
e) Only **(a)** and **(b)** take place.

2 Source documents serve which of the following purposes?

a) To serve as a record of the completed transactions.
b) To communicate the results of operations for a period of time.
c) To communicate information about transactions.
d) To serve as a source of data for reports to management.
e) To show the details of the system of internal control.

3 Interim statements or reports—

a) Are always more detailed than those covering the accounting year.
b) Are issued to the stockholders at regular intervals.
c) Are available to stockholders upon request.
d) Are prepared to provide data as the basis for management decisions.
e) Accomplish none of the above functions.

4 Concerning internal control, which of the following statements is incorrect?

a) An example of internal control is where one individual counts the day's cash receipts and a different person compares the total with the total of the cash register tapes.
b) Once an internal control system has been established, it should be effective as long as the formal organization remains unchanged.
c) Broadly speaking, internal control is the general methodology by which the management of an organization is carried on.
d) The purposes of internal control are to check the accuracy of accounting data, safeguard assets against theft, promote efficiency of operations, and ensure that management's policies are being followed.

5 Which of the following statements is not correct? The use of special journals—

a) Facilitates division of labor in journalizing and posting.
b) Systematizes the original entries of the major recurring transactions.
c) Saves time in journalizing and posting.
d) Has the major disadvantage that special journals make the use of accounting machines less feasible.
e) Eliminates detail in the general ledger.

6 When special journals are used, adjusting and closing entries are generally recorded in the—

a) Cash disbursements journal.
b) Cash receipts journal.
c) General journal.
d) Purchases journal.
e) Sales journal.
f) Payroll journal.

7 An entry to record the conversion of an account receivable into a note receivable would generally be made in—

a) The cash disbursements journal.
b) The cash receipts journal.
c) The general journal.
d) The purchases journal.
e) The sales journal.

8 Match each transaction in column A with the appropriate journal in which it would be recorded in column B. Assume each of the journals listed is used as a book of original entry and is designed as illustrated in the chapter.

Column A	*Column B*
1. Acquired merchandise on account.	a) Sales journal
2. Recorded the estimated amount of bad debts.	b) Cash receipts journal
3. Recorded the payment of wages.	c) Purchases journal
4. Sold merchandise on account.	d) Cash disbursements journal
5. Sold merchandise for cash.	e) General journal
6. Collected cash on account.	f) Payroll journal
7. Gave a note to a trade creditor.	
8. Received a stock dividend.	
9. Received a cash dividend.	
10. Sold land and received a note.	
11. Paid rent for the month.	
12. Received a credit memorandum from a trade creditor.	
13. Sent a purchase order to a trade creditor.	
14. Paid a trade creditor after the discount period had expired, thereby missing the discount.	
15. Recorded payroll for the month.	

9 Select the statement that is correct. The form of the journals used by the individual firms in an industry—

a) Must be identical to those used by every other firm in the industry.

b) Is closely related to the design and flow of the source documents used by the individual firms.

c) Will tend to differ according to the volume of transactions handled by the firms and the imagination of the person designing the journals.

d) Is none of the above.

e) Is as stated in **(b)** and **(c)**.

10 Which of the following statements is correct? When using a special sales journal—

a) The sales are always broken down by departments.

b) The sales may be broken down by sales territory, department, product, etc.

c) Cash sales of merchandise can be recorded in the cash receipts journal.

d) **(a)** and **(c)** are both correct.

e) **(b)** and **(c)** are both correct.

11 Choose the statement that is incorrect.

a) An account in the general ledger that is supported by a detailed classification of accounting data in a subsidiary record is known as a controlling account.

b) As a general rule, the individual accounts supporting a controlling account appear in the general ledger.

c) Individual accounts receivable provide an important source of data for firms which extend credit, and it is thus essential that they be kept up to date.

d) More than one controlling account may appear in the statement of financial position.

12 Subsidiary ledgers (select the correct response)—

a) Are standardized for all firms.

b) May be used by a company only if it uses them for both accounts receivable and accounts payable.

c) Are not even used by some firms.

d) Are useless for service type businesses.

e) Are used most extensively in manufacturing companies.

13 Which of the following figures would not be posted to a ledger account?

a) The cash credit column total in the cash disbursements journal.

b) The sundry debit column total in the cash disbursements journal.

c) The purchases debit column total in the purchases journal.

d) The accounts receivable debit column total in the sales journal.

14 Choose the correct statement.

a) Using a file of the copies of sales invoices as a subsidiary accounts receivable ledger is an example of direct posting.

b) The sale of a plant asset should not be recorded in the sales journal.

c) Postings to the subsidiary ledgers are made monthly.

d) If a firm makes a large number of charge sales each day and the dollar amount of each sale is small, it is advisable to enter the charge sales individually in the sales journal.

15 A documentary ledger is:
a) A file of legal documents such as contracts, insurance policies, etc.
b) The use of source documents or copies thereof in place of a subsidiary ledger of accounts.
c) Generally used as a supplement to the traditional subsidiary ledger.
d) Used only with electronic data processing.
e) The use of source documents in place of the general ledger accounts.

16 A voucher system is used in connection with transactions that involve only—
a) The receipt of cash.
b) The payment of cash.
c) The purchase and sale of merchandise.
d) Revenue and expense.
e) Bonds and capital stock.

17 Which of the following statements is not correct? A file of unpaid vouchers—
a) May be used to replace the accounts payable subsidiary ledger.
b) Is controlled by the Vouchers Payable account in the general ledger.
c) Shows during the year the total amount of all recorded outstanding liabilities for goods and services.
d) Shows only the total amount of outstanding liabilities for merchandise purchased.
e) Frequently shows the net discounted amounts due on the individual invoices payable.

18 The voucher is prepared and filed in the unpaid voucher file—
a) As soon as the goods are requisitioned.
b) As soon as the purchase order is sent out.
c) As soon as the invoice is received.
d) After the receipt of the materials has been verified by the receiving department and the prices and extensions on the invoice have been verified.
e) When payment is made.

19 Use of the Discounts Lost account in a voucher system—
a) Helps in implementing the principle of management by exception.
b) Requires the processing of a second separate voucher each time a payment is not made in time to take advantage of the cash discount.
c) Shows the same information as the Purchase Discounts account would show.
d) Does all of the above.
e) Does **(a)** and **(b).**

Now check your answer with the correct answers and explanations by turning to page 710.

Questions *chapter 5*

1 The processing of data is usually very costly. Why bother with this task?

2 You have applied for a position with a CPA firm in its management services division. Your role will be one of performing services for clients other than the normal auditing and tax services. The partner who is interviewing you asks, "What criteria will you use in deciding whether or not a particular client should be advised to mechanize (computerize) a major share of his data processing?" Your reply?

3 You are the manager of a chain department store. You have just received the annual financial statements. You are frustrated because the accountant has furnished nothing to compare the statements with. What might you like to have in your possession to use as a basis of comparison. How could these be obtained?

4 A department head in a chain department store comes to you (as manager) and complains as follows: "These annual reports I got do me no good. By the time I receive them it's too late. Things that happened 10 months ago can't be corrected at this late date. How do you expect me to run my department efficiently with this system?" How would you go about correcting this situation?

5 How are an organization chart and a system of internal accounting control related? Why might a firm, even if its management knew how to set up a foolproof system of internal accounting control, not choose to do so?

6 Describe the purpose of each of the following journals by giving the types of entries that would be recorded in each: sales, purchases, cash receipts, cash disbursements, payroll, and general. Assume the same formats as were illustrated in the chapter.

7 Is the balance of a controlling account equal to the total of its subsidiary accounts at all times? Explain.
8 Why don't the subsidiary accounts receivable and accounts payable accounts usually have account numbers?
9 How can you tell whether the special journal has been completely posted? Describe the posting marks which appear.
10 In the purchases journal illustrated in the chapter, purchases were recorded net of discount. If they had been recorded at gross, what changes would have been made in the design of the cash disbursements journal?
11 A fellow student remarks, "Whoever first thought of dividing the general journal into special journals did so in an effort to reduce posting time and to make data available to more persons at any one time. The next logical step in the process is to eliminate manual journalizing and posting altogether and use a retrieval system which makes information available to any person in the company at any time. In many firms computerized systems will probably be used to accomplish this." Do you agree?
12 What can be accomplished with a voucher system that is not accomplished through the use of a purchases journal and cash disbursements journal?
13 What two forms of vouchers were covered in the chapter? What usually determines which form is used? What information is normally included on a voucher?
14 What should the relationship be between the balance in the Vouchers Payable account, the "open" items in the voucher register, and the total of all vouchers in the unpaid voucher file?

Exercises *chapter 5*

1 You are employed by a company that has three selling departments. You are asked to design a sales journal which will provide a departmental breakdown of credit sales. Give the column headings that you would use and describe how postings would be made.
2 State whether each of the following is true or false. If a statement is false, correct the italicized words.

a) Posting is sometimes made directly from the source documents to the *subsidiary accounts.*
b) The use of documents in place of subsidiary accounts is referred to as the use of *direct posting.*
c) When entries in the journals and subsidiary accounts are entered simultaneously, the sorting function of the *subsidiary ledger* is all but eliminated.
d) When the controlling account balance and the total of the subsidiary accounts are in agreement, it means that *no errors exist in any of these accounts.*
e) The computer may someday greatly reduce the use of *journals and ledgers appearing in the form illustrated in the chapter.*

3 You are the chief accountant of the Magnuson Company. An invoice has just been received from the Arnott Company in the amount of $2,000, with terms of 2/10, n/30. List the procedures you would follow in processing this invoice up through the point of filing it in the unpaid vouchers file.
4 Refer to the situation described in Exercise 3. Assume that the time for payment of the voucher has arrived and the payment is to be made within the discount period. List the actions that would be taken if the company uses a Discounts Lost account.
5 What would be a reasonable procedure had the discount period elapsed before payment was made in Exercise 4 above?
6 List the posting steps that would be used to post the data shown in Illustration 5.8 (pages 200–201). How many numbers would actually be posted?

Problems, Series A *chapter* 5

5–1–A

During World War II a managerial accountant in the United States was called back to active duty with the Army. An acquaintance of his forged papers and assumed the identity of the accountant. He obtained a position in a small firm as the only accountant. Eventually he took over (from the manager) the functions of approving bills for payment, preparing and signing checks, and almost all other financial duties. On one weekend he traveled to some neighboring cities and prepared and mailed invoices made out to the company he worked for. On Monday morning he returned to work and began receiving, approving, and paying the invoices he had prepared. The following weekend he returned to the neighboring cities and cashed and deposited the checks in bank accounts under his own signature card. After continuing this practice for several months, he withdrew all of the funds and never was heard from again. Discuss some of the steps which could have been taken to prevent this theft. Remember that it is a small firm with limited financial resources.

5–2–A

On June 30, 1975, the Accounts Receivable controlling account on the books of the Grimes Company was equal to the total of the accounts in the subsidiary accounts receivable ledger. The balances were as follows: Accounts Receivable controlling account (Account No. 131), $8,590; Ferguson, Inc., $3,300; Hanson Products, Inc., $1,540; and Oliva Company, $3,750.

The purpose of this problem is to illustrate both the controlling account principle and the use of separate sales and cash receipts journals.

Prepare a sales journal (see Illustration 5.1, page 183) and cash receipts journal (Illustration 5.2, page 184). Also set up a general journal.

Required: Using the following information:

a) Completely journalize each of the transactions in the appropriate journals.

b) Post only the amounts pertaining to accounts receivable to the subsidiary accounts and to the controlling account. You will have to set up some additional subsidiary accounts. Keep all subsidiary accounts in alphabetical order. You will need accounts for the Cowden Company, Dorsey Company, and Wills Company.

c) Prepare a schedule of accounts receivable at July 31, 1975, and compare it with the balance of the controlling account at July 31, 1975.

Transactions (ignore the fact that usually the terms to all customers are the same):

July 1 Sales of merchandise on account to Oliva Company, $600; Invoice No. 306; terms, n/30.

3 Cash sales, $1,725.

5 Received cash for land sold at its original cost of $2,500.

5 Received $2,250 cash as partial collection of amount due today from Ferguson, Inc. No discount was allowed.

8 Received a 30-day, 6 percent note for $1,050 from Ferguson, Inc. in settlement of its account.

9 Sold merchandise to the Wills Company, $450; Invoice No. 307; terms, 3/10, n/30.

11 Received $1,509.20 from Hanson Products, Inc. A discount of 2 percent of the account balance was granted.

July 16 Sold merchandise to the Cowden Company, $500; Invoice No. 308; terms, n/30.

18 Sold merchandise to Hanson Products, Inc., $900; Invoice No. 309; terms, n/30.

20 Issued a credit memorandum to Hanson Products, Inc. for $125 on goods returned to Grimes on Invoice No. 309.

22 Sold $600 of merchandise to Ferguson, Inc.; Invoice No. 310; terms, n/10.

23 Received cash of $2,000 on balance due today from Oliva Company. No discount was taken.

25 Sold $750 of merchandise to Ferguson, Inc.; Invoice No. 311; terms, n/10.

27 Allowed Ferguson, Inc. credit of $50 on goods sold July 25 and damaged in transit due to faulty packing by Grimes Company.

31 Sold $650 of merchandise to the Dorsey Company; Invoice 312; terms, 2/10, n/30.

31 Cash sales, $10,300.

5–3–A

On June 30, 1975, the Accounts Payable controlling account on the books of the Grimes Company was equal to the total of the accounts in the subsidiary accounts payable ledger. The balances were as follows: Accounts Payable controlling account (Account No. 201), $7,750; Cote Company, $3,525; Larson Corporation, $1,225; and Richards Company, $3,000.

The purpose of this problem is to illustrate both the controlling account principle and the use of separate purchases and cash disbursements journals.

Prepare a purchases journal (see Illustration 5.4, page 190) and a cash disbursements journal (Illustration 5.5, page 191). Also set up a general journal.

Required: Using the data given below:

a) Completely journalize each of the transactions in the appropriate journal.

b) Post only the amounts pertaining to accounts payable to the subsidiary accounts and to the controlling account. You should arrange all subsidiary accounts in alphabetical order. You will need additional accounts for Aleo Corporation, Ball Company, Hodge Company, and Smith Corporation.

c) Prepare a schedule of accounts payable at July 31, 1975, and compare it with the balance of the controlling account at the same date.

Transactions:

July 1 Purchased merchandise costing $2,500 from the Ball Company; Invoice No. 562; terms, 2/10, n/30. All purchases are recorded net of discount.

2 Paid the Cote Company $2,500 on account with Check No. 101. No discount was available when the purchase was originally made.

3 Paid rent with Check No. 102 for the month of July, $300.

5 Gave the Larson Corporation a 60-day, 6 percent note for the amount owed. A 2 percent discount had been available, but was not granted. (The original purchase was for $1,250.)

6 Purchased merchandise costing $1,250 from the Cote Company; Invoice No. 261; terms, 2/10, n/30.

9 Paid $1,225 to the Ball Company on the July 1 purchase with Check No. 103.

11 Paid $1,000 for a life insurance policy on top executives to cover the period from August 1, 1975, to July 31, 1976. Used Check No. 104.

July 14 Paid $1,250 to the Ball Company on the July 1 purchase, Check No. 105.

17 Purchased merchandise costing $2,000 from the Ball Company; Invoice No. 581; terms, 2/10, n/30.

21 Received a credit memorandum from the Richards Company for $500 on merchandise returned to it. No discount was available as of the date of purchase.

23 Purchased merchandise costing $750 from the Aleo Corporation; Invoice No. 1031; terms, n/30.

25 Paid $1,500 to Richards Company on account with Check No. 106. No discount was allowed as of the date of purchase.

27 Purchased merchandise costing $1,750 from the Smith Corporation; Invoice No. 328; terms, 2/10, n/30.

29 Paid the Ball Company $1,000 on the purchase of July 17, Check No. 107.

31 Purchased merchandise costing $2,000 from the Hodge Company; Invoice No. 168; terms, 2/20, n/60.

5–4–A

The discussion in the chapter included an illustration of a combined sales and cash receipts journal and mentioned (but did not illustrate) the use of a combined purchases and cash disbursements journal.

Required:

a) Set up a *combined* sales and cash receipts journal similar to Illustration 5.3, page 189.
b) Design a *combined* purchases (Illustration 5.4) and cash disbursements (Illustration 5.5) journal, see pp. 190–91.
c) Set up a two-column general journal.
d) Journalize the transactions shown in Problems 5–2–A and 5–3–A in the journals you have created.
e) Post the amounts to the general ledger accounts shown below. You do not have to post to subsidiary accounts, but place the appropriate posting marks in the journals as if you had.
f) Prepare a trial balance as of July 31, 1975.
g) Why are combined journals not always used?

Account No.	*Account Title*	*Assumed June 30, 1975, Balances*
130	Cash	$ 7,500
131	Accounts Receivable	8,590
132	Notes Receivable	—0—
133	Unexpired Insurance	—0—
150	Land	2,500
		$18,590
200	Accounts Payable	$ 7,750
201	Notes Payable	—0—
250	Stockholders' Equity Accounts	10,840
		$18,590
300	Sales	
304	Sales Returns and Allowances	
307	Sales Discounts	
400	Purchases	
405	Purchase Returns and Allowances	
406	Discounts Lost	
407	Rent Expense	

5–5–A

The Stevens Company uses five journals as records of original entry. They are as follows: sales journal, purchases journal, cash receipts journal, cash disbursements journal, and general journal. At December 31, 1975, the column totals in the sales journal were:

	Sales					
Accounts Receivable	Men's Clothing	Women's Clothing	Appliances	Furniture	Bargain Basement	Other
225,500	40,000	45,000	35,000	60,000	30,000	15,500

The column totals in the purchases journal at December 31, 1975, were:

Purchases						
Men's Clothing	Women's Clothing	Appliances	Furniture	Bargain Basement	Other	Accounts Payable
52,500	54,000	27,500	51,000	37,500	21,750	244,250

The totals of the cash receipts journal columns were as follows:

		Sales							
Cash	Sales Discounts	Men's Clothing	Women's Clothing	Appli- ances	Furni- ture	Bargain Base- ment	Other	Accounts Receivable	Sundry Accounts
333,000	3,075	22,500	25,000	20,000	32,500	12,000	13,500	192,825	17,750

The entries in the Sundry Accounts column result from the collection of $13,000 of rental revenue, $4,500 on notes receivable, and $250 of interest revenue. The totals of the cash disbursements journal columns were:

Accounts Payable	Discounts Lost	Salaries Payable	Sundry Accounts	Cash
190,000	1,500	27,500	22,775	241,775

The entries in the Sundry Accounts column result from the payment of $1,275 for ordinary repairs to the buildings and $21,500 for the purchase of a warehouse.

The general journal includes the following entries at various dates during the year.

Notes Receivable	3,000	
Accounts Receivable		3,000
Office Equipment	4,000	
Notes Payable		4,000
Accounts Payable	250	
Notes Payable		250
Salaries Expense	34,000	
Federal Income Tax Withheld		5,575
FICA Tax Withheld		925
Salaries Payable		27,500

An abbreviated trial balance of the general ledger immediately prior to posting the above journals for the year was as follows:

STEVENS COMPANY
Trial Balance, December 31, 1975

	Debits	*Credits*
Cash	$ 35,000	
Accounts receivable	27,500	
Notes receivable	2,500	
Inventory—men's clothing	7,500	
Inventory—women's clothing	9,000	
Inventory—appliances	6,000	
Inventory—furniture	14,000	
Inventory—bargain basement	3,500	
Inventory—other	2,500	
Office equipment (combined)	6,000	
Buildings (combined)	112,500	
Accounts payable		$ 21,750
Notes payable		125
Stockholders' equity accounts (combined)		204,125
	$226,000	$226,000

Required:

a) Present the general ledger of the Stevens Company, including the balances in the above trial balance and postings based on the other data given in the problem. After posting, prepare a trial balance.

b) Given the following ending inventory figures, compute the gross margin for each of the departments:

Department	*Ending Inventory*
Men's clothing	$10,000
Women's clothing	7,500
Appliances	2,500
Furniture	5,000
Bargain basement	1,500
Other	2,000

5–6–A

The Crawford Company uses special journals for purchases, sales, cash receipts, and cash disbursements, as well as a general journal. These journals follow the same general design as those illustrated in this chapter.

Required:

a) Enter the following transactions in the proper journals. Purchases are to be recorded net. (All journals are to be numbered page 4.)
b) Post the entries to the general ledger accounts shown below. (There would be beginning balances in the accounts, but they may be ignored.)
c) Prepare a trial balance as of the end of the period.

General ledger accounts:

1. Cash
2. Accounts Receivable
3. Notes Receivable
4. Office Equipment
5. Accounts Payable
6. Salaries Payable
7. Federal Income Tax Withheld
8. FICA Tax Withheld
9. Notes Payable
10. Sales
11. Sales Discounts
12. Purchases
13. Discounts Lost
14. Salaries Expense
15. Advertising Expense
16. Rental Revenue

Transactions:

Dec. 1 Bought goods for resale from Mason Company, $2,800; Invoice No. C1109; terms, 2/10, n/30.
2 Purchased goods for resale from Lenz Company, $1,600; Invoice No. 1888Z; terms, 10 days.
3 Bought office equipment for use from Krogman Company, $3,880; Invoice No. 854. Gave a 30-day, 4 percent note in payment.
5 Bought goods for resale from Gordon Company, $2,200; Invoice No. X9784; terms, 2/10, n/30.
6 Cash sales, $2,840.
7 Collected rent revenue for December, $3,800.
8 Sold $2,000 of merchandise on account to Davitt, Inc.; Invoice No. 3345; terms, 2/10, n/30.
9 Collected $3,000 on an overdue account receivable from T. Raia.
10 Sold $2,800 of merchandise on account to Porter Company; Invoice No. 3346; terms, 2/10, n/30.
11 Sold $3,200 of merchandise on account to Zinn Company; Invoice No. 3347; terms, 2/10, n/30.
12 Paid Mason Company for purchase of December 1 with Check No. 201.
12 Paid Lenz Company for purchase of December 2 with Check No. 202.
14 Paid Gordon Company for purchase of December 5 with Check No. 203.
15 Received a 5 percent, 60-day note in settlement of an old account receivable from M. Conrad, $4,400.
16 Cash sales, $7,880.
17 Incurred salaries expense for first half of month of $8,200. Out of this gross amount $800 was withheld for federal income tax and $200 was withheld for FICA taxes. (Record this entry in the general journal.) The amount payable was paid with Checks No. 204–214.
18 Collected amount due on sale of December 8 to Davitt, Inc.
20 Collected amount due on sale of December 10 to Porter Company.
21 Collected amount due on sale of December 11 to Zinn Company.
22 Received a 5 percent, 60-day note in settlement of an old account receivable from T. Elliot, $2,820.
23 Cash sales, $5,000.

Dec. 24 Paid *Jamestown Post Journal* for advertising expense, $3,020 (Check No. 215).

26 Sold $2,400 of merchandise on account to Zinn Company; Invoice No. 3348; terms, 2/10, n/30.

26 Sold $5,600 on account to Baker Company; Invoice No. 3349; terms, 2/10, n/30.

27 Sold $11,880 on account to Cole Company; Invoice No. 3350; terms, 2/10, n/30.

31 Incurred salaries expense of $12,000. Out of this amount $900 was withheld for federal tax and $300 for FICA tax. The amounts due were paid with Checks No. 216–226. (Journalize the expense incurred in the general journal and the payment in the cash disbursements journal.)

5–7–A

The Dexter Company was organized January 1 of the current year. It uses a voucher register and a check register with the same column headings as in Illustrations 5.8 and 5.9 (pages 200–202), except that there are only four debit columns headed Merchandise Purchases, Transportation-In, Discounts Lost, and General Ledger Accounts. Enter the following approved transactions for the month of January in both registers. Total and rule the registers. Start with Voucher No. 1 and Check No. 1. Vouchers are prepared for the net amount of the invoice. For discounts lost, a new voucher is prepared for the amount of the discount.

Transactions:

Jan. 1 Received an invoice from the Modern Company in the amount of $2,400 for office equipment. Terms were 2/10, n/30, f.o.b. shipping point.

3 Received an invoice from the Bailey Company for merchandise in the amount of $4,200. Terms were 2/10, n/30.

5 Received an invoice from the Simpson Company for merchandise in the amount of $2,700. Terms were 2/10, n/30.

7 Paid $360 to the Lund Advertising Service for services received in January.

10 Paid $270 of freight charges to the James Company. Of this, $60 was applicable to the office equipment received on January 1 and the rest to merchandise received from the Bailey Company.

14 Paid the Simpson Company the amount due.

20 Paid the Bailey Company the correct amount due.

31 Paid the Thomas Company the net amount of $24,210 for merchandise received today.

5–8–A

The Hultman Company has been organized for several years and uses a voucher register and a check register with the same column headings as in Illustrations 5.8 and 5.9 (pages 200–202), except that there are only four debit columns headed Merchandise Purchases, Transportation-In, Discounts Lost, and General Ledger Accounts. The last voucher number used was 9743, and the last check issued was No. 2096. As of August 31, 1975, there were three vouchers in the unpaid voucher file:

Voucher No. 9696............	$ 660
Voucher No. 9741............	1,330
Voucher No. 9742............	570
	$2,560

The total of the unpaid voucher file agreed with the credit balance in the Vouchers Payable control account.

The following transactions occurred during September, 1975. Enter these transactions in the voucher register and the check register. Vouchers are prepared for the net amount of the invoice. For any discounts lost a new voucher is prepared for the amount of the discount.

Transactions:

Sept.	3	Paid a $600 note that matured this date plus $10 interest to the Citizens Bank.
	5	Received an invoice for $700 from the Reese Company for merchandise. Terms were 2/10, n/30.
	6	Paid Voucher No. 9696 to the Tims Company, $660.
	10	Received an invoice for $294 from the Zink Company for merchandise. Terms were 2/10, n/30.
	15	Paid the Reese Company the amount owed it on its invoice of September 5.
	17	Paid $130 to the Jacklin Company for advertising placed in September.
	30	Paid $8,900 to the Arlin Company. This included $178 chargeable to the Transportation-In account. The balance paid was the net cost of merchandise received today. Terms were 2/10, n/30.
	30	Paid the Zink Company the amount due on the purchase of September 10.

Total and rule the registers as of September 30. List the unpaid vouchers at September 30 and compare the total with the balance in the Vouchers Payable control account (Account No. 250) at that date after posting the proper amounts thereto.

5–9–A

Jim Brunswick, the owner and operator of the Strike-Spare Bowling Lanes, has been using a general journal to record all business transactions. The posting task has taken an increasing amount of his time. He asks your assistance in designing special journals which would make the task less time consuming.

His wife is to handle all of the credit purchases, cash disbursements, and adjusting entries in her office at home. The husband or his assistant will record all sales and cash receipts at the bowling lanes.

Sales are classified as follows: Bowling Fees, Equipment, Supplies, Shoe Rental, and Miscellaneous Services. (The adjoining restaurant and bar are owned and operated by another party.) Sales are made for both cash and credit. No sales discounts are offered.

Purchases are made from various suppliers. They are recorded at gross invoice price. Perpetual inventory procedure is used for bowling equipment. The entries debiting Cost of Goods Sold and crediting Merchandise Inventory—Equipment are to be made in the general journal. The periodic inventory procedure is used for supplies.

The assistant is paid once a week. The entry establishing the amount payable is to be made in the general journal.

Required:

a) Determine which special journals should be used.

b) Show the column headings which could be used in each of the special journals. Illustrate the use of the special journals by journalizing a sufficient number of assumed transactions so that at least one number appears in each of the columns you have designed.

c) Describe the posting of each of the special journals you have designed.

Problems, Series B *chapter 5*

5–1–B

You are the manager of a restaurant which serves liquor. Your accountant comes in once a year and prepares financial statements and the tax return. In the current year you have a feeling that even though business seems good, net earnings are going to be lower. You ask the accountant to prepare interim condensed statements on a monthly basis. All sales are priced to yield an estimated gross margin of 40 percent. You and your accountant and several of his assistants take physical inventories at the end of each of the four months indicated below. The resulting sales, cost of goods sold, and gross margins are:

	March		*April*		*May*		*June*	
	Restaurant	*Bar*	*Restaurant*	*Bar*	*Restaurant*	*Bar*	*Restaurant*	*Bar*
Sales.......	$29,040	$42,400	$31,240	$34,200	$30,480	$31,200	$33,000	$28,400
Cost of goods sold.....	18,620	25,200	19,040	24,800	18,380	24,600	20,400	24,900
Gross margin...	$10,420	$17,200	$12,200	$ 9,400	$12,100	$ 6,600	$12,600	$ 3,500

Of what use are the interim reports? What would you suspect after analyzing these reports? What sales control procedures would you recommend to correct the bad situation? How could the interim reports have been summarized so that the relationships would have been more obvious?

5–2–B

On August 31, 1975, the Accounts Receivable controlling account on the books of the Colt Company was equal to the total of the accounts in the subsidiary accounts receivable ledger.

The balance on August 31, 1975, in the Accounts Receivable controlling account (Account No. 120) is $45,000. The balances in the Accounts Receivable subsidiary ledger accounts are: Ball Corporation, $18,000; Sanders Company, $15,000; and West Corporation, $12,000.

The purpose of this problem is to illustrate both the controlling account principle and the use of separate sales and cash receipts journals.

Prepare a sales journal (see Illustration 5.1, page 189) and cash receipts journal (Illustration 5.2, page 190). Then set up a general journal.

Required: Using the following information:

a) Journalize completely the transactions in the appropriate journals.

b) Post only the amounts pertaining to accounts receivable to the subsidiary accounts and to the controlling account. You will have to prepare additional subsidiary accounts and should keep them all in alphabetical order. You will need additional accounts for Allen Company, Niles Corporation, and York Company.

c) Prepare a schedule of accounts receivable at September 30, 1975, and compare it with the balance of the controlling account at that same date.

Transactions (ignore the fact that normally the terms to all customers are the same):

Sept. 1 Received $6,860 from the Sanders Company. A discount of $140 had been taken.

2 On this date, merchandise was sold for $11,000 to the Allen Company; Invoice No. 501; terms, 2/20, n/30.

4 Cash sales, $25,000.

7 Received $9,000 on account from the Ball Corporation. No discount was taken.

8 Received $20,000 cash for land sold at a gain of $5,000.

10 Received a 60-day, 5 percent note from Ball Corporation for the remainder of the amount due.

12 Sold merchandise to the Sanders Company, $9,000; Invoice No. 502; terms, n/30.

15 Received payment for $5,000 worth of the merchandise purchased on September 2 by the Allen Company. The discount was taken on this payment.

18 Sold merchandise to the Niles Corporation, $34,000; Invoice No. 503; terms, n/30.

21 Cash sales, $57,000.

23 Issued a credit memorandum to Niles Corporation for $1,000 for goods returned.

26 Sold merchandise to the York Company, $10,000; Invoice No. 504; terms, 2/20, n/30.

29 Received $10,000 cash from the Niles Corporation to apply against the amount due on Invoice No. 503.

30 Cash sales, $39,000.

5–3–B

On August 31, 1975, the Accounts Payable controlling account on the books of the Colt Company was equal to the total of the accounts in the subsidiary accounts payable ledger. The balances were as follows: Accounts Payable controlling account (Account No. 220), $39,000; Frewsburg Company, $16,000; Maplehurst Corporation, $12,160; and Warren Corporation, $7,840.

The purpose of this problem is to illustrate both the controlling account principle and the use of separate purchases and cash disbursements journals.

Prepare a purchases journal (see Illustration 5.4, page 190) and cash disbursements journal (Illustration 5.5, page 191). Also set up a two-column general journal.

Required: Using the data given below:

a) Completely journalize each of the transactions in the appropriate journals.

b) Post only the amounts pertaining to accounts payable to the subsidiary accounts and to the controlling account. You will have to create some additional subsidiary accounts. You should arrange all subsidiary accounts in alphabetical order. You will need additional accounts for Bemus Point Corporation, Celeron Company, Jamestown Corporation, Kane Company, and Moonbrook Company.

c) Prepare a schedule of accounts payable at September 30, 1975, and compare it with the balance of the controlling account at the same date.

Transactions:

Sept. 1 Purchased merchandise costing $15,000 from the Celeron Company; Invoice No. 542; terms, 2/10, n/30. All purchases are recorded net of discount.

3 Paid the Warren Corporation $8,000 with Check No. 451. The original discount of 2 percent was not taken, as the discount period had expired.

4 Paid rent for the month of September, $500, with Check No. 452.

5 Paid the Frewsburg Company $9,000 on account with Check No. 453. No discount was available as of the date of purchase.

6 Gave the Frewsburg Company a $7,000, 30-day, 5 percent note for the balance due.

7 Purchased merchandise costing $8,000 from the Jamestown Corporation; Invoice No. 982; terms, 2/10, n/30.

8 Purchased merchandise costing $9,000 from the Warren Corporation; Invoice No. 1522; terms, 2/10, n/30.

9 Received a credit memorandum from the Jamestown Corporation for $1,000 of the $8,000 of merchandise purchased.

12 Paid the Celeron Company the amount due on the purchase of September 1 with Check No. 454.

15 Purchased merchandise costing $12,000 from the Bemus Point Corporation; Invoice No. 841; terms, n/30.

17 Paid Warren Corporation the amount due on the purchase of September 8 with Check No. 455.

20 Purchased merchandise costing $13,000 from the Warren Corporation; Invoice No. 1566; terms, 2/10, n/30.

22 Purchased merchandise costing $7,000 from the Moonbrook Company; Invoice No. 1910; terms, n/30.

25 Paid $8,000 on account to the Bemus Point Corporation on the purchase of September 15 with Check No. 456.

29 Received a credit memorandum for $3,000 from the Warren Corporation relating to the purchase of September 20.

30 Purchased merchandise having a cost of $5,000 from the Kane Company; Invoice No. 2125; terms, n/60.

5–4–B

The discussion in the chapter included an illustration of a combined sales and cash receipts journal and mentioned (but did not illustrate) the use of a combined purchases and cash disbursements journal.

Required:

a) Set up a *combined* sales and cash receipts journal similar to Illustration 5.3, page 189.
b) Design a *combined* purchases (see Illustration 5.4, page 190) and cash disbursements (Illustration 5.5, page 191) journal.
c) Set up a two-column general journal.
d) Journalize the transactions shown in Problems 5–2–B and 5–3–B in the journals you have created.
e) Post the amounts to the general ledger accounts shown below. You do not have to post to subsidiary accounts, but place the appropriate posting marks in the journals as if you had.
f) Prepare a trial balance as of September 30, 1975.
g) Why are combined journals not always used?

Account No.	Account Name	Assumed Balances on August 31, 1975
110	Cash	$ 40,000
120	Accounts Receivable	45,000
132	Notes Receivable	—0—
150	Land	15,000
		$100,000
220	Accounts Payable	$ 36,000
221	Notes Payable	—0—
250	Stockholders' Equity Accounts	64,000
		$100,000
300	Sales	
303	Sales Returns and Allowances	
307	Sales Discounts	
400	Purchases	
404	Purchase Returns and Allowances	
406	Discounts Lost	
407	Rent Expense	
408	Gain on Sale of Land	

5–5–B

The Jeffries Company uses five journals as records of original entry. They are as follows: sales journal, purchases journal, cash receipts journal, cash disbursements journal, and general journal. At December 31, 1975, the column totals in the sales journal were:

	Sales					
Accounts Receivable	Men's Clothing	Women's Clothing	Shoes	Cosmetics and Jewelry	Sporting Goods	Miscellaneous
40,500	10,000	12,500	4,200	4,000	7,800	2,000

The column totals in the purchases journal at December 31, 1975, were:

Purchases						
Men's Clothing	Women's Clothing	Shoes	Cosmetics and Jewelry	Sporting Goods	Miscellaneous	Accounts Payable
14,000	19,000	6,000	7,500	13,900	4,000	64,400

The totals of the cash receipts journal columns were as follows:

		Sales							
Cash	Sales Discounts	Men's Clothing	Women's Clothing	Shoes	Cosmetics and Jewelry	Sporting Goods	Miscel- laneous	Accounts Receivable	Sundry Accounts
70,100	560	6,000	8,000	3,300	6,000	3,200	4,000	36,000	4,160

The entries in the Sundry Accounts column result from the collection of $3,000 on notes receivable, $160 of interest revenue, and $1,000 of revenue from the operation of a delivery service for other companies. The totals of the cash disbursements journal columns were:

Accounts Payable	Discounts Lost	Salaries Payable	Sundry Accounts	Cash
55,700	1,400	9,700	7,900	74,700

The entries in the Sundry Accounts column result from the payment of $960 for a delivery truck and $6,940 for the purchase of a garage.

The two-column general journal includes the following summarized entries during the fiscal year:

Notes Receivable	4,040	
Accounts Receivable		4,040
Buildings	8,700	
Notes Payable		8,700
Salaries Expense	12,060	
Federal Income Tax Withheld		2,050
FICA Tax Withheld		310
Salaries Payable		9,700

An abbreviated trial balance of the general ledger immediately prior to posting the above journals for the year was as follows:

JEFFRIES COMPANY
Trial Balance, December 31, 1975

	Debits	*Credits*
Cash	$17,500	
Accounts receivable	12,000	
Notes receivable	4,400	
Inventory—men's clothing	6,000	
Inventory—women's clothing	10,000	
Inventory—shoes	1,000	
Inventory—cosmetics and jewelry	4,000	
Inventory—sporting goods	5,500	
Inventory—miscellaneous	1,300	
Office equipment (combined)	3,300	
Buildings (combined)	30,300	
Accounts payable		$10,100
Notes payable		1,000
Stockholders' equity accounts (combined)		84,200
	$95,300	$95,300

Required:

a) Present the general ledger of the Jeffries Company, including the balances in the above trial balance and postings based on the other data given in the problem. After posting, prepare a trial balance.

b) Assuming the following ending inventory amounts, prepare a statement showing the gross margin of each department:

Department	Ending Inventory
Men's clothing	$ 7,500
Women's clothing	5,000
Shoes	2,000
Cosmetics and jewelry	7,000
Sporting goods	10,000
Miscellaneous	1,000

5–6–B

Roxa, Inc. uses special journals for purchases, sales, cash receipts, and cash disbursements as well as a general journal. These journals follow the same general design as those illustrated in this chapter.

Required:

a) Enter the following transactions in the proper journals.
b) Post the entries to the general ledger accounts shown below. (All journal pages are to be numbered page 5. There would be beginning balances in the accounts but they may be ignored.)
c) Prepare a trial balance as of the end of the period.

General ledger accounts:

1. Cash
2. Accounts Receivable
3. Notes Receivable
4. Office Equipment
5. Accounts Payable
6. Salaries Payable
7. Federal Income Tax Withheld
8. FICA Tax Withheld
9. Notes Payable
10. Sales
11. Sales Discounts
12. Purchases
13. Discounts Lost
14. Salaries Expense
15. Delivery Expense
16. Advertising Expense
17. Rental Revenue

Transactions:

Aug. 1 Sold Allen, Inc., $3,000 of merchandise; terms, 2/10, n/30; Invoice No. WI-A1.
3 Bought merchandise from the Dunn Company; Invoice No. 33-NP; terms, 10 days, $2,100.
5 Cash sales, $9,500.
9 Rent revenue received, $400.
10 Salaries expense incurred was $2,750. Amounts withheld were $150 for federal income tax and $100 for FICA tax. (Record this in the general journal.) The net amount payable was also paid on this date with Checks No. 121–131.
11 Collected from Allen, Inc., for sale of August 1. Discount allowed.
11 Paid for office equipment received today, $1,200 (Check No. 132).
12 Paid Dunn Company for purchase of August 3 (Check No. 133).
14 Sold $2,000 of merchandise to Landry, Inc.; Invoice No. WI-A2; terms, 2/10, n/30.
15 Sold $700 of merchandise to Franks Company; Invoice No. WI-A3; terms, 2/10, n/30.
15 Bought merchandise from Dunn Company, $990; Invoice No. 34-VX; terms, 2/10, n/30.

Aug. 17 Bought merchandise from Green Company, $1,500; Invoice No. 98-VX; terms, 2/10, n/30.

18 Bought office equipment today for $950 and gave a 30-day, 4 percent note in payment.

19 Received a note receivable (6 percent, 90 days) for an old account receivable (Fred Williams) in the amount of $350.

19 Cash sales, $1,800.

20 Collected $770 on an overdue account receivable from James Lynn.

21 Cash sales, $1,120.

22 Cash sales, $300.

23 Collected net amount due from Landry, Inc. on sale of August 14.

24 Collected net amount due from Franks Company on sale of August 15.

26 Paid Dunn Company on invoice of August 15 (Check No. 134).

26 Paid Green Company on invoice of August 17 (Check No. 135).

26 Incurred salaries expense of $3,000. Amounts withheld were $200 for federal income tax and $100 for FICA tax (Record this in the general journal.) The net amount payable was paid on this date with Checks No. 136–146.

28 Paid delivery expense in cash, $400 (Check No. 147).

28 Paid advertising expense in cash, $800 (Check No. 148).

29 Sold $3,700 worth of merchandise to the Franks Company; Invoice No. WI-A4; terms, 2/10, n/30.

30 Sold $4,900 worth of merchandise to Landry, Inc.; Invoice No. WI-A5; terms, 2/10, n/30.

31 Bought merchandise from the Dunn Company, $890; Invoice No. 137-NP; terms, 10 days.

5–7–B

The Sven Company was organized January 1 of the current year, 1975. It uses a voucher register and a check register with the same column headings as in Illustrations 5.8 and 5.9, pages 200–202, except that there are only four debit columns headed Merchandise Purchases, Transportation-In, Discounts Lost, and General Ledger Accounts. Enter the following approved transactions for the month of January in both registers and total and rule the registers. Start with Voucher No. 1 and Check No. 1. Vouchers are prepared for the net amount of the invoice. For discounts lost, a new voucher is prepared for the amount of the discount.

Transactions:

Jan. 2 Received merchandise from the Lind Company on terms of 2/10, n/30. The invoice received was in the amount of $10,400.

3 Paid transportation charges to Moyer Trucking Company on purchase of January 2, $174.

6 Paid Wilson Display Company $6,600 for billboard advertising for a three-month period beginning February 1, 1975.

15 Paid the Lind Company for the purchase of January 2.

17 Received merchandise from Bradly Company on terms of 2/10, n/30. The invoice received was for $8,400.

18 Received merchandise from Burns Company on terms of 2/10, n/30. The invoice received was for $36,400. Paid net amount today to establish a good credit rating.

23 Received invoice for $3,600 from Office Equipment, Inc., for office equipment recently received. Terms are 2/10, n/30.

5-8-B

The Byrnes Company has been organized for several years and uses a voucher register and a check register with the same column headings as in Illustrations 5.8 and 5.9, pages 200–201, except that there are only four debit columns headed Merchandise Purchases, Transportation-In, Discounts Lost, and General Ledger Accounts. The last voucher used was No. 432, and the last check issued was No. A727. As of December 31, 1974, there were three vouchers in the unpaid voucher file:

Voucher No. 388...........	$ 5,760
Voucher No. 401...........	11,200
Voucher No. 431...........	3,280
	$20,240

The total of the unpaid voucher file agreed with the credit balance in the Vouchers Payable control account. The following transactions occurred during January, 1975. Enter the transactions in the voucher register and the check register. Vouchers are prepared for the net amount of the invoice. For discounts lost, a new voucher is prepared for the amount of the discount.

Transactions:

Jan. 2 An invoice in the amount of $5,600 was received from the Drake Company for office equipment already received. Terms were 2/10, n/30, f.o.b. shipping point.

3 Paid a $3,200 note that matured this date plus $64 interest. Payee: Citizens' Bank.

4 Received an invoice for $4,000 from the Dundee Company for merchandise recently received. Terms were 2/10, n/30.

5 Paid Voucher No. 388 to the Engle Company, $5,760.

7 Paid $560 to the Rapid Service for transportation. Of this amount $160 applied to the purchase from the Dundee Company and the balance applied to the purchase of office equipment from the Drake Company.

11 Paid the Drake Company for the purchase of January 2.

14 Paid Voucher No. 431 to the Baker Company, $3,280.

15 Paid $880 to the Ericson Company for advertising services received in January.

20 Paid the Dundee Company for the purchase of January 4.

22 Received an invoice for $12,000 from the Dundee Company for merchandise; terms, 2/10, n/30.

31 Paid the Hanley Company $70,400. This included $1,408 chargeable to Transportation-In. The balance paid was the net cost of merchandise received today. Terms were 2/10, n/30.

Total and rule the registers at January 31. List the unpaid vouchers at January 31 and compare the total with the balance in the Vouchers Payable control account (Account No. 250) at that date, after posting has been completed.

5-9-B

Bill Strausbaugh, the golf professional at the Plushmore Country Club, has been using a general journal to record all business transactions. But the volume of business has been increasing, and he seeks your assistance in devising some special journals. He wants his wife to keep track of all receipts, disbursements, and adjusting entries in her office at home. He and his assistant are to record all credit sales and purchases at the golf shop.

Sales are classified as follows: Golf Equipment, Golf Supplies, Apparel, Lessons, Cart Rental, and Miscellaneous Services. Sales are made both for cash and on account. No sales discounts are offered.

Purchases are made from many different suppliers. They are recorded at gross invoice price. The periodic inventory procedure is used for apparel and golf supplies; the perpetual inventory procedure is used for golf equipment. The entries debiting Cost of Goods Sold and crediting Merchandise Inventory—Equipment are to be made in the general journal.

The golf pro's assistant is paid each week. The general journal is to be used to record the amount payable.

Required:

a) Determine which special journals should be used.

b) Show the column headings which could be used in each of the special journals. Illustrate the use of each special journal by journalizing enough assumed transactions so that at least one number appears in each of the columns you have designed.

c) Describe the posting of each of the special journals you have designed.

Cash; Temporary and stock investments

Learning objectives

Study of the material presented in this chapter is designed to achieve a number of learning objectives. These include an understanding of:

1. The objectives sought by management in administering the cash resources of the company.
2. The nature of cash and the types of bank accounts.
3. The procedures for controlling cash receipts and disbursements.
4. The preparation of the bank reconciliation statement and the necessary actions to take on the basis of the reconciliation.
5. How to set up and administer a petty cash fund.
6. The nature of and accounting for temporary investments in deposit accounts and short-term marketable securities.
7. Accounting for stock investments.

Frame 1[6]

Business organizations hold cash primarily to finance their daily activities, although minimum amounts may be held on deposit to satisfy bank requirements. Even medium-sized firms often hold balances running into the millions of dollars. But the objectives sought by management in its administration of the cash resources of a company are actually threefold in nature: (1) making sure that normal operations are not disrupted by a shortage of cash; (2) ensuring that opportunities to earn additional revenues from investments are not lost by holding resources idle in the form of excessive cash balances; and (3) preventing the loss of cash due to theft or fraud.

In seeking these objectives, management's information needs will vary substantially. The first and second objectives will usually embrace an appraisal of the overall cash position of the company, which may be recorded in dozens of separate cash accounts. On the other hand, adequate control of cash against possible loss can only be instituted at the individual account level.

In appraising the financial position of a company, stockholders, creditors, and other outsiders need information as to total cash resources rather than the balances of individual accounts. Yet these outsiders fully expect that management will introduce proper controls to safeguard cash from loss and that the balances reported as cash actually consist of immediately spendable funds. It is the purpose of this chapter to deal with the nature and control of cash and the investing of temporarily unneeded cash balances. Certain long-term investments are also discussed.

Nature and control of general cash

Composition of cash

Cash is composed of those items commonly acceptable as a medium of exchange. To constitute cash, the item also must be immediately convertible into money at face amount.

Cash on hand includes:

1. Currency.
2. Coin.
3. Negotiable instruments, composed of:
   a) Undeposited checks—personal, cashier's, and certified.
   b) Undeposited bank drafts.
   c) Undeposited money orders—postal and express.

Cash in bank includes:

1. Demand deposits maintained in checking accounts.
2. Savings accounts, usually carried as cash, although the bank may request notification preceding withdrawal.
3. Demand certificates of deposit.

More than one account may be maintained for each of these three types of cash in bank.

Time certificates of deposit should not be considered as cash in the current asset section of a statement of financial position if they represent funds not available for immediate disbursement. But if they are of sufficiently short maturity, they are properly classified as current assets. Deposits in financial institutions other than banks, such as stockbrokerage firms, should be reported as current assets other than cash because they may not be available for immediate withdrawal or because they must be converted before they can be disbursed for general purposes. Deposits in closed banks should not be considered as cash; they should be set forth separately in the statement of financial position as noncurrent assets at their estimated liquidation value.

The preceding concept of cash excludes postage stamps, IOUs, notes receivable, bonds, and other negotiable or nonnegotiable instruments.

In the statement of financial position cash usually is presented as follows:

Cash in banks......................	$117,210
Cash on hand......................	1,420

or simply,

Cash on hand and in banks..........	$118,630

Which of the following items should be included within the classification cash on hand and in banks in the statement of financial position?

1. Undeposited money orders.
2. IOUs.
3. Time certificates of deposit.
4. Deposits in closed banks.

Now turn to Answer Frame 1[6] on page 236 to check your answer.

Frame 2[6]

Controlling cash receipts

From the moment cash is received until it is deposited in the bank, it should be completely safeguarded. While cash is of no more importance than inventory, it is more easily misappropriated because it can be concealed and because it is not readily identifiable.

The methods used to control cash receipts vary with each individual business concern. Therefore, the following description of the internal control of cash receipts may be varied in practice to suit individual necessities of each business. A few basic principles of controlling cash receipts follow.

(1) A record of all cash receipts should be prepared as soon as the cash is received. Most misappropriations of cash receipts occur before

Answer frame 1⁶

The first answer is correct. Undeposited money orders are cited in Frame 1⁶ as falling within the cash classification in the statement of financial position.

If you answered incorrectly reread Frame 1⁶ before turning to Frame 2⁶ on page 235.

2⁶
continued

a record is made of the receipt. Once a record is made, misappropriations are more readily traceable.

(2) All cash receipts should be deposited intact in the bank, preferably on the next business day or in the bank's night depository on the same day. Cash disbursements should not be made from cash receipts but only by check or from controlled petty cash funds. In many retail stores refunds for returned merchandise are made from the cash register; if this practice is followed, refund tickets should be prepared.

(3) The person who handles the cash receipts should not record them in the accounting records, and the company accountant should not have access to the cash receipts.

(4) If possible—and it is possible in all but small concerns—the internal function of receiving cash should be separated from the internal function of disbursing cash.

Determine whether each of the following statements describes a procedure which should be followed to safeguard cash receipts.

1. To avoid getting too many persons involved, one person should handle both cash receipts and cash disbursements.
2. To avoid the cost and time involved, as many cash disbursements as possible should be made before cash receipts are deposited in the bank.
3. The firm's bookkeeper should count the cash receipts daily and then enter the totals into the accounting records.
4. As soon as cash is received, a record of the receipt should be made.

Now turn to Answer Frame 2⁶ on page 238 to check your answers.

Frame 3⁶

Cash received at the time of sale. In order to safeguard cash received "over the counter" at the time of sale:

1. Visible cash registers should be used. It is preferable, but not always possible, to have a central cashier ring the register.
2. Prenumbered sales tickets should be used, controlled, and accounted for. A cash register may or may not be used in conjunction with the sales tickets, but it is preferable to do so. Also, it is preferable to have one person prepare the sales ticket and another person ring the register.

If cash registers (not accompanied by sales tickets) are used, at the end of each day or at the end of each cashier's shift:

1. One person should count the cash.
2. A second person should secure the totals contained in the register; that person should prepare the daily cash register report as shown in Illustration 6.1.
3. A third person should prepare the deposit ticket and deposit the cash in the bank; that person should not be the bookkeeper.
4. The bookkeeper should record the cash received. In many instances (2) and (4) are the same person, thereby reducing the personnel to three.

If sales tickets are used (with or without a cash register), at the end of each day or at the end of each cashier's shift:

1. One person should count the cash and should not have access to the sale tickets.
2. A second person should total the tickets and should not have access to the cash; that person should prepare the daily report. If a cash register is used, this person should read the register and reconcile the ticket total with the register total.
3. A third person should prepare the deposit ticket and deposit the cash in the bank.
4. The bookkeeper should record the cash received.

In all cases a duplicate bank deposit slip signed by the bank teller or an entry in a passbook should be obtained by the person depositing the cash. It should be inspected by the person preparing the daily report and by the bookkeeper to assure agreement of the three records—the daily report, the deposit tickets, and the entries of the bookkeeper.

A daily cash register report (Illustration 6.1) should be prepared; it becomes the record of the cash received and the sales made, and serves as the basis for the accounting entries. The report is almost self-explanatory. The top section is used as a record of cash count and deposit; the

Illustration 6.1, *Daily Cash and Sales Report*

Daily Cash and Sales Report

Date July 6, 1975

Cash Register Report

Register Reading, End of Day		5665	45
Register Reading, Beginning of Day		4103	28
Difference		1562	17
Corrections (+ or −)	+	2	00
Gross Cash		1564	17
Deduct: Cash Sales Refunds		20	80
Cash To Be Accounted For		1543	37
Cash Short (−) or Over (+)			
Cash To Be Deposited		1543	37

ANALYSIS OF SALES	SALES		SALES TAX		TOTAL	
Cash Sales Tickets	1504	01	60	16	1564	17
Deduct: Refunds	20	00		80	20	80
Net Cash Sales	1484	01	59	36	1543	37
Cash Short (−) or Over (+)						
Cash, Sales, and Tax	1484	01	59	36	1543	37

Prepared By *Bill Johns*

Checked By *Grace Beck*

Entered By *Jerry Leonard*

Answer frame 2[6]

1. No. Control over cash receipts is strengthened if the function of receiving cash is separated from the function of disbursing cash.
2. No. Effective control of cash receipts and disbursements requires that cash receipts be deposited intact in the bank.
3. No. An effective division of labor in the handling of cash receipts requires that the bookkeeper not have access to the cash receipts.
4. Yes. If a record of all cash receipts is prepared, misappropriations are more readily traceable.

If you missed any of the above, reread Frame 2[6] before beginning Frame 3[6] on page 236.

3[6] *continued*

bottom section serves as an analysis of sales and sales tax. The correction may be the result of underringing a sale as determined from a comparison of cash register tapes and copies of sales tickets. The report may be expanded to accommodate cash registers subdivided by sales classifications and by clerks or register drawers.

Decide whether each of the following statements is true or false.

1. If sales tickets are used, they should be prenumbered so that the duplicate copies can be checked to be sure there are no tickets missing and unaccounted for.
2. The daily cash and sales report provides the basis for entries in the journal.
3. The person who prepares the deposit ticket and deposits the cash in the bank should be the person who records the cash receipts in the accounting books.
4. If sales tickets are used, the person who counts the cash should also total the tickets to be sure the two totals are in agreement.

Now turn to Answer Frame 3[6] on page 240 to check your answers.

Frame 4[6]

Cash received from credit sales. Cash received from charge sales may come through the mail or from direct payment by the customer. Cash received through the mail and directly from customers paying on account in person must be so controlled that the work of receiving the cash and accounting for it is divided between two or more persons. Then, in order to misappropriate cash, two or more employees must be in collusion; division of labor significantly reduces the opportunity for embezzlement.

Currency received from customers paying on account in person should not be rung on a cash register used to record sales. A central receipts desk should be established for customers paying in person, either in currency or by check. Customers paying in person in currency and drafts should be given a receipt. Customers paying by check, either in person or by mail, normally are not given a receipt, since the paid checks serve this purpose. When currency, coin, and drafts are received from customers in person and a receipt is given to the customer, the receipt should be prepared in triplicate. The original copy is given to the customer, the duplicate is routed to the bookkeeper for the posting of the credit to the customer's account, and the triplicate is summarized daily and reconciled with the total of the cash count. The triplicate serves as the basis for the daily cash debit for cash receipts from this source. In this way, the one operation of preparing the customer's receipt provides all the data necessary for controlling the cash and accounting for it; it is not necessary to prepare a separate remittance list. If a customer remits in person in currency or by draft and does not want a receipt, it should still be prepared and the original copy destroyed.

When currency, checks, and drafts are received through the mail, the following procedure—or a variation of it—should be adopted.

1. One responsible employee should open the mail and list the remittances. This should be the same employee who reads the cash registers, totals the sales tickets, or totals copies of receipts given to customers, then his total cash will be composed of receipts from daily cash sales, receipts on the premises from charge customers, and receipts through the mail. After the remittance lists are prepared, one copy should be retained, one copy should be routed to the bookkeeper for posting to the customers' accounts, and one copy (together with the cash) should be routed to the person who will prepare the bank deposit.

2. The cashier should prepare the bank deposit and deposit the money in the bank. The cashier should obtain from the bank a duplicate deposit ticket, signed or machine-receipted by the bank teller. The person who prepares the remittance lists and the cash receipts totals should compare those totals with the duplicate copy of the deposit ticket and initial it. All funds received should be deposited daily and intact. Daily deposits minimize the amount of idle cash and facilitate reconciliation of the bank statement with the cash transactions.

3. The bookkeeper will record the cash receipts from the remittance lists. The total daily receipts recorded by the bookkeeper must equal the remittance totals, which in turn must equal the total of the cash deposited.

If this procedure is followed, an embezzlement cannot be effected unless at least two persons enter into collusion. The first person has no access to the books and, therefore, cannot conceal a misappropriation by record manipulation. For example, if that person withholds funds received from the customers, the customers will object to the subsequent excessive billing. If the cashier alone misappropriates money, his deposit records will not agree with the remittance lists of the first person or with the records of the bookkeeper. The theft of funds might, however, be temporarily concealed if in an act of collusion the first person were to understate cash register readings by a given amount with a cashier removing exactly this amount of cash.

Answer frame 3⁶

1. True. This is a desirable procedure to follow in maintaining a program of effective control over cash receipts.
2. True. The daily cash and sales report is the basis for journal entries recording the cash receipts and the sales.
3. False. An effective control measure in the handling of cash receipts requires that the bookkeeper not have access to the cash receipts.
4. False. If the same person counts the cash and also totals the sales tickets, the system of internal control over cash is weakened considerably. The performance of these functions by different persons enables one total to be used as a check on the other total. If one person performs both functions, the totals may be easily manipulated.

If you missed any of the above, reread Frame 3⁶ before beginning Frame 4⁶ on page 238.

4⁶
continued

Since the bookkeeper does not have access to the cash, he has no incentive to falsify the records pertaining to cash transactions. The bookkeeper and the cashier should never have access to each other's records.

At the end of each month, a bank reconciliation statement (discussed later in this chapter) should be prepared by the bookkeeper, and it should be verified by the person who prepares the cash remittance and receipt lists; the latter person should check deposit totals according to the bank statement with the total of the daily remittance lists and the cash receipts reports.

Determine whether each of the following statements is correct or incorrect.

1. Internal control over cash receipts is greatly weakened by the division of labor.
2. The duplicate deposit ticket signed by the bank teller provides evidence as to the amount of cash deposited.
3. The separation of the functions of preparing the cash remittance list and depositing the cash reduces the opportunity available to the cashier for misappropriating cash.
4. It is essential that the cash receipts recorded by the bookkeeper equal the totals from the remittance list, although the cash deposit total need not necessarily be in agreement with these figures.

Now turn to Answer Frame 4⁶ on page 242 to check your answers.

Frame 5⁶

Controlling cash disbursements

The functions of handling cash receipts and cash disbursements should be separated to the greatest extent possible. The following procedures are suggested to control cash disbursements effectively:

1. With the exception of authorized petty cash disbursements, all disbursements should be by check. No cash receipts should be disbursed.
2. All checks should be prenumbered—consecutively—and all should be controlled and accounted for.
3. Preferably, two signatures should appear on all checks.
4. If possible, the person who authorizes payment should not be one of those who sign the checks.
5. Each check should be supported by approved invoices or approved vouchers (authorizations to draw the checks).
6. The person authorizing the disbursement of cash should be certain that payment is in order and that it is made to the proper payee.
7. Invoices and vouchers should be indelibly stamped "paid," together with the date and check number. This minimizes duplicate payments of a debt.
8. The person signing the checks should not have access to returned checks paid by the bank.
9. The bookkeeper should obtain the bank statement and the paid checks and prepare the bank reconciliation statement.
10. All voided and spoiled checks should be retained and mutilated to prevent their unauthorized use.

Decide whether each of the following procedures is an aid to the effective control of cash disbursements (answer yes or no).

1. Requiring all checks to be prenumbered consectively.
2. Requiring all checks to be signed by one person and countersigned by another.
3. Requiring approved supporting documents for each check issued.
4. Requiring disbursements to be made in cash from daily receipts prior to their deposit in the bank.

Now turn to Answer Frame 5[6] on page 242 to check your answers.

Frame 6[6]

The bank checking account

Money deposited in a bank is subject to certain laws, rules, and regulations with which the depositor should become familiar; for example, a check given to a creditor in payment of an account is merely a conditional settlement dependent upon the sufficiency of funds in the bank account against which the check is drawn.

Because a bank must account accurately to its depositors for all funds received and disbursed on their individual accounts, the use of certain business papers is essential. These papers are discussed in the following pages of this section.

The signature card. A bank requires a new depositor to sign a signature card exactly as checks will be signed. The signature card is retained at the bank as a means of identifying the depositor's signature as it appears on returned checks drawn on the bank. If the depositor is a corporation,

Answer frame 4[6]

1. Incorrect. It is strengthened. If the work of handling cash receipts is effectively divided, cash cannot be misappropriated unless at least two persons enter into collusion.
2. Correct. The duplicate deposit ticket does provide evidence as to the amount of cash deposited.
3. Correct. If the cashier misappropriates cash, the amount on his duplicate deposit ticket will not agree with the total shown on the remittance list.
4. Incorrect. The cash deposit total must also equal the remittance list total and the amount recorded by the bookkeeper.

If you missed any of the above, reread Frame 4[6] before continuing to Frame 5[6] on page 240.

Answer frame 5[6]

1. Yes. Prenumbering checks and accounting for all numbers prevent the extraction and unauthorized use of an unnumbered check.
2. Yes. Requiring two signatures on all checks does aid in the control over cash disbursements.
3. Yes. Requiring checks to be issued only if supported by approved invoices or vouchers does aid in the control over cash disbursements.
4. No. All disbursements except those from the petty cash fund should be made by check. Cash disbursements should not be made out of daily cash receipts. The use of checks provides a more effective means of controlling disbursements. Furthermore, effective control over cash receipts requires that they be deposited intact in the bank.

If you missed any of the above, reread Frame 5[6] before starting Frame 6[6] on page 241.

6[6] *continued*

the bank will require the board of directors of the corporation to pass a resolution authorizing named persons to sign checks. The resolution is filed with the bank.

Bank deposits. When a deposit is made in the bank, the depositor prepares a deposit ticket. Deposit tickets assume a variety of forms; one is shown in Illustration 6.2. The checks should be listed individually, with accompanying identification, such as the bank identification number of the American Bankers' Association, which appears on each check. This number indicates the Federal Reserve District in which the bank is located and the specific identity of the bank. Notice the number $\frac{74\text{-}1174}{764}$ printed on the deposit ticket and also on the check in Illustration 6.4. The 74 is the code number for Michigan. The 1174 is the code number of the specific bank involved. The 7 of the 764 number is the code for the seventh Federal Reserve (Chicago) district. The 64 indicates that the check is to be routed through the Detroit branch of the Chicago Federal Reserve Bank on its way back to the bank on which drawn if it is sent outside of the local clearinghouse area by the drawer. On the deposit ticket the number 307–640–6 is the customer's account number.

In modern machine-based bank accounting systems, each depositor is given a number of deposit tickets, as shown in Illustration 6.2, imprinted with his name and account number. When he makes a deposit, he receives a machine-imprinted receipt such as that shown in Illustration 6.3. This

Illustration 6.2, *Deposit Ticket*

Front

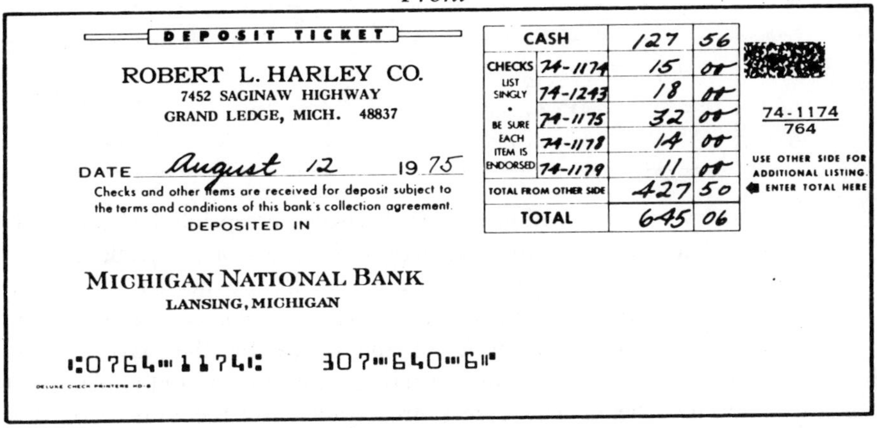

DEPOSIT TICKET

ROBERT L. HARLEY CO.
7452 SAGINAW HIGHWAY
GRAND LEDGE, MICH. 48837

DATE August 12 19 75

Checks and other items are received for deposit subject to the terms and conditions of this bank's collection agreement.

DEPOSITED IN

MICHIGAN NATIONAL BANK
LANSING, MICHIGAN

⑆0764⑉1174⑆ 307⑉640⑉6⑈

DELUXE CHECK PRINTERS HD-6

CASH		127	56
CHECKS LIST SINGLY	74-1174	15	00
	74-1243	18	00
BE SURE EACH ITEM IS ENDORSED	74-1175	32	00
	74-1178	14	00
	74-1179	11	00
TOTAL FROM OTHER SIDE		427	50
TOTAL		645	06

[redacted]

74-1174
764

USE OTHER SIDE FOR ADDITIONAL LISTING.
ENTER TOTAL HERE

Back

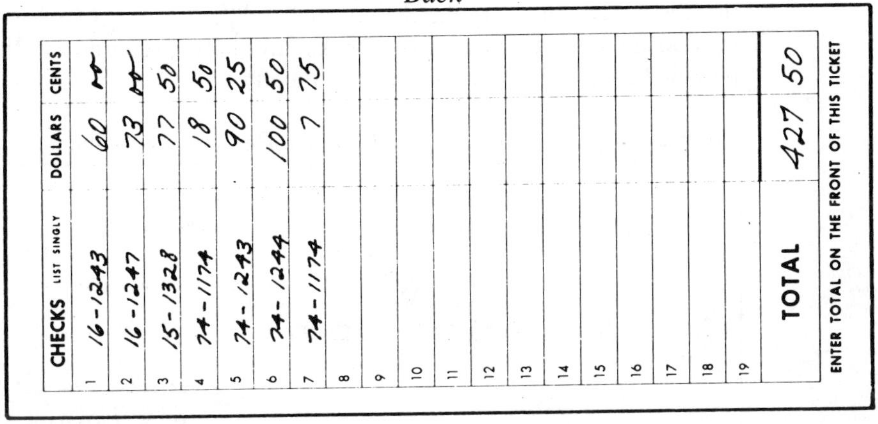

	CHECKS LIST SINGLY	DOLLARS	CENTS
1	16-1243	60	00
2	16-1247	73	00
3	15-1328	77	50
4	74-1174	18	50
5	74-1243	90	25
6	74-1244	100	50
7	74-1174	7	75
8			
9			
10			
11			
12			
13			
14			
15			
16			
17			
18			
19			
	TOTAL	427	50

ENTER TOTAL ON THE FRONT OF THIS TICKET

receipt for the Robert L. Harley Company's deposit shows the deposit was made in bank number 74-1174 in the year 1975, and that the deposit was transaction number 177, made on August 12, in the amount of $645.06, with teller DI.

The bank check. There are three parties to every bank check transaction: (1) the drawer, the depositor issuing the check; (2) the drawee, the bank on which the check is drawn; and (3) the payee, the party to whose order the check is made payable.

A check is a written order on a bank (the drawee) to pay a specific sum of money to the party designated (the payee) or to his order; it is signed by the person issuing the check (the drawer).

A type of check commonly used by modern business organizations is

Illustration 6.3, *Machine-Imprinted Deposit Receipt*

Mortgage Loans

This is the Receipt for your Deposit

AT

MICHIGAN NATIONAL BANK

LANSING, MICHIGAN

ALL ITEMS SUBJECT TO FINAL PAYMENT

BANK SYMBOL. TRANSACTION NUMBER. DATE AND AMOUNT OF YOUR DEPOSIT ARE SHOWN BELOW

74
1174   75   1 7 7 AUG 12 .   645•06 DI

5-31   ALWAYS OBTAIN A MACHINE PRINTED RECEIPT FOR YOUR DEPOSIT

shown in Illustration 6.4. Such checks are printed as illustrated, prenumbered when printed, and prepared in sets of an original and a duplicate or an original and as many copies as are needed by the drawer. The lower section of the check is known as a *remittance advice* and is detached prior to the depositing of the check by the payee. The remittance advice section presents the payee with information explaining the amount of the check. The copies are retained by the drawer of the check and may be used for a number of purposes, including use as the source of the disbursement entry in the journal. With the advent of modern data processing equipment, many checks are now prepared in the form of punched cards and processed automatically.

Illustration 6.4, *Check with Attached Remittance Advice*

HATZEL & BUEHLER, INC.
LANSING, MICHIGAN

VOUCHER Nº 1232   74-1174/764

SPECIMEN

DATE July 12, 1975   CHECK NO. 4207   AMOUNT OF CHECK $ 3,920.00

PAY TO THE ORDER OF   3920 DOLS 00 CTS

Blaine Manufacturing Company

William Hatzel   AUTHORIZED SIGNATURE

R. G. Buehler   AUTHORIZED SIGNATURE

MICHIGAN NATIONAL BANK - LANSING, MICHIGAN

⑆0764⑈1174⑆ 329⑈470⑈2⑈

DETACH BEFORE PRESENTING FOR PAYMENT   REMITTANCE ADVICE

PURCHASE ORDER NUMBER	VENDOR'S INVOICE NUMBER	INVOICE DATE	INVOICE AMOUNT	DISCOUNT	NET AMOUNT
1655	3781	7/2/75	$4,000.00	$80.00	$3,920.00

HATZEL & BUEHLER, INC.
LANSING, MICHIGAN

Indicate whether each of the following statements is true or false.

1. In a bank check transaction, the drawee is the party who issues the check.
2. Since a corporation is not a natural person, an authorized signature is not required for checks which are to be drawn on the corporation's deposits.
3. A deposit ticket is a written order drawn on a bank to pay a specific amount of money to a designated party.
4. The payee is the party to whose order a check is made payable.

Now turn to Answer Frame 6[6] on page 246 to check your answers.

Frame 7[6]

The checking account statement. It is customary for the bank to furnish each checking account depositor with a checking account statement, one form of which is shown in Illustration 6.5. The statement is

Illustration 6.5, Checking Account Statement

THIS STATEMENT PREPARED BY AUDITING DEPARTMENT

MICHIGAN NATIONAL BANK

CHECKING ACCOUNT STATEMENT

THIS STATEMENT COVERS THE PERIOD FROM JULY 31, 1975 TO AUGUST 31, 1975

ACCOUNT NO.	BEGINNING BALANCE		TOTAL ADDED FOR DEPOSITS		TOTAL DEDUCTED FOR CHECKS		SERVICE CHARGE*		CURRENT BALANCE
307-640-6	2,606 15	+	5,308 43	−	7,783 22	−	3 80	=	127 56

INCLUDED IN STATEMENT: NO. DEPOSITS	NO. CHECKS	FIRST LOW BALANCE: DATE	AMOUNT
5	38	AUG. 27	299 28

ROBERT L. HARLEY COMPANY
7452 SAGINAW HIGHWAY
GRAND LEDGE, MICHIGAN

*AMOUNT OF SERVICE CHARGE SHOULD BE DEDUCTED FROM YOUR CHECKBOOK BALANCE

PLEASE RECONCILE YOUR STATEMENT PROMPTLY (SEE REVERSE SIDE)

EPCC 308 REV 6-64

often referred to simply as the bank statement or the bank statement of account, is usually issued once each month, and covers a period of approximately one month. But the statement may not cover exactly one calendar month. It may cover a period from July 3 to August 3 or from the 14th of one month to the 14th of the next month. Many banks have adopted such a procedure simply to avoid having to prepare and mail thousands of bank statements as of the end of every calendar month.

The statement of account shows the account number, the beginning balance, the total of the deposits, the total of the checks paid by the bank, the service charges deducted, if any, and the ending balance. Also shown is the total number of deposits made in the period covered by the statement, as well as the number of checks paid in the period. The "First Low Balance" section of the statement informs the depositor of the date when his account first fell below a stated level, such level being

Answer frame 6[6]

1. False. The drawee is the bank upon which the check is drawn. The party who issues the check is known as the drawer.
2. False. The board of directors will designate certain persons to sign the corporation's checks.
3. False. A *check* is a written order drawn on a bank to pay a specific amount of money to a designated party. Deposit tickets describe the items deposited in the bank.
4. True. The party to whose order a check is made payable is known as the payee.

If you missed any of the above, reread Frame 6[6] before starting Frame 7[6] on page 245.

7[6]
continued

the minimum balance to be maintained in the account for the month in order to avoid the levying of charges by the bank for its services. For example, a number of banks follow a policy of levying no service charges on checking accounts if a minimum balance of $300 is kept in the account during the month. If it is not, a service charge of 10 cents is levied for each check paid by the bank during the month.

At the time of rendering a statement to the depositor, the checks paid by the bank during the month will also be returned to the depositor.

Reconciling the bank statement and Cash account balances. Comparison of the balance shown by the bank statement with the balance for the same date in the depositor's ledger account for cash in bank usually reveals a difference in the two amounts. This difference will usually consist of one or more of the following items:

1. Items that will cause a greater balance to be shown on the bank's statement than in the depositor's ledger account are as follows:
   a) Checks issued by the depositor which are still outstanding; the payees or endorsees have not presented the checks to the bank for payment.
   b) Deposits that have been made to the depositor's account by the bank for which corresponding entries have not been made on the depositor's books. For example, the bank may collect a note or a draft for the depositor, add it to his balance, and advise the depositor of the collection immediately; the depositor will not yet have recorded the amount in his account.
2. Items that will cause a smaller balance to be shown on the bank's statement than in the depositor's ledger account are as follows:
   a) Deposits recorded on the depositor's books which are in transit at the end of the month. They are picked up as deposits on the subsequent month's bank statement.
   b) Charges for services rendered which have been levied by the bank against the depositor and have been deducted from his bank balance but which have not been credited to cash on the books of the depositor. Notice of these deductions accompanies the bank statement in the form of debit memoranda. Examples of these deductions are service charges (when the daily balance in an account is below the minimum required by the bank) and charges for collecting notes or drafts.

Erroneous entries on the bank's books or on the depositor's books may cause misstatements in either balance. The net effect of these various items is that neither the bank statement nor the depositor's ledger account shows the exact expendable balance of cash that should appear in the statement of financial position. Correcting entries should be made to reflect items 1(*b*) and 2(*b*) on the depositor's records.

Indicate whether each of the following statements is correct or incorrect.

1. The checking account statement is a report rendered to a depositor by a bank showing the activity in his checking account for a period of time, usually a month.
2. Deposits in transit will cause the balance shown in the depositor's Cash ledger account to be less than the balance reported in the bank statement, all other things being equal.
3. Bank service charges not yet entered in the depositor's accounting records will cause his balance of cash to be higher than that reported by the bank, all other things being equal.
4. Outstanding checks of a depositor will cause the balance of the Cash account in his books to be greater than the balance reported by the bank, all other things being equal.

Now turn to Answer Frame 7[6] on page 248 to check your answers.

Frame 8[6]

The bank reconciliation statement. A bank reconciliation statement is prepared in order to account for the difference between the cash balance on the books and on the bank statement, and it concludes with the properly adjusted Cash account balance. In preparing the reconciliation statement, both the bank statement balance and the balance in the Cash ledger account are adjusted to the true balance of expendable cash that should appear on the statement of financial position, as shown in Illustration 6.6.

Illustration 6.6

WASHINGTON COMPANY
Bank Reconciliation Statement
August 31, 1975

Balance per bank statement, August 31, 1975	$23,195.85	Balance per ledger, August 31, 1975	$22,009.85
Add: Deposit in transit	1,057.05	Add: Note collected by bank	600.00
	$24,252.90		$22,609.85
Less: Outstanding checks	1,645.55	Less: Bank charges	2.50
Adjusted Ledger Balance, August 31, 1975	$22,607.35	Adjusted Ledger Balance, August 31, 1975	$22,607.35

Answer frame 7[6]

1. Correct. The statement properly defines a checking account statement.
2. Incorrect. Deposits in transit have been debited to the firm's Cash ledger account but have not yet been recorded in the bank's records. Thus, they will cause the ledger balance to be greater than the balance reported in the bank statement.
3. Correct. The bank service charges have already been deducted from the depositor's account at the bank, so the depositor's cash balance in his own ledger will be greater until he makes a corresponding reduction in his books.
4. Incorrect. Outstanding checks of a depositor will cause the cash balance shown in his ledger account to be smaller, not greater, than the balance reported by the bank. This is because the outstanding checks represent items that have already been deducted in the depositor's books (when they were issued) but have not yet been deducted in the bank's records, since they have not yet cleared.

If you missed any of the above, reread Frame 7[6] before starting Frame 8[6] on page 247.

8[6] *continued*

The first step in preparing the reconciliation statement is to examine the bank statement and the debit and credit memoranda, if any, returned with the statement. The depositor's records should be examined to note whether the items to which these memoranda pertain have been recorded. If not, they must be added to or deducted from the balance in the ledger account, as shown by the adjustments for $600 for the note collected and for $2.50 for bank service charges in Illustration 6.6.

The second step is to sort the canceled checks returned by the bank into numerical order. The outstanding checks are identified by a process of elimination. The numbers of the checks cleared and returned by the bank are compared with the numbers of the checks issued. Distinctive tick marks (√) are used in the books or on the copies of the checks issued to indicate those which are returned. The checks issued for which no canceled checks have been returned from the bank are the outstanding checks, which are beyond the control of the depositor. Checks outstanding at the beginning of the month which have cleared during the month may be traced to the reconciliation statement prepared at the end of the preceding month. Any checks outstanding at the end of the preceding month and not returned during the current month are, of course, outstanding at the end of the current month.

The next step in preparing the reconciliation statement is to determine whether there are any deposits in transit to the bank. The receipts for the last day of the month might be deposited in the night depository box at the bank and, thus, will not be considered a deposit by the bank until the next day. If all receipts are deposited, the total debits to the Cash account can be compared with the total deposits per the bank statement. If the two agree, it is quite unlikely that there is a deposit in transit. If the two do not agree but the number of deposits shown by the bank agrees with the number of days' receipts which are deposited daily, as shown by the books, then the bank has included in its deposits for the current month the deposit in transit at the end of the prior month and has not included as a deposit the receipts of the last day of the current month. For example, a bank statement may show deposits of $10,500, while the cash receipts per the ledger account total $10,350. If a deposit of $1,500 were in transit at the end of the prior month and the cash receipts for the last day of the month were $1,350, then there is a deposit in transit at the end of the current month of $1,350. The receipts per the Cash account can be reconciled with the deposits per the bank statement as follows:

Deposits per bank statement	$10,500
Less: Deposit in transit at the end of last month	1,500
	$ 9,000
Add: Receipts of last day of current month	1,350
Receipts per Cash account	$10,350

Deposits in transit and outstanding checks, together with the bank service charges indicated on the bank statement, will often account entirely for the difference between the balance in the bank statement and the balance in the Cash account. Any omissions and errors in the depositor's books are, of course, corrected by proper entries. These entries should be made prior to the preparation of the statement of financial position and the earnings statement. If any errors made by the bank are discovered in preparing the reconciliation statement (such as charging a check against the wrong account), they are called to the attention of the bank.

To illustrate the preparation of a bank reconciliation statement, assume that the bank statement of the Washington Company at August 31, 1975, showed a balance of $23,195.85; the Cash account balance of the depositor at the same date was $22,009.85. By comparing the canceled checks returned by the bank with the copies of the checks issued, the following checks were found to be outstanding at the end of the month:

Check No.	*Amount*
556	$ 840.00
570	354.25
571	451.30
	$1,645.55

An examination of the debit and credit memoranda returned with the bank statement reveals a credit memorandum showing that the bank had collected a customer's note for the Washington Company and had credited the amount collected, $600, to the company's account. (A credit memorandum is evidence of an addition to a depositor's account which arises from a transaction other than a normal deposit.) For this service, the bank charged the Washington Company $2.50 and so advised the company by including a debit memorandum for that amount with the canceled checks returned on August 31, 1975.

After deducting the $600 representing the collection of the note from the deposits shown on the bank statement, the remaining amount was less than the cash receipts for the month by exactly the amount of the cash receipts for August 31, $1,057.05. An examination of the deposit receipt ticket shows that the deposit was actually made on September 1. In other situations the deposits per bank statement may be larger than the cash receipts per the books even after taking into consideration the above-mentioned items. Generally, this difference will be caused by the deposit of receipts of the prior month (July in this instance) in the month for which the reconciliation is being prepared.

The statement reconciling the balance per the bank statement with the balance per Cash account as of August 31, 1975, (Illustration 6.6) shows that the cash available for immediate disbursement is not $22,009.85 or $23,195.85, but $22,607.35. Consequently, the following journal entries must be prepared and posted:

Cash	600.00	
Notes Receivable		600.00
To record note collected by bank.		
Bank Service Charges	2.50	
Cash		2.50
To record bank collection charges.		

The earnings statement for the period ended August 31, 1975, should include the expense of $2.50; the statement of financial position as of August 31, 1975, should show a cash balance of $22,607.35.

Indicate whether each of the following statements is true or false.

1. An error made by the bank in crediting an amount to a depositor's account requires a correcting journal entry in the depositor's own accounting records.
2. The cash amount shown in a corporation's statement of financial position must be the balance reported to the corporation in the bank statement of account.
3. Outstanding checks are the canceled checks which are returned by the bank with each statement of account.
4. Outstanding checks which were included in a bank reconciliation statement at January 31, 1975, must be included in the February 28, 1975, bank reconciliation statement if they are still outstanding.

Now turn to Answer Frame 8[6] on page 252 to check your responses.

Frame 9[6]

The data needed to prepare a bank reconciliation statement follow:

Balance per bank statement October 31, 1975	$3,290,00
Balance per Cash account of the Wilton Company at October 31,	

1975	3,681.00
Checks outstanding at October 31, 1975	805.00
Receipts of October 31 placed in bank's night depository	480.00
Check of Walton Company included in canceled checks returned by bank	105.00
Credit memorandum covering collection of note by bank for Wilton Company (not recorded by Wilton Company as of October 31)	570.00
Debit memorandum for collection fees charged by bank for collecting above note	3.00
Check of customer of Wilton Company deposited on October 25 but returned by bank marked N.S.F. (not sufficient funds). No entry has been made for the return by the Wilton Company	168.00
Wilton Company note payable to bank, charged at maturity by the bank to the Wilton Company's account, including interest of $10	1,010.00

Using the above data and a separate sheet of paper, provide the missing items in the following illustration of a bank reconciliation statement.

Illustration 6.7

WILTON COMPANY
Bank Reconciliation Statement
October 31, 1975

Balance per bank statement, October 31, 1975		$3,290.00
Add: Check of Walton Company deducted in error	$105.00	
?		
Less:		
Adjusted Ledger Balance, October 31, 1975		$3,070.00
Balance per ledger, October 31, 1975		$3,681.00
Add: ?		
Less: Not sufficient funds check	$168.00	
?	?	
?	?	?
Adjusted Ledger Balance, October 31, 1975		$3,070.00

Check your answers in Answer Frame 9[6] on page 252.

Frame 10[6]

The available cash balance is $3,070. The entry to adjust the Cash account in the ledger is:

Collection Fee Expense	3.00	
Accounts Receivable	168.00	
Notes Payable	1,000.00	
Interest Expense	10.00	
Notes Receivable		570.00
Cash		611.00

To record adjustments to correct Cash account. ($1,181 − $570 = $611 net cash outlay.) For details see reconciliation statement for October.

Answer frame 8[6]

1. False. Since the error was made by the bank, the correction must be made by the bank on its records.
2. False. The exact expendable balance of cash at the statement of financial position date is the amount that should appear in that statement. Due to such factors as deposits in transit and outstanding checks, this might not be the balance which is reported in the bank statement.
3. False. Outstanding checks are those checks which have been issued by the corporation but have not yet cleared the bank and been charged against the corporation's account.
4. True. The checks are still outstanding, so they still represent a source of difference between the cash balance on the books and on the bank statement. As such, they must still be included in the reconciliation statement.

If you missed any of the above, reread Frame 8[6] before beginning Frame 9[6] on page 250.

Answer frame 9[6]

The completed bank reconciliation is as follows:

WILTON COMPANY
Bank Reconciliation Statement
October 31, 1975

Balance per bank statement, October 31, 1975		$3,290.00
Add: Check of Walton Company deducted in error	$ 105.00	
Deposit in transit	*480.00*	*585.00*
		$3,875.00
Less: *Outstanding checks*		*805.00*
Adjusted Ledger Balance, October 31, 1975		$3,070.00
Balance per ledger, October 31, 1975		$3,681.00
Add: *Note collected by bank*		*570.00*
		$4,251.00
Less: Not sufficient funds check	$ 168.00	
Collection fees	*3.00*	
Wilton Company note charged against account	*1,010.00*	*1,181.00*
Adjusted Ledger Balance, October 31, 1975		$3,070.00

If you answered incorrectly, study your errors carefully before proceeding to Frame 10[6] on page 251.

10[6] *continued*

Alternate form of statement of account. The forms shown in Illustrations 6.2, 6.3, and 6.5 are similar to those employed by banks which process their data electronically. In many areas, especially smaller cities, bank data are not processed electronically. For such banks, the form of statement of account employed will contain information similar to that presented in Illustration 6.8—that is, virtually every individual item debited or credited to the account will be listed separately on the statement. The depositor will receive supporting documents for every transaction in his account—canceled check, returned customer's check, debit memorandum, credit memorandum, and deposit ticket. And it fol-

Illustration 6.8

THIS STATEMENT PREPARED BY AUDITING DEPARTMENT

MICHIGAN NATIONAL BANK

COMPLETE BANK AND TRUST SERVICE

ACCOUNT NUMBER 312 097 6

XYZ Bowling Company
% John Boles, Treas.
19261 S. Washington Ave.
Lansing, Michigan 48933

CHECKING ACCOUNT STATEMENT
THIS STATEMENT COVERS THE PERIOD

FROM 5-31-75 TO 6-30-75

DATE	DEBITS	TRANS. CODE	DATE	DEBITS	TRANS. CODE	DATE	DEPOSITS	TRANS. CODE
6 01 75	190 51		6 09 75	62 90		6 03 75	3045 85	
6 01 75	76 80		6 12 75	5 00		6 03 75	153 79	
6 01 75	3 96		6 12 75	33 00	60	6 03 75	390 86	
6 01 75	29 10		6 14 75	11 02		6 03 75	2004 17	
6 01 75	15 00		6 16 75	1571 15	29	6 04 75	3174 14	
6 01 75	25 96		6 16 75	459 64		6 04 75	1843 54	
6 02 75	85 85		6 21 75	12 95		6 04 75	3219 00	
6 02 75	13 67		6 21 75	2 07		6 05 75	448 27	
6 03 75	7 50		6 21 75	5308 39	8	6 05 75	2291 90	
6 03 75	50 83		6 24 75	19 58		6 07 75	45 00	
6 03 75	45 60		6 24 75	178 06		6 07 75	1723 02	
6 04 75	1 10	10	6 25 75	16 21		6 09 75	214 45	
6 04 75	27 46		6 25 75	458 00		6 09 75	62 90	12
6 04 75	19 76		6 28 75	7074 17	8	6 14 75	83 40	
6 05 75	90 92		6 28 75	2966 67	8	6 14 75	640 01	
6 05 75	50 00		6 28 75	413 88		6 14 75	729 20	
6 05 75	159 23		6 28 75	19 80		6 16 75	546 81	
6 05 75	5 84		6 30 75	77 52		6 17 75	524 60	
6 05 75	10 51		6 30 75	3 56		6 21 75	79 45	
6 07 75	57 94					6 24 75	409 83	
6 07 75	2 76	SC				6 25 75	522 54	
6 07 75	4 84					6 28 75	565 02	

INCLUDED IN STATEMENT		FIRST LOW BALANCE		
NO OF DEPOSITS 22	NO OF DEBITS 41	DATE	AMOUNT	BEGINNING BALANCE 18,492.68
TOTAL ADDED FOR DEPOSITS 22,717.75	TOTAL DEDUCTED FOR CHECKS AND CHARGES 19,668.71			CURRENT BALANCE 21,541.72

TRANSACTION CODES

BLANK - CHECK
BLANK - DEPOSIT
SC - SERVICE CHARGE
3 - CREDIT MEMO
5 - DEPOSIT CORRECTION
7 - LIST CORRECTION
8 - LIST
10 CHECK CORRECTION
12 CHARGE CORRECTION
29 CERTIFIED CHECK MEMO
40 MISC BANK CHARGE
60 DEBIT MEMO
OD OVERDRAWN BALANCE

EPCC - 309 REV 6/64

PLEASE RECONCILE YOUR STATEMENT PROMPTLY
(SEE REVERSE SIDE)

lows that since the same information is received regardless of the form of bank statement of account received, the reconciliation procedures are the same.

Certified checks. Illustration 6.8 shows that on June 16, 1975, a certified check (transaction code 29) in the amount of $1,571.15 was charged against the XYZ Bowling Company's account. Because of the possibility that a check may not be paid when presented to the bank upon which drawn, a payee may demand that the check be certified. A certified check is a regular check drawn by a depositor and taken by him to his bank for certification. The bank will stamp "certified" across the face of the check and insert the name of the bank and the date; the certification will be signed by a bank official. The bank will do this only after ascertaining that the depositor's balance is sufficient to cover the check, and the check will be deducted from the depositor's balance immediately. The check then becomes a liability of the bank and for this reason will be accepted without question as to its value.

Certified checks are usually retained by the bank after they have cleared and (since they are not returned to the drawer) may, if care is not exercised, be included in the list of outstanding checks. Such listing would be improper, because outstanding checks are deducted from the balance per the bank statement and the certified check has already been deducted from the balance in the bank's records.

Maintaining several checking accounts

Many business organizations maintain a number of bank accounts, not only to establish a favorably relationship with a bank but also for specialized purposes. In such cases, the ledger must contain separate cash accounts for each bank account as, for example, Cash—First National Bank, Cash—Michigan National Bank, and Cash—First State Bank. Each of these accounts must be reconciled separately with the statement received from the bank covering the account.

The amount of cash on hand and in banks is significant information to top management. Decisions must be made daily with regard to cash expenditures, and cash balances larger than needed to sustain day-to-day operations should be invested to secure revenue from them. At current interest rates, $1,000,000 invested in short-term, interest-bearing securities will yield over $100 of earnings per day.

Because of the significance of the information, virtually all businesses determine their daily cash balances. Such balances may be determined crudely on adding machine tapes of receipts, disbursements, and previous balances. They may even be reported to top management by a forwarding of these tapes. Or computer printouts may be run of the receipts, disbursements, and balances in many cash accounts with the balances summed into one final total.

Transfer bank accounts. A company operating in many widely scattered locations and maintaining accounts with many local banks must adopt special procedures in order to avoid the accumulation of excessive amounts of idle cash. One such procedure, entailing the use of special-instruction bank accounts, is to establish transfer accounts in the local banks whereby these banks automatically transfer (by wire or bank draft) all amounts on deposit in excess of a stated amount (which may be zero) to a central bank. In this way funds not needed to sustain local operations are quickly forwarded to the company's headquarters where they can be invested temporarily if not needed for general corporate purposes.

Indicate whether each of the following statements is true or false.

1. The procedures followed in preparing a bank reconciliation statement will differ depending upon whether a printed-out or abbreviated statement of account is received from the bank.
2. A certified check should never be shown as outstanding on a bank reconciliation statement, since it has already been deducted from the company's balance with the bank.
3. A separate reconciliation statement must be prepared for each bank account maintained by a business organization.

4. Transfer bank accounts which require the automatic forwarding of balances in excess of a stated amount to a central location are used in an attempt to reduce the amount of idle cash held by a company.

Now check your answers by turning to Answer Frame 10⁶ on page 256.

Frame 11⁶

Payroll checking accounts

Many concerns maintain a separate payroll bank account, especially when a large number of employees is paid by check. In general, a payroll checking account is employed in the following fashion. Prior to each pay date, the net payroll is computed, a check is drawn on the general commercial bank account for that amount, and the check is deposited in the payroll bank account. Individual payroll checks are issued to the employees, and when cashed they are cleared against the payroll bank account. It may be desirable to deposit an even-dollar amount larger than the net current payroll in the payroll account so that during the period between regular payroll dates there will be an available balance for such payroll checks as may be issued for advances to employees or for final pay upon termination of employment.

The maintenance of a payroll bank account has several advantages, as follows.

(1) A distinctive payroll check form may be adopted, with spaces provided on an attached apron for the amounts of gross earnings, the various payroll deductions, and the net cash paid.

(2) Payroll checks, evident as such, are easily cashed by employees.

(3) The work of reconciling the bank balances may be divided among employees. One check is drawn against the general commercial bank account. The hundreds or thousands of payroll checks issued each payday are drawn on the payroll bank account. Occasionally, payroll checks are lost or negotiated many times before clearing the bank. Localization of these items in the payroll reconciliation simplifies the reconciliation of the general Cash account.

(4) Only one authorization is prepared, calling for one check drawn against the general commercial bank account; therefore, payroll checks are issued without separately prepared and signed authorizations.

(5) The individual payroll checks need not be entered in the regular cash disbursements record; the payroll check numbers are inserted in the payroll journal or record, and a repetition of the entering of the checks is avoided.

Separate checking accounts are often used to pay dividends, periodic bond interest, and executives' salaries. They are occasionally used to pay for construction expenditures.

Answer frame 10[6]

1. False. Since both forms of bank statement contain the same summary information, there is no reason for the reconciliation procedures to differ.
2. True. Certified checks are deducted from the company's balance at the bank at the time of certification and therefore should not be treated as an item that will be deducted from this balance in the future.
3. True. Because of the possibility of offsetting errors, it would make little sense to reconcile a number of bank accounts simultaneously on one reconciliation statement.
4. True. This is exactly the reason why transfer bank accounts are established and maintained.

If you missed any of the above, reread Frame 10[6] before starting Frame 11[6] on page 255.

11[6] *continued*

Assume a company maintains a separate payroll bank account. Determine whether each of the following statements is correct or incorrect.

1. Separate authorizations need not be prepared for each payroll check.
2. The payroll checks must be entered individually in the cash disbursements journal or record and also in a payroll journal or record.
3. The payroll check form must conform to that of the checks issued for general cash disbursements.
4. The reconciliation of the general Cash account is simplified.

Now check your answers with those in Answer Frame 11[6] on page 258.

Frame 12[6]

Cash short and over

Occasionally, errors are made in returning change to customers. In these cases the amount of cash will be short of, or in excess of, the computed amount shown by the total of a cash register tape or an adding machine tape total of sales slips for a day.

Assume that a store clerk accidentally shortchanges a cash customer to the extent of $1. Total cash sales for the day were $704.50. At the end of the day, the total actual cash will be $1 over the sum of the sales tickets or the total of the cash register tape. The journal entry to record the day's business is as follows:

Cash	705.50	
Sales		704.50
Cash Short and Over		1.00

The Cash Short and Over account is a miscellaneous expense (debit balance) or revenue (credit balance) account. It is credited if the cash received is greater than the correct amount and debited if the cash received is less than the correct amount. The balance of the account at the end of the period will be treated as either Other Expense or Other Revenue.

Indicate whether each of the following statements is true or false.

1. It would be impossible to have a cash overage or shortage if employees were paid in cash rather than by check.
2. The entry to account for daily cash sales for which a small cash shortage existed would include a debit to Cash Short and Over.
3. If the Cash Short and Over account has a debit balance at the end of a period, it is classified as an expense.
4. A credit balance in a Cash Short and Over account should be considered a liability, because the shortchanged customer will demand return of this amount.

Check your answers with those in Answer Frame 12[6] on page 258.

Frame 13[6]

Petty cash funds

While it is desirable that all cash disbursements be made by check, most concerns find it necessary to make certain small payments in currency and coin. Disbursements for delivery charges, postage stamps, taxi fares, employees' supper money when working overtime, and other small items usually require a small amount of currency on hand.

To permit such small disbursements to be made in cash and at the same time to maintain adequate control over cash disbursements, business concerns often establish a petty cash fund of some round dollar amount such as $50 or $100. One individual in the company is placed in charge of the fund and is responsible for the entire sum.

Imprest petty cash funds

A petty cash fund could be established on a basis whereby an entry would be made to record every change in the fund. Thus, when the fund is established an entry could be made debiting Petty Cash and crediting Cash. If cash is expended for delivery charges, an entry could be made debiting Transportation-In (or Transportation-Out, as the case may be) and crediting Petty Cash. If maintained on this basis, the records of the company would soon be cluttered with numerous entries for relatively nominal amounts. For this reason, petty cash funds are almost invariably maintained on an imprest basis, which means that only periodically is the petty cash fund reimbursed out of general cash and the expense re-

Answer frame 11[6]

1. Correct. The authorization prepared at each pay date supporting the transfer of funds from the general Cash account to the payroll bank account eliminates the need to prepare separate authorizations for each paycheck.
2. Incorrect. The total of all individual payroll checks is entered as one item in the cash disbursements journal or record when the funds are transferred to the payroll bank account. It is not necessary to detail the individual payroll checks in the cash disbursements journal, since the payroll journal or record shows the details of the checks and their numbers.
3. Incorrect. The establishment of a separate payroll bank account enables the firm to use a distinctive payroll check form which includes a detachable section detailing the employee's gross earnings, the various payroll deductions, and the net cash paid.
4. Correct. The reconciliation of the general Cash account is simplified since any discrepancies associated with payroll checks are localized in the payroll bank account and thus do not affect the reconciliation of the general Cash account.

If you missed any of the above, reread Frame 11[6] before beginning Frame 12[6] on page 256.

Answer frame 12[6]

1. False. In any instance where cash is handled and a record is available as to the exact amount of cash which should be disbursed, received, or on hand, it is possible that a cash overage or shortage may occur.
2. True. Cash shortages are recorded by a debit to Cash Short and Over.
3. True. The Cash Short and Over account is an expense if it has a debit balance.
4. False. The customer does not realize that his change is incorrect. If he did, he would demand payment of the amount due him. The error would be corrected immediately, and no balance would appear in the account. Obviously, there would never be a cash overage if the customer were aware of the error. Consequently, it is assumed that no claim will be made for the cash over, and it is treated as an element of revenue.

If you missed any of the above, reread Frame 12[6] before turning to Frame 13[6] on page 257.

13[6] *continued*

corded. All future discussion will assume the establishment and maintenance of petty cash funds on this basis.

When the petty cash fund is established, a check is prepared, payable to the order of the person who is to be the petty cash cashier, and an entry is made as follows:

Petty Cash Fund	100	
Cash		100
To record drawing a check to establish a petty cash fund of $100.		

The amount of the fund depends upon the extent to which petty cash will be used. If possible, the fund should be sufficiently large to care for petty cash disbursements for a reasonble period of time, for example, one month. The fund in the preceding entry was established in the amount of $100. The check is cashed, and the cash placed in the petty cash box. The fund now is ready for disbursements to be made from it.

A *petty cash voucher* should be prepared for each disbursement from the petty cash fund. A petty cash voucher is shown in Illustration 6.9.

Illustration 6.9, *Petty Cash Voucher*

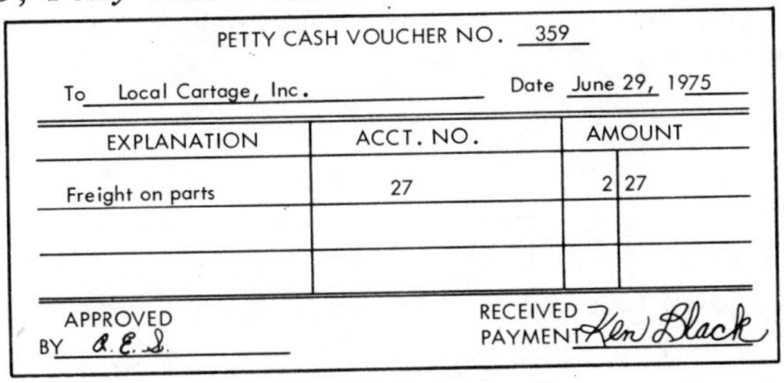
PETTY CASH VOUCHER NO. 359

To Local Cartage, Inc. Date June 29, 1975

EXPLANATION	ACCT. NO.	AMOUNT
Freight on parts	27	2 27

APPROVED BY A. E. S.

RECEIVED PAYMENT Ken Black

If the recipient of the cash disbursed can furnish an invoice, it should be stapled to the petty cash voucher. Thus, the petty cash cashier at all times is accountable for cash and petty cash vouchers totaling to the amount of the fund.

Is each of the following statements correct or incorrect?

1. Each disbursement from the petty cash fund should be supported by a petty cash voucher.
2. The creation of a petty cash fund does not require a journal entry to reflect the transfer of funds out of the general Cash account.
3. At any time, the sum of the cash in the petty cash fund and the total of the petty cash vouchers should equal the total amount for which the petty cash fund was established.
4. With the establishment of an imprest petty cash fund, one person is given the authority and responsibility for issuing checks to cover minor cash disbursements.

Turn to Answer Frame 13^{6} on page 260 to check your answers.

Frame 14^{6}

Replenishing the fund

Whenever the balance in the petty cash fund is at a relatively low level it is replenished. Each time the fund is to be replenished it is checked

Answer frame 13[6]

1. Correct. Each petty cash disbursement should be supported by a petty cash voucher in order to maintain effective control over the operation of the fund.
2. Incorrect. The creation of a petty cash fund does involve a transfer of funds out of the general Cash account, and the journal entry must reflect the transfer.
3. Correct. This is one of the means used to maintain internal control over the operation of the petty cash fund.
4. Incorrect. The purpose of an imprest petty cash fund is to provide a means for making small payments in coin and currency. The petty cash disbursements are not made by check.

If you missed any of the above, reread Frame 13[6] before starting Frame 14[6] on page 259.

14[6] *continued*

for accuracy. The total of the actual cash on hand is added to the total of the various petty cash vouchers, and this total should equal the amount of the fund. The person (someone other than the petty cash cashier) who examines the fund for accuracy should also review the vouchers to see that all disbursements appear to be for legitimate purposes. Thus, control is introduced in two ways: the cash and vouchers must sum to a known amount, and the expense vouchers are audited periodically by someone other than the person making the disbursements.

After the fund has been audited, or as part of the audit, the petty cash vouchers are separated and summarized according to the purpose of the expenditure. A check is drawn, payable to the cashier of the fund, for the amount of the vouchers and is charged to the various expense accounts (and occasionally other accounts) indicated by the summarization previously made.

To illustrate, assume that when summarized, the vouchers in a given fund show petty cash fund expenditures of $22.75 chargeable to transportation-in, $50.80 for postage stamps, and $19.05 chargeable to delivery expense, for a total of $92.60. A check in that amount would be drawn, payable to the cashier of the fund, and would be charged to the accounts indicated above. The entry would read:

Transportation-In	22.75	
Stamps and Stationery	50.80	
Delivery Expense	19.05	
Cash		92.60
To record check drawn to replenish petty cash fund.		

After the check for $92.60 has been endorsed and cashed and the money placed in the petty cash box, the fund is restored to the established amount, $100.

After the petty cash vouchers have been audited and approved and the fund replenished, they should be stamped or mutilated so that they cannot be reused.

Indicate whether each of the following statements is correct or incorrect.

1. Entries to record the replenishment of the petty cash fund result in debits to the various expense accounts and a credit to the Petty Cash account.
2. The amount of coin and currency in the petty cash fund is the same before the fund is reimbursed as it is afterward.
3. The balance in the Petty Cash ledger account is the same before the petty cash fund is reimbursed as it is after.

Now turn to Answer Frame 14[6] on page 262 to check your answers.

Frame 15[6]

At the end of the accounting period it is necessary to bring all expenses for the period into the accounts for earnings determination purposes and for proper statement of financial position reporting. Therefore, at the end of the year, if the fund is not at the established amount, the following entry should be made:

Various expense accounts	xxx	
Petty Cash		xxx

The amount of the entry is for the total of the expense vouchers in the petty cash fund. The statement of financial position at the end of the period will show a petty cash balance of less than the imprest amount as a separately listed current asset or as part of one total representing all of the company's cash balances.

Assuming that additional expenditures have been paid out of the petty cash fund prior to its replenishment in the following period, the journal entry to record the replenishment would read as follows:

Various expense accounts	xxx	
Petty Cash	xxx	
Cash		xxx

The Petty Cash account will be debited for the amount for which it was credited in the adjusting journal entry made at the end of the preceding accounting period.

Answer frame 14⁶

1. Incorrect. Entries to record the replenishment of petty cash do not result in the Petty Cash account being credited. The general Cash account is credited, since this is the source of the funds for reimbursing petty cash.
2. Incorrect. The amount of coin and currency in the petty cash fund is smaller before the fund is replenished than after. In fact, this is the reason for replenishing the fund.
3. Correct. As illustrated in Frame 14⁶, no entries are made in the Petty Cash account for disbursements or reimbursements, so the ledger account balance remains unchanged.

If you missed any of the above, reread Frame 14⁶ before starting Frame 15⁶ on page 261.

15⁶
continued

Assume a petty cash fund of $50 has been established by a firm. The fund is replenished at a time when it contains petty cash vouchers amounting to $12 for office supplies and $18 for delivery expenses. Which of the following entries properly reflects the drawing of a check to replenish the fund?

1.	Office Supplies Expense	12	
	Delivery Expense	18	
	Petty Cash		30
2.	Petty Cash	30	
	Cash		30
3.	Office Supplies Expense	12	
	Delivery Expense	18	
	Cash		30
4.	Petty Cash	30	
	Office Supplies Expense		12
	Delivery Expense		18

Now turn to Answer Frame 15⁶ on page 264 to check your answer.

Frame 16⁶

Temporary investments

At times a company may find that it has cash which is temporarily in excess of that needed for current operations. When this occurs the company is reluctant to leave those funds in a bank checking account which pays no interest. Other resting places can be found which may be as safe or almost as safe and yet pay a return. Before utilizing any of these means of earning a return on temporarily excess cash, one should consider three factors—safety (against loss), liquidity (getting the money immediately when it is needed), and rate of return.

Time deposit-type accounts

A company may choose to leave the cash in a bank or savings and loan institution, but in a savings account which will earn a rate of return. In the early 1970s, commercial bank time deposit accounts paid between 4 and 5 percent interest, and savings and loan accounts around 5 percent interest. (These rates are subject to change and are used for illustrative purposes only.) These outlets for temporary investment are very safe when the amount in any one account is not in excess of $20,000, since they are insured by an agency of the federal government up to that amount. But there can be a liquidity problem. The bank or savings and loan institution can require notification and impose a waiting period before funds can be withdrawn. They normally do not do this except in a period of unforeseen crisis (such as when a large number of depositors all want to withdraw their deposits over a short period of time).

When the company is notified of the interest it has earned, the following entry should be prepared (assume $200 interest has been earned):

Cash—Savings Account	200	
Interest Revenue		200
To record interest credited to our account at the Citizens' Federal Bank.		

Short-term marketable securities

Short-term marketable-securities include certificates of deposit, 91-day Treasury bills, Treasury tax anticipation notes, commercial paper of other companies, and other federal, state, and local governmental securities.

Certificates of deposit are purchased at a bank or savings and loan institution, and in the early 1970s paid 5½ to 7½ percent interest, in comparison to ordinary time deposits. They normally are in $1,000 or larger denominations, and the money must be left on deposit for a minimum period of time (for example, three months or two years) in order to earn the stipulated rate of interest. The rate of interest varies with the amount invested and the time to maturity. For example, in late 1973 a major savings and loan institution which paid 5¼ percent interest on regular deposit accounts offered three-month certificates at 5¾ (no minimum amount), one-year certificates at 6½ ($1,000 minimum), and four-year $1,000 certificates at 7½ percent. True annual rates also vary slightly upward when such interest is compounded quarterly, or even daily. Safety and rate of return are at least as good as with regular time deposits, but liquidity may be a problem in that the waiting period for withdrawal of the funds is longer.

Purchases of 91-day Treasury bills may also be made from commercial banks. These bills are normally issued at a discount (at an amount less

Answer frame 15[6]

The third entry is the proper one for the reimbursement of the petty cash fund. It properly records the expense amounts and reduces general cash. Petty Cash would only be credited if the fund were not replenished at the end of an accounting period.

If you answered incorrectly, reread Frame 15[6] before starting Frame 16[6] on page 262.

16[6] *continued* than face value) and collected at face value, with the difference being interest revenue. For instance, assume that 91-day Treasury bills having a $20,000 face value are acquired at $19,600 on January 1, 1975. The entries required to account for the transaction would be:

1975			
Jan. 1	Marketable Securities—91-Day Treasury Bills.......	19,600	
	Cash..		19,600
Apr. 4	Cash..	20,000	
	Marketable Securities—91-Day Treasury Bills...		19,600
	Interest Revenue............................		400

If a statement of financial position date occurred before the bills matured, it would be necessary to prepare an adjusting entry debiting Marketable Securities—91-Day Treasury Bills and crediting Interest Revenue for the amount of interest earned to that date. This situation is illustrated later when commercial paper is discussed.

Tax anticipation securities are also issued by the U.S. Treasury. They are purchased at a discount, mature shortly after the quarterly due date for corporate income taxes, and are accepted at face value when used to pay these taxes. The accounting for these transactions is similar to that illustrated for the 91-day Treasury bills. Both of these investments provide safety, a fair degree of liquidity, and a reasonable rate of return which varies according to supply and demand conditions in the money markets.

Longer term U.S. government securities may be purchased, but there is greater risk if they must be liquidated before their maturity date. As interest rates fluctuate in the money market, the current market prices of these securities fluctuate. Assume that a given security has an interest rate of 5 percent and is selling at face amount ($10,000). If the market rate of interest then goes up to 7 percent, investors would be willing to pay less than $10,000 for this security since the amount it pays is fixed at 5 percent. Thus, market prices vary inversely with the market rate of interest. A given company may have to take a substantial loss in order to obtain its funds when it needs them. It is much more common for companies with temporarily idle cash to stay with 91-day Treasury bills and to "roll them over" (acquire new ones every 91 days) than it is to purchase the longer term government securities.

Commercial paper (a short-term note) is also available as a temporary investment. This is a form of debt issued by other companies. The rate on high-grade commercial paper is only slightly higher than that on 91-day Treasury bills. It is not as safe as U.S. government securities, but safety and rate of return vary depending on the company issuing it. These notes can be sold at any time before maturity, but there is risk of loss since the market prices vary inversely with the market rate of interest. Illustrative of this type of security was the commercial paper issued in 1973 by one major U.S. corporation. Purchasers of these notes had to invest at least $25,000 and could specify any maturity date they wished. The note was written for the maturity value (that is, the interest was included in the face of the note).

To illustrate this situation, assume that a company sends a check for $47,000 to Apex Corporation to purchase commercial paper with a maturity value of $50,000. The note signed by Apex, payable to the company, is dated June 30 and is due in one year. The entries required to reflect the transactions (assuming a December 31 accounting year-end) are:

1975			
June 30	Marketable Securities—Apex notes	47,000	
	Cash		47,000
Dec. 31	Marketable Securities—Apex notes	1,500	
	Interest Revenue		1,500
1976			
June 30	Cash	50,000	
	Marketable Securities—Apex notes		48,500
	Interest Revenue		1,500

The adjusting entry on December 31, 1975, is necessary to record the interest earned through that date and to assign it to the proper year (1975). On the statement of financial position dated December 31, 1975, the Apex commercial paper would be shown as follows:

Current Assets:	
Cash	$ xxx
Marketable securities (at cost plus discount earned to date—which approximates market value)	48,500
Accounts receivable	xxx
Inventories	xxx

A company may also choose to invest in securities issued by states and municipalities. Obligations of states and municipalities are generally tax-free that is, any interest revenue is exempt from federal income taxes. Because of this desirable feature, the interest rates tend to be quite low. These securities are not as safe as U.S. government securities, but the degree of risk depends on who issues them. They may be resold in the market before maturity, but once again there is risk of loss since market prices fluctuate.

Determine whether each of the following statements is true or false.

1. Time deposit-type accounts are very safe, pose no liquidity problem, and earn a high rate of return.
2. Certificates of deposit may not be a good vehicle for short-term investment of seasonally idle cash.
3. When marketable securities are purchased at a discount and are collected at face value, the difference between these two amounts eventually becomes interest revenue.
4. Commercial paper paying a 7 percent rate of interest is necessarily more desirable than City of Baltimore bonds yielding 5 percent.

Now turn to Answer Frame 16[6] on page 268 to check your answers.

Frame 17[6]

Stock investments

Sometimes companies invest in the stocks of other companies. Such investments may actually consist of marketable securities in that the stocks may be readily marketable. But these are rarely purchased as temporary investments of idle cash. When acquired, they are more likely to be either long-term investments or an attempt to speculate in the stock market.

The long-term reasons for investing in the securities of others include the desire (1) to establish an affiliation with another business, (2) to acquire control over another business, or (3) to secure a continuing stream of revenue from the investment over a period of years.

Reporting securities in the statement of financial position

The generally stated guides as to how securities should be classified in the statement of financial position tend to emphasize intent and may be summarized as follows.

(1) If the securities held are readily marketable, they should be shown as current assets if they *will* be converted into cash in the normal operating cycle of the business. If they will not be converted, they should be considered noncurrent assets and reported in the investments section of the statement.

(2) If the securities are not readily marketable, they may not be classified as current assets, unless they mature in the coming operating cycle and there is no doubt as to their redemption.

The primary classification criterion is the intent of management.

Valuation of securities held

Cost basis. For investments in common stock which represent less than 20 percent of the outstanding shares of the issuing company or for bonds, the most common basis of valuation is cost, whether they are classified as current assets or long-term investments. Cost usually consists of price paid plus broker's commission. This is true even for those securities for which a ready alternative—market value—exists. An exception to this practice is found when a substantial and apparently permanent decline in the value of the securities has occurred. Then these investments are written down to market by debiting Loss on Market Decline of Securities and crediting either Marketable Securities or Investments, whichever is applicable.

Once securities have been written down, it is considered tantamount to recognizing unrealized revenue to write them back up even to their original cost should market prices advance in the future. Gain or loss is simply recorded for the difference between the sales proceeds and the amounts at which the securities are carried in the accounts when they are sold.

Equity basis. When a company holds 20 percent or more of the voting stock (common stock) of another company, it normally has the ability to exercise significant influence over the operations of that company. In situations where ownership is between 20 and 50 percent, the company is required[1] to use the equity method of accounting for its investment. Under the equity method, the investor initially records the investment at cost and then adjusts the carrying amount to recognize his share of the other company's earnings or losses after the date of acquisition. The receipt of dividends reduces the carrying value. We shall not deal with this method further in this text. We shall assume that investments in the common stock of others represent less than 20 percent of the outstanding shares.

Entry to record acquisition

When the common or preferred stocks of other corporations are acquired, they should be recorded at cost, which is the cash outlay or the fair value of the asset given in exchange. Since the stock acquired will usually be purchased from another investor through a broker, cost will normally consist of the price paid for the stock plus a commission to the broker. For example, assume that Brewer Corporation purchased 1,000 shares of Cowen Corporation common stock at $15 per share through a broker who charged $100 for his services in acquiring the stock. Brewer would record the transaction as follows:

Stock Investments..................................	15,100	
Cash..		15,100
To record purchase of 1,000 shares of Cowen common at $15 plus $100 brokers' commission.		

Cash dividends on investments. The usual accounting procedure followed in recording the receipt of dividends on stock investments is to debit Cash and credit Dividend Revenue when the cash dividend check

[1] Accounting Principles Board, "The Equity Method of Accounting for Investments in Common Stock," *Opinion 18* (New York: AICPA, March 1971).

Answer frame 16[6]

1. False. They are very safe in amounts up to $20,000, may pose a liquidity problem in times of crisis, and earn only a moderate rate of return.
2. True. Generally the funds must remain invested for a minimum period of time, such as 3 months to 4 years. With seasonally idle cash, time periods such as these may be too long. And a penalty in the form of a reduced interest rate is often exacted for "getting out early."
3. True. For instance, if 91-day Treasury bills are purchased for $9,800 and collected at $10,000, the interest revenue recognized will be $200.
4. False. Interest earned on commercial paper is subject to federal income tax, while interest earned on state and municipal securities is not. Also, the commercial paper may be riskier than the municipal bonds.

If you missed any of the above, reread Frame 16[6] before going on to Frame 17[6] on page 266.

17[6]
continued

is actually received. This is the method of accounting for dividends which is acceptable for tax purposes and is widely followed by investors.

An alternative will be required when a dividend is declared in one accounting period which will not be paid until the following period. Assume that the Cowen Corporation declared a cash dividend of 20 cents per share on December 1, 1975, payable on January 15, 1976, to stockholders of record as of December 20, 1975. Under these circumstances an entry should be made either on December 20 or as an adjusting entry on December 31 as follows:

Dividends Receivable	200	
Dividend Revenue		200
To record dividend of 20 cents per share on Cowen common stock due January 15, 1976.		

When the dividend is collected on January 15, the entry would be a debit to Cash and a credit to the Dividends Receivable account. In this manner the dividend is recorded as revenue in the period in which it is earned.

Stock dividends and stock splits. A stock dividend consists of the distribution by a corporation of additional shares of its stock to its stockholders. Usually the distribution consists of additional common stock to common stockholders. Such a distribution is not considered to be a revenue-producing transaction to the holders of the stock. A stock dividend is viewed simply as having the effect of dividing the stockholders' equity into a larger number of smaller pieces. It simply increases the number of shares a stockholder holds, but it does not change his percentage of ownership of the outstanding shares.

Thus, the accounting for stock dividends consists only of a notation in the accounts of the number of shares received and a change in the average per share cost of the shares held. For example, if 100 shares of A Company common stock are held, which cost $22 per share, and the A Company distributes a 10 percent stock dividend, the number of shares held is increased to 110 and the cost per share is now $20 ($2,200 ÷ 110 shares = $20 per share).

Similarly, when a corporation splits its stock, the only accounting entry required is a notation indicating the receipt of the additional shares. If Smith Company owned 1,000 shares of Jones Company common stock and Jones Company split its stock on a two-for-one basis, Smith would own 2,000 shares after the split and the cost per share would be halved.

Sale of stock investments. When stock holdings are sold, the gain or loss on the sale is the difference between the net proceeds received and the carrying value of the shares sold. Assume, for example, that 100 shares of Thacker Company common stock are sold for $75 per share. The broker deducted his commission and other taxes and charges of $62 prior to making remittance to the seller. If the seller's cost was $5,000, the required entry is:

Cash	7,438	
Stock Investments		5,000
Gain on Sale of Investments		2,438

The gain on sale of investments is shown in the earnings statement.

A company can also invest in the bonds of others. If these are marketable securities and will be converted into cash within the normal operating cycle, they should be carried at cost (unless there is a dramatic and seemingly permanent decline in their market value). Interest earned on these obligations will result in a credit to Interest Revenue. Any difference between carrying value and proceeds received upon sale should be recognized as a gain or loss. Chapter 10 deals extensively with bond investments as long-term assets. Much of the discussion in that chapter relates to bonds as temporary investments also. Thus, the discussion here has been kept to a minimum.

Decide whether each of the following statements is correct or incorrect.

1. If securities are readily marketable, they should be reported as current assets.
2. Securities should be reported at the lower of cost or market each time financial statements are prepared.
3. If a company holds more than 20 percent of the outstanding shares of a company, it might report this investment at an amount greater than cost.
4. Cash dividends received result in dividend revenue, but stock dividends received do not.

Now turn to Answer Frame 17[6] on page 270 to check your answers.

Summary *chapter* 6

Information on cash position and cash movement supplied by the accounting system is used by management in fulfilling its cash management

Answer frame 17[6]

1. Incorrect. Only if they will be converted into cash within the normal operating cycle of the business should they be shown as marketable securities among current assets. If they will not be converted within that time, they should be reported among noncurrent assets in the investments section. The primary classification criterion is the intent of management.
2. Incorrect. Only when a substantial and apparently permanent decline in the value of the securities has occurred should they be written down to market. Cost is the normal basis for carrying investments (for common stock which represents less than 20 percent of the outstanding shares of the issuing company or for bonds).
3. Correct. In situations where a company owns between 20 and 50 percent of the outstanding shares, it is required by APB *Opinion 18* to use the equity method of accounting for its investment. If the company in which it has invested has been profitable since acquisition, the investment would be carried at an amount greater than cost (assuming dividends have not exceeded earnings during this period). If the investment has been unprofitable, or if dividends received have exceeded a proportionate share of earnings, it would be carried at less than cost.
4. Correct. Cash dividends received are viewed as revenue, but stock dividends are not. A stock dividend simply increases the number of shares a stockholder holds but does not change his percentage of ownership of the outstanding shares.

If you missed any of the above, reread Frame 17[6] before turning to the chapter summary, page 269.

---

function and by outsiders in appraising the overall financial position of a business organization.

Adequate control over receipts and disbursements is necessary to protect cash. Defalcations are quite numerous and often involve stealing cash when it is flowing in or out of the business.

The balance on the monthly statement presented by the bank showing the activity in a checking account will usually differ from the balance maintained in the ledger account. The usual causes of this difference are outstanding checks, deposits in transit, and bank service charges which have not been recorded by the depositor. A statement should be prepared reconciling these differences. An entry is often needed to record items uncovered in reconciling the two amounts.

A company operating in many widely scattered locations may establish transfer accounts in local banks which require the immediate forwarding by the bank of any funds in excess of a stated amount to a central bank. There the funds can be quickly invested if not needed for other purposes.

Control over payroll checks is often established, at least in part, through use of a separate payroll checking account. The location of errors is also facilitated if the possible thousands of payroll checks are not intermingled with other checks in one account.

To overcome the inconvenience of writing checks for minor disbursements such as taxi fares, stamps, and delivery charges, a petty cash fund may be established and maintained on an imprest basis for control purposes. Vouchers are required to support disbursements made. Control is exercised through ascertaining that the balance in the fund and the sum of the vouchers paid is equal to the amount at which the fund is carried in the ledger and through audit of the petty cash vouchers.

When a company has cash in excess of that needed for current operations, it may decide to invest these funds in deposit accounts in a bank or savings and loan institution. Or it may decide to invest in temporary short-term securities such as certificates of deposit, 91-day Treasury bills, Treasury tax anticipation notes, commercial paper of other companies, or other government securities. Each of these sources of investment has certain characteristics regarding safety, liquidity, and rate of return which may make it more attractive than others in a given situation.

Stock investments are rarely purchased as temporary investments but rather are purchased for long-term reasons of affiliation, control, or to secure revenue over a period of years. Such securities are normally carried at cost. Cash dividends, stock dividends, and stock splits may be received on these investments.

To complete your review of this chapter study the terms in the Glossary which follows. Then go on to the Student Review Quiz for a self-administered test of your comprehension of the material in this chapter.

Glossary *chapter* 6 ✓

Bank reconciliation statement—a statement which shows the items and amounts which cause a bank's record of a depositor's account balance to differ from the depositor's record.

Bank service charges—amounts deducted by a bank from a depositor's account as payment for services rendered, usually checks paid or deposits processed.

Cashier's check—a written order drawn on a bank by an official of the bank to pay a specific amount of money to a designated party; a check in which the drawer and drawee are the same.

Checking account statement—a statement issued (usually monthly) by a bank describing the activities in a depositor's checking account.

Demand deposit—a balance maintained with a bank subject to withdrawal on demand; a checking account balance.

Deposit receipt—a written acknowledgment of the receipt of a deposit by a bank. It may be in the form of a stamped or initialed copy of the deposit ticket or a separate machine-imprinted receipt.

Deposit ticket—a document showing the name and number of the account into which the deposit is made, the date, and the items comprised in the deposit.

Deposit in transit—cash receipts of a depositor recorded as receipts in one month but recorded as a deposit by the bank in a succeeding month.

Deposit-type accounts—time deposit accounts with commercial banks and saving and loan institutions which earn interest on the balance.

Dividends—amounts paid to owners of the shares of stock of a corporation. These are usually paid in cash (called cash dividends) or in additional shares of stock (called stock dividends).

Marketable securities (short-term)—securities which can and will be converted into cash within one year or one current operating cycle, whichever is longer. Included among these securities are certificates of deposit, 91-day Treasury bills, Treasury tax anticipation notes, commercial paper of other companies, and other governmental securities.

Money order—a written promise on the part of the U.S. postal system or an express company that it will pay a specified sum of money to a designated party upon demand.

Outstanding checks—checks issued by a depositor which have not yet been paid by the bank upon which drawn.

Petty cash fund—a usually nominal sum of money established as a separate fund from which minor cash disbursements for valid business purposes are to be made. When established on an *imprest* basis, the cash in the fund plus the vouchers covering disbursements must always equal the balance at which the fund was established and at which it is carried in the ledger accounts.

Remittance advice—a form attached to a check informing the payee why the drawer of the check is making this payment.

Stock investments—purchases of stock securities issued by other companies.

Stock split—a division by which the owner of stock of a corporation receives some multiple of the number of shares he currently holds in place of the original shares. For instance, Mr. X might receive 2,000 shares of Corporation B's shares in place of the 1,000 shares he formerly held.

Temporary investments—deposit-type accounts and marketable securities (see the definitions of those terms).

Transfer bank account—a bank account controlled by special instructions which require the bank to forward immediately any funds in excess of a stated amount to a central bank.

Student review quiz *chapter 6*

To develop a permanent record of your responses you may write them on the answer sheet provided in the *Work Papers* or on a separate sheet of paper.

1 Which of the following statements is false?

a) Effective cash management includes safeguarding cash from loss.

b) Effective cash management embraces supplying sufficient cash to prevent disruptions of normal operations due to a cash shortage.

c) Stockholders need a more detailed classification of cash than does top management.

d) Management seeks to avoid the accumulation of excessive amounts of idle cash because such cash produces no earnings.

e) The establishment of effective controls over petty cash is a part of the plan of effective cash management.

2 Which of the following items is *not* classifiable as cash in the current asset section of the statement of financial position?

a) Undeposited checks.

b) Savings accounts.

c) Time certificates of deposit.

d) Demand certificates of deposit.

e) None of the above would be excluded.

3 Which of the following situations is *not* desirable in establishing a system of internal control over cash?

a) The bookkeeper secures the daily totals from the cash registers.

b) The person who opens the mail and lists the cash remittances also reads the totals from the cash registers.

c) The person who totals the sales tickets and reads the cash registers also prepares the monthly bank reconciliation statement.

d) The bookkeeper prepares the bank reconciliation statement.

e) The person who signs the checks issued by the company prepares the bank reconciliation statement.

4 Which of the following are desirable procedures to follow in the management and control of cash?

a) The person who authorizes payment of invoices should not be the one who signs the checks.

b) The cashier should not record the cash receipts in the customers' accounts.

c) The function of receiving cash should be separated from the function of disbursing cash.

d) All checks should be prenumbered consecutively.

e) All of the above.

5 The bank reconciliation statement—

a) Has as its basic purpose the disclosing of errors made by the bank in accounting for the depositor's funds.

b) Is prepared monthly by the bank for each of its depositors.
c) Begins with the balance per the bank statement and the balance per the ledger for cash and reconciles both balances with the adjusted ledger balance.
d) Need not be prepared when a daily bank statement is prepared.
e) Serves no useful purpose in the system of internal control over cash.

6 Which of the following items must be deducted from the bank statement balance in preparing a bank reconciliation statement which ends with adjusted cash balance?

a) Bank service charges.
b) Outstanding checks.
c) Checks returned marked "not sufficient funds."
d) Deposits in transit.
e) Notes collected by the bank for the depositor.
f) None of the above.

7 Given the following information for N. Parkinson & Company, determine which of the journal entries shown is necessary to adjust the Cash account balance.

Balance per bank statement, October 31, 1975	$22,220
Balance per Cash account in ledger, October 31, 1975	13,993
Outstanding checks at October 31, 1975	13,000
Deposit in transit dated September 30, 1975	1,525
Deposit in transit dated October 31, 1975	3,670
Bank service charges for October	3
Check from a customer returned by bank marked N.S.F.	1,100

a)	Accounts Receivable	1,100	
	Cash in Bank		1,100
b)	Accounts Receivable	1,100	
	Bank Service Charges	3	
	Cash in Bank		1,103
c)	Cash in Bank	3,670	
	Accounts Receivable		3,670
d)	Cash in Bank	1,103	
	Accounts Receivable		1,100
	Bank Service Charges		3
e)	None of the above.		

8 The accountant for the Anselman Company was able to prepare the bank reconciliation statement for August 31, 1975, using the unadjusted ledger balance for cash and the following information:

Deposit in transit	$1,200
Balance per bank statement	2,750
Bank service charges	5
Checks outstanding	1,625
N.S.F. check returned	500
Deposit of $550 recorded by company as $505	45

What must have been the unadjusted balance in the Cash account in the ledger?

a) $2,325.
b) $2,875.
c) $2,830.
d) $3,630.
e) None of the above.

9 The Petty Cash account is debited—

a) Only when the fund is established.
b) When the fund is established and every time it is replenished.
c) When the fund is established and when the size of the fund is increased.
d) When the fund is established and when the size of the fund is decreased.
e) When the fund is established, replenished, or increased in size.

10 J. F. Knauf Company employs an imprest petty cash fund in the amount of $100. On August 14, a count of the fund discloses the following:

Voucher for postage stamps	$18
Vouchers for transportation-in	36
Vouchers for sales returns	23
Currency	11
Coins	9
Total	$97

The correct entry to record replenishing the fund is:

a)	Postage Expense	18	
	Transportation-In	36	
	Sales Returns and Allowances	23	
	Accounts Payable		77
b)	Postage Expense	18	
	Transportation-In	36	
	Sales Returns and Allowances	23	
	Cash Short and Over	3	
	Cash in Bank		80
c)	Petty Cash	80	
	Cash in Bank		80

d) Postage Expense..........	18	
Transportation-In.........	36	
Sales Returns and Allowances..................	23	
Cash Short and Over..		3
Cash in Bank.........		74
e) Postage Expense..........	18	
Transportation-In.........	36	
Sales Returns and Allowances..................	23	
Cash in Bank.........		77

11 Which of the following statements is false?

a) A certified check is a liability of the bank certifying it.
b) A certified check will be accepted by many persons who would not otherwise accept a personal check.
c) A certified check is one drawn by a bank upon itself.
d) A certified check which has not been returned with the canceled checks at the end of the month need not be included in the outstanding checks.

12 Which one of the following temporary investments could not result in Interest Revenue being credited?

a) Time deposit in a commercial bank.
b) 91-day Treasury bills.
c) Andrews Company capital stock.
d) Baxter Company commercial paper.
e) Certificates of deposit.

13 Which of the following statements regarding temporary investments is false?

a) Time deposit accounts are insured against loss up to a certain amount by the federal government.
b) Long-term commercial paper may be held by a company as a short-term marketable security.
c) Treasury tax anticipation notes are purchased at a discount and may be used to pay corporate income taxes.
d) There is little or no risk of loss when long-term commercial paper is held for short-term purposes, since one can always wait and realize the maturity value.
e) Short-term marketable securities usually are carried at cost unless there has been a substantial and apparently permanent decline in the value of the securities.

14 On August 8, Sugar Candy Company acquired 300 shares of Standard Manufacturing $80 par value capital stock at $98 per share plus a brokerage commission of $700. The proper entry to record this transaction is:

a) Investment in Stock—Standard Mfg......	30,100	
Cash........		30,100
b) Investment in Stock—Standard Mfg......	29,400	
Stock Acquisition Expense.......	700	
Cash........		30,100
c) Investment in Stock—Standard Mfg......	24,000	
Premium on Stock of Standard Mfg......	5,400	
Stock Acquisition Expense.......	700	
Cash........		30,100
d) Investment in Stock—Standard Mfg......	24,000	
Premium on Stock of Standard Mfg......	6,100	
Cash........		30,100
e) Investment in Stock—Standard Mfg......	24,700	
Premium on Stock of Standard Mfg......	5,400	
Cash........		30,100

15 Jefferson Plywood Company holds 500 shares of the capital stock of United Electric Company. On December 1, 1975, United declared a cash dividends of $3 per share and a stock dividend of 10 percent, both payable on January 15, 1976, to stockholders of record on December 27, 1975. At the date of declaration, the stock of United was selling in the market at $60 per share. Jefferson Plywood Company must make which of the following entries before closing the books for 1975 to reflect these dividends?

a) No entry required.		
b) Cash..............	1,500	
Dividend Revenue.....		1,500
c) Cash..............	1,500	
Dividend Revenue.....		1,500
Stock Investments..	3,000	
Dividend Revenue.....		3,000
d) Dividends Receivable	1,500	
Dividend Revenue.....		1,500

e) Dividends Receivable 4,500
Dividend Revenue..... 4,500

Now compare your answers with the correct answers and explanations on page 711.

Questions *chapter 6*

1 What are the three objectives sought in effective cash management?
2 Cite four essential features in a system of internal control over cash receipts.
3 The bookkeeper of a given company was stealing remittances received from customers in payment of their accounts. To cover his abstractions, he made out false credit memoranda indicating returns and allowances made by or granted to the customers. What feature of a system of internal control, if operative, would have prevented this defalcation?
4 Cite six essential features in a system of internal control over cash disbursements.
5 The difference between a company's Cash ledger account balance and the balance in the bank statement is usually a matter of timing. Do you agree or disagree? Why?
6 Indicate the manner in which a payroll bank account is operated.
7 Indicate the method of operation of and the advantages obtained through the use of an imprest petty cash fund. Be sure to indicate exactly how control is effected through the use of the imprest system.
8 Why might a company's management wish to determine the cash position daily?
9 Explain how the use of transfer bank accounts can bring about effective cash management.
10 Discuss the alternatives a company has to leaving temporarily idle cash in a checking account.
11 If certificates of deposit generally pay a higher rate of interest than deposit-type accounts, why does anyone leave his money in a time deposit account?
12 What risk is there in making a temporary investment in marketable securities, such as commercial paper, which matures in the distant future (over one year from date of purchase)?
13 Explain the main problem encountered in classifying marketable securities in the statement of financial position.
14 The December 31, 1975, statement of financial position of the BMI Corporation shows, under a section heading entitled "investments and advances," U.S. government securities (at cost less amortized premium) in the amount of $100,780. What might be the reason for classifying these securities as "investments" rather than as "current assets"?
15 Explain briefly the accounting for stock dividends and stock splits from the investor's point of view.

Exercises *chapter 6*

1 The Howard Company's Cash account balance was $70,175 at the end of August. The bank statement showed a balance of $68,600 for the same date. Checks outstanding totaled $21,000, and deposits in transit totaled $30,500. If these are the only pertinent data available to you, what was the correct amount of cash against which the Howard Company could have written checks as of the end of August?
2 From the following data prepare a bank reconciliation statement and determine the correct available cash balance for the Folkers Company as of October 31, 1975:

Balance per bank statement, October 31, 1975	$4,658
Ledger account balance	3,676
Note collected by bank not yet entered in ledger	1,000
Bank charges not yet entered by Folkers Company	6
Deposit in transit	560
Outstanding checks:	
No. 327	128
No. 328	96
No. 329	240
No. 331	84

3 From the following information for the Faubus Company:
a) Prepare a bank reconciliation statement as of September 30, 1975.
b) Give the necessary journal entries to correct the Cash account.

Balance per bank statement, September 30, 1975	$16,300
Ledger account balance as of September 30, 1975	14,650
Note collected by bank	1,000
Bank charges	10
Deposits in transit	924
N.S.F. check deposited and returned	84
Check of Faubis Company deducted in error	$ 50
Outstanding checks	1,718

4 As of March 1 of the current year the Venturi Company had outstanding checks of $15,000. During March the company issued an additional $57,000 of checks. As of March 31 the bank statement showed that $51,000 of checks had cleared the bank during the month. What is the amount of outstanding checks as of March 31?

5 The Foster Company's bank statement as of August 31, 1975 shows total deposits into the company's account of $25,670 and a total of 14 deposits. On July 31 deposits of $1,350 and $1,050 were in transit. The total cash receipts for August amounted to $26,375 and the company's records show 13 deposits made in August. What is the amount of deposits in transit at August 31?

6 On August 31, 1975, the Blake Company's petty cash fund contained:

Coin and currency	$42.50
IOU from office boy	5.00
Vouchers covering expenditures for:	
Postage	20.00
Taxi fares	8.50
Entertainment of a customer	23.00

The Petty Cash account shows a balance of $100. If financial statements are prepared for each calendar month, what journal entry is required on August 31?

7 Use the data in Exercise 6 above. If the fund were replenished on August 31, 1975, what journal entry would be required?

8 On March 1, 1975, $10,000 face value, 91-day Treasury bills are acquired at $9,810. Give the entries required to show the purchase and the conversion back to cash on the maturity date, May 31.

9 Assume that on June 1, 1975, the Driscal Company purchased 120-day commercial paper of ABC Corporation. Maturity value is $40,000 and the paper is purchased for $39,200. Driscal's accounting year ends on July 31. Prepare entries to show the acquisition of the commercial paper, the necessary adjusting entry on July 31, and the conversion back to cash on the maturity date, September 29.

10 Book Company purchased on July 1, 1975, 100 shares of Case Company capital stock at $47 per share plus a commission of $50. On July 15 a 10 percent stock dividend was received. Book received a cash dividend of 50 cents per share on August 12, 1975. On November 1 Book sold all of the above shares for $58 per share, less commissions and taxes of $55. Prepare entries to record all of the above in Book Company's accounts.

Problems, Series A *chapter* 6

6–1–A

The bank statement for Williams Company's account with the First National Bank for the month ended April 14, 1975, showed a balance of $6,886. On this date the company's Cash account balance was $5,527. Returned with the bank statement were (1) a debit memo for service charges of $10; (2) a debit memo for a customer's N.S.F. check of $250; and (3) a credit memo for a $2,200 wire transfer of funds on April 14 from the State Bank, the local bank used by the company's branch office. Further investigation revealed that outstanding checks amounted to $1,300, the cash receipts of April 14 of $1,621 did not appear as a deposit on the bank statement, and the canceled checks included a check for $260 (drawn by the president of the company to cover travel expenses on a recent trip) which the company has yet to record.

Required:

a) Prepare a bank reconciliation statement for the month ended April 14, 1975.
b) Prepare any necessary journal entries.

6–2–A

The following information pertains to the Guthrie Corporation. The June 30 bank reconciliation statement was:

		Cash Account	*Bank Statement*
Balances on June 30		$21,524.48	$21,744.48
Add: Deposit not credited by bank			371.40
Total			$22,115.88
Deduct: Outstanding checks:			
No. 724	$ 24.60		
No. 886	20.00		
No. 896	191.40		
No. 897	250.20		
No. 898	105.20		591.40
Adjusted Cash Balance, June 30		$21,524.48	$21,524.48

The July bank statement was as follows:

Balance on July 1		$21,744.48	
Deposits during July		6,370.52	$28,115.00
Canceled checks returned:			
No. 724	$ 24.60		
No. 896	191.40		
No. 897	250.20		
No. 898	105.20		
No. 899	25.14		
No. 900	1,914.00		
No. 902	1,262.56		
No. 904	58.68	$ 3,831.78	
N.S.F. check of Gordon Company		72.04	3,903.82
Bank Statement Balance, July 31			$24,211.18

The cash receipts deposited in July, including receipts of July 31, amounted to $7,904.40. Checks written in July:

No. 899	$ 25.14
No. 900	1,915.00
No. 901	37.00
No. 902	1,262.56
No. 903	79.60
No. 904	58.68
No. 905	1,458.00
No. 906	20.00

The cash balance per the ledger on July 31 was $24,573.90.

Required: Prepare a bank reconciliation statement and any necessary adjusting entries.

6–3–A

The following information is taken from the books and records of the White Company.

Balance per ledger, July 31, 1975	$14,242
Collections received on the last day of July and debited to "Cash in Bank" on books but not entered by bank until August	5,312
Debit memo for customer's check returned unpaid (uncollectible check is on hand but no entry for the return has been made on the books)	500
Debit memo for bank service charge for July	15
Checks issued but not paid by bank	5,034
Credit memo for proceeds of a note receivable which was left at the bank for collection but which has not been recorded on the books as collected ($8 is interest revenue)	800
Check for an account payable entered on books as $480 but issued and paid by the bank in the correct amount of $840.	
Balance per bank statement, July 31, 1975	$13,889

Required: Prepare a bank reconciliation statement and the necessary journal entries to adjust the accounts.

6–4–A

The following data for March, 1975, are summarized from the accounts of Blackwell, Inc. The accountant also acts as cashier.

Cash Receipts		*Cash Disbursements*	
Mar. 2	$1,100	Check No. 911	$ 884
4	3,200	No. 912	1,226
5	1,300	No. 913	1,458
11	2,800	No. 914	888
13	3,500	No. 915	1,614
14	4,200	No. 916	2,400
19	1,000	No. 917	3,800
20	800	No. 918	2,700
27	60	No. 919	750
29	320	No. 920	700

At March 1 the checks outstanding were:

No. 209	$ 90
No. 792	1,600
No. 796	558
No. 910	1,262

There were no deposits in transit. The balance of the Cash in Bank account per books was $12,350 at March 31. The bank statement for the month of March is as follows:

BANK STATEMENT

Date	*Checks*	*Deposits*	*Balance*
Mar. 1			14,000
3		1,100	15,100
4	884		
4	1,226		12,990
6		4,500	17,490
9	1,614		
9	888		14,988
16		10,500	25,488
19	2,400		
19	2,700		20,388
24		1,800	22,188
25	558		
25	1,262		20,368
26	3,800		
26	1,000 N.S.F.		15,568
27	1,000 D.M.		14,568
29		380	14,948
31	4 D.M.		14,944

The debit memoranda are for the payment of a company note and for the monthly service charge.

Required:

a) Prepare a bank reconciliation statement as of March 31, 1975.
b) Journalize the entry or entries necessary to correct the books.
c) Comment on the company's control of cash receipts.

6–5–A

The following information pertains to the bank reconciliation statement to be prepared for the Rocket Company as of May 31, 1975:

a) Balance per bank statement as of May 31, 1975, was $4,980.
b) Balance per the Rocket Company's Cash account at May 31, 1975, was $5,914.
c) A late deposit on May 31 did not appear on the bank statement, $950.
d) Outstanding checks as of May 31 totaled $1,100.
e) During May the bank credited Rocket Company with the proceeds, $1,510, of a note which it had collected for the company. Face of the note was $1,500.
f) Service and collection charges for the month amount to $4.
g) Comparison of the canceled checks with copies of these checks reveals that one check in the amount of $234 had been recorded in the books at $342. The check had been issued in payment of an account payable.

h) A review of the deposit slips with the bank statement showed that a deposit of $500 of Ricket and Company has been credited to the Rocket Company account.

i) A $60 check received from a customer, H. Larry, was returned with the bank statement marked N.S.F.

j) During May the bank paid a $3,000, 6 percent, 60-day note of the Rocket Company and charged it to the company's account per instructions received. Rocket Company had not recorded the payment of this note.

k) An examination of the cash receipts and the deposit tickets revealed that the bookkeeper erroneously recorded a customer's check of $324 as $432.

Required:

a) Prepare a bank reconciliation statement as of May 31, 1975.

b) Prepare the journal entries necessary to adjust the accounts as of May 31, 1975.

6–6–A

The bank reconciliation statement for the Simonds Corporation for April 30, 1975, was as follows:

		Cash Account	*Bank Statement*
Balance as of April 30, 1975		$ 62,252	$104,424
Deposit in transit			2,900
			$107,324
Outstanding checks			52,400
Service charges	$ 48		
Note paid on demand	7,280	7,328	
Adjusted Balance on April 30, 1975		$ 54,924	$ 54,924

The bank statement for May shows:

Balance, May 1, 1975		$104,424
Deposits		141,448
		$245,872
Checks cleared	$243,800	
Service charges	60	243,860
Balance, May 31, 1975		$ 2,012

The total cash receipts for May amount to $140,836. The total checks drawn amount to $155,000. This total does not include one check drawn and signed by and payable to the treasurer of the company, who has disappeared. No record of this check appears anywhere in the company's records. Checks outstanding on May 31 total $38,600.

Required:

a) Compute the balance in the Cash account as shown by the company's records, excluding the check drawn payable to the treasurer.

b) Compute the amount of receipts for May not deposited, if any.

c) Compute the amount of the check drawn payable to the treasurer.

d) Prepare a bank reconciliation statement as of May 31, 1975.

e) Prepare any required adjusting entries.

f) What one procedure, if followed, might have prevented the theft of funds by the treasurer?

6–7–A

Maywell Company employes a special checking account upon which its payroll checks are drawn. Employees are paid on the 5th and the 20th of each month the salaries earned in the preceding half-month. The following transactions occur in December:

a) A check for $1,000 is drawn and deposited in the payroll checking account to cover advances to employees and checks issued to employees whose services are terminated. The payroll checking account is to be operated on an imprest basis.
b) The payroll for the last half of November consists of the following:

Gross wages of employees		$24,200
Less: Income taxes withheld	$3,500	
FICA taxes withheld	400	3,900
Net Payroll		$20,300

c) On December 4, a check is drawn in the amount of the net payroll and deposited in the payroll checking account.
d) Payroll checks aggregating the amount of the net payroll are issued to employees.
e) A payroll check in the amount of $40 is issued to Don Proudhon as an advance on the wages he will be receiving on December 20.
f) The payroll for the first half of the month of December is the same as given above. The advance to Don Proudhon is deducted from his payroll check.
g) A general account check is drawn and deposited in the payroll account.
h) The payroll checks are issued.

Required: Present in general journal form all entries which must be journalized in the records of the Maywell Company as a result of the above transactions.

6–8–A

The following data pertain to the petty cash fund of the Nicholson Company:

Nov. 2 A $400 check is drawn, cashed, and the cash placed in the care of the assistant office manager to be used as a petty cash fund maintained on an imprest basis.

Dec. 17 The fund is replenished. An analysis of the fund shows:

Coins and currency	$ 88.27
Postage stamps	4.80
Petty cash vouchers for—	
Delivery expenses	125.65
Freight-in	174.08
Postage stamps purchased	10.00

31 The end of the accounting period falls on this date. The fund was not replenished. Its contents on this date consist of—

Coins and currency	$353.27
Petty cash vouchers for—	
Delivery expenses	28.63
Postage stamps	23.10
Employee's IOU	15.00

The assistant office manager states that included in the cash on hand is the sum of $20 which has been collected from various employees to purchase a gift for an employee who is leaving to be married.

Required: Present journal entries to record the above transactions.

6–9–A

The bank statement of the Byron Corporation's checking account with the First National Bank shows:

Balance, June 30, 1975		$19,610
Deposits		36,400
		$56,010
Less: Checks deducted	$36,000	
Service charges	10	36,010
Balance, July 31, 1975		$20,000

The following additional data are available:

a) A credit memorandum included with the canceled checks returned indicates the collection of a note by the bank for the Byron Corporation, $2,000.
b) An N.S.F. check in the amount of $920 is returned by the bank and included in the total of checks deducted on the bank statement.
c) Deposits in transit as of July 31, $5,000, and as of June 30, $2,400.
d) Checks outstanding as of June 30, all of which cleared the bank in July, $3,400; checks outstanding as of July 31, $8,200.
e) Balance per ledger account as of July 31, $14,094.
f) Deposit of Bryan Corporation credited to Byron Corporation account by bank, $2,000.
g) Check of Bryan Corporation charged against Byron Corporation account by bank, $400.
h) Deposit of July 21 recorded by the company as $637, and by the bank at actual amount of $673. The receipts for the day were from collections on account.

Required:

a) Prepare a bank reconciliation statement as of July 31, 1975, for the Byron Corporation.
b) Determine the amount of cash receipts for the month of July shown by the Byron Corporation's accounts prior to adjustment.
c) Determine the amount of checks drawn by Byron in the month of July.
d) Prepare any adjusting journal entries needed at July 31, 1975.

6–10–A

Gambrel Corporation purchased on July 2, 1973, 100 shares of White Company $50 par value capital stock at $60 per share, plus broker's commission of $60. A 20 percent stock dividend was received on December 15, 1974.

On July 15, 1975, a dividend of 60 cents per share was received. On September 15, 1975, the White Company split each of its $50 par value shares of capital stock into two $25 par value shares of capital stock.

On November 2, 1975, the Gambrel Corporation sold 100 shares of White capital stock at $40, less commissions and taxes of $28.

Required:

a) Present journal entries to record all of the 1975 transactions.
b) In light of the above information, how would you recommend that the remaining shares of stock be classified in the December 31, 1976, statement of financial position if still held at that date?

6–11–A

On September 1, 1975, Shelby Company purchased the following securities, employing seasonally idle cash:

a) $50,000 of Black Company commercial paper due January 1, 1977, at a cost of $49,200.
b) 1,000 shares of Blue Chip Company capital stock at $61 plus broker's commission of $400.
c) 500 shares of Atlas Company capital stock at $98 plus broker's commission of $350.

Cash dividends of $1.25 per share on the Blue Chip capital stock and $1 per share on the Atlas capital stock were received on December 7 and December 10, respectively.

Market prices at December 31, 1975, are Black commercial paper, 99 percent of face value; Blue Chip stock, $65; and Atlas stock, $91.

Required:

a) Prepare journal entries to record the above transactions.
b) Prepare the necessary adjusting entries at December 31, 1975, assuming each security is to be valued at cost or market, whichever is lower.
c) Explain why it is logical to expect the market value of the Black commercial paper to rise while the price of the capital stock went up in one case and down in the other.

Problems, Series B *chapter* 6

6–1–B

The bank statement for the Monmouth Company's general checking account with the First National Bank for the month ended August 12, 1975, showed an ending balance of $5,509, service charges of $10, an N.S.F. check returned of $210, and the collection of a $1,000 note plus interest of $10. Further investigation revealed that a wire transfer of $1,800 from the bank account maintained by a branch office of the company had not been recorded by the company as having been deposited in the First National Bank account. In addition, a comparison of deposits with receipts showed a deposit in transit of $2,100. Checks outstanding amounted to $1,506, while the cash ledger balance was $3,513.

Required:

a) Prepare a bank reconciliation statement for the First National Bank account for the month ended August 12, 1975.
b) Prepare all necessary journal entries.

6–2–B

The following data pertain to the Nador Company:

a) Balance per the bank statement dated June 30, 1975, is $39,760.
b) Balance of the Cash in Bank account on the company books as of June 30, 1975, is $10,980.
c) Outstanding checks as of June 30, 1975, are $24,000.
d) Bank deposit of June 30 for $3,140 was not included in the deposits per the bank statement.
e) The bank had collected a $30,000, 6 percent, 30-day note which it credited to the Nador Company account. The bank charged the company a collection fee of $20 on the above note.
f) The bank erroneously charged the Nador Company account for an $18,000 check of the Nader Company. The check was found among the canceled checks returned with the bank statement.
g) Bank service charges for June, exclusive of the collection fee, amounted to $100.
h) Among the canceled checks was one for $690 given in payment of an account. The bookkeeper had recorded the check at $960 in the company records.
i) A check of Mr. Casey, a customer, for $4,200, deposited on June 20, was returned by the bank marked N.S.F. No entry has been made to reflect the returned check on the company records.
j) A check for $1,680 of Mr. Martin, a customer, which had been deposited in the bank, was erroneously recorded by the bookkeeper as $1,860.

Required: Prepare a bank reconciliation statement as of June 30, 1975. Also prepare any necessary adjusting journal entries.

6–3–B

The following data pertain to the Bakke Company. The reconciliation statement as of June 30, 1975, showed a deposit in transit of $1,350 and three checks outstanding:

No. 553	$ 450
No. 570	900
No. 571	1,200

During July the following checks were written and entered in the Cash account:

No. 572	$1,020	No. 578	$1,350
No. 573	1,320	No. 579	1,260
No. 574	810	No. 580	180
No. 575	,500	No. 581	2,427
No. 576	1,170	No. 582	2,724
No. 577	2,121	No. 583	900

As of July 31, all the checks which were written, except No. 578, were mailed to the payees. Check No. 578 was kept in the vault pending receipt of a statement from the payee. Four deposits were made at the bank as follows:

July 7	$7,500
14	9,600
21	5,700
28	6,900

The bank statement, which was received on August 2, correctly included all deposits and showed a balance as of July 31 of $31,260. The following checks were returned: Nos. 570, 571, 572, 573, 574, 575, 576, 577, 580, and 581. With the paid checks there were three debit memoranda for:

a) Fee of $3 for the collection on July 30 of a $900 note payable to the Bakke Company for which a credit memorandum was enclosed.
b) Monthly service charge of $6.
c) Payment of $750 note of the Bakke Company.

The bank statement included a credit for $3,000 dated July 29. The bank telephoned the company on the morning of August 3 to explain that this credit was in error because it represented a transaction between the bank and the Balke Company.

The balance in the Cash account on the books of the Bakke Company after posting is $21,435.

Required: Prepare a bank reconciliation statement for the Bakke Company as of July 31, 1975. Also prepare any necessary adjusting entries.

6–4–B

Horton Company's bank reconciliation statement of July 13, 1975, was as follows:

Bank balance, July 13, 1975		$20,850
Outstanding checks:		
No. 423	$ 350	
No. 425	1,225	
No. 430	1,400	
No. 442	1,505	4,480
		$16,370
Deposit in transit		875
Balance per Cash account, July 13, 1975		$17,245

Horton Company's records show the following receipts and disbursements for the month ended August 13, 1975:

Cash Receipts		*Cash Disbursements*	
July 18	$ 350	Check No. 443	$1,750
26	3,500	444	2,100
Aug. 10	7,000	445	1,575
13	5,250	446	3,500
		447	1,750

The bank statement covering the month ended August 13 showed:

Balance, July 13, 1975		$20,850
Deposits (4)		11,725
		$32,575
Checks deducted (6)	$8,505	
Service charges	7	8,512
Balance, August 13, 1975		$24,063

The checks returned by the bank were Nos. 423, 425, 442, 443, 444, and 445.

Required:

a) Compute the unadjusted cash balance per books as of August 13, 1975.
b) Prepare a bank reconciliation statement as of August 13, 1975.
c) Prepare any necessary adjusting journal entries as of the same date.

6–5–B

The outstanding checks of the Wilbur Company at November 30, 1975, are:

No. 229..........	$250.00
No. 263..........	272.25
No. 3678..........	169.75
No. 3679..........	201.00
No. 3680..........	350.50

During the month checks numbered 3681–3720 are issued and all of these checks clear the bank except Nos. 3719 and 3720 for $240.75 and $181.50, respectively. Checks No. 3678, 3679, and 3680 also clear the bank.

The bank statement on December 31 shows a balance of $5,586. Service charges amount to $5 and two checks are returned by the bank, one marked N.S.F. in the amount of $28.50 and the other marked "No account" in the amount of $500.

Mr. Hand recently retired as the office manager-cashier-bookkeeper for the company and was replaced by Mr. Jones. Mr. Jones noted the absence of a system of internal control but was momentarily deterred from embezzling for lack of a scheme of concealment. Finally, he hit upon several schemes. The $500 check marked "No account" by the bank is the product of one scheme. Mr. Jones abstracted cash receipts and replaced them with a check drawn upon a nonexistent account to make it appear that a customer had given the company a worthless check.

The other scheme was more subtle. He pocketed cash receipts to bring them down to an amount sufficient to enable him to prepare the following reconciliation statement:

Balance, Cash account, December 31, 1975............		$6,406.70
Less: Undeposited receipts...........................		709.45
		$5,697.25
Add: Outstanding checks No. 3719.....................	$240.75	
No. 3720.....................	181.50	422.25
		$6,119.50
Less: Worthless check................................	$500.00	
N.S.F. check................................	28.50	
Service charges................................	5.00	533.50
Balance per Bank Statement, December 31, 1975........		$5,586.00

Required:

a) State the nature of the second scheme hit upon by Mr. Jones. How much in total does it appear he has stolen?
b) Prepare a correct bank reconciliation statement as of December 31, 1975.
c) Suggest procedures which would have defeated the attempts of Mr. Jones to steal funds and conceal these actions.

6–6–B

The treasurer of the Shafer Corporation prepared the following bank reconciliation statement as of April 30, 1975:

Balance per bank statement, April 30	$55,795
Deposit in transit	3,670
	$59,465
Outstanding checks	18,100
	$41,365
N.S.F. check	1,000
Service charges	15
Balance per Books, April 30	$42,380

The bank statement for the month of May shows:

Balance, May 1, 1975		$ 55,795
Deposits		110,400
		$166,195
Checks cleared	$165,040	
Service charges	35	165,075
Balance, May 31, 1975		$ 1,120

The May deposits include the proceeds of a $30,000 note payable drawn by the treasurer of the Shafer Corporation payable to the bank in 60 days. The total cash receipts as shown by the Shafer Corporation records amount to $81,800 and the total checks recorded amount to $76,640. This latter total does not include one check drawn and signed by the treasurer payable to himself. The treasurer has disappeared. No record of this check appears anywhere in the company's records. Checks outstanding on May 31, 1975, total $16,700.

Required:

a) Compute the corrected cash balance as of April 30.
b) Compute the unadjusted cash balance as of May 31 shown by the company's records.
c) Compute the amount of the undeposited receipts, if any, as of May 31.
d) Compute the amount of the check drawn payable to the treasurer.
e) Prepare a bank reconciliation statement as of May 31.
f) Prepare any necessary adjusting entries.
g) State the particular feature of a good system of internal control which is designed to prevent abstractions of funds such as illustrated here.

6–7–B

Tex Corporation uses an imprest payroll checking account, with a $1,000 balance. This balance is used for payroll advances and to pay employees whose services are terminated between payroll payment dates. Following are selected transactions of the Tex Corporation during 1975:

Nov. 15 Payroll department determines that the payroll and payroll deductions for the first half of the month of November are:

Officers' salaries		$25,000
Office salaries		19,000
Salesmen's salaries and commissions		31,000
Sales office salaries		15,000
		$90,000
Payroll deductions:		
Federal income taxes withheld	$11,000	
FICA taxes withheld	2,000	
Community Fund contributions withheld	3,000	16,000
Net Payroll		$74,000

17 A check in the amount of the net payroll is drawn on the general checking account and deposited in the payroll checking account.
20 Payroll checks are issued.
24 One employee's services are terminated. The salary of this office employee for the partial period is $300, and the only deduction is for $45 of income taxes to be withheld. A payroll check is issued.

The bank statement for the payroll account shows a balance of $1,350.63. Checks outstanding are for $278.25 and $327.38.

Required:

a) Prepare general journal entries to record those transactions which would be formally recorded in the records of the Tex Corporation.
b) Determine the actual (not the book) balance in the payroll checking account at November 30. Why is it not the imprest balance of $1,000?
c) Prepare a bank reconciliation statement for the payroll checking account as of November 30, 1975.

6–8–B

Following are selected transactions of the Spray Company during 1975:

Mar. 1 Established a petty cash fund of $200 which will be under the control of the assistant office manager and is to be operated on an imprest basis.

Apr. 3 Fund is replenished on this date. Prior to replenishment, the fund consisted of the following:

Coin and currency	$ 9.58
Payroll check issued by Spray Company to part-time office boy, John Williams, properly endorsed by Williams	27.98
Petty cash vouchers indicating disbursements for—	
Postage stamps	50.00
Supper money for office employees working overtime	24.00
Office supplies	21.80
Window washing service	35.00
Flowers for wedding of employee	10.00
Flowers for hospitalized employee	10.00
Employee IOU	10.00

The employee's IOU is to be deducted from his next paycheck.

Required: Present journal entries for the above transactions.

6–9–B

Robert Richman was set up in business by his father, who purchased the business of an elderly acquaintance wishing to retire. One of the few changes in personnel made by Robert was to install a college classmate as the office manager-bookkeeper-cashier-sales manager.

During the course of the year, Robert found it necessary to borrow money from the bank (with his father as co-signer) because although the business seemed profitable, there seemed to be a continuous shortage of adequate cash. The investment in inventories and receivables grew substantially during the year. Finally, after a year had elapsed, Robert's father employed a certified public accountant to audit the records of Robert's business. The CPA reported that the office manager-bookkeeper-cashier-sales manager had been stealing funds and had been using a variety of schemes to cover his actions. More specifically he had:

a) Pocketed cash receipts from sales and understated the cash register readings at the end of the day or altered the copies of the sales tickets retained.
b) Abstracted checks mailed to the company in payment of accounts receivable, credited the proper accounts, and then created fictitious receivables to keep the records in balance.
c) Issued checks to fictitious suppliers and deposited them in accounts bearing these names with himself as signer of checks drawn on these accounts; the books were kept in balance by charging the purchases to the inventory account.
d) Abstracted petty cash funds by drawing false vouchers purporting to cover a variety of expenses incurred.
e) Prepared false sales returns vouchers indicating the return of cash sales to cover further thefts of cash receipts.

Required: For each of the above items, indicate at least one feature of a good system of internal control which would have prevented the losses due to dishonesty.

6–10–B

The Bosse Company acquired on July 15, 1975, 200 shares of Holm Company $100 par value capital stock at 97 plus a broker's commission of $120. On August 1, 1975, Bosse Company received a cash dividend of 60 cents per share. On November 3, 1975, it sold 100 of these shares at 105 less a broker's commission of $80. On December 1, 1975, the Holm Company issued shares comprising a 100 percent stock dividend declared on its capital stock November 18.

On December 31, 1975, the end of the calendar-year accounting period, the market quotation for Holm's common stock was 46.

Required:

a) Present journal entries to record all of the above data, assuming the securities are considered temporary investments and are to be valued at the lower of cost or market.
b) If the remaining shares are to be held for affiliation purposes—Holm Company has become a major customer—indicate how they should be shown in the statement of financial position.

Inventories

Learning objectives

Study of the material in this chapter is designed to achieve the following learning objectives:

1. A comprehension of the nature of inventory and its significance in both the earnings statement and the statement of financial position.
2. A knowledge of the application of the perpetual and periodic inventory procedures.
3. An understanding of the costs properly included in inventory, including both the theoretical and practical considerations of inventory costing.
4. A basic comprehension of the methods of accounting for purchase discounts.
5. An understanding of the practical and theoretical considerations of the various methods of inventory measurement under varying prices.
6. A comprehension of and the ability to apply the lower-of-cost-or-market rule under the various methods of inventory measurement.
7. An understanding of the various methods of estimating inventory.
8. Development of the student's ability to analyze the effect of transactions involving inventory on the financial statements.

Frame 1[7]

In earlier chapters the amount of merchandise on hand at any moment in time was referred to as the inventory of that particular business. The basis of its measurement was noted as being cost, as is true for most assets. Illustrations were presented showing how the inventory amount was used to determine cost of goods sold and how inventory was to be portrayed among the assets in a statement of financial position. Left to be considered at that time were a number of important questions such as, What should be included in inventory? At what dollar amount is the ending inventory to be reported?

The nature and significance of inventory

Inventory defined

For all business organizations except those which render services, the inventory is one of the largest and most important assets. In many instances, its size dwarfs the size of other assets. This is especially true in those industries in which there is an extended period of time between acquisition of inventory and final sale, such as in the tobacco and distilling industries.

The exact nature of the items included in inventory varies according to the nature of the business. Merchandising businesses, both retail and wholesale, acquire merchandise from others and sell it in the same condition in which it is acquired; they therefore have only one important inventory item—merchandise held for resale.

In manufacturing companies the inventory consists of raw materials, work in process, and finished goods. All exist for the same purpose—sale to customers—but are in different stages of readiness for sale, since the raw materials and work in process must be processed further prior to sale.

Since it is customary to list current assets in the statement of financial position according to liquidity (with the most liquid first), inventories are usually listed immediately after accounts receivable. It is also becoming customary to list other items such as factory supplies, store and office supplies, and similar items as a separate supplies inventory, even though none of these items are specifically offered for sale to customers.

Broadly speaking, inventory may be defined then as the aggregate of those items of tangible personal property which (1) are held for sale in the ordinary course of business, (2) are in process of production for such sale, or (3) are to be currently consumed in the production of goods or services which will be available for sale.[1]

[1] Committee on Accounting Procedure, American Institute of Certified Public Accountants, *Accounting Research and Terminology Bulletins,* Final Edition (New York, 1961), p. 27.

Importance of proper inventory measurement

The portion of the cost of goods available for sale that is not carried forward to the next period as an asset (inventory) is deducted (as cost of goods sold) from revenues in computing net earnings. Therefore, an accurate measurement of the ending inventory is necessary in order to reflect the proper net earnings for the period. And because the inventory amount appears in the statement of financial position, any misstatement in its measurement means that this statement is also in error.

If the ending inventory is overstated, then current assets are overstated, total assets are similarly overstated, and cost of goods sold is understated with a resulting overstatement of gross margin, net earnings, and retained earnings. To illustrate (assuming the periodic procedure):

For the Year Ended December 31, 1975

	Ending Inventory Correctly Stated		*Ending Inventory Overstated*	
Sales		$500,000		$500,000
Cost of goods available for sale	$400,000		$400,000	
Ending inventory	40,000	360,000	60,000	340,000
Gross Margin		$140,000		$160,000

Since the ending inventory is overstated by $20,000, current assets and total assets will also be overstated by $20,000.

Similarly, an understatement of ending inventory would have a number of effects. If ending inventory is understated, the result is to (place "over" or "under" in the blanks below):

1. __?__ state cost of goods sold. Overstate
2. __?__ state gross margin. Understate
3. __?__ state net earnings for the period. understate

Turn to Answer Frame 1[7] on page 294 to check your answers.

Frame 2[7]

The misstated net earnings are closed to Retained Earnings, misstating this account in an amount and direction which brings the statement of financial position into balance even though the inventory is misstated.

Suppose the ending inventory for the year ended December 31, 1975, were overstated. Would this error have an impact on the matching of expenses and revenues in any period other than the year 1975?

1. Yes. It would also affect the net earnings for 1976.
2. No. The only year affected is 1975.

To check your responses, turn to Answer Frame 2[7] on page 294.

Answer frame 1[7]

An understated ending inventory would:

1. Overstate cost of goods sold.
2. Understate gross margin.
3. Understate net earnings for the period.

If you answered incorrectly, reread Frame 1[7] before proceeding to Frame 2[7] on page 293.

Answer frame 2[7]

The first answer is the correct response. The ending inventory of one period is the beginning inventory of the succeeding period. Hence, an inventory error affects the net earnings of two periods. Since the beginning inventory is part of the cost of the goods available for sale, when it is overstated the cost of the goods available for sale is overstated.

If you answered incorrectly, restudy Frames 1[7] and 2[7] before going on to Frame 3[7] below.

Frame 3[7]

Assuming a correct ending inventory for the next year (ending December 31, 1976), the preceding illustration is continued:

	Beginning Inventory			
	Correct		*Overstated*	
Sales		$500,000		$500,000
Beginning inventory, January 1	$ 40,000		$ 60,000	
Purchases	360,000		360,000	
Costs of goods available for sale	$400,000		$420,000	
Less: Ending inventory, December 31	50,000		50,000	
Cost of goods sold		350,000		370,000
Gross Margin		$150,000		$130,000

An overstated beginning inventory understates gross margin by an equal amount. Similarly, an understated beginning inventory overstates gross margin. The overall result of the two periods (1975 and 1976) is summarized as follows:

	1975 and 1976 Inventories Correct	*1975 Inventory Overstated*
Gross margin, 1975	$140,000	$160,000
Gross margin, 1976	150,000	130,000
Gross margin, 1975 and 1976	$290,000	$290,000

Obviously, then, an error in inventory distorts the periodic determination of net earnings. Accounting for inventory is a key factor in earnings determination. This relationship emphasizes the importance of a correct measurement of all inventories.

If both the December 31, 1975, and the December 31, 1976, inventories are overstated by $50,000, indicate whether each of the following statements is correct or incorrect.

1. Net earnings for 1975 are understated by $50,000.
2. Net earnings for 1976 are understated by $100,000.
3. Net earnings for 1977 are understated by $50,000.
4. Total net earnings for the period 1976–77 are not affected.

Check your answers in Answer Frame 3[7] on page 296.

Frame 4[7]

The cost of inventory

Possible inclusions

The cost of inventory, like that of any other asset, consists of all outlays necessary to acquire the goods. Thus, cost includes:

1. The price on the invoice received from vendors.
2. Insurance in transit (when incurred by the buyer).
3. Transportation charges from the seller to the buyer (when incurred by the buyer).

Under periodic inventory procedure, the Purchases account is normally debited for the invoice price of the goods acquired. Preferably, the cost of insurance in transit and transportation-in should be debited to separate accounts, although some companies charge such costs directly to the Purchases account. In this latter instance, the earnings statement will not show separate amounts for these costs.

Because of the clerical difficulty in prorating insurance and transportation costs over dissimilar items of merchandise shipped together but separated on the invoice, it is not an uncommon practice to omit such costs when computing the cost of the ending inventory. But such an omission can be justified only on the basis of expediency or immateriality. Assets are misstated, as are the expenses of the period. Consider the following example covering a one-year period:

Invoice price of merchandise purchased	$100,000
Transportation-in and insurance in transit	20,000
Ending inventory at invoice price	40,000

If the cost of goods sold is computed by deducting the ending inventory (stated at $40,000) from the total cost of goods available for sale of $120,000, cost of goods sold is overstated by $8,000. The $8,000 is explained as follows: if $20,000 of transportation-in and insurance in transit costs were incurred in the purchasing of $100,000 of goods and

Answer frame 3[7]

1. Incorrect. The overstated 1975 ending inventory means that $50,000 too much was deducted from cost of goods available for sale, leaving cost of goods sold understated by $50,000 and gross margin and net earnings for 1975 overstated by $50,000.
2. Incorrect. The overstated inventory on December 31, 1975, results in an overstated beginning inventory for 1976 which, by itself, would cause net earnings to be understated by $50,000 for the year. The overstated ending inventory in 1976, however, has just the opposite effect on net earnings. In this case, both inventories are overstated by the same amount, and hence the effects of the two errors exactly offset one another and net earnings are correct in spite of the errors in the inventory amounts.
3. Correct. The overstatement of the December 31, 1976, inventory, which is the beginning inventory in 1977, results in a $50,000 overstatement of the cost of goods available for sale in 1977 and consequently an overstatement of cost of goods sold. By deducting $50,000 too much cost from sales revenue, gross margin and net earnings for 1977 are both automatically understated by that amount.
4. Incorrect. While it is true that the overstatement of the beginning inventory is exactly offset by the overstatement of the ending inventory in the computation of 1976 net earnings, the net earnings for 1977 are understated by virtue of the fact that the 1977 beginning inventory is overstated. Consequently, the total earnings for 1976–77 are understated by $50,000. The reported earnings for 1975–77 will not be affected in total although the 1975 earnings are overstated by $50,000 and the earnings for 1977 are understated by $50,000.

If you missed any of the above, restudy Frame 3[7] before continuing to Frame 4[7] on page 295.

4[7] *continued*

40 percent of these goods are in inventory, then presumably approximately 40 percent of the $20,000, or $8,000, should also be in inventory. Thus, the ending inventory should be stated at $48,000 and cost of goods sold at $72,000 ($120,000 – $48,000).

The amount of the error in net earnings will, of course, be reduced by the understatement of cost of goods available for sale through omission of transportation charges in the beginning inventory if this practice is followed consistently.

Inventory and purchase discounts. The accounting treatment accorded purchase discounts affects the cost of goods sold and the measurement of the inventory. Assume that a company purchases $20,000 of merchandise under terms of 2/10, n/30. The buyer may record the purchase at (*a*) gross or (*b*) net invoice price.

a) If the acquisition is recorded at gross invoice price, the entry is:

Purchases	20,000	
Accounts Payable		20,000

When the invoice is paid within the discount period, the $400 of purchase discounts will be recorded as follows:

Accounts Payable	20,000	
Cash		19,600
Purchase Discounts		400

(Under the perpetual procedure, the Merchandise Inventory account would be credited with the $400 of discounts taken.)

As illustrated in Chapter 4, treating Purchase Discounts as a contra account to Purchases has the effect of reducing purchases from gross invoice price to net invoice price—the price actually paid. Under this procedure, however, the cost of goods available for sale is still overstated slightly because the discounts available on unpaid accounts have not been deducted. It should also be noted that even when the discounts are deducted from purchases, some companies fail to reduce the invoice price of the ending inventory by the amount of discounts taken on the goods in inventory. This results, of course, in a slight overstatement of the Inventory account, with the resulting effect upon cost of goods sold, gross margin, net earnings, and retained earnings; but the amount of misstatement can usually be ignored on grounds of immateriality.

b) If the acquisition is recorded at net invoice price, the entry is:

Purchases	19,600	
Accounts Payable		19,600

If the invoice is paid within the discount period, the entry is:

Accounts Payable	19,600	
Cash		19,600

If the invoice is not paid within the discount period, the entry is:

Accounts Payable	19,600	
Discounts Lost	400	
Cash		20,000

Although discounts lost are technically losses, they are usually treated as an element of financial expense and classified among the "other expenses" in the earnings statement. Thus, under this method, the recorded cost of the merchandise is its net invoice price, regardless of whether the discounts are taken or not. This method can be used under both the perpetual and the periodic procedures. Only the account debited when the merchandise is acquired would differ.

When the net invoice price method is used to record purchases, the Accounts Payable account is credited at the time of purchase with:

1. The gross invoice price of the merchandise.
2. The net invoice price of the merchandise.
3. The gross or net invoice price depending upon whether the discount is taken or not.

Check your answer by turning to Answer Frame 4[7] on page 298.

Answer frame 4[7]

The second answer is the correct response. The credit to Accounts Payable on the date the purchase of the merchandise is recorded is at the net invoice price. The entry to record payment of an invoice paid after the discount period has elapsed debits Accounts Payable for the amount previously credited to that account (the net price) and debits the amount of the discount not taken to the Discounts Lost account. It should be noted that the only credit to Accounts Payable is made at the time the invoice is recorded. The fact that the company does or does not take advantage of the cash discount does not affect the credit to Accounts Payable.

If you chose the incorrect answer, restudy Frame 4[7] before going on to Frame 5[7] below.

Frame 5[7]

Inventory measurement under varying prices

Even though it is widely agreed that inventories should be reported at cost, many problems remain unresolved. For example, suppose a retailer has three units of a given product on hand, one acquired at $10, another at $11, and the third at $12. Now he sells two of them for $15 each. Is the cost of the two units sold $21, the cost of the first and second units; $22, the cost of the first and third units; or $23, the cost of the second and third units? Or is it $22, determined as two units at an average cost of $11? What if the market value of the unit on hand at the end of the accounting period has fallen to $9? Should this influence the amount at which the inventory is measured? Problems such as these and others have resulted in the development of a number of methods of inventory measurement. These include:

Actual cost methods:
1. Specific identification.
2. Methods based on assumed cost flows:
   a) First-in, first-out.
   b) Last-in, first-out.
   c) Average.

Cost modified for market value fluctuations:
1. Cost of market, whichever is lower.

Methods approximating cost:
1. Gross margin method.
2. Retail method (see Chapter 8, *Accounting II*).

The data in Illustration 7.1 are assumed with regard to the beginning inventory, purchases, and sales of a given product in order to illustrate the application of the actual cost methods. The total of the goods available for sale consists of 80 units with a total cost of $854. Of the units available, 60 were sold, producing sales revenue of $940, and 20 units were left on hand in inventory.

Illustration 7.1

BEGINNING INVENTORY, PURCHASES, AND SALES

Beginning Inventory and Purchases				Sales			
Date	Units	Unit Cost	Total Cost	Date	Units	Price	Total
January 1........	10	$10.00	$100.00	March 8.........	10	$15.00	$150.00
March 2.........	10	10.40	104.00	July 5...........	10	15.00	150.00
May 28..........	20	10.50	210.00	September 7.....	20	16.00	320.00
August 12........	10	11.00	110.00	November 27....	20	16.00	320.00
October 12.......	20	10.90	218.00				
December 21.....	10	11.20	112.00				
	80		$854.00		60		$940.00

Actual cost methods

Specific identification. The application of this method calls for the assignment of a known actual cost to a particular identifiable unit of product. The specific product involved is usually identifiable through the use of a serial number plate or identification tag. The method is quite appropriately applied when large, readily identifiable units of product are purchased and sold, for example, automobiles. The method may be applied under either the perpetual or the periodic inventory procedure. All that is required is some means of knowing that a particular cost attaches to a specific product.

To illustrate, assume that the 20 units of product on hand at the end of the year in the above illustration are definitely known to consist of 10 from the August 12 purchase and 10 from the December 21 purchase. The ending inventory then is shown in Illustration 7.2. The $222 cost

Illustration 7.2

ENDING INVENTORY UNDER SPECIFIC IDENTIFICATION

Purchased	Units	Unit Cost	Total Cost
August 12................	10	$11.00	$110.00
December 21............	10	11.20	112.00
Total....................	20		$222.00

of the ending inventory is deducted from the total goods available for sale of $854 to get the cost of goods sold of $632.

Assume that instead of the units being identified as being from the August 12 and December 21 purchases, 10 were from the December 21 purchase and 10 from the May 28 purchase. Under these assumptions, the cost of goods sold for the year for this product is __?__

Turn to Answer Frame 5[7] on page 300 to check your answer.

Answer frame 5[7]

The ending inventory is 10 at $11.20 ($112) plus 10 at $10.50 ($105) or total of $217. Deducting this amount from $854 leaves $637 as the cost of goods sold.

If you answered incorrectly, restudy Frame 5[7] before proceeding with Frame 6[7] below.

Frame 6[7]

The specific identification method results in cost of goods sold and inventory being stated in terms of the actual cost of the actual units sold or on hand, to the extent that actual cost is literally obtainable. Some criticize the method because it may result in relatively homogeneous units of product being included in inventory at different prices. For example, television sets varying only in the different numbers on the serial number tag may be carried at different costs if purchased at different times. Similarly, cost of goods sold may show homogeneous units of product sold entered at different costs. Others would argue that this is entirely logical under the cost method of accounting and that this method is the most theoretically sound of all the methods.

The specific identification method is also indicted by some as theoretically unacceptable because earnings may be manipulated when it is used. Actually this indictment misses the mark, since it should be directed at the accounting concept of earnings as the excess of realized revenues over the historical costs matched against those revenues. To illustrate the nature of the alleged theoretical deficiency, consider the following example.

A company has three units of a given product on hand, identical in every respect except for attached tags bearing serial numbers. These units of product cost $1,000, $1,100, and $1,200, respectively, since they were acquired at different times in a rising market. Now one is sold for $1,800. Since the units are identical, the customer is indifferent as to which one he receives. But the earnings reported on the sale will differ, being either $800, $700, or $600 depending upon which unit is shipped. The opportunity for manipulation should be obvious. If higher earnings are desired, ship the unit costing $1,000. If lower earnings are desired, ship the unit costing $1,200.

Note that if the growth in value of the units costing $1,000 and $1,100 is recognized as it accrues, the earnings reported from the sale of a unit will be $600 regardless of which unit is actually shipped. But the accounting convention of conservatism, expressed in the requirement of revenue realization before recognition, prevents the recognition of this growth in value prior to sale of the unit.

The major deficiency in the specific identification method in many cases is that it simply cannot be applied. Either the units cannot be identified or attempting to identify them would be too costly. For instance, it would be too difficult and costly to apply the method to the nails sold by a hardware store if the nails are purchased in hundred-pound kegs and sold by the pound, or to an ice cream parlor purchasing ice cream in five-gallon cans and selling it in cones, pints, and quarts. These difficulties cause the accountant to resort to making assumptions relative to the flow of costs through a business.

First-in, first-out (FIFO). When specific identification of the units sold or remaining is not possible or desirable, assumptions must be made as to how their costs flow through the business. Good merchandising policy calls for handling merchandise in such a fashion as to move the oldest stock first, if at all possible. In reality, in most businesses, the actual physical flow of goods is first-in, first-out in order to avoid substantial losses from spoilage. Fresh dairy products and fresh produce are excellent examples. Therefore, if business management actually seeks to make goods flow physically in a first-in, first-out manner, the accountant believes that an acceptable scheme of accounting for the costs of the goods is one in which the flow of costs parallels the physical flow of goods. Thus, the first-in, first-out method of inventory measurement results. The method may be applied under either the periodic or perpetual procedure.

FIFO applied under the periodic procedure. The application of this method under the periodic procedure involves pricing the inventory at the latest purchase prices, since it is believed that these are the goods still on hand. The older goods are the first out; that is, they have been sold, while the newer goods remain on hand. But it should be clearly understood that, according to accepted practice, the method may be applied even when the physical flow of goods is not first-in, first-out.

To apply the method using the data in Illustration 7.1, begin by listing the latest purchases and continue back through the year listing purchases until enough units have been listed to agree in total with the number of units in inventory. The inventory here is shown in Illustration 7.3.

Illustration 7.3

FIFO COST OF ENDING INVENTORY UNDER PERIODIC PROCEDURE

Purchased	*Units*	*Unit Cost*	*Total Cost*
December 21	10	$11.20	$112.00
October 12	10	10.90	109.00
Total	20		$221.00

The ending inventory thus consists of the latest purchases, and the balance of the cost of the goods available for sale (consisting of older costs) is charged to cost of goods sold. The ending inventory is $221, and this sum will be deducted from the total goods available for sale of $854 to get the cost of goods sold of $633.

Assume the records of the Barrett Company provide the following information for the month of October, 1975:

Inventory on October 1	600 units @ $2.00
Purchases:	
October 2	500 units @ 1.80
11	1,800 units @ 1.50
18	800 units @ 1.70
25	400 units @ 1.90

A physical count reveals that there are 1,400 units on hand at the end of the period.

The October 31, 1975, inventory priced under FIFO using the periodic procedure is:

1. $2,660.
2. $2,550.
3. $2,420.
4. $1,440.

Check your answer in Answer Frame 6[7] on page 304.

Frame 7[7]

FIFO applied under perpetual procedure. In the application of FIFO under the continuous or perpetual procedure, as merchandise is sold it is priced out of the Inventory account at the cost of the oldest items in stock. When the first lot of merchandise is sold, subsequent units sold are charged to cost of goods sold at the cost of the second lot purchased until the second lot is completely gone. As in the application of FIFO under the periodic procedure, the ending inventory will thus consist of the cost of the latest units purchased.

Illustration 7.4 shows the application of FIFO under the perpetual procedure using the data from Illustration 7.1. Note that the ending inventory of 20 units with a total cost of $221 is exactly the same as the ending inventory determined when FIFO was applied under the periodic procedure (Illustration 7.3).

If, in Illustration 7.4, another 15 units had been sold on December 28, the Cost of Goods Sold account would have been debited for another:

1. $163.50.
2. $165.00.
3. $168.00.

Refer to Answer Frame 7[7] on page 304 to check your answer.

Frame 8[7]

Last-in, first-out, (LIFO). Under LIFO, the costs of the last goods purchased are charged against revenues as the cost of the goods sold,

Illustration 7.4

FIFO COST OF ENDING INVENTORY
UNDER PERPETUAL PROCEDURE

Date		*Units*	*Unit Cost*	*Cost*
January 1	Inventory	10	$10.00	$100.00
March 2	Purchased	10	$10.40	104.00
	Balance	20:10	$10.00	
		10	10.40	$204.00
March 8	Sold	10	$10.00	100.00
	Balance	10	10.40	$104.00
May 28	Purchased	20	$10.50	210.00
	Balance	30:10	$10.40	
		20	10.50	$314.00
July 5	Sold	10	$10.40	104.00
	Balance	20	10.50	$210.00
August 12	Purchased	10	$11.00	110.00
	Balance	30:20	$10.50	
		10	11.00	$320.00
September 7	Sold	20	$10.50	210.00
	Balance	10	11.00	$110.00
October 12	Purchased	20	$10.90	218.00
	Balance	30:10	$11.00	
		20	10.90	$328.00
November 27	Sold	20:10	$11.00	
		10	10.90	219.00
	Balance	10	$10.90	$109.00
December 21	Purchased	10	$11.20	112.00
	Balance	20:10	$10.90	
		10	11.20	$221.00

while the inventory is composed of the costs of the oldest goods acquired. LIFO may be applied under either the perpetual or the periodic procedure for tax purposes. But, generally, inventories under the perpetual LIFO procedure are adjusted, as a practical matter (lower taxes), to the lower amounts (because of generally rising prices) often obtainable from application of LIFO under the periodic procedure. The regulations also provide that if LIFO is used for tax purposes it must be used in general financial reports. Note that although the costs of the goods purchased are assumed to flow in a last-in, first-out manner, this does not mean that the goods physically flow in this manner.

In order to determine the cost of the ending inventory, it is necessary to list the goods in the beginning inventory and continue listing subsequent purchases until enough units have been listed to equal the number in the ending inventory. Illustration 7.5 shows the determination of the ending inventory for the data in Illustration 7.1. The cost of the ending inventory of $204 is deducted from the cost of the goods available for sale of $854 to show a cost of goods sold of $650. Note that in this example, the costs charged against revenues as the cost of the goods sold are all fairly current or recent costs. The inventory consists of a March 2 purchase and the cost of the beginning inventory, which may actually have been incurred many years ago.

Answer frame 6[7]

3. $2,420 is the correct answer. Under the FIFO periodic method of pricing inventory, the October 31, 1975, inventory is computed by actual count. The cost of the 1,400 units in inventory in this problem is determined as follows:

Remaining purchases of October 25	400 units @ $1.90	=	$ 760
Remaining purchases of October 18	800 1.70	=	1,360
Remaining purchases of October 11	200 1.50	=	300
Total	1,400 units		$2,420

If you did not choose the correct answer, restudy Frame 6[7] before going on to Frame 7[7] on page 302.

Answer frame 7[7]

$165 is correct. In recording the sale of the 15 units, the remaining 10 units of those purchased on October 12 are considered to be sold first; the balance of 5 units is taken from the lot purchased on December 21. The computation of the cost of the goods sold on December 28 is:

10 units at $10.90	$109
5 units at 11.20	56
Total	$165

The new balance in the inventory account is five units at $11.20, or $56.

If you answered incorrectly, restudy Frame 7[7] before going on to Frame 8[7] on page 302.

8[7]
continued

Illustration 7.5

LIFO COST OF ENDING INVENTORY

Purchased	*Units*	*Unit Cost*	*Total Cost*
Beginning inventory	10	$10.00	$100.00
March 2	10	10.40	104.00
Total	20		$204.00

Assume that Barker-Hershe Company purchased merchandise as follows during 1975. There was no beginning inventory.

Feb. 1	1,000 units	@ $2.90	$ 2,900
June 9	500	2.60	1,300
Aug. 20	1,700	3.00	5,100
Dec. 26	800	3.10	2,480
	4,000 units		$11,780

There are 1,100 units remaining in ending inventory. The cost of goods sold for the year under LIFO is:

1. $8,620.
2. $3,380.

3. $3,160.
4. $8,400.

Check your answer by turning to Answer Frame 8[7] on page 306.

Frame 9[7]

FIFO and LIFO compared. Much has been written in recent years concerning the relative merits of FIFO and LIFO as methods of inventory measurement. LIFO's appeal can be tied directly to the nearly constant upward trend in prices experienced in this country since the early 1930s. An example will make this point clear.

Suppose that Company A has one unit of a given product on hand which cost $10. The unit is sold for $15, other expenses of sale amount to $3.50, the tax rate is 50 percent, and the unit is replaced for $11 prior to the end of the accounting period. Under FIFO accounting, net earnings are computed as follows:

Net sales	$15.00
Cost of goods sold	10.00
Gross margin	$ 5.00
Expenses	3.50
Net operating margin	$ 1.50
Federal income taxes (50 percent rate)	0.75
Net Earnings	$ 0.75

According to the above schedule the company is selling this product at a price sufficient to produce net earnings. But consider the following:

Cash secured from sale	$15.00
Expenses and taxes paid ($3.50 + $0.75)	4.25
Cash available for replacement and dividends	$10.75
Cost to replace	11.00
Additional cash required to replace inventory	$ 0.25

Thus, Company A, which is reporting net earnings of $0.75, finds itself unable to replace its inventory without securing additional funds. Note, by way of contrast, what happens when LIFO is used as the method of inventory measurement:

Net sales	$15.00
Cost of goods sold	11.00
Gross margin	$ 4.00
Expenses	3.50
Net operating margin	$ 0.50
Federal income taxes	0.25
Net Earnings	$ 0.25

Cash secured from sale	$15.00
Expenses and taxes paid ($3.50 + $0.25)	3.75
Cash available for replacement and dividends	$11.25
Cost to replace	11.00
Cash available for dividends	$ 0.25

Answer frame 8[7]

$8,620 is correct. Under the LIFO periodic procedure, the ending inventory of 1,100 units is priced as follows:

1,000 units at $2.90	$2,900
100 units at $2.60	260
Total	$3,160

The cost of goods sold with no beginning inventory is:

Total purchases	$11,780
Less ending inventory	3,160
Cost of goods sold	$ 8,620

If you answered incorrectly, restudy Frame 8[7] before going on to Frame 9[7] on page 305.

9[7] *continued*

Tax effect of LIFO. We have seen from the above example that the use of LIFO increased cost of goods sold by $1 and decreased taxes by $0.50. The $0.25 of net earnings can be distributed as dividends because the cost of replacing the inventory has already been deducted from sales revenue. This illustration indicates why many companies, in view of some rather prolonged periods of price increases experienced in this country, have changed to the LIFO method of inventory measurement.

Unfortunately, an important point is often overlooked in the LIFO versus FIFO controversy, namely, that a different concept of net earnings underlies each method. Under FIFO, if the assets received from the sale are sufficient to cover the historical cost of the unit sold and the other expenses, there are net earnings to be reported. Under LIFO, net earnings exist only if the sales revenue (measured by the assets received upon sale) is sufficient to cover all expenses and the cost of replacing the unit sold, provided replacement occurs before the end of the accounting period.

The more traditional arguments for LIFO are that it tends to match costs and revenues more precisely than does FIFO. The earnings statement reports sales and the most recent cost of making those sales when LIFO is used. Thus, the earnings reported reflect operating results and do not include gains from general price level increases.

Manipulation possible under LIFO. On the other hand, FIFO advocates point out that LIFO matches the cost of unsold goods against sales revenue and leaves inventory rather badly understated in a period of rising prices. They also point out that net earnings under LIFO can be manipulated by management. If smaller net earnings are desired, management may increase the amount of purchases at current high costs and, under LIFO, these costs will be charged to cost of goods sold. If higher earnings are desired, management can delay making purchases and charge to cost of goods sold some of the older, lower costs in inventory.

Assume that the acquisition price of a product sold by Gross Retailers, Inc. rose steadily throughout the year 1975. Indicate whether each of the following statements is true or false.

1. The sales for the year would be higher under FIFO than under LIFO.
2. The December 31, 1975, inventory would be higher if priced under LIFO rather than FIFO.
3. The gross margin would be less if the ending inventory is priced under LIFO rather than FIFO.

Check your answer in Answer Frame 9[7] on page 308.

Frame 10[7]

Weighted average method. This method may be applied under either the perpetual or the periodic inventory procedure. The method of calculation differs according to the procedure employed. Under the periodic procedure it is called simply the weighted average method. Under the perpetual procedure it is called the moving average method, although it would be technically more correct to call it a weighted moving average method.

Under the periodic inventory procedure, the total number of units purchased plus those on hand at the beginning of the year is divided into the total of the cost of the purchases plus the cost of the beginning inventory in order to derive a weighted unit cost. This unit cost is then multiplied by the number of units in the ending inventory in order to arrive at the cost of the inventory. Illustration 7.6, using the data from Illustration 7.1, shows the application of this procedure.

Illustration 7.6

APPLICATION OF WEIGHTED AVERAGE METHOD

Purchased	*Units*	*Unit Cost*	*Total Cost*
January 1	10	$10.00	$100.00
March 2	10	10.40	104.00
May 28	20	10.50	210.00
August 12	10	11.00	110.00
October 12	20	10.90	218.00
December 21	10	11.20	112.00
	80		$854.00
Weighted average unit cost is $854 ÷ 80, or $10.675.			
Ending inventory then is $10.675 × 20			213.50
Cost of Goods Sold			$640.50

Answer frame 9[7]

1. False. The amount of sales is unaffected by the method of inventory measurement and will be the same under FIFO or LIFO.
2. False. Under LIFO the inventory is priced at the earliest prices, which in this case means the inventory would include the lowest prices, since the purchase price of the product rose steadily throughout the year.
3. True. Under LIFO, cost of goods sold is charged with the most recent costs. In a period of constantly rising prices this means that the Cost of Goods Sold account is charged with the highest prices paid for the merchandise. It follows then that under LIFO the gross margin will be less than under FIFO.

If you answered any of the above incorrectly, restudy Frame 9[7] before continuing to Frame 10[7] on page 307.

10[7]
continued

Would you agree that the same result could be obtained simply by multiplying the number of units in the ending inventory by the average of the unit costs of this merchandise?

1. Yes.
2. No.

Check your answer in Answer Frame 10[7] on page 310.

Frame 11[7]

The weighted average method assigns to each homogeneous unit the same amount of cost regardless of whether the cost is to be charged to cost of goods sold or carried forward in inventory. But its implication that all goods sold are drawn from one big pool of goods is often not literally true. Also, use of the method involves delaying the determination of inventory and cost of goods sold amounts until the end of the year. When this delay is impractical or impossible (as with the perpetual inventory procedures), a similar method, the moving average method is used.

Moving average method. This method may be applied only on a continuous basis. Weighted average costs are computed after each purchase by dividing the total cost of units on hand by the number of units on hand. This information is contained in a perpetual inventory record. The effect of this method is to move unit costs upward or downward in accordance with quantities purchased and price fluctuations. Only purchases affect the moving average unit costs; the cost of units sold is always the last-established unit cost. Using the data from Illustration 7.1, the application of the method, using a perpetual inventory record, is shown in Illustration 7.7.

Note that with the purchase of March 2, a new unit cost is computed by adding together the cost of the first 10 units and the March 2 purchase of 10 units to secure a total cost to date of $204. This sum divided by

Illustration 7.7

PERPETUAL INVENTORY RECORD

	Purchased			*Sold*			*Balance*		
Date	*Units*	*Unit Cost*	*Total Cost*	*Units*	*Unit Cost*	*Total Cost*	*Units*	*Unit Cost*	*Total Cost*
Jan. 1							10	10.00	100.00
Mar. 2	10	10.40	104.00				20	10.20	204.00
8				10	10.20	102.00	10	10.20	102.00
May 28	20	10.50	210.00				30	10.40	312.00
July 5				10	10.40	104.00	20	10.40	208.00
Aug. 12	10	11.00	110.00				30	10.60	318.00
Sept. 7				20	10.60	212.00	10	10.60	106.00
Oct. 12	20	10.90	218.00				30	10.80	324.00
Nov. 27				20	10.80	216.00	10	10.80	108.00
Dec. 21	10	11.20	112.00				20	11.00	220.00

20 units gives a unit cost of $10.20. Note also that all units sold are charged out at the previously determined unit cost. The ending inventory in Illustration 7.7 can be compared with the inventory computed under the periodic weighted average method ($213.50) to indicate the difference caused by different weights given to the various prices paid. The unit prices in this perpetual inventory record can also be compared with the unit prices under FIFO perpetual procedure in Illustration 7.4 to see how the effect of averaging tends to slow the rise of the unit cost.

Any business desiring up-to-date information relative to its inventory will use records similar to the inventory record card shown in Illustration 7.7. In this way, the quantity and cost of the goods on hand are readily available. The actual form employed may vary somewhat from company to company depending upon the exact needs of each company.

If an additional 10 units were purchased at $11.60 per unit on December 28, these units would have been included in the inventory in Illustration 7.7 at a unit cost of:

1. $11.60.
2. $11.30.
3. $11.20.

Turn to Answer Frame 11[7] on page 310 to check your calculations.

Frame 12[7]

Would a company which kept its inventory under the periodic procedure have the choice of using FIFO, LIFO, specific identification, or a moving average as the basis for pricing its inventories? Choose the correct answer of the four listed on page 310.

Answer frame 10^7

The correct response is no. The method illustrated employs a weighted average of the prices paid for the merchandise rather than a simple average. Thus, the relative quantity purchased at each price may have a significant impact on the unit cost used in computing the cost of goods sold and the cost of the ending inventory. In Illustration 7.6, for example, the simple average price per unit would be $10.667 computed by simply summing the six unit costs and dividing by six. This is a relatively nominal difference and results from the fact that there were no marked variations in the quantities purchased. Consider, however, the following example:

100 units @	$1	$ 100
900	$2	1,800
1,000 units		$1,900

The weighted average unit cost is $1.90 ($1,900 ÷ 1,000), while the simple average cost is $1.50 [($1 + $2) ÷ 2].

If you answered incorrectly, restudy Frame 10^7 before going on to Frame 11^7 on page 308.

Answer frame 11^7

The correct response is $11.20. This new moving average cost per unit is determined as follows:

Dec. 28 balance	20 units @	$11.00 =	$220.00
Purchase	10	$11.60 =	116.00
Total	30 units		$336.00

$336.00 ÷ 30 = $11.20 per unit.

Reread Frame 11^7 if you answered incorrectly; otherwise proceed to Frame 12^7 on page 309.

12^7 *continued*

1. Yes; all four of these methods are consistent with keeping inventory records under the periodic procedure.
2. No; although the FIFO, LIFO, and specific identification methods would be acceptable, the moving average method is used only under the perpetual procedure.
3. No; although FIFO and LIFO would be acceptable, the specific identification method of pricing is not consistent with the periodic procedure.
4. No; the moving average and LIFO methods are not applicable under the periodic procedure.

Check your answer in Answer Frame 12^7 on page 312.

Frame 13^7

Differences in cost methods summarized. Illustration 7.8 summarizes the cost of goods sold, ending inventories, and gross margins which will

Illustration 7.8

SUMMARY OF EFFECTS OF EMPLOYING DIFFERENT INVENTORY METHODS WITH SAME BASIC DATA	*Specific Identification*	*FIFO*	*LIFO*	*Weighted Average*	*Moving Average*
(*Frame which discusses*)	(5^7)	(6^7, 7^7)	(8^7, 9^7)	(10^7)	(11^7)
Sales	$940.00	$940.00	$940.00	$940.00	$940.00
Cost of goods sold:					
Beginning inventory	$100.00	$100.00	$100.00	$100.00	
Purchases	754.00	754.00	754.00	754.00	
Goods available for sale	$854.00	$854.00	$854.00	$854.00	
Ending inventory	222.00	221.00	204.00	213.50	
Cost of goods sold	$632.00	$633.00	$650.00	$640.50	634.00
Gross Margin	$308.00	$307.00	$290.00	$299.50	$306.00

result from the application of the five basic cost methods of measuring ending inventory, using the data shown in Illustration 7.1.

Because the moving average method is applied only under the perpetual procedure, information relative to the amount of purchases during a period normally is not readily available. Only the ending inventory and the cost of goods sold are contained in the accounts.

Note that each of the above methods produces a different inventory measurement and gross margin. As might be expected, since the trend of prices is upward during the period, LIFO shows the highest cost of goods sold and the lowest gross margin.

Which is the "correct" method? All of the five methods are considered acceptable, and no one of them can be considered the only correct one. Each method possesses an attribute which makes it attractive in particular circumstances. The application of LIFO results in matching current cost with current revenue, and any net earnings can be distributed as dividends without impairing the level of operations. LIFO is actually a partial answer to the problems encountered in accounting under inflationary conditions. Also, LIFO reduces the amount of taxes payable currently under these conditions.

On the other hand, LIFO often charges against revenues the cost of goods not sold. And it permits manipulation of net earnings simply by changing the time at which additional purchases of merchandise are made. If precision in the matching of historical cost with revenue is desired, FIFO or specific identification are to be preferred. But earnings may also be manipulated under the specific identification method, as they may be under the simple weighted average method. Under the latter method, the purchase of a large amount of goods at a relatively high price after the last sale of the period will change the average unit cost of the goods charged to the Cost of Goods Sold account. Only under FIFO and the moving average methods is the manipulation of earnings not possible. But because net earnings under both of these methods, es-

Answer frame 12⁷

The second answer is the correct response. The FIFO, LIFO, and specific identification inventory methods may be used with either the perpetual or the periodic inventory procedure. The moving average method is definitely geared to the perpetual procedure, while the weighted average method is used only under the periodic procedure.

If you answered incorrectly, reread Frame 12⁷ before continuing to Frame 13⁷ on page 310.

13⁷ *continued* pecially under FIFO in periods of rising prices, may have to be reinvested in inventory in order to maintain a given level of sales volume, these earnings are considered fictitious by many accountants and dubbed "paper profits."

Would you agree with the following statement? Reducing the amount of taxes payable currently is a valid objective of business management, and since LIFO does this, all businesses should use LIFO.

1. Yes.
2. No.

Refer to Answer Frame 13⁷ on page 314 to check your choice.

Frame 14⁷

The lower-of-cost-or-market method

Pricing inventories at the lower-of-cost-or-market price has a long history of acceptance in accounting. The method is based, in part, upon the assumption that if the purchase price in the market in which the firm buys has fallen, the selling price has fallen or will fall. This is not always a valid assumption.

The term market as used in this context means replacement cost in terms of the quantity usually purchased (within certain limits described below). In the application of the method, it is still necessary to determine cost (by specific identification, FIFO, LIFO, or an average method).

The method embraces market values only to the extent that these values are less than cost. If the inventory at year-end has a cost of $20,000 and a market value of $21,000, this increase in market value is not recognized. To do so would be to recognize revenues prior to the time of sale.

On the other hand, if market value is $19,400, the inventory may be written down to market value from cost and the $600 loss recognized on the grounds that the inventory has lost some of its revenue-generating ability. Thus, the entry made anticipates a reduced selling price when the goods are actually sold.

By pricing merchandise in the ending inventory at the lower of cost or market ($19,400 in this case) the loss in the revenue-generating ability of the goods is reflected as a loss:

1. In the period in which the goods were purchased.
2. In the period in which the goods are sold.
3. In the period in which the price decline occurs.

Check your answer in Answer Frame 14[7] on page 314.

Frame 15[7]

Because of the shifting of earnings possible under the lower-of-cost-or-market method and because selling prices do not always vary with market prices, several modifications of the strict lower-of-cost-or-market method have been adopted. These modifications, in effect, set limits on the extent to which the market price may vary and still be used. Market must not (1) exceed net realizable value (NRV), nor (2) be less than net realizable value less an allowance for normal profit (NRV — NP). Net realizable value is defined as estimated selling price less estimated costs of completion and disposition. The term normal profit is not defined, but is generally considered to be the normal markup of similar products.

Market value under the lower-of-cost-or-market rule may not exceed:

1. Replacement cost.
2. Net realizable value less a normal profit.
3. Net realizable value.
4. Cost.

Check your answer in Answer Frame 15[7] on page 314.

Frame 16[7]

Application of the lower-of-cost-or-market method. In the accounting records, the lower-of-cost-or-market method may be applied to each item in inventory, to each class in inventory, or to total inventory. Illustration 7.9 shows the application of the method to individual items and to total

Illustration 7.9

APPLICATION OF LOWER-OF-COST-OR-MARKET METHOD

Item	*Unit Cost*	*Unit Market*	*Total Cost*	*Total Market*	*Lower of Cost or Market*
1........100 units........	$8.00	$6.90	$ 800	$ 690	$ 690
2........200 units.......	5.00	5.25	1,000	1,050	1,000
3........500 units.......	3.00	3.00	1,500	1,500	1,500
			$3,300	$3,240	$3,190

Answer frame 13^7

No is the answer we believe is appropriate. LIFO will not always reduce the amount of taxes payable currently, because reported net earnings will be higher under LIFO than under other methods if prices decline through a period. Furthermore, LIFO does not seem appropriate for a company dealing in real estate or automobiles, where specific identification of units sold is readily possible. Also, there are other uses for accounting information than reducing the amount of currently payable taxes.

If you answered incorrectly, restudy Frame 13^7 before going on to Frame 14^7 on page 312.

Answer frame 14^7

Answer 3 is correct. The goal of the method is to charge off the loss in usefulness of goods in the period in which the loss actually occurs. If you answered incorrectly, restudy Frame 14^7 before going on to Frame 15^7 on page 313.

Answer frame 15^7

Net realizable value is the correct answer.

If you answered incorrectly, reread Frame 15^7 before going on to Frame 16^7 on page 313.

16^7 *continued*

inventory. The market values employed are assumed to be those derived after applying the above limits.

Fill in the blanks with the correct figures.

1. If each item is priced at the lower of cost or market, the inventory in Illustration 7.9 is \$ ___?___
2. If the total inventory is priced at the lower of cost or market, the inventory is \$ ___?___

Turn to Answer Frame 16^7 on page 316.

Frame 17^7

Financial statement treatment of declines to market. The measurement of the ending inventory at the lower of cost or market raises questions as to how the inventory should be reported in the statement of financial position and in the earnings statement. In the statement of financial position the inventory should be shown among the current assets at the appropriate amount determined by applying the lower-of-cost-or-market criteria, with adequate disclosure of the inventory-costing and measurement methods.

In the earnings statement, many accountants prefer to show the inventory in the cost of goods sold section at actual cost. Then the decline to market can be shown as a separate item near the bottom of the earnings statement.

To illustrate the above procedure, assume that during the year 1975 the Fenton Company purchased merchandise at a cost of $300,000 and later returned $10,000 of the merchandise. The beginning inventory was $40,000, and the cost of the merchandise sold was $280,000. Sales for the period amounted to $400,000. The cost of the ending inventory thus is $50,000.

As of December 31, 1975, the market value of this inventory is $48,000. Thus, under the lower-of-cost-or-market method a decline of $2,000 must be recognized. Selling and administrative expenses for the year total $100,000. The earnings statement based on these data is given

Illustration 7.10

FENTON COMPANY
Earnings Statement
For the Year Ended December 31, 1975

Sales			$400,000
Cost of goods sold:			
Inventory, January 1		$ 40,000	
Purchases	$300,000		
Less: Returns	10,000	290,000	
Total goods available for sale		$330,000	
Less: Inventory, December 31 (at cost)		50,000	
Cost of goods sold			280,000
Gross margin			$120,000
Selling and administrative expenses			100,000
Net earnings from operations			$ 20,000
Less: Loss from market decline of inventory			2,000
Net Earnings			$ 18,000

in Illustration 7.10. The inventory would appear in the current asset section of the statement of financial position as follows:

Inventory, at lower-of-FIFO-cost-or-market (cost, $50,000)	$48,000

The required entries to record the above data relative to inventory are:

Inventory	50,000	
Cost of Goods Sold		50,000
Loss from Market Decline of Inventory	2,000	
Inventory		2,000

Other companies prefer not to separate the loss from market decline. Instead they simply deduct the ending inventory at the lower-of-cost-or-market amount from the total of the goods available for sale. In this manner the amount of market decline recognized is buried in cost of goods sold. The entry should be:

Inventory	48,000	
Cost of Goods Sold		48,000

Answer frame 16[7]

1. If each item is priced at lower of cost or market, the inventory is $3,190.
2. If the total inventory is priced at lower of cost or market, the inventory is $3,240.

If you answered incorrectly, restudy Frame 16[7] before going on to Frame 17[7] on page 314.

17[7] *continued*

With respect to the lower-of-cost-or-market method, indicate whether each of the following statements is true or false.

1. The method may be applied to individual items, to groups, or to total inventory for financial reporting purposes.
2. Write-downs to market value should not be recorded if selling prices are not expected to fall.
3. Merchandise may be stated at more than net realizable value if its cost and market value are greater than net realizable value.

Check your answer in Answer Frame 17[7] on page 318.

Frame 18[7]

Gross margin method of estimating inventory

The gross margin method is an estimating procedure used to approximate the amount of an inventory for the following purposes:

1. To obtain an inventory cost at the end of each month of a fiscal period except the last. The inventory cost so computed is used in the monthly financial statements.
2. As a method of verifying a previously determined ending inventory amount.

The gross margin method is a substitute method used to arrive at an inventory amount and is based on the assumption that the rate of gross margin realized is highly stable from period to period. The method is satisfactory only if this assumption is correct.

To illustrate the gross margin method of computing the inventory, assume that the Sweet Company has for several years maintained a rate of gross margin on sales of 40 percent. The following data for 1975 are available: the January 1 inventory was $30,000; purchases of merchandise were $390,000; and sales of merchandise were $600,000. The approximate inventory for December 31, 1975, can be computed as follows:

Inventory, January 1, 1975		$ 30,000
Purchases		390,000
Cost of merchandise available for sale		$420,000
Less estimated cost of sales:		
Sales	$600,000	
Gross margin (40% of $600,000)	240,000	
Estimated cost of sales		360,000
Inventory, December 31, 1975		$ 60,000

Indicate the correct figures for the first question below and answer yes or no to the second.

1. If the Sweet Company's sales had been $525,000 instead of $600,000, what would the cost of sales have been and what amount would have been shown for inventory on the December 31, 1975, statement of financial position?
2. Is it advisable for a company to rely exclusively on the gross margin method to determine the ending inventory and cost of goods sold for the end-of-year financial statements?

Check your responses by turning to Answer Frame 18[7] on page 318.

Frame 19[7]

Inventory destroyed or stolen

If inventory is destroyed by fire or is stolen and if perpetual inventory records are kept, it is possible to determine a reasonable estimate of the loss. If perpetual inventory records are not maintained or if they are destroyed, it may be necessary to estimate the amount of the inventory destroyed or stolen by applying the gross margin method.

After the cost of the destroyed inventory is estimated, the amount recoverable from the insurance company, if the goods are insured, should be set up as a receivable. To illustrate, assume that $7,750 of inventory is destroyed by fire. The journal entry to record the destruction of the goods will be as follows:

Receivable from Insurance Company	7,750	
Inventory		7,750

Later, if the insurance company settles the claim for $7,100, the journal entry to record the recovery will be as follows:

Fire Loss	650	
Cash	7,100	
Receivable from Insurance Company		7,750

Thus, the net loss from the fire will be $650, and the Fire Loss account will be closed to the Expense and Revenue Summary account at the end of the fiscal period. If the inventory were not insured, however, the entry would be as follows:

Fire Loss	7,750	
Inventory		7,750

Answer frame 17[7]

1. True. These are the ways in which the method may be applied.
2. True. If such write-downs are recognized, they serve only to increase the amount of gross margin recognized in a subsequent period to a larger than normal amount.
3. False. Goods should never be carried at more than their net realizable value, as this would mean losses are included in inventory. The net realizable value of a particular good may be less than the going market value of similar goods because of damage, deterioration, or handling.

If you answered any of the above incorrectly, restudy Frame 17[7] before going on to Frame 18[7] on page 316.

Answer frame 18[7]

1. The correct cost of sales is $315,000; the December 31, 1975, inventory would be shown as $105,000. These are computed as follows:

Inventory, January 1, 1975		$ 30,000
Purchases		390,000
Cost of merchandise available for sale		$420,000
Less estimated cost of sales:		
Sales	$525,000	
Gross margin (40% of $525,000)	210,000	315,000
Inventory, December 31, 1975		$105,000

2. The correct response is no. The gross margin method provides only an estimate of the cost of goods sold and the ending inventory. It is not usable by itself for year-end statements because it assumes that the gross margin rate in the current period is the same as in prior periods. It is necessary to use a physical inventory in conjunction with one of the previously described methods of determining the actual inventory, cost of goods sold, gross margin, and net earnings for the current year. Without so doing, the gross margin method is not valid for future years because there would be no way to determine the "normal" rate of gross margin earned to be used in future computations. But an actual physical count is usually performed only at the end of the year, not during the year.

If your answers were incorrect, study Frame 18[7] again before going on to Frame 19[7] on page 317.

19[7] *continued*

On February 23, 1975, a fire destroyed a warehouse owned by J. L. Kiley Company. By applying the gross margin method, the cost of the merchandise destroyed was estimated at $127,000. The company was fully covered by insurance, and it submitted a claim to the insurance company for the full cost of the goods destroyed. The claim was settled for $119,500. Which of the following journal entries correctly records the settlement of the claim for fire loss on the Kiley Company books?

1.	Cash	119,500	
	Receivable from Insurance Company		119,500
2.	Cash	119,500	
	Fire Loss		119,500
3.	Cash	119,500	
	Fire Loss	7,500	
	Receivable from Insurance Company		127,000

4.	Cash	119,500	
	Fire Loss	7,500	
	Inventory		127,000

Check your answer in Answer Frame 19[7] on page 320.

Summary *chapter* 7

This chapter is concerned with what items should be included in inventory and with the dollar amount to be attached to the ending inventory.

Inventories consist of those items which are being held for sale to customers (merchandise or finished goods inventories), are in the process of production for future sale (work in process inventories), or are to be consumed in the production of goods or services for sale (raw materials and supplies inventories).

In principle, the cost of inventory includes the net invoice price plus all costs necessary to secure the merchandise and place it in a condition and location ready for sale (or use, in the case of a manufacturer). Only such factors as extra clerical expense, inconvenience, and immateriality excuse omitting costs of insurance and transportation-in and including the gross rather than net invoice prices in determining the cost of inventory.

There are a number of methods of inventory measurement. The ones which involve the use of actual cost include specific identification, FIFO, LIFO, and average cost. Another method often used is the lower-of-cost-or-market method. Two other methods which estimate cost are the gross margin method and the retail inventory method (the latter is dealt with in Chapter 8 of *Accounting II*).

The specific identification method involves the assignment of a known actual cost to a specifically identified unit of product.

Both FIFO and LIFO involve assumptions concerning the flow of costs. FIFO assumes that the cost of the goods first acquired is the cost of the first goods sold. In other words, the cost of the goods remaining in ending inventory is assumed to be the cost of the last units acquired. Under LIFO just the opposite is assumed. The cost of the last units acquired is considered to be the first to be charged to cost of goods sold, and the cost remaining in ending inventory is assumed to be the cost of the first units acquired. These two methods involve assumptions concerning costs and may be used regardless of the actual physical flow of units.

FIFO can be applied under either the periodic or the perpetual procedure, with the same end result. LIFO also may be applied under either procedure, but generally inventories are adjusted to the amounts obtainable from application of LIFO under the periodic procedure. If LIFO is used for tax purposes it must also be used for general financial reporting purposes.

The weighted average method is employed under the periodic proce-

Answer frame 19[7]

Answer 3 is the correct response. A receivable in the amount of $127,000 should have been set up when the amount of the claim was determined. The full amount of the receivable is canceled by the payment received even though the cash received is less than the full amount of the claim. The unrecovered cost of the destroyed merchandise is charged to the loss account.

The fourth entry would be acceptable if insurance companies paid for losses on the same date they occur, but this is seldom the case.

If you answered incorrectly, reread Frame 19[7] before going on to the chapter summary, page 319.

---

dure. The total of the number of units purchased plus those in the beginning inventory is divided into the total cost of goods available for sale to derive a weighted average unit cost. The units in ending inventory are then priced at this weighted unit cost.

The moving average method is applied only under the perpetual procedure. Weighted average costs are computed after each purchase by dividing the total cost of the units on hand by the number of units on hand. Units sold during the period are removed from inventory at the last-established unit cost.

All of the above methods are considered acceptable and no one of them can be considered the only correct one. Each method possesses an attribute which makes it attractive in certain circumstances.

The lower-of-cost-or-market method originated at a time when statements of financial position were used largely for short-term credit purposes and the grantor of credit liked to see a "conservative" statement of financial position. In applying lower-of-cost-or-market, market is defined as current replacement cost, but market may not exceed net realizable value nor be less than net realizable value less an allowance for normal profit. Net realizable value is defined as the estimated selling price less estimated costs of completion and disposition.

In the accounting records the lower-of-cost-or-market method may be applied to each item of inventory, to each class of inventory, or to total inventory.

Two methods of estimating ending inventory are the gross margin method and the retail method. The gross margin method is quite crude and is usually used only for interim statement purposes and as a very rough check on the accuracy of the ending inventory determined through a physical count. It is based on the assumption that the rate of gross margin realized is highly stable from period to period. The method is only as valid as this assumption. To find the ending inventory, the estimated cost of goods sold is deducted from the cost of goods available for sale (the estimated cost of goods sold is found by subtracting the estimated gross margin from sales). It is advisable to take a physical inventory to determine the year-end inventory, since the gross margin percentage for the current period may have changed from previous years.

The retail inventory method is discussed in Chapter 8 of *Accounting II*.

To complete your review of this chapter, study the definitions of new terms contained in the glossary which follows. Then go on to the Student Review Quiz for a self-administered test of your comprehension of the material in the chapter.

Glossary *chapter 7*

FIFO (first-in, first-out)—a method of pricing inventory under which the costs of the first goods acquired are the first costs charged to cost of goods sold when goods are actually sold.

Gross margin method—a method for estimating inventory. Gross margin percentages from previous periods are applied to sales of the current period to arrive at an estimated amount of gross margin and cost of goods sold. Cost of goods sold is deducted from cost of goods available for sale to arrive at estimated ending inventory.

LIFO (last-in, first-out)—a method of pricing inventory under which the costs of the last goods acquired are the first costs charged to cost of goods sold when goods are actually sold.

Lower-of-cost-or-market method—a method of pricing inventory under which cost or market, whichever is lower is selected for each item, each group, or for the whole inventory.

Moving average method—a method of pricing inventory under which a new unit cost is determined after each purchase by dividing total cost of units on hand by the number of units on hand. The cost of each sale is recorded at the latest computed unit cost. This method can only be used with the perpetual inventory procedure.

Net realizable value—estimated selling price of merchandise less estimated cost of completion and disposition.

Specific identification—an inventory method which involves the assignment of a known actual cost to a particular identifiable unit of product.

Weighted average method—a method of pricing inventory under which the total number of units purchased plus those in the beginning inventory is divided into the total cost of goods available for sale to arrive at a weighted unit cost. The ending inventory is carried at this cost per unit.

Student review quiz *chapter 7*

To develop a permanent record of your responses, you may write them on the answer sheet provided in the *Work Papers* or on a separate piece of paper.

1 In 1975 the Sun Company had an ending inventory of $2,800. Its average inventory for 1975 was $2,400. The following is a trial balance at December 31, 1975:

	Debits	*Credits*
Cash	$ 9,532	
Accounts receivable . . .	1,600	
Merchandise inventory, Jan. 1	2,000	
Accounts payable		$ 900
Capital stock		11,000
Sales		8,850
Sales returns, allowances	50	
Sales discounts	22	
Purchases	7,100	
Purchase returns and allowances		400
Purchase discounts		64
Transportation-in	160	
Freight-out	200	
Sales salaries	550	
	$21,214	$21,214

Considering the above data, the cost of goods sold for the year is:

a) $7,596.
b) $6,396.
c) $6,196.
d) $5,996.
e) $5,836.
f) None of the above.

2 As a matter of proper accounting theory, which of the following costs should not be included in inventory?

a) Amount paid to railroad for hauling goods to place of business.

b) Amount paid to local trucking company to haul goods to warehouse from railroad station.
c) Cost of handling, unpacking, checking, and pricing merchandise received.
d) Cost of storing goods until they are sold.
e) Cost of hauling goods from place of business to customers' warehouses.

3 If the inventory on December 31, 1975, is understated by $100,000, which of the following would result?
a) Expenses of 1975 would be overstated.
b) Net earnings of 1976 would be understated.
c) Net earnings of 1975 would be overstated.
d) Expenses of 1976 would be overstated.
e) None of these.

4 The use of a Discounts Lost account implies that—
a) The cost of inventory is the invoice price of the inventory items.
b) The cost of inventory is the list price of the inventory items.
c) Purchase discounts lost are a part of the cost of merchandise.
d) Purchase discounts lost are penalties for inefficiency rather than additions to cost of merchandise purchased.
e) Purchase discounts taken are part of the cost of the inventory.

5 A company has, for a given year, a beginning inventory of 200 units at $2.50; purchases of 600 units at $3.50, and 1,100 units at $4; and sales of 700 units and 1,000 units. What is the cost of the ending inventory under the FIFO method of determining inventory?
a) $0.
b) $500.
c) $700.
d) $800.
e) None of these.

6 Which of the following statements is false? When the general price level is rising, the inventory on the statement of financial position at the end of the year—
a) Would be lower under the LIFO method of costing than under the FIFO method.
b) Would more nearly approximate current replacement cost under FIFO than under LIFO.
c) Would be the same whether FIFO were applied under the periodic or the perpetual procedure.
d) Would be higher under the weighted average method than under the moving average method.

7 Given the following data, which of the statements below are true? Assume there is no beginning inventory.

Feb.		*Units*	*At ($)*
2	Purchase	1,000	1.10 = $1,100
10	Purchase	600	1.50 = $ 900
12	Sell	400	
20	Purchase	300	2.00 = $ 600
25	Sell	200	
28	Balance	1,300	

a) Under the weighted average method, the units sold on February 12 would have a unit cost of $1.368 ($2,600 ÷ 1,900).
b) Under the LIFO method applied on the periodic basis, the 400 units sold on February 12 would be charged to cost of goods sold at $1.50 each for a total of $600.
c) Under the moving average method, the 400 units sold on February 12 would be costed at $1.25 ($2,000 ÷ 1,600).

8 With respect to the various methods of inventory measurement, which of the following statements is false?
a) The application of the FIFO method will usually result in fairly current costs being included in the cost of goods sold.
b) LIFO may often result in the cost of goods not sold being charged to cost of goods sold.
c) A company can manipulate its net earnings to a certain extent if it employs the LIFO method.
d) A company can manipulate its net earnings to a certain extent if it employs the specific identification method.
e) In applying the lower-of-cost-or-market method, cost must still be determined through the use of FIFO, LIFO, specific identification, or by means of some average method.

9 The Doll Company has three different products in its inventory at December 31, 1975, which have costs and current market values as follows:

Item	*Cost*	*Market*
A.......	$3,000	$3,200
B.......	4,000	3,900
C.......	6,000	5,800

With respect to the above inventory, which of the following statements are true?

a) The inventory could be reported at $12,900 under the lower-of-cost-or-market method.
b) The inventory could be reported at $12,700 under the lower-of-cost-or-market method.
c) If item C, which was purchased for sale at a price of $7,500, can still be sold for $7,500, it should be included in inventory at $6,000 under the lower-of-cost-or-market method.
d) If item B has a selling price of $4,200 and additional costs of $400 are yet to be incurred in disposing of this item, it should be included in inventory at $3,800 under the lower-of-cost-or-market method.

10 Under the lower-of-cost-or-market method the determination of the "market" figure to compare with cost is which of the following?
a) The price at which the inventory can be sold to customers.
b) The replacement cost of the inventory.
c) The net realizable value of the inventory.
d) The net realizable value less normal profit.
e) It is **(b)** above only if **(b)** falls between **(c)** and **(d)**. If **(b)** is higher than **(c)**, then **(c)** becomes market. If **(b)** is lower than **(d)**, then **(d)** becomes market.
f) None of the above statements fully describes the approach.

11 The gross margin method of computing inventory (choose the false statement)—
a) Assumes a stable rate of gross margin from period to period.
b) May indicate possible inventory shortages when used in conjunction with a physical inventory.
c) May be used in lieu of a physical inventory at year end.

12 Holt & Son, Inc. for several years has maintained a 30 percent average gross margin on sales. Given the following data for 1975 for cost price and normal retail price, what is the approximate inventory on December 31, 1975, computed by the gross margin method of estimating inventory?

	Cost	*Retail*
Inventory, Jan. 1....	$13,000	$ 21,000
Purchases..........	52,000	79,000
Total...............	$65,000	$100,000

Sales in 1975 were $70,000.
a) $30,000.
b) $16,000.
c) $19,500.
d) $21,000.
e) $ 9,000.

Now compare your answers with the correct answers and explanations on page 712.

Questions *chapter* 7

1 Why does an understated ending inventory understate net earnings for the period by the same amount?
2 Why does an error in ending inventory affect two accounting periods?
3 What does "cost" of inventory include?
4 How should purchase discounts lost be shown in the earnings statement?
5 What is the effect of a failure to include in inventory the cost of transportation, insurance in transit, and other handling?
6 What does it mean to "take a physical inventory"?
7 Indicate how a company can manipulate the amount of net earnings it reports if it uses the LIFO method of inventory measurement. Why is the same manipulation not possible under FIFO?
8 In the measurement of inventory at the lower of cost or market, what is the effect on the cost of goods sold if the ending inventory is shown in the earnings statement: (*a*) at market, if that figure is below cost? (*b*) at cost, if that figure is below market?
9 Why is it considered acceptable accounting practice to recognize a loss by writing down an item of merchandise in inventory to market, but unacceptable to recognize a gain by writing up an item of merchandise in inventory?

10 Under what operating conditions will the gross margin method of computing an inventory produce approximately correct amounts?

Exercises *chapter 7*

1 The Jacksonian Corporation uses the periodic inventory procedure, maintains an account to show discounts lost, and records purchases at their net prices. Prepare entries for the following:

May	1	Received merchandise from the Mead Corporation, $2,000; terms, 2/10, n/30.
	3	Received merchandise from the Byron Corporation, $1,200; terms, 2/10, n/30.
	8	Paid the Mead Corporation invoice.
	15	Paid the Byron Corporation invoice.

2 The Look Company uses the net invoice price in its statements and records. Journalize the following selected daily transactions:

a) Purchased on account and received six units of merchandise at $200 each; terms, 2/10, n/30.

b) Received and paid cash for a large supply of sales tickets, letterheads, etc.; invoice price, $500 less 2 percent cash discount.

c) Ordered four units of merchandise at $100 each; terms, 2/10, n/30.

d) Paid cash for one unit of office equipment; terms, 2/10, n/30. The invoice read:

One checkwriter	$300	
Less 2% discount	6	$294
Express charges		4
Cash paid		$298

e) Paid transportation charges of $36 on the six units of merchandise received in **(a)**.

f) Paid the invoice for transaction **(a)** after the discount period had expired.

g) Sold one unit of merchandise acquired in transaction **(a)** for $320 cash.

3 The Chairn Company inventory records show a January 1 inventory of 500 units at $6 (total $3,000) and purchases of:

	Units	*At ($)*
Feb. 14	300	5.40 = $1,620
Mar. 18	800	5.25 = 4,200
July 21	600	5.70 = 3,420
Sept. 27	600	5.40 = 3,240
Nov. 27	200	5.85 = 1,170

The December 31 inventory was 1,200 units.

a) Present a short schedule showing the measurement of the ending inventory using the FIFO method.

b) Do the same using the LIFO method.

4 The Irvine Company's inventory of a certain product was 8,000 units with a cost of $11 each on January 1, 1975. During 1975 numerous units of this product were purchased and sold. Also during 1975 the purchase price of this product fell steadily until at year-end it was $9. The inventory at year-end was 12,000 units. State which of the two methods of inventory calculation, LIFO or FIFO, would have resulted in the higher reported net earnings and explain briefly.

5 Using the lower-of-cost-or-market method of inventory measurement, determine the appropriate inventory price for each of the following items:

	A	*B*	*C*	*D*
Unit cost	$17	$ 8	$34	$76
Replacement cost	16	6	35	80
Estimated selling price	20	11	40	90
Cost to complete and sell	3	3	7	12
Normal profit margin	2	1	5	7

6 The Martin Company had the following inventory transactions during 1975:

a) January 1 inventory on hand, 100 units at $4 = $400.

b) January sales were 20 units.

c) February sales totaled 30 units.

d) March 1, purchased 50 units at $4.20.

e) Sales for March through August were 40 units.

f) September 1, purchased 10 units at $4.80.

g) September through December sales were 45 units.

Record the journal entries affecting the Inventory account if the periodic inventory procedure is used and a physical inventory on December 31, 1975, showed 25 units on hand. Price the ending inventory at its weighted average cost.

7 Your assistant has compiled the following schedule to assist you in determining the decline in inventory from cost to the lower of cost or market, item by item.

	A	*B*	*C*	*D*
Units	200	200	600	1,000
Unit cost	$ 18	$ 8	$ 6	$ 10.20
Unit market	17	9	6	10.40
Total cost	3,600	1,600	3,600	10,200
Total market	3,400	1,800	3,600	10,400

Total cost is $19,000, total market $19,200.

a) What is the amount of inventory write-down?

b) Present the entry to reflect this decline in the accounting records.

c) Illustrate how the year-end inventory would be presented in a statement of financial position.

8 From the following 1975 data for the Hanson Company prepare an earnings statement for the year ended December 31, 1975, under each of the two acceptable methods of reporting under the lower-of-cost-or-market method (one method is to show inventory at cost and a loss from market decline of inventory after earnings from operations; the other is to show inventory at market in the earnings statement).

Sales	$560,000
Inventory, Jan. 1	26,000
Purchases	340,000
Selling expense	80,000
Administrative expense	50,000
Purchase returns	14,000
Purchase discounts lost	1,400

The December 31, 1975, inventory at cost is $24,000; at lower of cost or market, $18,800.

9 Roll Company follows the practice of taking a physical inventory at the end of each calendar year accounting period to establish the ending inventory amount for financial statement purposes. Its financial statements for the past few years indicate a normal gross margin of 30 percent. On July 18, a fire destroyed the entire store building and contents. The records were in a fireproof vault and are intact. These records, through July 17, show:

Merchandise inventory, Jan. 1	$ 50,000
Merchandise purchases	1,250,000
Purchase returns	15,000
Transportation-in	85,000
Sales	1,550,000
Sales returns	50,000

The company was fully covered by insurance and asks you to determine the amount of its claim for loss of merchandise.

Problems, Series A *chapter 7*

7–1–A

Fritzwell Company has followed a policy of not including in ending inventory any freight or insurance in transit costs on merchandise purchased. The justification offered is that the failure to include these costs in the ending inventory is approximately offset by a similar failure to include such costs in the beginning inventory. These costs average approximately 25 percent of the invoice cost of the merchandise. The inventories and net earnings for the past several years are:

For Year Ending	*Inventory*	*Net Earnings*
December 31, 1973.	$120,000	$100,000
December 31, 1974.	96,000	104,000
December 31, 1975.	160,000	112,000

Required:

a) State the amount of net earnings that would have been reported for the years 1974 and 1975 if the company had properly inventoried these freight and insurance costs.

b) State the circumstances under which the company's policy would have a nominal effect upon net earnings for the year.

7–2–A

Following are selected transactions and data of the Davis Company:

1976

Mar.	1	Bought merchandise, invoice amount, $4,000; terms, 2/10, n/30; from X Company.
	5	Bought merchandise, invoice amount, $5,000; terms, 2/10, n/30; from Y Company.
	11	Paid X Company for purchase of March 1.
	21	Paid Y Company for purchase of March 5.
	31	The goods bought from both X Company and Y Company make up the complete physical inventory.

Required (you may assume there were no opening inventory and no sales for March):

a) Present journal entries to record the above transactions and to set up the ending inventory at March 31, following a procedure which shows discounts taken. Assume the periodic inventory procedure is used.

b) Repeat **(a)** above under a procedure which shows discounts lost.

c) Which procedure would you recommend, and why?

7–3–A

Following are data relating to the beginning inventory and purchases of a given item of product of the Star Company for the year 1976:

January 1 inventory............	1,400 @	$1.05
February 2....................	1,000	1.00
April 5.......................	2,000	0.87
June 15.......................	1,200	0.85
September 30..................	1,400	0.80
November 28...................	1,800	0.90

During the year 6,600 units were sold. The periodic inventory procedure is employed.

Required:

Compute the ending inventory and cost of goods sold under each of the following methods:

a) FIFO.
b) LIFO.
c) Weighted average.

7–4–A

The Steele Corporation was organized on January 1, 1973, to deal in a product whose resale price reacted promptly to fluctuations in cost. Unit prices rose during the three years ended December 31, 1975. Selected data for 1973–75 are:

Year Ended December 31	*Inventory*		*Annual Data*	
	FIFO	*LIFO*	*Purchases*	*Sales*
1973............	$1,600	$1,200	$7,200	$8,100
1974............	2,000	1,400	6,000	9,500
1975............	3,300	2,000	7,400	8,200

Required: Compute the gross margin for each of the three years under FIFO and under LIFO.

7–5–A

The Adams Company determines its net earnings using the FIFO method of inventory measurement and reported net earnings for 1973 of $58,000; 1974, $42,000; and 1975, $52,000. Inventories on the FIFO and LIFO bases were:

December 31	*FIFO*	*LIFO*
1972............	$15,000	$14,000
1973............	17,200	15,800
1974............	16,800	15,600
1975............	18,300	16,700

Required: Compute the net earnings that would have been reported in 1973, 1974, and 1975 by the Adams Company had it employed the LIFO method of inventory measurement.

7–6–A

Given below are data relating to the ending inventory of the Trotter Company at December 31, 1975.

Item	*Quantity*	*Unit Cost*	*Unit Market*
1.	6,000	$1.00	$0.95
2.	12,000	0.80	0.90
3.	4,000	0.75	0.80
4.	10,000	1.40	1.25
5.	8,000	1.25	1.30
6.	2,000	0.90	0.80

Required:

a) Compute the ending inventory applying the lower-of-cost-or-market method to the total inventory.
b) Repeat **(a)** above applying the method to individual items.
c) Assume that the selling price, including normal margin, of item 6 is $1.25 and that the 2,000 units are to be delivered under a contract of sale at a price of $1.20 each. At what price should they be included in the ending inventory? Why?

7–7–A

Hayes Company employs a fiscal year ending September 30. At this time inventories are usually at a very low level because of reduced activity. The management of the company wishes to maintain full insurance coverage on its inventory at all times. The company has earned approximately 35 percent gross margin on net sales over the last several years. Given below are data taken from the accounting records of the company for the seven months ending April 30, 1976:

Sales.	$330,000
Sales returns.	20,000
Sales discounts.	6,000
Inventory October 1, 1975.	26,000
Purchases.	262,000
Purchase returns.	12,000
Purchase discounts.	5,000
Transportation-in.	10,000
Selling expenses.	30,000
Administrative expenses.	25,000

Required:

a) Indicate, in general, how the company can estimate its inventory at any given date.
b) State the amount of insurance coverage the company should obtain on its inventory in order to be fully covered at all times if the inventory is at its highest level on April 30 of each year (assuming inventory levels will not increase in the future).

7–8–A

The sales and cost of goods sold for the Pine Company for the past five years were as follows:

Year	Sales (Net)	Cost of Goods Sold
1970	$693,400	$464,578
1971	749,600	502,232
1972	857,400	565,884
1973	820,600	558,008
1974	885,600	593,352

For the seven months ended July 31, 1975, the following information is available from the accounting records of the company:

Sales	$645,680
Purchases	382,400
Purchase returns	2,400
Sales returns	14,480
Inventory January 1, 1975	79,000

In requesting the extension of credit by a new supplier, the Pine Company has been asked to present current financial statements. It does not wish to incur the cost nor devote the time necessary to take a complete physical inventory at July 31, 1975.

Required:

a) Indicate how financial statements can be prepared without taking a complete physical inventory.
b) From the data given, estimate the inventory at July 31, 1975.

Problems, Series B *chapter 7*

7–1–B

Jolley Company reported net earnings in 1973 of $119,200, in 1974 of $128,800, and in 1975 of $108,600. Analysis of its inventories shows that certain clerical errors were made, so that inventory figures were:

	Incorrect	*Correct*
December 31, 1973	$24,200	$28,400
December 31, 1974	28,000	23,400

Required:

a) Compute the amount of net earnings for each of the three years assuming that the clerical errors in computing the inventory had not been made.
b) Determine the total net earnings for the three years with the use of the incorrect inventories and compare this with the total net earnings determined when correct inventories were used.

7–2–B

Gibson Company, a newly organized corporation, embarked upon an extensive purchasing program in November, 1975. It opened its doors for business on December 15, 1975. The company decided to employ a calendar year accounting period, and as of December 31, 1975, its accounts show:

Sales	$ 42,000
Purchases	720,000
Transportation-in	96,000
Purchase discounts	14,400

All purchases were subject to discount terms of 2/10, n/30. The cost of the inventory on December 31, 1975, at vendor's gross invoice prices was $690,000.

Required: Present a schedule showing the correct computation of cost of goods sold and the gross margin for the period ending December 31, 1975.

7–3–B

The purchases and sales of a certain product for the Hamilton Company for April, 1975, are shown below. There was no inventory at April 1.

Purchases			*Sales*	
Apr. 3	1,000 units @	$2.50	Apr. 4	600 units
10	800	2.60	11	500
22	1,600	2.30	16	500
28	900	2.40	26	400
			30	600

Required:

a) Compute the ending inventory of the above product as of April 30 under each of the following methods: (1) FIFO, (2) LIFO, (3) weighted average, and (4) moving average.

b) Give the journal entries to record the purchases and the cost of goods sold for the month under both FIFO and LIFO methods applied under the periodic procedure.

7–4–B

Listed below are the purchases and sales of a certain product made by the Thomas Company during 1974 and 1975. The company had 10,000 units of this product on hand at January 1, 1974, with a cost of $1 per unit.

Purchases			*Sales*		
1974			1974		
Feb. 18	2,000 @	$1.00	Feb. 1	3,000 @	$1.60
Apr. 16	5,000	0.95	Apr. 21	4,000	1.50
Aug. 26	5,000	0.90	Sept. 1	4,000	1.40
Dec. 21	4,000	0.92	Dec. 23	3,500	1.45
1975			1975		
Jan. 26	3,000 @	$0.95	Jan. 7	2,500 @	$1.50
Mar. 6	5,000	1.00	Mar. 21	4,000	1.60
Aug. 12	3,000	1.10	Sept. 8	2,500	1.60
Nov. 15	4,000	1.20	Dec. 2	4,500	1.75

The company employs the periodic inventory procedure.

Required:

a) Compute the cost of the ending inventory and the cost of goods sold for both years assuming the use of the FIFO method of inventory measurement.

b) Repeat (a) above assuming the use of LIFO.

7–5–B

Given below are the net earnings and inventories of the Robinson Corporation as reported for the years indicated:

December 31	FIFO	LIFO	Net Earnings
1974..........	$360,000	$294,000	$ 950,000
1975..........	372,000	348,000	980,000
1976..........	414,000	408,000	1,020,000

The Robinson Corporation has employed the FIFO method of inventory measurement.

Required (ignore the possible effects of federal income taxation):

a) State the amount of net earnings that the company would have reported in 1975 and 1976 if it had employed the LIFO method rather than FIFO.

b) State the amount of net earnings that the company would have reported in 1976 had it changed from FIFO to LIFO in 1976.

7–6–B

The accountant for the Hill Corporation prepared the following schedule of the company's inventory at December 31, 1975, and used the lower of the total cost or total market value in determining cost of goods sold.

				Total Value	
Item	Quantity	Cost per Unit	Market Value per Unit	Cost	Market
A..........	2,000	$1.50	$1.50		
B..........	1,500	1.00	0.90		
C..........	3,000	0.50	0.40		
D..........	4,000	0.25	0.30		

Required:

a) State whether this is an acceptable method of inventory measurement, and determine the amounts computed.

b) Compute the amount of the ending inventory on an alternative application of the lower-of-cost-or-market method.

c) State the effect upon net earnings in 1975 if the alternative in **(b)** was used rather than the method in **(a)**.

7–7–B

As part of a loan agreement with a local bank, the Larson Company is required to present quarterly and cumulative earnings statements for the year 1975. The company employs the periodic inventory procedure and customarily marks its merchandise to sell at a price which will yield a gross margin of 40 percent. Selected data for the first six months of 1975 are:

	First Quarter	Second Quarter
Sales	$310,000	$315,000
Purchases	200,000	225,000
Purchase returns and allowances	12,000	13,000
Purchase discounts	3,800	3,900
Sales returns and allowances	10,000	5,000
Transportation-in	8,800	8,900
Selling expenses	31,000	30,000
Administrative expenses	21,000	19,000

The cost of the physical inventory taken December 31, 1974, was $38,000.

Required:

a) Indicate how the earnings statements may be prepared without taking a physical inventory at the end of each of the first two quarters of 1975.

b) Prepare earnings statements for the first quarter, the second quarter, and the first six months of 1975.

7–8–B

Following are selected transactions and data of the Forest Company for 1975:

June 1 Bought merchandise, invoice amount, $6,500; terms, 2/10, n/30; from the Birch Company.

6 Bought merchandise, invoice amount, $7,000; terms, 2/10, n/30; from the Pine Company.

12 Paid the Birch Company for the purchase of June 1.

15 Paid the Pine Company for the purchase of June 6.

30 The entire physical inventory consists of the goods bought from the Birch Company and the Pine Company.

Required:

a) Assuming use of the periodic inventory procedure, present journal entries to record the above transactions and to set up the ending inventory at June 30 following a procedure which shows discounts taken.

b) Repeat **(a)** above under a procedure which shows discounts lost.

c) Which method would be of more value to the management of the Forest Company? Why?

chapter 8

Receivables and payables; payroll accounting

Learning objectives

Study of the material in this chapter is designed to achieve various learning objectives. These include an understanding of:

1. The nature of receivables and payables and their related accounts.
2. The process of accounting for bad debts.
3. Other possible contra accounts to accounts receivable.
4. The nature of and accounting for notes payable, notes receivable, and notes receivable discounted.
5. Accounting for payables which arise from sales taxes and property taxes.
6. Payroll accounting and the various payables that arise from having employees.

Frame 1[8]

The term "receivables" is often used in a broad sense in accounting to encompass any sum of money due to be received from any party for any reason resulting from a past transaction.

The term "payables" similarly is used to describe any amount of money due to be paid to any party for any reason resulting from a past transaction.

The purpose of this chapter is to discuss the aspects of receivables and payables which are not discussed in other parts of this text. Special attention is given to the contra accounts affecting accounts receivable (there usually are no such accounts affecting accounts payable), notes receivable and notes payable (and the interest receivable and interest payable which result from them), and payroll accounting.

Illustration 8.1 summarizes receivables and payables which commonly appear in statements of financial position. All of the items mentioned except the bonds and some of the notes would normally appear as current assets or liabilities in the statement of financial position. Of course there are other receivables and payables that could have been included, but they are less common and are left to texts designed for more advanced courses.

Determine whether each of the following statements is correct or incorrect.

1. There are usually contra accounts for both accounts receivable and accounts payable.
2. Notes payable and notes receivable result only from loans involving a bank or an individual and are long-term.
3. Interest receivable and interest payable normally result from notes and bonds; while dividends receivable, dividends payable, and subscriptions receivable result from the existence of capital stock.
4. The employment of persons creates several liabilities on the books of the employer.

Now turn to Answer Frame 1[8] on page 336 to check your answers.

Frame 2[8]

Accounts receivable

Revenue from sales is usually recorded at the time of the completion of the sale, which is generally assumed to be the time of delivery of the goods to the customer. There are two main reasons for this: (1) the revenue is earned, that is, the seller has usually completed or substantially completed his part of the agreement; and (2) the revenue is realized, that is, an exchange has taken place with an outsider and the amount

Illustration 8.1, *Summary of Receivables and Payables*

Receivables	*Payables*	*Comments*
Accounts receivable	Accounts payable	Result from the sale of goods or performance of services where payment is deferred. These were discussed in Chapters 3 and 7. This chapter focuses on the contra accounts associated with accounts receivable. There normally are no contra accounts to accounts payable.
Notes receivable	Notes payable	May result from the sale of goods or performance of services, but may also be the result of loans involving a bank or an individual. A note is a formal document signed by the maker. These may be short-term or long-term.
Bond investments	Bonds payable	Bonds are almost always long-term and are discussed in Chapter 10.
Interest receivable	Interest payable	Interest normally results from notes and bonds.
Dividends receivable	Dividends payable	Dividends result from the existence of capital stock and are discussed in Chapter 13.
Subscriptions receivable		Result from the issuance of capital stock and are discussed in Chapter 12.
Rent receivable	Rent payable	Result from the use of a building or other asset by someone other than the owner; covered in Chapter 4 and elsewhere.
	Federal income taxes payable	Result from federal income tax legislation and are discussed in Chapter 12, in *Accounting II*.
	Real and personal property taxes payable	Result from taxation of property by local (and some state) governmental units.
	Sales taxes payable	Many states (and some cities) levy a flat rate tax on retail sales.
	Payroll liabilities: Salaries and wages payable FICA taxes payable Employees' income tax withheld Federal unemployment taxes payable State unemployment taxes payable	These all result from the employment of persons by the entity.

Answer frame 1[8]

1. Incorrect. There are normally contra accounts to accounts receivable, but not to accounts payable.
2. Incorrect. They may also result from the sale of goods or performance of services involving customers and supplies. They are usually short-term, but may be long-term.
3. Correct. Interest does normally come from notes and bonds, although it can also result from such sources as savings accounts at banks. Dividends and subscriptions receivable do result from capital stock.
4. Correct. Included among payroll liabilities are salaries and wages payable, FICA taxes payable, employees' income tax withheld, federal unemployment taxes payable, and state unemployment taxes payable. There could also be union dues withheld and local income taxes withheld.

If you missed any of the above, reread Frame 1[8] before beginning Frame 2[8] on page 334.

2[8] *continued*

of revenue is ascertainable because of the receipt of cash or the customer's promise to pay cash. The asset usually received is an account receivable, although cash or occasionally a note may be received.

The recording of revenue at the time of the receipt of a promise to pay is the source of a number of special accounting problems not found in companies selling for cash only. These include sales discounts and uncollectible accounts, as well as the expenses of operating a credit and collection department. Additionally, any company selling merchandise is apt to experience sales returns and sales allowances. Since a number of these items may not be encountered until the period following the period of sales, a question arises as to how to secure the proper matching of these items against the recognized sales revenue which causes them to come into existence.

Uncollectible accounts or bad debts

An inescapable fact of life for companies doing business on a credit basis is that certain accounts will not be collected. The desired matching of uncollectible accounts or bad debts against sales revenue is accomplished through the use of an allowance for doubtful accounts. One purpose of the allowance for doubtful accounts is to reduce accounts receivable to their proper amount for statement of financial position purposes, that is, the amount that will ultimately be collected—their net realizable value.

Of even greater importance today is the use of the allowance to bring about a proper matching of the bad debts against revenue. For example, this proper matching consists of matching against the revenues of 1975 all accounts arising from 1975 sales which will ultimately prove uncollectible in 1975, 1976, or some other year. Thus, the purposes of establishing an allowance for doubtful accounts are twofold: (1) to bring about (by debiting Bad Debts Expense) a proper matching of expense and revenue so as to secure a fair determination of net earnings and (2) to secure (by crediting the Allowance for Doubtful Accounts) a proper valuation of the asset, accounts receivable, in the statement of financial position.

A question of accounting theory centers around the proper interpretation of the account debited when the allowance for doubtful accounts is established or increased. Describing it as a loss is unacceptable, since it is known in advance that it will be encountered and thus cannot be considered involuntary. A strong case can be made for treating the account as a deduction from sales revenue (through the use of a sales contra account) on the grounds that the receivables should be valued at the same amount for earnings statement purposes as for statement of financial position purposes. Practice today, however, almost universally treats the account as an operating expense, and this text will follow common practice and treat the account as one of the costs of conducting a business on a credit basis, classifiable as an operating expense.

Estimating bad debts expense

There are two basic methods of directly or indirectly estimating the amount of bad debts to be charged to a given accounting period, plus a variation of one of the methods.

Percentage of sales method. This method involves accumulating statistics relative to the amount which has proven uncollectible from each year's credit sales. This ratio of uncollectible accounts to credit sales is then employed in estimating directly the amount of bad debts expense to be charged to the current accounting period. If cash sales are nominal or are a fairly constant percentage of total sales, the entry may be based on total net sales.

To illustrate, assume that the Brice Company consistently has found that one half of 1 percent of its net sales are ultimately uncollectible. On the basis of this experience, it may, each month, each quarter, or each year, charge an amount equal to one half of 1 percent of the net sales for the period to expense and add a like amount to the Allowance for Doubtful Accounts. If net sales for 1975 are $400,000, the entry will read:

Bad Debts Expense..	2,000	
Allowance for Doubtful Accounts........................		2,000
To record bad debts expense.		

The $2,000 debit to Bad Debts Expense increases the expense for the period by exactly one half of 1 percent of $400,000, and the credit to the allowance account increases the contra asset account and thus causes net accounts receivable to show the estimated realizable cash value of the receivables. Assuming that the gross amount of accounts receivable is $100,000 and there was no previous balance in the allowance account, net accounts receivable would appear as follows on the statement of financial position:

Accounts receivable	$100,000
Less: Allowance for doubtful accounts	2,000
Net accounts receivable	$ 98,000

In published financial statements, sometimes the gross accounts receivable and the allowance are shown parenthetically:

Accounts receivable (gross $100,000 less allowance for doubtful accounts, $2,000)	$98,000

At the date of setting up the allowance, the specific accounts that will become uncollectible are not known. The use of the allowance permits charging expense at the end of the period for open accounts that may become uncollectible in the future.

If the Allowance for Doubtful Accounts account has a balance before adjustment for possible uncollectible accounts from the current period's sales, it presumably relates to accounts of prior periods which are not yet collected. In any event, under this method the amount in the allowance account will not influence the size of the periodic charge to expense.

Since this method bases the estimate of expense solely on the sales revenue of the same period, it is theoretically preferable because it yields the most precise matching of expense and revenue.

Percentage of accounts receivable method. This method may use a different percentage for each age category of receivable or may use one overall percentage.

A DIFFERENT PERCENTAGE FOR EACH AGE CATEGORY (AGING METHOD). An aging schedule is presented in Illustration 8.2, showing how the age of each customer's account is determined. The time intervals

Illustration 8.2

CARROL COMPANY
Analysis of Accounts Receivable, December 31, 1975

			Number of Days Past Due				
		Not Due	1–30	31–60	61–90	91–180	
		Estimated Uncollectible Percentage					
Customer	Debit Balance	1%	5%	10%	25%	50%	Amount Needed in Allowance
X	$ 8,000					$ 8,000	$ 4,000
Y	16,000		$ 12,000	$4,000			1,000
Z	4,000				$800	3,200	1,800
All others	800,000	$560,000	240,000				17,600
	$828,000	$560,000	$252,000	$4,000	$800	$11,200	$24,400

used to classify customer account balances will vary according to the credit terms granted. Credit terms of 30 days are assumed in the illustration. The column headings indicate the number of days elapsed since the accounts were due for payment by the customers.

As can be seen from Illustration 8.2, under this method the age of the accounts is the basis for estimating uncollectibility. For example, only 1 percent of the accounts not yet due (sales made less than 30 days prior to the end of the accounting period) is expected to be uncollectible, while at the other extreme 50 percent of all accounts 91–180 days past due is expected to become worthless. Aging schedules appropriate for other circumstances may require additional columns for accounts more than 180 days overdue, depending upon company policy with regard to the write-off of apparently uncollectible accounts.

Assume that the Allowance for Doubtful Accounts in the December 31, 1975, trial balance of the Carrol Company (Illustration 8.2) has a credit balance of $8,000. Prepare the entry needed to adjust the allowance account up to the required credit balance and to recognize the bad debts expense.

Check your answer by turning to Answer Frame 2[8] on page 340.

Frame 3[8]

Note carefully that under the aging method the primary goal is to secure an accurate measure of the net realizable value of the receivables. Thus, emphasis is placed on determining the proper balance in the Allowance for Doubtful Accounts account rather than upon the amount in the Bad Debts Expense account. The amount in the adjusting entry consequently will be the difference between the balance in the allowance and the newly determined required balance.

Normally, additional information (such as the financial habits of the customer) must be taken into consideration. An account long past due may be collectible; an account receivable arising from a very recent sale may be uncollectible. The aging schedule also keeps management currently informed concerning collections, collectible and uncollectible accounts, and the tendency of customers to accelerate or decelerate their rates of payment.

When specific accounts are actually determined to be uncollectible, the necessary entry to record this involves a debit to the Allowance for Doubtful Accounts account (see Frame 5[8]). In those cases where the debits to the Allowance for Doubtful Accounts to write off uncollectible accounts have exceeded the amounts credited to the allowance in prior years, the adjustment must be large enough to produce the desired credit balance. For example, in the preceding case, if the allowance had a debit balance of $3,000, the adjustment would be for $27,400. If the $3,000 balance was not the result of writing off accounts arising from 1975 sales,

Answer frame 2[8]

The required entry to record the information presented is:

Bad Debts Expense	16,400	
Allowance for Doubtful Accounts		16,400
To adjust the Allowance for Doubtful Accounts of $8,000 to the estimated necessary balance of $24,400.		

If you answered incorrectly, reread Frame 2[8] before beginning Frame 3[8] on page 339.

3[8] *continued*

at least $3,000 of the amount is a mismatching of uncollectible accounts of prior years against current revenues.

As of December 31, 1975, Austin Corporation has outstanding accounts receivable of $200,000, all from 1975 sales, and an Allowance for Doubtful Accounts with a debit balance of $2,500, of which $1,500 was caused by the write-off of accounts receivable arising from sales made in 1975. Through an aging of the accounts and the application of estimated rates of uncollectibility, the accountant for the company estimates that $6,000 of the outstanding receivables will never be collected.

Determine whether each of the following statements about the Austin Corporation is true or false.

1. The balance in the allowance account after proper adjustment will be $6,000.
2. The amount in the entry adjusting for bad debts will be $8,500.
3. The amount of mismatching of expense and revenue resulting from the application of the aging procedure in estimating bad debts will be $2,500.

Now turn to Answer Frame 3[8] on page 342 to check your answers.

Frame 4[8]

ONE OVERALL PERCENTAGE. This is a crude variation of the aging technique. The mechanics of its application are also similar. To illustrate, assume that on the basis of past experience the Ball Company estimates that 5 percent of its outstanding receivables of $100,000 as of December 31, 1975, will ultimately prove to be uncollectible. The Allowance for Doubtful Accounts has a debit balance of $1,000. The journal entry to adjust for bad debts is as follows:

Bad Debts Expense	6,000	
Allowance for Doubtful Accounts		6,000
To adjust allowance for possible uncollectible accounts.		

The application of this method does not embrace the rather careful analysis of customers' accounts found in the aging method. It also suffers from the deficiencies of the aging method.

With regard to the method of estimating bad debts, indicate whether each of the following statements is correct or incorrect.

1. As far as accuracy of the estimates is concerned, there is little difference between using an aging schedule and using one overall percentage of accounts receivable.
2. The percentage of sales method matches most closely the uncollectible accounts arising from a given year's sales with the sales revenue of that year.
3. The balance in the Allowance for Doubtful Accounts before adjustment may be ignored in determining the amount in the period-end adjusting entry for bad debts when an aging schedule is used.

Now turn to Answer Frame 4[8] on page 342 to check your answers.

Frame 5[8]

Write-off of uncollectible accounts

Once a company has established an allowance for doubtful accounts, accounts which are deemed definitely uncollectible are charged against the allowance. Using the assumed account receivable of B as an example and assuming that $4,000 of the account ultimately proves to be uncollectible, the entry to record this fact in January, 1976 is:

Allowance for Doubtful Accounts	4,000	
Accounts Receivable		4,000

Posting this entry does not change the estimated net collectible amount of the asset, accounts receivable. To illustrate: If accounts receivable amount to $20,000 and the allowance is $2,000, the net receivables are $18,000. If a $1,000 account is written off, the receivables and allowance balances are $19,000 and $1,000, respectively, or $18,000 net.

It should also be noted that it is quite possible for the Allowance for Doubtful Accounts to have a debit balance if it is adjusted only once a year. Companies do not often carry accounts receivable which are one year or more old in their accounts. Consequently, by the end of 1975, all accounts arising from 1974 sales will often be collected or written off. If estimates were exact, the allowance balance would be zero. Some accounts arising from 1975 sales, however, have probably been charged off; the result is a debit balance before adjusting, unless estimates of prior years have been excessive.

Answer frame 3[8]

1. True. The aging method focuses on the required balance in the Allowance for Doubtful Accounts account. The entry brings this balance up to the total of the estimated uncollectibles.
2. True. The required balance for the allowance is $6,000. It now has a debit balance of $2,500. Thus, an entry crediting the allowance for $8,500 is needed.
3. False. The mismatching is for only $1,000 and not $2,500, since $1,500 of the debit balance was caused by the write-off of current-year (1975) receivables. A charge to expense in 1975 to cover $1,500 of the debit balance would thus be quite proper matching.

If you missed any of the above, reread Frame 3[8] before starting Frame 4[8] on page 340.

Answer frame 4[8]

1. Incorrect. Using one overall percentage of accounts receivable lacks the careful analysis of accounts found using the aging schedule. So it cannot be as accurate.
2. Correct. This is the method which directly relates the expense to the sales of the period. Both variations of the other method base the estimate of bad debts on the accounts receivable balance, which may include some accounts which arose in prior accounting periods.
3. Incorrect. The balance in the allowance may not be ignored. The percentage of accounts receivable method (of which the aging schedule is one variation) is designed primarily to determine the proper balance for the allowance for possible losses from existing receivables. The adjustment made must consider the existing balance in the allowance or the allowance after adjustment will not contain the desired balance.

If you missed any of the above, reread Frame 4[8] before starting Frame 5[8] on page 341.

5[8] *continued*

In the above entry charging off $4,000 of B's account, an expense is *not* recognized because (choose the correct answer):

1. The customer may still pay the account later in the year.
2. The expense will be recognized when the adjusting entry is made to record bad debts expense at the end of 1976.
3. The expense was recognized sometime prior to 1976.

Now turn to Answer Frame 5[8] on page 344 to check your answer.

Frame 6[8]

Bad debts recovered

The first indication that an account has been charged off in error usually occurs when a check is received in the mail. The cash receipt will be recorded in the normal fashion of debiting Cash and crediting

Accounts Receivable. When the credit is posted, the lack of a balance in the specific customer's account will be noted or the customer's account will not be in the current accounts receivable file. Further investigation will then reveal its prior write-off to the allowance, and an entry reinstating the account will be required.

To illustrate, assume that on October 8, 1976, B's check for $4,000 is received in the mail. The entry is:

Cash	4,000	
Accounts Receivable		4,000

When it is discovered that B's account had been written off to the allowance, the following entry is required:

Accounts Receivable	4,000	
Allowance for Doubtful Accounts		4,000

The entry charging off the account as uncollectible is reversed for two reasons. Which of the following is *not* a reason for this action?

1. The write-off of the account resulted from an erroneous assumption that it was uncollectible; the ultimate collection of the account is evidence that it should not have been written off.
2. After the entry is posted, the customers' account reflects the actual history of the transactions entered into with him.
3. The allowance for doubtful accounts was incorrectly estimated on December 31, 1975.

Now check your answer in Answer Frame 6[8] on page 344.

Frame 7[8]

If only a part of a previously written off account is collected, the preferable procedure is to reinstate only that portion of the account actually collected, unless there is concrete evidence that the entire account will be collected. There will be ample opportunity to reinstate the balance of the account when actual collection is effected. Furthermore, the total reinstatement of the account would not change the net amount of accounts receivable reported in the statement of financial position, since the reinstatement entry serves to increase both the accounts receivable and the allowance by a like amount.

Other accounts receivable valuation accounts

Occasionally, a published annual report will show accounts receivable reduced by an allowance for freight. Such an account shows the estimated amount of freight costs paid by the buyer for the seller (goods shipped f.o.b. destination, freight collect), which the buyer will deduct before making remittance to the seller.

Answer frame 5[8]

The third answer is correct. At the date of charging off $4,000 of B's account (the original sale having been made in a prior year), an expense is not recognized because under the accrual basis of accounting the expense element was recorded in the same period as the sale. At that time, possible uncollectible accounts were estimated and an entry was made recording the bad debts expense and adding a similar amount to the allowance for doubtful accounts.

If you answered incorrectly, reread Frames 4[8] and 5[8] before beginning Frame 6[8] on page 342.

Answer frame 6[8]

Statement 3 is correct. The fact that B happened to pay his account eventually does not mean that the allowance was incorrect; it merely means that B's account is not one of those which proved to be or will prove to be uncollectible.

If you answered incorrectly, restudy Frame 6[8] before beginning Frame 7[8] on page 343.

7[8] *continued*

Similarly, in rare instances, a published annual report will show accounts receivable valuation accounts entitled Allowance for Collection Costs, Allowance for Sales Discounts, and Allowance for Sales Returns. These allowances are established for the same two reasons—to get a proper matching of freight and collection expenses against revenues and to present accounts receivable at their net realizable value. But, as a practical matter, such allowances are seldom set up for one of the following reasons:

1. It is believed that these expenses are fairly constant from period to period, with the result that there is no material effect upon reported net earnings from failure to accrue them.
2. The amount to be accrued is difficult to estimate with any reasonable degree of accuracy.
3. Of all of the possible adjustments which have theoretical justification as valuation contra accounts to accounts receivable and as items to be considered in determining net earnings, only the deduction for possible uncollectible accounts is permitted in determining taxable earnings under present regulations.

Receivables in the statement of financial position

The gross amount of accounts receivable should be stated in the statement of financial position. This gross amount, shown as an asset, is equal to all subsidiary accounts with debit balances. (The total of all accounts with credit balances should be shown under current liabilities under the caption "credit balances in customers' accounts.") From this asset total should be deducted any allowances established, including the allowances for doubtful accounts, sales discounts, sales returns and allowances, transportation, and so on. These allowances reduce the gross receivables to the amount expected to be collected—the net realizable value—which is the proper amount for statement of financial position purposes. More importantly, the entries establishing these allowances serve to bring about a higher degree of precision in the matching process of assigning expenses against revenues or in refining the estimate of net revenue from sales.

Assume that the total current assets and the total current liabilities in the Y Company's June 30, 1975, statement of financial position are $250,000 and $125,000, respectively. Offset against the total amount of accounts receivable are $5,000 of customers' credit balances. Decide whether each of the following statements is true or false.

1. Total current assets are understated.
2. Total current liabilities are understated.
3. The ratio of current assets to current liabilities is correct.
4. The amount of working capital (current assets minus current liabilities) is overstated.

Now turn to Answer Frame 7[8] on page 346 to check your answers.

Frame 8[8]

Notes receivable and notes payable

A promissory note is an unconditional promise in writing, made by the borrower (the maker) and signed by him, obligating him to pay the lender (the payee) or someone else who legally acquires the note a certain sum of money on demand or at a definite time. Normally, only the maker and the payee are parties to the instrument, but sometimes others who legally acquire the note or guarantee payment also become parties.

A company may have notes receivable or notes payable arising from transactions with suppliers or customers. When a company is the maker of a note, with a supplier as the payee, the company has received short-term financing from that supplier. When a company is the payee of a note and a customer is the maker, the company has supplied short-term financing to that customer. Notes may also arise from loans involving a bank or an individual associated with the entity. The accounting for these transactions is covered in this section.

Most notes bear an explicit charge for interest. Interest is the fee charged for use of money through time. It is an expense to the maker of the note and revenue to the payee of the note. For the sake of convenience, in commercial transactions interest is commonly calculated on the basis of 360 days per year. The elapsed time in a fraction of a year between two stated days is computed by counting the exact number of days, omitting the day the money is borrowed but counting the day it is paid back. A note falling due on a Sunday or a holiday is due on the following business day.

Answer frame 7[8]

1. True. Total current assets are understated because $5,000 worth of liabilities is offset against them.
2. True. Total current liabilities are understated because $5,000 worth of current liabilities is offset against current assets.
3. False. The ratio of $250,000/$125,000 is larger than the correct ratio of $255,000/$130,000.
4. False. There is no effect upon the amount of working capital, as both current assets and current liabilities are understated by the same amount.

If you missed any of the above, reread Frame 7[8] before starting Frame 8[8] on page 345.

8[8] *continued*

Assume that we desire to calculate the interest on a $1,000 note; the interest rate is 6 percent and the life of the note is 60 days. The calculation is as follows:

$$\text{PRINCIPAL} \times \text{RATE OF INTEREST} \times \text{TIME} = \text{INTEREST}$$
$$\$1{,}000 \times \frac{6}{100} \times \frac{60}{360} = \$10$$

Notice that when the interest rate is 6 percent and the life of the note is 60 days you can find the amount of interest by moving the decimal point in the principal two places to the left. This is often referred to as the 6 percent, 60-day rule. For instance, assuming that the following notes are all 6 percent, 60-day notes, the interest on each is:

Principal	*Interest*
$ 1,000	$ 10.00
1,250	12.50
168,000	1,680.00

Now assume that a $2,000 note is a 6 percent, 30-day note. Show:

1. How the interest would be calculated using the formula.
2. The calculation using the 6 percent, 60-day rule. (This method can be used even if the note is not a 6 percent, 60-day note.)

Now turn to Answer Frame 8[8] on page 348 to check your answers.

Frame 9[8]

Determination of maturity date

Since a note is a promise to pay a certain sum in money on demand or at a definite time, it is necessary to know the rules used to determine the maturity date—the due date—of the note. The maturity date may be indicated by one of several methods.

1. On demand. "On demand, I promise to pay. . . ." In this case, the maturity date is at the option of the holder and cannot be computed.

2. *On a stated date.* "On July 18, 1976, I promise to pay. . . ." The date is designated, and a computation is not necessary to determine it.

3. *At the end of a stated period.* (*a*) "One year after date, I promise to pay. . . ." If the maturity is expressed in years, the note matures on the same day of the same month as the date of the note in the year of maturity.

(*b*) "Four months after date, I promise to pay. . . ." If the maturity is expressed in months, the note will mature on the same day in the month of maturity. For example, one month from July 18, 1976, is August 18, 1976; two months from July 18, 1976, is September 18, 1976; three months from July 18, 1976, is October 18, 1976. If a note is issued on the last day of a month and the month of maturity has fewer days than the month of issuance, the note matures on the last day of the month of maturity. A one-month note dated January 30, 1976, matures on February 29, 1976. A five-month note dated January 31, 1976, matures on June 30, 1976.

(*c*) "Ninety days after date, I promise to pay. . . ." If the maturity is expressed in days, the exact number of days must be counted. The first day (date of origin) is omitted and the last day (maturity date) is included in the count; for example, a 90-day note dated October 19, 1976, matures on January 17, 1977.

October 20 to October 31, 1976	12 days
November, 1976	30
December, 1976	31
January 1 to January 17, 1977	17
	90 days

Notes arising from business transactions

Sometimes a note results from the conversion of an open account. To illustrate, assume that on October 6, 1975, Fox (the payee) receives from Kent (the maker) a 60-day, $18,000 note; the interest rate is 5 percent, and the note results from the earlier sale (on October 4) of merchandise by Fox to Kent. The interest will be earned over the life of the note and will not be paid until maturity, December 5, 1975. The entries for both the payee and the maker are as follows:

Fox, Payee

Oct. 4:		
Accounts Receivable	18,000	
Sales		18,000
To record sale.		
Oct. 6:		
Notes Receivable	18,000	
Accounts Receivable		18,000
To record receipt of note.		
Dec. 5:		
Cash	18,150	
Notes Receivable		18,000
Interest Revenue		150
To record receipt of principal and interest.		

Answer frame 8[8]

1. Using the formula, the calculation is as follows:

$$\text{PRINCIPAL} \times \text{RATE OF INTEREST} \times \text{TIME} = \text{INTEREST}$$
$$\$2{,}000 \times \tfrac{6}{100} \times \tfrac{30}{360} = \$10$$

2. Using the 6 percent, 60-day rule, the reasoning is as follows:

Interest on $2,000 at 6% for 60 days = $20
Interest on $2,000 at 6% for 30 days = $10

If you do not understand these answers, restudy Frame 8[8] before starting Frame 9[8] on page 346.

9[8]

continued

Kent, Maker

Oct. 4:		
Purchases	18,000	
Accounts Payable		18,000
To record purchase.		
Oct. 6:		
Accounts Payable	18,000	
Notes Payable		18,000
To record giving of note.		
Dec. 5:		
Notes Payable	18,000	
Interest Expense	150	
Cash		18,150
To record payment of principal and interest.		

A note is dishonored if the maker fails to pay it at maturity. The payee of the note may debit either Accounts Receivable or Dishonored Notes Receivable and credit Notes Receivable for the face of the note. If interest is due, he should debit the uncollected interest to the same account to which the dishonored note is debited and credit Interest Revenue. The maker should merely debit the amount of interest incurred to Interest Expense and credit Interest Payable.

To illustrate, assume that Kent did not pay the note at the maturity date. The entries on the books of the payee and the maker are as follows:

Fox, Payee

Dec. 5:		
Dishonored Notes Receivable	18,150	
Notes Receivable		18,000
Interest Revenue		150

Kent, Maker

Dec. 5:		
Interest Expense	150	
Interest Payable		150

Sometimes when a note cannot be paid at maturity, the maker either pays the interest on the original note or includes it in the face of a new note given to take the place of the old note. When it becomes obvious that the maker will never pay the note, the amount in the Dishonored Notes Receivable account pertaining to that note should be written off to Bad Debts Expense, Loss on Dishonored Notes, or some similar account. If notes were taken into account when making the annual provision for doubtful accounts, the debit should be to the Allowance for Doubtful Accounts account.

Assume that Galway gives a $10,000, 6 percent, 60-day note to Kelley on June 1. On the maturity date the note is dishonored. Give the entry required on each set of books on that date.

Now turn to Answer Frame 9[8] on page 350 to check your answers.

Frame 10[8]

Notes payable arising from need for short-term financing

There are various reasons why a business may need short-term financing, that is, why it may need to use the bank's or some other creditor's money for short periods of time. A business usually expects the cash inflow resulting from the sale of goods or services to exceed the cash outflow resulting from the purchase of goods for resale or the purchase of supplies, labor services, utilities, and so on. This is especially true because some expenses, such as depreciation expense, do not involve the current outflow of cash. But at certain times in the life of a business the inflow of cash may not exceed the outflow of cash from operations. Included among the factors which can cause this to happen are: (1) delay in the receipt of cash due to granting customers credit terms on amounts due (although this is at least partially offset by the use of credit on its purchases to delay the payment of cash); (2) seasonal buildup of inventory, such as that occurring in department stores just before the Christmas holidays and (3) expansion in operations caused by the expectation of a future increase in sales. We shall discuss some of the ways in which a business can acquire short-term financing.

Giving a note to the bank. In instances when a borrower presents his noninterest-bearing note to a bank with a request for a loan, the bank computes the amount of interest it charges for the use of its money on the face value of the note, deducts the amount computed from the face value, and gives the balance, the proceeds, to the borrower. The amount deducted is often called a bank discount, and the process of computing the amount is referred to as discounting. To illustrate this process, assume that a bank discounts a customer's $20,000, 90-day, noninterest-bearing note at 6 percent. The 6 percent interest is the bank's

Answer frame 9[8]

The required entries are as follows:

Kelly, Payee

July 31	Dishonored Notes Receivable	10,100	
	Notes Receivable		10,000
	Interest Revenue		100

Galway, Maker

July 31	Interest Expense	100	
	Interest Payable		100

If you answered incorrectly, restudy Frame 9[8] before beginning Frame 10[8] on page 349.

10[8] *continued* charge for the use of its money. The discount is $300, and this sum is deducted from the $20,000 and the remainder of $19,700 given to the customer.

To illustrate how this is recorded in the accounts, assume that the above transaction occurred on December 1, 1975. It could be recorded by the borrower as follows:

Dec. 1	Cash	19,700	
	Notes Payable—Discount	300	
	Notes Payable		20,000

Note that the borrower does not receive $20,000, but $19,700. Since he will pay $300 for the use of this sum for a period of 90 days, he is actually paying a rate of interest higher than 6 percent. (If $300 is the interest on $20,000 at 6 percent for 90 days, then $300 is more than 6 percent on $19,700 for 90 days.) Note also that the bank must discount this note in order to introduce interest into the transaction. If the bank advanced $20,000 on this note, it would not earn any interest from this loan because at maturity it would receive only $20,000. The Notes Payable—Discount account is used as a valuation contra account to reduce notes (traditionally carried at face value) to their net present value.

Assuming that December 31, 1975, is the end of the borrower's accounting period, interest expense for the month of December is recorded as follows:

Dec. 31	Interest Expense	100	
	Notes Payable—Discount		100

In the current liability section on the December 31, 1975, statement of financial position, the note and the discount appear as follows:

Notes Payable	$20,000
Less: Discount	200
	$19,800

When the note is paid at maturity, the entry is as follows (maturity date is February 29, 1976):

Feb. 29	Notes Payable	20,000	
	Interest Expense	200	
	Cash		20,000
	Notes Payable—Discount		200

This entry reduces the Notes Payable—Discount and Notes Payable accounts to zero balances. Notice that the difference between the cash paid out ($20,000) and that originally received ($19,700) is equal to the total interest expense ($300). The interest relates to a 90-day period, 30 days of which fall in the year ending December 31, 1975, and 60 days in the following year. Thus, the amount charged to interest expense should be $100 in 1975 and $200 in 1976.

The practice of discounting notes in the manner just described has been discontinued by many banks simply because under the procedure the customer does not receive the amount of funds requested. Presumably he should receive the amount he requests. An alternative approach is to compute interest on the amount requested, add this to the amount requested, and draw a note for the total of the two. Thus the customer would sign a 90-day, noninterest-bearing note for $20,300 and would receive $20,000. At the date of borrowing the entry would be:

Cash	20,000	
Notes Payable—Discount	300	
Notes Payable		20,300

Note that the borrower actually is paying 6 percent on the amount he receives when this method is used. Under the method illustrated earlier, he paid more than a 6 percent rate of interest.

The borrowing could alternatively be effected by giving a $20,000, 90-day, 6 percent interest-bearing note. At the date of borrowing the required entry is as follows:

Cash	20,000	
Notes Payable		20,000

At maturity the borrower pays both the face amount of the note and interest at the rate stated in the note on the face amount (a total of $20,300). When this method is used, the borrower also is paying the actual stated percentage rate of interest.

Assume that on November 1, 1976, John Akron discounts his own $10,000, 90-day note at the bank. The bank discount rate is 6 percent. Akron signs a note for $10,000 but receives that amount less interest from the bank. Give the entry Akron would make on November 1 to record receipt of the proceeds, and then give the adjusting entry required on December 31 to recognize interest expense incurred to date.

Now check your answers in Answer Frame 10[8] on page 352.

Answer frame 10[8]

The required entries are:

Nov. 1	Cash	9,850	
	Notes Payable—Discount	150	
	Notes Payable		10,000
Dec. 31	Interest Expense	100	
	Notes Payable—Discount		100

If you answered incorrectly, reread Frame 10[8] before beginning Frame 11[8] below.

Frame 11[8]

Discounting notes receivable. When a borrower issues his own note payable to a bank, he is directly liable to the bank at the maturity date of the loan. Such notes payable are shown in the statement of financial position as liabilities.

Instead of borrowing directly, a borrower may use another method of obtaining short-term financing from a bank. He may select a note receivable held by him, endorse it, and receive cash by discounting it at his bank if the instrument meets the requirements of the bank. Thus, a note receivable discounted arises. The borrower who discounts the note receivable is contingently, instead of directly, liable to the lending bank; that is, he must pay the bank the amount due at maturity only if the maker of the note fails to pay the obligation.

The cash proceeds of notes receivable discounted are computed as follows:

1. Ascertain the maturity value of the note (face value plus interest). This is the amount the bank will collect at maturity. For a noninterest-bearing note, the face of the note equals the maturity value. For an interest-bearing note, the face of the note plus interest for the life of the note equals the maturity value.
2. Ascertain the discount period; that is, count the exact number of days from the date of discounting to the date of maturity. Exclude the date of discounting, but include the date of maturity in the count. The discount period, of course, can never be longer than the life of the note.
3. Using the rate of discount charged by the bank, compute the discount on the maturity value (principal plus interest) for the discount period.
4. Deduct the bank discount from full value at maturity. The result is the cash proceeds.

The contingent liability is usually shown in the accounts by recording the notes receivable discounted in a Notes Receivable Discounted account at the face value of the note, even though the contingent liability extends to the interest also. If the original maker does not pay the bank at the maturity date, the borrower who discounts the note will be held liable.

EXAMPLE. Assume that on May 4, 1975, Carlson received a $10,000 note from Thomas bearing interest at 6 percent and maturing in 60 days from May 4. On May 14, 1975, Carlson discounted the note at the Michigan National Bank at 8 percent. The discount and the cash proceeds are determined as follows:

Face value of note	$10,000.00
Add: Interest at 6 percent for 60 days	100.00
Maturity value	$10,100.00
Less: Bank discount on $10,100 at 8 percent for 50 days	112.22
Cash proceeds	$ 9,987.78

The entry is as follows:

May 14	Cash	9,987.78	
	Interest Expense	12.22	
	Notes Receivable Discounted		10,000.00

If the proceeds exceed the book value of the note, the difference is credited to an Interest Revenue account.

Now assume that on June 1 Eric Jackson receives a $20,000, 6 percent, 90-day note dated June 1. He discounts it at the bank on July 1. The bank's rate of discount is 8 percent.

1. What is the note's maturity value?
2. What is its maturity date?
3. What is the discount period?
4. What is the discount amount charged by the bank?
5. How much are the cash proceeds?
6. What is the entry to record the receipt of the proceeds?

Now check your answers in Answer Frame 11[8] on page 354.

Frame 12[8]

Statement of financial position presentation of notes receivable discounted. In the above example, a statement of financial position prepared for Carlson as of December 31, 1975, should show a contingent liability in the amount of $10,000 for notes receivable discounted. Assume that the total of all notes receivable is $70,000. One acceptable method of presenting this information in the statement of financial position is:

ASSETS

Current Assets:	
Cash	$xx,xxx
Accounts receivable	xx,xxx
Notes receivable (Note 1)	60,000

Notes to Financial Statements:

Note 1: At December 31, 1975, the company is contingently liable for $10,000 of customers' notes receivable (in addition to the $60,000 shown) which it has endorsed and discounted at the local bank.

Answer frame 11[8]

The correct answers are as follows:

1. The maturity value is the face value plus the interest, or $20,300.

$$\text{Interest} = \$20{,}000 \times 6/100 \times 90/360 = \$300$$

2. The maturity date is August 30.

Days in June	30	
Less date of note	1	29
Days in July		31
Days in August needed to total 90 days		30
Total		90

3. The discount period is 60 days.

Days in July	31	
Less date of discounting	1	30
Days in August, including maturity date		30
Total		60

4. The discount charged by bank is $270.67.

$$\text{Maturity Value} \times \text{Discount Rate} \times \frac{\text{Discount Period}}{360}$$

$$\$20{,}300 \times 8/100 \times 60/360 = \$270.67$$

5. The cash proceeds are $20,029.33—the maturity value, $20,300, less the discount, $270.67.
6. The required entry is:

July 1	Cash	20,029.33	
	Notes Receivable Discounted		20,000.00
	Interest Revenue		29.33

If you answered incorrectly, reread Frame 11[s] before beginning Frame 12[s] on page 353.

12[8] *continued*

Although the contingent liability is actually for the note plus the accrued interest to maturity ($10,100), for convenience it is customarily shown only for the face of the note ($10,000).

Discounted notes receivable paid by maker. When a note receivable has been discounted, it is usually the duty of the endorsee (the holder) to present the note to the maker for payment at maturity. Sometimes the note designates the place of payment. If the maker pays the endorsee (the bank in the above illustrations) at maturity, the endorser is thereby relieved of his contingent liability. If the note is not paid at maturity, the endorsee can collect from the endorser who, in turn, can try to collect from the maker.

Assume that Thomas (in the example) pays his $10,000 note plus interest of $100 to the Michigan National Bank on July 3, 1975, the note's maturity date. Carlson, who discounted the note at the bank, has been relieved of the possibility of being held liable on the note and, therefore, will make the following entry:

July 3	Notes Receivable Discounted	10,000	
	Notes Receivable		10,000

This entry reduces the balance of each of these accounts to zero.

Discounted notes receivable not paid by maker. If Thomas dishonors his note at maturity rather than paying it, the Michigan National Bank will collect the principal ($10,000), interest ($100), and any protest fee (assume it to be $5) from Carlson. Carlson will have to make two entries as follows:

July 3	Notes Receivable Discounted	10,000	
	Notes Receivable		10,000
	To remove the note and the contingent liability from the accounts.		
July 3	Dishonored Notes Receivable	10,105	
	Cash		10,105
	To record the cash deducted from our account by the bank on the note dishonored by Thomas.		

Carlson will then try to collect $10,105 from Thomas. If he finds that he cannot do this, he will remove the $10,105 from the Dishonored Notes Receivable account and treat it as a loss from bad debts.

Assume that Jones (the maker) dishonors a $5,000 note that Fiorello had discounted at the bank. On August 20 the bank deducts $5,010 (maturity value plus protest fee) from Fiorello's account at the bank. Give the entries that Fiorello would make on his books.

Now check your answers in Answer Frame 12[8] on page 356.

Frame 13[8]

Long-term notes

Notes may be either short-term or long-term. They are usually short-term, but when they are long-term (have maturities exceeding approximately one year) they are to be recorded at their present cash value.[1] To illustrate, assume the existence of a $1,000 face value note, bearing no explicit rate of interest, which is due one year from its date. (Even though this does not "exceed approximately one year" and technically would not have to be recorded at its present value, it is assumed the

[1] Accounting Principles Board, "Interest on Receivables and Payables," *Opinion 21* (New York: AICPA, August, 1971).

Answer frame 12[8]

The required entries are:

Aug. 20	Notes Receivable Discounted	5,000	
	Notes Receivable		5,000
Aug. 20	Dishonored Notes Receivable	5,010	
	Cash		5,010

If you answered incorrectly, restudy Frame 12[8] before starting Frame 13[8] on page 355.

13[8] *continued*

company chooses to do so.) Assume that the rate of interest to be used in reducing this note to its present value is 6 percent. To solve for the present value we ask, What amount if invested at 6 percent would grow to $1,000 one year from now? If x equals that amount, the calculation is:

$$x + 0.06x = \$1{,}000$$
$$1.06x = \$1{,}000$$
$$x = \frac{\$1{,}000}{1.06} = \$943.40$$

Assuming the notes payable results from the purchase of a machine on December 31, 1975, it is recorded as follows:

Machinery	943.40	
Notes Payable—Discount	56.60	
Notes Payable		1,000.00

At the due date, $1,000 is paid to the payee and $56.60 is recorded as interest expense. The required entry at the due date, December 31, 1976. is:

Notes Payable	1,000.00	
Interest Expense	56.60	
Notes Payable—Discount		56.60
Cash		1,000.00

The accounting for the interest in this type of transaction is quite similar to that used when a company discounts its own note at the bank.

Most long-term notes do bear an explicit rate of interest. When such a note arises from an arm's-length transaction, it is assumed that the rate of interest stipulated by the parties represents fair and adequate compensation to the supplier of funds. In these instances, the note payable is recorded at the purchase price of the asset acquired. An example of such a transaction is the mortgage note payable.

Mortgage note payable. Sometimes individuals or companies give their own notes to finance the acquisition of a plant asset. Such a note is usually a long-term liability and is secured by a mortgage on the property acquired. A mortgage is an obligation to give up the property that has been pledged to the payee in case the maker defaults on his payments. Most of us become familiar with this form of financing when we purchase a home. Business firms also sometimes use this method of financing when they acquire assets such as buildings.

This form of financing can be illustrated by looking at a home mortgage, but it is equally applicable to a business acquiring a building. Most mortgages on homes run for a period of 25 or 30 years. The homeowner makes a constant lump-sum payment each month (exclusive of real estate taxes), which at first pays mostly interest and very little principal. Assume that the mortgage on your home is $35,000, the interest rate is 8 percent, and the life of the note is 25 years. There are mortgage payment schedule books which indicate that the monthly payment for principal and interest is $271. Here is how the first two month's and the last month's payments are applied:

	Monthly Payment	*Interest*	*Principal*	*Principal Balance*
Date of purchase..........	—	—	—	$35,000.00
First month..............	$271	$233.33	$ 37.67	34,962.33
Second month............	271	233.08	37.92	34,924.41
300th month.............	271	2.00	269.00	—0—

Notice that interest is calculated on the latest principal balance. For instance, when you make the first $271 payment interest is calculated as follows:

$$\frac{\$35{,}000 \times 0.08}{12} = \$233.33$$

It is necessary to divide by 12 because the interest rate is 8 percent per year and the calculation of the amount is for one month. The excess of the payment over the interest is applied against the principal ($37.67 in the first payment above). Thus, the principal balance decreases slowly (but more rapidly each month), so that the last $271 payment at the end of 25 years pays interest (approximately $2) on the remaining principal balance (approximately $269) and reduces the principal balance to zero.

Assume that on January 1, 1975, Company X acquires a building for $35,000 and gives its 8 percent note payable to a bank to finance the purchase. The January entries pertaining to the mortgage note would be as follows (see table above):

Jan.	1	Building..................................	35,000.00	
		Mortgage Note Payable...............		35,000.00
	31	Interest Expense..........................	233.33	
		Mortgage Note Payable....................	37.67	
		Cash..................................		271.00

What entry is made at the end of February 1975?

Now check your answer in Answer Frame 13[8] on page 358.

Answer frame 13[8]

The required entry on February 28, 1975, is:

Interest Expense	233.08	
Mortgage Note Payable	37.92	
Cash		271.00

This can be seen from the sample mortgage schedule book illustrated in Frame 13[8]. If you answered incorrectly, reread Frame 13[8] before beginning Frame 14[8] below.

Frame 14[8]

Other payables

The remaining payables that will be discussed all arise from tax legislation in one form or another.

Sales taxes

Many states (and some cities) levy a flat rate tax upon retail sales, with the tax usually levied upon the consumer but collected by the retailer. Exceptions exist, as in Michigan and Illinois, where the tax is actually levied upon the retailer, who passes it on to the consumer.

Entries can readily be made to record the collection of sales taxes on such big-ticket items as automobiles, where each sale is recorded separately. Even retail stores selling numerous smaller items can account for the taxes on sales by ringing such taxes up separately in a cash register. Thus, the register readings for Department K of a given department store for a particular day might require that the following entry be made:

Cash	4,124.68	
Accounts Receivable	6,094.68	
Sales—Department K		9,826.48
Sales Tax Liability		392.88

The amount of tax collected may not be exactly equal to the amount of tax due, if the tax is levied upon the retailer, because of the rounding of fractions involved.

As a practical matter, many concerns record the entire amount received in the Sales account and isolate the amount of tax collected only at the end of the month. For example, the Sales account of the Wynn Stores, Inc. for the month ending May 31, 1976, shows a balance of $56,278.91. This amount is equal to 104 percent of actual sales, assuming a 4 percent sales tax. The actual sales can be determined simply by dividing the $56,278.91 by 1.04. The result is $54,114.34, and the sales taxes on this amount are $2,164.57 (computed either as the difference between the two amounts or as 0.04 × $54,114.34).

Real and personal property taxes

Most local governmental units—counties, townships, and cities—depend upon real and personal property taxes as their chief source of revenue. In some cases, states levy real property taxes. In other cases, states participate in the distribution of revenues raised through the levying of personal property taxes.

Legally, property is divided into two categories: real property and personal property. Real property includes land and all other items permanently attached to the land, such as buildings, sewers, fences, and sidewalks. Personal property includes furniture, machinery, delivery equipment, inventories, and in many states such items as security investments and accounts and notes receivable.

Normally, real property taxes are based upon the assessed value of the property. The assessed value is determined by the county tax assessor (or commission).

Personal property taxes are usually based upon the book value (cost minus depreciation) of the property. In a few states personal property taxes are based on assessed value.

Real and personal property taxes are expenses of the owner of the property. There are many dates involved in the levying of these taxes. Several of these are the assessment date, beginning of taxing authority's fiscal year, date tax is levied, date or dates tax is payable, and tax period appearing on tax bill. Some of these dates may coincide for any particular case. A question arises as to which period the tax expense should be charged. A publication of the American Institute of Certified Public Accountants states, "Generally, the most acceptable basis of providing for property taxes is monthly accrual on the taxpayer's books during the fiscal period of the taxing authority for which the taxes are levied. . . ."[2]

The monthly accruals will in many cases be based upon estimates, since the actual tax statements are not received until later in the year. The exact entries made will vary according to whether the taxes have been paid.

To illustrate, assume that the taxpayer and the taxing authority both employ fiscal years ending on December 31. The taxpayer bases his monthly accrual of taxes on an estimated $480 of annual taxes until the actual amount of taxes is known, which occurs in May when tax statements are mailed. The tax is due by June 15. Thus, the monthly entry to be made at the end of each of the first four months in 1975 reads:

Real Property Tax Expense	40	
Real Property Taxes Payable		40

The tax statement received on May 10 shows actual taxes for 1975 of $492, due by June 15, 1975. Thus, the correct tax expense for each of the past four months is $41 ($492 ÷ 12). An adjustment for the underaccrual can be made in May by accruing $41 for May plus $4 ($1 for

[2] *Accounting Research and Terminology Bulletins,* Final Edition (New York: AICPA, 1961), pp. 83–84.

each of the prior four months), or a total of $45. The entry for May reads:

Real Property Tax Expense	45	
Real Property Taxes Payable		45

The entry to record the payment of taxes on June 15 is:

Real Property Taxes Payable	205	
Prepaid Real Property Taxes	287	
Cash		492

The adjusting entry to record real property tax expense for each of the remaining seven months in 1975 is:

Real Property Tax Expense	41	
Prepaid Real Property Taxes		41

In this instance there is neither a liability for taxes nor an asset account showing prepaid taxes at year-end, since the fiscal years of the taxpayer and the taxing authority coincide and the taxes for the year are paid.

The accounting for personal property taxes is similar to that for real property taxes. Personal property taxes may be levied in advance and, if so, a Prepaid Personal Property Taxes account should be debited at the time of payment. Periodically—each month, for example—a Personal Property Tax Expense account should be debited and the Prepaid Personal Property Taxes account credited for the proportionate part of the expired prepayment. If not paid in advance, monthly accruals will be needed.

Assume that the Harrington Company's fiscal year ends on June 30, 1976, while the local taxing authority has a fiscal year ending on December 31, 1976. The company estimated its total property taxes for the calendar year 1976 at $3,600 and made the following entry at the end of each of the first five months of 1976 (January through May):

Real Property Tax Expense	300	
Real Property Taxes Payable		300

The actual tax statement was received in June, and a check for $1,860 (one half of the total taxes for the year) was mailed on June 30 to the taxing authority. On a separate sheet of paper write:

1. The entries necessary to record the accrual of property taxes for June and the payment of the $1,860 of taxes.
2. The required entry to record the accrual of property taxes for each of the remaining six months in the calendar year ending December 31, 1976.

Check your answers in Answer Frame 14[8] on page 362.

Frame 15[8]

Payroll accounting

Payables arising from payroll accounting include: salaries payable, federal (and sometimes state and city) income tax withheld, FICA tax liability, federal unemployment tax liability, and state unemployment tax liability.

Federal income tax withheld

Under the federal pay-as-you-go income tax collection system, most individuals must pay (partially or in full) their federal income taxes on wages as they are received throughout the year rather than waiting until they file an income tax return and at that time paying the entire annual amount of the tax. The tax is withheld by the employer from the wages of employees at the time wage payments are made; the withheld taxes are periodically remitted by the employer to a depositary bank or to the Internal Revenue Service.

The amount of the income tax to be withheld from the pay of each employee depends upon (1) the amount of the employee's earnings, (2) the frequency of the payroll period, and (3) the income exempt from taxation as determined by the number of exemptions claimed by the employee. The amount of each personal exemption is $750 and is built into the withholding tax rates and tables. (Exemptions are explained more fully in Chapter 12 of *Accounting II,* but a fuller explanation is not necessary at this point.)

Every employer is required to maintain payroll records for his employees, setting forth (among other items) the names and addresses of persons employed during the year, their social security numbers, exemptions, gross wages earned, taxes withheld, other deductions, and dates and amounts of net take-home pay.

After the end of each calendar year, an employer must furnish each employee certain information necessary to aid him in preparing his personal federal income tax return; this information also serves the purpose of providing the Internal Revenue Service with data for determining whether taxpayers have filed proper income tax returns.

Accounting for federal income tax withheld. To illustrate the accounting entries for federal income tax withheld from employees, assume that there is one employee whose gross wages during the first six months of 1974 are $1,000 per month, and that the tax to be withheld is $110.40 each month, determined from a withholding table supplied by the Internal Revenue Service. The monthly accounting entries will be as follows:

Salary Expense	1,000.00	
Accrued Salaries Payable		889.60
Federal Income Tax Withheld		110.40
Accrued Salaries Payable	889.60	
Cash		889.60

Answer frame 14[8]

1. The entries on June 30 are:

June 30	Real Property Tax Expense	360	
	Real Property Taxes Payable		360
	Taxes for six months are $1,860, of which $1,500 is already accrued, leaving a balance of $360 to be accrued in June.		
	Real Property Taxes Payable	1,860	
	Cash		1,860
	Payment of one half of annual taxes.		

2. The monthly adjusting entry for the last six months of 1976 is:

Real Property Tax Expense	310	
Real Property Taxes Payable		310

If you answered incorrectly, restudy Frame 14[8] before beginning Frame 15[8] on page 361.

15[8] *continued*

See if you can give the correct entry to be made when the tax withheld is remitted to a depositary bank or to the Director of the Internal Revenue Service.

Now check your answer in Answer Frame 15[8] on page 364.

Frame 16[8]

Federal Insurance Contributions Act taxes

The basic plan for management of the FICA fund is simple. During their years of employment covered by the Act, employed persons, their employers, and self-employed persons pay a certain percentage of their earnings (up to the limit specified in the Act) into a special fund. This fund is used to pay retirement and other benefits to the covered persons. When earnings stop because the covered worker has retired or died, or in certain cases has been disabled, benefit payments are made from the fund to take the place of the earnings the worker has lost. Certain hospital and post-hospital care costs for almost everyone over 65 also are payable out of social security funds. Additional voluntary medical insurance is also available for those individuals 65 and over who enroll for it.

FICA taxes are levied against both the employer and the employee. The amount of tax withheld from the salary of each covered employee for 1974 is 5.85 percent of the first $13,200 of wages paid in any one year. This rate (5.85%) and base ($13,200) are subject to frequent change but will be used as illustrative in our discussion of FICA taxes.

In addition to withholding 5.85 percent of the first $13,200 of wages paid to each covered employee, the employer must bear as one of his costs a tax equal to that withheld from each employee. Thus, the total FICA tax in 1974 amounts to 11.7 percent of the first $13,200 of the wages of each covered employee—half borne by the employee and half by the employer. The employee's FICA account with the government increases by the total of the two. If eligible for coverage under the Act, a self-employed person pays the entire FICA tax at a rate approximately one and one-half times that paid by an employee. But the program, rates, coverage, and benefits may—at any time—be changed by an act of Congress.

An employer under the old-age benefits provisions of the Federal Insurance Contributions Act is any person, partnership, corporation, trust, estate, or other association employing one or more individuals in nonexempt employment. If the employer fails to deduct the employee's portion, he is liable to the federal government for the entire tax.

If an employee works for more than one employer during the course of a year, each employer must pay his own tax and deduct the employee's portion of the tax from each paycheck on the first $13,200 of wages paid the employee during the calendar year. If Employee A works for Employer No. 1 for the first six months of the year and receives wages of $14,000, 5.85 percent of $13,200 ($772.20) of FICA taxes will be deducted from his wages. This constitutes his full year's contribution. If, during the last six months of the same year, he works for Employer No. 2 and receives wages of $10,000, 5.85 percent of $10,000 ($585) will be deducted from his wages. When he files his personal income tax return at the end of the year, he will obtain an overpayment refund by taking a credit of $585 against his income tax for that year. Employers cannot recover any of the amounts they have paid on this employee.

Accounting entries required for FICA taxes. In order to illustrate the accounting entries for FICA taxes, assume that an employee receives a salary of $1,000 per month, paid monthly. The amount to be deducted from the salary of the employee each month is 5.85 percent of $1,000 ($58.50). Also assume that his income tax withholding is $110.40. The entries to record the accrual and payment of the employee's salary on the records of the employer are:

Salary Expense	1,000.00	
FICA Tax Liability		58.50
Federal Income Tax Withheld		110.40
Accrued Salaries Payable		831.10
Accrued Salaries Payable	831.10	
Cash		831.10

Both the FICA Tax Liability account and the Federal Income Tax Withheld account represent amounts owed to the federal government which are payable to the Internal Revenue Service.

In addition to the amounts withheld for each employee, the employer is liable for his portion of the FICA tax. In this case his expense also

Answer frame 15[8]

The correct entry is:

Federal Income Tax Withheld	110.40	
Cash		110.40

If you answered incorrectly, reread Frame 15[8] before beginning Frame 16[8] on page 362.

16[8] *continued*

is 5.85 percent of $1,000 or $58.50. To record the employer's portion of the FICA tax, the following entry is made:

FICA Tax Expense	58.50	
FICA Tax Liability		58.50

This entry normally is part of the month-end adjustment procedure. Therefore, it is not necessary to record the employer's expense and liability every time a payroll entry is made; it may be done only at the end of a month or before financial statements are to be prepared.

The FICA Tax Liability account accumulates both the employer's and the employee's portions of the tax. The balance in the account is carried on the records as a current liability until remittance is made to the Internal Revenue Service.

Using the three following accounts and amounts, set up the journal entry that would be made when the taxes are remitted.

1. Cash, $227.40.
2. Federal Income Tax Withheld, $110.40.
3. FICA Tax Liability, $117.00.

Now turn to Answer Frame 16[8] on page 366 to verify your answer.

Frame 17[8]

Unemployment taxes

The Federal Unemployment Tax Act (FUTA) provides for a cooperative federal-state system of unemployment compensation. The federal unemployment tax is a tax imposed on salaries and wages to help finance the joint federal-state unemployment program.

Unemployment benefits to qualified unemployed persons are paid by each of the states and territorial governments. The unemployment laws of the several states and territories vary only in minor respects; their general similarity is due to the fact that the Federal Unemployment Tax Act sets forth certain minimum standards that must be met by each state.

Federal unemployment tax rate. The federal unemployment tax rate generally has varied between 3 and 3.5 percent. In recent years it has been 3.1 percent, levied on the first $3,000 of earnings per employee. This rate will be used as an example in all further discussion. The Federal Unemployment Tax Act provides that each employer may have a credit of up to 2.7 percentage points against his federal unemployment tax for amounts paid to the state. This, in effect, leaves the federal unemployment tax at 0.4 of one percent on the first $3,000 of wages paid to each employee.

The entire federal unemployment tax is borne by the employer; no tax is levied on the employee. The tax is based upon the wages paid to covered employees during each calendar year. As noted, it is levied on only the first $3,000 of wages paid per employee per year, as compared with $12,000 in the case of the FICA tax.

State unemployment taxes. Most states set the state unemployment tax rate at 2.7 percent of the first $3,000 of earnings per employee. It is assumed in the illustrations and problems in this text that the state rate is 2.7 percent.

Almost all state unemployment insurance tax laws levy a state unemployment tax only against the employer.

Each pay period, or once each month, the employer should prepare accounting entries for the federal and state unemployment taxes in the following form:

Federal Unemployment Tax Expense	xxx	
State Unemployment Tax Expense	xxx	
Federal Unemployment Tax Liability		xxx
State Unemployment Tax Liability		xxx

The state unemployment tax borne by the employer, like the federal unemployment tax, is an expense on the records of the employer.

Adjustments of rates due to experience ratings. Practically all states grant a state unemployment insurance tax reduction to employers who maintain stabilized employment. Thus, the state unemployment insurance tax rate for any employer may vary from year to year; this rate is called the employer's "experience" rate. The federal act allows a company paying a rate lower than 2.7 percent to the state (as a result of a record of stable employment) to continue to credit 2.7 percent against the federal tax as long as some employer in the state is paying the 2.7 percent rate.

Other payroll taxes

Many governmental units such as cities and states depend upon payroll taxes as a source of revenue. The accounting for city and state payroll taxes withheld is very similar to the accounting for the withholding of federal taxes. Most states and cities which levy payroll taxes have their own peculiarities as to exempt wages, tax rates, and so forth. The accountant must study each state or local tax law or ordinance in order to understand what may or may not be involved.

Answer frame 16[8]

The correct entry is:

FICA Tax Liability	117.00	
Federal Income Tax Withheld	110.40	
Cash		227.40

If you answered incorrectly, reread Frame 16[8] before starting Frame 17[8] on page 364.

Summary of payroll taxes

17[8] *continued*

It is important to maintain thorough and accurate payroll records. In accounting for the payroll, it is advisable to have (1) a record summarizing the wages and deductions of each pay period; and (2) a record of the earnings of each employee, by pay periods and collectively by months, calendar quarters, and annually.

An individual earnings record is desirable in order to maintain a record of details such as number of exemptions, time worked, gross earnings, deductions, and net pay for each employee. There should be a separate earnings record for each employee for each year.

Individual earnings records are useful in the following instances:

1. In the preparation of the statements given to each employee each pay period setting forth his gross earnings and determining the amounts withheld for income tax and other purposes.
2. In the preparation of the returns (W-2) submitted to the Internal Revenue Service for annual gross earnings, wages subject to the FICA tax, and income tax withheld.
3. To determine the proper cutoff when wages of an employee reach the $3,000 level for federal unemployment insurance tax purposes and the $13,200 level for FICA tax purposes.
4. In the settlement of disputes between employer and employee concerning earnings, amounts withheld for income tax, and other deductions.
5. In order to prepare payroll analyses for governmental agencies or authorities.

Journal entries must be prepared for the periodic payroll. A payroll journal (illustrated in Chapter 5) may be used to do this. Normally, if postings are not made directly from a payroll journal the payroll information of each pay period is summarized and entered in total as one entry in the general journal in the following format:

Salaries Expense	xxxx	
Federal Income Tax Withheld		xxxx
FICA Tax Liability		xxxx
City Tax Withheld		xxxx
State Tax Withheld		xxxx
Union Dues Liability		xxxx
Accrued Salaries Payable		xxxx

This entry indicates that the gross amount of the salary is entered as an expense. The net cash disbursed, however, is less than the gross salary by the amount of the deductions. These deductions are recorded as liabilities in the accounts of the employer, indicating amounts owed to the various taxing authorities and the union.

As a review of payroll accounting, work out the following problem on a separate sheet of paper. (Assume the illustrative rates used in the text apply.) The Bishop Company has 13 employees and an annual payroll of $98,000: three employees each earn $14,000 per year and 10 employees each earn $5,600 per year. (None of the employees holds another job.)

1. What is the annual FICA tax (*a*) for the employees, and (*b*) for the employer?
2. What are the amounts of the federal and state unemployment tax per year?
3. What is the total expense borne by the employer for these items?

Now turn to Answer Frame 17[8] on page 368 to check your answers.

Summary *chapter* 8

Receivables encompass any sum of money due to be received from any party for any reason resulting from a past transaction. Included among receivables are such items as accounts receivable, notes receivable, interest receivable, rent receivable, dividends receivable, and subscriptions receivable.

Payables are amounts to be paid to any party for any reason resulting from a past transaction. Included among payables are such items as accounts payable, notes payable, bonds payable, interest payable, rent payable, dividends payable, and various types of taxes payable.

The most common type of contra account to accounts receivable is an allowance for doubtful accounts. The other side of the entry establishing the allowance is a debit to Bad Debts Expense. Two methods of establishing the amount of the entry are the percentage of sales method and the percentage of accounts receivable method. The latter method may involve the use of one overall percentage or the aging technique. Other contra accounts to accounts receivable could be established but seldom are.

Notes receivable and notes payable may arise from business transactions or from borrowing or lending for some specific purpose. When in need of short-term financing, a borrower may either issue his own note to a bank or may discount a note receivable. He is directly liable for paying his own note, but is only contingently liable for paying the note receivable discounted (he must pay if the maker does not).

Long-term receivables and payables should be recorded at their present cash values.

Answer frame 17[8]

1. The correct answers are:
   a) For the employees:

3 × $13,200 × 0.0585	$2,316.60
10 × $ 5,600 × 0.0585	3,276
	$5,592.60

   b) For the employer:

Same as for the employees	$5,592.60

2. Federal and state unemployment tax:

Federal: 13 × $3,000 × 0.004	$ 156
State: 13 × $3,000 × 0.027	1,053
	$1,209

3. Total expense borne by the employer:

FICA (employer's share)	$5,592.60
Federal and state unemployment taxes	1,209
	$6,801.60

If you answered incorrectly, review Frames 16[8] and 17[8] before turning to the chapter summary on page 367.

Payroll accounting exists whenever an entity hires employees. A summary of taxes based on employee earnings is as follows:

SUMMARY OF TAXES BASED ON EMPLOYEE EARNINGS

Tax	*Paid by*	*Rate*
Social Security (FICA, FOAB)	Both employer and employee pay at current rate	5.85% of first $13,200 each employee earns annually*
Income tax†	Employee	Varies with earnings and exemptions
State unemployment	Employer	2.7% of first $3,000 each employee earns annually‡
Federal unemployment	Employer	0.4% of first $3,000 each employee earns annually§

* This rate is the rate for 1974. The rate and base may be expected to increase in subsequent years.

† If combined FICA and withholding taxes exceed $100 per month, they must be deposited monthly with a federal depository bank.

‡ Some states have a higher rate than this. Also, most states allow a reduction from the basic rate to firms with low labor turnover.

§ The federal rate varies, but in this text an assumption is made that it is 3.1 percent. An allowance of 2.7 percent is granted for amounts paid to the state, thus reducing the effective rate to 0.4 percent. The credit granted to firms in some states is reduced because the state has borrowed funds from the federal government.

Whenever any of these amounts have been incurred but remain unpaid at the time financial statements are to be prepared, payables for these items must be shown.

Study the new terms introduced in this chapter in the glossary which follows. Then go on to the Student Review Quiz for a self-administered test of your comprehension of the material in this chapter (page 370).

Glossary *chapter* 8

Aging (of accounts receivable)—a process of classifying accounts receivable according to their age in appraising the accounts for purposes of establishing or adding to the balance in an Allowance for Doubtful Accounts account.

Allowance for doubtful accounts—a contra account to accounts receivable designed to reduce gross accounts receivable to their net realizable value.

Assessed value—a valuation placed on property by a tax assessor or commission. It serves as a base upon which to calculate the amount of real (and sometimes personal) property taxes due.

Bad debts expense—an operating expense a business incurs when it sells on credit. It results from nonpayment of accounts receivable.

Discounting notes receivable—the act of transferring a note receivable with recourse to a bank. The proceeds are equal to the maturity value less the discount (amount charged by the bank). The discount is computed as: the maturity value times the annual discount rate times the number of days the bank must hold the note to maturity divided by 360. In computing the number of days, the maturity date is included while the date of discount is excluded.

Dishonored notes receivable account—an account showing notes which the makers failed to pay at maturity and which have not yet been written off.

Earnings record—a record showing details such as number of exemptions, time worked, gross earnings, deductions, and net pay for an employee.

Exemption—an amount which may be deducted from gross earnings (gross income) in arriving at taxable income.

Experience rating—a measure of a firm's history with respect to the number and periods of time its employees draw unemployment compensation; used in reducing unemployment taxes for firms with a stable history of employment.

FICA—the Federal Insurance Contributions Act.

Maker—the person preparing and signing a promissory note.

Maturity value—the amount the holder of a negotiable instrument is entitled to receive at the due date. Included in the amount are the principal and accrued interest, if any.

Note, promissory—an unconditional promise made in writing by one person to another, signed by the maker, engaging to pay on demand or at a definite time a sum certain in money to order or to bearer.

Notes Payable—Discount—a contra account used to reduce Notes Payable to their net present value. The amount in the discount account is converted into interest expense as time passes.

Payable—any amount of money due to be paid to any party for any reason resulting from a past transaction.

Payee—the person to whose order payment is promised or ordered on a note or other negotiable instrument.

Percentage of accounts receivable—a method of determining the desired size of the allowance for doubtful accounts and, indirectly, the bad debts expense for the period. This method has two variations. One is to use an overall percentage and the other is to use the aging technique.

Percentage of sales—a method of estimating the expected amount of uncollectible accounts from a given period's credit sales and, indirectly, of determining the balance in the allowance for doubtful accounts.

Personal property—property such as furniture, machinery, delivery equipment, inventories, and in many states such things as security investments and accounts and notes receivable.

Property taxes payable—obligations which arise from taxes on real property and personal property.

Real property—land and all other items permanently attached to land, such as buildings, sewers, fences, and sidewalks.

Receivable—any sum of money due to be received from any party for any reason resulting from a past transaction.

Student review quiz *chapter* 8

To develop a permanent record of your responses, you may write them on the answer sheet provided in the *Work Papers* or on a separate sheet of paper.

1 Which of the following methods of determining bad debts expense most closely matches expense to revenue?

a) Charging bad debts only as accounts are written off as uncollectible.
b) Charging bad debts with a percentage of sales for that period.
c) Estimating the allowance for doubtful accounts as a percentage of accounts receivable.
d) Estimating the allowance for doubtful accounts by aging the accounts receivable.

2 In March, 1975, after trying unsuccessfully to collect for nearly two years, Ellis Sport Shop wrote off the $87.50 account of John F. Poole as uncollectible. In August, 1975, Mr. Poole remitted a check for $50 with the terse notation "had a good day at the track." Which of the following entries should be made on the books of the Ellis Sport Shop?

a)	Cash	50.00	
	Accounts Receivable (Poole)		50.00
b)	Cash	50.00	
	Allowance for Doubtful Accounts		50.00
c)	Cash	50.00	
	Accounts Receivable (Poole)		50.00
	Accounts Receivable (Poole)	50.00	
	Allowance for Doubtful Accounts		50.00
d)	Cash	50.00	
	Accounts Receivable (Poole)		50.00
	Accounts Receivable (Poole)	87.50	
	Allowance for Doubtful Accounts		87.50
e)	Cash	50.00	
	Bad Debts Expense		50.00

3 The accounts of the Jellis Corporation on December 31, 1975, show accounts receivable of $202,000, an allowance for doubtful accounts (Cr.) of $500, sales of $980,000, and sales discounts of $13,500. At this time, the company decides to write off the account of the Backus Corporation, $2,000. The allowance for doubtful accounts is then to be adjusted to 2 percent of the outstanding receivables. The amount of bad debts expense recognized for the year is:

a) $19,330.
b) $19,600.
c) $4,040.
d) $3,540.
e) $5,500.

4 Conceptually, valuation contra accounts to accounts receivable could be established for all of the following except (choose the exception)—

a) Uncollectible accounts.
b) Freight allowances granted customers.
c) Possible sales returns.
d) Customers' credit balances.
e) Sales discounts customers are expected to take in making remittances.

5 Which of the following items should not be classified as a current asset in the statement of financial position?

a) A $5,000, five-year note receivable which matures in six months for which there is no ready market. Collection at that time is expected.
b) An amount due from an officer of the company for merchandise purchased on account.

c) A wage advance to an employee.
d) Semiannual rent receivable on a building owned and leased to another party.
e) A note receivable from an officer of the company who has left the company and cannot be traced.

6 The maturity date of a 90-day note dated February 15, 1975, is—
a) April 15, 1975.
b) May 14, 1975.
c) May 15, 1975.
d) May 16, 1975.
e) On demand.

7 The Lambert Company issued an $1,800, 60-day, 4 percent note to Omsted Wholesalers for merchandise purchased. The journal entry at time of sale on the books of the *payee* is:

a)	Notes Receivable	1,800	
	Sales		1,800
b)	Notes Receivable	1,872	
	Sales		1,800
	Interest Revenue		72
c)	Purchases	1,800	
	Notes Payable		1,800
d)	Purchases	1,800	
	Interest Expense	72	
	Notes Payable		1,872
e)	Notes Receivable	1,800	
	Interest Receivable	72	
	Sales		1,800
	Interest Revenue		72

8 Drehmel & Company accepted a 90-day, 5 percent note having a face value of $400 from T. R. Baxter in settlement of his account receivable. The note was dishonored at maturity. The correct entry on the books of Drehmel & Company to record the default on the note is:

a)	Dishonored Notes Receivable	400	
	Notes Receivable		400
b)	Dishonored Notes Receivable	405	
	Notes Receivable		400
	Interest Revenue		5
c)	Dishonored Notes Receivable	420	
	Notes Receivable		400
	Interest Revenue		20
d)	Notes Payable	400	
	Accounts Payable—Drehmel & Company		400
e)	Notes Payable	400	
	Interest Expense	5	
	Accounts Payable—Drehmel & Company		405

9 Referring to Question 8, prepare the entry on Drehmel's books which would be correct if T. R. Baxter subsequently—
a) Gave a new note for the amount owed.
b) Paid cash for the amount owed.

10 V. R. Graves arranged a loan at the bank. He gave the bank a 60-day note on which both the face value and the maturity value are $18,000. The bank discounted the note at 6 percent. Which of the following statements is not correct?
a) Mr. Graves received $17,820 in cash ($18,000 − $180).
b) This type of note is often called a noninterest-bearing note.
c) The effective rate of interest on the loan is greater than 6 percent.
d) The effective rate of interest on the loan is less than 6 percent.

11 On April 1 Lubenow Brothers received a $300, 60-day, 6 percent note from J. I. Holden. On May 10 they discounted it at the bank at 3 percent. Which of the following statements regarding this set of transactions are *true?*
a) Face value of the note is $300.
b) Maturity value of the note is $303. [$300 + ($300 × 0.06 × $^{60}/_{360}$)].
c) The discount period is 20 days.
d) The discount is $300 × 0.03 × $^{20}/_{360}$

12 On June 10 Bradley Shops received a $1,000, 60-day, 3 percent note from Mrs. C. L. Weber. This note was discounted at the bank at 6 percent on the day it was received. The journal entry which would be used in practice to record the discounting transaction is:

a)	Cash	994.95	
	Interest Expense	5.05	
	Notes Receivable Discounted		1,000.00
b)	Cash	1,000.00	
	Interest Expense	5.00	
	Notes Receivable		1,005.00
c)	Cash	994.95	
	Interest Revenue	5.05	
	Notes Receivable Discounted		1,000.00
d)	Cash	1,000.00	
	Interest Expense	5.00	
	Notes Receivable Discounted		1,000.00
	Interest Revenue		5.00

e) Cash.	994.95	
Interest Expense.	10.05	
Notes Receivable Discounted.		1,000.00
Interest Revenue . . .		5.00

13 At the date of discounting a note receivable from R. T. Johns, the Arbuckle Company made the following entry:

Cash.	2,950	
Interest Expense.	50	
Notes Receivable Discounted.		3,000

The maturity value of the note is $3,050. R. T. Johns did not pay the note. The bank deducted the amount due from the Arbuckle Company's account. The protest fee was $10. Which of the following *correctly* records the default transaction on Arbuckle Company's books?

a) Dishonored Notes Receivable.	3,010	
Cash.		3,010
b) Dishonored Notes Receivable.	3,060	
Cash.		3,060
c) Accounts Receivable. . .	3,010	
Cash.		3,010
d) Dishonored Notes Receivable.	3,060	
Cash.		3,060
Notes Receivable Discounted.	3,000	
Notes Receivable. .		3,000
e) Notes Receivable Discounted.	3,050	
Notes Receivable. .		3,050
Dishonored Notes Receivable.	3,060	
Cash.		3,060

14 Mr. Burne worked for A Company from January 1 to August 30, 1974, and earned a total of $14,000 from that company. In addition, he worked for B Company from October 5 to the end of the year, earning a total of $2,400 from B Company. Which of the following deductions for FICA taxes should have been made from his paychecks?

a) Company A should have deducted 5.85 percent of $14,000, and Company B should have deducted 5.85 percent of $2,400.

b) Company A should have deducted 5.85 percent of $13,200, and Company B should have deducted 5.85 percent of $2,400.

c) Company A should have deducted 5.85 percent of $3,000, and Company B should have deducted nothing.

d) Company A should have deducted 5.85 percent of $3,000, and Company B should have deducted 5.85 percent of $2,400.

e) Company A should have deducted 5.85 percent of $13,200, and Company B should have deducted nothing.

15 The January 18, 1974, gross payroll for salaries of the Mateer Corporation is $1,600. The total federal income tax withheld is $325. Which of the entries would be correct at the time of payment, assuming no prior recording of salaries?

a) Salary Expense.	1,217.00	
Cash.		1,217.00
b) Salary Expense.	1,600.00	
Cash.		1,600.00
c) Salary Expense.	1,600.00	
Federal Income Tax Withheld		325.00
FICA Tax Liability.		93.60
Cash.		1,181.40
d) Salary Expense.	1,600.00	
FICA Tax Expense.	93.60	
FICA Tax Liability.		93.60
Federal Income Tax Withheld		325.00
Cash.		1,275.00
e) Salary Expense.	1,600.00	
FICA Tax Expense.	93.60	
FICA Tax Liability.		187.20
Federal Income Tax. Withheld		325.00
Cash.		1,181.40

16 Harold Jackson is trying to decide whether to hire four men at $14,000 each per year, or 28 men on a part-time basis at $2,000 each per year, to operate four of the concessions at his amusement park. The employees' wages will be subject to FICA and unemployment taxes. Compare the FICA tax expense and unemployment tax expense in 1974 under the two alternatives. (The state unemployment tax rate is 2.7 percent and the federal rate is 3.1 percent, both on $3,000.) The difference is:

a) $5,012.
b) $3,180.
c) $1,551.20.
d) $1,364.

Now compare your answers with the correct answers and explanations on page 713.

Questions *chapter* 8

1 What are the two major purposes to be accomplished in establishing an allowance for possible uncollectible accounts?
2 In view of the fact that it is impossible to estimate the exact amount of uncollectible accounts receivable for any one year in advance, what exactly does the Allowance for Doubtful Accounts account contain after a number of years?
3 How might information in an aging schedule prove useful to management for purposes other than estimating the size of the required allowance for doubtful accounts?
4 In view of the difficulty in estimating future events, would you recommend that accountants wait until collections are made from customers before recording sales revenue? Or wait until known accounts prove to be uncollectible before charging an expense account?
5 The credit manager of a company has established a policy of seeking to eliminate completely all losses from uncollectible accounts. Is this a desirable objective for a company? Explain.
6 For a company using the allowance method of accounting for uncollectible accounts, which of the following affects its reported net earnings: (1) the establishment of the allowance, (2) the writing off of a specific account, (3) the recovery of an account previously written off as uncollectible?
7 What are the major theoretical arguments supporting the establishment of allowances for sales discounts, sales returns, freight, and collection expenses?
8 Explain why an account receivable might have a credit balance. What is the proper treatment of such an item in the financial statements?
9 Differentiate between dishonored notes receivable and notes receivable discounted. How is each shown in the statement of financial position?
10 Describe the three ways involving a note payable in which amounts can be borrowed from a bank.
11 Why might a situation arise in which the bank rate of discount is less than the rate in a customer's note which the holding company discounts at the bank?
12 At what amount should long-term notes payable be recorded?
13 How is interest calculated on a mortgage note payable each month?
14 What is the most acceptable method of accounting for property taxes?
15 What are the various payables that arise from payroll accounting?
16 Which payroll taxes are incurred by the employer? What are the applicable rates and bases for computation of these taxes?

Exercises *chapter* 8

1 How should the following situation be shown in the statement of financial position? The subsidiary accounts receivable ledger of the Matson Company shows a total of $124,000. An examination of the accounts shows one account of $15,000 due from the president of the company. The composition of this account is as follows:

a) Due from sale of merchandise, $4,000.
b) A loan of $5,000.
c) Stock subscriptions receivable of $6,000.

2 How should the following appear in the statement of financial position of the Bee Corporation on December 31, 1975? Why?

Accounts receivable (including credit balances of $700)	$123,000
Accounts payable (including advance payments to vendors of $500)	87,000

3 On December 28, 1975, Jordan Corporation received a check for $2,500 as a 10 percent down payment on an order for merchandise from the Argonne Company. Argonne is not indebted to Jordan at this time. The receipt was recorded by debiting Cash and crediting Argonne's Accounts Receivable account. The merchandise was not delivered until January 5, 1976. On December 31, 1975, the trial balance amount of accounts receivable was $172,000. Indicate the proper statement of financial position presentation of the above data.

4 The accounts of the Baldon Company as of December 31, 1975, show Accounts Receivable, $90,000; Allowance for Doubtful Accounts, $500; Sales, $540,000; and Sales Returns and Allowances, $10,000. Prepare journal entries to adjust for possible uncollectible accounts under each of the following assumptions:

a) Uncollectible accounts are estimated at one half of 1 percent of net sales.

b) The allowance is to be increased to 3 percent of accounts receivable.

5 On April 1, 1975, Brackton Company, which employs the allowance method of accounting for uncollectible accounts, wrote off Bill Combs' account receivable of $352. On December 14, 1975, the company received a check for that amount from Combs marked "in full of account." Prepare the necessary entries for all of the above.

6 The statement of financial position of the Owens Company as of December 31, 1975, shows accounts receivable of $428,500 from which is deducted, among other deductions, the amount of $3,750. This amount is described as "estimated freight allowances." Explain the nature of this $3,750 item. Give the entry that probably was made to establish the allowance.

7 Compute the required size of the allowance for doubtful accounts for the following receivables:

Accounts Receivable	*Age (Months)*	*Probability of Collection*
$100,000	Less than 1	0.95
40,000	1 to 3	0.80
20,000	3 to 6	0.70
5,000	6 to 12	0.40
1,000	12 and over	0.10

8 You have read the rule that when the terms of an obligation are 6 percent for 60 days you can look at the face amount of the obligation and move the decimal point two places to the left to find the dollar amount of interest. Prove that this rule is true.

9 Bauer gives his 90-day, $15,000, 4 percent note to Beebe in exchange for merchandise. Give the entry that each will make on the maturity date, assuming payment is made.

10 Give the entries that Bauer and Beebe (see Exercise 9) would make at the maturity date assuming that Bauer defaults.

11 Determine the maturity dates for notes with each of the following lives:

Issue Date	*Life*
January 13, 1976	1 year
January 31, 1976	1 month
June 4, 1976	30 days
December 1, 1976	90 days

12 Austin Company gives a 120-day, $5,000, 6 percent note to Chase Company on July 6, 1976. Chase Company discounts the note at the bank on August 20, 1976. The rate of discount is 6 percent. Determine the entries each company would make on the date of discounting.

13 In Exercise 12, if Austin Company fails to make payment on the maturity date, what entry is required on the books of each company?

14 Day Kreuzburg goes to the bank and asks to borrow $1,000 at 6 percent for a 60-day period. Give the entry which should be made to record the proceeds received for each of the following alternatives:

a) He signs a note for $1,000. Interest is deducted from the face amount in determining the proceeds.

b) He receives $1,000 and signs a note for the interest plus the amount borrowed.

c) He receives $1,000 and signs a note for that amount. The interest is to be paid at the maturity date.

15 Give the entry or entries which would be made at the maturity date for each of the alternatives given in Exercise 14 assuming the loan is repaid before the end of the accounting period.

16 Barry Erskine had two employers during the year. He earned $10,000 while working for one and $4,200 while working for the other. Using 1974 rates, determine the amount which will be withheld from his total wages for FICA taxes. How much will his two employers have to pay for FICA taxes as a result of employing Erkskine? Does the FICA fund receive more by Erskine's working for two employers than if he had earned the same amount working for only one employer?

17 You live in a state that imposes a 2.7 percent unemployment tax, levied on the same amount of income as is taxed by the federal government under FUTA. Due to a history of relatively stable employment, your company is granted a 0.3 percent credit or allowance by the state in its unemployment tax rate. During 1975 you employ 10 persons and pay each of them $4,500. How much do you incur as federal and state unemployment tax expense? How much would the employees' share normally be?

18 The Weston Company operates in a state having a 4 percent tax on retail sales. During the year the company credits the Sales account for the total amount of each sales transaction (including the sales tax portion). If the balance in the Sales account is $832,000 for the year, how much should be reclassified and transferred to the Sales Tax Payable account?

Problems, Series A *chapter* 8

8–1–A

As of December 31, 1975, the Carney Company's accounts prior to adjustment show:

Accounts receivable	$ 70,000
Allowance for doubtful accounts	2,000
Sales	800,000

Carney Company follows a practice of estimating uncollectible accounts at 1 percent of sales.

On February 23, 1976, the account of Harold Pastor in the amount of $2,100 is considered uncollectible and is written off. On August 12, 1976, Pastor remits $300 and indicates that he intends to pay the balance due as soon as possible. By December 31, 1976, no further remittance has been received from Pastor.

Required:

a) Prepare journal entries to record all of the above transactions and adjusting entries.
b) Give the entry necessary as of December 31, 1975, if the Carney Company estimated its uncollectible accounts at 8 percent of outstanding receivables rather than at 1 percent of sales.

8–2–A

The accounts receivable (all arising under sales terms of n/30) of the Max Corporation as of December 31, 1975, total $300,000. The age composition of $270,000 of these accounts is:

Age	*Amount*
Not yet due	$225,000
Past due:	
1–30 days	30,000
31–60 days	8,000
61–90 days	2,000
91–120 days	1,000
Over 120 days	4,000
	$270,000

Given below are the three other accounts which account for the remaining $30,000 of accounts receivable:

Jill, Inc.

Date	Explanation	L.F.	Debit	Credit	Balance
1/1/75	Balance forward (12/28/74 sale)				3,000
1/8/75		CR 1		3,000	—0—
1/11/75		S 1	4,000		4,000
2/5/75		CR 2		4,000	—0—
9/18/75		S 9	5,000		5,000
9/26/75	Adjustment granted	J 9		700	4,300
10/5/75		CR 10		4,000	300
10/8/75		S 10	2,500		2,800
11/3/75		CR 11		2,500	300
11/15/75		S 11	3,200		3,500
12/4/75		CR 12		3,200	300
12/18/75		S 12	4,300		4,600
12/21/75		S 12	2,000		6,600

Kessel Company

Date	Explanation	L.F.	Debit	Credit	Balance
4/5/75		S 4	2,200		2,200
5/5/75		CR 5		2,200	—0—
8/3/75		S 8	2,100		2,100
9/5/75	Return	J 9		500	1,600
9/11/75		CR 9		1,600	—0—
10/15/75		S 10	6,300		6,300
11/7/75		CR 11		1,500	4,800
11/10/75		S 11	500		5,300
12/15/75		CR 12		1,000	4,300

Tanner Company

Date	Explanation	L.F.	Debit	Credit	Balance
1/1/75	Balance forward				6,200
1/8/75		CR 1		6,200	—0—
2/18/75		S 2	11,000		11,000
3/6/75		CR 3		11,000	—0—
5/19/75		S 5	2,200		2,200
6/1/75		S 6	1,100		3,300
6/7/75		CR 6		2,200	1,100
6/23/75		S 6	20,500		21,600
7/5/75		CR 7		21,600	—0—
10/15/75		S 10	23,000		23,000
11/3/75		CR 11		4,000	19,000
11/9/75		S 11	5,400		24,400
11/18/75	Return 10/15 sale	J 11		300	24,100
12/5/75		CR 12		8,000	16,100
12/17/75		S 12	3,000		19,100

Required:

a) Prepare an aging schedule classifying the accounts as per the age groups given above.

b) Assuming the allowance for doubtful accounts has a debit balance of $2,100, prepare the necessary adjusting journal entry for estimated uncollectible accounts as of December 31, 1975, if the amount of uncollectible accounts is estimated at ½, 1, 2, 5, 10, and 25 percent, respectively, of the age groups given above.

c) What has apparently happened with regard to $300 of the balance of the Jill, Inc., account? What is the probability of collecting this balance?

8–3–A

On June 1, 1976, the Weis Company received a $6,000, 120-day, 8 percent note from the Mayer Company dated June 1, 1976. On August 15, 1976, the note was discounted at the bank. The rate of discount was 6 percent.

Required: Determined:

a) The maturity value of the note.

b) The number of days from the discount date to the maturity date.

c) The dollar amount of the discount.

d) The cash proceeds received by the company.
e) The proper entry to record the receipt of proceeds at the date of discount.

8–4–A

Following are selected transactions of the Flynn Company:

Oct. 31 Discounted its own 30-day, $10,000, noninterest-bearing note at the First State Bank at 6 percent.

Nov. 8 Received a $5,000, 30-day, 3 percent note from the Schultz Company in settlement of an account receivable. The note is dated November 8.

15 Purchased merchandise by issuing its own 90-day note for $4,800. The note is dated November 15 and bears interest at 4 percent.

20 Discounted the Schultz Company note at 6 percent at the First State Bank.

30 The First State Bank notified the Flynn Company that it had charged the note of October 31 against the company's checking account.

Required: Assume that all notes falling due after November 30 were paid in full on their due dates by the respective makers. Prepare dated journal entries for the Flynn Company for all of the above transactions and all necessary adjusting entries assuming a fiscal year accounting period ending on November 30.

8–5–A

The Moseley Company is in the power boat manufacturing business. As of September 1, the balance in its Notes Receivable account is $46,000. The balance in the Notes Receivable Discounted account is $14,000, and the balance in Dishonored Notes Receivable is $10,120. A schedule of the notes (including the dishonored note) is as follows:

Face Amount	*Maker*	*Date*	*Life*	*Interest Rate*	*Comments*
$20,000	J. Reid Co.	6/1/76	120 days	6%	
12,000	R. Barr Co.	6/15/76	90 days	4	
14,000	M. Gray Co.	7/1/76	90 days	5	Discounted 8/16/76 at 6%
10,000	A. Egan Co.	7/1/76	60 days	6	Dishonored, Interest $100, Protect fee $10
$56,000					

Required: Prepare dated journal entries for the following transactions.

Transactions:

Sept. 5 The J. Reid Company note is discounted at the Garret County Bank. The discount rate is 5 percent.

10 Received $6,110 from the A. Egan Company as full settlement of the amount due from it. The company does not charge losses on notes to the Allowance for Doubtful Accounts account.

? The R. Barr Company note is collected when due.

? The J. Reid Company note is not paid at maturity. The bank deducts the balance from the Moseley Company's bank balance. A protest fee of $8 is also deducted.

Sept. ? M. Gray Company pays its note at maturity.
30 Received a new 60-day, 6 percent note from the J. Reid Company for the total balance due on the dishonored note. The note is dated as of the maturity date of the dishonored note. The Moseley Company accepts the note in good faith.

8–6–A

The Wilmot Company has an annual payroll of $440,000 in 1974. There are 10 employees who earn $14,000 each and 80 part-time employees, each of whom earns an equal amount.

Required:

a) What are the total employee and employer portions of the FICA tax for the year?
b) What are the amounts of federal and state unemployment tax per year, assuming that the federal rate is 3.1 percent and the state rate is 2.7 percent for this company?
c) What is the total expense incurred by the employer for these items?

8–7–A

The Oragoo Company pays its employees once each month. The payroll data for May are as follows:

Gross payroll	$37,200	(One employee is above the $3,000 limit. Prior to May his gross salary was $14,000 and his gross May salary was $3,000.)
Income tax withheld	4,260	
FICA tax	?	
State income tax	3% of gross salary	

Required: Prepare entries to record:

a) The May payroll.
b) The employer's FICA tax for May (use 1974 rates).
c) The employer's federal and state unemployment taxes assuming that the federal rate is 3.1 percent and that the state has granted a reduction of 0.2 percentage points in the rate applicable to Oragoo because of a record of stable employment. The normal state rate is 2.7 percent.
d) Payment of the various taxes.

Problems, Series B *chapter* 8

8–1–B

Presented below are selected accounts of the Jackson Company as of December 31, 1975. Prior to closing the accounts, the $3,000 account of Rick Company is to be written off (this was a credit sale of February 12, 1975).

Accounts receivable	$ 160,000
Allowance for doubtful accounts	2,000 Dr.
Sales	1,120,000
Sales returns and allowances	20,000

Required:

a) Present journal entries to record the above and to record the bad debts expense for the period, assuming the estimated expense is 2 percent of net sales.

b) Give the entry to record the estimated expense for the period if the allowance is to be adjusted to 5 percent of outstanding receivables instead of as in **(a)** above.

8–2–B

The accounts receivable (all arising under sales terms of n/30) of the Arends Corporation at December 31, 1975, total $200,000. The age composition of $180,000 of these accounts is:

Age	*Amount*
Not yet due	$142,000
1–30 days past due	18,000
31–60 days past due	8,000
61–90 days past due	6,000
91–120 days past due	4,000
Over 120 days past due	2,000
	$180,000

Given below are the four other accounts which account for the remaining $20,000 of accounts receivable:

Jones, Inc.

Date	Explanation	L.F.	Debit	Credit	Balance
1/1/75	Balance forwarded (12/27/74 sale)				2,000
2/7/75		S 14	8,000		10,000
2/10/75		CR 3		2,000	8,000
3/1/75		CR 6		2,000	6,000
7/5/75		S 17	1,200		7,200
7/8/75		CR 20		2,000	5,200
11/3/75		CR 31		400	4,800

Smith Company

Date	Explanation	L.F.	Debit	Credit	Balance
1/10/75		S 5	5,000		5,000
2/1/75		CR 3		2,500	2,500
3/4/75	Allowance granted 1/10 sale	J 5		1,000	1,500
6/2/75		CR 16		500	1,000
6/6/75		S 16	300		1,300
7/3/75		CR 19		500	800
9/12/75		S 30	900		1,700
9/15/75		CR 22		200	1,500
11/30/75		CR 32		400	1,100

White Corporation

Date	Explanation	L.F.	Debit	Credit	Balance
7/5/75		S 17	1,500		1,500
8/2/75		CR 20		500	1,000
8/28/75		S 28	1,000		2,000
9/5/75		CR 21		500	1,500
10/5/75		CR 28		500	1,000
10/6/75		S 32	12,700		13,700
11/3/75		CR 31		2,000	11,700

Zellor Corporation

Date	Explanation	L.F.	Debit	Credit	Balance
8/22/75		S 26	1,000		1,000
9/5/75		CR 21		1,000	—0—
9/12/75		S 30	1,200		1,200
9/30/75		S 31	500		1,700
10/5/75		CR 28		1,700	—0—
10/28/75		S 34	1,300		1,300
11/2/75	Adjustment granted	J 17		100	1,200
11/7/75		CR 31		1,000	200
11/10/75		S 36	1,800		2,000
12/5/75		CR 34		1,800	200
12/11/75		S 38	2,200		2,400

Required: Prepare an aging schedule for the accounts receivable of the Arends Corporation. Compute the required allowance for doubtful accounts balance assuming estimated percentages of uncollectible accounts of ½, 1, 2, 5, 10, and 25 percent, respectively, for the six classifications given above. Prepare the necessary adjusting journal entry assuming the allowance has a debit balance of $750.

8–3–B

The Boyer Company received on July 14, 1976, a note from the Austin Company with the following description:

Face amount	$30,000
Life of note	90 days
Date of note	7/14/76
Interest rate on note	5%
Date of discounting note at the bank	8/23/76
Rate of discount charged by the bank	6%

Required: Determine:

a) The maturity date of the note.
b) The maturity value of the note.
c) The number of days from the discount date to the maturity date.
d) The dollar amount of the discount.
e) The cash proceeds received by the company.
f) The entry to record the receipt of the proceeds at the date of discount.

8–4–B

Using the simplified method illustrated in the text on page 346, compute the interest when the terms are as follows:

Interest Rate	*Life*	*Face Amount*
6%	60 days	$ 8,500
2	90 days	10,000
1	50 days	3,000
9	40 days	8,000
12	20 days	4,500

8–5–B

The Pratt Company has an accounting period of one year, ending on July 31. On July 1, 1976, the balances of certain ledger accounts are: notes receivable, $24,800; notes receivable discounted, $12,000; and notes payable, $40,000. The balance in notes receivable consists of the following:

Face Amount	*Maker*	*Date of Note*	*Life*	*Interest Rate*	*Date Discounted*	*Discount Rate*
$12,000	Rivera Co.	5/15/76	60 days	6%	6/1/76	6%
4,000	Shaw Co.	6/1/76	60 days	6%	—	—
8,800	Reilly Co.	6/15/76	30 days	5%	—	—
$24,800						

The note payable is a 60-day bank loan dated May 20, 1976. Interest Expense was debited for the discount, which is at a rate of 6 percent.

Required: Prepare dated journal entries for the following transactions and necessary July 31 adjustments.

Transactions:

July 1 The Pratt Company discounted its own $12,000, 60-day, noninterest-bearing note at the State Bank. The discount rate is 5 percent and the note is dated today.

3 Received a 20-day, 6 percent note, dated today, from the Jensen Company in settlement of an account receivable of $2,400.

6 Purchased merchandise from the Rivera Company, $19,200, and issued a 60-day, 6 percent note, dated today, for the purchase.

8 Sold merchandise to the Todd Company, $16,000. A 30-day, 6 percent note, dated today, is received to cover the sale.

14 The $12,000 note discounted on June 1, 1976, is paid by the Rivera Company directly to the holder in due course.

15 The Reilly Company sent a $4,000, 30-day, 6 percent note, dated today, and a check to cover its note of June 15, 1976, and interest in full to this date.

18 The Todd Company note of July 8 is discounted at the State Bank for the remaining life of the note. The discount rate is 6 percent.

19 The note payable dated May 20, 1976, is paid in full.

23 The Jensen Company dishonored its note of July 3, due today.

26 The Jensen Company sent a check for the interest on the dishonored note and a new 30-day, 6 percent note dated July 23, 1976.

30 The Shaw Company note dated June 1, 1976, is paid with interest in full.

8–6–B

a) The Mermack Company has 36 employees and an annual payroll in 1974 of $243,600; eight employees earn $14,000 each per year and 28 employees earn an equal amount each per year. What is the annual FICA tax (1) for the employees and (2) for the employer?

b) What is the amount of the federal and state unemployment tax per year, assuming a federal rate of 3.1 percent and a state rate of 2.7 percent for this employer?

c) Which of the preceding items would constitute expenses on the records of the Mermack Company?

8–7–B

Throughout the first quarter of 1974 the Groft Company employed seven machinists at $3,600 each per quarter year and an assistant manager at $4,500 per quarter year. The monthly payroll was paid on the last day of each month. On January 31 the company withheld $1,230 of federal income taxes from the employees, along with the proper FICA tax and a 2 percent city income tax.

Required: Journalize:

a) The payroll for January.

b) The employer's FICA tax for January.

c) The employer's federal and state unemployment taxes, assuming a federal rate of 3.1 percent and a state rate of 2.7 percent for this company.

d) The entry or entries to record payment of the various taxes.

Plant and intangible assets; depreciation, depletion, and amortization

Learning objectives

The study of the material in this chapter is designed to achieve these learning objectives:

1. A basic understanding of the nature of long-term assets, including the general characteristics of the various types of long-term assets.
2. An understanding of the nature of depreciation, depletion, and amortization, especially the similarities and differences among these concepts.
3. An understanding of the nature of the transactions involving long-term assets.
4. Theoretical and practical knowledge of the various methods of determining depreciation.
5. Development of the student's ability to trace the effects of transactions involving long-term assets through the accounts to the financial statements. This is of particular importance in the correction of errors involving the accounting for long-term assets.

Frame 1[9]

General nature of long-term assets

Long-lived assets (assets whose useful lives are expected to extend over several accounting periods) and their effects on periodic net earnings are considered in this chapter.

In order to match periodic revenues and related expenses as accurately and logically as possible, measurement must be made of the part of the service-rendering abilities of these assets that expired during the period. While it is often difficult to predict with a high degree of accuracy the exact length of the useful lives of these assets, some estimate must be made so that the amount of the expense (the amount of the service expiration) may be determined.

Long-lived assets are comprised of plant assets and intangible assets. Plants assets are those tangible assets which are acquired for use in the operations of the business rather than for resale; intangible assets also possess this attribute but cannot be seen or touched.

Types of plant assets

Plant assets may be classified as follows:

1. Land. The category of land includes that acquired for the purpose of future expansion or for which there are current plans for constructing office buildings, factory buildings, or parking facilities; rights-of-way, as those owned by railroads and other utilities; sites acquired for natural resource content; residential land or speculative land; and land devoted to agricultural purposes. Because land does not deteriorate with age and use, it is considered nondepreciable or nondepletable. One possible exception is recognized—agricultural land may lose its fertility and may be subject to erosion.

2. Natural resources. Mines, quarries, oil deposits, gas deposits, and timber stands are known as *wasting assets*. These tangible assets are exhausted through the extraction or removal of their physical properties and are thus subject to depletion.

3. Depreciable plant assets. Buildings, machinery, tools, delivery equipment, office equipment and furniture, and leasehold improvements are plant assets. All possess the physical characteristic of tangibility, and all eventually have reduced utility because of physical wear and tear or obsolescence.

Types of intangible assets

Intangible assets are usually classified as follows:

1. Those that are specifically identifiable and can be acquired singly as well as in groups of assets, such as patents, trademarks, and franchises.
2. Those that are individually unidentifiable and may be acquired only as part of a group of assets. Because they are not identifiable individually they are often lumped together and called goodwill.

These intangible assets possess no physical characteristics but have value because of the business advantages or exclusive privileges and rights they confer upon their owners.

Expenses related to plant and intangible assets

Plant assets, except land and natural resources, are subject to depreciation. Depreciation in accounting is an estimate, usually expressed in terms of cost, of the amount of service potential of an asset which expired in a given period. It is caused by wear and tear, physical deterioration, inadequacy relative to future needs, obsolescence, the passage of time, and the action of the elements. Depreciation accounting seeks to distribute in a systematic and rational manner over the estimated useful life of a plant asset its cost less salvage value. The depreciation on any depreciable asset should be recorded periodically by debiting the Depreciation account and crediting the Allowance for Depreciation account. The subsequent accounting treatment of the amounts of recorded depreciation depends upon the nature of the services received from the asset involved. If services received are functionally classified as selling or administrative, the depreciation is typically expensed in the period recognized. If manufacturing services are received, the depreciation may be treated as an element of manufacturing cost (see Chapters 2–4 in the companion text, *Accounting II*) and considered a cost of the goods manufactured. When so treated, it becomes an expense (as part of cost of goods sold) when the goods manufactured are delivered to customers. The depreciation recorded on one asset may be considered a part of the cost of another—as, for example, when a truck is used in the construction of a building.

Depletion is the exhaustion of a natural resource, such as a copper mine, brought about by the physical removal of a part of the resource. Because such resources are usually recorded at cost, the depletion recognized in a period is an estimate of the cost of the quantity of the resource extracted or mined in that period. It is recorded as a debit to the Depletion account and a credit either directly to the resource account or to the Allowance for Depletion account. This depletion cost is combined with other mining or extractive costs to arrive at the total cost of the ore mined. This total cost is, in turn, allocated between cost of goods sold and inventory of ore on hand according to the amount of ore sold. Thus it is conceivable that all, some, or none of the depletion recognized in a period will be expensed in that period. That portion not considered expense will undoubtedly be treated as a part of the cost of a current asset—inventory.

As discussed later, all intangible assets are subject to amortization. Amortization is an estimate, usually expressed in terms of cost, of the services received from an intangible asset in a given period. It is recorded as a debit to an amortization account and a credit directly to the intangible asset account involved, although allowances for amortization may be established. The possible subsequent treatments of the amortization account are the same as those given above for depreciation.

Generally, plant and intangible assets are first recorded at acquisition cost. Depreciable plant assets subsequently are carried at this cost, with the portion of the cost which has been allocated to current and past periods carried in the corresponding Allowance for Depreciation account. Depletable plant assets and intangible assets, on the other hand, usually are carried at acquisition cost less the portion of cost which has been allocated to current and past periods.

Frequently evidence exists which suggests that plant and intangible assets could be sold at various times at prices differing substantially from their recorded costs. The accounting requirement of realization typically bars the recording of market prices greater than cost until the asset is sold. On the other hand, it is generally considered inappropriate to recognize a loss by writing down an asset from cost to a lower market value if the cost of the asset is expected to be recovered fully from the future revenues produced by the asset. Consequently, plant and intangible assets are seldom reported at amounts other than cost or cost less an amortized or depreciated portion thereof.

On a separate piece of paper, state whether each of the following statements correctly or incorrectly expresses the purpose of depreciation accounting.

1. To adjust the accounts to show the current market value of plant assets at statement of financial position dates.
2. To set up a fund of money from which the plant assets can be replaced at the end of their useful lives.
3. To match the cost of plant assets against the revenue produced by the use of those assets.
4. To measure the amount of physical deterioration of plant assets which has occurred during the accounting period.

Check your answers against Answer Frame 1⁹ on page 390.

Frame 2⁹

Can you distinguish between depreciation and depletion? Indicate whether each of these statements is correct or incorrect.

1. Depletion is related to assets which are used up in a physical sense (for example, a mineral deposit), depletion being the charge for the physical quantity extracted; depreciation is related to assets which remain physically intact as a unit over their entire lives (for example, a building or a piece of machinery).
2. Depletion is related to intangible assets, while depreciation is related to tangible assets.

3. Depletion is more closely related to time than to the use of the asset, whereas depreciation is a function more of use than of time.

Now check your responses by turning to Answer Frame 2[9] on page 390.

Frame 3[9]

Plant assets

Cost basis of measurement

Plant assets usually are recorded initially at cost, which includes all expenditures necessary to place the asset in condition for use.

Cost of land. The cost of land includes the contract purchase price, option cost, attorney fees, cost of title search, fees for recording the transfer of title, taxes in arrears assumed by the purchaser, cost of grading, and local assessments for sidewalks, streets, sewers, and water mains.

Cost of building. If a building is purchased, its cost includes the contract purchase price, the costs of remodeling and repairing the building for the purposes of the new owner, unpaid taxes assumed by the purchaser, legal costs, and real estate brokerage commissions. When land and buildings thereon are purchased for one lump sum, the total cost should be apportioned so that separate ledger accounts may be established for land and for buildings; this may be accomplished by a competent appraiser. One of the reasons why the separation is made is to establish the proper balances in the respective accounts. Because the buildings will be depreciated and the land will not, establishing the proper balances is especially important. Reported earnings are affected.

If a building is constructed rather than purchased outright, the cost may be more difficult to determine. But it generally includes payments to contractors, architects' fees, building permits, taxes during construction, salaries of officers supervising construction, and insurance during construction. Interest on borrowed funds during construction is usually added to the building account, although some accountants believe that it is a financing cost (to be debited to expense).

As part of its expansion program, Tyler Corporation purchased an old farm on the outskirts of Bridgeport, Connecticut as a factory site. The company paid $75,000 for this property. An appraisal made shortly before the sale indicated that the land was worth approximately two thirds of the total value, the buildings one third. In addition, the company agreed to pay back taxes of $4,000 on this property. The attorneys' fees and other legal costs related to the purchase of the farm amounted to $630. The farm buildings were demolished at a net cost of $5,000 (cost of removal less salvage value), and a factory was constructed at a cost of $100,000. Building permits and architects' fees amounted to another $12,000. Finally, the company paid an assessment of $3,500 to the city

Answer frame 1⁹

1. Incorrect. Depreciation is a process of cost allocation, not a process of valuation. Remember that accounting is usually based on cost.
2. Incorrect. Depreciation accounting does not involve the transfer of any money to a special bank account or to a little tin box in the president's office. While all accounting records are kept in money terms, the only transactions which affect the firm's money holdings are those which include a debit or credit to cash or to some bank account.
3. Correct. Depreciation is a concept misunderstood by many. If you answered this question correctly, you have done well in recognizing that the aim of depreciation accounting is to allocate systematically the cost of plant assets to the same period that revenue is produced with those assets.
4. Incorrect. The rate of expected physical deterioration of the asset is one of the factors which determines the expected useful life of the asset and thus has an impact on the rate at which the cost of the asset is charged to expense. But depreciation is not determined solely by the physical deterioration of the asset. Other factors such as obsolescence and inadequacy are equally, and often more, important.

If you answered any question incorrectly, reread Frame 1⁹ before going on to Frame 2⁹ on page 388.

Answer frame 2⁹

1. Correct. Depreciation, depletion, and amortization are terms you will come across often, and it is important that you be able to distinguish among them.
2. Incorrect. Both depreciation and depletion are related to tangible assets. The allocation of the cost of intangible assets to periods is called amortization.
3. Incorrect. Depletion is related to the physical removal of a quantity of a resource. Time enters only in setting the interval for which physical removal must be determined. Depreciation, on the other hand, is generally related to the passage of time and to physical use.

If you got any answer wrong, restudy Frame 2⁹ before going on to Frame 3⁹ on page 389.

3⁹ *continued*

for water mains, sewers, and street paving. What is the depreciable cost of the new factory building?

The correct answer may be found by checking Answer Frame 3⁹ on page 392.

Frame 4⁹

Cost of machinery. If machinery is acquired by purchase, its cost includes the invoice price, transportation charges, insurance in transit, cost of installation, and other costs needed to put it into condition and location for use. If a machine is constructed by a company for its own use, the cost should include material, labor, and an amount equal to the increase in other factory costs caused by the construction of the machine. This cost of the machine should be so recorded in the Machinery account (even if such cost is below the price that would have been paid had the machine been purchased from another concern), since it represents the resources sacrificed to acquire the machine.

Cost of delivery equipment. The cost of delivery equipment includes all costs necessary to place the equipment in use in accordance with the order of the purchaser. Included in the cost are the f.o.b. shipping point price, transportation charges, accessories' cost, and special paint and decoration costs.

Cost of office equipment. The cost of office equipment includes the net invoice purchase price and all costs necessary to place the equipment in condition and location for use.

After pricing machinery of the type needed, the Hainer Foundry decided to build its own machine. The cost of construction was $14,000. The f.o.b. shipping point price of a similar machine purchased from the usual source is $17,500, and transportation charges to the Hainer plant amount to another $800. The machine constructed should be recorded in the accounts at which of the following amounts?

1. $14,000.
2. $17,500.
3. $18,300.

Now check your response in Answer Frame 4[9] on page 392.

Frame 5[9]

Noncash exchanges and gifts of plant assets

Plant assets usually are acquired by purchases either for cash or on account. They also may be acquired by other methods for example, by exchange for other assets, by giving stocks or bonds held as investments, or as gifts. When plant assets are acquired under the latter conditions, a question arises concerning the "cost" at which the asset should initially be recorded in the accounts. Several possible bases may be available, including book value, fair market value, and appraised value.

Book value. The book value of an asset surrendered is an acceptable basis of measurement for a newly acquired asset only if a better basis is not available. This is true even if an amount of cash is received or given in the exchange.

Fair market value. If noncash assets are acquired in an exchange for securities having a ready market value, the cost of the assets acquired is deemed to be the fair market value of the securities surrendered. If the securities surrendered do not have a ready market value, the cash purchase price at which the asset could have been acquired should be

Answer frame 3[9]

The depreciable cost is $112,000. All of the costs relating to the purchase of the farm and the razing of the old buildings are assignable to the land account in this case, because none of the old buildings purchased with the land is to be used. The real objective was to purchase the land, but the land was not available without taking the buildings also. If, instead of the situation described, one or more of the existing buildings had been adapted through a remodeling program for use by Tyler Corporation, it would have been necessary to determine what part of the cash purchase price of the farm, the back taxes, and the legal fees was allocable to such buildings and what portion of the cost plus remodeling costs would have been included in the cost of the new factory. Land improvements such as sewers, water mains, and paving are usually considered a part of the cost of the land. Thus, the depreciable cost of the factory building is the construction cost of $100,000 plus the architects' fees and building permit costs of $12,000.

If you did not respond correctly, reread Frame 3[9] before proceeding to Frame 4[9] on page 390.

Answer frame 4[9]

The correct answer is the first one, $14,000. The accountant uses the actual cost incurred. Estimates of what an item would cost are used only when objective cost figures are not available.

If you answered incorrectly, restudy Frame 3[9] before going on to Frame 5[9] on page 391.

5[9] *continued*

used as the cost of the asset and also as the amount considered to be received for the securities.

Appraised value. Noncash assets are sometimes acquired by outright donation. Although such assets have no cost to the recipient, they usually are recognized and recorded in the accounting records. If similar assets are not regularly traded, so that a market value cannot be determined for the assets received, they are usually recorded at their appraised value as determined by a professional appraiser.

In any exchange of noncash assets the accountant's task is that of finding the most appropriate measurement to assign to the assets received. The general rule that he follows is that of using the fair market value of the assets received or of the assets surrendered, whichever is the more clearly evident.

On July 14, 1975, in exchange for 100 shares of its common stock, the Ogden Company acquired land adjacent to its factory for use as a parking lot. At the beginning of negotiations, the owner of the property quoted a price of $7,500 for this land. The common stock of the Ogden Company has a par value of $60 per share and a market value on July 14, 1975, of $71.50 per share. Similar plots of land in the city are selling for $6,900. At what amount should this land be recorded in the accounts? You may check your response in Answer Frame 5[9] on page 394.

Frame 6[9]

Continuing expenditures on plant assets

Expenditures which are directly related to plant assets are often made during the period of ownership and operation of such assets at times other than the date of acquisition. The accounting treatment accorded such expenditures consists of charging the amount expended to (1) an asset account, (2) an allowance for depreciation account, or (3) an expense account.

Expenditures which are added to the asset account or are charged to the allowance for depreciation account are frequently called capital expenditures because they increase the net book value of the plant or capital assets, while expenditures expensed immediately are described as revenue expenditures. Distinctions between capital and revenue expenditures will be developed and explained as this chapter progresses.

Expenditures capitalized in asset accounts

Expenditures for new or used assets, additions to existing assets, or betterments or improvements to existing assets are capital expenditures properly chargeable to asset accounts because they add to the total service-rendering ability of the assets. For example, the $30,000 cash cost of a used press, as well as the $300 of transportation charges incurred in hauling the press to the company's plant, is properly charged to an asset account, Machinery.

If shortly after purchase the company spent $2,650 to recondition the press and $950 to install it, these expenditures are properly charged to the Machinery account. They are a part of the total cost incurred to secure the services to be received from the machine throughout its entire life.

Assume that a few weeks later the company spent $700 for additional electrical controls for the press. This expenditure has the effect of improving the asset (presumably increasing its efficiency). What is the correct entry to record the expenditure?

The correct entry is presented in Answer Frame 6[9] on p. 394.

Frame 7[9]

Assuming this press has an estimated life of 10 years and no expected salvage value at the end of that time, what is the annual depreciation on this item of machinery under the straight-line method?

Turn to Answer Frame 7[9] on page 394 to check your answers.

Answer frame 5⁹

The land should be recorded at $7,150. Since the stock given in exchange for the land has a determinable market price at the time of the exchange, that price is the best measure of the cost of the land to Ogden Company. The fact that similar property in the city is selling for less is not important; Ogden Company obviously wanted the adjacent property enough to be willing to give up stock which it could sell in the market for $7,150. Also, every tract of land is unique—there is none other exactly like it.

If you did not answer correctly, reread Frame 5⁹ before going on to Frame 6⁹ on page 393.

Answer frame 6⁹

The correct entry to record the installation of additional electrical controls on the press is:

Machinery	700	
Cash (or Accounts Payable)		700
Electrical controls installed on press.		

If you do not understand that expenditures such as this should be capitalized, read Frame 6⁹ again. Then go on to Frame 7⁹, page 393.

Answer frame 7⁹

The annual straight-line depreciation on the press is $3,460. This is computed by summing the invoice price, transportation charges, reconditioning, installation costs, and the cost of the electrical controls ($30,000 + $300 + $2,650 + $950 + $700 = $34,600) and dividing by 10 years.

If you answered incorrectly, restudy this answer frame before going on to Frame 8⁹ below.

Frame 8⁹

Expenditures capitalizable as charges to allowance for depreciation

Occasionally, during the life of a plant asset, expenditures are made as a result of a decision that it is more economical to overhaul and repair an existing machine rather extensively than to replace it at that particular time. Such expenditures usually extend the life of the asset, that is, they change the *quantity* but not the *quality* of the services rendered by the asset. Because they will benefit future periods, these expenditures are properly capitalizable. But because there is no visible, tangible addition to or improvement of the asset, they are often charged to the allowance for depreciation. Such expenditures are viewed as canceling a part of the past accumulated depreciation.

Similarly, expenditures for major repairs which do not extend the life of an asset are often charged to the allowance for depreciation (with an increase in subsequent depreciation charges) in order to avoid distorting periodic net earnings by expensing them. In this manner the cost of major repairs is spread over a number of years.

To illustrate, assume that after operating the press for four years, the company in the preceding illustration spent $4,020 to recondition it. The effect of the reconditioning is to extend the life of the machine to a total of 14 years from an original estimate of 10 years. The journal entry to record the major repair is:

Allowance for Depreciation of Machinery	4,020	
Cash (or Accounts Payable)		4,020
Cost of reconditioning press.		

At acquisition the press had an estimated life of 10 years with no salvage value expected. At the end of the fourth year the balance in its allowance for depreciation account under the straight-line procedure is $13,840 ([$34,600 ÷ 10] × 4). After the $4,020 debit to the allowance for depreciation, the balances in the asset account and its related allowance account are:

Cost of press	$34,600
Allowance for depreciation	9,820
Net book value (end of four years)	$24,780

The remaining book value of $24,780 is allocated to the remaining 10 years in equal amounts of $2,478 per year under straight-line procedure, assuming that no salvage value is expected at the time of disposal. Note that the effect of the expenditure is to increase the carrying amount of the asset by reducing its contra account, the allowance for depreciation.

If the expenditure did not extend the life of the asset but was still charged to the allowance for depreciation because of its size, the $24,780 would be spread over the remaining six years of life with annual charges of $4,130 ($24,780 ÷ 6) under straight-line procedure.

The accounting procedure of charging the cost of major repairs to the allowance for depreciation has validity in theory only when the annual depreciation charges are increased to take such expected cost into consideration. Assume, for example, that a company acquired a machine at a total cash cost of $10,000, that this machine would last 10 years if it was given a major overhaul at the end of 5 years, and that the cost of the overhaul is estimated at $5,000. Under such circumstances, an entry debiting depreciation and crediting the allowance for depreciation for $1,500 per year is appropriate ([$10,000 + $5,000] ÷ 10 = $1,500). Also, under the circumstances outlined, the only proper treatment to be accorded the costs of the major overhaul is to charge them to the allowance for depreciation.

The practical difficulties of estimating the dollar amount of repairs well in advance of their incurrence frequently preclude employment of this technique in a manner as precise as that illustrated. The actual procedures followed may approximate those of the preceding illustration regarding the $4,020 repair to the press.

Expenditures charged to periodic expense

Expenditures for expected amounts of ordinary repair and part replacement are treated as periodic expenses because of their recurring nature and because they neither add to the service-rendering ability of the asset above that acquired at acquisition nor extend its life. Also, estimates of the annual depreciation charge on an asset are usually based on the assumption that the asset will be adequately maintained and that the ordinary repair costs will be expensed as incurred. Thus, regular maintenance (lubricating a machine) and ordinary repairs (replacing a broken fan belt) are usually charged to expense as incurred, as revenue expenditures. To illustrate, if the company above spends $240 to repair the press after using it for some time, the journal entry is:

Maintenance Expense	240	
Cash		240
To record payment of repair cost on press.		

Differentiating capital from revenue expenditures. In many instances it is exceedingly difficult to distinguish clearly between capital and revenue expenditures, since the distinction lies primarily in the length of the period of time benefited by the expenditure. But if a revenue expenditure is capitalized by charging it to an asset account rather than to its proper expense account, asset costs are overstated, expenses in the period of expenditure are understated, and net earnings and retained earnings are currently overstated. For all succeeding periods of the asset's life, net earnings will be understated through incorrect depreciation charges. If a capital expenditure is incorrectly charged to an expense account, the book value of the assets is misstated, acquisition period expenses are overstated, and net earnings and retained earnings are understated in the period of acquisition. For succeeding periods, expenses will be understated and net earnings overstated because depreciation expense will be understated in those periods.

On January 2, 1975, Zee Company purchased a machine for cash at an invoice price of $25,000. In addition, the company paid $300 freight charges and $540 installation charges. The invoice price of the machine was charged to the Machinery account, while the freight and installation costs were debited to Maintenance Expense. This machine has an estimated useful life of seven years. If this error is not discovered and corrected, which of the following correctly states the effect on net earnings for 1975 and 1976?

1. Net earnings for 1975 will be understated by $840; net earnings for 1976 will be unaffected.
2. Net earnings for 1975 will be understated by $840; net earnings for 1976 will be overstated by $120.
3. Net earnings for 1975 will be understated by $720; net earnings for 1976 will be overstated by $120.

4. Net earnings for 1975 will be overstated by $960; net earnings for 1976 will be overstated by $120.

Now check your responses in Answer Frame 8[9] on page 398.

Frame 9[9]

Company policy and expenditures on plant assets

Unit of property concept. A major concept guiding the accounting for plant assets, especially partial replacements of plant assets, is that of a unit of property. Under this concept, an expenditure on a plant asset for anything less than a complete replacement of the unit of property is charged to expense. Thus, a building may be a unit of property and the cost incurred in replacing its roof will be charged to expense in the year incurred. An automobile may be a unit of property, with the cost of replacing its transmission charged to expense when incurred.

While the size of the unit of property is usually a matter of company policy, the dangers in the use of this approach must be recognized. If the unit of property is considered to be, say, a machine and its electric motor, the replacement of the motor in one year and of the machine in the next year can result in the entire asset being replaced and charged to expense. The accounts of the company will continue to carry the cost of the old motor and machine, and may show these items to be nearly fully depreciated when in reality both assets are quite new.

On the other hand, it would hardly be feasible to set up all of the various parts of an automobile (such as tires, muffler, engine, transmission, spark plugs, battery, and fan belt) as separate assets and depreciate and account for each of them individually, even though they may very well have different useful lives.

The unit of property concept in accounting for plant assets is applied with a high degree of precision in public utility accounting because the rates charged by the utility are set by the state to enable the utility to earn a fair return upon the property employed. Here, relatively small items (cross-arms on transmission line poles, for example) are considered separate units of property subject to depreciation. This practice has much in theory to commend it.

Arbitrary minimums. As a matter of managerial policy, expenditures for plant assets, such as the $4.95 cost of a wastebasket, may be expensed immediately simply because the benefits resulting from the application of depreciation accounting procedures to such items do not equal or exceed the cost involved. Similarly, a firm may decide to capitalize all repair costs incurred on a specific asset in a single act of repair if it exceeds an arbitrary amount, say $500, while expensing those of a lesser amount. The arbitrary nature of these practical rules should be recognized. They have little, if any, support in theory, primarily because they tend to understate assets.

Answer frame 8[9]

Answer 3 is correct. The $840 overstatement of maintenance expense caused by charging to expense some of the costs attributable to the new machine will cause 1975 net earnings to be understated by that amount. But the asset account has been understated, and hence depreciation has been based on too small a figure. If the asset costs were properly capitalized, the depreciation charge for 1975 would be $120 larger ($840/7 = $120) and net earnings for the year are therefore understated by the net amount of $840 − $120 = $720. Of course the 1976 depreciation also will be understated by $120 if the error is not corrected, thus resulting in a $120 overstatement of 1976 net earnings.

If you did not respond correctly, restudy Frame 8[9] before continuing to Frame 9[9] on page 397.

Rearrangement costs

9[9]
continued

In order to facilitate production, machinery and other plant assets may be rearranged within a factory. Theoretically, the cost of rearranging the assets should be added to the assets' cost, and the original cost of installation already capitalized in the asset accounts (along with the related accumulated depreciation) should be removed. But, as a practical matter, if the cost of rearrangement can reasonably be absorbed into expense in the period of rearrangement, that procedure is usually followed. If the rearrangement cost is too large to be absorbed currently, resulting in a material distortion of periodic net earnings, it should be set up as an asset and written off over a period of time not to exceed the future accounting periods expected to benefit from the rearrangement.

Depreciation of plant assets

As indicated in Frame 1[9], depreciation is the allocation of the cost of a plant asset to expense over its useful life in a reasonable and systematic manner. Depreciation expense is one of the expenses of operating a business. The use of plant assets in business operations represents the conversion of a plant asset cost to an operating expense. The expense related to the use of plant assets in the operations for the period is recognized by charging to expense a proper portion of the original cost of the asset. Depreciation expense is a noncash expense, because the asset being depreciated presumably is not being paid for in any manner paralleling the depreciation expense charges appearing in an earnings statement. In effect, plant asset cost is recovered from customers by charging them enough for the product to cover all expenses, including depreciation. It is important to remember, however, that the charge to expense by itself is not sufficient evidence that the cost has been recovered. Costs are recovered only when total revenue is at least equal to total expenses, which of course is the normal situation for firms which remain in business.

Factors affecting depreciation estimates. In order to estimate periodic depreciation, the following three factors must be considered:

1. Cost.
2. Estimated salvage value. Salvage or scrap value is the amount estimated to be recoverable (less disposal cost) on the date on which the asset will be retired or otherwise disposed of.
3. Estimated life. This may be expressed in years, months, working hours, or units of production.

When depreciation is recorded, a depreciation expense account should be debited. The depreciation expense account appears in the earnings statement as one of the expenses of obtaining revenue. The periodic depreciation is credited to an Allowance for Depreciation account. The Allowance for Depreciation account is used in order that the original cost of the asset will continue to be shown in the asset account and the total accumulated depreciation will be presented separately in the allowance account.

Straight-line depreciation. There are many methods of computing depreciation. One of the most commonly used is the straight-line method. The straight-line method allocates the same dollar amount of depreciation to expense each period. Under this method the passage of time is considered the predominant factor in cost allocation. It assumes that wear, obsolescence, and deterioration of the plant asset are all directly proportional to elapsed time, even though such proportionality may not in fact exist.

The formula for the straight-line method of computing depreciation is as follows:

$$\text{Depreciation per Period} = (\text{Cost} - \text{Estimated Salvage Value}) \div \text{Number of Accounting Periods in Estimated Life}$$

To illustrate, for a machine costing $17,000 with an estimated life of 10 years and an estimated salvage value of $1,000, the depreciation per year is ($17,000 — $1,000) ÷ 10, or $1,600. The schedule in Illustration 9.1 presents the annual depreciation entries, the balance of the allowance for depreciation, and the book (or carrying) value of this machine. Book value is the difference between original cost and the balance of the allowance account.

On the basis of Illustration 9.1, indicate whether each of the following statements is true or false in regard to the straight-line method of computing depreciation.

1. The annual depreciation charge is a constant amount.
2. Book value at the end of the last year of an asset's estimated life should be equal to the estimated salvage value.
3. The credit balance in the allowance for depreciation account at the end of the 10th year is equal to the cost of the asset.

Now check your responses in Answer Frame 9[9] on page 402.

Illustration 9.1

STRAIGHT-LINE METHOD DEPRECIATION SCHEDULE

End of Year	*Depreciation Expense Dr.; Allowance for Depreciation Cr.*	*Total Allowance*	*Book Value*
			$17,000
1....................	$ 1,600	$ 1,600	15,400
2....................	1,600	3,200	13,800
3....................	1,600	4,800	12,200
4....................	1,600	6,400	10,600
5....................	1,600	8,000	9,000
6....................	1,600	9,600	7,400
7....................	1,600	11,200	5,800
8....................	1,600	12,800	4,200
9....................	1,600	14,400	2,600
10....................	1,600	16,000	1,000*
	$16,000		

* Estimated salvage value.

Frame 10[9]

Units of production depreciation. If usage is the dominant factor causing expiration of the asset, it may be desirable to base depreciation on physical output. A depreciation charge per unit of output may be obtained by dividing the original asset cost less salvage value by the estimated number of units to be produced during the life of the asset. The periodic depreciation expense is obtained by multiplying the rate per unit by actual output each period.

For example, on March 1, 1975, Jay Corporation purchased a stamping machine at a total cost of $60,000. The machine is expected to have an eight-year life, during which time it will produce approximately five million units of product. Its scrap value at the end of that time is estimated to be negligible. During 1975, 900,000 units of product are processed by using this machine. Depreciation for the year under the units of production method is:

1. $7,500.
2. $6,250.
3. $10,800.

The correct answer is in Answer Frame 10[9] on page 402.

Frame 11[9]

Accelerated depreciation. The 1954 Revenue Act permitted taxpayers to use a fixed percentage declining-balance method or a sum-of-the-years'-

digits method of computing depreciation. These methods are often referred to as accelerated depreciation. Subsequent amendments have continued the use of accelerated depreciation methods. Under these methods larger amounts of depreciation are recorded in the early years of the life of an asset than in the later years. Businessmen often prefer these methods because the increased depreciation charges in the early years reduce taxable earnings and thereby reduce the amount of federal income taxes which must be paid in those years.

Theoretical support for these methods also exists. Their use seems especially appropriate where the service-rendering or revenue-producing ability of the asset declines through time, where the value of the asset declines more in early years and less in later years of its life, and where repairs and other maintenance costs increase through time.

Double declining-balance depreciation. Under this method the straight-line rate of depreciation is doubled, and the doubled rate is applied to the declining balance of the asset—its net book value. Salvage value is ignored. Illustration 9.2 gives an example of an asset costing

Illustration 9.2

DOUBLE DECLINING-BALANCE METHOD
DEPRECIATION SCHEDULE

End of Year	*Depreciation Expense Dr.: Allowance for Depreciation Cr.*	*Total Allowance*	*Book Value*
			$16,000.00
1. (20% of $16,000.00)....	$3,200.00	$ 3,200.00	12,800.00
2. (20% of $12,800.00)....	2,560.00	5,760.00	10,240.00
3. (20% of $10,240.00)....	2,048.00	7,808.00	8,192.00
4. (20% of $ 8,192.00)....	1,638.40	9,446.40	6,553.60
5. (20% of $ 6,553.60)....	1,310.72	10,757.12	5,242.88
6. (20% of $ 5,242.88)....	1,048.58	11,805.70	4,194.30
7. (20% of $ 4,194.30)....	838.86	12,644.56	3,355.44
8. (20% of $ 3,355.44)....	671.09	13,315.65	2,684.35
9. (20% of $ 2,684.35)....	536.87	13,852.52	2,147.48
10. (20% of $ 2,147.48)....	429.50	14,282.02	1,717.98*

* The remaining amount of $1,717.98 will be the basis for computing gain or loss upon the disposition of the asset after 10 years.

$16,000 with an estimated life of 10 years. In this example the 10 percent straight-line rate of depreciation (100% ÷ 10 years = 10% per year) is doubled, yielding a depreciation rate of 20 percent.

When the double declining-balance method is used to compute the annual depreciation amount, the annual amount is allocated to the months within the year on a straight-line basis. For example, the depreciation per month in the first year for the asset in Illustration 9.2 is $266.67 ($3,200 ÷ 12). In the second year, it is $213.33 ($2,560 ÷ 12).

Answer frame 9[9]

1. True. The charge for depreciation is a constant—in this case, $1,600 each year over the life of the asset.
2. True. The depreciation charge is computed on the basis of cost minus salvage. It follows that total depreciation will equal this difference, and the final book value must be equal to the salvage value.
3. False. The credit balance in the allowance account at the end of the 10th year is the total amount of depreciation charged over the life of the asset, which is equal to cost less estimated salvage value. In this case the balance of the account is $16,000 ($17,000 – $1,000), not the $17,000 original cost of the asset. But the statement would be true if the estimated salvage value were zero.

If you answered any of the above incorrectly, restudy Frame 9[9] before going on to Frame 10[9] on page 400.

Answer frame 10[9]

Answer 3, $10,800, is correct. The 1975 depreciation on the machine is computed as follows: the cost of the machine divided by estimated total output is the depreciation per unit; depreciation per unit times output per period is the depreciation expense for the period. Thus for 1975:

$$\frac{\$60{,}000}{5{,}000{,}000 \text{ units}} = \$0.012 \text{ per unit; } \$0.012 \times 900{,}000 \text{ units} = \$10{,}800.$$

$7,500 is the regular straight-line depreciation based on years of life, not usage. The second answer ($6,250) correctly recognized that the machine was in use for only 10 months, but is still based on time rather than usage.

If you did not get the correct answer, reread Frame 10[9] before going on to Frame 11[9] on page 400.

11[9]
continued

Indicate whether each statement is correct or incorrect. Under the double declining-balance method the annual depreciation charge:

1. Is constant over the life of the asset.
2. Increases over the life of the asset.
3. Is computed by multiplying the book value of the asset at the beginning of the year by a fixed percentage.
4. Is computed by multiplying the original cost of the asset by a smaller and smaller percentage each successive year.

Check your responses in Answer Frame 11[9] on page 404.

Frame 12[9]

Sum-of-the-years'-digits depreciation. This method also produces larger depreciation charges in the early years of the life of an asset. The years of estimated life of an asset are added together and used as the denominator in a fraction, of which the number of years of life remaining (from the beginning of the year) is the numerator. Cost less estimated salvage value is then multiplied by this fraction to compute the periodic depreciation. This is illustrated below for a plant asset costing $19,000, with an estimated life of five years and salvage value of $1,000:

Sum of the years' digits: 1 + 2 + 3 + 4 + 5 = 15.

Depreciation:	
Year 1: 5/15 of $18,000	$ 6,000
Year 2: 4/15 of $18,000	4,800
Year 3: 3/15 of $18,000	3,600
Year 4: 2/15 of $18,000	2,400
Year 5: 1/15 of $18,000	1,200
Total depreciation	$18,000

At the beginning of Year 1 there are 5 years of life remaining. Thus, the ratio used to compute the depreciation charge for Year 1 is 5/15.

The mathematical formula to find the sum of the digits for any given number of periods is:

$$S = \frac{n(n + 1)}{2}$$

where S is the sum of the digits and n is the number of periods in the asset's life. Thus, the sum of the years' digits for 5 years is 15, computed as $5(5 + 1)/2$.

If, on January 2, 1975, a company purchased an asset costing $60,000 with an estimated life of 10 years and salvage value of $5,000, under which of the following methods would the 1975 depreciation be the largest?

1. Straight-line method.
2. Double declining-balance method.
3. Sum-of-the-years'-digits method.

To check your response, turn to Answer Frame 12[9] on page 404.

Frame 13[9]

Melrose Corporation follows a policy of channeling production through the newest machinery in the plant whenever possible so that the most recently acquired machinery is utilized most fully, the next oldest is used almost as much, and so on until finally the oldest machinery is placed in a standby capacity.

Answer frame 11[9]

1. Incorrect. It decreases over the life of the asset.
2. Incorrect. It decreases over the life of the asset.
3. Correct. Salvage value is not deducted. Notice one more thing, however. When using the fixed percentage on a declining balance method, there will always be a remaining book value—an "automatic" salvage value. In Illustration 9.2 this amounts to $1,717.98 at the end of the 10th year.
4. Incorrect. The same percentage is used each year.

If you missed any of the above, reread Frame 11[9] before going on to Frame 12[9] on page 402.

Answer frame 12[9]

Answer 2, double declining-balance, is correct. The 1975 depreciation for the plant asset computed under each of the three methods is:

1. Straight-line method: $60,000 less $5,000, divided by 10 years, is $5,500.
2. Double declining-balance method: 20 percent of $60,000 is $12,000. The straight-line depreciation rate is 10 percent (100% ÷ 10 years = 10%); and 20 percent is used because it is double the straight-line rate.
3. Sum-of-the-years'-digits method: 10/55 × $55,000 = $10,000.

If you answered incorrectly, reread Frames 9[9]–12[9] before turning to Frame 13[9] on page 403.

13[9] *continued*

If you were asked to decide whether the Melrose Corporation should use the straight-line or the sum-of-the years'-digits method for depreciating machinery, which of the following methods would result in the best matching of its cost and revenues?

1. Straight-line method.
2. Sum-of-the-years'-digits method.

Check your answer in Answer Frame 13[9] on page 406.

Frame 14[9]

Revisions of life estimates

When events disclose that the original estimate of the life of an asset is incorrect, the annual depreciation charge under the straight-line procedure may be revised as follows: the net book value of the asset at the beginning of the current period (less salvage) is divided by the number of life periods estimated to remain; the result is the revised annual depreciation charge applicable to the current and succeeding years.

For example, assume that a machine has a cost of $16,000, an estimated salvage value of $2,000 at the end of its useful life, and that the balance in the Allowance for Depreciation account (based on a life estimate of 10 years) stands at $5,600 at the end of the fourth year of the asset's life. At the beginning of the fifth year it is estimated that the asset will last another 10 years (salvage value remains at $2,000). What is the revised annual depreciation charge?

Check your computation in Answer Frame 14[9] on page 406.

Frame 15[9]

Disposition of plant assets

Sale of plant assets. When a plant asset is sold, the balances in the asset account and its related allowance for depreciation account must be eliminated from the records. The difference between the net book value of the asset and the amount received from its sale represents a gain or loss on the sale.

For example, assume that at the date of the sale the account balances, selling price, and gain are as shown below:

Machine cost	$24,000
Allowance for depreciation	10,000
Book value	$14,000
Sales price	15,500
Gain realized	$ 1,500

The journal entry to record the sale is as follows:

Cash	15,500	
Allowance for Depreciation of Machinery	10,000	
Machinery		24,000
Gain on Sale of Plant Assets		1,500

If an asset is sold for less than its net book value, a loss is incurred. Thus, if the above machine was sold for $13,000, a debit of $1,000 would be entered in a Loss on Sale of Plant Assets account.

Accounting for depreciation. When a plant asset is sold or otherwise disposed of, entries should be made to record the depreciation from the date on which it was last recorded to the date of sale. If depreciation is not recorded for the partial period, operating costs will be understated and the gain on the sale of the asset understated or the loss overstated.

Answer frame 13[9]

Answer 2, sum-of-the-years'-digits method, is correct. The aim of matching costs and revenue is better accomplished by one of the accelerated methods of depreciation than by the straight-line method in this case because the machines are used more intensively during their early years and presumably produce more revenue in the first few years, producing successively less revenue as they grow older. The sum-of-the-years'-digits method results in matching a larger proportion of the cost of the machine to the first year's revenue, with successively smaller charges for depreciation in the following years. This pattern approximates the revenue-producing pattern of the machines owned by the Melrose Corporation.

If you answered incorrectly, reread Frames 9[9]–13[9] before going on to Frame 14[9] on page 404.

Answer frame 14[9]

The computation of the revised annual depreciation charge is:

$$(\$16{,}000 - \$5{,}600 - \$2{,}000) \div 10 = \$840$$

The book value at the beginning of the fifth year is $10,400 ($16,000 – $5,600), salvage value is still $2,000, and the life of the asset remaining at the beginning of the fifth year is 10 years, which results in the revised annual depreciation charge of $840.

If you did not answer correctly, reread Frame 14[9] before advancing to Frame 15[9] on page 405.

15[9]
continued

As of December 31, 1975, after closing, the Office Equipment account balance for Company X was $7,200 and the Allowance for Depreciation of Office Equipment account balance $2,880. The rate of depreciation is 12 percent per year. The office equipment was sold for $4,000 cash on January 31, 1976. The following entry was made to record the depreciation applicable to January, 1976:

Depreciation of Office Equipment	72	
Allowance for Depreciation of Office Equipment		72
Depreciation on $7,200 at 12 percent per year for one month.		

What is the journal entry to record the sale?

Turn to Answer Frame 15[9] on page 408 to check your answer.

Frame 16[9]

Does the recording of a gain or a loss when the plant asset is sold indicate that an error was made in setting the rate of depreciation for the asset?

1. Yes.
2. No.
3. Not necessarily.

Check your response in Answer Frame 16[9] on page 408.

Frame 17[9]

Asset retirements without sale. When an asset is retired from productive service and is not sold, it is necessary to remove the retired asset from the plant asset accounts. If the retired asset is scrapped for salvaged material—even though the material will not be sold immediately—the value of the salvaged material should be debited to a Salvaged Materials account. To illustrate, assume that a machine with an original cost of $6,000 and an allowance for depreciation of $5,100 is retired from service and the scrap value of the machine is estimated at $150. The journal entry to record the retirement is:

Salvaged Materials	150	
Allowance for Depreciation of Machinery	5,100	
Loss on Retirement of Plant Assets	750	
Machinery		6,000

Assets destroyed. Assume that an uninsured building costing $32,000 with an allowance for depreciation of $8,000 is completely destroyed by fire. The journal entry is:

Fire Loss	24,000	
Allowance for Depreciation of Building	8,000	
Building		32,000

If the building was insured, only the net fire loss in excess of the amount recoverable from the insurance company would be debited to the Fire Loss account. To illustrate, assume that in the preceding illustration the building was partially insured and that $18,000 was recoverable from the insurance company. The journal entry is as follows:

Receivable from Insurance Company	18,000	
Fire Loss	6,000	
Allowance for Depreciation of Building	8,000	
Building		32,000

Asset exchanges. Certain types of plant assets, such as automobiles and trucks, are often acquired in circumstances involving the trade-in of an old asset. Questions arise as to the amount at which the asset received is to be recorded and the amount of gain or loss, if any, to be recognized.

To illustrate, assume that Delivery Truck No. 1, which cost $2,400 and on which $1,600 of depreciation has accumulated, is exchanged for Delivery Truck No. 2, which has a suggested list price of $3,600; Delivery Truck No. 1 and $3,000 are given in exchange. Using the suggested list price as a base, the exchange might be recorded as follows:

Delivery Trucks (No. 2)	3,600	
Allowance for Depreciation of Delivery Trucks	1,600	
Loss on Exchange of Plant Assets	200	
Delivery Trucks (No. 1)		2,400
Cash		3,000

Answer frame 15[9]

The journal entry to record the sale is:

Cash	4,000	
Allowance for Depreciation of Office Equipment	2,952	
Loss on Sale of Plant Assets	248	
Office Equipment		7,200

The debit to Cash, of course, is equal to the cash received; the credit balance in the Allowance for Depreciation of Office Equipment account is eliminated by the debit to that account; and Office Equipment is decreased by the cost of the machine. Since the selling price of the asset ($4,000) was less than the book value of the asset at date of disposition ($7,200 – $2,952 = $4,248), the company incurred a loss of $248 on the sale.

If you did not record the correct journal entry, reread Frame 15[9] before going on to Frame 16[9] on page 406.

Answer frame 16[9]

Not necessarily. An error in estimating the useful life of the asset may cause the book value at the date of sale to be over- or understated and thus affect the determination of the gain or loss on the sale. But the difference between the selling price and the book value of the asset is related to many other factors which are frequently of more importance. Examples are: (1) changes in the price level (remember that the book value of the asset is in terms of its original cost) and (2) the abundance or shortage of supply and demand for this particular kind of asset—for example, the increased demand for used machinery of certain types during wartime.

Also, an asset may be disposed of after the occurrence of a completely unexpected event, such as damage to the asset or the introduction by a competitor of a new product rendering the product produced by the asset sold completely obsolete.

If you answered incorrectly, reread Frames 15[9] and 16[9] before going on to Frame 17[9] on page 407.

17[9] *continued*

The loss is computed as the difference between book value, $800 ($2,400 – $1,600), and the trade-in allowance granted by the dealer, $600 ($3,600 – $3,000). Depreciation on the newly acquired truck would be based on the $3,600.

The Internal Revenue Code does not permit recognition of gains or losses for tax purposes in these situations. The amount (basis) at which the newly acquired asset is recorded is the sum of the net book value of the asset given up plus any additional expenditure made. The additional cash expenditure required is referred to as "boot." The entry to record the above exchange in accordance with tax law is as follows:

Delivery Trucks (No. 2)	3,800	
Allowance for Depreciation of Delivery Trucks	1,600	
Delivery Trucks (No. 1)		2,400
Cash		3,000

The refusal to recognize gains or losses on certain exchanges of assets for tax purposes bars the door to the manipulation of their amounts. For example, in the first illustration above, the size of the loss can be changed substantially if the dealer and the buyer agree that the selling price of the new truck and the trade-in allowance granted for the old truck are both to be reduced by $500. The buyer would still pay $3,000 cash plus the old truck for the new truck, but his loss would be computed as follows:

Cost of old truck	$2,400
Accumulated depreciation	1,600
Net book value	$ 800
Trade-in allowance granted	100
Loss	$ 700

Depending on the actual values involved, a part of the $700 loss is fictitious. It is rather unlikely that an automotive vehicle with a book value of $800 would have a cash or actual value of only $100.

The loss will be recognized for tax purposes, however, if the old asset is sold outright for cash and a new asset purchased for cash in separate transactions unrelated to each other.

In recent years, especially (but not only) in the automobile industry, suggested list prices have been notoriously inaccurate representations of actual selling prices. Discounts in the neighborhood of 20 percent on such prices have been widely available, although often concealed through the granting of unreasonably high trade-in allowances. Suppose that in the above trade-in situation, the fair cash value of the truck traded in was $400 as determined from sales of similar trucks in auction sales of used cars and trucks. By granting a $600 trade-in allowance for the old truck, the dealer has actually given the buyer a discount of $200 on the purchase of the new truck. The entry to record the exchange in the light of the above information, ignoring federal income tax regulations, would read:

Delivery Trucks (No. 2)	3,400	
Allowance for Depreciation of Delivery Trucks	1,600	
Loss on Exchange of Plant Assets	400	
Delivery Trucks (No. 1)		2,400
Cash		3,000

Of the various possible entries made to record this exchange, this entry reflects the theoretically preferable approach. Under this approach the asset received is recorded at the fair cash value of the old asset at the time of the exchange plus the amount of cash given to boot: $400 + $3,000 = $3,400.

On June 16, 1975, the Mirmac Company traded in office equipment which originally cost $8,000 for newer models having a suggested total list price of $11,500. The equipment dealer agreed to allow $4,500 on the trade, so Mirmac issued a check for $7,000 for the balance due. The old equipment had a cash market value of $4,000 at the time of the trade; its book value adjusted to June 16, 1975, was $4,300. Calculate the amount at which these new assets would be shown on the Mirmac Company books under:

1. The income tax method.
2. The theoretically correct accounting method.

Check your answers in Answer Frame 17⁹ on page 412.

Frame 18⁹

Subsidiary plant ledgers

A controlling account should be maintained in the general ledger for each class of plant assets—buildings, machinery, delivery equipment, and office equipment—and a subsidiary ledger account or card should be maintained for each individual asset of each class. Each subsidiary account should contain full information relating to the asset.

If subsidiary ledger accounts are carried for each asset in each class, not only is control exercised over the assets, but when one asset is disposed of the proper total cost to be credited to the asset account is readily determinable, as is the total amount to be charged to the allowance for depreciation account. If all assets of one class were carried in one account and if only one account existed for the total of the depreciation allowance, it would be difficult to determine the portion of the totals applicable to the asset being sold, retired, or exchanged.

Leaseholds and leasehold improvements

A lease is a contract which gives the lessee the right to operate and use property during the life of the lease contract in exchange for payments to the lessor. If the terms of the lease specify only periodic rentals, an asset account usually will not appear for the leasehold and the periodic rentals will be charged to the Rent Expense account.

If the terms of the lease specify an advance lump-sum payment, the advance payment will be charged to the Leasehold account and will be amortized over the life of the lease by a debit to Rent Expense and a credit to Leasehold. Straight-line amortization is commonly employed, although accelerated methods may be used if it is believed that a better matching of expense and revenue will result.

In recent years considerable controversy has centered around whether better disclosure of financial position might not follow if an entry were made at the time of the signing of a long-term lease agreement.[1] The entry recommended calls for a debit to a Rights to Use Leased Property account and a credit to a Liability on Long-Term Leases account for an amount equal to the present value of the expected stream of rental payments. (Present value concepts are explained in the next chapter.) These recommendations have, to date, been largely ignored in practice in spite of their theoretical merit.

On July 1, 1975, Sliger Company leased a tract of land and a building for 25 years at an annual rental of $10,000 payable each June 30. The first annual rent payment will be made on June 30, 1976. In addition, the lessor required Sliger Company to make an initial lump-sum payment of $50,000 at the date of signing the lease.

Which of the following entries is the correct journal entry to be made on July 1, 1975?

Leasehold	50,000	
Cash		50,000
Rent Expense	50,000	
Cash		50,000

Turn to Answer Frame 18[9] on page 412 to check your answers.

Frame 19[9]

On December 31, 1975, two entries will be made, one to accrue rent under the terms of the contract and the other to adjust the Leasehold account. One entry is:

Rent Expense	5,000	
Accrued Rent Payable		5,000

What is the other entry?

Check your responses by turning to Answer Frame 19[9] on page 412.

Frame 20[9]

If the lessee improves the leased property, the leasehold improvements will usually revert to the owner at the termination of the lease. Improvements are assets and initially should be debited to an account entitled Leasehold Improvements.

[1] John H. Myers, "Reporting of Leases in Financial Statements," *Accounting Research Study No. 4* (New York: American Institute of Certified Public Accountants, 1962).

Answer frame 17[9]

The cost of the new office equipment acquired by Mirmac Company under the two methods is:

1. Under the income tax method: $4,300 + $7,000 = $11,300.
2. Under the theoretically correct accounting method: $4,000 + $7,000 = $11,000.

The entry to record the trade-in under each of the methods is:

1. Income tax method:

Office Equipment (new)	11,300	
Allowance for Depreciation of Office Equipment	3,700	
Office Equipment (old)		8,000
Cash		7,000

2. Theoretically correct method:

Office Equipment (new)	11,000	
Allowance for Depreciation of Office Equipment	3,700	
Loss on Exchange of Plant Assets	300	
Office Equipment (old)		8,000
Cash		7,000

Notice again that under the income tax method, no gain or loss is recognized and the dealer's suggested list price is of no significance in computing the cost of the new equipment. It is meaningful only in determining the amount of "boot" required by the seller. But it does not follow that the suggested list price is always to be ignored. In some cases the actual selling price of an asset may be its suggested list price. And it should be recognized that in many exchanges no objective evidence exists as to the fair cash value of the asset given up. Yet the accountant must be alert to the possibility that assets are overstated.

Note also that the income tax method used in the first journal entry above may lead to material misstatements for purposes of earnings determination and asset measurement. This is true because (1) a loss is not recognized and (2) depreciation expense is improperly stated in future periods because it is not based upon the actual cost of the newly acquired asset.

If you answered incorrectly restudy Frame 17[9] before continuing in Frame 18[9] on page 410.

Answer frame 18[9]

The first entry is correct. The $50,000 advance payment is recorded as a long-term asset by debiting the Leasehold account, with the appropriate portion of this asset transferred to Rent Expense at the end of each accounting period. The entire lump-sum payment is not an expense for 1975. That portion applicable to 1975 will be recorded as an expense at the close of the accounting period.

If you answered incorrectly, review Frame 18[9] before going on to Frame 19[9] on page 411.

Answer frame 19[9]

The December 31, 1975, entry to amortize the Leasehold account is:

Rent Expense	1,000	
Leasehold		1,000
To record as rent expense one half of a year's amortization of the leasehold down payment ([$50,000 ÷ 25 years] × ½).		

If you answered incorrectly, reread Frames 18[9] and 19[9] before going on to Frame 20[9] on page 411.

Ignoring the possibility of renewing the lease, the balance in the Leasehold Improvements account should be written off to periodic expense over which of the following?

1. The life of the lease.
2. The life of the improvements.
3. Whichever of (1) and (2) is shorter.

Check your response in Answer Frame 20[9] on page 414.

Frame 21[9]

Natural resources

Natural resources, such as mines, quarries, and timber stands, should be recorded in the accounts at either (*a*) the cost of acquisition plus the cost of development, or (*b*) the discovery value plus the cost of development.

Discovery value may be used under certain circumstances when the purchase cost bears no reasonable relationship to the value of the resources. For tax purposes, discovery value is the fair market value of the property at the date of discovery or within 30 days thereafter. Discovery value arises when land is acquired at the cost of the land alone, followed by the subsequent discovery of a natural resource with a value greater than its cost. To illustrate, assume that land was purchased for cattle grazing purposes at a cost of $20,000. Shortly after the purchase, it was discovered that valuable oil deposits lay under the land surface. A geological survey indicated that the oil deposits were worth, at market, $500,000. The discovery value, therefore, is $500,000. Not to reflect an asset worth $500,000 in the statement of financial position obviously would understate asset values materially. Assuming the $20,000 land cost has already been recorded, the entry to place the discovery value in the accounts is:

Oil Deposits—Discovery Value........................	500,000	
Capital from Appreciation—Discovery Value Increment..................................		500,000

Natural resources are carried in the accounts at total cost minus depletion or total discovery value minus depletion. Depletion is a cost allocation brought about by extraction of physical quantity, whereas depreciation is a cost allocation brought about by wear, obsolescence, inadequacy, and action of the elements.

Depletion charges may be computed by dividing the cost or the discovery value by the estimated number of units—tons, barrels, or board feet—in the property. This is known as the unit method of computing depletion. To illustrate, assume that $800,000 was paid for a mine estimated to contain 800,000 tons of ore. The unit (per ton) depletion

Answer frame 20[9]

Answer 3 is correct. The useful life of the leasehold improvements to the lessee is the shorter of the life of the improvements or the life of the lease; hence, this is the period over which the cost of the leasehold improvements should be spread. To illustrate, assume that on January 2, 1975, X leases a building for 25 years under a nonrenewable lease at an annual rental of $20,000 payable on each December 31; X immediately incurs a cost of $80,000 for improvements to the building, which are estimated to have a life of 40 years. The $80,000 should be amortized over 25 years, since the period of the lease is shorter than the life of the improvements and X will not be able to use the improvements beyond the life of the lease. If only annual statements are prepared, the following journal entries will properly record the expense for the year ended December 31, 1975:

Rent Expense (or Leasehold Improvement Expense).......	3,200	
Leasehold Improvements..........................		3,200
To charge off 1/25th of $80,000.		
Rent Expense....................................	20,000	
Cash..		20,000
To record annual rent of $20,000.		

The total rental expense is thus $23,200 per year.

Leaseholds and leasehold improvements are ordinarily in under the intangible assets section of the statement of financial position.

If you answered incorrectly, review Frame 20[9] and the above illustration before proceeding to Frame 21[9] on page 413.

21[9] *continued*

charge would be $1 per ton ($800,000 divided by 800,000 tons). If 90,000 tons of ore were extracted in 1975, the depletion charge would be 90,000 times $1, or $90,000. The journal entry to record the depletion charge would be:

Depletion.......................................	90,000	
Allowance for Depletion—Mineral Deposits...........		90,000

As an alternative, the Mineral Deposits account could be credited directly. The Depletion account is the material cost of the ore mined. It is combined with labor and other mining costs to arrive at the total cost of the ore mined. This total cost is then allocated between cost of goods sold and inventory. The situation should be presented in the statement of financial position as follows:

Mineral deposits.................	$800,000
Less: Allowance for depletion......	90,000
	$710,000

Depreciation of plant assets. Buildings, machinery, tipples, derricks, and other plant assets subject to depreciation erected on extractive industry property are depreciated in the same manner as other depreciable assets. If, however, it is expected that such assets will be abandoned when the natural resource at a given location is exhausted, they should be depreciated over the shorter of (*a*) the life of the physical asset or (*b*) the life of the natural resource. In some cases the periodic depreciation charge is computed on the basis of the units of mineral extracted.

Reese Mining Company owns mining property acquired on May 1, 1975, at a cost of $3,400,000. The mine is estimated to contain ore deposits totaling two million tons, of which 85 percent can be economically extracted. The company expects to work the mine for approximately 10 years from the date it starts mining operations. The buildings completed just prior to the start of mining operations on January 1, 1976, cost $54,000 and have an expected physical life of 30 years with no net salvage value. The mining equipment installed on the property cost $300,000 and is expected to have a $10,000 salvage value at the end of an estimated four-year life. During 1976, 200,000 tons were mined. The company employs the straight-line method of computing depreciation on its buildings and the sum-of-the-years'-digits method on machinery. Which of the following correctly states the depletion and depreciation for the year ended December 31, 1976?

1. Depletion, $400,000.
   Depreciation—buildings, $5,400.
   Depreciation—equipment, $116,000.
2. Depletion, $400,000.
   Depreciation—buildings, $1,800.
   Depreciation—equipment, $116,000.
3. Depletion, $340,000.
   Depreciation—buildings, $5,400.
   Depreciation—equipment, $120,000.

Check your calculations in Answer Frame 21[9] on page 416.

Frame 22[9]

Intangible assets

Sources of intangible assets. Intangible assets arise from (1) superior entrepreneurial capacity, reputation, or management know-how—goodwill; (2) exclusive privileges granted by governmental authority—trademarks, patents, copyrights, and franchises; or (3) exclusive privileges gained by private initiative—formulas and processes.

All intangible assets are nonphysical, but not all nonphysical assets are commonly classified as intangible assets. For example, an account receivable is intangible, but it is a current asset.

Goodwill. Goodwill is best viewed as an intangible value attached to an entity (or, perhaps, a division of an entity) which results primarily from its management's entrepreneurial capacity, skill, or know-how and from favorable relations with customers over a number of years. The

Answer frame 21[9]

Answer 1 is correct. The computation of the depletion and depreciation is as follows:

Depletion: Expected total production = 85% of 2,000,000 tons = 1,700,000 tons.

$$\frac{\$3,400,000}{1,700,000} = \$2 \text{ per ton; } \$2 \times 200,000 \text{ tons} = \$400,000.$$

Depreciation:

$$\text{Buildings: } \frac{\$54,000}{10 \text{ years}} = \$5,400 \text{ per year.}$$

The economic life of the buildings to the mining company is only the period during which they are used; in this case the life of the mine, since it is shorter than the physical life of the structures.

Equipment: 4/10 ($300,000 – $10,000) = 4/10 of $290,000 = $116,000. In other cases the life of the mine may be shorter than the life of the equipment; depreciation is computed using the shorter period of time if the equipment must be abandoned at the end of the life of the mine.

If you chose an incorrect answer, restudy Frame 21[9] before continuing to Frame 22[9] on page 415.

22[9] *continued*

value of an entity is often greater than the sum of the fair market values attached to its discernible assets because its management has the ability to use the resources of the entity to produce an above-average rate of earnings per dollar of investment. This means that the proof of the existence of goodwill can be found only in the ability of a company to generate superior or above-average earnings. But to define goodwill as the excess of the value of an entity over the sum of the value of its parts, or as the present value of its expected above-average earnings, is to confuse the measurement of goodwill with its nature.

A Goodwill account will normally appear in the records only if the goodwill has been purchased and paid for in cash, capital stock, or other property of the purchaser. Goodwill cannot be purchased independently; an entire business or a portion of it must be purchased in order to acquire the accompanying intangible asset, goodwill.

To illustrate, assume that A Company purchases all of the assets of B Company, consisting of accounts receivable, inventories, land, buildings, equipment, and patents, for $500,000 cash in addition to assuming responsibility for the $250,000 of debts owed by B Company. With assumed market values (not costs from B's books) as follows, the unidentifiable intangible value attaching to B and purchased by A is:

Cash paid		$500,000
Liabilities assumed		250,000
Total price paid		$750,000
Less fair market values of individually identifiable assets:		
Accounts receivable	$ 80,000	
Inventories	100,000	
Land	100,000	
Buildings	200,000	
Equipment	150,000	
Patents	20,000	650,000
Goodwill		$100,000

The $100,000 is called and recorded in an account entitled Goodwill largely because of an inability to identify the specific reasons for its existence, which might include good reputation, product leadership, valuable human resources, and a good information system.

AMORTIZATION OF GOODWILL. Although goodwill cannot be amortized in the determination of taxable earnings, current accounting practice generally requires its amortization. The write-off of goodwill acquired when a business organization was purchased can be readily justified when superior earnings are not forthcoming. If the level of superior earnings declines, the goodwill is losing its productive ability and amortization is justified. There is no questioning the complete write-off of goodwill if it does not continue to have a favorable effect on earnings.

The current controversy centers around whether goodwill which is being maintained in value should be left on the books in total, amortized periodically, or written off in its entirety. Current practice permits the recording of goodwill only when it is purchased. A policy consistent with this practice would call for the amortization of goodwill, since purchased goodwill cannot last forever. If goodwill exists long after the entity was purchased, it is self-created and not purchased goodwill. If A Company, in the previous example, decided that the goodwill attached to B would last 10 years, an annual adjusting entry that debits Goodwill Amortization Expense and credits Goodwill for $10,000 would be required.

Identify whether each of the following statements is true or false.

1. A company may possess goodwill even though it does not show goodwill on the statement of financial position.
2. The existence of goodwill is evidenced by superior earnings of the firm in comparison to the normal industry earnings average.
3. Purchased goodwill is the price paid for expected future earnings at a level above that which is considered normal.
4. The periodic amortization of goodwill to an earnings statement account is not an acceptable accounting practice.
5. Goodwill is one asset which, if purchased, must be acquired as one of a number of assets acquired simultaneously.

To check your responses, turn to Answer Frame 22[9] on page 418.

Answer frame 22[9]

1. True. Goodwill is usually shown in the accounts only if it has been purchased. Since the seller of a business often receives a payment for goodwill, this asset must have existed before sale even though it was not shown on the statement of financial position.
2. True. Goodwill is evidenced by the superior earning capacity of an enterprise.
3. True. Goodwill purchased does represent payment for superior earning power.
4. False. Goodwill must be amortized through periodic charges to an earnings statement account.
5. True. How could you purchase the earning power of a business without buying the business itself, or at least a portion of it?

If you missed any of the answers, reread Frame 22[9] before going on to Frame 23[9] on page 417.

Frame 23[9]

Trademarks. Trademarks are symbols, designs, brand names, or any other indication of easy recognition attributed to a product. Trademarks should be protected by registration, even though they are valid under common law. Trademarks do not expire at the end of a time interval; priority of use and continuity of use are requirements for the perpetuity of the privilege. Trademarks should be recorded in the accounts at cost, which is composed of the cost of developing the trademark and the cost of legal protection.

Patents. A patent is an exclusive privilege granted by a government, conferring upon the owner of the patent the exclusive right to manufacture, sell, lease, or otherwise benefit from the patent. The real worth of a patent arises from its ability to produce earnings. The legal life of a patent is 17 years, and protection under it starts at the time of application for the patent and extends for 17 years from the date it is granted.

If a patent is acquired by purchase, the purchase price is the cost. If it is acquired by development, the cost of all experimentation and development, legal fees, filing fees, and the cost of drawings and models should be charged to the Patents account.

A patent may have no proven value until it has withstood the test of an infringement lawsuit. If an infringement lawsuit is successfully defended, the cost of the lawsuit should be capitalized; if the infringement lawsuit is lost, the cost of the lawsuit plus the cost of the patent should be charged to expense.

The cost of a patent should be amortized over the shorter of 17 years or the estimated useful life of the patent. If a patent cost $34,000 and is to be amortized ratably over an economic life of 10 years, the journal entry to record the amortization at the end of each year is:

Patent Amortization Expense	3,400	
Patents		3,400

Allowances for patent amortization are seldom used. If, after a number of years, the patent becomes worthless, the unamortized balance should be charged to expense and set forth separately in the earnings statement, if material in amount.

On January 2, 1975, the G. O. Nye Company applied for and was subsequently granted a patent for which it had incurred a total of $40,000 of legal and development costs. In the same year the company instituted a patent infringement suit which was settled in favor of the Nye Company. The costs related to this suit amounted to $2,500. On the basis of this information, which of the following entries does not represent a possibly correct amortization policy?

1. Patent Amortization Expense	2,125	
Patents		2,125
To charge off 1/20th of $42,500.		
2. Patent Amortization Expense	2,500	
Allowance for Patent Amortization		2,500
To charge off 1/17th of $42,500.		
3. Patent Amortization Expense	5,000	
Patents		5,000
To charge off 2/17ths of $42,500.		

The correct answer is in Answer Frame 23[9] on page 420.

Frame 24[9]

Copyrights. A copyright confers an exclusive privilege upon its owner protecting writings, designs, and literary productions from unauthorized reproduction. A copyright affords protection for 28 years, with the privilege of renewal for an additional 28 years. Because the majority of publications have only a limited existence, it is advisable to charge the cost of the copyright against the first edition published through charges to expense over the period of its publication.

Franchises. A franchise is usually a contract between a government subdivision and a private company, usually a public utility, granting the latter certain rights (ranging from those of a nominal nature to that of complete monopoly to service a given territory) while placing on it certain restrictions, especially regarding rates charged. If periodic payments to the grantor of a franchise are required, they should be debited to a Franchise Expense or Rent Expense account. Where a lump-sum payment is made to obtain a franchise, the grantee should amortize the cost over the expected useful life of the franchise or (as explained below) 40 years, whichever is less, by periodic expense charges.

Amortization of intangible assets. If an intangible asset legally expires on a specific date, its cost should be amortized over a period no longer than its legal life. *Opinion No. 17* of the Accounting Principles Board

Answer frame 23[9]

The first entry is one which cannot be correct. The maximum life of any patent is 17 years; hence the cost of the patent is not correctly amortized over 20 years under any circumstances. Amortization of the total patent cost of $42,500 over the legal life of the patent would result in annual amortization of $2,500 of the cost (as indicated in entry 2). While the Allowance for Patent Amortization account is generally not used, it is not incorrect.

Entry 3 gives a possible correct answer because the problem did not specify the expected useful life of the patent. If the patent is likely to be effective in producing revenue for a period shorter than its legal life, the cost should be amortized over this shorter period. This entry assumes a life of 8.5 years. It could be a correct amortization.

If you did not select the right entry, restudy Frame 23[9] before going on to Frame 24[9] on page 419.

24[9] *continued* requires that any intangible asset acquired after October 31, 1970, be amortized over a period not to exceed 40 years.[2]

On January 2, 1975, the Big City Bus Line, a privately owned company which employs a calendar-year accounting period, obtained a franchise from the city for the use of city streets and designated bus-stop areas. The franchise was granted for a 12-year period at an annual fee of $1,800 payable on January 2 of each year. Which of the following entries for 1975 correctly illustrates the treatment of the franchise in the accounts of the Big City Bus Line?

1.	Jan. 2	Rent Expense	1,800	
		Cash		1,800
2.	Jan. 2	Franchise	21,600	
		Cash		1,800
		Franchise Rentals Payable		19,800
	Dec. 31	Rent Expense	1,800	
		Franchise		1,800

Check your answer in Answer Frame 24[9] on page 422.

Frame 25[9]

Plant and intangible assets and the changing value of the dollar

The changing dimension of the unit of measure

Discussion of the topic of accounting for plant assets as related to the changing value of a dollar appears in the *Accounting Review,* the *Journal of Accountancy,* and in newspapers frequently enough to justify a brief

[2] Accounting Principles Board, "Intangible Assets," *Opinion 17,* (New York: AICPA, August, 1970).

reference in an elementary text. This chapter has shown that through the processes of depreciation, depletion, and amortization, the costs of various plant and intangible assets are allocated to the accounting periods during which the assets are used to produce revenue. Costs are recorded in the accounts in terms of dollars at the price level of the years in which the assets were acquired. Periodic cost allocations (expenses) are fractional amounts of these acquisition-cost dollars. But since current revenue is usually expressed in dollars of the current year, it seems inappropriate to match expenses and revenues without adjusting for different price levels.

Adjusting historical cost for price level change

To illustrate assume that depreciation and amortization of $40,000 are based on costs of assets acquired in 1954. Net earnings for 1975 before depreciation and amortization are $90,000 and are expressed largely in 1975 dollars. Ignoring income taxes, the net earnings for 1975 under conventional accounting would be $90,000 minus $40,000, or $50,000. But reliable indices of the general price level may indicate that the 1975 dollar has only 50 percent of the purchasing power of the 1954 dollar. In other words, $200 in 1975 has the same purchasing power that $100 had in 1954. Therefore, it is alleged that in allocating the 1954 cost of $40,000 to the year 1975, the cost should be expressed in terms of 1975 dollars in order to provide proper comparability of the figures on the 1975 earnings statement. The $40,000 of 1954 cost is the equivalent of $40,000 times 200 percent, or $80,000, of cost during 1975. In other words, the cost inherent in the use of the plant assets during the year 1975 amounts to $80,000 worth of 1975 dollars. To the extent that 1975 revenue does not provide an equivalent sum, the total costs incurred are not being recovered. The net earnings of $50,000 are misleading because they are computed on the assumption that the utility of capital assets consumed during 1975 equals $40,000 of revenue when, in terms of 1975 dollars, it equals $80,000. In order to reflect the net earnings after the charge for consumption of capital assets, the computation is expressed in terms of 1975 dollars as $90,000 less $80,000, or $10,000. To obtain meaningful net earnings figures, it may be considered advisable to recognize the changing value of the dollar.

Opposition to adjusting historical cost

While the reasoning above is logical, its application to double-entry accounting is difficult because of conflicting opinions relative to such matters as (*a*) the reliability of index numbers, (*b*) the manner in which entries should be recorded and amounts shown on statements, and (*c*) the frequency of making such adjustments. Some interested parties feel that the computation of depreciation on the replacement cost of each specific asset solves the dilemma. Others feel very strongly that the accountant should adhere to original historical costs only and permit the

Answer frame 24[9]

Number 1 is the correct response. Franchises are treated in much the same way as leaseholds. An initial lump-sum payment is recorded as an asset and then amortized over the life of the franchise or 40 years, whichever is shorter. Annual payments are treated as rent expense in the period in which they apply. The Franchise account is debited only if a lump-sum payment is made to obtain the franchise. Annual future rental payments are not set up as a liability at the time the franchise is obtained. Each payment is treated like any other rental payment.

If you answered incorrectly, reread Frame 24[9] before continuing to Frame 25[9] on page 420.

25[9] *continued*

user of financial statements to apply index numbers, if he chooses, in his interpretations.

At the present time there is substantial authoritative support for retaining cost as the basis of measurement of assets in the books of account and for computing periodic depreciation and amortization on historical cost. But it is also recommended that the effects of changing price levels be disclosed as supplemental information in conventional financial statements, although little has been done in practice in the United States to date toward carrying out this recommendation.

Indicate whether each of the following statements is true or false.

1. If an index of the general level of prices stood at 100 in 1960 and 150 in 1975, then $10,000 of costs in terms of 1960 dollars when expressed in 1975 dollars would amount to $15,000.
2. Financial statements adjusted for change in the general level of prices are required as supplemental statements to the regular financial statements, which are based largely on historical cost.
3. Computation of depreciation on a replacement cost basis has the same effect as adjusting the statements for changes in the general price level.
4. One of the objectives of making adjustments for changes in the general level of prices is to state costs and revenues in terms of dollars of the same period.

Check your answer in Answer Frame 25[9] on page 424.

Summary *chapter* 9

Plant assets are broadly classified as land, natural resources, and depreciable property. Intangible assets are often classified according to whether they are individually identifiable or unidentifiable. Plant assets, except land and natural resources, are subject to depreciation. Natural resources, and in some instances land, are subject to depletion. All intangible assets are subject to amortization.

The primary basis of valuation of plant and intangible assets is cost. Cost usually consists of all expenditures made (or obligations incurred) to secure and place the asset in operating condition. Assets acquired in noncash exchanges for securities are recorded at the fair market value of the asset received or the securities surrendered, whichever is more clearly evident. Assets received as gifts are frequently valued at appraised values in the absence of clear-cut evidence of their fair market value.

Subsequent expenditures on plant assets are classifiable as capital expenditures, chargeable to the asset or allowance for depreciation accounts, or revenue expenditures, chargeable to expense accounts. Capital expenditures are those which in some way improve an asset or extend its life. Revenue expenditures are the normal, recurring costs which must be incurred to keep the assets in operating condition and which do not increase the service-rendering ability of the asset nor extend its life.

Many companies employ arbitrary minimums in determining whether the expenditure to acquire an asset (such as a wastebasket) or to repair an asset is to be capitalized. The concept of unit of property is also employed in determining whether the cost of replacing a part of an asset is to be expensed or capitalized.

Theoretically, the amount of depreciation charged to a given period should bear some relationship to the services received from the asset during the period.

Four commonly used depreciation methods are straight-line, units of production, double declining-balance, and sum-of-the-years'-digits.

When an existing asset such as an automobile is traded for another, the newly acquired asset may be recorded at (1) its suggested list price, (2) an amount equal to the net book value of the old asset plus the additional cash paid, or (3) an amount equal to the fair market value of the old asset plus the additional cash paid (the preferred alternative).

Typically, leases are not recorded unless an advance lump-sum payment is made which is subsequently amortized over the life of the lease. The periodic payments required under the provisions of a lease agreement are usually expenses in the period for which payment was made. Leasehold improvements revert to the owner of the leased property at the end of the lease and for this reason should be amortized over the life of the lease or the life of the asset, whichever is shorter.

Natural resources are usually recorded at the cost of development plus their cost of acquisition or their discovery value. Such resources should be recorded at discovery value if the land containing them was acquired for the cost of the land alone and the resources subsequently are discovered. Depletion charges on natural resources are usually based upon the number of physical units (pounds, tons, barrels) involved.

Goodwill is an intangible value attached to an entity resulting primarily from the entrepreneurial skill or capacity of its management to produce an above-average rate of earnings on investment.

Trademarks seemingly do not expire at the end of a time interval but

Answer frame 25[9]

1. True. The adjustment is computed as follows: $150/100 \times \$10{,}000 = \$15{,}000$.
2. False. Financial statements adjusted for general price level change are recommended as supplemental statements. Presently they are not required.
3. False. Depreciation based on replacement cost in most cases differs from that computed when adjusting for general price level changes. This difference occurs because changes in the specific prices of individual assets may increase (or decrease) by an amount greater (or less) than the changes in the general price level. The general price level change is an average of all price level changes in the economy.
4. True. This is one of the primary objectives of adjusting historical data for changes in the general price level.

If you answered any of the above incorrectly, reread Frame 25[9] before proceeding to the chapter summary on page 422.

---

must be amortized over a period not to exceed 40 years. Patents should be recorded at cost—including the cost of an infringement suit, if any—and, since they are of limited life, should be amortized over their useful life or legal life, whichever is shorter.

The cost of a copyright should be amortized over its useful life, which is often considerably shorter than its legal life. If a lump-sum payment was made to secure a franchise, it should be amortized over a period not to exceed 40 years.

To complete your review, study the definitions of new terms introduced in this chapter in the glossary which follows. Then go on to the Student Review Quiz for a self-administered test of your comprehension of the material in the chapter (see page 425).

Glossary *chapter* 9

Accelerated depreciation—an accounting procedure under which the amounts of depreciation recorded in the early years of an asset's life are greater than those recorded in later years.

Amortization—an estimate, usually expressed in terms of cost, of the service potential of an intangible asset that expired in a period, which is accounted for by periodically charging a portion of the cost of an intangible asset to expense.

Betterment—replacement of an existing asset or part of an asset with a superior or improved asset or part.

Boot—the amount of cash paid in addition to the asset surrendered in order to acquire another asset.

Capital expenditure—an expenditure made, usually with regard to plant assets, which is to be capitalized because of the benefits it will render in subsequent periods.

Capitalization—as used in discussions of intangible assets, the finding of the asset value equivalent to a given stream of earnings with a known interest rate; thus, a continuing stream of net earnings of $50,000 has a capitalized value of $500,000 if the interest rate is 10 percent.

Copyright—an exclusive privilege conferred upon the owner protecting writings, designs, and literary productions from unauthorized reproduction.

Depletion—the amount deducted from the cost (or other basis) of an asset of the natural resource type because of a removal of a part of the resource.

Depreciation—an estimate, usually expressed in terms of cost, of the amount of service potential of a plant asset that expired in a period. The double declining-balance method of computing annual depreciation consists of finding the straight-line rate, doubling it, and applying it to the net book value which the asset had at the beginning of the year. The straight-line method assigns equal amounts of depreciation to equal periods of time. The sum-of-the-years'-digits method assigns depreciation in decreasing amounts to successive periods of time; the formula used consists of multiplying cost (less estimated salvage) by a fraction, the denominator of which is the sum of the numbers from one to the number of years of useful life expected from an asset and the numerator of which is the number of periods of life remaining from the beginning of the year. The units of production method assigns equal amounts of depreciation to each unit of product produced by an asset.

Franchise—usually a contract between a government subdivision and a private company, often a public utility, granting the latter certain privileges (ranging from those of a minor nature to that of complete monopoly to service a given territory) while placing on it certain restrictions, especially in the matter of rates charged.

Goodwill—an intangible value attaching to an entity resulting primarily from the expectation that its management has the ability to produce an above-average rate of earnings per dollar of investment.

Improvement—an alteration or structural change in a depreciable asset which results in a better asset, that is, one which has greater durability, productivity, or efficiency. Costs of improvements are properly capitalizable.

Lease—a contract under which the owner of property (the lessor) grants to another (the lessee) the right to operate and use the property for a stated period of time in exchange for stipulated payments.

Leasehold—the down payment, other than first year's rent, made at the time of signing of a lease agreement.

Leasehold improvement—any physical alteration to leased property from which benefits are expected to be secured beyond the current accounting period.

Obsolescence—the decline in usefulness of an asset brought about by invention and technological progress.

Patent—an exclusive privilege granted by a government conferring on the owner of the patent the exclusive right to manufacture, sell, lease, or otherwise benefit from the patented invention.

Revenue expenditure—a normal, recurring expenditure made on plant assets to keep them in operating condition which is expected to benefit only the current period.

Trademark—a symbol, design, brand name, or any other indication of easy and ready recognition attributed to a product.

Unit of property—a concept employed in determining whether a given expenditure to replace part of an asset is to be capitalized or expensed, with capitalization to be undertaken only when a complete unit of property is replaced.

Wasting assets—depletable natural resources such as mineral and petroleum deposits and timber stands.

Student review quiz *chapter* 9

To develop a permanent record of your responses, you may write them on the answer sheet provided in the *Work Papers* or on a separate sheet of paper.

1 The chief purpose of depreciation accounting is to:

a) Provide a fund for financing the replacement of depreciable assets.

b) Show conservative figures on the financial statements.

c) Provide a deduction for income tax purposes.

d) Revalue assets whose value has declined.

e) Systematically allocate the service potential of depreciable assets, usually as measured in terms of cost, against the revenue produced over the estimated useful lives of those assets.

2 The Walker Department Store purchased land with a building thereon from William Ring for the purpose of building a parking ramp for its customers. The purchase contract specified that Walker Department Store would pay Mr. Ring $20,000 in cash and would assume the present real estate mortgage note of $5,000. Walker also agreed to assume payment of $180 worth of property taxes in arrears. The $230 in legal fees incurred by the store in connection with this transaction included: $150 for title search, $30 for drawing up necessary documents, $40 of transfer taxes, and $10 in recording fees. As soon as it gained title to the property, Walker Department Store demolished the existing building and graded the property in preperation for the erection of the parking ramp. The cost of tearing down the old structure and grading was $3,200. On the basis of the above data, at what cost should this land be recorded in Walker's accounts?

a) $20,230.
b) $25,180.
c) $25,230.
d) $25,410.
e) $28,610.

3 Baker Company owns a tract of land acquired over 40 years ago at a cost of $40,000. On this tract of land stands a fully depreciated building which is still in use and which cost $500,000. Baker Company purchased the adjoining tract of land and intends to erect one large manufacturing building over both tracts of land. An old, occupied tenement building is located on the adjoining land. With regard to the following statements regarding expenditures made by the Baker Company, choose the one which is incorrect.

a) The cost of demolishing the old fully depreciated building should be charged to the land account.
b) The cost of demolishing the old tenement building should be charged to the land account.
c) Payments made to the occupants of the tenement building to induce them to surrender their leases should be charged to the land account.
d) The cost of the fully depreciated building should be removed from the Building and Allowance for Depreciation accounts when the building is demolished.
e) The cost of excavation of the land in order to construct a basement for the building should be charged to the building account.

4 Which of the following expenditures made by the Rothe Millwork Company relative to its plant assets should be charged to expense immediately upon incurrence? Assume the company has been operating for a number of years.

a) Transportation and insurance costs on a new lathe.
b) Sales tax on a new lathe.
c) The cost of safety guards installed on all table and band saws.
d) Interest paid on an installment contract to purchase a new band saw.
e) Cost of testing and breaking in a new machine.

5 On January 2, 1971, Erv's Bootery purchased office equipment at a cost of $1,800 which had an estimated life of six years with no salvage value. On March 1, 1975 the equipment is sold for $560 cash. At the close of the annual accounting period on December 31, 1974, the Office Equipment account had a balance of $1,800 and the Allowance for Depreciation of Office Equipment account, $1,200. Which of the following entries should be made on March 1, 1975?

a)	Cash	560	
	Allowance for Depreciation of Office Equipment	1,200	
	Loss on Sale of Plant Assets	40	
	Office Equipment		1,800
b)	Depreciation Expense..	50	
	Allowance for Depreciation of Office Equipment.........		50
	Cash	560	
	Allowance for Depreciation of Office Equipment	1,250	
	Office Equipment		1,800
	Gain on Sale of Plant Assets....		10

c)

Depreciation Expense..	50	
Allowance for Depreciation of Office Equipment..........		50
Cash................	560	
Allowance for Depreciation of Office Equipment..............	1,200	
Loss on Sale of Plant Assets............	40	
Office Equipment		1,800

d)

Depreciation Expense..	75	
Allowance for Depreciation of Office Equipment..........		75
Cash................	560	
Allowance for Depreciation of Office Equipment..............	1,275	
Office Equipment		1,800
Gain on Sale of Office Equipment..........		35

e) None of the above.

6 On July 1, 1975, the Brinkman Toy Company purchased a machine invoiced at $8,000 (terms 2/10, n/30, f.o.b. shipping point). The invoice was paid within the discount period. Freight charges amounted to $190 and installation costs to $570. The estimated useful life of the machine is eight years, at which time it will have an estimated salvage value of $200. It is further estimated that this machine will produce a total of 100,000 units during its lifetime. Assuming that 9,000 units have been produced by December 31, 1975, the close of the accounting period, depreciation for 1975 based on usage would be:

a) $8,560 × ⅛ × ½ = $535.
b) $0.0876 × 9,000 = $788.40.
c) $0.086 × 9,000 = $774.
d) $0.0856 × 9,000 = $770.40.
e) $0.084 × 9,000 = $756.

7 On July 1, 1975, the Vollrath Machine Company built and installed a machine for its own use. Direct costs of the machine were materials, $3,000, and labor, $2,200. It was estimated that supplies and other factory costs applicable to the construction of this machine totaled $900. The estimated life of the machine was five years; estimated salvage value, $100. It would have cost Vollrath Machine Company $7,000 to buy a comparable machine, installed. Which of the following statements are true?

a) The charge for depreciation for the year ended June 30, 1976, (first year) would be greater under the double declining-balance method than under the sum-of-the-years'-digits method.
b) The charge for depreciation for the year ended June 30, 1977, (second year) would be greater under the sum-of-the-years'-digits method than under the double declining-balance method.
c) The charge for depreciation for the year ended June 30, 1976, (first year) under the sum-of-the-years'-digits method would be $2,000.
d) Statements **(a)**, **(b)**, and **(c)** are true.
e) Only **(a)** and **(c)** are true.

8 Mobile Furniture Company owns one delivery truck, which it purchased on October 1, 1972, at a cost of $3,200. The estimated life of the truck at that time was four years. On June 30, 1975, the close of the fiscal year, the Allowance for Depreciation account had a balance of $2,200. On July 1, 1975, the company trades this vehicle for a new one having a suggested retail price of $3,700. The dealer allows a $900 trade-in for the old truck, and the company pays the balance in cash. The old truck has a fair market value of $750. The journal entry to record the trade-in (do not use the income tax method) is:

a)

Delivery Truck No. 2..	3,700	
Allowance for Depreciation on Delivery Truck.............	2,200	
Loss on Exchange of Plant Assets........	100	
Delivery Truck No. 1..........		3,200
Cash............		2,800

b)

Delivery Truck No. 2..	3,550	
Allowance for Depreciation on Delivery Truck.............	2,200	
Loss on Exchange of Plant Assets........	250	
Delivery Truck No. 1..........		3,200
Cash............		2,800

c)

Delivery Truck No. 2..	3,800	
Allowance for Depreciation on Delivery Truck.............	2,200	
Delivery Truck No. 1..........		3,200
Cash............		2,800

d)

Delivery Truck No. 1..	3,800	
Allowance for Depreciation on Delivery Truck..............	2,200	
Delivery Truck No. 2..........		3,200
Cash............		2,800

e)

Delivery Truck No. 2..	2,800	
Allowance for Depreciation on Delivery Truck..............	2,200	
Loss on Exchange of Plant Assets........	1,000	
Delivery Truck No. 1..........		3,200
Cash............		2,800

9 On October 15, 1975, the firm of Tweedle & Dee traded in an old typewriter for a newer model. The cost of the old machine was $225 and its book value (adjusted to October 15, 1975) $45. The new machine was priced at $385 but was acquired for $300 plus the old machine. According to income tax regulations, the basis for depreciation of the new machine was:

a) $385.
b) $365.
c) $345.
d) $300.
e) None of these (must know fair market value of the old machine at date of trade-in).

10 Wagner, Inc. leased a building for 30 years. The lease contract called for an advance lump-sum payment of $90,000 (30 percent of the total payments due under the lease) plus $7,000 annual rent payable at the end of each year. The Wagner company immediately remodeled the building at a cost of $18,000. The building has an estimated useful life of 40 years. Which of the following entries should be made at the end of each year?

a)

Leasehold Improvement Expense....	600	
Leasehold Improvements...		600
Rent Expense......	10,000	
Leasehold......		3,000
Cash..........		7,000

b)

Leasehold Improvement Expense....	450	
Leasehold Improvements...		450
Rent Expense......	10,000	
Leasehold......		3,000
Cash..........		7,000

c)

Leasehold Improvement Expense....	450	
Rent Expense......	10,000	
Leasehold Improvements...		3,000
Cash..........		7,450

d)

Leasehold Improvement Expense....	600	
Rent Expense......	10,000	
Leasehold......		600
Cash..........		10,000

e)

Leasehold Improvement Expense....	600	
Leasehold Improvements...		600
Rent Expense......	7,000	
Cash..........		7,000

11 On June 1, 1974, Bates Metals Company acquired ore deposits estimated at two million tons, of which 1,700,000 tons are expected to be economically extractable. The property on which the ore is situated was acquired at a cost of $850,000. Special equipment, capable of being used only on this property, is installed at a cost of $63,000 and has an estimated average life of 15 years. In the fiscal year ended May 31, 1975, Bates mined 200,000 tons of the ore. Annual production in succeeding years is expected to be 300,000 tons or more. Possibly correct adjusting entries to be made on May 31, 1975 are:

a)

Depletion................	85,000	
Allowance for Depletion...............		85,000
Depreciation.............	4,200	
Allowance for Depreciation of Mining Equipment.........		4,200

b)

Depletion................	100,000	
Allowance for Depletion...............		100,000
Depreciation.............	10,500	
Allowance for Depreciation of Mining Equipment.........		10,500

c)

Depletion................	107,412	
Allowance for Depletion...............		100,000
Allowance for Depletion of Mining Equipment.........		7,412

d)

Depletion................	100,000	
Allowance for Depletion...............		100,000
Depreciation.............	4,200	
Allowance for Depreciation of Mining Equipment.........		4,200

e) None of the above.

12 Barry Drug Company developed a patent on a new drug. The total cost of experimentation and research was $140,000. Legal fees in securing the patent amounted to $1,000. It was estimated that the patent would have a useful life of about five years. Shortly after the patent was acquired, Barry Drug Company became involved in a lawsuit in which it successfully defended itself against the claim of patent infringement. The cost of this litigation was $3,500. The correct journal entry to reflect the patent amortization for each fiscal year is:

a) Patent Amortization Expense	28,000	
Patents		28,000
b) Patent Amortization Expense	28,200	
Allowance for Amortization of Patents		28,200
c) Patent Amortization Expense	28,900	
Patents		28,900
d) Patent Amortization Expense	8,500	
Patents		8,500
e) No entry; patents are not amortized.		

13 Which of the following statements are false?

a) Goodwill is recorded only when purchased for cash.

b) The goodwill of a business can be purchased separately from the rest of its assets.

c) Goodwill, once recorded, should not be amortized.

d) The existence of goodwill can be determined without reference to the earnings of a business.

e) All of the above are false.

14 Which of the following statements is not true?

a) Cost is the basis of accounting for plant assets largely because the accountant has no ready alternative.

b) Generally, plant assets are recorded at their fair value at the time of acquisition; in cases where cash is not involved, cost is assumed to be the fair value of the asset received or given up, whichever is more clearly evident.

c) Historical cost is used as a basis of valuation of assets in accounting because the accountant does not really care what the value of an asset is.

d) To obtain an accurate reflection of cost in recording depreciation, many accountants believe that the changing value of the dollar must be taken into consideration.

e) The goal in accounting for plant assets and intangible assets is actually the same—to spread the cost of these assets over the periods in which they produce benefits.

Now compare your answers with the correct answers and explanations on page 714.

Questions *chapter* 9

1 Barnes Corporation recently bought, for $100,000, a plot of land on which to construct a new warehouse at some future date. Legal fees connected with the transaction were $1,200. Back taxes on the property amounted to $5,000, for which Barnes Corporation assumed the liability. Estimates from various demolition crews indicate that the cost of razing the old warehouse currently on the property will be $7,000. What is the cost of the land?

2 Why should periodic depreciation, depletion, or amortization be recorded on virtually all plant assets?

3 For each of the following, state whether the expenditure made should be charged to an expense, an asset, or an allowance for depreciation account:

a) Cost of installing air conditioning in a leased building.

b) Biennial painting of an owned factory building.

c) Cost of installing a new transmission in a three-year-old truck which was purchased new. The truck is considered a unit of property.

d) Cost of replacing the roof on a 10-year-old building which was purchased new and has an estimated total life of 40 years. Replacement of the roof was anticipated in setting the annual depreciation charge on the building.

e) Cost of rewinding the armature of an electric motor.

4 **(a)** Distinguish between depreciation, depletion, and amortization. Name

two assets which are subject to depreciation; to depletion; to amortization.
(b) Distinguish between tangible and intangible assets and classify the above-named assets accordingly.

5 **(a)** When plant assets are sold for cash, how is the gain or loss determined? **(b)** Assume that a plant asset is disposed of by exchanging it for a new asset of a similar type. Describe the three different bases at which the new asset may be recorded. Which basis has the most support in accounting theory?

6 What is the difference between a leasehold and a leasehold improvement? Is there any difference in accounting procedures applicable to each?

7 Brush, Inc. leased a tract of land for 40 years at an agreed annual rental of $10,000. The effective date of the lease was July 1, 1975. During the last six months of 1975 Brush constructed a building on the land at a cost of $250,000. The building was placed in operation on January 2, 1976, at which time it was estimated to have a physical life of 50 years. Over what period of time should the building be depreciated? Why?

8 What four factors must be considered in determining a periodic depreciation charge?

9 You note that a certain store seems to have a steady stream of regular customers, a favorable location, courteous employees, high-quality merchandise and a reputation for fairness in dealing with customers, employees, and suppliers. Does it follow automatically that this business has goodwill?

10 In any exchange of noncash assets, the accountant's task is that of finding the most appropriate valuation to assign to the assets received. What is the general rule for determining the most appropriate valuation in such a situation?

Exercises *chapter* 9

1 Bison Company acquired, for $160,000 cash, real property consisting of a tract of land and two buildings. The company intended to raze the old factory building and remodel and use the old office building. In order to allocate the cost of the propery acquired, the company had the property appraised. The appraised values were: land, $60,000; factory building, $60,000; office building, $80,000. The factory building was demolished at a net cost of $8,000. The office building was remodeled at a cost of $16,000. The cost of a new identical office building was estimated to be $90,000. Present a schedule or schedules showing the determination of the amounts at which the assets acquired should be carried in the Bison Company accounts. Show calculations.

2 The Martin Company purchased some office furniture on March 1, 1975, for $12,400 cash. Cash of $200 was paid for freight and cartage costs. The furniture is being depreciated over an eight-year life under the straight-line method, assuming $600 of salvage value. The company employs a calendar-year accounting period and records depreciation for the full month in which an asset is installed. On July 1, 1978, $40 was spent to refinish the furniture. All of the furniture was sold on October 1, 1979, for $4,000. Prepare journal entries for the Martin Company to record all of the above data, including the annual depreciation adjustments.

3 Elliot Company purchased a new machine on January 2, 1975, at a cash cost of $60,000. The machine is estimated to have a life of five years, with no salvage value at the end of that time. If federal income taxes are levied at a rate of 50 percent of net earnings, how much would the income taxes payable for the years 1975 and 1976 be reduced if the company chose the double declining-balance method of computing depreciation rather than the straight-line method?

4 Plant equipment originally costing $18,000 on which $12,000 of depreciation has been accumulated is sold for $4,500. Prepare the journal entry to record the sale.

5 Ace Company owns an automobile acquired on July 1, 1974, at a cash cost of $5,200; at that time it was estimated to have a life of four years and $400 salvage value. Depreciation has been recorded through June 30, 1977, on a straight-line basis. On July 1, 1977, the auto is traded for a new auto having a list price of $6,600. The dealer allows a $2,000 trade-in allowance for the old auto, and Ace Company pays the balance due in cash. The old auto has a cash value of $1,000 on this date. Prepare the journal entry to record the trade-in, using that method which most clearly portrays the current value of the new auto.

6 King Company paid $600,000 for the right to extract all of the mineral-bearing ore, estimated at three million tons, from a certain tract of land. During the first year, King Company extracted 300,000 tons of the ore and sold 200,000 tons. What part of the $600,000 should be charged to expense during the first year?

7 Stone Company leased a building and a tract of land for a 20-year period beginning January 1, 1975, paying $40,000 in cash and agreeing to make annual payments equal to 1 percent of the first $500,000 of sales and half of 1 percent of all sales over $500,000. Sales for 1975 amounted to $1,200,000. Payment of the annual amount will be made on January 14, 1976. Prepare journal entries to record the cash payment of January 1 and the proper expense to be recognized for the use of the leased land and building for 1975.

8 Jones Corporation leased a building for a 30-year period beginning January 1, 1975, at an agreed annual rental of $10,000, payable each January 1 for the year in advance. Jones made the following entry on January 1, 1975:

Leasehold........	300,000	
Cash........		10,000
Rent Payable		290,000

Do you believe the entry is correct? If not, give the correct entry.

9 The James Company developed a new product at a cost of $34,000. A patent was granted on the product on January 2, 1959. In January 1970 the company successfully prosecuted an infringement of these rights. The legal fees amounted to $6,000. What will be the amount of patent cost amortized in 1975?

Problems, Series A *chapter* 9

9–1–A

The Lampert Building Corporation purchased a one-square-mile farm from the owner under the following terms: cash paid, $125,000; mortgage note assumed, $100,000; interest accrued on mortgage note assumed, $2,500. Lampert was to issue to the owner 1,000 shares of its $20 par common stock, which at this time had a market value of $40 per share although its book value was only $36 per share.

The company paid $23,000 for brokerage and legal services to acquire the property and secure clear title. It planned to subdivide the property into residential lots and construct homes on these lots. Clearing and leveling costs of $9,000 were paid. Crops on the land were sold for $6,000. A house on the land, to be moved by the buyer, was sold for $2,100. The other buildings were razed at a cost of $4,000 and salvaged material was sold for $4,200.

Approximately three acres of the land were deeded to the township for roads, and another five acres were deeded to the local school district as a site for a future school. After the subdivision was completed, this land would have an approximate value of $800 per acre. The company secured a total of 600 salable lots from the remaining land.

Required: Present a schedule showing in detail the composition of the cost of the 600 salable lots.

9–2–A

Jill Company acquired a machine on July 1, 1975, at a cash cost of $24,000 and immediately spent $1,000 to install it. The machine was estimated to have a useful life of eight years and a scrap value of $2,000 at the end of this time. It was further estimated that the machine would produce 500,000 units of product during its life. In the first year the machine produced 100,000 units.

Required: Prepare journal entries to record depreciation for the fiscal year ended June 30, 1976, if the company employed:

a) The straight-line method.
b) The sum-of-the-years'-digits method.
c) The double declining-balance method.
d) The units of production method.

9–3–A

Bessemer Company purchased a machine on January 2, 1973, at an invoice price of $61,400. Transportation charges amounted to $500, and $1,100 was spent to install the machine. Costs of removing an old machine to make room for the new amounted to $600, and $100 was received for the scrapped material from the old machine.

Required:

a) State the amount of depreciation that would be recorded on the machine for the first year on the straight-line basis, on the double declining-balance basis, and on the sum-of-the-years'-digits basis, assuming an estimated life of eight years and no salvage value expected.

b) Give the journal entry needed at December 31, 1975, to record depreciation assuming a revised total life expectancy for the machine of 12 years; assume that depreciation has been recorded through December 31, 1974, on a straight-line basis.

9–4–A

When you were hired as manager of the Andover Company on January 1, 1976, the company bookkeeper gave you the following information regarding one of its equipment accounts:

Equipment—Machine B

1975			1975		
Jan. 1	Disposition cost of machine A	500	Jan. 1	Cash from sale of machine A	400
1	Material used in building machine B	10,000	Dec. 31	Depreciation on machine B for year ended 12/31/75 (10% of $20,000)	2,000
1	Labor used in building machine B	8,000			
1	Cost of installing machine B	900			
1	Net earnings from building machine B rather than purchasing it	1,500			

Required: Construct the theoretically correct Equipment account for machine B.

9–5–A

Sharon Company purchased a new 1975 model automobile on September 1, 1975. The list price of the new car was $3,300 and the company received a trade-in allowance of $1,200 for a 1973 model. The 1973 model had been acquired on September 1, 1973, at a cost of $2,400, and depreciation had been recorded through December 31, 1974, on a double declining-balance basis, with four years of useful life expected. At the time of the trade, the 1973 automobile had a cash value of $900.

Required: Prepare journal entries to record the exchange of the automobiles under **(a)** the tax method and **(b)** the theoretically correct accounting method.

9–6–A

Bing Company purchased a machine at a cash cost of $24,000. An electric motor was purchased for cash and attached to the machine at a total cost of $16,000, The machine was installed in a production center on the first floor at a cost of $8,000 on July 1, 1974. Its estimated life was 15 years, with no salvage value expected. On July 1, 1979, the machine and motor unit was moved from its first-floor location to the second floor and the entire unit installed at a cost of $12,000. The estimated life of the unit in its second-floor location is 10 years, with no salvage value expected.

Required: Compute the depreciation charge for the year ending June 30, 1980, using the straight-line method.

9–7–A

a) Newberry Company purchased a tract of land and a building having appraised values of $80,000 and $160,000, respectively. The terms of the sale were that Newberry would pay $122,000 in cash, and assume responsibility for an $80,000 mortgage note, with $2,000 of accrued interest, and $9,000 of unpaid property taxes. Newberry intends to use the building as an office building.

Required: Prepare journal entries to record the purchase.

b) Percy Company secured a lease on a building and a tract of land for a 40-year period beginning July 1, 1965, by paying $40,000 immediately in cash and agreeing to make annual payments each June 30 of $10,000. Effective July 1, 1975, Percy Company subleased this property to the Acme Company at an annual rental of $24,000, payable each July 1 for the year in advance, for the remaining 30 years of its lease.

Required: Assuming a fiscal year ending June 30, prepare journal entries for the Percy Company for all of the above for the year ending June 30, 1976.

9–8–A

Senac Company owned a mine, acquired at a total cost of $2,350,000, which contained an estimated 2.4 million tons of ore. It was further estimated that the land would have a value of $200,000 when the mine was exhausted and that only two million tons of ore could be economically extracted. A building was erected on the property at a cost of $400,000. The building had an estimated physical life of 35 years, with no scrap value because removal costs would equal any salvaged material value. Specialized mining equipment was installed at a cost of $625,000. This equipment had an estimated life of six years and an estimated $16,000 salvage value. The company commenced operations on July 1, 1974, and during the year ended June 30, 1975, extracted 200,000 tons of ore. The company decided to employ the units of production basis of recording depreciation on the building and the sum-of-the-years'-digits method of recording depreciation on the equipment.

Required: Prepare journal entries to record the depletion and depreciation charges for the year ended June 30, 1975. Show calculations.

9–9–A

The Racine Company incurred various costs aggregating to $33,000 in developing a patentable process. On January 2, 1974, it applied for a patent on the process, incurring additional costs (largely legal in nature) of $1,500. The patent was estimated to have a useful life of 10 years. The total of $34,500 was properly charged to an asset account and amortized property in 1974. On July 1, 1975, the company incurred legal and court costs of $8,550 in a successful defense of the patent in an infringement suit.

Required: Compute the patent amortization cost for 1975.

Problems, Series B *chapter* 9

9–1–B

Black Company planned to erect a new factory building and a new office building in Ithaca, New York. Preliminary studies showed two possible sites as available and desirable. Further studies showed the second site to be preferable. A report on this property showed an appraised value of $160,000 for land and orchard and $80,000 for a building.

After considerable negotiation the company and the owner reached the following agreement: Black Company was to pay $78,000 in cash, issue to the owner 1,000 shares of its common stock, assume a $60,000 mortgage note on the property, assume the interest accrued on the mortgage note of $1,800, and assume unpaid property taxes of $4,000. Black Company's common stock had a book value of $44, a par value of $40, and a market value of $56 per share on the date the agreement was signed. Black Company paid $18,000 cash for brokerage and legal services in acquiring the property.

Shortly after acquisition of the property, Black Company sold the fruit on the trees for $2,200, remodeled the building into an office building at a cost of $32,000, and removed the trees from the land at a cost of $5,000. Now, construction of the factory building is to begin in a week.

Required: Prepare schedules showing the proper valuation of the assets acquired by the Black Company.

9–2–B

The Mason Company has the following entries in its Building account:

1974			*Debits*
May	5	Cost of land and building purchased	$270,000
	5	Broker fees incident to purchase	12,000
1975			
Jan.	3	Contract price of new wing added to south end of building	70,000
	15	Cost of new machinery, estimated life 10 years	300,000
June	10	Real estate taxes for six months ended 6/30/75	6,000
Aug.	10	Cost of landscaping and building parking lot for employees in back of building	8,300
Sept.	6	Replacement of broken windows	200
Oct.	10	Repairs due to regular usage	2,400
1974			*Credits*
Dec.	31	Transfer to Land account, as per allocation of purchase cost authorized in minutes of board of directors	$ 45,000
1975			
Jan.	5	Proceeds from lease of second floor for six months ended 12/31/74	5,000

The original property was acquired on May 5, 1974. The Mason Company immediately engaged a contractor to construct a new wing on the south end of the building. While the new wing was being constructed, the company leased the second floor as temporary warehouse space to the Goodman Company. During this period (July 1 to December 31, 1974) the company installed new machinery costing $300,000 on the first floor of the building. Regular operations commenced on January 2, 1975.

Required:

a) Compute the correct balance for the Building account as of December 31, 1975. The building is expected to last 40 years. The company employs a calendar-year accounting period.

b) Prepare the necessary journal entries to correct the records of the Mason Company at December 31, 1975. No depreciation entries are required.

9–3–B

The Kost Company's fiscal year ends September 30. The company has its own fleet of delivery vehicles, all acquired new. Included are the following:

Description	*Date Acquired*	*Cost*	*Expected Life*	*Expected Resale Value*
Sedan No. 1.............	Oct. 1, 1973	$ 5,000	4 years	$1,200
Truck No. 4.............	Jan. 1, 1975	14,000	100,000 miles	1,500
Truck No. 2.............	Oct. 1, 1969	6,000	100,000 miles	800
Trailer No. 16...........	Mar. 1, 1972	7,700	350,000 miles	—0—

Mileage readings at September 30 show the following:

	1974	*1975*
Sedan No. 1............	10,000 miles	22,000 miles
Truck No. 4............	—0—	16,000
Truck No. 2............	312,000	326,000
Trailer No. 16..........	115,000	130,000

Required: Set up schedules showing in full detail the amount of depreciation to be recorded for the year ended September 30, 1975, on each of the above assets. (Use the straight-line method for Sedan No. 1.)

9–4–B

A machine belonging to the McGuire Company that cost $20,000 has an estimated life of 20 years. After 10 years an extremely important machine part, representing about 30 percent of the original cost, is worn out and replaced. The replacement cost is $7,000 and the useful life of the new part is the same as the remaining useful life of the machine.

Required:

a) Prepare journal entries to record the replacement of the old with the new part. (Assume depreciation has already been brought up to date.)

b) Compute the annual depreciation charge after replacement, using the straight-line method.

9–5–B

On January 1, 1975, the Swenson Company had the following balances in its plant asset and allowance accounts:

	Asset	Allowance for Depreciation
Land	$ 20,000	
Leasehold	90,000	
Buildings	130,300	$ 6,290
Equipment	178,000	82,600
Trucks	24,800	11,900

Additional information:

a) The leasehold covers a plot of ground leased on January 1, 1971, for a period of 40 years.
b) Building No. 1 is on the owned land and was completed on July 1, 1974, at a cost of $75,000. Life is set at 50 years. Building No. 2, quite similar to Building No. 1, is on the leased land and was completed on July 1, 1971, at a cost of $55,300. Life is also set at 50 years.
c) Equipment is depreciated at 12.5 percent per year.
d) Truck A, purchased on January 1, 1973, at a cost of $8,000, was given a life of two and a half years and a scrap value of $500. Truck B, purchased on July 1, 1973, at a cost of $7,200, was given a life of two years and a scrap value of $1,200. Truck C, purchased on July 1, 1974, at a cost of $9,600, was given a life of three years and a scrap value of $1,200.

The following events occurred in 1975:

Jan. 2 Rent for 1975 on leased land is paid, $4,200.
Apr. 1 Truck B is traded in on Truck D. List price of the new truck is $8,500. Allowance for Truck B is $1,600. Balance is paid in cash. Truck D is given a life of two and a half years and a scrap value of $1,250. (Do not use tax method.)
1 Truck A is sold for $1,500 in cash.
Dec. 31 At this time it is decided that Truck C will have a life of only two and a half instead of three years, while its scrap value remains unchanged.

Required: Prepare journal entries to record the 1975 transactions and the necessary December 31, 1975, adjusting entries, assuming a calendar-year accounting period. Use the straight-line depreciation method.

9–6–B

On January 2, 1975, Lansing Company signed a nonrenewable lease agreement on a tract of land giving it the right to occupy the land for the next 40 years. The company paid the owner of the land $25,500 by check, representing the annual rental charge for the first and the last two years of the lease, and charged it to the Leasehold account. On December 31, 1975, the company completed construction of a building on the leased property at a cost of $150,150. The life of the building was estimated at 50 years.

Required: Prepare the adjusting entries applicable to the leasehold for 1975 and to record the building depreciation for 1976.

9–7–B

The accounts of the Paulson Company with respect to one automobile owned as of September 30, 1975, (the close of the company's fiscal year) show: Automobile, cost $4,500; Allowance for Depreciation—Automobile, $3,500. On October 1, 1975, Paulson Company traded this automobile for another having a manufacturer's list price of $6,200. The dealer allowed a $1,900 trade-in allowance for the old car. The company remitted a check for the difference between list price and trade-in allowance, plus $56 of sales taxes and $12 for an auto license for the balance of the calendar year. The old car had a fair market value of $950 at the time of the exchange.

Immediately after purchasing the new automobile the company installed heavy-duty premium tires on the automobile, exchanging the regular tires on the auto for new ones having a list price of $330. The company received a trade-in allowance for the regular tires of $145. The company could have purchased the new heavy-duty premium tires for $275 in cash. Cash was also paid out in the amount of $50 for special advertising painting on the auto.

Required: Prepare journal entries to record the acquisition of the new auto and the new heavy-duty tires and to record the cost of the special painting. Do not use the tax method.

9–8–B

The Klee Mining Company on January 2, 1975, acquired ore deposits at a cash cost of $1,275,000. The ore deposit contains an estimated two million tons, but present technology will allow the economical extraction of only 85 percent of the total deposit. Machinery, equipment, and temporary sheds are installed at a cost of $168,000. These assets will have no further value to the company when the ore body is exhausted; they have a physical life of 12 years. In 1975, 200,000 tons of ore are extracted. The company expects the mine to be exhausted in 10 years.

Required:

a) Compute the depletion charge for 1975.

b) Compute the depreciation charge for 1975 under each of the following methods: (1) straight-line, (2) sum-of-the-years'-digits, (3) double declining-balance, and (4) units of production.

c) Which depreciation method do you believe to be most appropriate in the circumstances cited?

9–9–B

The Madison Company accumulated valid experimental and research costs of $25,500 in developing a process for which a patent was obtained on January 2, 1974. It is assumed that the patent will be useful during its full legal life. In January, 1975, the company successfully prosecuted an infringement of these patent rights at a cost of $1,000. In late December, 1975, the company paid $7,000 to obtain patents that could, if used by competition, make the earlier Madison patents useless. The purchased patents will never be used.

Required: Give the entries to record the information relative to the patents in 1974 and 1975.

Compound interest, bonds, leases, and pensions

Learning objectives

Study of the material in this chapter is designed to achieve these learning objectives:

1. A basic comprehension of the nature of compound interest, future value, and present value.
2. An understanding of the nature of long-term debt.
3. An understanding of the theory and application of financial leverage in the management decision-making process.
4. An awareness of the possibilities of corporate bonds as an investment opportunity.
5. An understanding of the process of accounting for bonds by both the issuing corporation and the investor.
6. An understanding of the nature of bond discount and premium, as well as the methods of accounting for each.
7. A knowledge of the use of sinking funds as a device for debt retirement.
8. A basic understanding of leases and pensions as long-term debts and the accounting for each.

Frame 1[10]

Compound interest, future value, and present value

A knowledge of compound interest, future value, and present value concepts is helpful in understanding the accounting for bonds, leases, and pensions. Interest was discussed in Chapter 8, but now the discussion needs to be expanded.

Compound interest

Would you prefer to have $1,000 given to you today or the promise of a gift of $1,000 a year from today? The choice is obvious: $1,000 today is preferable. Why is this so? Two reasons are apparent: (1) there is a risk that the $1,000 gift promised will not be received, and (2) the $1,000 received today can be invested, say at 8 percent, so that a year from now it will be worth $1,080, which will make you $80 better off than if you did receive the promised $1,000. Money has time value, which is usually expressed in terms of interest.

Suppose the choice is $1,000 today or the promise of $1,100 two years from now, that there is no doubt the $1,100 will be received, and that the money can be invested to earn 5 percent per year with certainty. What is your choice in this situation? If you choose to invest the $1,000 received today at 5 percent per year you will have $1,050 at the end of the first year. This amount can be invested at the start of the second year so that you will earn $52.50 ($1,050 × 0.05) in interest during the second year. In total you will accumulate $1,102.50 by the end of the second year, which is larger than the $1,100 promised at that time.

It was assumed that the 5 percent interest rate is earned on all funds invested at the start of the year. Thus, at the start of the second year, the amount invested consisted of the $1,000 principal amount plus the $50 of interest earned during the first year. This is the assumption behind compound interest calculations.

Future value

Interest is said to be compounded when periodically its amount is computed and added to the base to form a new amount upon which the interest for a later period is computed. For example, an investment of $1,000 at 6 percent compound interest will grow to $1,123.60 in two periods of one year each at compound interest, but only to $1,120 at simple interest. At simple interest, the interest for each period is $60, for a total of $120. At compound interest, the interest for the first period is $60 and the amount of the investment at the end of the first period is $1,060 ($1,000 × 1.06). Interest for the second period is then $63.60 ($1,060 × 0.06), and the amount of the investment is $1,123.60 ($1,060 × 1.06) at the end of the second period.

Note that the \$1,123.60 amount was derived by multiplying \$1,000 × 1.06 × 1.06. Since 1.06 times 1.06 is equal to $(1.06)^2$, a shortcut can be employed in the calculation. The amount of the investment at the end of the second period is simply \$1,000 $(1.06)^2$, which equals \$1,000 times 1.1236, or \$1,123.60. From this the formula for the compound amount of 1 can be derived as being $(1 + i)^n$ where i is the interest rate per period and n is the number of periods involved.

The task of computing the sum to which any invested amount will grow at a given rate for a stated number of periods is facilitated through the use of interest tables. From Table I on page 721, the amount to which an investment of \$1 at 6 percent for three periods will grow can be determined as being \$1.191016. The amount to which an investment of \$1,000 will grow is simply 1,000 times this amount.

Now assume that \$500 is invested for 10 years at 8 percent compounded semiannually. What amount of money is available after 10 years? The answer is \$1,095.56. Interest is computed semiannually and therefore there are 20 interest periods. Since the 8 percent interest rate is expressed on an annual basis but is computed semiannually, it is necessary to take one half (4 percent) as the basis for computation. Therefore, using Table I, the amount to which \$1 invested at 4 percent for 20 periods will grow is \$2.191123. Multiplying by \$500 results in an amount of \$1,095.56.

What is the correct answer to each of the following?

1. Mr. Jones' son intends to go to college five years from now. Mr. Jones figures that he will need \$20,000 at that time in order to finance his son's college education. Mr. Jones can invest money today at a rate of 10 percent compounded semiannually. Will Mr. Jones have enough money to send his son to college if he invests \$12,500 today?
2. If Tom Brown invests \$6,000 today in securities having an interest rate of 8 percent compounded semiannually, will he have at least \$10,000 at the end of six years?

Check your responses in Answer Frame 1[10] on page 442.

Frame 2[10]

Present value

How much would you be willing to pay for a promise of \$1,080 to be received one year from today if the rate of interest is 8 percent? Essentially, this question may be rephrased to ask how much you would have to invest today in order to have \$1,080 at the end of the year. Since

Answer frame 1[10]

1. Yes. If Mr. Jones invests \$12,500 today at 10 percent compounded semiannually, he will have \$20,361.19 (\$12,500 × 1.628895). The 1.628895 is obtained from Table I (5 percent for 10 periods).
2. No. He will have only \$9,606.19 (\$6,000 × 1.601032). The 1.601032 is obtained from Table I (4 percent for 12 periods) and represents the amount that a dollar invested today at 8 percent compounded semiannually will accumulate to at the end of six years.

If you missed either of the above, it is important to review Frame 1[10] before going on to Frame 2[10] on page 441.

2[10] *continued*

the interest rate is 8 percent, the problem may be expressed as follows, with x being the required investment.

$$x + 0.08x = \$1{,}080$$
$$1.08x = \$1{,}080$$
$$x = \frac{\$1{,}080}{1.08} = \$1{,}000$$

Note that this is simply the reverse of asking how much \$1,000 will amount to at the end of a year if invested at 8 percent. Present value problems, then, are simply the reverse of future amount problems. Since present value is exactly the reverse of a future sum, it is found by dividing the future sum by $(1 + i)^n$. Thus at 8 percent the present value of \$1,000 due in one period is equal to \$1,000 × 1/1.08, which is equal to \$1,000 × 0.9259 or \$925.90. Likewise, the present value at 8 percent of \$1,000 due in two periods is obtained by \$1,000 × $1/(1.08)^2$ = \$1,000 × 0.857 = \$857. The inverse relationship can be seen by asking to what amount an investment of \$857 at 8 percent will grow in two years. The answer is obtained by multiplying \$857 by 1.08 to obtain \$925.56 and then multiplying \$925.56 by 1.08 to obtain \$1,000.

Suppose that \$100,000 is promised to you in 10 years time and that the interest rate is 6 percent, compounded annually. How much are you willing to accept now instead? Again, the use of the appropriate table is helpful. The appropriate table is Table II shown in the appendix on page 722, entitled "Present Value of 1 (at Compound Interest)." The relevant cell of this table is in the 6 percent column, row 10, which gives a figure of 0.558395. Multiplying this figure by \$100,000 results in a present value of \$55,839.50. This means that \$55,839.50 invested today drawing compund interest at the rate of 6 percent annually will accumulate to \$100,000 at the end of 10 years. In other words, the investment earns a 6 percent return.

Now assume that the interest in this example is to be compounded semiannually. What is the resulting present value? Under this assumption it is necessary to use the 3 percent column (because interest is semiannual) and row 20 (because there are now 20 interest periods). Therefore, the present value is \$55,367.60 (\$100,000 × 0.553676).

Present value of an annuity

Instead of being promised a lump-sum payment at the end of a stipulated number of years, it is quite possible that you may enter into an agreement which promises to pay you an equal amount of money at the end of each year (or other specified time period) for a stated length of time. Such an agreement is called an annuity. For example, you may have the opportunity to pay an amount of money today for the guaranteed receipt of $1,000 at the end of each of the next eight years. If the current rate of interest is 8 percent, how much are you willing to pay for the future receipts? This can be solved by using the Present Value of 1 table and computing the value for each period as follows:

Periods	*Present Value of $1 @ 8%*	*Present Value of $1,000 @ 8%*
1	0.926	$ 926
2	0.857	857
3	0.794	794
4	0.735	735
5	0.681	681
6	0.630	630
7	0.583	583
8	0.540	540
		$5,746

Such a procedure could become quite tedious if the annuity consisted of 50 to 100 or more payments. Fortunately, tables are available showing the present values of an annuity of $1 per period for varying interest rates and periods. An example is Table III on page 724 which is called "Present Value of an Annuity of 1." Basically, this table gives the amount that must be invested today to allow the investor to withdraw $1 at the end of every period for various periods at different interest rates. Looking under the column for 8 percent and the row for eight periods, the figure is 5.747. The present value of the $1,000 annuity then is simply 1,000 times this figure, or $5,747. (The $1 difference in the two figures is caused by using rounded amounts in Table II.) The future amount of an annuity also could be computed but will not be illustrated here since it is not needed in solving the problems discussed.

Indicate whether each of the following statements is correct or incorrect.

1. The present value of an annuity of $500 for 10 years is $5,000 if the interest rate is 6 percent compounded annually.
2. N. Richard is in dire need of cash. He presently owns a contract which requires a financial institution to pay him $24,000 in a lump sum 10 years from now and quarterly payments of $600 during each of the 10 years. He realizes that the current market rate of interest on such contracts is 12 percent compounded quarterly. If Richard sells the contract today for $21,250 he will be no worse off than if he holds the contract for 10 years.

Check your solutions in Answer Frame 2[10] on page 444.

Answer frame 2^{10}

1. Incorrect. $5,000 is the total amount received over the 10 years, but the payments comprising this total must be discounted at 6 percent in order to find their present value. The present value is $3,680.04 ($500 × 7.360087) and represents the amount that must be invested today at 6 percent to permit the payment or withdrawal of $500 at the end of each of the next 10 years.
2. Correct. The present value of the contract may be computed as follows:

Present value of $24,000 due in 10 years at 12% compounded quarterly, i.e., 3% per quarter (Table II): $24,000 × 0.306557	$ 7,357.37
Present value at 3% of an annuity of $600 per period for 40 periods (Table III): $600 × 23.114772	13,868.86
Total present value	$21,226.23

Since he can sell the contract for $21,250 today, he will be slightly better off if the sale is made. Notice also that the calculation of the present value of the contract is made by computing the present value of the lump-sum payment and the present value of the $600 annuity. This is the same method by which the selling price of a bond is computed.

If you did not answer correctly, carefully restudy Frame 2^{10} before going on to Frame 3^{10} below.

Frame 3^{10}

Bonds

A bond is one of the most common forms of long-term debt financing. When these bonds are issued, often other companies purchase them as long-term investments. A bond is a written unconditional promise made under seal wherein the borrower promises to pay to the holder of the bond (1) the face value of the bond at the maturity date, and (2) interest at a specified rate on the face value at specified dates (usually semiannually).

Bonds may be secured or unsecured. Secured bonds are those which have a claim against certain property of the issuer if the bonds are not paid at the maturity date. The property pledged (or mortgaged) may be real estate, machinery, merchandise, investments, or personal property. A mortgage is a conditional transfer of certain property given by the borrower (the mortgagor) to the lender of funds (the mortgagee) in order to secure the payment of a loan. Bonds which have first claim on a certain asset are called first mortgage bonds, while those which have second claim on that same asset are called second mortgage bonds, and so on.

Unsecured bonds are generally called debenture bonds—they are issued against the general credit of the corporation. Another form of unsecured bonds which is quite rare are income bonds. They are different from other bonds in that interest need be paid only to the extent of the earnings of the issuer. For instance, if interest on the bonds is $20,000 for a given year and the issuer only earns $5,000 before interest expense is deducted, only $5,000 of interest must be paid. (If there are no earnings or if a loss is sustained, no interest need be paid).

For interest-paying purposes bonds may be either registered bonds or coupon bonds. Interest is paid to the owner of registered bonds by check. The owner's name is registered on the records of the issuing corporation. Interest is paid on coupon bonds when the appropriate coupon is detached and cashed at the interest date or thereafter. The registered type of bond is most frequently used by corporations today. An unregistered bond is transferred to another party by mere delivery, whereas transfer of a registered bond requires the owner's endorsement, assignment, and registration.

Any type of bond may be convertible if such a provision is stated in the bond indenture. Such bonds are convertible, at the bondholder's option and under stated conditions, into stock of the issuing corporation. For example, a $1,000 convertible debenture bond might be convertible (for a stated period of its life) into 20 shares of the issuing company's common stock.

Indicate whether each of the following statements is correct or incorrect.

1. Debenture bonds are not secured by a pledge of any specific property.
2. It is easier to transfer an unregistered bond than it is to transfer one that is registered.
3. A bondholder with a bond secured by a second mortgage is in a less favorable position than a first mortgage bondholder in the event of a seizure and sale of the property (called a foreclosure).
4. The same property may be used as security for more than one issue of bonds.
5. The issuing corporation determines whether it will accept the request of a holder of convertible bonds that his bonds be converted into the stipulated number of common shares.

Turn to Answer Frame 3[10] on page 446 to check your answer.

Frame 4[10]

Why a company might decide to issue bonds

When a corporation needs additional long-term funds, it must decide between the issuance of additional capital stock or borrowing by issuing evidences of indebtedness in the form of notes or bonds. The issuance of notes and bonds may be advantageous if the present stockholders pre-

Answer frame 3[10]

1. Correct. Debenture bonds are issued against the general credit of the issuer and are not secured by a pledge of any specific property or collateral.
2. Correct. An unregistered bond is transferable by mere delivery, whereas the transfer of a registered bond requires the owner's endorsement, assignment, and registration.
3. Correct. The claims of the first mortgage bondholders must be satisfied before any proceeds from the foreclosure sale are available to meet the claims of the second mortgage bondholders.
4. Correct. For example, a second mortgage bond issue is secured with the same property pledged as security on the first mortgage bond issue. But it constitutes only a secondary lien on the property, while the first mortgage bond issue constitutes the senior (or primary) lien.
5. Incorrect. On issuing the convertible bonds, the corporation commits itself to accepting a conversion request if it is within the constraints of the convertible bond contract.

If you missed any of the above, restudy Frame 3[10] before advancing to Frame 4[10] on page 445.

4[10] *continued*

fer not to share ownership and corporate earnings with additional shareholders.

A bondholder is a creditor; a stockholder is an owner; but both can be viewed as investors. Since many bonds are secured by the plant assets of the borrower and rank ahead of the stock as claims on assets in liquidation, the owner of a bond is provided with greater protection for his investment than is a stockholder.

Interest expense on a note or bond is a fixed cost to the borrower that must be met when it is due if default on the loan is to be avoided. Interest on bonds must be paid on dates specified by the bond contract; dividends on stock are declared at the discretion of the board of directors. Therefore, when a company issues notes or bonds, it should be reasonably certain that the use of the borrowed money will result in net earnings larger than the interest cost of the loan.

Advantages and disadvantages of borrowing

The advantages of operating a business with borrowed funds may be illustrated with the use of the data contained in Illustration 10.1. Both companies began operations on January 1, 1975. They were equally efficient in employing assets, as both were able to earn a 20 percent rate of return from operations (before interest and taxes) on assets acquired as of the beginning of 1975 ($4,000,000 ÷ $20,000,000). Company B, because of the bonds in its capital structure, earned 16.5 percent on its initial stockholders' equity, as contrasted with Company A's 10 percent. The earnings per share differed also, with A earning $1 while B earned $1.65.

Illustration 10.1, *Favorable Financial Leverage*

COMPANIES A AND B, CONDENSED STATEMENTS
Statement of Financial Position
January 1, 1975

	Company A	*Company B*
Total Assets	$20,000,000	$20,000,000
Bonds payable, 7%		$10,000,000
Stockholders' Equity (Capital Stock)	$20,000,000	10,000,000
	$20,000,000	$20,000,000

Earnings Statement
Year Ended December 31, 1975

Net earnings from operation for 1975	$ 4,000,000	$ 4,000,000
Interest expense		700,000
Net earnings before income taxes	$ 4,000,000	$ 3,300,000
Income taxes at 50%	2,000,000	1,650,000
Net Earnings for 1975	$ 2,000,000	$ 1,650,000
Number of shares	2,000,000	1,000,000
Earnings per share	$1.00	$1.65
Rate of earnings on initial stockholders equity (net earnings ÷ stockholders' equity)	10%	16.5%
Ratio of net earnings from operations to assets employed	20%	20%

Financial leverage. The differences can be explained as follows: Company B borrowed $10 million at a rate of 7 percent, which cost the company $350,000 after income taxes. Interest of $700,000 was incurred, but the $700,000 of interest reduced the amount of federal income taxes levied by $350,000. Thus, the net cost after tax is $350,000. Both companies operated equally efficiently, earning $4 million (before interest and taxes) on $20 million worth of total assets. Company B, however, was able to finance one half of its assets at a cost before taxes of 7 percent, while the assets secured through borrowing were earning a return of 20 percent before taxes. This additional return of $1,300,000 ($2,000,000 – $700,000) yielded an additional $650,000 of net earnings after taxes (at a 50 percent rate) to the stockholders of Company B. The additional earnings were sufficient to increase earnings per share in Company B to $1.65 as contrasted to $1 for Company A.

Company B is employing what is known as financial leverage, or is said to be "trading on the equity." That is, it is using the existence of stockholders' equity as a basis for securing borrowed funds, the use of which is intended to enhance the amount of earnings of the common stockholders. The situation given above, where the use of leverage increased the earnings per share, is called favorable financial leverage.

Unfavorable financial leverage can exist also, and would for Company B if earnings from operations of each company amounted to only $1 million instead of $4 million. In this case the earnings per share for Companies A and B, respectively, would be $0.25 and $0.15 (you may want to prove this to yourself).

Since the market price of a share of stock is dependent, in part at least, upon earnings per share, the price of a leveraged company's stock will fluctuate more sharply because of similar changes in earnings before interest and taxes than that of an unleveraged company.

A disadvantage of borrowing is that it reduces the ability of a company to absorb losses. Suppose that both A and B sustain losses amounting to $11 million. Company A will still have $9 million worth of stockholders' equity at the end of the year and can continue operations with a chance to recover. Company B will be insolvent at the end of the year (its liabilities will exceed its assets), and the stockholders of B may lose their entire investment through bankruptcy proceedings.

State whether each of the following statements is correct or incorrect.

1. The market price per share of the capital stock of a company with substantial amounts of debt outstanding is likely to fluctuate more widely than that of a company with little or no debt outstanding.
2. For most levels of earnings, the financial structure of a corporation influences the amount of earnings per share of capital stock.
3. Paying 6 percent dividends on capital stock has the same effect on earnings as paying 6 percent interest on bonds.
4. Issuing bonds has a beneficial effect on earnings per share regardless of the level of earnings from operations.

Now check your answers in Answer Frame 4[10] on page 450.

Frame 5[10]

Why a company might decide to invest in bonds

A company can only issue bonds when someone else is willing to acquire them. There are both short-term and long-term reasons for deciding to invest in bonds.

The main short-term reason is to earn at least a nominal rate of return on cash that would otherwise be temporarily idle. As emphasized in Chapter 8, there may be vehicles for investment which involve less risk, but regardless of this some companies do acquire bonds as a temporary investment. The primary risk is that the investor will have to sell the bonds at a time when the market price is relatively low (because of an increase in the market rate of interest).

Long-term reasons for investing in bonds include the desire to secure a continuing stream of revenue from the investment over a period of years and the desire to establish a financial affiliation with another company. Insurance companies often acquire bonds for the former reason. They receive insurance premiums from customers and must earn a return on these until the time comes to pay claims. Investing in capital stock is too risky, while investing in bonds is not. The insurance companies can usually wait until the maturity date if need be and collect the face value of the bonds. They can usually refrain from having to sell the bonds before maturity at a temporarily depressed market price. Also, interest on bonds must be paid, while dividends on capital stock need not be declared.

The purpose for which a corporation acquires bonds, which usually must be determined on the basis of management intent, has a determining influence on accounting for the bonds and the way they are shown in the statement of financial position. If bonds are held as a temporary investment they should be classified as current assets. Otherwise, they should be considered to be long-term and reported as noncurrent assets, under the caption "Investments."

This chapter deals primarily with the accounting treatment for the long-term type of investment in bonds by corporations.

Indicate whether each of the following statements is true or false.

1. The marketability of bonds owned is the basis for showing them in the statement of financial position as either a current or noncurrent asset.
2. The purchaser of a bond must hold the bond to its maturity date.
3. One purpose for holding bonds is to secure some revenue from cash that would otherwise be idle.
4. To an insurance company interested in securing a steady stream of revenue for a number of years, an investment in bonds is subject to less risk than an investment in capital stock of the same company.

Check your responses in Answer Frame 5[10] on page 450.

Frame 6[10]

Determining the price of a bond

The price a bond issue will bring when offered to investors, or the price at which a bond sells in the market when sold to another investor before maturity, often differs from its face or maturity value. Before the reasons for this can be understood it is necessary to know the meaning of the terms contract rate of interest, market rate of interest, and effective rate of interest.

The *contract rate* on the face value of a bond is often called the *nominal* rate of interest or the *coupon* rate of interest. It is the rate of interest that is printed on the face of the bonds. For instance, if a company is authorized to issue $1 million face value of bonds with an interest rate of 6 percent, this means that each year the amount of the checks sent out as interest will be equal to $1 million times 0.06, or $60,000. The contract rate of interest is 6 percent and will remain so for the entire

Answer frame 4^{10}

1. Correct. This results because the market price per share of capital stock is at least partly dependent on earnings per share. Such earnings are subject to greater fluctuation for a leveraged company than for an unleveraged company.
2. Correct. This is one of the points which is apparent from an examination of Illustration 10.1. The firm's financial or capital structure affects the amount of earnings which is available to common stockholders and thus also influences the amount of earnings per share of common stock.
3. Incorrect. Bond interest is deductible in arriving at taxable earnings, but dividends on capital stock are not.
4. Incorrect. The deductibility of bond interest expense for tax purposes is often mentioned as one advantage of issuing bonds as opposed to stock. But if earnings from operations are very low, the fixed interest may even exceed those earnings. Thus, whether or not issuing bonds will increase earnings per share depends on the level of earnings from operations.

If you missed any of the above, restudy Frame 4^{10} before continuing in Frame 5^{10} on page 448.

Answer frame 5^{10}

1. False. The basis for such classification is management's intention concerning the purpose for which the bonds are held. A bond that is intended to be held to its maturity date is a noncurrent asset (unless the maturity date is within the coming year) even though it may be readily marketable.
2. False. The owner of the bond can usually sell the bond whenever he wishes, to another investor willing to buy it. But the owner runs the risk of having to sell at a time when the market price is temporarily depressed.
3. True. Although bonds are generally long-term in nature to the issuer, the holder of the bonds can buy and sell them as desired and earn interest during the period in which they are held. Bonds are, however, only one type of security in which temporarily idle cash may be invested, and they may be riskier than others if the bonds must be sold before maturity. (Prices may be temporarily depressed at the time of sale.)
4. True. Bond interest has to be paid, whereas dividends can be declared at the option of the issuing company's board of directors. Also, at the maturity date the investor normally will receive the face value of the bonds. There is no maturity date for capital stock and one cannot be sure of the amount of money that will be obtained from its future sale.

If you answered any of the above incorrectly, reread Frame 5^{10} before proceeding to Frame 6^{10} on page 449.

6^{10} *continued*

life of the bond issue. It cannot be changed, since it is printed right on the face of each bond.

The *market rate* of interest for a particular bond issue is that minimum rate of interest which investors in the market are willing to accept on bonds of this particular risk category on any given date. For instance, on January 1, 1975, because of a limited supply of money in the economy and other factors, investors may be willing to buy ABC Corporation bonds only if they can earn 7 percent or more on them. On July 1, 1975, because of a drastic increase in the supply of money in the economy and other factors, they may be willing to buy these bonds even if they can earn only 5 percent or more. (For General Motors Corporation bonds, which are not as risky, the rates may have been 6½ percent on January 1 and 4½ percent on July 1). The market rate of interest varies almost daily because of changing conditions in the money markets. These changing conditions include such things as actions of the Federal Reserve Board, open market operations of the Treasury Department, the balance of foreign trade, other domestic and foreign investment opportunities (including swings in the stock market), and so on (the list is almost endless).

The *effective rate* of interest is the rate of interest that an investor can earn on a particular bond issue by paying a certain price for it. In theory, it should be equal to the market rate of interest that exists on the day the securities are purchased. For instance, if the XYZ Company bought all of the ABC Corporation bonds (mentioned above) on January 1, 1975, when the market rate of interest was 7 percent, it would be willing to pay less than the face value of $1 million for the bonds so that by receiving $60,000 per year interest plus $1 million at maturity it could earn 7 percent on its investment. It would be said that the XYZ Company paid a price that would yield it an effective rate of interest of 7 percent and that the bonds sold at a discount. If, on the other hand, the XYZ Company bought the bonds on July 1, 1975, when the market rate of interest was only 5 percent, it would be willing to pay more than the face value for the bonds so that by receiving $60,000 per year interest and $1 million at the maturity date, it could earn an effective rate of interest of 5 percent. It would be said that the bonds sold at a premium.

The relationships among these three types of interest rates should now be obvious. By paying more or less than the face value of the bonds, the investor can change the effective rate of interest that he will earn on the bonds from the contract rate to the market rate which exists on the day of purchase. The contract rate of interest cannot be changed, and is used to determine how much cash (as interest) must be paid to the owner of the bonds each year (one half of the annual amount is usually paid each six months). The market rate of interest is subject to change at any time due to changing conditions in the economy. Securities purchased on any given date are exchanged at a price which will yield an effective rate of interest that is equal to the market rate of interest on that date. Once the purchase has been made, the investing company is locked into that effective rate of interest if it holds the bonds to the maturity date. It may, of course, sell to someone else in the market before the maturity date.

The price at which a bond sells can be computed using the present value techniques illustrated at the beginning of this chapter. Assume that on January 1, 1975, the ABC Corporation offered $1 million of 6 percent, 10-year bonds calling for semiannual interest payments each

January 1 and July 1 (beginning July 1, 1975, and ending January 1, 1985) to the XYZ Company at a price to yield an effective rate of interest of 5 percent. What sum of money would the ABC Corporation receive?

The answer is computed as follows (using the interest tables in the appendix):

Present value of the promise to pay principal is $1 million times the present value of $1 due in 20 interest periods at 2½ percent, or $1,000,000 × 0.610271 (from Table II on page 722)........	$ 610,271
Present value of the promise to pay periodic interest is $30,000 (the semiannual cash payment based on the contract rate of interest) times the present value of an annuity of $1 for 20 interest periods at 2½ percent, or $30,000 × 15.589162 (from Table III on page 724)..	$ 467,675
Total price..	$1,077,946

Therefore, the bonds would be sold at a premium of $77,946, since the contract rate of interest is greater than the market rate of interest for bonds of this risk category on this particular date.

In determining the price of a bond, the life of the bond is always stated in terms of interest payment periods and the effective rate used in seeking amounts from the interest tables is the annual effective rate divided by the number of interest periods in one year.

To test your understanding, compute the issue price of $500,000 maturity value, 6 percent bonds which call for semiannual interest payments on October 1 and April 1 and mature on April 1, 1985. The bonds are issued on April 1, 1975, to yield 8 percent.

Check your answer in Answer Frame 6[10] on page 454.

Frame 7[10]

Accounting for bond transactions

Bonds may be issued either on an interest date or between interest dates. As illustrated in the previous frame, they may be issued at face value, at a discount (below face value), or at a premium (above face value). These various combinations will be illustrated.

To show the accounting for bond transactions in each of the situations illustrated, it will be assumed that the Issuer Corporation issues $1 million face value, 6 percent bonds. The bonds pay interest on January 1 and July 1, are dated January 1, 1975, and mature on January 1, 1985. A private placement is arranged with the Purchaser Insurance Company for the entire issue; that is, all of the bonds are acquired by the insurance company and no brokerage fee is involved. If the purchasing company did pay a brokerage fee, the fee would be debited to the Bond Investment account and would reduce the discount or increase the premium on the purchaser's books.

Bonds issued without accumulated interest

The agreement between the issuer of bonds and the trustee representing the bondholders usually stipulates that at every interest date an entire six months of interest will be paid by the issuer to the owner of the bonds. The amount of cash to be paid is calculated by multiplying the face value of the bonds by the contract rate of interest and then dividing by two. In the cases to be illustrated, this is $1,000,000 $\times$ 0.06 = $60,000 per year, or $30,000 per one-half year.

When bonds are issued on the date of the bonds (January 1, 1975, in this illustration) or on an interest payment date (any January 1 or July 1 between July 1, 1975, and January 1, 1985), the purchaser of the bonds is entitled to receive the six months of interest due at the next interest date. Thus, no accumulated interest needs to be recognized at the issuance date.

Bonds issued on the date of the bonds at face value. Assume the bonds are issued on January 1, 1975, at their $1 million face value. The required entries on the books of both the Issuer Corporation and the Purchaser Insurance Company at the date of issue, the first interest date, and the end of the accounting (and calendar) year are as follows:

Issuer Corporation			*Purchaser Insurance Company*		
Jan. 1, 1975:			Jan. 1, 1975:		
Cash	1,000,000		Bond Investments......	1,000,000	
Bonds Payable		1,000,000	Cash..............		1,000,000
To record issue of bonds at face value.			To record purchase of bonds at face value.		
July 1, 1975:			July 1, 1975:		
Interest Expense........	30,000		Cash..................	30,000	
Cash..............		30,000	Interest Revenue...		30,000
To record payment of six months' interest.			To record receipt of six months' interest.		
Dec. 31, 1975:			Dec. 31, 1975:		
Interest Expense........	30,000		Accrued Interest Receivable.	30,000	
Accrued Interest Payable........		30,000	Interest Revenue...		30,000
To record accrual of six months' interest.			To record accrual of six months' interest.		

Notice that the entries are like two sides of the same coin. The $60,000 of interest expense on the Issuer Corporation's books is represented by $60,000 of interest revenue on the books of the Purchaser Insurance Company.

On a separate sheet of paper see if you can give the entry required on January 1, 1976, on each set of books.

Now turn to Answer Frame 7[10] on page 454 to check your response.

Answer frame 6[10]

The issue price of the bonds is computed as follows:

Present value of principal is \$500,000 times the present value of \$1 due in 20 interest periods at 4 percent, or \$500,000 × 0.456387	\$228,193.50
Present value of periodic interest payments is \$15,000 times the present value of an annuity of \$1 for 20 interest periods at 4 percent, or \$15,000 × 13.590326	203,854.89
Total price	\$432,048.39

These bonds would therefore sell at a discount of \$67,951.61, since the coupon rate of interest is less than the market rate of interest required by investors on that particular date.

If you answered incorrectly, restudy Frame 6[10] before proceeding to Frame 7[10] on page 452.

Answer frame 7[10]

The correct entries for January 1, 1976, are:

Issuer Corporation

Accrued Interest Payable	30,000	
Cash		30,000
To record payment of interest.		

Purchaser Insurance Company

Cash	30,000	
Accrued Interest Receivable		30,000
To record payment of interest.		

Issuer merely pays its liability for accrued interest payable and Purchaser collects its receivable.

If you answered incorrectly, restudy Frame 7[10] before beginning Frame 8[10] below.

Frame 8[10]

Bonds issued on the date of the bonds at a discount. Now assume that the going market rate of interest on January 1, 1975, for bonds of this risk class is greater than the contract rate of interest (6 percent). This would make the Purchaser Insurance Company willing to pay less than the face value of the bonds. (It is only willing to pay an amount which equates the effective yield on the bonds to the market rate of interest, as illustrated earlier.) Assume that the issuance price is \$922,000, or \$78,000 below the face value of \$1 million. The bonds are described as selling at 92.2 (which means 92.2 percent of face value).

The entries on both sets of books for January 1, July 1, and December 31, 1975, are:

Issuer Corporation

Jan. 1:		
Cash	922,000	
Bonds Payable—Discount	78,000	
Bonds Payable		1,000,000
To record issue of bonds at 92.2.		

Purchaser Insurance Company

Jan. 1:		
Bond Investments	922,000	
Cash		922,000
To record purchase of bonds at 92.2.		

July 1:		
Interest Expense..........	30,000	
Cash................		30,000
To record payment of six months' interest.		
Dec. 31:		
Interest Expense..........	30,000	
Accrued Interest Payable..............		30,000
To record accrual of six months' interest.		
Interest Expense..........	7,800	
Bonds Payable—Discount		7,800
To accumulate the discount for one year.		

July 1:		
Cash....................	30,000	
Interest Revenue.....		30,000
To record receipt of six months' interest.		
Dec. 31:		
Accrued Interest Receivable..............	30,000	
Interest Revenue.....		30,000
To record accrual of six months' interest.		
Bond Investments........	7,800	
Interest Revenue.....		7,800
To accumulate the discount for one year.		

There are several things that need to be explained regarding these entries. First, notice that Issuer records its liability in two parts. It credits Bonds Payable at the face amount of the bonds, $1 million and debits the discount of $78,000 to the Bonds Payable—Discount account. (Discount on Bonds Payable is also an acceptable title.) This is a contra account to bonds payable. That is, on the statement of financial position to be prepared as of December 31, 1975, the long-term liabilities section would contain the following:

Bonds payable......................................	$1,000,000
Less bonds payable—discount ($78,000 − $7,800) ...	70,200
Bonds payable, net................................	$ 929,800

Notice that the net amount of bonds payable is higher (by $7,800) than it was on the issue date. This is caused by the entry crediting the Bonds Payable—Discount account. The discount is accumulated (some would say amortized) in this manner over the time period running from the date of issuance to the maturity date. In this illustration that time period is from January 1, 1975, to January 1, 1985, a period of 10 years or 120 months. Since the total discount was $78,000, the amount of discount to be accumulated each month is:

$$\frac{\text{Discount}}{\text{Months between issue and maturity dates}} = \frac{\$78{,}000}{120 \text{ months}} = \$650/\text{month or } \$7{,}800/\text{year}$$

The discount may be accumulated at each interest date as well as at the end of the accounting year. The goal in accumulating the discount is to reduce it to zero by the maturity date of the bonds, so that the net amount of bonds payable will have grown to equal the $1 million face amount of the bonds. The discount can be viewed as being extra interest, in that the issuer receives $922,000 at the issue date and must pay back $1 million at the maturity date. This difference of $78,000 should be spread over the 10-year life of the bonds (at $7,800 per year), thus increasing the interest from $60,000 per year to $67,800 per year.

The Purchaser Insurance Company does not utilize a contra account in recording its investment. It merely debits Bond Investments for the price paid for the investment. It is traditional in accounting to record assets at cost. Thus, over the years it has been customary to use a method which does not involve a contra account (although logically it could be done). The discount is accumulated by increasing the interest revenue and increasing the balance in the Bond Investments account. At the maturity date the Bond Investments account has been built up to the maturity value of $1 million. Interest revenue per year has been $67,800, which is equal to the face amount of $60,000 plus one tenth of the discount of $78,000. The discount of $78,000 is accounted for as if earned in 10 equal annual amounts of $7,800. (When bonds are acquired as a temporary investment, the discount is not accumulated.)

To test your understanding, how much interest will be recognized each year on these bonds if they are issued at 95 instead of at 92.2?

Now turn to Answer Frame 8^{10} on page 458 to check your answers.

Frame 9^{10}

Bonds issued on the date of the bonds at a premium. If the market rate of interest on January 1, 1975, for bonds in this risk category is less than the contract rate of interest (6 percent), the Purchaser Insurance Company will be willing to pay a premium (more than the face value) for these bonds. (It will be willing to pay an amount which equates the effective rate to the market rate.) Assume that the bonds are issued at $1,078,000, which is described as being issued at 107.8 (percent of face value).

The entries on both sets of books during 1975 are:

Issuer			*Purchaser*		
Jan. 1:			Jan. 1:		
Cash..................	1,078,000		Bond Investments......	1,078,000	
Bonds Payable — Premium........		78,000	Cash..............		1,078,000
Bonds Payable.....		1,000,000	To record purchase of bonds at 107.8.		
To record issue of bonds at 107.8.					
July 1:			July 1:		
Interest Expense.......	30,000		Cash..................	30,000	
Cash..............		30,000	Interest Revenue...		30,000
To record payment of six months' interest.			To record receipt of six months' interest.		
Dec. 31:			Dec. 31:		
Interest Expense.......	30,000		Accrued Interest Receivable.......	30,000	
Accrued Interest Payable.........		30,000	Interest Revenue...		30,000
To record accrual of six months' interest.			To record accrual of six months' interest.		
Bonds Payable—Premium........	7,800		Interest Revenue.......	7,800	
Interest Expense...		7,800	Bond Investments..		7,800
To amortize the premium for one year.			To amortize the premium for one year.		

Notice that the entries are quite similar to those made when a discount is involved except that the amortization of a premium has an opposite effect on the amount of interest to that of the accumulation of a discount. (The premium can be amortized at July 1 and December 31, but the method illustrated seems less complicated.) The interest recognized for each year is reduced by $7,800 (one tenth of the $78,000 premium), thus causing interest to be recorded at $52,200 each year. By the maturity date of the bonds, the Bonds Payable—Premium account (Premium on Bonds Payable is also an acceptable title) has a zero balance, so that the net amount of bonds payable is the face value of $1 million. The Bond Investments account on Purchaser's books is similarly reduced to $1 million by the maturity date. (When bonds are acquired as a temporary investment, the premium is not amortized on the books of the purchasing company.)

To test your understanding, calculate the total interest to be recorded on each set of books for the entire life of the bonds.

Now check your answer by turning to Answer Frame 9^{10} on page 458.

Frame 10^{10}

Bonds issued with accumulated interest

When bonds are issued between interest dates (at any time other than on January 1 or July 1, in our illustration) the purchaser of the bonds is not entitled to receive the full six months of interest due at the next interest date. Therefore, the seller charges the purchaser for that portion of the interest that he will receive but has not earned.

Bonds issued at face value between interest dates. To illustrate this situation, assume that Issuer Corporation issues the bonds to the Purchaser Insurance Company on March 1, 1975, at face value. The entries on both sets of books during 1975 are:

Issuer

Mar. 1:		
Cash	1,010,000	
Bonds Payable		1,000,000
Accrued Interest Payable		10,000
To record issue of bonds at face plus accrued interest.		
July 1:		
Accrued Interest Payable	10,000	
Interest Expense	20,000	
Cash		30,000
To record payment of six months' interest.		

Purchaser

Mar. 1:		
Bond Investments	1,000,000	
Accrued Interest Receivable	10,000	
Cash		1,010,000
To record purchase of bonds at face value plus accrued interest.		
July 1:		
Cash	30,000	
Accrued Interest Receivable		10,000
Interest Revenue		20,000
To record receipt of six months' interest.		

Answer frame 8[10]

The total interest is calculated as follows:

Face value	$1,000,000
Less: Issue price	950,000
Discount	$ 50,000

$$\frac{\text{Discount}}{\text{Life of bonds in years}} = \frac{\$50,000}{10 \text{ years}} = \$5,000/\text{year extra interest}$$

Since the face amount of interest is $60,000, the total interest per year is $65,000.

If you answered incorrectly, restudy Frame 8[10] before beginning Frame 9[10] on page 456.

Answer frame 9[10]

The total interest on each set of books is calculated as follows:

Issuance price	$1,078,000
Less face value of bonds	1,000,000
Premium to be deducted from interest	$ 78,000

The total contract amount of interest is $1,000,000 × 0.06 × 10 years = $600,000. Thus the interest to be recognized by each company is:

Contract amount of interest	$600,000
Less premium to be deducted	78,000
	$522,000

This translates into $52,200 per year, which agrees with the illustration in Frame 9[10].

If you answered incorrectly, review Frame 9[10] before beginning Frame 10[10] on page 457.

10[10]

continued

Dec. 31:			Dec. 31:		
Interest Expense	30,000		Accrued Interest Receivable	30,000	
Accrued Interest Payable		30,000	Interest Revenue		30,000
To record the accrual of six months' interest.			To record the accrual of six months' interest.		

Notice that the interest recognized is only $50,000 ($1,000,000 × 0.06 × 10/12). The actual amount of cash distributed on the interest dates is $60,000. The difference, $10,000, represents the amount that the issuer charges the purchaser on the date of issue for the unearned interest that will be paid to the owner of the bonds on July 1, 1975.

Bonds issued at other than face value between interest dates. The most complex situation involving bonds occurs when bonds are issued between interest dates at either a premium or a discount. Accumulated interest must be accounted for at the issuance date and a discount must be accumulated or a premium amortized at year-end.

Assume that Issuer Corporation issues the bonds to the Purchaser Insurance Company at 92.2 on March 1, 1975. The necessary entries during 1975 are:

Issuer

Mar. 1:		
Cash	932,000	
Bonds Payable—Discount	78,000	
Bonds Payable		1,000,000
Accrued Interest Payable		10,000
To record the issue of bonds at 92.2 plus accrued interest.		
July 1:		
Accrued Interest Payable	10,000	
Interest Expense	20,000	
Cash		30,000
To record the payment of six months' interest.		
Dec. 31:		
Interest Expense	30,000	
Accrued Interest Payable		30,000
To record the accrual of six months' interest.		
Interest Expense	6,610	
Bonds Payable—Discount		6,610
To record the accumulation of 10 months' discount at $661 per month.		

Purchaser

Mar. 1:		
Bond Investments	922,000	
Accrued Interest Receivable	10,000	
Cash		932,000
To record the purchase of bonds at 92.2 plus accrued interest.		
July 1:		
Cash	30,000	
Accrued Interest Receivable		10,000
Interest Revenue		20,000
To record receipt of six months' interest.		
Dec. 31:		
Accrued Interest Receivable	30,000	
Interest Revenue		30,000
To record the accrual of six months' interest.		
Bond Investments	6,610	
Interest Revenue		6,610
To record the accumulation of 10 months' discount at $661 per month.		

With the bonds issued at a discount, entries are required to allocate the discount to the periods of remaining life of the bonds. Since the amount of the discount ($78,000) is the same as that illustrated earlier, one might expect the amount accumulated each month to be the same as in the previous illustration (see Frame 8^{10}) and thus be $650 per month. But the time over which the discount is spread has been shortened from 120 months to 118 months. Thus the amount to accumulate per month is:

$$\frac{\text{Discount}}{\text{Months between issuance and maturity dates}} = \frac{\$78{,}000}{118 \text{ months}} = \$661 \text{ per month}$$

To test your understanding, assume that the Issuer Corporation sells the bonds to the Purchaser Insurance Company on March 1, 1975 at 107.8. Using the entries above as a guide, prepare the entries as of March 1, July 1, and December 31 on both sets of books.

Now check your answers with those in Answer Frame 10[10] on page 462.

Frame 11[10]

Effective interest rate method for accumulating a discount or amortizing a premium

The straight-line method of accumulating a discount or amortizing a premium is not theoretically correct, in that it incorrectly states interest expense from period to period. But it is used by many companies because it does not materially misstate net earnings. Thus, it is the method used in this chapter.

But a brief illustration of the theoretically correct method seems to be called for. Refer to the situation portrayed in Frame 9[10] where the bonds were issued at a premium of $78,000. This represents an effective rate of interest of about 5 percent.[1]

The proper amount of interest expense applicable to each period should be the effective rate of interest times the net liability (maturity value plus the remaining premium) that exists at the beginning of each interest period. Since there are two interest periods per year, the calculation has to be made each six months. In the case illustrated in Frame 9[10], the net liability of the bonds on January 1, 1975, is $1,078,000, which is the face value plus the unamortized premium. Therefore, under the effective rate method, the interest to be recognized for the first two years is as shown in the following table:

	*Debit to Interest Expense (2.5 % × Carrying Value)**	*Debit to Bonds Payable—Premium ($30,000 − Interest Expense)*		*Credit to Cash or Accrued Interest Payable*	*Carrying Value (Face Value plus Unamortized Premium)*
At issuance date.......					$1,078,000
1975 July 1...........	$26,950	$3,050	$6,176	$30,000	1,074,950
Dec. 31..........	26,874	3,126		30,000	1,071,824
1976 July 1...........	26,796	3,204	$6,488	30,000	1,068,620
Dec. 31..........	26,716	3,284		30,000	1,065,336

* The $26,950 is calculated by multiplying $1,078,000 by 2.5 percent; $26,874 is obtained by multiplying $1,074,950 by 2.5 percent; and so on.

[1] This can be verified by studying the example in Frame 6[10] where the premium was shown as $77,946 for bonds with similar characteristics and represented an effective rate of interest of 5 percent.

If both Issuer Corporation and the Purchaser Life Insurance Company use the effective rate method, the December 31, 1975, entries on their books for amortizing the premium are:

Bonds Payable—		
Premium	6,176	
Interest Expense		6,176

Interest Revenue	6,176	
Bond Investments		6,176

All the other entries are the same as in Frame 9[10]. Thus, the misstatement of earnings is only $1,624 ($7,800 less $6,176).

To test your understanding, determine the amount of misstatement of earnings for 1976 which is caused by using the straight-line method illustrated in Frame 9[10].

Now check your answer in Answer Frame 11[10] on page 462.

Frame 12[10]

Redeeming outstanding bonds

Bonds payable maturing within a year should be transferred to the current liability section of the statement of financial position if they are to be retired by the use of current assets. Bond issues may be redeemed as follows.

1. Bonds may be redeemed in total at maturity by direct payments from the cash of the issuing company. The entry to record the retirement reads (assuming accrued interest due on this date has been previously recorded):

Bonds Payable	xxxx	
Accrued Bond Interest Payable	xxx	
Cash		xxxx

2. They may be redeemed in whole or in part at a date preceding the maturity date, at the option of the issuing company—a typical provision found in modern bond indentures (the agreement between the issuer and the trustee for the purchasers). In such circumstances, the bond indenture may call for payment to the bondholder of a sum greater than the maturity amount of the bonds—a redemption premium (commonly referred to as a *call premium*). Why might a company want to retire a bond issue before it is due? There are a number of reasons, but one of the most important may be the opportunity to issue new bonds at a lower interest rate than those currently on the market. A review of the past 15 years indicates how much interest rates in general may change. To guard against this calling in of bonds and issuance of new bonds at

Answer frame 10[10]

The correct entries for 1975 are:

Issuer

Mar. 1:		
Cash	1,088,000	
Bonds Payable		1,000,000
Bonds Payable—Premium		78,000
Accrued Interest Payable		10,000
To record the issue of bonds at 107.8 plus accrued interest.		
July 1:		
Accrued Interest Payable	10,000	
Interest Expense	20,000	
Cash		30,000
To record the payment of six months' interest.		
Dec. 31:		
Interest Expense	30,000	
Accrued Interest Payable		30,000
To record the accrual of six months' interest.		
Bonds Payable—Premium	6,610	
Interest Expense		6,610
To amortize 10 months' premium at $661 per month.		

Purchaser

Mar. 1:		
Bond Investments	1,078,000	
Accrued Interest Receivable	10,000	
Cash		1,088,000
To record the purchase of bonds at 107.8 plus acrued interest.		
July 1:		
Cash	30,000	
Accrued Interest Receivable		10,000
Interest Revenue		20,000
To record the receipt of six months' interest.		
Dec. 31:		
Accrued Interest Receivable	30,000	
Interest Revenue		30,000
To record the accrual of six months' interest.		
Interest Revenue	6,610	
Bond Investments		6,610
To amortize 10 months' premium at $661 per month.		

The entries are quite similar to those for the situation in which there was a discount. The only difference is that the amortization of the premium has an effect on interest recognized opposite to that of the accumulation of the discount.

If you answered incorrectly, restudy Frame 10[10] carefully before going on to Frame 11[10] on page 460.

Answer frame 11[10]

Since the amortization of premium in 1976 is $6,484 under the effective rate of interest method and $7,800 under the straight-line method, the difference is only $1,316. This certainly is an immaterial amount for most companies large enough to issue $1 million in bonds. The difference will get smaller and smaller until about the end of the fifth year, and then the effective rate method will yield larger amounts than the straight-line method by an ever-increasing amount. Amortization under either method must total to $78,000. For ease of calculation, you should use the straight-line rate in the exercises and problems unless otherwise indicated.

If you answered incorrectly, restudy Frame 11[10] before beginning Frame 12[10] on page 461.

a lower interest rate, the investor has generally demanded that he be paid a premium for redeeming the bonds before maturity. Higher premiums are often required for redemption in the early years of the life of a bond issue than for redemption in later years. For example, the redemption price may be 104.25 in the first year, 104.05 in the second, and may gradually decrease to 100 several years prior to maturity date.

To illustrate, assume that the Box Company calls for redemption of $200,000 (face value) of its outstanding bonds on an interest payment date (after making the payment) during a year in which the redemption price is 103.50. (The bonds were issued face value.) The entry to record this transaction is:

Bonds Payable	200,000	
Loss on Bond Redemption	7,000	
Cash		207,000

The redemption premium of $7,000 [($200,000 × 103.50%) − $200,000] is charged to a Loss on Bond Redemption account. If any bond premium or discount remains after adjustment to the date of redemption, it must be written off. Assuming now that $4,000 of the balance in a Bonds Payable—Discount account relates to the $200,000 worth of bonds retired, the following entry is also required:

Loss on Bond Redemption	4,000	
Discount on Bonds Payable		4,000

The total loss on redemption is $11,000. If material, this amount is reported separately in the earnings statement.

3. Bond issues may be redeemed by means of a sinking fund, as explained in Frame 13[10].

4. Bonds may be redeemed in a series in accordance with the provisions of the indenture. These bonds are known as serial bonds. They differ from the bonds described in (2) above because the redemption time of every bond is specified before the bonds are issued. This allows investors to choose a bond with the desired time period to meet their needs. (Note that the effective interest rate for the shorter period bonds may be lower than for the longer term part of the issue because many investors consider them less risky.) Quite often serial bonds are issued by governmental units, such as municipalities.

To illustrate the accounting for these bonds, assume a total issue of $2 million of 20-year bonds is to be redeemed at the rate of $200,000 per year starting at the end of the 10th year from the date of the bonds. At the end of the 10th year, and each year thereafter, the following entry is made for the face value of the bonds redeemed:

Bonds Payable	200,000	
Cash		200,000

Interest does not accrue on a bond beyond the scheduled redemption date.

From the investor's point of view, he must make sure that any accrued interest receivable and premium or discount applicable to the period in which redemption takes place is recorded. If properly accounted for, there should be no gain or loss on the redemption of a serial bond.

Specify whether each of the following statements is true or false.

1. Bonds may be redeemed in total at maturity, in total at a date preceding maturity, or serially throughout the life of the bond issue, according to the specific provisions of the bond indenture.
2. The accounts of a given company show Bonds Payable, $50,000, and Discount on Bonds Payable, $3,000, at a time when all of the bonds are called and redeemed at 104. Ignoring accrued interest, the required entry is:

Bonds Payable	50,000	
Loss on Bond Redemption	5,000	
Cash		52,000
Bonds Payable—Discount		3,000

3. Bonds payable of $100,000 which mature on August 1, 1976, should be classified as a current liability in a statement of financial position dated December 31, 1975, if it is expected that they will be redeemed out of current assets.
4. The accounts of a given company show Bonds Payable, $80,000, and Premium on Bonds Payable, $3,000, at a time when all of the bonds are redeemed at 105. Ignoring the accrued interest, the required entry is:

Bonds Payable	80,000	
Loss on Bond Redemption	7,000	
Cash		84,000
Bonds Payable—Premium		3,000

Check your answers in Answer Frame 12[10] on page 466.

Frame 13[10]

Redeeming bonds through sinking funds

The manner in which a sinking fund has been employed to redeem bonds has changed through the years. Traditionally, a sinking fund consisted of an accumulation of cash and securities (and earnings thereon) which were readily marketable. The use of these funds was restricted to the redemption of the entire bond issue at the maturity date.

Provisions in more modern indentures require that payments be made on or before a given date to a sinking fund which will be used to immediately redeem a stipulated amount of bonds and to pay the accrued interest on them. If a trustee is used in such sinking fund arrangements, he will determine by specific identification which bonds will be called for redemption. The expenses of the sinking fund trustee are not to be reimbursed from the sinking fund. Thus, the modern sinking fund brings about the serial redemption of outstanding bonds without actually issuing serial bonds.

To illustrate current practices regarding the use of a sinking fund, assume that on October 1, 1971, the Bradley Company issued $1 million of 25-year, 6 percent semiannual coupon bonds at face value. Under the terms of the indenture, the company is to deliver to the trustee on September 30, 1976, and each September 30 thereafter as long as any bonds are outstanding, an amount sufficient to redeem $50,000 of the principal amount at 100 and to pay any accrued interest on the bonds called for redemption through the sinking fund. The entry to record the required payment on September 30, 1976, is:

Sinking Fund	51,500	
Cash		51,500
Payment to trustee of funds to call $50,000 of bonds at face value plus accrued interest of $1,500 ($50,000 × 0.06 × ½).		

The trustee calls $50,000 of bonds, pays for the bonds and the accrued interest, and notifies the company. Assuming that the accrued interest has been recorded, the entry is:

Accrued Bond Interest Payable	1,500	
Bonds Payable	50,000	
Sinking Fund		51,500
To record payment by trustee of accrued interest on, and redemption of, bonds through sinking fund.		

Indicate whether each statement is correct or incorrect:

1. The primary purpose of a sinking fund is the payment of periodic interest on outstanding bonds.
2. During that period of the life of a bond issue when the company is required to make annual payments into a sinking fund, a portion of the bonds outstanding should be shown as a current liability in the statement of financial position.
3. The journal entry made by the company when its sinking fund trustee reports the purchase of securities he is required to make according to the terms of the indenture consists of a debit to Bond Investments and a credit to Sinking Fund Cash.

To check your responses, turn to Answer Frame 13[10] on page 466.

Answer frame 12[10]

1. True. The statement notes a number of ways in which bond issues may be redeemed. The manner in which a specific bond issue may be redeemed depends, of course, upon the provisions of the bond indenture.
2. True. This is the proper entry to record the bond redemption described. The call premium is $50,000 × 0.04 = $2,000. The remaining bond discount accounts for the other $3,000 of the loss.
3. True. Since the bonds payable are to mature within a year and are to be paid with current assets accumulated for the purpose, they should be classified as current liabilities.
4. False. To write off the Premium on Bonds Payable account when the bonds are redeemed, the account must be debited, not credited, since the account normally has a credit balance. The correct entry is thus:

Bonds Payable	80,000	
Bonds Payable—Premium	3,000	
Loss on Bond Redemption	1,000	
Cash		84,000

Normally, the payment made on redemption includes an amount to pay the interest accrued to the redemption date.

If you missed any of these answers, restudy Frame 12[10] before going on to Frame 13[10] on page 464.

Answer frame 13[10]

1. Incorrect. The periodic deposits made with the sinking fund trustee are not primarily for the payment of the bond interest.
2. Correct. If you answered correctly, you are doing quite well, since nothing has been said about the classification of outstanding bonds when periodic sinking fund payments are required. An amount equal to the value of the bonds which will be redeemed through the operation of the sinking fund in the coming operating cycle should be shown as a current liability.
3. Incorrect. The journal entry made when the sinking fund trustee reports the acquisition of securities debits Bonds Payable and credits Sinking Fund. A company cannot invest in its own bonds.

If you did not answer correctly, reread Frame 13[10] before proceeding to Frame 14[10] below.

Frame 14[10]

Statement of financial position illustration

The liabilities portion (current and long-term) of the statement of financial position of the Michaels Corporation (Illustration 10.2) presents certain accounts discussed in this chapter.

Illustration 10.2

THE MICHAELS CORPORATION
Partial Statement of Financial Position
December 31, 1975

LIABILITIES AND STOCKHOLDERS' EQUITY

Current Liabilities:			
Accounts payable		$160,000	
Accrued bond interest payable		4,000	
Current portion of long-term debt		10,000	$174,000
Long-Term Liabilities:			
Debenture bonds, 7 percent, due 1983	$200,000		
Less: Discount	4,000	$196,000	
First-mortgage bonds, 6 percent, due 1984	$190,000		
Add: Premium	2,000	192,000	388,000
Total Liabilities			$562,000

With reference to the information pertaining to bonds contained in this partial statement of financial position, indicate whether each of the following statements is true or false.

1. At the time the 7 percent debenture bonds were issued, the prevailing market rate of interest for similar bonds was greater than 7 percent.
2. The semiannual interest payment date of at least one of the bond issues does not fall on December 31, 1975.
3. The stated interest rate of 6 percent on the first mortgage bonds was lower at the time of their issuance than the prevailing market rate for similar bonds.
4. Both of the corporation's bond issues are secured by pledges of specific property.

Check your answers in Answer Frame 14[10] on page 468.

Frame 15[10]

Other long-term liabilities: Leases

During the past 25 years the long-term lease has become a common method of financing operating assets. The contracts usually call for rental payments over a period of years. Often the lease will extend over a significant portion of the expected life of the leased asset, or it may extend over a shorter period with an option to either renew the lease or purchase the asset, sometimes at a nominal price. The terms of the contracts may be individually tailored to the needs of the lessee. Often, such leases stipulate that taxes, insurance, and maintenance costs be paid by the lessee.

Answer frame 14[10]

1. True. The fact that the debenture bonds were issued at a discount indicates that the market rate prevailing at the time was greater than the 7 percent rate offered on the bonds.
2. True. The presence of the Accrued Bond Interest Payable account among the current liabilities indicates that not all of the bond interest expense accrued at December 31, 1975, was paid by that date.
3. False. The fact that the first mortgage bonds were issued at a premium indicates that the nominal rate of interest (6 percent) was higher, not lower, than the market interest rate for similar bonds at the time they were issued.
4. False. The first mortage bonds are secured by a pledge of specific property while the debenture bonds are unsecured. The term "mortgage" reveals that the bonds are secured.

If you answered any of the above incorrectly, reread Frame 14[10] before turning to Frame 15[10] on page 467.

15[10] *continued*

Leasing may be advantageous to a particular firm because of its flexibility, tax implications, and the possibility of obtaining financing when other means are not readily available. One of the disadvantages of leasing is that it may cost more than borrowing from other sources. But the total contract and services involved must be evaluated in order to make such a determination.

How leases should be treated on the statement of financial position has been the subject of considerable debate. It has been proposed that leasing an asset is no different than purchasing the asset—that only the method of financing differs. This line of argument states that the lease payments should be discounted at the current rate of interest applicable to the firm and their present value recorded as a liability, with a corresponding debit to an asset account. Then as each payment is made, a portion of the recorded liability is canceled, interest expense is recognized, and a credit is made to cash. Proponents of this theory believe that such a treatment shows all assets on a comparable basis in the statement of financial position and avoids mixing operating expenses with the cost of financing.

But the Accounting Principles Board refused to go so far as to require that all leases be recorded. Rather the Board, in *Opinions No. 5* and *7*, chose to distinguish between financial (or financing) leases and operating leases. The financing lease, as its name implies, is simply a means of financing the purchase of an asset. A noncancellable lease containing one or more of the following provisions is considered a financing lease: (1) the initial term of the lease is for the expected useful life of the asset (or the lessee has the right to renew for periods up to the useful life of the asset), with the lessee to bear the cost of all repairs, maintenance, insurance, and taxes; (2) the initial term of the lease is for less than the useful life of the asset and the lessee has the option to purchase the asset at a price substantially below market value or renew the lease for the balance of the asset's useful life at substantially reduced periodic rental payments.

When these conditions are not present, the lessee is simply renting the asset rather than buying it—as one might rent an automobile for several days from one of the large auto leasing firms. There is clearly no intention to purchase the asset, although in some cases the asset leased may ultimately be purchased.

Generally, no liability is recorded for future payments under an operating lease. The cost of the rent is simply charged to the period in which it is incurred (recall that rent is usually prepaid) and the terms of the lease disclosed in the footnotes to the financial statements.

The assets and liabilities implicit in financial leases are, on the other hand, generally recorded at the discounted value of the future rental payments. To illustrate, assume that the Brand J Company enters into a noncancellable 10-year lease on January 1, 1975, and agrees to pay $5,000 immediately and another $5,000 at the end of each of the first 9 years of the lease. At the end of the 10th year, the company can purchase the machine, which is estimated to have a useful economic life of 15 years, for $1. The lease is to be treated as a financing lease. The company currently has to pay 8 percent on borrowed funds used to finance the purchase of similar assets.

The value to be recorded in the Equipment account is equal to the immediate payment of $5,000 plus the present value of an annuity of $5,000 for nine years at 8 percent. Using Table III on page 725, the debit to the Equipment account is computed as: $5,000 + ($5,000 × 6.247) = $36,235. The appropriate entry on signing the lease and paying the first lease payment of $5,000 is:

Jan. 1	Equipment	36,235	
	Long-Term Lease Liability		31,235
	Cash		5,000
	To record the "purchase" of equipment under a 10-year lease at $5,000 plus the discounted value (8%) of the future lease payments.		

The long-term lease liability can be viewed as the balance of the "principal" of a loan obtained to acquire the property which is being leased. To find the interest expense that has accrued on this loan by the end of 1975, it is necessary to multiply 8 percent by the outstanding balance ($31,235) as of the beginning of the year. Since (0.08 × $31,235) = $2,498.80, this is the amount of interest that is being paid at the end of 1975 when the second lease payment is made. The remainder of the $5,000 payment made on December 31, 1975, is applied against the principal ($31,235) to reduce it as follows:

Principal balance before Dec. 31 payment	$31,235.00
Less portion of $5,000 which is not interest ($5,000 − $2,498.80)	2,501.20
Principal balance after Dec. 31 payment	$28,733.80

Thus the correct entry to record the payment on December 31, 1975, is:

Interest Expense	2,498.80	
Long-Term Lease Liability	2,501.20	
Cash		5,000.00
To record payment on lease in accord with terms of lease.		

Also on December 31, 1975, it is necessary to record the adjusting entry for depreciation of the equipment acquired. Assuming that the straight-line rate is to be used and that the estimated salvage value at the end of 15 years is \$235, the amount each year is:

$$\frac{\text{Cost} - \text{Salvage value}}{\text{Life in years}} = \frac{\$36{,}235 - \$235}{15} = \$2{,}400 \text{ per year}$$

The entry on December 31, 1975, and every year thereafter through the 15th year is thus:

Depreciation Expense	2,400	
Allowance for Depreciation—Equipment		2,400
To record depreciation expense on equipment acquired under long-term lease.		

It is desirable to construct a table such as that shown in Illustration 10.3 to show the portion of each \$5,000 payment that should be debited

Illustration 10.3

	Entry Required on December 31			
	(a)	(b)	(c)	(d)
	Debit to Interest Expense (8% of Previous Balance in Long-Term Lease Liability Account)	*Debit to Long-Term Lease Liability Account (\$5,000 − Amount in Column a)*	*Credit to Cash*	*Balance in Long-Term Lease Liability Account after Dec. 31 Entry*
Beginning				\$31,235.00
1975	\$2,498.80	\$2,501.20	\$5,000	28,733.80
1976	2,298.70	2,701.30	5,000	26,032.50
1977	2,082.60	2,917.40	5,000	23,115.10
1978	1,849.21	3,150.79	5,000	19,964.31
1979	1,597.14	3,402.86	5,000	16,561.45
1980	1,324.92	3,675.08	5,000	12,886.37
1981	1,030.91	3,969.09	5,000	8,917.28
1982	713.38	4,286.62	5,000	4,630.66
1983	370.45	4,629.55	5,000	1.11*

* Difference is due to rounding. The difference is eliminated by increasing the debit to Long-Term Lease Liability by \$1.11 and decreasing the debit to Interest Expense by this amount.

to Interest Expense and the portion that should be debited to the Long-Term Lease Liability account.

Using Illustration 10.3, determine the correct entry to record the $5,000 lease payment made on December 31, 1976.

Now check your answer by turning to Answer Frame 15[10] on page 472.

Frame 16[10]

Pensions

One of the long-term liabilities on the books of some firms is for obligations under an employee pension plan. Pension plans typically provide that each employee with a certain number of years of service can begin receiving a specific sum from a pension fund each year, beginning at a certain age or upon disability. For instance, such a plan may state that an employee with 5 to 10 years of service will receive an amount each year after age 65 which is equal to 30 percent of his highest annual salary; an employee with 10 to 20 years of service, 40 percent; and an employee with over 20 years of service, 50 percent. Since these plans are usually the result of extensive bargaining between the firm and a labor union, the provisions of various plans are subject to wide variation.

A pension plan may be funded or unfunded. It is a funded plan if periodic payments are made by the firm to a trustee or to some other outside agency, such as an insurance company, which has taken over the obligation to pay benefits when due. Then the firm has no future control over the cash paid into the pension fund. Unfunded plans are those where the company retains its obligation to pay future benefits under the plan and, therefore, does not make payments to an outside agency. Under some such plans the firm need not even set aside funds to pay these future benefits. Because of sad stories about 64-year old workers losing their pensions because they were not funded and the company went bankrupt, there is an increasing pressure, and thus an increasing tendency, toward funded plans.

Under funded plans the accounting is not very complex. The pension expense to be recognized for a given accounting period is the amount which the firm is obligated to pay into the fund as a result of meeting the terms of the pension plan. For instance, if the pension plan formula is applied and it is determined that $248,000 must be paid into the fund, this is the amount of pension expense for the period. The amount of any pension plan liability is simply the amount that is due to be paid into the fund but has not yet been paid. For firms that are delinquent in their payments, this liability can grow to substantial amounts. Once the amount has been paid, the cash is out of the control of the firm and is usually invested by the outside agency to accumulate enough earnings

Answer frame 15[10]

The correct entry on December 31, 1976, is:

Interest Expense	2,298.70	
Long-Term Lease Liability	2,701.30	
Cash		5,000.00
To record the Dec. 31, 1976, payment on the long-term lease.		

The amounts for this entry are obtained from the 1976 line in Illustration 10.3. Notice that after the December 31, 1983, entry has been made, the balance in the Long-Term Lease Liability account has been reduced to zero since the "loan" has been completely paid off.

If you answered incorrectly, restudy Frame 15[10] before beginning Frame 16[10] on page 471.

16[10] *continued*

to meet the payments to former employees when they come due. The benefits to be paid under some such plans depend on the success of the investments made by the trustee (or other outside agency).

The accounting entries for an unfunded plan are more complex. The accountant will usually seek the advice of a professional actuary in estimating the amounts involved. Such factors as estimates of how long people will work for the company, how long they will live after retirement, and so on, are involved. The pension plan expense is equal to the present value of future pension benefits that have been incurred that year.[2] The Pension Plan Liability account is credited for this amount. When benefits are paid to retired former employees, the Pension Plan Liability account is debited. As long as the present value of the future pension benefits incurred each year exceeds the payment of benefits, the liability continues to grow. The detailed actuarial methods used to arrive at the amounts involved in accounting for unfunded pension plans are beyond the scope of this text.

To test your understanding, assume that the Leisure Corporation incurred an obligation to pay future pension benefits with a present value of $160,000 in 1975 and actually paid out benefits of $70,000 during the year. Prepare the necessary entries to reflect these events (prepare a summary entry for the payments). Assume there is no past service cost to amortize.

Now turn to Answer Frame 16[10] on page 474 to check your answers.

[2] This is complicated somewhat by the fact that a special problem is encountered initially when a pension plan is adopted. Some method must be used to recognize the pension liability (which can be substantial in amount) created by the fact that the pension an employee will become eligible to receive is often based on years of service and that some of these years fall before the plan is adopted. The cost of providing such pension benefits is referred to as past service cost. APB *Opinion No. 8* requires that past service costs be allocated to future periods of not less than 10 nor more than 40 years.

Summary *chapter* 10

An exposure to the concepts of compound interest, future value, and present value is necessary to understand the accounting for bonds, leases, and pensions.

A bond is one of the most common forms of long-term debt financing. Because of the interest expense on such debt and its deductibility in arriving at taxable net earnings, the issuance of debt will have an effect, known as financial leverage, on the earnings available for stockholders. Favorable financial leverage results when borrowed funds generate more earnings per share than if the funds had been raised by issuing additional shares of capital stock. When the reverse is true, unfavorable financial leverage is present.

When bonds are issued by a company, other companies often purchase them as long-term investments. Long-term investments in bonds are made to establish an affiliation with another company or to secure a continuing stream of revenue over a period of years. Alternatively, they may be acquired as a temporary investment. The intent of management is the determining factor as to whether an investment in bonds is short-term or long-term in nature.

Bonds may be secured or unsecured, and they may or may not be convertible into stock of the issuing corporation.

The price a bond will bring often differs from its face value and is dependent on the relationship between the contract rate of interest and the current market rate of interest for bonds of the same risk category. The contract rate of interest determines how much cash will be paid as interest on each interest date during the life of the bonds. The bonds sell at a premium or a discount to make the effective (or yield) rate of interest equal to the market rate of interest which exists at the time of issuance. The price a bond issue will bring can be determined by finding the present value of the promise to pay the principal at maturity and the present value of the promise to pay the periodic interest throughout the life of the bonds. These present values are determined by discounting the future cash flows at the effective rate of interest. Any discount or premium is recorded in a separate account by the issuing company, but the amount paid by the investor is usually recorded in a single account on his books. The discount represents interest which will be paid at the maturity date of the bonds and must be assigned to the time periods within the bond's life. The discount is additional interest expense to the issuer and interest revenue to the investor. In paying a premium for a bond, investors actually pay in advance for a part of each of the periodic interest payments they will receive. The effect of issuing or purchasing bonds at a premium or discount on periodic interest can be computed using the effective interest rate method or the straight-line method.

When bonds are issued between interest dates, the investor will pay for both the bond and the interest accrued from the last interest payment date to the date of acquisition. This is because the issuer is obligated to issue interest checks which cover a full interest period, whereas the

Answer frame 16[10]

The correct entry on December 31, 1975, is:

Pension Plan Expense	160,000	
Pension Plan Liability		160,000
To record the obligation to pay future benefits under the pension plan at their present value.		

The entry for payments to be made at various dates during 1975 is:

Pension Plan Liability	70,000	
Cash		70,000
To record the payment of benefits under the pension plan.		

If you answered incorrectly, restudy Frame 16[10] before turning to the Chapter summary on page 473.

---

investor is entitled to interest only for that period during which he holds the bonds.

Bond indenture provisions relative to redemption of the bonds vary. Bonds may be redeemed in their entirety at maturity, in whole or in part at a date preceding maturity (usually at a specified premium, through the operation of a sinking fund), or serially according to the maturity dates specified on the various blocks of bonds. Any difference between the book value of the long-term bond investment (or liability) and the amount received (or paid) will be treated as either a gain or a loss.

When a lease agreement has the characteristics of a purchase, the asset and corresponding liability should be set up on the books even if the arrangement is legally a lease. The amount to be recorded is the present value of the total of the unpaid installments due on the lease. Interest should be imputed at a reasonable rate, taking into account the lessee company's costs of borrowing from other sources.

Pension plans can result in a fairly substantial liability on the books of a company, especially where the plan is unfunded. Under funded plans, the pension expense to be recognized for a given period is the amount which the company is obligated to pay into the fund as a result of meeting the provisions of the pension plan. Under unfunded plans, the pension expense is equal to the present value of the future benefits that have been incurred that period (plus any amortization of past service costs that may be involved). The services of an actuary are often required in determining the amounts involved in accounting for pension plan transactions.

To complete your review, study the defiitions of new terms introduced in this chapter contained in the glossary which follows. Then go on to the Student Review Quiz for a self-administered test of your comprehension of the material in the chapter.

Glossary *chapter* 10

Annuity—a series of equal payments spaced equally in time.

Bond indenture—the overall contract between the issuer of bonds and the bondholders or the trustee representing the bondholders.

Bond redemption fund—a fund established to bring about the gradual redemption of outstanding bonds; usually called a sinking fund.

Call premium—the price in excess of face value which a bond issuer may be required to pay to redeem bonds prior to maturity date.

Compound interest—interest calculated on the principal plus the interest earned in previous periods, as compared to simple interest in which interest is computed only on the principal.

Contract rate of interest—the rate of interest printed on the face of the bonds.

Debenture bonds—unsecured bonds whose value depends upon the general credit of the issuer and which are a general lien against all unpledged property.

Effective interest rate method—a method in which interest expense (revenue) for a period is calculated by multiplying the book value of the bonds payable (investment in bonds) by the effective interest rate at the bond issue (purchase) date. The difference between the actual expense (revenue) and the amount paid (received), based on the nominal bond interest rate, represents the accumulation of discount or amortization of premium for the period.

Effective rate of interest—the rate of interest that an investor can earn on a particular bond issue by paying a certain price for it and that the issuer will incur by issuing it at that price.

Favorable financial leverage—effect on earnings per share resulting from the generation of a larger amount of net earnings by borrowed funds than the cost incurred to use them.

Financial leverage—the effect upon earnings of the introduction, or existence, of long-term debt (or other instrument with a fixed payout) as a means of financing a business; results from the fact that interest on debt is fixed in amount regardless of the level of earnings and is deductible in arriving at taxable earnings.

Income bonds—unsecured bonds for which the payment of periodic interest is contingent upon its being earned.

Lease—a contract calling for periodic rental payments for the use of an asset.

Market rate of interest—the minimum rate of interest which investors are willing to accept on bonds of a particular risk category.

Mortgage—a conditional transfer of title to property to secure a debt.

Present value—the value today of a specified future cash flow (an annuity or a lump-sum amount) discounted at a stipulated rate of interest.

Redemption premium—see call premium.

Registered bonds—bonds for which the names of the owners are recorded by the issuer or trustee.

Senior lien—a first mortgage, or the first claim or lien upon property.

Sinking fund—a fund into which periodic cash deposits are made for the purpose of redeeming outstanding bonds.

Straight-line method—a method of accumulating a discount or amortizing a premium which results in the same amount being assigned to each month of the life of a bond.

Trading on the equity—the securing of a portion of the needed capital of a business through the use of securities which limit the amount of interest (or dividends) paid periodically on them (see finaicial leverage).

Trustee—usually a bank or trust company selected to represent the bondholders in a bond issue and enforce the provisions of the bond indenture made by the issuing company.

Unfavorable financial leverage—the reverse of favorable financial leverage.

Unsecured bonds—bonds for which no specific property is pledged as security and whose value, as a result, depends on the general credit of the issuer.

Student review quiz *chapter* 10

To develop a permanent record of your responses, you may write them on the answer sheet provided in the *Work Papers* or on a separate sheet of paper.

1 The present value of $1 due in 40 periods at 2 percent is 0.45289042. The present value of $1 due in 20 periods at 4 percent is 0.45638695. The present value of $1 due at the end of each of 40 periods at 2 percent is 27.35547924. The present value of $1 due at the end of each of 20 periods at 4 percent is 13.59032634. If $100,000 of 20-year, 5 percent bonds issued and dated on July 1, 1975, and calling for semiannual interest payments on January 1 and July 1 are issued to yield 4 percent, their issue price is—

a) $114,027.40.
b) $79,614.52.
c) $113,677.74.
d) $79,264.86.
e) None of the above.

2 A bond issued at a discount indicates that at the date of issue—

a) Its contract rate was lower than the prevailing market rate of interest on similar bonds.
b) Its contract rate was higher than the prevailing market rate of interest on similar bonds.
c) The bonds were issued at a price greater than their face value.
d) The bonds are noninterest-bearing.
e) None of the above.

3 On October 1, 1975, the Heide Company issued $1 million of 6 percent bonds due on October 1, 1985, at a discount of $120,000. The adjusting entry on December 31, 1975, the end of the company's accounting year, is:

a)	Bond Interest Expense	18,000	
	Bonds Payable—Discount		3,000
	Accrued Bond Interest Payable		15,000
b)	Bond Interest Expense	15,000	
	Bonds Payable—Discount	3,000	
	Accrued Bond Interest Payable		18,000
c)	Bond Interest Expense	15,000	
	Bonds Payable—Discount	3,000	
	Cash		18,000
d)	Bond Interest Expense	15,000	
	Cash		15,000
e)	Bond Interest Expense	27,000	
	Bonds Payable—Discount		12,000
	Accrued Bond Interest Payable		15,000

4 The Stanhope Corporation issued 6 percent first mortgage bonds having a face value of $500,000 for $575,000. What entry is required?

a)	Cash	500,000	
	Bonds Payable		500,000
b)	Cash	575,000	
	Bonds Payable		575,000
c)	Cash	575,000	
	Bond Interest Payable		75,000
	Bonds Payable		500,000
d)	Cash	575,000	
	Bonds Payable—Discount		75,000
	Bonds Payable		500,000
e)	Cash	575,000	
	Bonds Payable—Premium		75,000
	Bonds Payable		500,000

5 G.K., Inc. issued 20-year bonds at a premium of $40,000. The entry to record the semiannual amortization of the premium is:

a)	Bond Interest Expense	1,000	
	Bond Interest Payable		1,000
b)	Bonds Payable—Premium	1,000	
	Bonds Interest Payable		1,000
c)	Bonds Payable—Premium	2,000	
	Bonds Interest Expense		2,000
d)	Bonds Payable—Premium	1,000	
	Bond Interest Expense		1,000
e)	Bond Interest Expense	1,000	
	Bonds Payable—Premium		1,000

6 The Ebenworth Company issued \$100,000 of 6 percent bonds on September 1, 1975, and received a total of \$100,750. Interest on these bonds is payable on January 1 and July 1 of each year. The correct entry to record the issuance of the bonds is:

a)	Cash	100,750	
	Bonds Payable		100,750
b)	Cash	100,750	
	Bonds Payable		100,000
	Bonds Payable—Premium		750
c)	Cash	100,750	
	Bonds Payable		100,000
	Accrued Bond Interest Payable		750
d)	Cash	100,750	
	Bonds Payable—Discount	250	
	Bonds Payable		100,000
	Accrued Bond Interest Payable		1,000
e)	Cash	100,750	
	Bonds Payable—Discount	250	
	Bonds Payable		100,000
	Interest Revenue		1,000

7 Marshall Corporation issued \$300,000 of 5 percent, 20-year bonds on July 1, 1975, at 97. The bonds are dated July 1, 1975, mature on July 1, 1995, and call for semiannual interest payments on July 1 and January 1. The bond indenture provides that upon proper notice, the issuing corporation may redeem its bonds, in whole or in part, on any date after December 31, 1977, at 105. In 1985 the corporation notifies holders of \$100,000 face value of bonds that their bonds will be called for redemption on July 1, 1985. Interest coupons for the interest payment due on July 1, 1985, are to remain attached to the bonds called for redemption. The company's accounting year ends on June 30. Assuming all of the bonds called are surrendered, the entry to record the redemption of the bonds is:

a)	Bonds Payable	100,000	
	Accrued Bond Interest Payable	2,500	
	Loss on Bond Redemption	5,000	
	Cash		107,500
b)	Bonds Payable	100,000	
	Accrued Bond Interest Payable	2,500	
	Loss on Bond Redemption	6,500	
	Cash		107,500
	Bonds Payable—Discount		1,500
c)	Bonds Payable	100,000	
	Loss on Bond Redemption	6,500	
	Cash		105,000
	Bonds Payable—Discount		1,500
d)	Bonds Payable	100,000	
	Accrued Bond Interest Payable	2,500	
	Loss on Bond Redemption	9,500	
	Cash		107,500
	Bonds Payable—Discount		4,500
e)	Bonds Payable	100,000	
	Loss on Bond Redemption	9,500	
	Cash		105,000
	Bonds Payable—Discount		4,500

8 The Marsohn Corporation issued \$100,000 of 5 percent, 10-year bonds at face value. The bond indenture provides that a sinking fund be established by the company through annual payments each June 30 sufficient to enable the trustee to call and retire \$10,000 of the bonds at face value plus accrued interest on July 1. The bonds call for semiannual interest payments on January 1 and July 1. The entry to be made by the company at the time of making its first deposit with the trustee is:

a)	Sinking Fund	10,000	
	Cash		10,000
b)	Sinking Fund	10,000	
	Bond Interest Payable	250	
	Cash		10,250

c)

Bonds Payable.	10,000	
Cash.		10,000

d)

Bonds Payable.	10,000	
Interest Expense. . . .	250	
Cash.		10,250

e) None of the above.

9 On July 1, 1975, Cosgrove Corporation issued $500,000 of 5 percent serial bonds at 100. The bond indenture provides that $50,000 of these bonds mature each July 1, beginning in 1978. The bonds are registered as to the principal and interest, and interest payments are made directly by the company by check. The company's accounting period ends on June 30. Which of the following entries properly records the transactions entered into by the company on July 1, 1978, assuming that all of the bonds maturing on this date are surrendered for redemption?

a)

Bonds Payable.	50,000	
Accrued Bond Interest Payable. .	12,500	
Cash.		62,500

b)

Bonds Payable.	50,000	
Cash.		50,000

c)

Bonds Payable.	50,000	
Accrued Bond Interest Payable. .	1,250	
Sinking Fund. . .		51,250

d)

Bonds Payable.	50,000	
Accrued Bond Interest Payable. .	12,500	
Sinking Fund. . .		62,500

e) None of the above.

10 Any balance in a bond sinking fund of a modern business corporation would probably best be classified in the statement of financial position as part of the—

a) Current assets.
b) Current liabilities.
c) Long-term liabilities.
d) Long-term assets.
e) Stockholders' equity.

11 James Company purchased $100,000 face value of Carol Corporation bonds on April 30. The interest rate was 9 percent, payable semiannually on January 1 and July 1. James Company paid $102,000 in the transaction. The journal entry to record the purchase is:

a)

Investment in Bonds.	102,000	
Cash.		102,000

b)

Investment in Bonds.	100,000	
Accrued Interest Receivable.	2,000	
Cash.		102,000

c)

Investment in Bonds.	100,000	
Premium on Investment in Bonds.	2,000	
Cash.		102,000

d)

Investment in Bonds.	99,000	
Accrued Interest Receivable.	3,000	
Cash.		102,000

e)

Investment in Bonds.	99,000	
Premium on Investment in Bonds.	3,000	
Cash.		102,000

12 Which of the following statements are incorrect?

a) Entering into a long-term lease agreement can result in the recording of an asset and a liability on the books of the lessee.
b) When a long-term lease amounts to an installment purchase of a depreciable asset, it is necessary to record interest expense and depreciation expense for the first and several subsequent accounting periods.
c) All long-term leases are to be treated as installment purchases.
d) Pension plans which are funded are easier to account for than are unfunded pension plans.
e) When benefits are paid to persons under an unfunded pension plan, the company should debit Pension Expense and credit Cash.

Now compare your answers with the correct ones on page 715.

Questions *chapter* 10

1 What is meant by the term "trading on the equity"?

2 What are the advantages of obtaining long-term funds by the issuance of bonds rather than additional shares of capital stock? What are the disadvantages?

3 Ace Corporation was authorized to issue $1.5 million of 7 percent, 10-year bonds. On a certain statement of financial position date, only $1 million of the bonds had been issued. How should these facts be displayed in the statement of financial position? Why should they be disclosed?

4 If a corporation can obtain funds at a net cost of 3 percent to buy an asset which will produce a series of annual net cash flows of $1,000 at the end of each of the next 10 years, should it make the investment in this asset if its cost is $8,750? (The present value of an annuity of $1 due for 10 periods at 3 percent is 8.53020284.)

5 When bonds are issued between interest dates, why is it appropriate that the issuing corporation should receive cash equal to the amount of accrued interest in addition to the issue price of the bonds?

6 Why might it be more accurate to describe a sinking fund as a bond redemption fund?

7 Indicate how each of the following items should be classified in a statement of financial position on December 31, 1975:

a) Cash balance in a sinking fund.
b) Accrued interest on bonds payable.
c) Debenture bonds payable due in 1985.
d) Premium on bonds payable.
e) First mortgage bonds payable, due July 1, 1976.
f) Discount on bonds payable.
g) First National Bank—Interest account.
h) Estimated accrued pension costs.

8 Why would an investor whose intent is to hold bonds to maturity pay more for the bonds than their face value?

9 In what way may long-term leases be similar to installment purchases of property?

10 Is the pension plan liability likely to be larger at any given time under a funded plan or an unfunded plan? Why?

Exercises *chapter* 10

1 Conceptually, what is the present worth of a lump-sum payment of $10,000 due in five years? If the going market rate of interest of investments of a certain type is 5 percent per year and the present value of $1 due in five years at 5 percent is 0.78352617, what is its specific worth?

2 Conceptually, what is the present worth of a series of annual payments of $1,000 due at the end of each of the next five years? If the going market rate of interest on investments of this type is 5 percent per year and the present value of an annuity of $1 for five periods at 5 percent is 4.32947667, what is its specific worth?

3 Interest on Martin Corporation's coupon bonds is paid by a trustee, the Third National Bank. Assuming the semiannual interest amounts to $25,000 and all of the coupons are cashed, prepare the entries to record the deposit of the interest with the trustee, the accrual of the interest, and the cashing of the coupons.

4 The Bailey Company issued $100,000 of 10-year, 6 percent bonds dated June 1, 1975, on August 1, 1975, at 99. Prepare the entry necessary to record the issuance. Wonder Company bought one-tenth of these bonds. Prepare the journal entry to record this long-term investment.

5 Thayer Company issued $200,000 of 10-year, 5 percent bonds at 102 on January 1, 1975, the date of the bonds.

a) Was the market rate of interest for these bonds higher or lower than 5 percent?
b) What is the amount of bond interest expense for 1975, assuming straight-line amortization of the bond premium?
c) What is the amount of bond interest recognized for 1975 assuming the effective interest rate method is used? (Assume the effective rate is 4.8 percent.)

6 If Baxter Corporation bought $40,000 of the bonds issued by Thayer Company (see Exercise 5) as a long-term investment, what amount of interest revenue was earned in 1975, assuming straight-line amortization was used? Give the journal entry required at December 31, 1975, to amortize the premium.

7 If, in Exercise 5, the bonds were issued at 95, what would the interest expense be for 1975 assuming use of the straight-line method?

8 The Wixon Company, pursuant to provisions of its bond indenture, acquired $20,000 of its outstanding bonds on the open market at 97 plus accrued interest. These bonds were originally issued at face and carry a 6 percent interest rate payable semiannually. The acquisition was made on September 1, and the bonds are dated December 1, 1964. Prepare the entries required to record the acquisition and the accrual of the interest to the acquisition date on the bonds acquired.

9 The K Company is required to make an annual deposit of $40,000 plus accrued interest of $1,200 on April 30, 1976, to the trustee of its sinking fund so that the trustee can redeem $40,000 of the bonds on May 1, 1976. Prepare the entries required on April 30 to record the interest accrual and sinking fund deposit and the entries on May 1 to record the bond retirement, payment of interest, and payment of trustee expenses, assuming the latter amount to be $125. (The bonds were issued at 100.)

10 Equipment is acquired under a long-term lease. The terms of the lease state that $10,000 must be paid on January 1, 1975, and each January 1 thereafter for the next nine years. The equipment has an estimated life of 20 years and no salvage value. Give the following:

a) The entry to record the initial lease payment (use 6 percent as a reasonable rate of discount).

b) The adjusting entries on December 31, 1975, to accrue the interest on the lease and for depreciation on the equipment.

c) The entry required for the second lease payment on January 1, 1976.

11 Dexter Corporation has a funded pension plan and is obligated to pay $32,250 to the Bengston Insurance Company (the outside agent) for the year 1975. It makes the payment on January 15, 1976. Give the entries to accrue the expense on December 31, 1975, and to record the payment on January 15, 1976.

12 Ryberg Corporation has an unfunded pension plan. During 1975 it incurs the obligation to pay future benefits having a present value of $42,536. It also pays $18,400 to retired and disabled employees as pension benefits. Give the entries to record these transactions.

Problems, Series A *chapter* 10

10–1–A

On June 1, 1975, Sullivan Corporation issued $600,000 of 10-year, 8 percent bonds dated April 1, 1975, at 100. Interest on the bonds is payable semiannually upon presentation of the appropriate coupon. All of the bonds are of $1,000 denomination. The company's accounting period ends on June 30, with semiannual statements prepared on December 31 and June 30.

All of the first coupons on each of the bonds are presented to the company's bank and paid by October 2, 1975. All but two of the second coupons on the bonds are similarly received and paid on April 1, 1976.

Required:

a) Present all necessary journal entries for the above transactions, including all adjusting entries needed at June 30, 1975.

b) Shaft Company purchased $300,000 of Sullivan Corporation's bonds on June 1, 1975, as a long-term investment. The company prepares financial statements on September 30. Present all journal entries for Shaft Company relating to the bonds through September 30, 1975.

10–2–A

Preston, Inc., issued $100,000 of 8 percent, 10-year bonds at 98. Interest is payable semiannually. Janson Corporation also issued $100,000 of 8 percent, 10-year bonds, but received a price of 102 for its bonds. These bonds also call for semiannual interest payments. Both bond issues are dated and issued on July 1, 1975.

Required: Prepare journal entries to record the issuance of both bond issues, the interest expense, and the payment of interest for the first semiannual period. Assume both companies have a calendar-year accounting period and that straight-line amortization is acceptable. Which company is actually paying the lower interest rate? Why?

10–3–A

The Flynn Company, on July 1, 1975, issued $100,000 of 10-year, 6 percent bonds dated July 1, 1975, at face value. Bond interest coupons are to be submitted semiannually on July 1 and January 1 for payment. The company is required to deposit with the trustee on each June 30, beginning in 1976, a sum sufficient to enable the trustee to call $10,000 face value of bonds for redemption on July 1 at face value plus accrued interest. The company also has the right to deliver bonds acquired in the open market to the trustee in lieu of making a cash payment. The company's accounting period ends on December 31, and semiannual statements are prepared.

The following transactions were entered into by the Flynn Company:

1976
Jan. 2 Bank reports that it paid all of the semiannual interest coupons.
June 30 Paid the required deposit to trustee.
July 1 Trustee reports $10,000 of bonds acquired at face value as well as payment of accrued interest on these bonds.

3 Bank reports that it paid semiannual interest coupons in the amount of $2,700.

Dec. 31 Paid $75 of trustee's expenses.

1977

Jan. 2 Report from bank shows that it paid all of the outstanding coupons due for payment on January 1, 1977.

June 1 Purchased $10,000 of outstanding bonds in the market at 99½ and delivered them to the trustee in lieu of the cash deposit required on June 30.

Required: Prepare journal entries to record the issuance of the bonds and to record the data in the above transactions, including whatever adjusting entries are needed at December 31, 1975, June 30, 1976, and December 31, 1976.

10–4–A

On December 1, 1975, Mason Company issued $200,000 of 6 percent, 10-year first mortgage bonds for $193,040 cash plus accrued interest. The bonds are dated August 1, 1975, and call for semiannual interest payments on August 1 and February 1.

Gordon Corporation issued $200,000 of 6 percent, 10-year first mortgage bonds on August 1, 1975, for $209,520 cash plus accrued interest. The bonds are dated July 1, 1975, and call for semiannual interest payments on January 1 and July 1.

Required: Assume the accounting period ends for both companies on March 31 and present entries to record the issuance of both bond issues, the first interest payment, and the necessary adjusting entries at March 31, 1976. Straight-line amortization is appropriate.

10–5–A

The Harrison Corporation purchased one-tenth of the bonds of each company in Problem 10–4–A as a long-term investment. Its year-end is also March 31. Present the journal entries to record the acquisition of the bonds, the first interest payment, and any necessary adjusting entries at March 31, 1976.

10–6–A

Following are selected transactions of the Hinson Company, which employs a fiscal-year accounting period ending on June 30:

1975

July 1 Received authorization to issue $200,000 of 6 percent, 10-year bonds dated July 1, 1975. Interest is payable semiannually on January 1 and July 1.

Aug. 1 Issued, for cash, $100,000 of the bonds at 103.57.

1976

Jan. 1 Paid semiannual interest.

Mar. 1 Issued the remaining bonds for $97,760 plus accrued interest since the last interest date.

July 1 Paid semiannual interest on all bonds.

Required: Prepare journal entries to record all of the above transactions including the adjusting entries needed at June 30, 1976. Also present the long-term liability section of the company's June 30, 1976, statement of financial position. Straight-line amortization is acceptable.

10–7–A

On January 1, 1975, Roberts, Inc. issued $200,000 of 7 percent, 20-year bonds dated January 1, 1975, at 106. Interest is payable on January 1 and July 1. The bond indenture provides that the company may retire any or all of the bonds on any interest payment date subsequent to July 1, 1979, at a price equal to 105 percent of face value. On January 1, 1980, Roberts, Inc. redeemed $80,000 of its outstanding bonds. The company's accounting period ends on December 31.

Required: Prepare journal entries to record the issuance of the bonds, the first semiannual interest payment (the company decided on semiannual straight-line amortization of the premium), and the entries necessary on January 1, 1980.

10–8–A

Blakely Company issued $100,000 of 8 percent serial bonds on July 1, 1975, at face value. The bonds are dated July 1, 1975; call for semiannual interest payments on July 1 and January 1; and mature at the rate of $20,000 per year, with the first maturity falling on July 1, 1980. The company's accounting period ends on September 30, with quarterly statements prepared.

Required: Present journal entries to record the interest payment of July 1, 1980; the maturing of $20,000 of bonds on July 1, 1980; and the adjusting entries needed on September 30, 1980. Also, show how the bonds will be presented in the company's statement of financial position for September 30, 1980.

10–9–A

Tilson Company issued $100,000 of 7 percent, 20-year bonds on October 1, 1975. The bonds are dated October 1, 1975, call for semiannual interest payments on October 1 and April 1, and are issued to yield 8 percent (4 percent per period).

Walker Company issued $100,000 of 9 percent, 20-year bonds on October 1, 1975. The bonds are dated October 1, 1975, call for semiannual interest payments on October 1 and April 1, and are issued to yield 8 percent (4 percent per period).

Required:

a) Compute the amount received by each company for the bonds issued. (Use the tables in the appendix).

b) Present entries to record the issuance of the bonds.

c) Present entries to recognize the interest expense and payment for the first six months using the effective interest rate method of allocation of premium or discount to the periods of life in the bonds. Assume a fiscal year accounting period ending May 31.

10–10–A

Maxwell Company bought one-tenth of the Tilson Company's bonds (see Problem 10–9–A) as a long-term investment. Record the journal entries for the acquisition of the bonds; receipt of interest on April 1, 1976; and the adjusting entry required on September 30, 1976, the company's year-end. Use the effective interest rate method for the entries required on April 1 and September 30 for amortizing any premium or accumulating any discount.

10–11–A

The Huntington Corporation entered into a long-term lease agreement in which it agreed to pay $30,000 at the end of each year for 25 years for the use of equipment. (Leases usually require advance payment at the beginning of the year, but this one does not). The terms of the lease clearly indicate that the lease agreement is, in effect, a purchase. The company currently is paying interest at 8 percent on some installment contracts.

Required: Compute the amount at which the equipment is to be recorded. Show the original journal entry recognizing the asset and the liability, and the entry to record the first year's payment.

Problems, Series B *chapter* 10

10–1–B

On December 1, 1975, Huntly Company issued $500,000 of 10-year, 6 percent bonds dated July 1, 1975, at 100. Interest on the bonds is payable semiannually on July 1 and January 1. All of the bonds are registered. The company's accounting period ends on March 31. Quarterly financial statements are prepared.

The company deposits a sum of money sufficient to pay the semiannual interest on the bonds in a special checking account in the First National Bank and draws interest payment checks upon this account. The deposit is made the day before the checks are drawn.

Required:

a) Present journal entries to record the issuance of the bonds; the December 31 adjusting entry; the January 1, 1976, interest payment; and the adjusting entry needed on March 31, 1976.

b) The Cronkite Corporation bought $100,000 of the Huntly Company bonds on December 1, 1975, as a long-term investment. The company's year-end is December 31. Present all journal entries for Cronkite Corporation for these bonds through December 31, 1975.

10–2–B

Meade Corporation issued $100,000 of 6 percent, 10-year bonds at 95. Interest is payable semiannually. Lee Company also issued $100,000 of 6 percent, 10-year bonds, but received a price of 105 for its bonds. These bonds also call for semiannual interest payments. Both bond issues are dated and issued on July 1, 1975.

Required: Prepare journal entries to record the issuance of both bond issues, the interest expense, and the payment of interest for the first semiannual period. Both companies have a fiscal-year accounting period ending on June 30 and straight-line amortization is applicable. (Amortize any premium and accumulate any discount on the interest date.) Which company is actually paying the lower interest rate? Why?

10–3–B

On October 1, 1975, Bernard Corporation issued $200,000 of 10-year, 6 percent debenture bonds at face value. The bonds are registered, and interest is payable semiannually on October 1 and April 1. The company is required by the bond indenture to deposit with the trustee each September 30 an amount sufficient to retire at face value $20,000 of the outstanding debenture bonds plus accrued interest. Such bonds are to be called for redemption on October 1 of each year, beginning in 1976. The company has the right to deliver bonds acquired in the market in lieu of making a cash deposit, with the required deposit reduced by $1,000 plus interest of $30 for each bond so delivered.

The first three interest payments were made according to provisions of the bond indenture, and the first sinking fund deposit was made as scheduled. The trustee reported on October 1, 1976, that the required number of bonds had been called. Trustee expenses of $100 were paid on December 1, 1976.

On August 1, 1977, the company purchased $20,000 of its outstanding bonds in the market at 99¾ plus accrued interest and delivered these to the trustee in lieu of making a cash deposit on September 30, 1977.

Required: Prepare journal entries to record all transactions on the above bonds from October 1, 1975, through August 1, 1977, including the necessary adjusting entries. The company has a calendar-year accounting period and prepares quarterly statements.

10–4–B

King Company issued $200,000 of 6 percent, 10-year first mortgage bonds at 102.36 on September 1, 1975. The bonds are dated July 1, 1975, and call for semiannual interest payments on July 1 and January 1.

Voss Company issued $200,000 of 8 percent, 10-year first mortgage bonds at 96.55 on December 1, 1975. The bonds are dated July 1, 1975, and call for semiannual interest payments on July 1 and January 1.

Required: Assuming that the accounting period ends on March 31 for both companies, present journal entries to record the issuance of the bonds, the payment of the first semiannual interest payment, and the adjusting entries needed on March 31. Use the straight-line method for amortizing the premium and accumulating the discount and do so only at year-end.

10–5–B

Queen Corporation bought $100,000 face value of the bonds of each company in Problem 10–4–B as a long-term investment. Queen's accounting year ends on March 31.

Required: Present all journal entries necessary to record the purchases, interest payments, and any adjusting entries needed through March 31, 1976. Amortize the premium or accumulate the discount only at the accounting year-end.

10–6–B

Following are selected transactions relating to the bonds of the White Company.

1975
July 1 Authorized issue of $200,000 of 6 percent, 10-year bonds dated July 1, 1975, interest payable semiannually on January 1 and July 1.
Sept. 1 Issued $100,000 face value of the bonds at 92.92.
1976
Jan. 1 Paid the semiannual interest.
Feb. 1 Issued the remaining bonds at 102.26.
July 1 Paid semiannual interest.

Required: Present journal entries to record all of the above transactions, including the adjusting entry needed at June 30, 1976, the end of the company's accounting period. Also, present the long-term liability section of the company's June 30, 1976, statement of financial position. Use the straight-line method in accounting for the discount and premium, and amortize any premium or accumulate any discount only at the end of the accounting year.

10–7–B

Howell, Inc. issued $1 million of bonds on January 1, 1975, at 105 percent of their face value. The bonds bear interest at the rate of 6 percent, payable semiannually, and mature on January 1, 1995. The bond indenture provides that the issuing corporation may, on any interest date subsequent to December 31, 1979, redeem all or any part of its outstanding bonds by call by paying a redemption price equal to 105 percent of face value. On January 1, 1980, after due notification as to which bonds are being called, the corporation calls and cancels $400,000 of its outstanding bonds. The company employs a calendar-year accounting period.

Required: Prepare journal entries to record the issuance of the bonds, the accrual of the first six months' interest expense and the payment thereof (also amortize the premium on this date), and the entries necessary on January 1, 1980.

10–8–B

Walden Company issued $200,000 of 6 percent bonds on July 1, 1975, at face value. The bonds are dated July 1, 1975; call for semiannual interest payments on July 1 and January 1; and mature at the rate of $20,000 per year on July 1, beginning in 1980. The company's accounting period ends on September 30.

Required:

a) Present journal entries to record the interest expense and payment for the six months ending July 1, 1980; the maturing of the bonds on July 1, 1980; and the adjusting entries needed on September 30, 1980.
b) Show how the bonds will be presented in the company's statement of financial position for September 30, 1980.

10–9–B

May Company issued $100,000 of 8 percent, 20-year bonds on July 1, 1975. Anderson Company issued $100,000 of 5 percent, 20-year bonds on July 1, 1975.

Both bond issues are dated July 1, 1975, call for semiannual interest payments on July 1 and January 1, and are issued to yield 6 percent (3 percent per period).

Required:

a) Compute the amount received by each company for the bonds issued. (Use the tables in the appendix.)

b) Present entries to record the issuance of the bonds.

c) Using the effective interest rate method, present entries to recognize the interest expense and payment of the interest for the first six months. Assume a fiscal-year accounting period ending December 31.

10–10–B

Larry Corporation purchased one-tenth of the May Company bonds (see Problem 10–9–B) as a long-term investment.

Required: Present the journal entries for the purchase and the interest payment of January 1, and the adjusting entry required on June 30, 1976, the company's year-end. Use the effective interest rate method to amortize any premium or accumulate any discount, and do so at each interest date and at the end of the accounting year.

10–11–B

Ko-Rad Company entered into a lease agreement on January 1, 1975, covering some equipment and calling for payments of $25,000 a year at the beginning of each of the 10 years of the lease. The terms of the lease clearly indicate that it is in effect a purchase of the equipment. The company currently is paying 10 percent for borrowing used to finance asset purchases.

Required: Give the journal entries to record the first lease payment and the signing of the lease on January 1, 1975; the interest accrued for 1975; the depreciation expense for 1975 on the equipment, assuming a 15-year life and no salvage value; and the second lease payment on January 1, 1976.

Single proprietorships; partnerships

Learning objectives

Study of the material presented in this chapter is designed to achieve a number of learning objectives. These include an introductory level comprehension of:

1. The nature of sole proprietorships and partnerships. There is a good likelihood that a high percentage of persons reading this text will at some time be involved as an owner, employee, or auditor of a single proprietorship or partnership. These two forms of business organization are barely mentioned elsewhere in this text.
2. The accounting techniques associated with sole proprietorships and partnerships.
3. The methods of dividing the earnings in a partnership.
4. The differences between the financial statements and the closing processes of these two forms of organization and those of the corporation.
5. How to open the books of a new corporation when a single proprietorship or partnership is transformed into a corporation.

Frame 1[11]

Common types of business organizations

There are three familiar types of business organizations. They are the:

1. Single proprietorship.
2. Partnership.
3. Corporation.

There are more unincorporated businesses (single proprietorships and partnerships) than corporations in the United States, but corporations far outdistance the unincorporated forms as a group in the total dollar volume of output of goods and services.

Single proprietorships and partnerships are quite similar in that they do not issue capital stock, and their existence is not separated from the owners. The difference between these two types is that a single proprietorship is owned by one person, whereas a partnership is an association of two or more persons to carry on a business as co-owners.

A corporation issues capital stock, and the stockholders own the capital stock rather than the assets of the corporation. It has an existence separate from that of its owners and is treated as a separate "being" under the law.

In accounting for these types of business organizations, the major differences are found in the accounts maintained for the owners' equity. This chapter is concerned with accounting for single proprietorships and partnerships. Chapters 12 and 13 deal with accounting for corporate stockholders' equity.

Owners' equity accounts

The owner's equity accounts of a single proprietorship consist of a capital account and a drawing (also called current) account with the owner, as follows:

Henry Childs, Capital
Henry Childs, Drawing

The owners' equity accounts of a partnership consist of a capital account and a drawing account with each partner, as follows:

John Parsons, Capital
John Parsons, Drawing
Peter Carson, Capital
Peter Carson, Drawing

The owners' equity accounts of a corporation consist of at least two accounts: Capital Stock and Retained Earnings.

The procedures for accounting for the owners' capital contributions, earnings and losses, and earnings withdrawals in a single proprietorship, a partnership, and a corporation may be summarized as shown in Illustration 11.1.

Illustration 11.1

SUMMARY OF PROCEDURES FOR ACCOUNTING FOR OWNERS' CAPITAL

	Capital Investment	Earnings and Losses	Withdrawals
Single proprietorship	Credited to proprietor's capital account	Closed to proprietor's drawing account at the end of each year	Debited to proprietor's drawing account
Partnership	Credited to each partner's capital account in accordance with the assets contributed	Closed to the partners' drawing accounts at the end of each year	Debited to each partner's drawing account
Corporation	Credited to Capital Stock account	Closed to Retained Earnings at the end of each year	Debited to Retained Earnings as dividends are declared payable to the stockholders

The equity accounts of which two of the common types of business organization most closely resemble each other?

1. The partnership and the corporation.
2. The single proprietorship and the corporation.
3. The single proprietorship and the partnership.

Now turn to Answer Frame 1[11] on page 492 to check your answer.

Frame 2[11]

Single proprietorships

The characteristics of the capital account and the drawing account of a single proprietorship are set forth below, based on the trial balance shown in Illustration 11.2.

The inventory for Peter Clark's business at December 31, 1976, was $10,200. When the trial balance was taken at December 31, 1976, the capital and drawing accounts of Clark were as follows:

Peter Clark, Capital

Date		Explanation	Folio	Debit	Credit	Balance
1976						
Jan.	2	Cash investment			17,000	17,000
July	8	Additional investment			9,000	26,000

Answer frame 1[11]

The third response is the correct one. Not only are the equity account titles of the single proprietorship and the partnership identical, but both the single proprietorship and the partnership accounts contain a capital and a drawing account for each contributor of capital, whereas the Capital Stock account and the Retained Earnings account in the corporate ledger do not separate the capital balances and withdrawals (dividends) of each individual owner.

If you answered incorrectly, reread Frame 1[11] before beginning Frame 2[11] on page 491.

2[11]

continued

Peter Clark, Drawing

Date		Explanation	Folio	Debit	Credit	Balance
1976						
Mar.	8	Cash		1,400		1,400
June	17	Cash		1,800		3,200
Sept.	9	Cash		1,600		4,800
Dec.	16	Cash		3,200		8,000

End of period entries

The ending inventory is set up and the expense and revenue accounts are closed to the Expense and Revenue Summary account exactly as they are for a corporation. The Expense and Revenue Summary account then appears as follows:

Expense and Revenue Summary

Date		Explanation	Folio	Debit	Credit	Balance
1976						
Dec.	31	Net sales			106,000	106,000
	31	Expenses		92,400		13,600

Illustration 11.2

PETER CLARK
Trial Balance, December 31, 1976

	Debits	*Credits*
Cash	$ 16,400	
Accounts receivable	22,000	
Accounts payable		$ 17,000
Peter Clark, capital		26,000
Peter Clark, drawing	8,000	
Sales		108,000
Sales returns	2,000	
Purchases	78,000	
Rent expense	3,600	
Delivery expense	4,800	
Store expense	16,200	
	$151,000	$151,000

The balance of the Expense and Revenue Summary account—$13,600—representing the net earnings for the year, is now closed to the Peter Clark Drawing account:

Expense and Revenue Summary	13,600	
Peter Clark, Drawing		13,600

Finally, the balance of the drawing account is closed to the capital account:

Peter Clark, Drawing	5,600	
Peter Clark, Capital		5,600

In making the entries to determine the cost of goods sold and to close the revenue and expense accounts of a single proprietorship (indicate whether each is correct or incorrect):

1. The owner's drawing account is used in place of an Expense and Revenue Summary account.
2. The owner's capital account is used in place of the Expense and Revenue Summary account.
3. The revenue and expense accounts are closed directly to the Retained Earnings account.
4. The entries are identical to those prepared for a firm doing business in the corporate form.

Now turn to Answer Frame 2[11] on page 494 to check your answers.

Frame 3[11]

To continue the Peter Clark illustration, assume that after closing the net earnings to the drawing account and after closing the drawing account to the capital account, the two accounts appear as follows:

Peter Clark, Capital

Date		Explanation	Folio	Debit	Credit	Balance
1976						
Jan.	2	Cash investment			17,000	17,000
July	8	Additional investment			9,000	26,000
Dec.	31	Balance of drawing account			5,600	31,600

Answer frame 2[11]

1. Incorrect. The owner's drawing account does enter into the closing process, but the revenue and expense accounts are not closed directly to this account.
2. Incorrect. The revenue and expense accounts are not closed directly to the owner's capital account.
3. Incorrect. There is no account with the title Retained Earnings in the books of a single proprietorship.
4. Correct. The process of closing the revenue and expense accounts is not changed by the type of business organization. The difference lies in the closing of the Expense and Revenue Summary account.

If you missed any of the above, reread Frame 2[11] before turning to Frame 3[11] on page 493.

3[11]
continued

Peter Clark, Drawing

Date		Explanation	Folio	Debit	Credit	Balance
1976						
Mar.	8	Cash		1,400		1,400
June	17	Cash		1,800		3,200
Sept.	9	Cash		1,600		4,800
Dec.	16	Cash		3,200		8,000
	31	Net earnings			13,600	5,600 Cr.
	31	To capital account		5,600		—0—

Financial statements were prepared for the single proprietorship of Peter Clark on December 31, 1976. These statements reflect the information shown in the capital and drawing accounts illustrated above. Which of the following do you think is the correct presentation of the proprietor's equity section of the statement of financial position?

1. *Proprietor's Equity:*

Peter Clark, Capital	$26,000	
Less: Peter Clark, Drawing	8,000	
Net Proprietor's Equity		$18,000

2. *Proprietor's Equity:*

Peter Clark, Capital	$26,000	
Plus 1976 Net Earnings	13,600	
Total Proprietor's Equity		$39,600

3. *Proprietor's Equity:*

Peter Clark, Capital	$31,600	
Peter Clark, Drawing	13,600	
Total Proprietor's Equity		$45,200

4. *Proprietor's Equity:*

Peter Clark, Capital		$31,600

5. *Proprietor's Equity:*

Peter Clark, Capital	$26,000	
Plus 1976 Net Earnings	5,600	
Total Proprietor's Equity		$31,600

Now check your answer by turning to Answer Frame 3[11] on page 496.

Frame 4[11]

Financial statements for a single proprietorship

The proprietor's equity section of Peter Clark's statement of financial position, dated December 31, 1976, is shown in Illustration 11.3. As the

Illustration 11.3

PETER CLARK — *Exhibit A*
Statement of Financial Position
December 31, 1976

ASSETS		LIABILITIES AND PROPRIETOR'S EQUITY	
Current Assets:		Current Liabilities:	
Cash	$16,400	Accounts payable	$17,000
Accounts receivable	22,000	Proprietor's Equity:	
Merchandise inventory	10,200	Peter Clark, capital—Exhibit C	31,600
		Total Liabilities and	
Total Assets	$48,600	Proprietor's Equity	$48,600

illustration shows, the statement of financial position of a single proprietorship differs from that of a partnership or corporation only in the owner's equity section.

The earnings statement of a single proprietorship (Illustration 11.4) is similar to that of any other type of business organization.

Illustration 11.4

PETER CLARK — *Exhibit B*
Earnings Statement
For the Year Ended December 31, 1976

Gross sales		$108,000
Less: Sales returns		2,000
Net Sales		$106,000
Cost of goods sold		
Purchases	$78,000	
Deduct: Merchandise inventory, December 31, 1976	10,200	
Cost of goods sold		67,800
Gross margin		$ 38,200
Deduct: Operating expenses:		
Rent expense	$ 3,600	
Delivery expense	4,800	
Store expense	16,200	24,600
Net Earnings		$ 13,600

But a new statement is also presented—the statement of proprietor's capital, which is prepared from the capital and drawing accounts. The statement shows the annual change in proprietor's equity and the causes of the change. See Illustration 11.5.

Answer frame 3[11]

Answer 4 is the correct one. Net earnings were closed to the drawing account and the drawing account in turn was closed to the capital account. Thus, the only proprietor's equity account with an open balance on December 31, 1976, the end of the accounting period, is Peter Clark's capital account.

If you answered incorrectly, reread Frame 3[11] before beginning Frame 4[11] on page 495.

4[11]
continued

Illustration 11.5

PETER CLARK *Statement of Proprietor's Capital* *For the Year Ended December 31, 1976*		*Exhibit C*
Investment, January 2, 1976		$17,000
Add: Additional investment	$ 9,000	
Net Earnings, 1976—Exhibit B	13,600	22,600
		$39,600
Deduct: Withdrawals, 1976		8,000
Capital Balance, December 31, 1976		$31,600

The withdrawals of cash or other assets made by the owner of a business operated as a single proprietorship are:

1. Shown on the earnings statement as a part of salary expense.
2. Viewed as withdrawals of earnings or capital and are not deductible expenses in the computation of the net earnings of the business.

Check Answer Frame 4[11] on page 498 to see if you selected the correct response.

Frame 5[11]

Advantages and disadvantages of a single proprietorship

The advantages of a single proprietorship include:

1. Ease of establishing the business. All that is required is the necessary capital. No legal contracts need be signed or provisions of certain laws adhered to as in the case of corporations.
2. No division of authority or of earnings. Both belong solely to the owner.
3. No separate taxation of the earnings of the business or of the withdrawals. All earnings are taxable to the owner whether he withdraws them or not.

The more important of the disadvantages of a single proprietorship include:

1. Unlimited liability. If business assets will not pay the debts of the business, the owner's personal assets will have to be used to pay them.

2. Limited capital. Only limited amounts of capital can usually be raised by one person.
3. Limited skills. Only limited skills are usually found in one person, while many are needed to operate a business successfully. Of course, the owner may be able to hire these skills.
4. Limited transferability. It may be more difficult to find a ready buyer for a single proprietorship than it would be for shares of stock in a corporation.

Partnerships

The Uniform Partnership Act defines a partnership as "an association of two or more persons to carry on as co-owners a business for profit."

The association of two or more persons should be effected by a written contract known as the *articles of copartnership*. Any natural person who possesses the right to enter into a contract may become a partner. Unless otherwise specified in the partnership contract, each partner has one vote in the management.

A partner is an agent (one who has the authority to act for another) of the partnership; as such, he has the power to bind the remaining partners. Therefore, it is the responsibility of each partner to act in the interest of the partnership and not in his personal interest in all matters pertaining to the partnership.

Partnerships are formed when (1) business capital requirements exceed the amount that may be raised by a single proprietor, or (2) a single proprietor desires to obtain the talents and services of other persons who will also share in the risks or rewards of the business, or (3) it is the desire of a single proprietor to offer inducement to an employee to stay with the business by making him a partner.

A business organization of the partnership type usually is relatively small (compared with most corporations) as measured by sales, capital, or earnings and is used where the capital contributions of a few persons are sufficient for the needs of the business. Partnerships also exist in the professional field—accounting, law, and medicine—where there is a personal responsibility between the firm and the client and where, because of this personal responsibility, the laws of the state may prohibit incorporation by those engaged in such professions. The limited liability feature of the corporation is often deemed to be contrary to public policy in these professional fields. Hence, a partnership type of organization is frequently employed.

A partnership commonly is known as a firm. But many partnerships end their names with the word "company," used in the sense of "associates." For example, James Hardin and Company could be the name of a partnership of certified public accountants.

Determine whether each of the following is true or false.

1. Partnerships are often formed when the capital required by a business is greater than can be raised by one individual but small enough to be provided by a few individuals.

Answer frame 4^{11}

The second response is correct. The owner of a business operated as a single proprietorship obtains the earnings of that business, not a salary. Only payments for services of others are deductible as salary or wage expense in arriving at the net earnings of the business. Therefore, the withdrawals are shown in the statement of proprietor's capital and not in the earnings statement.

If you answered incorrectly, reread Frame 4^{11} before beginning Frame 5^{11} on page 496.

5^{11} *continued*

2. Unless otherwise specified in the partnership agreement, each partner's vote in the managment of the firm is in relation to the amount of capital he has contributed to the firm.
3. Each partner is an agent of the partnership, and therefore a contract entered into by one in the name of the partnership is binding upon the other partners.
4. The unlimited liability feature of the partnership form of organization is one of the features which distinguishes it from the corporate form of doing business.
5. An individual must contribute capital to become a partner in a firm.

Now turn to Answer Frame 5^{11} on page 500 to check your answers.

Frame 6^{11}

Advantages of a partnership

The status of the partnership form of business organization is sufficiently flexible to permit reasonable accumulation of capital and talent, and a partnership is not required to observe as many formalities as a corporation. In general, the legal restrictions imposed on a partnership are not greater than those imposed on individuals.

Disadvantages of a partnership

Perhaps the greatest disadvantage of the partnership form of organization lies in the fact that *each* partner may be held liable for *all* the debts of the partnership. In general, a stockholder of a corporation is not liable for the payment of the debts of a corporation; his loss cannot exceed the price paid for his capital stock. Also, any one partner may bind the partnership by making contracts in the ordinary course of business; therefore, a partner not exercising good judgment can cause the loss of the assets of the firm and also of the personal wealth of the remaining partners. If one partner personally pays all of the legal debts of the firm, he has a right of action against the remaining partners. The only personal assets of a partner exempt from the claims of creditors of the partnership are those specifically exempt under the bankruptcy laws.

The unlimited liability feature frequently stands in the path of securing adequate capital by discouraging those who possess large private resources from investing in a partnership.

As a functioning organization, the partnership becomes unwieldy when the number of partners becomes large. A partnership is subject, at any time, to momentary discontinuance through the death, adjudged incapacity, or retirement of one of the partners.

Because partners are co-owners of the net assets of a partnership, the transfer of the capital investment of one partner, by sale or otherwise, to another person (either another partner or an outside person) may be difficult to accomplish. If one partner desires to sell his investment in a partnership, either (1) a new partner must be obtained, with the consent of the remaining partners, or (2) the remaining partners may purchase the investment of the partner who wishes to withdraw, assuming that the latter is willing to sell his share to the remaining partners.

Suppose that you are thinking of going into business and have an opportunity to join a partnership. Your prospective partner makes the following statements to you. Determine whether each is correct or incorrect.

1. As a member of a partnership, you will pay income taxes on your full share of the partnership net earnings for the year even though you do not withdraw an amount equal to your share of the earnings.
2. The loss an owner of corporate stock may suffer if the business fails is limited to the price he paid for the stock, but a partner runs the risk of losing far more than the capital he has contributed to the partnership.
3. It is just as easy to sell and transfer all or a part of your interest in the partnership to a willing buyer as it is to sell your interest in General Motors Corporation.
4. None of the partner's personal assets is exempt from the claims of creditors of the partnership in case the partnership defaults on its debts.

Now turn to Answer Frame 6^{11} on page 500 to check your answers.

Frame 7^{11}

Rights and duties of partners

The Uniform Partnership Act contains provisions relating to a partner's rights in specific partnership property, interest in the partnership, and right to participate in the management.

Specific partnership property. Specific partnership property—such as buildings and merchandise—is usually held by the partners as co-owners.

Answer frame 5[11]

1. True. This is a typical situation for the formation of a partnership.
2. False. Unless the partnership agreement specifically states otherwise, all partners have an equal voice in management.
3. True. This is why one has to be very careful in selecting partners with whom to go into business.
4. True. There is a risk of losing one's personal assets as well as business assets when one is in a business organized as a partnership.
5. False. An individual may become a partner in a firm without contributing capital if the other partners consider his talents and services crucial enough to the success of the firm.

If you missed any of the above, reread Frame 5[11] before turning to Frame 6[11] on page 498.

Answer frame 6[11]

1. Correct. The earnings of the partnership "flow through" to the partners and each pays income taxes on his share of earnings whether it has been distributed to him or not.
2. Correct. Each partner is liable for all the debts of the partnership. If partnership assets are not adequate to cover these, the partners' personal assets may have to be used to cover these debts.
3. Incorrect. A stockholder may sell all or part of his interest in a corporation to any willing buyer of his shares of stock. Transfer of ownership of the stock does not affect the life of the corporation or the liability of the other stockholders. A partnership, however, does not possess the characteristic of continuity which attaches to the corporate form of organization. A partnership is a personal relationship entered into by contract between the partners. Each partner is personally liable for all debts of the partnership. It is not surprising, therefore, to find the remaining partners are guaranteed by law the right to refuse acceptance as a partner to a purchaser of any one partner's investment in the partnership. When acceptance as a partner is refused, the purchaser only acquires the right to the share of earnings to which the partner would have been entitled and the right to effect a dissolution and liquidation.
4. Incorrect. Assets which are specifically exempt under the bankruptcy laws cannot be taken over by the creditors of the partnership. Generally speaking, the purpose of these laws is to avoid having a person stripped of all his possessions and thrown out in the street.

If you missed any of the above, restudy Frame 6[11] before turning to Frame 7[11] on page 499.

7[11]
continued

Under the partnership form of organization and subject to any specific agreement between the partners, the right of each partner to possess partnership property for partnership purposes is equal to the right of each of the other partners. Only by the consent of the other partners does one partner have any right to possess partnership property for other than partnership purposes. A partner cannot assign (transfer rights in ownership to another party) his proportionate interest in partnership property unless the other partners also assign; this is because no partner owns a particular part of the specific partnership assets. By the same reasoning, a partner's proportionate interest in the specific assets of the firm is not subject to attachment (confiscation by legal process). The partner does, however, have an interest in the firm as a whole, and this interest may be sold by the partner or acquired by his creditors through court action.

If a partner dies, his right in specific property rests in the surviving partners; but the surviving partners possess the partnership property for firm usage only. The surviving partners are liable to the estate of the deceased partner for the value of his right.

Interest in the partnership. The interest in the partnership refers to each partner's share of the earnings and share of the capital. The rights to share earnings and capital are personal property under the provisions of the Uniform Partnership Act.

The right to participate in management. Unless stated otherwise in the partnership agreement, each partner possesses an equal vote in the management of a partnership regardless of the amount of his capital in comparison with the capital of other partners. In matters of routine business, the voice of the majority of the partners governs. In addition to this specific right in management, the following implied rights are listed:

1. A partner has the right to inspect the accounting records of the firm.
2. If, in conducting partnership business, a partner makes advances for the benefit of the partnership, he is entitled to reimbursement.
3. The essential nature of the business can be changed only by the consent of all partners.
4. New partners may be admitted only upon the consent of all partners.
5. If a firm suffers losses through the negligence of a partner, the other partners possess the right of indemnity against the partner at fault.

As a member of a partnership, each partner is guaranteed certain rights. Which of the following rights is *not* held by a partner under the Uniform Partnership Act?

1. The right to inspect the accounting records of the firm.
2. The right to reimbursement for advances made by him in the course of partnership business.
3. The right to approve the admission of a new partner.
4. The right to assign his proportionate interest in specific partnership assets.
5. The right to possess partnership property for partnership purposes.

Now check with Answer Frame 7[11] on page 502.

Frame 8[11]

The partnership agreement

The partnership agreement or contract, known as the articles of copartnership, is the basis for the formation and operation of the partnership. The agreement should be in writing in order to avoid misunderstanding

Answer frame 7[11]

Only number 4 is not a right held by a partner under the Uniform Partnership Act. Partnership property is held by the partners as co-owners. Unless a specific agreement is entered into between the partners, no partner has a claim to any specific partnership asset or to any portion of any one asset, nor can he assign his proportionate interest in any partnership asset. A partner can assign his share of the earnings, but this is far different from the right to assign his interest in a specific asset.

If you answered incorrectly, reread Frame 7[11] before turning to Frame 8[11] on page 501.

8[11] *continued*

and consequent disagreement. Among other points, the partnership contract should contain the following:

1. The names of the partners and the partnership and the business location.
2. The nature of the business.
3. The effective date of the contract.
4. The types of partners—general, limited, silent, secret.
5. The capital contribution of each partner.
6. The duties of each partner.
7. The duration of the partnership.
8. The manner in which dissolution is to be effected.
9. The rights of the partners in the event of dissolution.
10. The location of the records and the manner of dividing the earnings and losses between the partners.
11. The salaries of the partners, if any.
12. The drawings allowed each partner.
13. Provisions for interest on drawings.
14. Interest credits on capital account balances.
15. The manner of arbitrating disputed questions.
16. Insurance provisions on the life of each partner.
17. The annual date of closing the financial records.
18. Restrictions on other work.

When a partnership agreement is prepared, it is difficult to anticipate all future events. If a point arises that is not covered by the contract, the provisions of the Uniform Partnership Act govern in those states which have adopted this act. Otherwise the common law governs.

To constitute a binding contract, the articles of copartnership must possess those qualities that make any contract valid, namely:

1. The object of its establishment must be legal.
2. The partners must possess the capacity to contract.
3. The contract must not have been made under fraud or duress.
4. There must be a meeting of the minds of the contracting parties.
5. There must be consideration, that is, something of value exchanged.

Assume that three men—Zilch, Zachary, and Scott—are partners. A dispute arises about something which is not covered in their articles of copartnership. The partnership agreement also does not set forth a manner of arbitrating disputed questions. Which of the following will occur?

1. The partnership contract becomes void and the partnership ceases to exist.

2. The common law governs the solution of the dispute.
3. In those states which have adopted the Uniform Partnership Act, it takes priority in providing the solution to partnership disputes. Otherwise the common law governs.
4. No law applies. The partners will have to come to some agreement as best they can and may then amend their partnership agreement to take care of this type of situation in case it should arise in the future.

Now check your answer in Answer Frame 8[11] on page 504.

Frame 9[11]

Unique features in partnership accounting

The need for adequate accounting records is greater in a partnership than in a single proprietorship because of the division of interests that exists and because of the complications that arise in the treatment of such matters as partners' drawings and the division of earnings.

Regardless of the form of business organization, the principles or concepts of accounting are the same; only the application of accounting principles varies among the different types of business organizations—the single proprietorship, the partnership, and the corporation. Where there are two or more proprietors of a business, the provisions of their contract must be carefully interpreted.

The partners' capital accounts. A capital account is maintained for each partner. The total in the partner's capital account after closing represents the partner's equity. Each partner's capital account is:

1. Credited with the original investment.
2. Credited with subsequent investments.
3. Debited with permanent capital reductions.
4. Debited or credited with the balance of his drawing account at the end of each fiscal period.

To illustrate the use of the capital accounts for original and subsequent investments, assume that James Law and Todd Hart, who have been in business as single proprietors, form a partnership. The formation of the partnership represents a new entity. As a matter of equity, the assets contributed by each partner are recorded at their current market values at the time they are contributed (usually the date when the partnership is formed). The contributions, so valued, of each partner to the partnership are listed below:

Law		*Hart*	
Cash	$ 5,600	Cash	$ 6,600
Accounts receivable	6,800	Merchandise	3,400
Merchandise	12,000	Land	8,000
Delivery equipment	3,000	Building	20,000
Accounts payable	(3,200)	Accounts payable	(2,200)

Answer frame 8[11]

The third response is the correct one. But you should recognize that good business judgment dictates that the partnership agreement be carefully prepared and put into writing so that all parties concerned are fully aware of their respective rights and responsibilities. Under these conditions, it is to be hoped that resort to the statutory or common law to resolve differences will be infrequent.

If you answered incorrectly, reread Frame 8[11] before turning to Frame 9[11] on page 503.

9[11]
continued

The journal entries on January 1, 1975, to record the investment of each partner are as follows:

Cash	5,600	
Accounts Receivable	6,800	
Merchandise Inventory	12,000	
Delivery Equipment	3,000	
Accounts Payable		3,200
James Law, Capital		24,200
To record the investment of Law in the partnership of Law and Hart.		
Cash	6,600	
Merchandise Inventory	3,400	
Land	8,000	
Building	20,000	
Accounts Payable		2,200
Todd Hart, Capital		35,800
To record the investment of Hart in the partnership of Law and Hart.		

If additional investments are made at a later date, they also are credited to the capital accounts. Assume that on August 1, 1975, additional investments are made as indicated by the following journal entry:

Cash	5,800	
James Law, Capital		2,400
Todd Hart, Capital		2,400
To record additional cash investments.		

On December 31, 1975, before closing the books, the capital accounts of the partners will appear as follows:

James Law, Capital

Date		Explanation	Folio	Debit	Credit	Balance
1975						
Jan.	1	Original investment			24,200	24,200
Aug.	1	Additional cash investment			2,400	26,600

Todd Hart, Capital

Date		Explanation	Folio	Debit	Credit	Balance
1975						
Jan.	1	Original investment			35,800	35,800
Aug.	1	Additional cash investment			2,400	38,200

The drawing account. During an accounting period, partners may withdraw cash or merchandise for their personal use. The partnership agreement should specify whether withdrawals of merchandise should be priced at cost or at selling price. These withdrawals are charged to the drawing account of each partner and credited either to Purchases (if priced at cost) or Sales (if priced at selling price). The drawings are made against earnings that presumably have been earned during the fiscal period but have not yet been closed to the drawing account. When the Expense and Revenue Summary account is closed at the end of the fiscal period, each partner's share of the earnings is credited to his drawing account. If earnings exceed withdrawals, there will be a credit balance in the drawing account. This balance is then closed to the partner's capital account.

As a rule, a partner cannot withdraw any part of his original investment without the consent of all the other partners. Whether or not he can draw against subsequent additions to his capital depends upon the partnership agreement. Drawings definitely identified as withdrawals of investments should be debited directly to the capital account.

To illustrate drawing accounts, assume that Law and Hart have made withdrawals as indicated below:

James Law, Drawing

Date		Explanation	Folio	Debit	Credit	Balance
1975						
Feb.	7	Cash		1,600		1,600
Apr.	8	Cash		1,700		3,300
July	31	Cash		1,750		5,050
Dec.	1	Cash		1,650		6,700

Todd Hart, Drawing

Date		Explanation	Folio	Debit	Credit	Balance
1975						
Mar.	1	Cash		1,900		1,900
June	7	Cash		1,700		3,600
Sept.	18	Cash		2,000		5,600
Dec.	4	Cash		1,600		7,200

To test your understanding of the material just covered, assume the following data. On June 1, 1975, John Tall and David Short, each of whom has been in business as a single proprietor, decide to form a partnership. The contributions of each partner are listed below at both the book values of the assets on the respective proprietorship books and their market values on June 1, 1975.

	J. Tall		*D. Short*	
	Book Values	*Market Values*	*Book Values*	*Market Values*
Cash	$ 4,000	$ 4,000	$ 2,000	$ 2,000
Accounts receivable	3,000	3,000	6,000	6,000
Merchandise	10,000	11,000	9,000	9,000
Office equipment (net)	5,000	8,000	1,000	800
Land	—	—	10,000	12,000
Building	—	—	20,000	25,000
Total	$22,000	$26,000	$48,000	$54,800

On September 15 the partners invest additional cash in the business: Tall, $3,700; Short, $2,100. During 1975 the partners make withdrawals as follows:

Tall			*Short*		
July 31	Cash	$ 800	June 27	Merchandise	$ 100
Aug. 15	Merchandise	300	Aug. 30	Cash	900
Nov. 30	Cash	700	Oct. 31	Cash	1,000
			Dec. 10	Merchandise	400
	Total	$1,800		Total	$2,400

Which one of the following statements is correct?

1. The original contributions should be credited to the capital accounts at market value, withdrawals should be debited to the capital accounts, and additional investments should be credited to the capital accounts.
2. Statement 1 is correct except that withdrawals should be debited to the drawing accounts rather than the capital accounts.
3. The original contributions should be credited to the capital accounts at the proprietor's book value, withdrawals should be debited to the drawing accounts, and additional investments should be credited to the capital accounts.
4. Statement 3 is correct except that the additional investments should be credited to the drawing accounts.
5. The original contributions should be credited to the capital accounts at market value, withdrawals of cash should be debited to the drawings accounts, withdrawals of merchandise should be debited to the capital accounts, and additional investments should be credited to the capital accounts.

Check your answer with Answer Frame 9[11] on page 508.

Frame 10[11]

End of period entries

At the end of the fiscal period, all adjusting journal entries are made and the expense and revenue accounts are closed to the Expense and Revenue Summary account in the customary manner. This account in turn is closed to the drawing accounts of the partners, and the drawing accounts are closed to the capital accounts, provided this method does not violate the partnership agreement.

To illustrate, assume that the net earnings of the partnership of Law and Hart for the year ended December 31, 1975, are $30,000 and that the partners divide the earnings equally. The journal entry to close the net earnings to the drawing accounts is:

Expense and Revenue Summary	30,000	
James Law, Drawing		15,000
Todd Hart, Drawing		15,000
To close the net earnings to the drawing accounts.		

Each partner's share of the net earnings may be carried directly to his capital account, but the preferred practice is to credit the net earnings of each partner to his drawing account, where it offsets the withdrawals. The latter practice causes drawings to appear to be made against current earnings, and the capital accounts are relieved of unnecessary detail.

The next step is to close the balance of the drawing accounts to the capital accounts by the following journal entries:

James Law, Drawing	8,300	
James Law, Capital		8,300
To close the December 31, 1975, drawing account balance.		
Todd Hart, Drawing	7,800	
Todd Hart, Capital		7,800
To close the December 31, 1975, drawing account balance.		

After the entries are posted, the drawing accounts and the capital accounts of Law and Hart appear as follows:

James Law, Drawing

Date		Explanation	Folio	Debit	Credit	Balance
1975						
Feb.	7	Cash		1,600		1,600
Apr.	8	Cash		1,700		3,300
July	31	Cash		1,750		5,050
Dec.	1	Cash		1,650		6,700
	31	Net earnings			15,000	8,300 Cr.
	31	To capital		8,300		—0—

Answer frame 9[11]

Statement number 2 is correct. All capital investments made by the partners should be credited to their capital accounts, and all withdrawals of merchandise and cash should be charged to the drawing accounts. The partners' capital accounts are credited at the current market value of the assets contributed to the partnership. The value of the contributions of each of the partners must be measured in terms of what the owner could receive if he chose to sell the assets and invest the cash. The dollar amounts at which these items were recorded in another set of books (such as the proprietorship books) are irrelevant.

If you answered incorrectly, reread Frame 9[11] before turning to Frame 10[11] on page 507.

10[11]
continued

James Law, Capital

Date		Explanation	Folio	Debit	Credit	Balance
1975						
Jan.	1	Original investment			24,200	24,200
Aug.	1	Additional cash investment			2,400	26,600
Dec.	31	From drawing			8,300	34,900

Todd Hart, Drawing

Date		Explanation	Folio	Debit	Credit	Balance
1975						
Mar.	1	Cash		1,900		1,900
June	7	Cash		1,700		3,600
Sept.	18	Cash		2,000		5,600
Dec.	4	Cash		1,600		7,200
	31	Net earnings			15,000	7,800 Cr.
	31	To capital		7,800		—0—

Todd Hart, Capital

Date		Explanation	Folio	Debit	Credit	Balance
1975						
Jan.	1	Original investment			35,800	35,800
Aug.	1	Additional cash investment			3,400	39,200
Dec.	31	From drawing			7,800	47,000

To test your understanding, assume that on December 31, 1975 the balances in the capital and drawing accounts of Andrews and Scott, a partnership, before closing are:

Arthur Andrews, capital	$50,000
Arthur Andrews, drawing	8,000 Dr.
Paul Scott, capital	20,000
Paul Scott, drawing	6,000 Dr.

Partnership net earnings for the year are $14,000. The partners share earnings and losses equally. Given this situation, which of the following sets of closing entries is the appropriate one?

1.	Expense and Revenue Summary	14,000	
	Arthur Andrews, Drawing		7,000
	Paul Scott, Drawing		7,000
	Arthur Andrews, Capital	1,000	
	Arthur Andrews, Drawing		1,000
	Paul Scott, Drawing	1,000	
	Paul Scott, Capital		1,000
2.	Expense and Revenue Summary	14,000	
	Arthur Andrews, Drawing		8,000
	Paul Scott, Drawing		6,000
3.	Expense and Revenue Summary	14,000	
	Arthur Andrews, Capital		7,000
	Paul Scott, Capital		7,000
	Arthur Andrews, Capital	8,000	
	Arthur Andrews, Drawing		8,000
	Paul Scott, Capital	6,000	
	Paul Scott, Drawing		6,000
4.	Arthur Andrews, Drawing	7,000	
	Paul Scott, Drawing	7,000	
	Expense and Revenue Summary		14,000
	Arthur Andrews, Drawing	1,000	
	Arthur Andrews, Capital		1,000
	Paul Scott, Drawing	1,000	
	Paul Scott, Capital		1,000

Now turn to Answer Frame 10[11] on page 510 to check your answer.

Frame 11[11]

Financial statements of a partnership

Partnership earnings statement. The earnings statement of a partnership is the same in form as that for any other type of organization engaged in a similar business. It is advisable to append a section to the earnings statement showing the division of the net earnings between the partners. This is illustrated in the earnings statement for the firm of Law and Hart for the year ended December 31, 1975 (see Illustration 11.6).

Partnership statement of financial position. The only distinctive feature of a statement of financial position for a partnership lies in the

Answer frame 10[11]

The first answer is the correct one. Although the same net result can be obtained by other procedures, the preferred way to handle the closing of the Expense and Revenue Summary account is through the drawing accounts. The entry to close Andrews' drawing account requires a debit to his capital account and a credit to his drawing account because his withdrawals of $8,000 during 1975 exceeded his share of the net earnings, resulting in a net decrease in his capital investment.

If you answered incorrectly, reread Frame 10[11] before starting Frame 11[11] on page 509.

11[11]
continued

Illustration 11.6

LAW AND HART
Earnings Statement
For the Year Ended December 31, 1975

Sales			$220,000
Less: Sales discounts			1,000
Net sales			$219,000
Cost of goods sold			
Inventory, January 1, 1975		$ 15,400	
Purchases	$147,000		
Less: Purchase discounts	1,000	146,000	
Cost of goods available for sale		$161,400	
Inventory, December 31, 1975		32,400	
Cost of goods sold			129,000
Margin on sales			$ 90,000
Deduct: Operating expenses:			
Selling expenses		$ 36,000	
Administrative expenses		24,000	
Total Operating Expenses			60,000
Net Earnings			$ 30,000

Distribution of Net Earnings

James Law, 50 percent	$15,000
Todd Hart, 50 percent	15,000
Total Net Earnings	$30,000

presentation of the capital accounts in the owners' equity section. This feature is shown in the statement of financial position for the partnership of Law and Hart at December 31, 1975. (See Illustration 11.7, page 511.)

Statement of partners' capital. At the close of each fiscal period, a statement of the capital accounts of the partners is prepared. This statement is a summary of the transactions affecting the capital of each partner and in total for all partners; it is obtained from the capital accounts in the general ledger. It starts with the capital account balance at the beginning of the year and ends with the capital account balance at the end of the same year. This statement is presented in Illustration 11.8.

It can be seen that the financial statements for a partnership are very similar in form to the financial statements for a single proprietorship.

Illustration 11.7

LAW AND HART
Statement of Financial Position
December 31, 1975
ASSETS

Current Assets:			
Cash		$17,800	
Accounts receivable		20,000	
Merchandise inventory		32,400	
Total Current Assets			$ 70,200
Property, Plant, and Equipment:			
Land		$ 8,000	
Delivery equipment	$ 3,000		
Less: Allowance for depreciation	600	2,400	
Building	$20,000		
Less: Allowance for depreciation	600	19,400	
Total Property, Plant, and Equipment			29,800
Total Assets			$100,000

LIABILITIES AND PARTNER'S EQUITY

Current Liabilities:		
Accounts payable		$ 18,100
Partners' Equity:		
Law, capital	$34,900	
Hart, capital	47,000	
Total Partners' Equity		81,900
Total Liabilities and Partners' Equity		$100,000

Illustration 11.8

LAW AND HART
Statement of Partners' Capital
For the Year Ended December 31, 1975

	Law	*Hart*	*Total*
Investment, January 1, 1975	$24,200	$35,800	$60,000
Investment, August 1, 1975	2,400	3,400	5,800
	$26,600	$39,200	$65,800
Add: Net earnings per earnings statement	$15,000	$15,000	$30,000
Less: Drawings	6,700	7,200	13,900
	$ 8,300	$ 7,800	$16,100
Capital Account Balances, December 31, 1975	$34,900	$47,000	$81,900

The changes in each partner's investment as well as the changes in the total capital investment are summarized in which of the following statements?

1. Earnings statement.
2. Statement of financial position.
3. Statement of partners' capital.

Now turn to Answer Frame 11[11] on page 512 to check your answer.

Answer frame 11[11]

Answer 3 is correct. The statement of partners' capital analyzes the changes in the partners' capital accounts and acts as a link between the earnings statement and the statement of financial position. It does so by using the net earnings and net earnings distribution amounts from the earnings statement in arriving at the new capital account balances shown in the statement of financial position.

If you answered incorrectly, reread Frame 11[11] before starting Frame 12[11] below.

Frame 12[11]

Division of partnership earnings

The ratio in which partnership earnings and losses are divided is known as the *earnings and loss ratio,* or, as it is frequently called, the profit and loss ratio. The earnings and losses are divided in accordance with the provisions of the partnership contract. If the contract is silent with respect to the division of earnings and losses, the law assumes an equal division for all partners; this is true even if there is inequality in investments, ability, time devoted to the business, or risks assumed.

If each of the partners invests an equal amount of assets, has approximately equal ability, devotes the same amount of time to the business, and incurs the same risks, the earnings and losses probably should be divided equally. If variations in the foregoing factors exist between partners, the partner devoting the most time to the business, for example, might be compensated by a salary (out of net earnings) preceding the division of the remaining net earnings. The salary is part of the earnings sharing agreement. It is not considered an expense of the partnership. For example, if A is to be given credit for a salary of $10,000 before the remaining earnings are divided equally with B and net earnings are $50,000, A is credited with $30,000 and B with $20,000 when the Expense and Revenue Summary account is closed. As another illustration, one partner may invest greater capital than another partner, in which case the partner with the greater investment may insist on an inclusion in the partnership agreement that interest be allowed on capital account balances in the division of net earnings before the remainder is divided in accordance with the earnings and loss ratio.

Common methods of dividing earnings are:

1. In a set ratio such as:
   a) Equally.
   b) In an agreed ratio other than equal.
   c) In the ratio of the partners' capital account balances at the beginning of the fiscal period.
   d) In the ratio of the average capital investment.
2. By allowing interest on the capital investments or salaries and dividing the remaining net earnings in an agreed ratio.

Assume that Rogers and Morgan have decided to form a partnership. Rogers' initial capital investment is $75,000; Morgan's is $25,000. The partners are equally capable of running the business they are starting and they expect to share equally in the management of the business. But Rogers has other business interests which of necessity occupy much of his time and attention. Consequently, the partners have agreed that Rogers will devote only half of his time to partnership business whereas Morgan will devote 100 percent of his.

Under these circumstances, which of the following methods of dividing earnings and losses between the partners appears to be most equitable for inclusion in the partnership agreement?

1. Equal division of earnings and losses.
2. An earnings and loss ratio of 3 to 1 (75 percent to Rogers and 25 percent to Morgan).
3. Allowing interest on the average capital investments of the partners and dividing the remaining net earnings equally.
4. Allowing salaries to the partners and dividing the remaining net earnings equally.
5. Allowing salaries for time devoted to the business and interest on the capital investments and dividing the remaining net earnings equally.

Now turn to Answer Frame 12[11] on page 514 to check your answer.

Frame 13[11]

Illustrations of distributions of partnership earnings

The illustrations which follow are based on these data about the partnership of Anders and Budd: net earnings for the year ended December 31, 1975, were $60,000. During 1975 Anders' drawings were $14,000 and Budd's drawings were $22,000. The capital account balances of the partners on December 31, 1975, before the accounts were closed, were Anders, $85,000, and Budd, $134,000.

Case 1. Earnings divided only in a set ratio. If the net earnings of $60,000 were divided equally between Anders and Budd, they would each be credited with $30,000 of earnings. If the partnership agreement instead called for a division of earnings of 60 percent to Anders and 40 percent to Budd, the entry to divide the $60,000 net earnings for 1975 would credit Anders with $36,000 and Budd with $24,000.

Answer frame 12[11]

Answer 5 is correct. This method adjusts for differences in capital and time contributed by the partners. The equal division of the remaining earnings also seems equitable, since the partners share equally in the management decisions and are equally competent in operating a business of this kind. If one of the partners brought special talents to the firm, the division of partnership earnings would no doubt take this into account. In any case, whatever division of earnings is agreed upon between the partners and set forth in the partnership agreement will be followed in closing the accounts. If no agreement is set forth in the articles of copartnership, net earnings must be divided equally regardless of differences in investment or time spent.

If you answered incorrectly, reread Frame 12[11] before going on to Frame 13[11] on page 513.

13[11]
continued

Suppose the partnership agreement called for a division of earnings in the beginning of period capital account ratio and Anders' beginning balance was $40,000 and Budd's was $80,000. The amount of earnings credited to the drawing accounts when the Expense and Revenue Summary account was closed would be:

1. Anders ___?___
2. Budd ___?___

Now check your response with the answers provided in Answer Frame 13[11] on page 516.

Frame 14[11]

Sometimes the earnings are divided in the average capital account ratio. Illustration 11.9 contains the assumed details in the partners' capital accounts.

The ratio of average capital amounts is computed by using the total average capital ($50,000 + $90,000 = $140,000) as the denominator of fractions having each partner's average capital as numerators. Thus, Anders is credited with $50,000/$140,000 or 35.71 percent of net earnings, and Budd with $90,000/$140,000 or 64.29 percent.

If the partners invest or withdraw capital on dates other than the first of the month, a unit of time other than a month (days or weeks) may be used to determine the average capital. If days are used, the month-dollars column becomes day-dollars and the total of the day-dollars column is divided by the number of days in the year to arrive at the average capital.

Assume that the January 1, 1975, balance and the changes in the capital account of Kaems, a member of the partnership of Kames and Mohr,

Illustration 11.9, *Computation of Average Capital*

Anders, Capital

Date	Debits	Credits	Balance	Months Unchanged	Month-Dollars (Weighted Equivalent)
Jan. 1			$40,000	6	$240,000
July 1		$15,000	55,000	5	275,000
Dec. 1		30,000	85,000	1	85,000
				12	$600,000

Average capital of Anders: $600,000 ÷ 12 = $50,000.

Budd, Capital

Date	Debits	Credits	Balance	Months Unchanged	Month-Dollars (Weighted Equivalent)
Jan. 1			$ 80,000	7	$ 560,000
Aug. 1		$ 4,000	84,000	3	252,000
Nov. 1		50,000	134,000	2	268,000
				12	$1,080,000

Average capital of Budd: $1,080,000 ÷ 12 = $90,000.

are as indicated below and that the partners divide earnings in the ratio of their average capital investments.

Kaems, Capital

Date	*Debits*	*Credits*	*Balance*	*Months Unchanged*	*Month-Dollars (Weighted Equivalent)*
Jan. 1			$32,000	?	?
May 1	$6,000		?	?	?
July 1		$14,000	?	?	?
Oct. 1	2,000		?	?	?
				?	?

What is Kaems' average capital investment for 1975?

Turn to Answer Frame 14[11] on page 516 to check your answer.

Frame 15[11]

Case 2. Interest allowed on investments before dividing the remainder. If interest is allowed on the partners' capital investments (the balance in the capital accounts) at the beginning of the year, or on their average capital amounts for the year, a portion of annual net earnings (equal

Answer frame 13[11]

1. Anders' drawing account would be credited with $20,000 ($40,000/$120,000 × $60,000).
2. Budd's would be credited with $40,000 ($80,000/$120,000 × $60,000).

The distribution of net earnings is computed by using fractions: each partner's beginning capital balance is a numerator and total beginning capital is the denominator.

If you answered incorrectly, reread Frame 13[11] before turning to Frame 14[11] on page 514.

Answer frame 14[11]

The computation of Kaems' average capital investment is:

Kaems, Capital

Date	*Debits*	*Credits*	*Balance*	*Months Unchanged*	*Month-Dollars (Weighted Equivalent)*
Jan. 1			$32,000	4	$128,000
May 1	$6,000		26,000	2	52,000
July 1		$14,000	40,000	3	120,000
Oct. 1	2,000		38,000	3	114,000
				12	$414,000

The average capital of Kaems is $414,000 ÷ 12 = $34,500.

If you answered incorrectly reread Frame 14[11] before starting Frame 15[11] on page 515.

15[11] *continued*

to the total capital account balances multiplied by the interest rate agreed upon) is divided in a capital investment ratio.

The interest allowed is a distribution of part of net earnings for the period rather than an expense to be deducted in arriving at net earnings. It is considered a distribution of net earnings. If there is a net loss for the year, the debit to Expense and Revenue Summary resulting from the distribution will further increase the debit balance in that account to be distributed to the partners.

To follow the illustration of this method of earnings distribution, it is necessary to recall that the partners' capital account balances on January 1, 1975, were Anders, $40,000, and Budd, $80,000, and their average capital investments for 1975 were $50,000 and $90,000, respectively.

If interest at 6 percent per year is allowed each partner on his capital investment at the beginning of the year, the interest allowed is:

Anders, $40,000 at 6%	$2,400
Budd, $80,000 at 6%	4,800
Total	$7,200

If interest at 6 percent per year is allowed each partner on the average of his capital account for the year 1975, the interest allowed is:

Anders, $50,000 at 6%.	$3,000
Budd, $90,000 at 6%.	5,400
Total.	$8,400

To test your understanding, assume the partnership agreement of Nye and Blackwell specifies that the partners are allowed interest at the rate of 8 percent per year on their average capital investments. Nye's average capital investment during 1975 was $50,000; Blackwell's was $40,000 On a separate sheet of paper calculate the amount of interest credited to each partner.

Now turn to Answer Frame 15[11] on page 518 to check your answer.

Frame 16[11]

Case 3. Salaries allowed before dividing the remainder. Partners also may agree to allow themselves salaries. Salaries may be allowed in order to compensate for differences in time devoted to the business or differences in ability. If the salary agreement is not specified in the articles of copartnership, no partner may receive a salary as a differential even if there are differences in time spent or differences in ability or risks assumed.

Salaries to partners are divisions of net earnings and are not operating expenses as are salaries paid to employees. If a salary agreement is in effect, the salaries are credited to the partners' drawing accounts as distributions of net earnings. The net earnings amount on a partnership's earnings statement is computed without deducting amounts for interest on partners' capital and salaries to partners. These are always considered to be part of the earnings-sharing mechanism instead of expenses to be deducted in arriving at net earnings. Salaries are allowed even if their total exceeds the amount of earnings.

In the case of Anders and Budd, suppose that partnership net earnings are only $20,800, that the earnings-sharing conditions are that Anders is allowed a salary of $16,000 per year and Budd a salary of $10,000 per year, and that the remaining net earnings or net loss is divided equally. What is the correct division of the $20,800 total between Anders and Budd?

Now check your answer by turning to Answer Frame 16[11] on page 518.

Frame 17[11]

Case 4. Interest and salaries allowed before dividing the remainder. If it is desired to compensate the partners for capital contributed, they

Answer frame 15[11]

The correct answer is:

Nye, $50,000 at 8%	$4,000
Blackwell, $40,000 at 8%	3,200
Total	$7,200

If you answered incorrectly, reread Frame 15[11] before turning to Frame 16[11] on page 517.

Answer frame 16[11]

The answer is that Anders receives $13,400 and Budd $7,400. This is determined as follows:

	Anders	*Budd*	*Both*	*Earnings to Be Distributed*
Net earnings				$20,800
Salaries	$16,000	$10,000	$26,000	(5,200)
Remainder (negative balance)	(2,600)	(2,600)	(5,200)	—0—
	$13,400	$ 7,400	$20,800	

Notice that the salaries are granted even though earnings are insufficient to cover them. The resulting negative balance is then distributed to the partners in the agreed ratio.

If you answered incorrectly, reread Frame 16[11] before turning to Frame 17[11] on page 517.

17[11] *continued*

may be allowed interest; if it is desired to compensate them for differences in time devoted to the business or in ability, they may be allowed salaries.

Assume that Anders and Budd are allowed interest at 6 percent per year on their capital account balances at January 1, 1975, and that Anders is allowed a salary of $16,000 and Budd a salary of $10,000; remaining net earnings or net loss is divided equally. Net earnings are $60,000. The division in this case is:

	Anders	*Budd*	*Both*	*Earnings to Be Distributed*
Net earnings				$60,000
Interest	$ 2,400	$ 4,800	$ 7,200	52,800
Salary	16,000	10,000	26,000	26,800
Remainder	13,400	13,400	26,800	—0—
Distribution	$31,800	$28,200	$60,000	

The entry to divide net earnings is:

Expense and Revenue Summary	60,000	
Anders, Drawing		31,800
Budd, Drawing		28,200
To divide the earnings between the partners.		

Even if the allowances for salaries or interest exceed net earnings, or if there is a net loss for the period, the partners still are given credit for their full amounts of interest and salary. For example, in the situation above if there was a net loss of $20,000 instead of net earnings of $60,000 for the year, the division would be:

	Anders	*Budd*	*Both*	*Earnings to Be Distributed*
Net loss				$(20,000)
Interest	$ 2,400	$ 4,800	$ 7,200	(27,200)
Salary	16,000	10,000	26,000	(53,200)
Remainder	(26,600)	(26,600)	(53,200)	—0—
Distribution	$ (8,200)	$(11,800)	$(20,000)	

The entry to divide the net loss would be:

Anders, Drawing	8,200	
Budd, Drawing	11,800	
Expense and Revenue Summary		20,000
To divide the net loss between the partners.		

The partnership of Robins and Caruso operates the R & C Shoe Store. The partners share equally in the making of management decisions and have approximately equal amounts of capital invested in the firm. But Robins devotes 100 percent of his time to partnership affairs, being in charge of day-to-day operation of the store, while Caruso spends no appreciable time with the daily operating aspects of the business. The partners therefore agree that Robins will be allowed a salary of $10,000 per year and that the remaining earnings or losses will be divided equally. In 1975 the firm suffers a net loss of $2,000. Which of the following statements correctly describes the effect on the partners' capital investments?

1. The two partners will each bear $1,000 of the net loss.
2. Robins will bear the entire net loss of $2,000 via a reduction in his salary for 1975.
3. Caruso will bear a loss of $6,000 and Robins will show a net gain of $4,000.

Now turn to Answer Frame 17[11] on page 520 to check your answer.

Answer frame 17[11]

The third answer is correct. A partner's salary is a distribution of net earnings and therefore does not enter into the determination of the net earnings or net loss for the period as reported on the earnings statement. The distribution of the net loss in the Robins-Caruso case is:

	Robins	*Caruso*	*Both*	*Earnings to Be Distributed*
Net loss...........				$ (2,000)
Salary.............	$10,000	—0—	$ 10,000	(12,000)
Remainder..........	(6,000)	$(6,000)	(12,000)	—0—
Distribution........	$ 4,000	$(6,000)	$ (2,000)	

The net effect is that Caruso bears a loss of $6,000, while Robins' salary has an offsetting effect against his share of the loss so that he still realizes a $4,000 increase in his capital account.

The entry to record the division of the net loss is as follows:

Caruso, Drawing.......................................	6,000	
Robins, Drawing....................................		4,000
Expense and Revenue Summary......................		2,000
To divide the net loss between the partners.		

If you answered incorrectly, reread Frame 17[11] before turning to Frame 18[11] below.

Frame 18[11]

Partners' loans to the partnership

A partner may advance money to his firm as a loan that is to be repaid in accordance with the terms of the loan agreement. It is natural that such loans bear interest; otherwise, the partnership would be using a partner's private funds without compensation. Interest paid on such loans is an expense which is deducted in arriving at net earnings on the earnings statement. Such interest should not be treated as a distribution of net earnings, because it is not interest on a partner's investment.

Partners' loans to the firm rank second to the claims of other creditors and, in case of liquidation, should not be paid until those debts are settled. The loan to the firm should appear in the statement of financial position as a separate current or long-term liability, depending upon the length of time before the loan is due.

Recording earnings distribution in the accounts

The Expense and Revenue Summary account for the partnership of Anders and Budd, basing the distribution of the net earnings on interest, salaries, and the equal division of the remainder (case 4 in Frame 17[11]), is presented below, followed by the earnings statement and the statement of the partners' capital accounts.

After all expenses and revenues have been closed to the Expense and Revenue Summary account, the distribution of the net earnings may be shown in that account as follows:

Expense and Revenue Summary

Date		Explanation			Folio	Debit	Credit	Balance
1975								
Dec.	31	Sales					600,000	600,000
		Expenses				540,400		59,600
		Interest revenue					400	60,000
		Net earnings distribution:				60,000		—0—
		Interest						
		Anders.......	$ 2,400					
		Budd........	4,800	$ 7,200				
		Salaries						
		Anders.......	$16,000					
		Budd........	10,000	26,000				
		Remainder						
		Anders.......	$13,400					
		Budd........	13,400	26,800				
				$60,000				

Presenting distribution of earnings in the earnings statement

The earnings statement for the partnership of Anders and Budd for the year ended December 31, 1975, is shown in Illustration 11.10.

Statement of partners' capital accounts

The statement of the partners' capital accounts, showing the distribution of the earnings and the capital changes, is presented in Illustration 11.11. The statement could, of course, show net earnings added to the beginning capital account balances before drawings are deducted, instead of after; either format is correct.

The purpose of the statement of partners' capital is to present details that could not readily be shown on the statement of financial position. The statement of financial position need indicate only the final balance of each partner's capital account when it is accompanied by this detailed analysis.

The statement of financial position of a partnership composed of many partners may show only a single item and amount called "Partners' Capital," with each partner's name and capital balance reported in a supporting schedule.

Illustration 11.10

ANDERS AND BUDD
Earnings Statement
For the Year Ended December 31, 1975

Sales			$600,000
Cost of goods sold:			
Inventory, January 1, 1975		$ 62,000	
Purchases	$364,000		
Less: Purchase discounts	1,600	362,400	
Total		$424,400	
Inventory, December 31, 1975		64,000	
Cost of goods sold			360,400
Gross margin on sales			$239,600
Deduct: Operating expenses:			
Selling expenses		$ 80,000	
Administrative expenses		100,000	
Total operating expenses			180,000
Net operating earnings			$ 59,600
Other revenue:			
Interest revenue			400
Net Earnings			$ 60,000

Distribution of Net Earnings

	Anders	*Budd*	*Total*
Interest	$ 2,400	$ 4,800	$ 7,200
Salary	16,000	10,000	26,000
Remainder equally	13,400	13,400	26,800
Net Earnings	$31,800	$28,200	$60,000

Illustration 11.11

ANDERS AND BUDD
Statement of Partners' Capital
For the Year Ended December 31, 1975

	Anders	*Budd*	*Total*
Balance, January 1, 1975	$ 40,000	$ 80,000	$120,000
Add: Additional investments	45,000	54,000	99,000
Capital account balances, December 31, 1975, before drawing charges	$ 85,000	$134,000	$219,000
Deduct: Drawings	14,000	22,000	36,000
Capital account balances before 1975 earnings distribution	$ 71,000	$112,000	$183,000
Net earnings 1975, per earnings statement:			
Interest	2,400	4,800	7,200
Salaries	16,000	10,000	26,000
Remainder equally	13,400	13,400	26,800
Capital Account Balances, December 31, 1975	$102,800	$140,200	$243,000

Incorporating an unincorporated business

In many instances a corporation is organized to continue the operations of a going business—a partnership or a single proprietorship. The corporate form of organization has the characteristics of limited liability for its owners, an increased availability of large sums of capital due to an expended ownership base, and a more permanent existence.

The procedure for incorporation involves the same initial step as the organization of any corporation. For example, if a partnership is to be incorporated, the charter of the proposed corporation must be secured from the state. Then a contract of sale is entered into by the corporation and the partners of the partnership. In this manner shares of stock in the new corporation are subscribed for, with payment to be made by turning over the assets and liabilities of the partnership. When payment is made and the shares issued, the corporation is engaged in operating a going business. The effect of the incorporation is to transfer the interest of the partners to the corporation, with the partners becoming stockholders in the corporation. Few of the customers and employees of the incorporated partnership are apt to be aware of the act of incorporation.

Is each of the following statements true or false?

1. Stockholders of a corporation can be held personally responsible for the debts of a corporation just as partners can be held personally liable for debts of the partnership.
2. The corporate form of organization is a less permanent form of business organization than is the partnership.
3. The corporation is well adapted to conditions that necessitate the investment of large sums of capital.
4. One possible motivation for incorporating a partnership is to expand the ownership base of the business.

Now turn to Answer Frame 18[11] on page 524 to check your answers.

Frame 19[11]

Illustration of the incorporation of a partnership

The partnership of Bonner and Donald is to be incorporated. The partnership's statement of financial position is as shown in Illustration 11.12.

The partners form a corporation, to be known as the Bondon Corporation, which receives authorization to issue $200,000 of common stock, consisting of 10,000 shares with a par value of $20 per share.

The partners, who share earnings and losses equally, agree to make the following adjustments preceding incorporation:

1. Charge off uncollectible accounts receivable of $4,000.
2. Write down merchandise inventory by $6,000.
3. Write up land by $4,000.
4. Place goodwill on the books at $16,000.

Answer frame 18[11]

1. False. Stockholders of a corporation usually cannot be held personally liable for the debts of the corporation. This feature of limited liability is at times a motivating force in the incorporation of a partnership.
2. False. Corporate existence is not affected by the death, incapacity, or withdrawal of a stockholder, whereas a partnership is dissolved by the death or withdrawal of a partner.
3. True. The ability to obtain funds from many investors through the issuance of capital stock makes the corporate form of organization well suited to conditions which require the investment of large sums of capital.
4. True. This is a possible motivation for incorporating a partnership. The ownership base is expanded through the issuance of capital stock to investors.

If you missed any of the above, reread Frame 18[11] before turning to Frame 19[11] on page 523.

19[11] *continued*

Illustration 11.12

BONNER AND DONALD
Statement of Financial Position
July 31, 1975

ASSETS		LIABILITIES AND PARTNERS' EQUITY	
Cash	$ 8,000	Accounts payable	$ 30,000
Accounts receivable	32,000	Notes payable	10,000
Merchandise inventory	40,000	A. M. Bonner, capital	80,000
Land	6,000	C. D. Donald, capital	40,000
Building	70,000		
Furniture and fixtures	4,000		
	$160,000		$160,000

Each partner is to contribute additional cash to raise the capital accounts to $100,000 for Bonner and $50,000 for Donald, and each will take capital stock of the corporation in that amount.

In order to adjust the assets and capital in accordance with the agreement, the following entries are made on the books of the partnership:

Land	4,000	
Goodwill	16,000	
Accounts Receivable		4,000
Merchandise Inventory		6,000
Bonner, Capital		5,000
Donald, Capital		5,000
To adjust in accordance with the agreement.		
Cash	20,000	
Bonner, Capital		15,000
Donald, Capital		5,000
To record the additional cash contributions to increase the capital of Bonner to $100,000 and that of Donald to $50,000.		

After these entries are posted, the statement of financial position of the partnership is as shown in Illustration 11.13. The next step is to close the records of the partnership and open the records of the corporation.

Illustration 11.13

BONNER AND DONALD
Statement of Financial Position
July 31, 1975

ASSETS		LIABILITIES AND PARTNERS' EQUITY	
Cash	$ 28,000	Accounts payable	$ 30,000
Accounts receivable	28,000	Notes payable	10,000
Merchandise inventory	34,000	A. M. Bonner, capital	100,000
Land	10,000	C. D. Donald, capital	50,000
Building	70,000		
Furniture and fixtures	4,000		
Goodwill	16,000		
	$190,000		$190,000

New records should be opened by the corporation; the old books of the partnership must be closed, although from the view of the corporation it is irrelevant whether this is done. New records should be opened because a new business entity exists. In the case of Bonner and Donald, the entries to accomplish these purposes will be as follows.

Entries in partnership records. Entries are needed to record the transfer of all assets and all liabilities to the corporation and the receipt and distribution of the capital stock of the corporation. The entries on July 31, 1975, are:

Stock of Bondon Corporation	150,000	
Accounts Payable	30,000	
Notes Payable	10,000	
Cash		28,000
Accounts Receivable		28,000
Merchandise Inventory		34,000
Land		10,000
Building		70,000
Furniture and Fixtures		4,000
Goodwill		16,000
To record the transfer of the partnership assets and liabilities to the corporation, and to record receipt of 7,500 shares of capital stock in payment.		
Bonner, Capital	100,000	
Donald, Capital	50,000	
Stock of Bondon Corporation		150,000
To record the closing of the partners' capital accounts and the distribution of the stock to the partners.		

After these entries are posted, the partnership books are closed. All of the accounts now have zero balances.

Entries in corporate records. Needed is an entry to record the acquisition of the assets and liabilities of the partnership and the issuance of capital stock after memorandum entries have been made for the authorized capital stock. The entry to accomplish this is made on August 1, 1975:

Cash	28,000	
Accounts Receivable	28,000	
Merchandise Inventory	34,000	
Land	10,000	
Building	70,000	
Furniture and Fixtures	4,000	
Goodwill	16,000	
Accounts Payable		30,000
Notes Payable		10,000
Capital Stock		150,000
To record the purchase of the assets and the assumption of the liabilities of the partnership of Bonner and Donald and the issuance of 7,500 shares of capital stock in payment.		

Determine whether each of the following statements about the preceding illustration is correct or incorrect:

1. It was not necessary to close the partners' capital accounts, since Bonner and Donald were the only ones who received any capital stock.
2. In essence, the effect of the entries was to transfer the interest of the partners to the corporation in exchange for the capital stock of the corporation.
3. Since the partners shared earnings and losses equally, they each received equal amounts of common stock.

Now turn to Answer Frame 19[11] on page 528 to check your answers.

Summary *chapter* 11

In the accounting for single proprietorships and partnerships, capital investments are credited to the capital accounts, earnings and losses are closed to the drawing accounts, and withdrawals are debited to the drawing accounts.

The adjusting and closing entries of a single proprietorship or a partnership are identical to those prepared for a corporation except for the closing of the Expense and Revenue Summary account. This account should be closed to the drawing accounts of the owners, where the withdrawals already recorded as debits will be offset against the earnings credited before the balance is closed to the capital accounts of the owners.

The statement of financial position for a proprietorship has only one account in the owner's equity section—the owner's capital account. A partnership's statement of financial position usually has one capital account for each partner, unless there are many partners.

The earnings statements of a single proprietorship, partnership, and corporation are quite similar except that the earnings statement of a partnership generally shows the distribution of net earnings among the partners.

Single proprietorships have as advantages (1) ease of establishing the business, (2) no division of authority or of earnings, and (3) no separate taxation of the earnings of the business or of the withdrawals (all earnings are taxed to the owner whether he withdraws them or not). Partnerships have the first and third of the above advantages, but not the second.

The more important disadvantages include unlimited liability, limited capital, limited skills, and limited transferability of ownership interests.

If the partnership agreement is silent with respect to the division of earnings and losses, they are shared equally. Although any conceivable scheme may be agreed upon, the granting of salaries or interest or both as part of the sharing of earnings is quite common. These salaries and interest amounts allowed partners are not expenses to be deducted in arriving at partnership net earnings. They are simply means for sharing earnings. The amount of earnings remaining after salaries and interest can be shared in any agreed-upon manner.

To complete your review, study the terms introduced in this chapter in the glossary which follows. Then go on to the Student Review Quiz for a self-administered test of your comprehension of the material in the chapter (page 528).

Glossary *chapter* 11

Agent—one who has the authority to act for another (the partnership) or in the place of another.

Articles of copartnership—see partnership agreement.

Assign—to transfer rights in ownership to another party, such as a creditor.

Attachment—confiscation of property by legal process. Creditors often have this right when the debtor does not perform on a contract.

Capital account—an owner's equity account used in proprietorship and partnership accounting. It is credited with the owner's initial and additional investments and when the drawing account for that owner has a credit balance and is closed to it. It is debited for reductions in the permanent investment of the owner and when the drawing account for that owner has a debit balance and is closed to it. A separate capital account is maintained for each owner.

Drawing account—an owner's equity account (although it has a zero balance after closing and might be considered a nominal account like the expense and revenue accounts). A drawing account is maintained for each owner. It is debited when the owner withdraws assets (usually merchandise or cash) from the partnership or when there is a debit balance in the Expense and Revenue Summary account and this particular owner must absorb part of that debit balance in the closing process. It is credited when the owner is credited with distributions of earnings.

Earnings and loss ratio—often called the profit and loss ratio. Earnings which are not divided through salary or interest allowances are divided among partners according to this ratio.

Interest granted to partner—a means often used in the sharing of earnings to give weight to the relative amounts of capital invested by the partners. The interest is sometimes based on the beginning of year balances in the capital accounts and sometimes on the average balances in the capital accounts. The interest is not an expense to be deducted in arriving at net earnings.

Partnership—an association of two or more persons to carry on a business as co-owners.

Partnership agreement—also known as articles of copartnership (when in written form): the conditions or provisions accepted by all of the partners to serve as the basis for the formation and operation of the partnership.

Answer frame 19[11]

1. Incorrect. The partners' capital accounts must be closed because the partnership no longer exists. A new business entity in the form of the corporation has taken its place.
2. Correct. This is basically the effect of the process of incorporating a partnership.
3. Incorrect. Each partner received capital stock in the amount of his respective capital account balance. These balances were not equal. The explanation of the journal entry recording the stock subscriptions also indicates that the partners did not receive equal amounts of stock. Banner received twice as many shares as Donald.

If you missed any of the above, reread Frame 19[11] before proceeding to the chapter summary, page 526.

Salary granted to partners—a means often used in the sharing of earnings to reward certain partners for spending more time than other partners in running the affairs of the business. The salary is not an expense of the partnership in determining net earnings.

Single proprietorship—a business organization owned by one person.

Statement of partners' capital—a financial statement analogous to the statement of retained earnings of a corporation. It is a summary of the transactions affecting the capital balance of each partner and in total for all partners. (For an example, see Illustration 11.8 or 11.11.)

Statement of proprietor's capital—a summary of the transactions affecting the capital balance of a single proprietor. It is quite similar to the statement of partners' capital. (For an example, see Illustration 11.5.)

Uniform Partnership Act—a written law adopted in many states which is applicable in resolving contested matters between partners which are not covered in the partnership agreement.

Unlimited liability—a characteristic of single proprietorships and partnerships under which owners are liable for more than merely the amounts invested in the business, as their personal assets may also be taken to satisfy the claims of business creditors.

Student review quiz *chapter* 11

To develop a permanent record of your responses, you may write them on the answer sheet provided in the *Work Papers* or on a separate sheet of paper.

1 Which of the following accounts would appear in the equity section of the annual statement of financial position of a single proprietorship?

a) John Dunn, Drawing.
b) John Dunn, Capital.
c) John Dunn, Current.
d) John Dunn, Capital Stock.
e) **(b)** and **(c)**.
f) **(a)** and **(b)**.

2 In closing the books of a single proprietorship, the Expense and Revenue Summary account is closed to—

a) Retained earnings.
b) The owner's capital account.
c) The owner's drawing account.
d) No account.
e) None of the above accounts.

3. Which of the following statements is false?

a) There are more single proprietorships and partnerships as a group than corporations in the United States.
b) Corporations are responsible for a greater dollar volume of output of goods and services than are single proprietorships and partnerships combined.
c) Salaries credited to partners are not expenses of the partnership.
d) Salaries paid to executives of a corporation are expenses of the corporation.
e) None of the above is true.

4 Charles Wade and James Parker are partners. They agree that Parker may withdraw $1,000 of his capital. The journal entry to record the withdrawal includes a—

a) Debit of $1,000 to James Parker, Capital.
b) Credit of $1,000 to James Parker, Capital.
c) Debit of $1,000 to James Parker, Drawing.
d) Credit of $1,000 to James Parker, Drawing.
e) Debit to Expense and Revenue Summary.

5 If the partnership contract is silent with regard to the division of earnings and losses, all earnings and losses are divided—

a) In the ratio of the partners' average capital investment.
b) In the ratio of the partners' capital investment at the beginning of the accounting period.
c) In the ratio of the partners' time devoted to the partnership business.
d) Equally.
e) In none of the above ways.

6 The partnership agreement between Wilke and Mitchell states that earnings and losses are to be divided on the basis of average capital investment for the year. Drawings up to $10,000 per year for Wilke and $15,000 per year for Mitchell are to be allowed and not considered reductions of capital. There were no other withdrawals during the year and no additional capital investments. Net earnings for 1975 are $28,000. The accounts at December 31, 1975, show:

Wilke, capital	$30,000
Mitchell, capital	50,000
Wilke, drawing	10,000 Dr.
Mitchell, drawing	14,000 Dr.

The entry needed to record the division of earnings for 1975 is:

a)	Expense and Revenue Summary	28,000	
	Wilke, Drawing		14,000
	Mitchell, Drawing		14,000
b)	Expense and Revenue Summary	28,000	
	Wilke, Drawing		10,500
	Mitchell, Drawing		17,500
c)	Expense and Revenue Summary	28,000	
	Wilke, Drawing		10,125
	Mitchell, Drawing		17,875
d)	Expense and Revenue Summary	28,000	
	Wilke, Drawing		10,000
	Mitchell, Drawing		18,000

e) None of the above.

7 The capital accounts of Hansen and Dunn show the following balances as of January 1, 1975: Hansen, $90,000; Dunn, $10,000. Hansen participates only in management decisions, whereas Dunn devotes all of his time to the operation of the partnership business. The articles of copartnership specify that the partners are allowed 5 percent per year interest on capital balances at the beginning of the period. In addition, Dunn is allowed a salary of $7,000, with the remaining net earnings or loss divided equally. Partnership net earnings for 1975 are $26,000. Which of the following entries is required by the above information?

a)	Expense and Revenue Summary	26,000	
	Hansen, Drawing		11,500
	Dunn, Drawing		14,500
b)	Salary Expense	7,000	
	Interest Expense	5,000	
	Cash		12,000
	Expense and Revenue Summary	14,000	
	Hansen, Drawing		7,000
	Dunn, Drawing		7,000
c)	Expense and Revenue Summary	5,000	
	Hansen, Drawing		4,500
	Dunn, Drawing		500
	Expense and Revenue Summary	19,000	
	Hansen, Drawing		11,500
	Dunn, Drawing		7,500
d)	Expense and Revenue Summary	26,000	
	Hansen, Drawing		13,000
	Dunn, Drawing		13,000
e)	Salary Expense	7,000	
	Interest Expense	5,000	
	Expense and Revenue Summary		12,000
	Expense and Revenue Summary	14,000	
	Hansen, Drawing		7,000
	Dunn, Drawing		7,000

8 The articles of copartnership of Arthur and Wilson specify that Arthur will receive a salary of $12,000 and that the remaining net earnings or net loss will be shared as follows: Arthur, 30 percent; Wilson, 70 percent. The partnership had a net loss of $2,000 for the year (before deduction of Arthur's salary). What entries are required?

a)	Expense and Revenue Summary....	14,000	
	Arthur, Drawing		12,600
	Wilson, Drawing		1,400
b)	Arthur, Drawing....	600	
	Wilson, Drawing....	1,400	
	Expense and Revenue Summary....		2,000
c)	Wilson, Drawing....	9,800	
	Arthur, Drawing		7,800
	Expense and Revenue Summary....		2,000
d)	Arthur, Drawing....	3,000	
	Wilson, Drawing....	7,000	
	Expense and Revenue Summary....		10,000
e)	Expense and Revenue Summary....	10,000	
	Wilson, Drawing....	1,400	
	Arthur, Drawing		11,400

9 Interest on loans made by partners to the partnership is:
a) A division of earnings.
b) Treated in the same manner as partners' salaries.
c) Treated in the same way as interest on capital account balances.
d) An expense to the partnership.
e) None of the above.

10 Comstock's partnership capital and drawing accounts are summarized below:

Comstock, Capital	*Debit*	*Credit*	*Balance*
January 1.......			10,000
January 16......		5,000	15,000

Comstock, Drawing	*Debit*	*Credit*	*Balance*
January 15......	500		500
January 31......	500		1,000

It is agreed by all of the partners that semimonthly drawings of $500 will be allowed all partners and will not be treated as charges against capital.

Comstock's average capital investment in the month of January is:

a) $\$12{,}500 = \dfrac{(\$10{,}000 + \$15{,}000)}{2}$

b) $\$12{,}250 = \dfrac{(\$10{,}000 + \$15{,}000 - \$500)}{2}$

c) $\$12{,}000 = \dfrac{(\$10{,}000 + \$15{,}000 - \$1{,}000)}{2}$

d) $\$7{,}500 = \dfrac{(\$10{,}000 + \$5{,}000)}{2}$

e) $\$7{,}250 = \dfrac{(\$10{,}000 + \$5{,}000 - \$500)}{2}$

Now compare your answers with the correct answers and explanations on page 716.

Questions *chapter* 11

1 Contrast briefly the differences in accounting for capital, earnings and losses, and distributions of earnings in a single proprietorship, a partnership, and a corporation.

2 In what respect do the accepted principles of accounting for a single proprietorship differ from those for a corporation?

3 A friend of yours, majoring in economics, insists that the net earnings of a single proprietorship actually consist of a wage for labor services rendered by the owner, interest on the capital investment of the owner, and a profit for risk taking and for providing the leadership for the business. Do you agree? If so, would you suggest that the accountant try to determine the amount of each of these rewards for furnishing various resources to the business?

4 Roberts is currently operating a small machine shop. He is considering forming a partnership with an employee whom he considers an excellent worker and foreman and with whom it is easy to associate. Prepare a brief list of the advantages and disadvantages to Roberts of the potential partnership.

5 Many matters are usually covered in the typical partnership agreement. Some of them are of little significance to the accountant, while others are quite crucial. What are some of the crucial provisions as far as the accountant is concerned?

6 Moser and Burgan are partners in a local grocery store. Both take home sufficient merchandise to feed their families. Would you suggest that the merchandise taken home be recorded at selling price or cost? Why?

7 Can you think of a set of circumstances in which you might be willing to enter into a partnership with another person, do all of the work needed to run the business, provide all of the capital, and yet be willing to allow the other person a substantial share of the net earnings?

8 Why should a partnership agreement be quite specific regarding the treatment of withdrawals by partners insofar as the sharing of earnings and losses is concerned?

Exercises *chapter* 11

1 Borman, Lovell, and Anders are partners. In 1975 net earnings are $90,000. With how much will each be credited in the earnings distribution if:

a) Nothing is said in the partnership agreement concerning the division of earnings?

b) The earnings and loss ratio is 50–30–20 respectively?

2 Give the entries to record the division of earnings in 1(**b**) above. Also give the entries to record the closing of the drawing accounts assuming drawings were $15,000, $20,000, $10,000, respectively.

3 Given the earnings and loss ratio in question 1(**b**), how would the three share a loss of $60,000?

4 Partner A was credited with a salary of $12,000 and interest of $6,000 on his capital account and charged with $1,000 as his share of the balance in the Expense and Revenue Summary account. He drew $14,000 during the year. What amount will he report on his tax return as his share of the partnership's earnings?

5 The capital account balances of X and Y stood at $10,000 and $50,000 throughout the entire year. X drew $3,000 and Y drew $3,600, and these drawings are not to be considered capital withdrawals. (Sometimes a limit is placed on drawings in any one time period and the excess drawings are debited to the capital accounts rather than the drawing accounts.) The net earnings for the year are $10,000. If salaries are to be allowed X and Y in the amounts of $4,000 and $3,000 and the balance of the earnings distributed equally, how much will each partner receive as his share of the earnings for the year?

6 From the following data in Cavett's capital account, compute his average capital investment for the current year:

Jan. 1	Balance..........	$32,000
Mar. 1	Withdrew.........	6,000
May 1	Invested..........	12,000
June 1	Invested..........	2,000
Aug. 1	Withdrew.........	1,000
Dec. 1	Withdrew.........	3,000

7 R and T are partners agreeing that salaries of $500 per month are to be allowed each partner, withdrawable on the last day of each month. Interest is to be credited to each partner at the rate of 6 percent on his actual capital balance less any withdrawals in excess of the allowed salaries. The remainder of the earnings or losses is to be shared equally.

R's capital account balance at January 1 was $50,000 and he drew his monthly salary at the end of each month. In addition, he withdrew $2,000 on July 1.

T's capital account balance at January 1 was $100,000. He drew his monthly salary at the end of each month. He also drew $5,000 on April 1 and $3,000 on October 1.

Prepare a short schedule showing the distribution of earnings for the current year of $30,000.

Problems, Series A *chapter* 11

11–1–A

Bob Kelley organized a mill supply business on January 4, 1975, by investing the following assets:

Cash	$10,000	
Office equipment	8,500	(Purchased January 3)
Delivery truck	4,500	(Purchased January 3)

Kelley owes $3,000 on the truck as of January 4, 1975.

During the year Kelley drew a total of $16,000. Net earnings for the year were $20,000. Prior to going into business for himself, Kelley had received an offer of a position at a salary of $18,000 plus fringe benefits worth $4,000 per year. If he had not organized his firm, he could have invested his savings in securities having a comparable risk which bear interest at 10 percent.

Required:

a) Prepare entries to close out the net earnings for the year and whatever other entries are needed.
b) Prepare a schedule of the proprietor's capital for Mr. Kelley for the year.
c) Based solely on the information given, does it appear that Mr. Kelley made a wise move in going into business for himself? Show support for your conclusion.

11–2–A

MIKE BRANDON
Trial Balance, December 31, 1975

	Debits	*Credits*
Cash	$ 37,500	
Accounts receivable	60,000	
Inventory, January 1	24,000	
Plant assets	150,000	
Accounts payable		$ 45,000
Mike Brandon, capital		219,000
Mike Brandon, drawing	13,500	
Sales		200,000
Purchases	80,000	
Purchase returns		6,000
Rent expense	22,500	
Delivery expense	30,000	
Store expense	45,000	
Other expense	7,500	
	$470,000	$470,000

The inventory at December 31, 1975, is $27,000. Brandon invested $7,500 of cash on July 17.

Required:

a) Prepare necessary entries at the year-end.
b) Prepare an earnings statement for the year.
c) Prepare a statement of proprietor's capital for the year.
d) Prepare a statement of financial position at the year-end.

11–3–A

An analysis of Sanders' capital account for the year 1975 shows a beginning balance of $30,000, a capital withdrawal of $10,000 on June 1, and an additional investment of $5,000 on November 1. A similar analysis of his partner Cannon's capital account shows a beginning balance of $5,000 and an additional investment of $20,000 on July 1. The balance in the Expense and Revenue Summary account shows net earnings for the year of $22,000.

Required: Prepare a schedule and the required journal entry to record the distribution of the net earnings to the partners under each of the following assumptions:

a) Sanders and Cannon are allowed annual salaries of $8,000 and $10,000; 6 percent interest on average capital balance is to be credited to each partner; balance of earnings and losses to be shared equally.
b) Equal annual salaries of $10,000 to each partner; 6 percent interest on capital balances at beginning of year; balance in a 3 to 2 ratio to Sanders and Cannon.

11–4–A

Blake's capital account shows a beginning balance of $72,000 and a July 1 withdrawal of $9,000. Rice's capital account shows a beginning balance of $90,000 and a November 1 withdrawal of $18,000. The Expense and Revenue Summary account shows a debit balance of $12,000 for the year 1975.

The partnership agreement calls for salaries of $12,000 and $18,000 to Blake and Rice; interest at 6 percent on average capital balances; balance to Blake and Rice in a 30 to 70 ratio.

Required: Prepare a schedule showing the distribution of the loss for the year to the partners. No excess drawings were charged against the capital accounts. Also prepare the necessary journal entry.

11–5–A

The balances in the capital accounts of C and D at June 30, 1975, are $120,000 and $60,000, and these balances were unchanged during the year. C drew $16,000 during the year and D drew $18,000. Net earnings for the year amount to $80,000.

Required: Compute the earnings to be distributed to each partner at the end of the year under each of the following conditions:

a) Salaries allowed are $12,000 and $20,000 to C and D; remaining earnings to be divided in capital account ratio as of the beginning of the year.
b) Salaries allowed are $38,000 and $32,000 to C and D; interest on capital account balances as of the beginning of the year at 6 percent; no other provisions are contained in the agreement with regard to sharing earnings and losses.

11–6–A

Slim and Fat formed a partnership on March 1, 1975, by investing $20,000 and $32,000. On July 1, 1975, Slim and Fat invested additional capital of $8,000 and $12,000. At this time the partners agreed that in dividing net earnings, interest on capital account balances would be allowed at 6 percent on the investment for the period of time actually invested.

On September 1 both partners invested an additional $20,000. No drawings were made except for the monthly withdrawal of salaries at the annual rate of $14,400 and $19,200 for Slim and Fat. The net earnings for the partial year ending December 31, 1975, amounted to $48,000.

Required: Prepare a short schedule showing the distribution of the net earnings to each of the partners.

11–7–A

Boy and Girl, as partners, have agreed to the following distribution of net earnings:

a) Salaries of $18,000 and $24,000 to Boy and Girl.
b) A bonus to Girl of 25 percent of net earnings in excess of salaries.
c) The remainder equally.

Net earnings for the years 1974, 1975, and 1976 were $90,000, $30,000, and a loss of $15,000.

Required: Prepare short schedules showing the distribution of earnings and losses to the partners.

11–8–A

BLUE AND GRAY
Trial Balance, December 31, 1975

	Debits	Credits
Cash	$ 20,500	
Accounts receivable	30,000	
Allowance for doubtful accounts		$ 500
Inventory	18,500	
Equipment	35,000	
Allowance for depreciation of equipment		8,500
Unexpired insurance	455	
Accounts payable		25,500
Blue, capital		18,500
Gray, capital		36,500
Blue, drawing	500	
Gray, drawing	6,000	
Sales		275,000
Purchases	220,000	
Selling expenses	20,000	
Administrative expenses	16,500	
Other revenue		2,955
	$367,455	$367,455

The articles of copartnership for Blue and Gray provide for the distribution of earnings and losses in the following manner:

a) Each partner is allowed 6 percent interest per year on his capital investment as of the beginning of the year.
b) Blue is allowed a salary of $15,000 and Gray a salary of $18,000 per year as a distribution of earnings.
c) The remaining earnings and losses are divided equally.

Your analysis of the books and records discloses the following data that require your consideration: the ending inventory is $15,500; 1 percent of sales is to be added to the allowance for doubtful accounts; depreciation on the equipment should be recorded at 10 percent of cost. Blue's capital account includes a credit for $2,000 invested on July 15 of the current year. Unexpired insurance at December 31, 1975, is $40.

Required: You are to prepare the following for the partnership:

a) Adjusting and closing journal entries.
b) An earnings statement for the year.
c) A statement of partners' capital for the year.

11–9–A

The Jack and Jill partnership trial balance of December 31, 1975, is:

	Debits	*Credits*
Accounts receivable	$ 7,500	
Sundry assets	150,000	
Sundry liabilities		$ 37,500
Jack, capital		30,000
Jill, capital		90,000
	$157,500	$157,500

On January 2, 1976, the partners incorporate their business. They agree to record goodwill of $7,000 on the books and to establish an allowance for doubtful accounts equal to 10 percent of the accounts receivable. Jack and Jill share earnings and losses in a 60 to 40 ratio, respectively.

The J and J Corporation is authorized to issue 4,000 shares of $50 par value stock. The partners' capital accounts after adjustment indicate the par value of the shares to be issued to Jack and Jill. The net assets of the partnership are transferred to the corporation on January 2.

Required:

a) Present the journal entries necessary to close the books of the partnership.
b) Present the journal entries necessary to open the books of the corporation. (Ignore the entry to record the authorized number of shares.)

Problems, Series B *chapter* 11

11–1–B

John Watson invested $40,000 in his own drugstore on January 4, 1975. On March 15, June 15, September 15, and December 15 he withdrew $1,000, $1,600, $1,300, and $3,000, respectively. On July 1 he invested an additional $5,000. At December 31 his records showed net earnings of $14,000 for the year.

Mr. Watson believed that he could have worked for a chain drug company and received a salary of $9,000 plus fringe benefits of $1,000. He also could have invested his money in securities earning 6 percent instead of investing in a drugstore.

Required:

a) Present the necessary end-of-period entries to close out the net earnings for the year.
b) Prepare a schedule of proprietor's capital for Mr. Watson for the year.

c) Based solely on the information given, does it appear that Mr. Watson made a wise move in opening his store?

11–2–B

STEVE CLINE
Trial Balance, December 31, 1975

	Debits	*Credits*
Cash	$ 10,100	
Accounts receivable	14,000	
Inventory, January 1	7,200	
Accounts payable		$ 10,200
Steve Cline, capital		12,000
Steve Cline, drawing	4,000	
Sales		82,000
Purchases	43,000	
Purchase returns		1,000
Rent expense	13,000	
Delivery expense	4,200	
Store expense	9,700	
	$105,200	$105,200

The inventory at December 31, 1975, is $8,300. At December 31, 1974, after closing the accounts, Cline's capital account had a $10,000 credit balance. He invested $2,000 cash on May 1, 1975.

Required:

a) Prepare the necessary entries at year-end.
b) Prepare an earnings statement for the year.
c) Prepare a statement of proprietor's capital for the year.
d) Prepare a statement of financial position at year-end.

11–3–B

An analysis of the capital accounts for 1975 of Mann and Sellers, partners, shows:

Mann

Jan. 1	Balance	$60,000
June 1	Capital withdrawal	10,000
Nov. 1	Additional investment	15,000

Sellers

Jan. 1	Balance	$10,000
July 1	Additional investment	20,000

The balance in the Expense and Revenue Summary account shows net earnings of $30,000 for the year 1975.

Required: Prepare a schedule showing the distribution of the net earnings under each of the following assumptions with regard to earnings distribution. Also prepare the entries to distribute the earnings and to close the drawings accounts. (Note: In each instance assume drawings equal to salaries allowed for each partner.)

a) Mann and Sellers are allowed annual salaries of $9,000 and $12,000; 6 percent interest on actual capital balances for actual periods the capital is invested; balance of earnings shared equally.

b) Equal annual salaries of $12,500 to each partner; interest at 8 percent on capital balances at beginning of year; balance in a 2 to 3 ratio to Mann and Sellers.

11–4–B

The E and H partnership had the following agreement concerning earnings sharing. E receives 8 percent on his capital account balance as of the beginning of each year. H receives a salary of $1,200 per month as a distribution of earnings. The remainder is divided equally. The net earnings for 1975 were $36,000.

Required:

a) Assuming that E's and H's capital account balances at January 1, 1975, were $120,000 and $30,000, respectively, prepare a schedule and the entry necessary to distribute the net earnings.

b) Prepare the entries necessary to close the drawing accounts after the distribution of the earnings. The drawing accounts of the partners had the following balances (before closing) at December 31, 1975: E, zero; H, $14,400.

c) Present a schedule showing the changes occurring in 1975 in the capital accounts of each partner.

11–5–B

The capital account balances (unchanged during the year) at December 31, 1975, for He and She, partners, are $120,000 and $60,000. He drew $12,000 and She drew $30,000 during the year, with all withdrawals charged to the respective drawing accounts. Net loss for the year amounts to $12,000.

Required: Prepare short schedules showing the distribution of earnings to each of the partners for the year 1975 under each of the following assumed provisions in the partnership agreement relating to earnings distribution:

a) Salaries allowed of $12,000 and $30,000 to He and She; remaining earnings divided according to capital account balances at the beginning of the year.

b) Salaries allowed of $18,000 and $30,000; interest on capital account balances at beginning of the year at 6 percent; no further provisions relating to earnings distribution included in the partnership agreement.

11–6–B

Fred and Harry formed a partnership on April 1, 1975, by investing $40,000 each. Later, on July 1, each partner invested another $12,000.

The partnership agreement calls for monthly salaries of $1,200 to Fred and $1,400 to Harry, withdrawable monthly. Drawings in excess of allowed salaries are to be charged interest at the rate of 6 percent per year until paid back or covered by undrawn salary allowances. Fred drew his regular monthly salary and also withdrew $6,000 on September 1, so that his drawing account has a debit balance at December

31, 1975, of $16,800. Harry drew his regular salary and an additional $4,000 on November 1, 1975.

The partnership agreement provides for sharing the balance in the Expense and Revenue Summary account equally after allowing for salaries and the recording of interest credits for excessive withdrawals, if any.

Required: Prepare a schedule and the necessary journal entry to record the distribution of the net earnings of the partnership at December 31, 1975, assuming earnings for the year of $35,000.

11–7–B

Duffey and Nally are partners in a retail hardware store. Their partnership agreement calls for salaries to Duffey and Nally of $9,000 and $18,000; interest on capital accounts at 6 percent on actual balances during the year, provided drawings are not in excess of monthly salaries allowed; a bonus to Nally of 20 percent of the earnings in excess of salaries and interest allowed; the balance of the net earnings or losses to be shared equally.

During 1975 each partner drew his allowed salary and there were no withdrawals in excess of allowed salaries. The capital accounts of the two partners remained unchanged during the year at $40,000 for Duffey and $60,000 for Nally.

Required: Present short schedules showing the distribution of net earnings to the partners assuming that the earnings statement for 1975 shows:

a) $36,000 of net earnings.
b) $20,000 of net earnings.
c) A loss of $8,000.

11–8–B

Poole and Rankin are partners operating a retail store. Their partnership agreement calls for annual salaries of $12,000 to Poole and $16,000 to Rankin, interest at 6 percent on capital accounts at actual balances throughout the year if drawings for the year do not exceed salaries allowed, and the balance of the earnings to be shared equally. Their June 30, 1975, trial balance follows:

	Debits	*Credits*
Cash	$ 40,400	
Accounts receivable	64,000	
Inventory, July 1, 1974	28,800	
Accounts payable		$ 40,800
Notes payable, Rankin		20,000
Poole, capital		28,000
Rankin, capital		20,000
Poole, drawing	8,000	
Rankin, drawing	10,000	
Sales		428,000
Purchases	272,000	
Purchase returns		4,000
Employee salaries and wages	12,000	
Rent expense	52,000	
Delivery expense	16,800	
Store expense	36,800	
	$540,800	$540,800

The $20,000 note payable to Rankin is a 90-day note dated May 1, 1975, and calls for interest at 6 percent per year. The inventory at June 30, 1975, is $33,200. The only change in the capital accounts during the year was an additional investment by Poole of $8,000 on January 1.

Required:

a) The necessary adjusting and closing entries.
b) An earnings statement for the year ended June 30, 1975.
c) A statement of partners' capital accounts for the year.
d) A statement of financial position at the end of the year.

11–9–B

Lewis and Clark are partners. At December 31, 1975, they decided to incorporate, as of January 2, 1976, under the name of L and C, Inc. They shared earnings and losses equally. At December 31, 1975, their statement of financial position was as follows:

LEWIS AND CLARK
Statement of Financial Position
December 31, 1975

ASSETS	
Cash	$ 15,000
Receivables	31,000
Merchandise inventory	25,000
Plant assets	49,000
Total Assets	$120,000
LIABILITIES AND PARTNERS' EQUITY	
Accounts payable	$ 10,000
Lewis, capital	55,000
Clark, capital	55,000
Total Liabilities and Partners' Equity	$120,000

The partners agreed to the following valuations of noncash assets for transfer to the corporation: receivables, $30,000; merchandise inventory, $15,000; and plant assets, $55,000. Each partner received capital stock with a par value equal to the balance in his capital account after adjustment; 4,000 shares of $100 par value stock were authorized.

Required:

a) Present the journal entries necessary to close the books of the partnership.
b) Present the journal entries necessary to open the books of the corporation. (Ignore the memorandum entry which is made to record the authorized shares.)

Corporations: Formation, administration, and classes of capital stock

Learning objectives

Study of the material presented in this chapter is designed to achieve a number of learning objectives. These include:

1. A general knowledge of the nature of corporations, including familiarity with the incorporation process, the corporate structure, and the advantages and disadvantages of doing business under the corporate form of organization.
2. An introductory level comprehension of the nature of capital stock, particularly the distinctions between common and preferred stock.
3. A working knowledge of the transactions relating to the issuance of capital stock.
4. Familiarity with the valuation problems involved in capital stock issues, especially when stock is issued in exchange for goods and services.
5. An understanding of the nature, significance, and accounting treatment of intangible assets generated by incorporation.

Frame 1[12]

Although fewer in number than single proprietorships and partnerships, corporations possess the bulk of our business capital and currently supply us with most of our goods and services. This chapter discusses the corporate form of business organization, its administration, and some of the unique problems encountered in accounting for and reporting on the ownership (stockholders' equity) interest in a corporation.

The corporation defined

A corporation is an association of individuals recognized by law as possessing an existence separate and distinct from any of these individuals. That is, it is a separate legal entity. It is an artificial, invisible, intangible being or person created by law. It is endowed with many of the rights and obligations possessed by natural persons. It can, for example, enter into contracts in its own name; buy, sell, or hold real or personal property; borrow money; hire and fire employees; sue and be sued. But it cannot vote.

Advantages of the corporation

Corporations have proved to be remarkably well-suited vehicles for marshaling the huge amounts of capital necessary to secure the economies attending large-scale mass production. The advantages individuals find in investing their savings in corporations include (1) ease of transferability of ownership simply by selling the shares owned; (2) limited liability, that is, stockholders are not personally responsible for the corporation's debts; (3) continuous existence; (4) professional management; (5) centralized authority and responsibility; and (6) stockholders are not agents of a corporation.

Assume that you are a wealthy person with many business interests who has agreed to provide the capital to finance an enterprise seeking to develop, manufacture, and sell a device recently developed by a nearly destitute inventor. You and the inventor are each to have a 50 percent interest in the enterprise. On a separate piece of paper or on the answer sheet provided in the *Work Papers* indicate whether each of the following statements is true or false.

1. You favor the corporate form of organization for your business enterprise primarily because of the ease with which the corporation's shares can be transferred.
2. The fact that a stockholder's responsibility for corporate debts is usually limited to his investment in the capital stock of the corporation is the main reason you favor the corporate form of business organization.
3. If you expected your business to have a very long life, you would prefer the partnership form of organization for your enterprise.

4. The fact that the corporation may secure the services of a team of highly skilled professional managers causes you to favor the corporate form.

Now turn to Answer Frame 1[12] on page 544 to check your answers.

Frame 2[12]

Disadvantages of the corporation

The corporate form of organization is not without its disadvantages. These include:

1. Taxation. Being a separate legal entity, the net earnings of a corporation are subject to taxation.

2. Government regulation. Because corporations are created by law, they are subject to greater regulation and control than other forms of organization.

3. Entrenched management. Such a management may become thoroughly entrenched because it can use corporate funds to solicit proxies (votes) from stockholders.

4. Limited ability to raise creditor capital. The limited liability of stockholders makes a corporation an attractive device for accumulating stockholder capital. At the same time, this limited liability feature limits the amount of creditor capital a corporation may amass because creditors cannot look to the personal assets of stockholders for satisfaction of their debts if the corporation cannot pay.

Incorporating

Each state has a corporation act which permits the formation of corporations by qualified persons. The requirements of the corporation act must be met by the persons—incorporators—who desire to form a corporation. Most state corporation laws require a minimum of three incorporators, each of whom must be a natural person of legal age, and a majority of whom must be citizens of the United States.

If a company intends to conduct business solely within one state, it normally seeks incorporation in the state in which the business will be conducted, because most state laws are less severe for domestic corporations. The law of each state views a corporation organized in that state as a domestic corporation and a corporation organized in any other state as a foreign corporation. Concerns conducting an interstate business usually incorporate in the state whose laws are considered most advantageous to the corporation being formed, especially as regards the powers granted the corporation, the taxes levied upon it, and the reports required of it.

Answer frame 1[12]

1. False. This is not the primary reason you would prefer the corporate form of business organization. See Answer 2.
2. True. You, being a wealthy person, undoubtedly wish to limit your responsibility for any debts the business might incur. The corporate form of organization provides such a limitation.
3. False. Continuous existence is one of the main advantages of the corporation, not the partnership. The corporate form of business organization is better suited for businesses that are long-lived.
4. True. The corporate form does have this advantage.

If you missed any of the questions, you are encouraged to reread Frame 1[12] before beginning Frame 2[12] on page 543.

Articles of incorporation

2[12] *continued*

The contract between the state and the incorporators and their successors is known as the charter. The application for the charter is known as the articles of incorporation. When the information requested in the application form is supplied, the articles are filed with the proper office of the state of incorporation. Upon approval by this office (frequently that of the secretary of state), the charter is granted and the corporation exists. Different states require different information in the articles of incorporation; the following list is representative of the information that must be supplied: (1) name of corporation; (2) location of principal office; (3) purposes of business; (4) number of shares authorized, class or classes of shares, and voting and dividend rights of each class of shares; (5) value of assets paid in by the original subscribers to shares; (6) subscription price for shares without par value; (7) limitations on authority of the management and owners of the corporation; and (8) such things as the duration of the corporation's existence.

As soon as the charter is obtained, the corporation is authorized to operate its business. The incorporators call the first meeting of the stockholders. Two of the purposes of the first meeting of the stockholders are to elect a board of directors and to adopt a code of regulations (bylaws) for the corporation.

In most states an incorporation fee is charged based upon a designated number of cents per share of authorized capital stock; the fee is usually on a sliding scale, decreasing on a per share basis as the number of shares authorized increases.

Indicate whether each of the following statements is true or false.

1. A corporation may conduct business only in the state in which it is incorporated.
2. The charter is the contract between the state and the incorporators which gives the corporation its separate legal existence.

3. Items which may influence the selection of the state of incorporation include the powers granted a corporation, the taxes levied against it, and the reports required of it.
4. A corporation which is a domestic corporation to one state will be considered a foreign corporation by all other states.

Now turn to Answer Frame 2^{12} on page 546 to check your answers.

Frame 3^{12}

Directing the corporation

The corporation is managed through the delegation of authority in a line from the stockholders to the directors to the officers. The stockholders elect the board of directors. The board of directors formulates the broad policies of the company and selects the principal officers, who execute the policies.

Stockholders. Stockholders, as such, do not have the right to participate actively in the management of the business, although they may serve as directors or officers, or both. But each stockholder does have certain basic rights; these include the right to (1) dispose of his shares (2) buy additional shares as they are issued on a proportional basis (the preemptive right), (3) share in dividends when declared, (4) share in assets in liquidation, and (5) share in management by voting his shares.

Normally, stockholders meet annually. At this meeting each stockholder is entitled to one vote for each share of voting stock held. If a stockholder does not personally attend meetings, he may vote by proxy. A proxy is a document of authority, signed by the stockholder, giving another person—usually the secretary of the corporation—the authority to vote his shares. At the annual meeting, the stockholders share in the management by voting on such questions as changing the charter, increasing capital stock issues, approving pension plans, selecting auditors, and others.

Determine whether each of the following is true or false.

1. One of a stockholder's basic rights is to dispose of his shares of capital stock.
2. Through the use of a proxy, a stockholder gives another person authority to vote his shares at a stockholders' meeting.
3. The preemptive right refers to a stockholder's right to receive dividends when they are declared by the board of directors.
4. When a corporation liquidates, stockholders have the right to receive the undistributed assets that are in excess of the claims of creditors.

Turn to Answer Frame 3^{12} on page 546 to check your answers.

Answer frame 2^{12}

1. False. A corporation is incorporated in only one state, but it need not restrict its business activities to that state.
2. True. The charter is as described.
3. True. These items should be considered in selecting the state in which to incorporate.
4. True. A corporation is only considered a domestic corporation in the state in which it is incorporated.

If you missed any of the above, reread Frame 2^{12} before beginning Frame 3^{12} on page 545.

Answer frame 3^{12}

1. True. This is one of the stockholder's basic rights.
2. True. A proxy does give another person the authority to vote a stockholder's shares at a stockholders' meeting.
3. False. The preemptive right is the right of the stockholder to subscribe for additional shares from new issues of capital stock of the class owned in proportion to his holdings at the date of the additional issue.
4. True. This is one of the basic rights of a stockholder.

If you missed any of the above, restudy Frame 3^{12} before beginning Frame 4^{12} below.

Frame 4^{12}

Board of directors. Stockholders elect a board of directors which is primarily responsible for the formulation of broad business policies and for the protection of both stockholder and creditor interests. The board in turn appoints administrative officers, and delegates to them the execution of the broad policies established by the board. The board also has more specific duties including (1) authorization of contracts, (2) declaration of dividends, (3) establishment of executive salaries, and (4) granting authorization to borrow money. The decisions of the board are recorded in the minutes of its meetings. These minutes are an important source of information to the accountant, as they serve as a basis for certain entries.

Corporate officers. Officers of a corporation usually are specified in the code of regulations and commonly are as follows:

The president is the chief executive officer of the corporation. He is empowered by the code of regulations to appoint all necessary employees except those appointed by the board of directors.

Vice presidents frequently are empowered to sign negotiable paper and are charged with the responsibility of specified functional operations, such as sales, engineering, production, and finance.

The secretary has charge of the official records of the company. He records the proceedings of meetings of stockholders and directors and usually is the duly appointed corporate agent upon whom processes, tax notices, and demands are served.

The treasurer is the custodian of company funds. He may be charged with general supervision of accounting. Usually he is one of the persons designated to sign checks.

Code of regulations (bylaws). At its first meeting, the board of directors, authorized by the stockholders, drafts and adopts a code of regulations, also known as the corporation's bylaws. The code contains, along with other information, provisions for the following: (*a*) the place, date, and manner of calling the annual stockholders' meeting; (*b*) the method of electing directors and the number of directors; (*c*) the duties and powers of the directors; and (*d*) the method of selecting officers of the corporation.

Determine whether each of the following is true of false.

1. The administrative officers of a corporation are elected by the stockholders.
2. The application for a charter is known as a code of regulations.
3. The board of directors is elected by the stockholders and exercises broad directional control over the affairs of the corporation.
4. The minutes of the meetings of the board of directors are not an item of interest to the corporation's accountant or auditor.

Now turn to Answer Frame 4[12] on page 548 to check your answers.

Frame 5[12]

Capital stock

Capital stock authorized

The corporate charter will state the number of shares and the par value, if any, per share of each class of stock that the corporation is permitted to issue. The corporation may not intend to issue all of its authorized stock immediately. It may hold some for issuance in the future when additional capital is needed. If all authorized stock is issued immediately, the consent of the state will be required to alter the charter in order to secure additional authorized shares for issuance if capital is needed later.

Capital stock outstanding

The total ownership of a corporation rests with the holders of the outstanding shares of stock—that is, the shares authorized and issued and currently held by stockholders. If, for example, a corporation is authorized to issue 10,000 shares of common stock but has issued only 8,000 shares, the holders of the 8,000 shares own 100 percent of the corporation.

Answer frame 4[12]

1. False. The board of directors selects the administrative officers of a corporation.
2. False. The application for a charter is known as the articles of incorporation.
3. True. Stockholders do elect the board of directors, which, in turn, represents the stockholders' interest in the overall management of the corporation.
4. False. Since these minutes contain the official decisions of the board of directors, they provide the basis for certain entries, especially those pertaining to corporate capital.

If you missed any of the above, reread Frame 4[12] before beginning Frame 5[12] on page 547.

5[12]
continued

Each outstanding share of stock of a given class is identical with any other outstanding share of that class with respect to the rights and privileges possessed. Shares authorized but not yet issued are referred to as unissued shares (there are 2,000 unissued shares in the above example). No rights or privileges attach to these shares until they are issued; they are not, for example, entitled to dividends, nor can they be voted at stockholders' meetings.

Classes of capital stock

The two ordinary classes of capital stock that may be issued by a corporation are (*a*) preferred stock and (*b*) common stock. If only one class of stock is issued, it is known as common stock, and the rights of the stockholder (listed in Frame 3[12]) are enjoyed equally by the holders of all shares. The common stock is usually referred to as the residual equity in the corporation. This means simply that all other claims rank ahead of the claims of the common stockholder.

A corporation may also issue preferred stock with different rights and privileges than those possessed by the common stock. And different classes of preferred stock may exist with slightly different characteristics.

Indicate whether each of the following statements is true or false.

1. A corporation may have several classes of preferred stock.
2. The number of shares of stock which a corporation has issued and outstanding may at times exceed the number of its authorized shares.
3. Shares of preferred stock and shares of common stock are both representations of ownership in a corporation and both always confer the same rights and privileges.
4. The number of a corporation's authorized shares of stock may exceed the number of its shares which are issued and outstanding.

Now turn to Answer Frame 5[12] on page 550 to check your answers.

Frame 6[12]

Preferred stock

Corporations generally issue preferred stock for one or more of three main reasons: (1) With several classes of stock available for issuance, more capital may be attracted from investors who have differing investment objectives. In fact some institutional investors (banks) are prohibited by law from owning common stocks but may own preferred stocks. (2) Since preferred stocks usually have no voting rights, their issuance does not dilute the control of the common stockholders over the corporation. (3) The return (dividend) on preferred stocks is usually fixed. Thus, considerable financial leverage is made possible by their use.

As an example of financial leverage, assume that the organizers of a corporation have two feasible ways of securing capital: (1) issue 20,000 shares of $10 par value common for $200,000, or (2) issue 10,000 shares of $10 par value common for $100,000 and 1,000 shares of $100 par value, 6 percent preferred stock for $100,000. Net earnings of $30,000 per year are expected. The earnings to the common stockholders on a per share basis (net earnings less preferred dividends divided by number of common shares outstanding) and as a percentage of original investment are:

	With Preferred	*Without Preferred*
Net earnings	$30,000	$30,000
Preferred dividends	6,000	—0—
Net earnings to common stock	$24,000	$30,000
Number of common shares outstanding	10,000	20,000
Earnings per share of common stock	$2.40	$1.50
Earnings to common as a percentage of original investment ($100,000 and $200,000)	24%	15%

The use of the preferred stock increases the expected earnings per share on the common stock from $1.50 to $2.40 and the rate of return expected on the original investment from 15 percent to 24 percent. Under these circumstances, if the common stock is regularly traded on an exchange, it will probably sell at a substantially higher price if the preferred is issued than if it is not.

When a corporation issues both preferred and common stock, the preferred stock may be:

1. Preferred as to dividends. If it is, it may be:
   a) Cumulative or noncumulative.
   b) Participating or nonparticipating.
2. Preferred as to assets in the event of liquidation.
3. Convertible or nonconvertible.
4. Callable.

Stock preferred as to dividends

If stock is preferred as to dividends, the holders thereof are entitled to a specified dividend per share before the payment of any dividend

Answer frame 5[12]

1. True. There can be several classes of preferred stock, each with different characteristics (such as dividend rates).
2. False. The number of shares which a corporation has issued and are outstanding cannot exceed the number of shares it is authorized to issue.
3. False. Shares of preferred stock and of common stock do not usually confer the same rights and privileges, although both are representations of ownership in the corporation.
4. True. For various reasons, a corporation may chose not to issue all of the stock it is authorized to issue.

If you missed any of the above, reread Frame 5[12] before beginning Frame 6[12] on page 549.

6[12]
continued

on the common stock. The required dividend may be stated as a specific dollar amount per share per year, such as $4.40, or it may be stated as a percentage of the par value of the preferred stock. Regardless of the manner in which they are stated, preferred stock dividends are usually paid quarterly. A dividend—in full or in part—can be paid on the preferred stock only if it is declared by the board of directors and, in some states, only if the corporation has retained earnings at least equal in dollar amount to the dividend declared.

A stock preferred as to dividends is cumulative if all dividends in arrears (required dividends not paid in prior years) and the current dividend on this stock must be paid before dividends can be paid on the common stock. For example, assume cumulative 4 percent preferred stock outstanding of $100,000, common stock outstanding of $100,000, and retained earnings of $10,000. No dividends have been paid for two years, including the current year. The preferred stockholders are entitled to dividends of $8,000 before any dividend can be paid to the common stockholders.

Dividends in arrears are never shown as a liability of the corporation, since they are not a legal liability until declared by the board of directors. But since the amount of dividends in arrears may influence the decisions of users of a corporation's financial statements, such dividends should be, and usually are, disclosed in a footnote. An appropriate footnote might read: "Dividends in the amount of $8,000, representing two years' dividends on the company's 4 percent cumulative preferred stock, were in arrears as of December 31, 1975."

If a preferred stock is noncumulative, a dividend omitted or not paid in any one year need not be paid in any future year. Because omitted dividends are usually lost forever, noncumulative preferred stocks hold little attraction for investors and are rarely issued.

A corporation has $100,000 par value of 5 percent preferred stock outstanding, $200,000 par value of common stock outstanding, and $50,000 of retained earnings. No dividends were paid last year because a net loss was sustained. Before the payment of any dividends to the common stockholders may be made at the current year-end, the preferred stockholders are entitled to dividends of:

1. How much if the stock is cumulative?
2. How much if it is noncumulative?

Now check your answers by turning to Answer Frame 6[12] on page 552.

Frame 7[12]

Participating preferred stock

Although it is a relatively uncommon offering, a preferred stock may possess the right to participate in dividends at a rate greater than its stated basic dividend according to carefully spelled-out provisions in the preferred stock contract. For example, a preferred stock may have a preference over common to a cumulative dividend of $5 per share per year. After the common stock has received a dividend of $2 per share in any fiscal year, the preferred may be entitled to participate in additional dividends on a share-for-share basis with the common. Thus, for every $1 of dividends paid to the common over the specified $2 per share, $1 must be paid to the preferred. If a dividend of $4 is to be paid to the common, $7 must be paid to the preferred.

If there is no limit on the amount of additional dividends a preferred stock may receive, it is called a fully participating preferred. If a maximum limit is placed on the annual dividend on a participating preferred stock, such as $8 in the above example, it is called a partially participating preferred stock.

If preferred stock is nonparticipating, as are most preferreds, it is entitled to its indicated dividend only, regardless of the size of the dividend paid on the common stock.

Stock preferred as to assets

Most preferred stocks are preferred as to assets in the event of dissolution and liquidation of the corporation. Typically, this means that the preferred stockholders are entitled to receive the par value (or a larger stipulated liquidating value) per share before the common stockholders receive any distribution of corporate assets. If there are cumulative preferred dividends in arrears at liquidation, they usually are payable regardless of whether there are retained earnings sufficient to meet them. Stock may be preferred as to assets or dividends, or both.

To illustrate the preference as to assets feature, assume a corporation has $100,000 par value of preferred stock outstanding; $200,000 par value of common stock outstanding; and, after paying its liabilities, cash of $240,000 remaining to distribute to its stockholders. If the preferred stock is preferred as to assets and there are no dividends in arrears, the preferred stockholders will receive $100,000, with $140,000 being paid to the common stockholders. If the preferred stock is not preferred as

Answer frame 6[12]

1. \$10,000 if the preferred stock is cumulative. The shareholders are entitled to dividends for two years, last year and this year, before the common shareholders may receive any dividends.
2. \$5,000 if the preferred stock is noncumulative. The preferred stockholders are entitled to only the current year's dividend before payments may be made to the common stockholders.

If you missed these answers, reread Frame 6[12] before beginning Frame 7[12] on page 551.

7[12] *continued*

to assets, the \$240,000 is prorated between the preferred and common stockholders in the ratio of the dollar total of the classes: \$80,000 [(\$100,000/\$300,000) × \$240,000] to the preferred stockholders and \$160,000 to the common stockholders.

Indicate whether each of the following statements is true or false.

1. Shareholders whose stock is preferred as to assets in the event of corporate liquidation are entitled to receive the par value of their shares before any amounts are distributed to creditors or common stockholders.
2. All stock preferred as to dividends is also preferred as to assets.
3. In the event of liquidation, holders of shares preferred as to assets and dividends are entitled to receive only the par value of their stock before common shareholders receive anything, even though cumulative preferred dividends are in arrears.
4. The common stockholders of a corporation would prefer that the corporation issue fully participating rather than partially participating preferred stock if a participation feature must be included in order to sell the preferred stock.

Now check your answers in Answer Frame 7[12] on page 554.

Frame 8[12]

Convertible preferred stock

In recent years substantial amounts of new preferred stock have been issued by corporations merging with or acquiring other corporations. The preferred stock issued is often convertible; that is, the holder of the stock may exchange it, at his option, for shares of common stock of the same corporation at a conversion ratio stated in the preferred stock contract.

Preferred stock is often issued in these mergers for two main reasons: (1) to avoid the use of bonds with their fixed interest charges which must be paid regardless of the amount of net earnings, and (2) to avoid issuing so many additional shares of common stock that earnings per share will be less in the current year than in prior years.

Investors find convertible preferred stock attractive because of the greater probability that the dividends on the preferred will be paid (as compared to dividends on common shares) and because the conversion privilege may be the source of substantial price appreciation. The latter is especially attractive to those institutional investors prohibited by law from owning common stocks.

To illustrate this latter attraction, assume that the Olsen Company issued 1,000 shares of 6 percent $100 par value convertible preferred stock at $100 per share. The stock is convertible at any time into four shares of Olsen common stock, which has a current market value of $20 per share. In the next several years the company reports sharply increased net earnings and increases the dividend on the common stock from $1 to $2 per share, with the result that the common stock now sells at $40 per share. The holder of one share of preferred stock can convert his stock into four shares of common stock and increase his annual dividend from $6 to $8. Or he can sell his preferred share at a substantial gain, since the preferred stock will sell in the market at approximately $160, the market value of the four shares of common into which it is convertible. Or he may continue to hold it in the expectation of realizing an even larger gain at a later date.

On the other hand, the issuing corporation may force conversion by calling the preferred stock for redemption. Virtually all preferred stocks, convertible or nonconvertible, are callable at the option of the issuing corporation. This means simply that the holders of nonconvertible preferred stock must surrender it to the company when requested to do so. Holders of convertible preferred may either surrender it or convert it into common shares. The preferred shares are usually callable at a small premium (the call premium) of 3 or 4 percent of the par value of the stock. If the stock is surrendered, the former holder receives par value, plus the call premium, plus any dividends in arrears and a prorated portion of the current period's dividend. If the market value of the common shares he can obtain by converting his shares into common is higher than the amount he would receive in redemption, he would be foolish not to convert.

The many reasons why a corporation might call its preferred stock include (1) the outstanding preferred stock may require a 7 percent annual dividend while capital to retire the stock can be secured by issuing a new 4 percent preferred; (2) the issuing company may have been sufficiently profitable to enable it to retire the preferred stock out of earnings; and (3) the company may wish to force conversion of a convertible preferred because the cash dividend on the equivalent common shares will be less than the dividend on the preferred.

Statement of financial position presentation

To illustrate the proper financial reporting of preferred and common stock, reporting of authorized and unissued shares, and a manner of describing the shares, assume that a corporation is authorized to issue

Answer frame 7[12]

1. False. The claims of the creditors take precedence over the claims of the stockholders, even those stockholders whose stock is preferred as to assets.
2. False. A stock may be preferred as to assets or dividends, or both. Preferred stocks are not automatically preferred as to both assets and dividends.
3. False. If there are cumulative preferred dividends in arrears at liquidation, they must also be paid in full before any distribution can be made to the common stockholders.
4. False. As a common stockholder, you would prefer to see some limit on the dividends going to preferred stock. You would, therefore, prefer that the corporation issue the partially participating preferred stock.

If you missed any of the above, reread Frame 7[12] before beginning Frame 8[12] on page 552.

8[12] *continued*

10,000 shares of $100 par value, 6 percent, cumulative, convertible preferred stock, all of which have been issued and are outstanding; and 200,000 shares of $10 par value common stock of which 80,000 shares have been issued and are outstanding. The stockholders' equity section of the statement of financial position (assuming $450,000 of retained earnings) is:

Paid-In Capital:		
Preferred stock—$100 par value, 6 percent, cumulative, convertible; authorized, issued, and outstanding, 10,000 shares	$1,000,000	
Common stock—$10 par value; authorized, 200,000 shares; issued and outstanding, 80,000 shares	800,000	$1,800,000
Retained earnings		450,000
Total Stockholders' Equity		$2,250,000

A footnote to the statement of financial position states the rate at which the preferred stock is convertible into common stock. If the preferred stock is participating, a footnote is included stating the terms of participation and the word "participating" is included in the description of the stock in the statement of financial position.

Indicate whether each of the following statements is true or false.

1. Use the data in the above illustration and assume that no dividends have been declared or paid for the years 1974 and 1975. If the board of directors declares $250,000 of dividends on January 2, 1976, $120,000 must go to the preferred stockholders.
2. The corporation in the above illustration could quite safely and properly issue the 120,000 of authorized but unissued common shares to its common stockholders for $10 per share.

3. A corporation can often force conversion of its convertible preferred stock even though holders of the stock would prefer not to convert it.
4. A corporation can issue a preferred stock that is cumulative, participating, convertible, callable, and possesses voting rights.

Now check your answers in Answer Frame 8^{12} on page 556.

Frame 9^{12}

Capital stock with par value

Each share of capital stock (common or preferred) is, according to the terms of the charter of the issuing corporation, of par value or without par value. The par value, if any, is stated in the charter and printed on the stock certificates issued. Par value may be of any amount—1¢, 10¢, 16⅔¢, $1, $5, or $100; low par values, $10 or less, are commonplace in our economy.

Par value per share is no indication of the amount of stockholders' equity per share (book value per share, as it is called) that is recorded in the accounting records of the corporation. The stockholders' equity consists of paid-in capital and retained earnings, and the latter may be either positive or negative. Nor does par value give any clue to the market value of the stock. Shares with a par value of $5 have sold in the market for well over $600, and many $100 par value preferred stocks have sold for considerably less than par. Par value is not even a reliable indicator of the price at which shares can be issued. Even in new corporations, shares are often issued at prices well in excess of par value and may even be issued for less than par value if state laws permit.

But par value does serve two purposes: (1) it is the amount per share that is credited to the capital stock account for each share outstanding, and (2) the par value of the outstanding shares is often the legal or stated capital of the corporation. A corporation is prohibited by law from declaring dividends or acquiring its own stock if such actions will reduce stockholders' equity below the legal capital of the corporation. For this reason, the par value of the outstanding shares does tend to serve as a buffer or cushion of capital to protect creditors from losses.

Indicate whether each of the following statements is true or false.

1. The par value of a share of capital stock is no indication of the market value or the book value of the share of stock.
2. The par value of a share of capital stock indicates the price at which the share must originally be issued.
3. The par value of a share of common stock must be $100.
4. Losses decrease and earnings increase the par value of stock.

Now check your answers by turning to Answer Frame 9^{12} on page 556.

Answer frame 8[12]

1. True. The preferred stock is entitled to dividends of $60,000 per year. Since the stock is cumulative, two years' dividends must be paid to the preferred before any dividends can be paid to the common stockholders.
2. False. The corporation cannot safely and properly issue the unissued common shares to its common stockholders. Some of the authorized but unissued shares must be reserved for issuance to the preferred stockholders when they present their convertible preferred shares for conversion.
3. True. A corporation can often force conversion of its preferred stock. If the market price of the preferred is largely a reflection of the market value of the common shares into which it can be converted, and if this market price is larger than the call price of the preferred, an investor would be foolish not to convert the preferred when it is called.
4. True. A corporation will usually put into a preferred stock contract those features necessary to make the stock attractive to investors. If all of these features are required to induce investors to acquire the stock, then they may be included. The callable feature is, of course, designed primarily to allow the corporation to terminate the investment.

If you missed any of the above, reread Frame 8[12] before beginning Frame 9[12] on page 555.

Answer frame 9[12]

1. True. The assignment of a par value to a share of stock is meaningless as far as indicating the market value or book value of the stock.
2. False. A share of stock may be issued for more than its par value and, if state laws permit, it may be issued for less than its par value.
3. False. Par value may be any amount.
4. False. Earnings and losses do not influence the par value of stock. They do, however, affect the book value of stock.

If you missed any of the above, reread Frame 9[12] before beginning Frame 10[12] below.

Frame 10[12]

Capital stock without par value

Laws permitting the issuance of shares of stock without par value (sometimes referred to as no par value stock) were first enacted in New York in 1912. Similar, but not uniform, legislation has since been passed in many states. Shares of stock without par value may or may not have a stated value.

Stated value stock. The board of directors of a corporation issuing stock without par value may assign a stated value to each share of capital stock. This stated value, like par value, may be set at any amount by the board, although some state statutes specify a minimum amount such as $5 per share. Stated value may be established either before or after the shares are issued, if not specified by applicable state law.

When shares without par value but with stated value are issued, the shares are carried in the capital stock account at a uniform amount per share—the stated value. Any amounts received in excess of the stated value per share, as well as the stated value itself, represent a part of the capital of the corporation and should be credited to a paid-in capital account. The stated or legal capital of a corporation issuing stated value shares is generally equal to the aggregate of the stated value of the shares issued.

As an illustration, assume that the DeWitt Corporation, which is authorized to issue 10,000 shares of capital stock without par value, assigns a stated value of $20 per share to its stock. The 10,000 authorized shares are issued at $22 per share. The stockholders' equity section of the statement of financial position is as follows:

Common stock without par value, stated value, $20; 10,000 shares authorized, issued, and outstanding	$200,000
Paid-in capital in excess of stated value	20,000
Total Stockholders' Equity	$220,000

The $20,000 received over and above the stated value of $200,000 is carried permanently as paid-in capital because it is a part of the capital originally contributed by the stockholders. The stated capital of the DeWitt Corporation, however, is generally held to be $200,000—the stated value of the shares issued.

Shares without par value or stated value. If a corporation issues shares without par value which have not been assigned a stated value, the entire amount received is credited to the capital stock account. Because shares may be issued at different times and at differing amounts, the credit to the capital stock account is not at a uniform amount per share, contrary to the case of par value or no par, stated value shares. The entire amount received for shares without par value, to which no stated value is assigned or required by state law, is the amount of stated capital. Some state laws specify that, as a minimum, a certain percentage of the amount received must be carried in a capital stock account.

If, in the above illustration of the DeWitt Corporation, no stated value is assigned to the shares, the stockholders' equity section of the company's statement of financial position is as follows:

Common stock without par or stated value; 10,000 shares authorized, issued, and outstanding	$220,000
Total Stockholders' Equity	$220,000

The actual capital contributed by stockholders is $220,000. In some states, the stated capital is also $220,000. In Michigan the stated capital is at least 50 percent of the amount received. But even if the DeWitt Corporation were organized under the laws of the state of Michigan, the stockholders' equity section of its statement of financial position would be as given above, since the shares have no stated value.

Some general guides to the legal concept of stated capital have been presented. In any actual situation the stated capital of a corporation is governed by the laws of the state of incorporation, and these laws vary considerably.

Dividends declared on shares without par value, whether with or without a stated value, are expressed in dollars per share; dividends on par value shares may be expressed either in terms of a percentage of the par value per share or in dollars per share.

There are several reasons for issuing capital stock without par value. (1) The use of a par value may cause confusion among some investors who are unable to reconcile the constant par figure with the changes in book value and the fluctuating prices at which the stock may be quoted in the stock market. When there is no par or stated value, this source of confusion is avoided. (2) If par value stock is issued at a discount, it often carries with it a contingent liability upon the shareholders to creditors of the corporation for the amount of the discount. Although this liability has not been enforced in many cases, the issuance of shares without par or stated value avoids the possibility of such a liability. (3) Most states prohibit the original issuance of stock at a discount. Use of shares without a par or stated value permits an issuance at whatever price the existing market conditions warrant. (4) In states that prohibit the original issuance of stock at a discount, subterfuges may be employed when par value stock is issued in exchange for property other than cash. For example, the board of directors may accept property in exchange for capital stock. The value of the property may be inflated to avoid disclosure of the discount on common stock. The issuance of shares without par or stated value removes one of the reasons for inflation of asset values.

Decide whether each of the following statements is true or false.

1. Shares without par or stated value cannot be issued at a discount.
2. The assignment of a stated value to each share of stock that is without par value results in the receipt of a uniform price per share for the stock.
3. The issuance of par value stock at a price less than the par value may create a contingent liability upon stockholders to creditors of the corporation.
4. The amount carried in the account Paid-In Capital in Excess of Stated Value represents part of a corporation's permanent capital.

Now turn to Answer Frame 10[12] on page 560.

Frame 11[12]

Recording capital stock issues

The steps in recording the issuance of capital stock usually are as follows:

1. Receipt of subscriptions for the issuance of the capital stock.
2. Collection of the subscriptions.
3. Issuance of the stock certificates.

In most states, authorized stock becomes legally issued at the time a subscription is accepted. A bona fide subscription contract may be regarded as an asset of the corporation. Thus, the subscriber is a shareholder. The subscriber's legal status as a shareholder is not dependent on the issuance of the stock certificate. Nevertheless, for accounting purposes capital stock is not recorded as issued until the time the stock certificate is delivered to the shareholder.

The authorization of a stock issue does not create an asset or a capital item; it merely establishes the possibility of obtaining assets through the issuance of the stock. Therefore, the authorization to issue stock is not a transaction to be recorded by journal entry. The authorization to issue stock is noted as a memorandum in the ledger (and often in the general journal) in order to avoid issuing shares in excess of the number authorized.

The Stock Subscribed account

When stock certificates are not issued until a subscriber has paid in full for his subscription, a separate account must be maintained to show the amount of stock subscribed but not yet outstanding. This is accomplished by setting up a Common (or Preferred) Stock Subscribed account.

To illustrate, assume that the Grayson Corporation was authorized to issue 100,000 shares of common capital stock without par value. On January 2, 1975, the corporation received subscriptions for 20,000 shares at $20 per share. The subscriptions were collected on January 10, 1975. The journal entries would be as follows:

January 2, 1975

On this day the corporation was authorized to issue 100,000 shares of common stock without par value.

1975			
Jan. 2	Subscriptions Receivable—Common	400,000	
	Common Stock Subscribed		400,000
	To record subscriptions to 20,000 shares of common stock without par or stated value at $20 per share.		
Jan. 10	Cash	400,000	
	Subscriptions Receivable—Common		400,000
	To record the collection of subscriptions in full.		
Jan. 10	Common Stock Subscribed	400,000	
	Common Stock		400,000
	To record issuance of stock certificates for 20,000 shares.		

Answer frame 10^{12}

1. True. Discounts cannot exist for stock without par value as there is no base figure (par) from which to compute a discount.
2. False. The assignment of a stated value to stock without par value results in a uniform amount per share being credited to the capital stock account; but shares issued at different times are still likely to be issued at different prices because of changing market conditions. Any excess over the stated value is credited to a paid-in capital account.
3. True. Stock issued at a discount (at a price less than its par value) may carry a contingent liability to creditors of the corporation for the amount of the discount.
4. True. Amounts received for stock without par value in excess of the stated value per share do represent a part of the permanent capital of the corporation.

If you missed any of the above, reread Frame 10^{12} before beginning Frame 11^{12} on page 558.

11^{12} *continued*

Indicate whether each of the following statements is true or false.

1. The entry to record the receipt of cash in payment for common stock subscriptions results in a debit to Subscriptions Receivable—Common and a credit to Cash.
2. The credit balance in the Common Stock Subscribed account represents the dollar amount of shares authorized but not yet issued.
3. The authorization of a stock issue is recorded in the journal by a debit to Subscriptions Receivable—Common and a credit to Common Stock Authorized.
4. The receipt of subscriptions to preferred stock without par or stated value is recorded by a debit to Subscriptions Receivable—Preferred and a credit to Preferred Stock Subscribed.

Now turn to Answer Frame 11^{12} on page 562 to check your answers.

Frame 12^{12}

To continue the Grayson Corporation illustration, assume that on January 15, 1975, subscriptions were received for 30,000 shares at $22 per share, and 80 percent of each of the subscriptions was collected on January 25, 1975. Certificates for these shares are to be issued when the subscriptions are collected in full.

Note that the subscriptions received January 2 were at $20 per share and those received January 15 were at $22 per share. On January 15 the corporation decided to assign a stated value of $20 to each share. This merely means that the corporation wished to credit the proper capital stock account at the uniform amount of $20 per share. Any amount received in the future or in the past in excess of $20 per share ($2 in this case) would be credited to a capital account called Paid-In Capital in Excess of Stated Value. This account represents a portion of the capital contributed by the stockholders, and it is capital just as is the amount credited to the capital stock accounts.

The journal entries would be as follows:

1975			
Jan. 15	Subscriptions Receivable—Common	660,000	
	Common Stock Subscribed		600,000
	Paid-In Capital in Excess of Stated Value		60,000
	Subscriptions received for 30,000 shares of stock without par value at $22 per share. The stated value is $20 per share.		
Jan. 25	Cash	528,000	
	Subscriptions Receivable—Common		528,000
	Received 80 percent on each of the subscriptions of January 15, 1975.		

What is the total stated value of the Grayson Corporation shares subscribed for but not issued at January 25, 1975?

Now turn to Answer Frame 12[12] on page 562 to check your answer.

Frame 13[12]

Presentation in statement of financial position

Illustration 12.1 shows the statement of financial position prepared from the accounts shown in Frames 11[12] and 12[12].

Illustration 12.1

THE GRAYSON CORPORATION
Statement of Financial Position
January 25, 1975

ASSETS

Current Assets:		
Cash		$ 928,000
Subscriptions Receivable—Common		132,000
		$1,060,000

STOCKHOLDERS' EQUITY

Paid-In Capital		
Common stock without par value, stated value, $20 per share; 100,000 shares authorized:		
Issued and outstanding, 20,000 shares	$400,000	
Subscribed but not issued, 30,000 shares (see subscriptions receivable)	600,000	$1,000,000
Paid-in capital in excess of stated value		60,000
		$1,060,000

Answer frame 11[12]

1. False. The entry is a debit to Cash and a credit to Subscriptions Receivable—Common.
2. False. The credit balance in the Capital Stock Subscribed account indicates the dollar amount of shares subscribed for but not issued to the subscribers.
3. False. No formal journal entry is made for the authorization to issue stock. The authorization is noted as a memorandum in the ledger (and often in the journal) in order to avoid issuing shares in excess of the number authorized.
4. True. These are the accounts which should be debited and credited. When subscriptions are accompanied by a full cash remittance and the shares subscribed for are issued immediately, there is no need to use the Subscriptions Receivable and Stock Subscribed accounts. For example, if common shares are involved, an entry debiting Cash and crediting the Common Stock account for the amount received is sufficient.

If you missed any of the above, reread Frame 11[12] before beginning Frame 12[12] on page 560.

Answer frame 12[12]

The value is $600,000. This is the balance in the Common Stock Subscribed account and represents the stated value of stock subscribed for but not yet issued to subscribers.

If you did not answer correctly, reread Frame 12[12] before beginning Frame 13[12] on page 561.

13[12] *continued*

Two accounts, Subscriptions Receivable—Common (or Preferred) and Common (or Preferred) Stock Subscribed, must be displayed on any statement of financial position prepared prior to collection in full of amounts owed by subscribers and issuance of the stock certificates.

The Common Stock Subscribed account should be regarded as a temporary capital stock account, with its balance representing the stated (or par) value or, for shares without par or stated value, the subscription price of shares subscribed for but not yet issued. It should be presented immediately below the Common Stock account. The two accounts should be combined to present the total of shares issued and to be issued. To this should be added the balance, if any, of the Paid-In Capital in Excess of Stated (or Par) Value account.

The reference to subscriptions receivable following the caption, "Subscribed but not issued, 30,000 shares" in Illustration 12.1 informs the reader that only $468,000, not $600,000, has been received on the 30,000 subscribed shares.

Subscriptions receivable normally will be collected within a matter of days or weeks. They are, therefore, properly classified as a current asset in the statement of financial position, although the account should be displayed separately and not included in the total of trade accounts receivable. In rare instances, collection of the subscriptions will not be effected within the coming operating cycle. The account is then properly classifiable as a noncurrent asset and preferably shown under the caption "Other assets" near the bottom of the assets section of the statement of financial position.

Decide whether the following statement is true or false.

The balance in the Subscriptions Receivable—Common account shown in Illustration 12.1 represents the cash collections on common stock.

Now turn to Answer Frame 13[12] on page 564 to check your answer.

Frame 14[12]

Issuance of par value stock

The following examples illustrate the conventional method of recording the issuance of par value stock. The method follows the practice indicated in accounting for shares with stated value, where it was assumed that the shares were issued when subscriptions are fully paid. The examples differ from each other in the degree of completion of the various steps of subscription of stock, collection of cash, and issuance of certificates. The data used concern the Lake Company, organized as a corporation with an authorized capital stock (all common) of $500,000, divided into 5,000 shares with a par value of $100 each. The authorization is noted in memorandum form in the general journal and in the Common Stock account.

If all the capital stock is subscribed at par the entry is:

Subscriptions Receivable—Common	500,000	
Common Stock Subscribed		500,000
To record the subscriptions to 5,000 shares at par.		

At the time of a 20 percent cash collection of the subscriptions, the entry is:

Cash	100,000	
Subscriptions Receivable—Common		100,000
To record the partial collection of the subscriptions.		

When subscriptions are collected in full, the certificates are issued and the following entry is prepared:

Common Stock Subscribed	500,000	
Common Stock		500,000
Certificates issued for 5,000 shares paid in full.		

Answer frame 13[12]

False. Subscriptions receivable represents the balance of the subscription price of all subscribed shares not yet collected.

If you answered incorrectly, review Frame 13[12] before turning to Frame 14[12] on page 563.

14[12]
continued

If all subscriptions accepted were accompanied by full cash payment and the shares were issued immediately, the following entry would suffice:

Cash	500,000	
Common Stock		500,000

If the stock is subscribed for at a $100,000 premium, the entry is:

Subscriptions Receivable—Common	600,000	
Common Stock Subscribed		500,000
Paid-In Capital in Excess of Par Value—Common		100,000
To record the subscriptions to 5,000 shares of common stock at $120 per share.		

When the common stock subscriptions are collected in full, an entry is made to record the issuance of the stock. If preferred stock is subscribed and fully paid, the entries are the same except that the corresponding preferred stock accounts are used.

To test your understanding of these entries, suppose that a company has authorized 2,000 shares of preferred stock at a par value of $100 per share; 1,400 shares are subscribed at $105 per share; 50 percent of each of the subscriptions is subsequently collected; no stock certificates are issued. The company has also authorized 10,000 shares of common stock at a par value of $100 per share; 8,000 shares are subscribed at $110 per share; 80 percent of each of the subscriptions is subsequently collected; no stock certificates are issued. Each class of capital stock must be specifically named in the journal entry and in the ledger accounts; in all other respects the entries are similar to those already illustrated. Thus the entries for the preferred stock subscriptions and their partial collection are as follows:

Subscriptions Receivable—Preferred	147,000	
Paid-In Capital in Excess of Par Value—Preferred		7,000
Preferred Stock Subscribed		140,000
To record subscriptions to 1,400 shares of $100 par value preferred stock at $105 per share.		
Cash	73,500	
Subscriptions Receivable—Preferred		73,500
To record the collection of 50 percent of the subscriptions.		

Prepare the entries to record the subscriptions to the common stock and their partial collection.

Check your answers by turning to Answer Frame 14[12] on page 566.

Frame 15[12]

Defaulted subscriptions. The possibility exists that a subscriber may be unable or unwilling to fulfill his subscription contract. Since these contracts often call for an immediate cash payment, with the balance payable in periodic installments, the further possibility exists that the subscriber may have paid a part of the total subscription price. The laws of the state of incorporation generally govern the disposition of the amount paid in and the balance of the contract. There are three possible courses of action: (1) the subscriber may receive as many shares as he has paid for in full, and the balance of the contract is canceled; (2) the amount paid in may be refunded (often after deducting any expenses and losses incurred in selling the shares to another party); and (3) the amount paid in may be declared forfeited to the corporation. In the latter case, the amount retained should be credited to a Paid-In Capital from Defaulted Subscriptions account to indicate the source of the capital.

Capital stock issued for property or services

When capital stock is issued for property or services a question arises: At what dollar amount should the exchange be recorded? In general, accountants seek to measure the economic significance of such exchanges by recording them at the fair value of the property or services received or of the stock issued, whichever is more clearly evident.

As an example, assume that the owners of a tract of land deed it to a corporation in exchange for 1,000 shares of $12 par value common stock which, at the time of the exchange, has a value of $14,000. The required entry is:

Land	14,000	
Common Stock		12,000
Paid-In Capital in Excess of Par Value—Common		2,000

When shares of stock are issued for property (or services), the board of directors has the right to value the property at any amount. In the absence of fraud, the courts are generally reluctant to interfere with the board's direction of corporate affairs. Consequently, in view of the legal prohibitions against issuing shares at a discount, a discount is not likely to be recorded when shares are issued for property. There have, in fact, been many recorded instances where the assets received were flagrantly overvalued by recording them at the par value of the shares issued. The accountant, especially the independent public accountant, has an obliga-

Answer frame 14[12]

The correct entries are:

Subscriptions Receivable—Common	880,000	
Common Stock Subscribed		800,000
Paid-In Capital in Excess of Par Value—Common		80,000
To record subscriptions to 8,000 shares of $100 par value common stock at $110 per share.		
Cash	704,000	
Subscriptions Receivable—Common		704,000
Collected 80 percent of the common stock subscriptions.		

If you answered incorrectly, review Frame 14[12] before turning to Frame 15[12] on page 565.

15[12] *continued*

tion to users of financial statements to determine whether the property received was overvalued and a discount improperly omitted from the accounts, and, if so, to require full disclosure of the determined discount.

Indicate whether each of the following statements is true or false.

1. A subscriber to capital stock who defaults on his subscription may, if applicable state laws so stipulate, be required to forfeit his right to any amounts paid on the subscription.
2. A subscriber to capital stock who defaults on his subscription may, if applicable state laws so stipulate, receive a partial refund of any amount paid in.
3. When shares of stock are issued for property other than cash, the exchange may be recorded at the fair value of the shares issued.
4. When shares of stock are issued for property other than cash, the exchange should generally be recorded at the par or stated value of the shares issued.

Now turn to Answer Frame 15[12] on page 568 to check your answers.

Frame 16[12]

Paid-In Capital in Excess of Par (Stated) Value accounts

Amounts received in excess of the par or stated value of shares issued should be credited to an account called Paid-In Capital in Excess of Par (or Stated) Value. The board of directors can dispose of this account in a number of ways, as discussed in the next chapter. But until such action is taken, the amounts received in excess of par or stated value should be carried in separate accounts for each class of stock issued and reported in the statement of financial position as follows:

Paid-in Capital:			
Preferred stock—$100 par value, 6 percent cumulative; 1,000 shares authorized, issued, and outstanding	$100,000		
Common stock—without par value, stated value $5; 100,000 shares authorized, 80,000 shares issued and outstanding	400,000	$500,000	
Paid-in capital in excess of par or stated value:			
From preferred stock issuances	$ 5,000		
From common stock issuances	20,000	25,000	$525,000
Retained Earnings			200,000
Total Shareholders' Equity			$725,000

Organization costs

Costs of organizing a corporation, such as state incorporation fees and legal fees applicable to incorporation, should be debited to an account called Organization Costs. Since these costs were incurred to benefit the corporation indefinitely, it is reasonable that they be carried as an asset. According to Accounting Principles Board *Opinion No. 17,* organization costs must be amortized. As long as the Organization Costs account is kept on the records, it should appear in the statement of financial position as an intangible asset. An organization cost is an example of a long-term prepayment of an intangible nature, therefore, it is excluded from current assets.

What is the proper entry if 100 shares of common stock with a par value of $40 per share are issued in exchange for legal services received in organizing a corporation, and the attorney providing the services previously agreed to a price of $5,000 for these services?

Turn to Answer Frame 16[12] on page 568 to check your response.

Frame 17[12]

Documents, books, and records relating to capital stock

Currently, as reported in the financial pages of most daily newspapers, millions of shares of corporate capital stock are traded every business day on organized stock exchanges such as the New York Stock Exchange and in the over-the-counter market. These sales (or "trades") seldom involve the corporation issuing the stock as a party to the exchange, but rather are made by existing stockholders to other individual or institutional investors. These trades are followed by the physical transfer of documents known as stock certificates.

When a stockholder sells his shares, the new owner receives the stock certificate, duly signed over to him, and presents it to the issuing corporation. The certificate is canceled and attached to its corresponding stub in the stock certificate book, and a new certificate is prepared for the

Answer frame 15[12]

1. True. Applicable state laws may require a subscriber who defaults on a subscription to forfeit any amount paid in.
2. True. Applicable state laws may stipulate that a subscriber to capital stock who defaults on his contract receive a refund (full or partial) of any amount paid in.
3. True. An exchange of shares of stock for property other than cash may be recorded at the fair value of the shares issued if this value is more clearly evident than the value of the property received.
4. False. Exchanges of stock for property other than cash should generally be recorded at the fair value of the shares or the property, whichever is more clearly evident. Recording the exchange at the par or stated value of the shares may improperly bury a discount in the asset accounts.

If you missed any of the above, reread Frame 15[12] before beginning Frame 16[12] on page 566.

Answer frame 16[12]

The correct entry is:

Organization Costs	5,000	
Common Stock		4,000
Paid-In Capital in Excess of Par Value—Common		1,000

The services should be valued at the price previously agreed on, and should be charged to an asset account because these services will benefit the corporation indefinitely. The amount by which the value of the services received exceeds the par value of the shares issued is properly credited to a Paid-In Capital in Excess of Par value—Common account.

If you answered incorrectly, reread Frame 16[12] before beginning Frame 17[12] on page 567.

17[12] *continued* new owner. The number of shares of stock outstanding at any time can be determined by summing the shares shown on the open stubs (stubs without certificates attached).

Stockholders' ledger

Among the more important records maintained by a corporation is the stockholders' ledger. This ledger is subsidiary to and contains the supporting detail for the common (or preferred) stock account contained in the general ledger. It contains an account for each stockholder and as a result may, in a large corporation, consist of more than a million individual accounts. Each stockholder's account shows the number of shares he owns, their certificate numbers, and the dates on which he acquired or sold shares. Entries are made in terms of the number of shares rather than dollars.

The stockholders' ledger contains the same information as the stock certificate book but summarizes it alphabetically by stockholder, since a stockholder may own a dozen or more certificates. When so summarized, a corporation can readily determine the number of shares a stockholder is entitled to vote at a stockholders' meeting, and dividend checks can be limited to one per stockholder rather than one per stock certificate.

Many large corporations with actively traded shares turn the task of maintaining reliable stock records over to an outside stock transfer agent and a stock registrar. The stock transfer agent, usually a bank or trust company, transfers shares between stockholders by canceling the certificates covering shares sold, issuing new stock certificates, and making appropriate entries in the stockholders' ledger. The new certificates are sent to the stock registrar, typically another bank, which maintains separate records of the shares outstanding. The control afforded by this type of system makes it highly unlikely that stock certificates can be fraudulently issued by an employee of a corporation and the proceeds stolen.

The minutes book

The minutes book, kept by the secretary of the corporation, is a written record of the actions taken at official meetings of the board of directors and at stockholders' meetings. It is the written authorization for many actions taken by corporate officers. All actions taken by the board of directors and the stockholders must be in accord with the provisions contained in the charter and in the code of regulations. The minutes book contains a variety of data, including the following:

a) A copy of the corporate charter.
b) A copy of the code of regulations (bylaws).
c) Dividends declared by the board of directors.
d) Authorization for the acquisition of major assets.
e) Authorization for borrowing.
f) Authorization for increases or decreases in capital stock.
g) Authorization for pension plans.

Indicate whether each of the following statements is true or false.

1. The minutes book is a special journal containing the debit and credit entries for transactions authorized by the board of directors.
2. A transfer of 50 shares of common stock from one stockholder, who has seen the market price of the shares decline since he acquired them, to another stockholder results in a reduction of the balance in the Common Stock account.
3. The stock transfer agent and the stock registrar of a corporation actively seek to find buyers for the corporation's stock.
4. Issuing corporations are typically not directly involved in the daily buying and selling of their shares on organized stock exchanges.

Now turn to Answer Frame 17[12] on page 570 to check your answers.

Answer frame 17[12]

1. False. The minutes book is not a journal, and the information contained in it is not in debit and credit entry form.
2. False. The market price of shares transferred from one stockholder to another has no effect upon the accounting records of the corporation.
3. False. The functions performed by the stock transfer agent and the stock registrar do not include seeking buyers for the issuing corporation's stock.
4. True. These exchanges or trades are usually made by stockholders and other investors. The next chapter will discuss circumstances in which an issuing corporation may be a party to an exchange on an organized stock exchange.

If you missed any of the above, reread Frame 17[12] before beginning Frame 18[12] below.

Frame 18[12]

Values commonly associated with capital stock

Par value. Par value is simply the nominal amount printed on a stock certificate. It is the amount per share at which par value stock is customarily recorded in the accounts. Under some state statutes the par value of the issued shares is the legal capital of the corporation—that is, the amount of capital which must be maintained unless formal procedures are employed to reduce this amount (reduction of par value, for example).

Stated value. Stated value is the amount per share at which the board of directors of a corporation may decide to record its capital stock if it does not have a par value. Any excess of issuance price over stated value is credited to Paid-In Capital in Excess of Stated Value. Stated value is similar to par value in that it is established arbitrarily and bears no necessary relationship to the market or book value of the capital stock.

Market value. Market value is the price at which shares of capital stock are bought and sold by investors in the open market. Market price is directly affected by all the factors that influence general economic conditions, investors' expectations concerning the corporation, the money market, and the earnings of the corporation. It is the value of greatest interest to most investors, assuming there is no expectation of dissolution of the corporation or of redemption of the stock involved.

Liquidation value. Liquidation value is the amount a stockholder will receive if a corporation discontinues operations and liquidates by selling its assets, paying its liabilities, and distributing the remaining cash among the stockholders. Since the assets may be sold for more or less than the amounts at which they are recorded in the corporation's accounts, liquidation value may be more or less than book value, which is discussed below. If only one class of common stock is outstanding, each stockholder will receive, per share, the amount obtained by dividing the remaining cash by the number of shares of stock outstanding. If both common and preferred stock are outstanding, liquidation values depend on the preference features of the preferred stock.

Redemption value. Preferred stock may be issued with the stipulation that the corporation has the right to redeem it. The redemption price may be par, par plus dividends in arrears, or par plus dividends to redemption date plus a premium of a few dollars (such as $1 to $5) per share. The excess of the call premium over the premium received on issuance is charged to retained earnings as a distribution to the retiring preferred stockholders.

Book value. The book value of all of a corporation's outstanding shares is the total of the recorded net asset values of the corporation—that is, total assets minus liabilities. Or, it is simply total stockholders' equity. When only common stock is outstanding, book value per share is computed by dividing stockholders' equity by the number of shares outstanding plus shares subscribed but not yet issued, if any.

Assume that the stockholders' equity of a corporation is:

Common stock without par value, stated value $10; authorized, 20,000 shares, issued and outstanding, 15,000 shares	$150,000	
Paid-in capital in excess of stated value	10,000	$160,000
Retained earnings		50,000
Total Stockholders' Equity		$210,000

Compute the book value per share.

Now turn to Answer Frame 18[12] on page 572 to check your answer.

Frame 19[12]

When two or more classes of capital stock are outstanding, the computation of book value per share is more complex. The usual approach is to assume that the assets and liabilities are liquidated at book value, which means that the corporation has cash equal to its stockholders' equity to distribute among its stockholders. How much cash would be distributed for each share of stock then depends upon the rights of the preferred shareholders. Preferred shareholders typically are entitled to a specified liquidation value per share, plus cumulative dividends, if any, since most preferred stocks are preferred as to assets and are cumulative. In each case, the specific provisions in the preferred stock contract will govern.

As an illustration, the Celoron Company's stockholders' equity is as follows:

Preferred stock, $100 par value, 5,000 shares	$ 500,000
Common stock, $10 par value, 200,000 shares	2,000,000
Paid-in capital in excess of par value—common	200,000
Retained earnings	400,000
Total Stockholders' Equity	$3,100,000

Answer frame 18[12]

The book value per share is $14 ($210,000 divided by 15,000 shares outstanding).

If you answered incorrectly, review Frame 18[12] before beginning Frame 19[12] on page 571.

19[12] *continued*

The preferred stock is 6 percent, cumulative, and nonparticipating, preferred as to dividends and as to assets in liquidation to the extent of liquidation value of $100 per share, plus cumulative dividends. Dividends for the current year and the preceding three years are unpaid on the preferred stock. The book values for each class of stock are:

		Total	*Per Share*
Total stockholders' equity		$3,100,000	
Book value of preferred stock (5,000 shares):			
Liquidation value	$500,000		
Dividends (four years at $30,000)	120,000	620,000	$124.00
Book value of common stock (200,000 shares)		$2,480,000	12.40

Suppose that all of the features attached to the preferred stock in the above example are the same except that the preferred stockholder has the right to receive $103 per share in liquidation. Compute the book value per share of preferred stock.

Check your response in Answer Frame 19[12] on page 574.

Frame 20[12]

Caution must be exercised not to attach too much significance to book value. The shares of many corporations are regularly traded at market prices many times larger than their book values. But book value computations may be of some significance in determining stock values in corporations whose stock is not regularly traded on an exchange or in a local market.

Indicate whether each of the following statements is true or false.

1. Stated value is the amount per share at which stock without par value is issued.
2. Liquidation value is the amount at which a corporation has the right to redeem its preferred stock.
3. The market value and the book value per share of capital stock of a corporation will automatically be equal.
4. An increase in its retained earnings from one year to the next may not increase the book value per share of the common stock of a cor-

poration which has an unchanged number of shares of common stock and preferred stock during the year.

Now check your answers by turning to Answer Frame 20[12] on page 574.

Summary *chapter* 12

A corporation is an association of individuals recognized by law as a separate legal entity. A corporation is granted legal existence when (among other requirements) a proper application for incorporation is submitted to and approved by the appropriate state agency and a charter is granted. Members of the board of directors are selected by the stockholders; the board formulates broad policies and selects officers to guide the corporation and execute policies.

The two ordinary classes of stock a corporation may issue are preferred and common. Preferred stock will usually possess some rights not granted common stockholders, such as a preference in receiving dividends. As to dividends, a preferred stock may be cumulative or noncumulative and participating or nonparticipating. Preferred stockholders are frequently denied the right to vote. Capital is often raised through issuance of preferred stock to enhance the return to common stock and to retain control of the corporation in the hands of common stockholders.

Par value is an arbitrary dollar amount assigned to a share of stock and may be more or less than book value or market value. But the stated or legal capital of a corporation issuing par value shares is usually the aggregate par value of the shares issued.

Stock without par value may, for accounting purposes, be assigned a stated value, which is a somewhat arbitrarily chosen amount similar to par value. The stated capital of a corporation issuing shares without par value may be equal to the stated value assigned.

The issuance of stock generally involves the receipt of subscriptions, the collection of the subscriptions, and the issuance of the stock certificates. Although the stock is often considered legally issued when a subscription is received, the accountant generally credits a capital stock account only when the actual stock certificates are issued. When a subscription is received, a subscriptions receivable account and a stock subscribed account will always be needed unless payment in full is received immediately and the stock is issued. Depending on the price agreed upon, an excess over par or stated value account may also be involved.

The subscriptions receivable account will be shown as a current asset if relatively immediate collection is expected and as an "other asset" in the noncurrent section of the statement of financial position if collection is expected in the distant future.

The stock subscribed account is shown immediately after the capital stock account, and the total of the capital and subscribed stock accounts is shown to indicate the total dollar amount assigned to shares issued

Answer frame 19^{12}

The book value per share of preferred stock is $127, computed as the liquidation value of $103 plus dividends of $6 per year in arrears for four years.

If you answered incorrectly, reread Frame 19^{12} before beginning Frame 20^{12} on page 572.

Answer frame 20^{12}

1. False. Stated value is the amount per share recorded in the capital stock account for stock if it has no par value. Any excess of the issuance price over the stated value is credited to a Paid-In Capital in Excess of Stated Value account.
2. False. Redemption value is the amount at which preferred stock may be redeemed by the corporation. Liquidation value is the amount a stockholder will receive if a corporation goes out of business, sells its assets, pays its liabilities, and distributes the remaining cash among the stockholders.
3. False. There is no reason why the book value and the market value per share of stock should be equal. Market value depends largely upon investor expectations, while book value reflects recorded asset values. Market value may thus be a reflection of the expectations of investors other than those who acquired stock from the issuing corporation.
4. True. The truth of the answer may be illustrated by means of an example. A corporation has outstanding 1,000 shares of $100 par value 6 percent cumulative preferred stock, entitled to par plus cumulative dividends at liquidation; and 10,000 shares of $10 par value common stock. Retained earnings at December 31, 1974, totaled $10,000, and no dividends were paid on the preferred stock in 1974. Net earnings for 1975 amount to $5,000. No dividends were paid in 1975. The book value of the common stock on December 31, 1974, and 1975 is:

	December 31	
	1974	*1975*
Stockholders' equity	$210,000	$215,000
Book value of preferred stock:		
Liquidation value	$100,000	$100,000
Dividends	6,000	12,000
Total book value of preferred stock	$106,000	$112,000
Book value of common stock	$104,000	$103,000
Book value per share of common stock	$10.40	$10.30

The reason for the decline in book value of the common stock is that net earnings for the year were less than the cumulative dividend on the preferred stock—the growth in the book value of preferred stock.

If you missed any of the above, reread Frame 18^{12} and 19^{12} before going on to the chapter summary on page 573.

---

or to be issued. Any amount paid in above stated value is added to this total.

A subscriber to stock may default on his contract. In this event, he may receive shares for the amount he has paid in, receive a refund of the amount paid in, or forfeit the amount paid in to the corporation.

When capital stock is issued for property or services, it is recorded in the accounts at the fair market value either of the property or services received or of the shares issued, whichever is more clearly evident.

When shares are issued for an amount greater than their par or stated value, this excess should be credited to an account called Paid-In Capital in Excess of Par (or Stated) Value, with separate accounts established for each class of stock. Such accounts should never be closed to the Expense and Revenue Summary account, since they record contributed capital, not elements of earnings.

Costs such as legal fees and corporate franchise fees incurred in organizing a corporation should be charged to an Organization Costs account and reported in the statement of financial position as an intangible asset.

To complete your review, study the definitions of new terms introduced in this chapter contained in the glossary which follows. Then go on to the Student Review Quiz for a self-administered test of your comprehension of the material in the chapter (see page 576).

Glossary *chapter* 12

Articles of incorporation—the form containing information about the proposed corporation that is filed with the state by incorporators seeking to organize the corporation.

Book value (per share)—stockholders' equity per share; computed as the amount per share each shareholder would receive if the corporation were liquidated without incurring any further expense and if assets were sold and liabilities liquidated at their recorded amounts.

Call premium—the difference between the amount at which a corporation may call its preferred stock for redemption and the par value of the stock.

Capital stock authorized—the stock that a corporation is entitled to issue as designated in its charter.

Capital stock, unissued—capital stock authorized for which stock certificates have not been issued.

Charter, corporate—the contract between the state and the incorporators of a corporation or their successors granting the corporation its legal existence.

Code of regulations (bylaws)—a set of rules or regulations adopted by the board of directors of a corporation to govern the conduct of corporate affairs within the general laws of the state and the policies and purposes stated or implied in the corporate charter.

Convertible preferred stock—preferred stock which is convertible into common stock of the issuing corporation.

Corporation—an association of individuals which, at law, is viewed as an artificial person. It is granted many of the rights and placed under many of the obligations of a natural person. As viewed through the eyes of the law of a given state, all corporations organized under the laws of that state are domestic corporations, all others are foreign.

Defaulted subscription—a contract to acquire stock on which a required installment payment has not been made.

Discount on capital stock—the amount by which the par value of shares subscribed for exceeds their subscription price. The issuance of shares at a discount is illegal in most states.

Dividends in arrears—cumulative unpaid dividends.

Incorporators—natural persons seeking to bring a corporation into existence.

Liquidation value—the amount to be paid per share of preferred stock upon liquidation of the corporation, often equal to par value, accumulated dividends, and a fixed premium.

Minutes book—the record book in which actions taken at stockholders' and board of directors' meetings are recorded.

Organization costs—an intangible asset consisting of the various costs incurred in bringing a corporation into existence, including legal and other service fees or costs and fees paid to the state.

Paid-in capital in excess of par (or stated) value—capital contributed to a corporation in addition to that assigned to the shares issued and recorded in capital stock accounts.

Par value—an arbitrary amount assigned to each share of a given class of stock and printed on the stock certificate.

Preemptive right—the right of a stockholder to subscribe to additional shares of the same class of stock he holds in any subsequent issuance of new shares. This right may be waived.

Preferred stock—corporate capital stock which carries certain privileges or rights not carried by all outstanding shares of stock. Preferred stock may be:

Cumulative—the right to receive a basic dividend each year accumulates if not paid; dividends in arrears must be paid before dividends can be paid on the common stock.

Noncumulative—the right to receive a dividend expires if not declared.

Participating—entitled to receive dividends above the stated preference rate under certain conditions which are carefully stated in the preferred stock contract.

Premium on capital stock—the amount by which the subscription price for shares exceeds the par value of the shares.

Proxy—a legal document which, when properly executed, grants to another the right to vote a given stockholder's shares at a stockholders' meeting.

Redemption value—the price per share at which a corporation may call its preferred stock for retirement.

Stated capital—an amount prescribed by law below which the stockholders' equity of a corporation will not be reduced through the declaration of dividends or other distributions of corporate assets to stockholders in exchange for their shares of stock.

Stated value—an arbitrary amount assigned by the board of directors to each share of a given class of no par value stock.

Stock certificate—a printed or engraved document serving as evidence of ownership of shares of capital stock.

Stock preferred as to assets—a stock which is entitled to receive assets in liquidation up to a stated amount before any assets may be distributed to the common stockholders.

Stock preferred as to dividends—a stock which is entitled to receive certain dividends prior to the payment of any dividends to common stockholders.

Stock registrar—an outside agency, typically a bank, which authenticates stock issues and maintains separate records of stock outstanding.

Stock transfer agent—an outside agency, typically a bank or trust company, employed by a corporation to transfer stock between buyers and sellers.

Stock without par value (no par value stock)—capital stock without par value, to which a stated value may or may not be assigned.

Stockholders' ledger—a group of subsidiary accounts showing the number of shares of stock held by each stockholder at any one moment.

Subscribed stock—stock for which subscriptions have been received, but for which stock certificates have not been issued.

Subscriber—a person contracting to acquire shares, usually in an original issuance of stock by a corporation.

Subscription—a contract to acquire shares of stock, usually in an original issuance of stock by a corporation.

Subscription price—the price at which a subscriber agrees to acquire shares of stock in a subscription agreement.

Student review quiz *chapter* 12

To develop a permanent record of your responses, you may write them on the answer sheet provided in the *Work Papers* or on a separate piece of paper.

1 Which of the following is not a characteristic of a corporation?

a) Limited liability of owners to creditors.
b) Difficult transferability of ownership because of wide diversification of ownership.
c) Separate legal existence.
d) Ability to enter into contracts.
e) Right to sue (and to be sued) in its own name.

2 A common stockholder does not process which of the following?

a) The right to share in the earnings of the corporation when dividends are declared.
b) The right to vote in the election of the board of directors of the corporation.
c) The right of direct ownership of the corporate assets.
d) The right to share proportionately in corporate assets in case of liquidation if such assets exceed the claims of creditors.
e) The right to transfer his ownership in the corporation.

3 Which of the following statements are true?

a) A corporation must usually have a minimum of three incorporators.
b) A corporation incorporated in one state is considered a foreign corporation by all of the other states.
c) A corporation may have a perpetual existence.
d) A corporation need not be incorporated in a given state in order to do business in that state.
e) All of the above are true.

4 The par value of a share of common stock is:

a) The amount for which the stock can be sold in the market.
b) The amount at which, according to some state laws, the share must be first issued.
c) The same thing as stated value.
d) A changing amount which varies according to earnings and losses of the issuing corporation.
e) Generally of little significance, being merely a nominal and arbitrary amount printed on a stock certificate.

5 B.P. Beck Company is organized with authorized capital stock of $100,000, consisting of 1,000 shares of $100 par value common stock. All of the capital stock is subscribed at par. In the following week, payment is received in full for 70 percent of the shares subscribed. No payment has been received from the persons who subscribed for the other 30 percent of the shares. Which of the following entries should be made to record receipt of the subscription payments?

a) Cash	70,000	
Subscriptions Receivable—Common		70,000
b) Cash	70,000	
Common Stock		70,000
c) Cash	70,000	
Common Stock		70,000
Common Stock Subscribed	70,000	
Subscriptions Receivable—Common		70,000
d) Cash	70,000	
Subscriptions Receivable—Common		70,000
Common Stock Subscribed	70,000	
Common Stock		70,000
e) Cash	70,000	
Common Stock Subscribed		70,000

6 Roehrig, Inc. is organized with authorized capital stock of $100,000 consisting of 2,000 shares of $50 par value common stock. Subscriptions are received for 600 shares at $60 per share and the subscriptions are collected in full. The correct set of entries for these transactions is which of the following?

a) Subscriptions Receivable—Common	36,000	
Common Stock Subscribed		36,000
Cash	36,000	
Subscriptions Receivable—Common		36,000
Common Stock Subscribed	36,000	
Common Stock		30,000
Paid-In Capital in Excess of Par Value		6,000
b) Subscriptions Receivable—Common	36,000	
Paid-In Capital in Excess of Par Value		6,000
Common Stock Subscribed		30,000

Cash	36,000	
Subscriptions Receivable—Common		36,000
Common Stock Subscribed	30,000	
Common Stock		30,000

c)

Subscriptions Receivable—Common	36,000	
Common Stock Subscribed		36,000
Cash	36,000	
Paid-In Capital in Excess of Par Value		6,000
Subscriptions Receivable—Common		30,000
Common Stock Subscribed	36,000	
Common Stock		36,000

d)

Subscriptions Receivable—Common	36,000	
Common Stock Subscribed		36,000
Cash	36,000	
Subscriptions Receivable—Common		36,000
Common Stock Subscribed	36,000	
Paid-In Capital in Excess of Stated Value		6,000
Common Stock		30,000

e)

Subscriptions Receivable—Common	36,000	
Common Stock Subscribed		30,000
Paid-In Capital in Excess of Stated Value		6,000
Cash	36,000	
Subscriptions Receivable—Common		36,000
Common Stock Subscribed	30,000	
Common Stock		30,000

7 The R. U. Hungry Restaurant Corporation issued 80 shares of common stock (par value $100 per share) to Richard S. Hoglund for real estate having a fair market value of $9,000 at the date of transfer. Which of the following is the required entry?

a)

Land	8,000	
Common Stock		8,000

b)

Land	9,000	
Common Stock		9,000

c)

Land	9,000	
Common Stock		8,000
Paid-In Capital in Excess of Par Value		1,000

d)

Land	9,000	
Common Stock		8,000
Paid-In Capital in Excess of Stated Value		1,000

e)

Land	9,000	
Common Stock		8,000
Discount on Stock		1,000

8 Babcock Furniture Company was incorporated with authorized capital of 100,000 shares of common stock without par value but with a stated value of $50 per share. The company issued 60,000 shares for cash at a price of $60 per share. Which of the following entries should be made?

a)

Cash	3,600,000	
Common Stock		3,000,000
Paid-In Capital in Excess of Stated Value		600,000

b)

Cash	3,600,000	
Common Stock		3,600,000

c)

Cash	3,600,000	
Common Stock		3,000,000
Paid-In Capital in Excess of Par Value		600,000

d)

Subscriptions Receivable—Common	3,600,000	
Common Stock		3,000,000
Paid-In Capital in Excess of Stated Value		600,000

e)

Subscriptions Receivable—Common	3,600,000	
Common Stock		3,000,000
Paid-In Capital in Excess of Par Value		600,000

9 With regard to common stock without par or stated value, which of the following statements are true?

a) The Common Stock account will show the total of the amount received for the stock issued plus the subscription price of the stock subscribed for but for which payment has not been received.

b) In the case of a subscription with a cash down payment, the Subscriptions Receivable and the Common

Stock Subscribed accounts will show the same dollar amount.
c) There may be a Paid-In Capital in Excess of Par Value account.
d) Depending on the price received, a Paid-In Capital in Excess of Stated Value account may be established when the shares are subscribed for.
e) The Common Stock account may be credited for varying amounts if shares are issued at different prices at different times.

10 When an individual who has subscribed to stock defaults on his installment payment (choose the true statements):
a) The total amount he has already paid in may be refunded to him.
b) The amount he has paid in, less losses and expenses necessary for reissue of the stock may be refunded to him.
c) He may forfeit the entire amount he has already paid in.
d) He may be called upon to pay the entire balance due immediately.
e) The procedure followed depends on the laws of the state of incorporation.

11 The stockholders' ledger is which of the following?
a) Another name for the general ledger.
b) A subsidiary ledger showing all transactions with regard to stock—subscriptions, issuance, and so on.
c) A subsidiary ledger containing an account for each stockholder showing his stock ownership—number of shares issued to him, transferred by him, and currently held.
d) A subsidiary ledger containing an account for each stockholder which records the stock transactions entered into by him in terms of both the number of shares exchanged and the amounts paid or received therefor.
e) None of the above.

12 Novacheck Machine Company has outstanding 10,000 shares of 4 percent, $100 par value preferred stock (noncumulative and nonparticipating) and 10,000 shares of $100 par value common stock. Retained earnings are $70,000. No dividends were paid last year. What amount of dividends are the preferred stockholders entitled to at the end of the current year before payment of any dividends to common stockholders?
a) No preference as to dividends.
b) $40,000.
c) $55,000.
d) $70,000.
e) $80,000.

13 Stielow Plumbing Ware Company has outstanding 10,000 shares of 3 percent, $100 par value, cumulative preferred stock and 10,000 shares of $100 par value common. Retained earnings are $98,000. No dividends were paid last year. Retained earnings available at the end of the current year for dividends on the common stock are:
a) None.
b) $19,000.
c) $34,000.
d) $38,000.
e) $68,000.

14 Ponton Chemical Company has 10,000 shares of 3 percent $100 par value preferred stock and 20,000 shares of common stock without par value outstanding. The preferred stock is cumulative and participates equally on a share-for-share basis with the common stock in any dividends in excess of $3 per share per year on the common stock. Retained earnings total $200,000. If no dividends are in arrears, what portion of a total of $96,000 in dividends to be declared by the board of directors would go to each class of stock?
a) $30,000 preferred, $66,000 common.
b) $32,000 preferred, $64,000 common.
c) $33,000 preferred, $63,000 common.
d) $60,000 preferred, $36,000 common.
e) $48,000 preferred, $48,000 common.

15 The book value of the common stock of a corporation which has both common and preferred stock outstanding is which of the following?
a) A constant value.
b) Synonymous with redemption value of the common stock.
c) Synonymous with liquidation value of the common stock.
d) Synonymous with par or stated value of the common stock.
e) None of the above.

16 If stockholder A sells 100 shares of stock in Corporation X to B, the record of Corporation X in which an entry will be made is which of the following?
a) The minutes book.
b) The general journal.
c) The general ledger.
d) The stockholders' ledger.
e) None of the above.

17 In accounting for stockholders' equity, the accountant is primarily concerned with which of the following?

a) Determining the total amount of stockholders' equity.

b) Distinguishing between realized and unrealized revenues.

c) Recording the source of each of the various elements of stockholders' equity.

d) Making sure that the board of directors does not declare dividends in excess of retained earnings.

e) Assigning proper amounts to the capital stock accounts.

Now compare your answers with the correct answers and explanations on page 717.

Questions *chapter* 12

1 What are the basic rights associated with a share of capital stock, if there is only one class of stock outstanding?

2 What are the differences between par value stock and stock with no par value?

3 Explain the nature of the Subscriptions Receivable account. How should it be classified in the statement of financial position? On what occasions is it debited? Credited?

4 Explain the nature of the account entitled Paid-In Capital in Excess of Par Value. Under what circumstances is an entry recorded in the account?

5 Explain the purpose of (*a*) the stockholders' ledger, (*b*) the minutes book, (*c*) the stock transfer agent, and (*d*) the stock registrar.

6 Cite the major advantages of the corporate form of business organization and indicate why each is considered an advantage.

7 What is meant by the allegation that corporate earnings are subject to double taxation? Cite several other disadvantages of the corporate form of organization.

8 Why is the title Organization Expense not a good one for the account which records the costs of organizing a corporation? Could you justify leaving the balance of an Organization Costs account intact throughout the life of a corporation?

9 With reference to preferred stock, what is the meaning of the terms (*a*) cumulative and noncumulative and (*b*) participating and nonparticipating?

10 Corporate capital stock is seldom, if ever, issued for less than par value. Give two reasons why this is true.

11 What is the general approach of the accountant in seeking the dollar amount at which to record the issuance of corporate stock for services or property other than cash?

12 A corporation has outstanding 1,000 shares of 4 percent $100 par value cumulative preferred stock. Dividends on this stock have not been declared for three years. Is the corporation liable to its preferred stockholders for these dividends? How should they be shown in the statement of financial position, if at all?

13 Explain why a corporation might issue a preferred stock that is both convertible into common stock and callable.

14 Assuming there is no preferred stock outstanding, how can the book value per share of common stock be determined? Of what significance is it? What is its relationship to market value per share?

15 Explain the terms liquidation value and redemption value. To what class of stock do they usually apply?

Exercises *chapter* 12

1 One hundred shares of $100 par value common stock are issued to the promoters of a corporation in exchange for land (which cost the promoters $7,000 one year ago) needed by the corporation for use as a plant site. Experienced appraisers have recently estimated the value of the land to be $8,500. What journal entry would be appropriate to record the acquisition of the land?

2 James Corporation owes a trade creditor $12,000 on open account which it does not have sufficient cash to pay. The trade creditor suggests that James Corporation issue to him 1,000 shares of the company's $10 par value common stock, which is currently selling on the market at $12. What might prevent the James Corporation from engaging in this apparently quite desirable and advantageous transaction? If this bar did not exist, and the James Corporation did issue the shares as suggested by the creditor, present the entry or entries that should be made on James Corporation's books.

3 Why would a corporation ever consider issuing stock having a par value of $10,000 as payment in full of a bill for legal services rendered of $7,500? If such a transaction occurred, give the journal entry to record it.

4 Blaine Corporation has 1,000 shares of $100 par value convertible preferred stock outstanding which was issued at par value. Each share is convertible into 3.5 shares of $10 stated value common stock. Give the entry to record the conversion of all 1,000 shares of preferred.

5 Parker Company called all of its 2,000 shares of outstanding $100 par value preferred stock. The stock was cumulative, nonparticipating, entitled to $100 per share plus cumulative dividends in liquidation, and callable at $105. Give the entry to record the calling of the preferred stock, assuming it was originally issued at par value. Give the entry required if the stock had originally been issued at $102. In each case assume there are no unpaid cumulative dividends.

6 The stockholders' equity section of the Aspen Company's statement of financial position is as follows:

Paid-In Capital:	
Common stock without par value, $5 stated value; authorized, 100,000 shares, issued and outstanding, 20,000 shares.	$100,000
Subscribed but not issued, 20,000 shares.	100,000
Paid-in capital in excess of stated value.	40,000
Paid-In Capital.	$240,000
Retained Earnings.	60,000
	$300,000

Compute the average price at which the common stock was subscribed. Compute the book value per share of common stock.

7 Baker Company has 1,000 shares of cumulative preferred stock with a $6 annual dividend per share and 5,000 shares of common stock without par value outstanding. No dividends were paid in 1973 or 1974. At the beginning of 1975 the company had a deficit of $12,000. During 1975 it had net earnings of $60,000. If a dividend of $3 per share is declared on the common stock, what is the ending balance in retained earnings?

Problems, Series A *chapter* 12

12–1–A

On July 1, 1975, the Walters Company was authorized to issue 10,000 shares of $25 par value common stock. On July 7, subscriptions for 1,000 shares at $30 per share were received. The subscription contract required a 10 percent immediate payment, with the remainder due on July 31. No stock certificates were to be issued until the subscriptions were paid in full.

Required:

a) Present the entries to record all transactions during July, 1975. Subscriptions were collected when due.
b) Present the July, 1975, entries assuming the stock is without par value.
c) Present the entries for July 7, 1975, if the subscriptions for the stock without par value were accompanied with cash payment in full and the stock was issued.

12–2–A

On July 3, 1975, the Dobbs Company was authorized to issue 10,000 shares of common stock, and 2,000 shares were immediately issued to the promoters of the company for cash at $20 per share. Another 200 shares were also issued to the promoters for services rendered in organizing the company.

On July 5, 1975, $500 worth of legal and printing costs were paid. These costs related to securing the corporate charter and the stock certificates.

On July 10 subscriptions were received from the general public for 3,000 shares at $18 per share, with one half of the subscription price paid in cash immediately. The balance is due August 10, 1975.

Required:

a) Prepare the statement of financial position of the Dobbs Company as of the close of July 10, 1975, assuming the authorized stock has a $10 par value.
b) Repeat **(a)** assuming the stock is without par value but is to have a $15 stated value.
c) Repeat **(a)** assuming the stock is without par or stated value.

12–3–A

The Cowles Company issued all of its 2,000 shares of authorized preferred stock on July 1, 1973, at $103 per share. The preferred stock is without par value, has a stated value of $2.50 per share, is entitled to a cumulative basic preference dividend of $6 per share, is callable at $105 beginning in 1979, and is entitled to $100 per share in liquidation plus cumulative dividends. Cowles also issued its 4,000 authorized shares of common stock without par value but with a $10 stated value on this date at $50 per share.

On June 30, 1975, the end of its second fiscal year of operations, the company's retained earnings amounted to $70,000. No dividends have been declared or paid on either class of stock since the date of issue.

Required:

a) Prepare the stockholders' equity section of the Cowles Company's June 30, 1975, statement of financial position.
b) Compute the book value in total and per share of each class of stock as of June 30, 1975, assuming the preferred stock is nonparticipating.

c) If $55,000 of dividends are to be declared as of June 30, 1975, compute the amount payable to each class of stock assuming the preferred stock is nonparticipating.

d) Repeat **(c)** assuming the preferred stock is entitled to participate equally on a share-for-share basis with the common stock in any dividends declared in any fiscal year in excess of $4 per share of common stock.

12–4–A

On July 1, 1975, the Suffock Corporation received authorization to issue 20,000 shares of common stock without par value. On that date subscriptions were received from the general public for 7,000 shares at $30 per share. Also, on the same date, 1,000 shares were issued to Mr. Suffock and his sons for services rendered and costs incurred in organizing the corporation. The following transactions occurred during the remainder of the month of July.

July	10	Received subscriptions for another 3,000 shares at $32 per share and collected one third of each of the July 1 subscriptions for 7,000 shares.
	11	Issued 2,000 shares in exchange for a tract of land.
	20	Collected the balance of each of the July 1 subscriptions and issued the shares. Also, collected one half of each of the July 10 subscriptions.
	30	Collected the balance of each of the July 10 subscriptions and issued the shares.

Required:

a) Assume that on September 1, 1975, the board of directors placed a stated value of $10 per share on the common stock. Present journal entries to record all of the July transactions and the entry needed on September 1.

b) Prepare journal entries to record all of the July transactions assuming that the stock issued was $25 par value stock.

12–5–A

The Wilde Company was authorized to issue 2,000 shares of preferred stock, par value $50, and 10,000 shares of common stock, par value $20.

WILDE COMPANY
Post-Closing Account Balances
December 31, 1975

Organization costs	$ 65,000
Inventory	48,000
Common stock subscribed, 4000 shares	80,000
Buildings and equipment	100,000
Allowance for depreciation	20,000
Cash	98,000
Accounts payable	12,000
Preferred stock, $50 par; 2000 shares authorized, issued, and outstanding	100,000
Accounts receivable	122,000
Common stock, $20 par; 10,000 shares authorized, 6000 shares issued and outstanding	120,000
Paid-in capital in excess of par—common	8,000
Notes payable (due June 30, 1976)	50,000
Unexpired insurance	11,500
Subscriptions receivable—common	38,400
Paid-in capital in excess of par—preferred	3,000
Retained earnings	?

Required: From the above list of accounts and balances, present in good form the December 31, 1975, statement of financial position.

12–6–A

Part 1. On January 1, 1971, the retained earnings of the Finlay Company were $70,000. Net earnings for the succeeding five years were as follows:

1971..............	$49,000
1972..............	30,000
1973..............	2,000
1974..............	11,000
1975..............	46,000

The outstanding capital stock of the corporation consisted of 2,000 shares of $4 preferred stock with a par value of $100 per share, and 8,000 shares of common stock without par value having a stated value of $50 per share. No dividends were in arrears as of January 1, 1971.

Required: Prepare schedules showing how the net earnings for the above five years were distributed to the two classes of stock if, in each of the years, the entire current earnings (and only these earnings) were distributed as dividends and the preferred stock was:

a) Cumulative and nonparticipating.
b) Cumulative and participating on the basis of $0.02 per share of dividends to the preferred stock for every $0.01 per share of dividends paid to the common stock over $4 per share per calendar year.
c) Noncumulative and participating as in **(b)**.
d) Noncumulative and nonparticipating.

Part 2. In 1976 the board of directors and stockholders decided to dissolve the Finlay Company. All of its assets were sold, its liabilities were liquidated, and $480,000 remained for distribution to stockholders. No dividends were in arrears and current dividends had been paid.

Required: Prepare short schedules showing how the cash was distributed to the stockholders if:

a) The preferred stock was preferred as to assets and entitled to $105 in liquidation.
b) The preferred stock was not preferred as to assets.

12–7–A

The McCord Company received its charter on April 1, 1975, authorizing it to issue 5,000 shares of $100 par value, $4 cumulative, convertible preferred stock; 10,000 shares of $1.50 cumulative preferred stock without par value having a stated value of $5 per share and a liquidation value of $25 per share; and 100,000 shares of common stock without par or stated value.

On April 2 promoters of the corporation acquired 50,000 shares of the common stock for cash of $10 per share, and 200 shares were issued to an attorney for services rendered in organizing the corporation. On April 3 the company issued all of its authorized shares of $4 convertible preferred stock for land valued at $200,000 and a building valued at $600,000. The property was subject to a mortgage of $300,000.

On April 4 subscriptions for 5,000 shares of the $1.50 preferred stock were received at $26 per share, with one half of the subscription price paid in cash. On April 8 the remaining 5,000 shares of $1.50 preferred stock were issued to an inventor for a patent. A subscription for 1,000 shares of common stock at $10 per share was also received, with a cash payment of $1,000 accompanying the subscription.

On April 25 the balance due on the April 4 subscriptions was collected and the shares issued. By April 30 the subscriber to 1,000 shares of common stock had failed to pay the balance of his subscription, which he had agreed to pay in 10 days. Shares were issued for his down payment, and the balance of the contract was canceled.

Required:

a) Prepare general journal entries for the above transactions.
b) Prepare the stockholders' equity section of the April 30, 1975, statement of financial position. Assume a deficit of $10,000.
c) Assume that each share of the $4 convertible preferred stock was convertible into six shares of common stock and that all of the preferred was converted on September 1, 1978. Give the required journal entry.

12–8–A

Littleton, Inc. is a corporation in which all of the outstanding preferred and common stock is held by four Littleton brothers. The brothers have an agreement stating that the remaining brothers will, upon the death of a brother, purchase from his estate his holdings of stock in the company at book value. The agreement also stipulates that the land owned by the company be valued at fair market value, that inventory be valued at its current replacement cost, and that whatever other adjustments are needed to place the accounts on a sound accounting basis be made prior to computing book value.

The stockholders' equity accounts of the company on June 30, 1975, the date of the death of William Littleton, show:

Preferred stock, 6%, $100 par value, liquidation value $100; 2,000 shares authorized, issued, and outstanding	$200,000
Paid-in capital in excess of par—preferred	10,000
Common stock without par value, stated value, $5; 30,000 shares authorized, issued, and outstanding	150,000
Paid-in capital from recapitalization	150,000
Retained earnings	20,000
	$530,000

The fair market value of the land held by the company and carried in its accounts at $20,000 is $50,000, and the current replacement cost of the inventory is $16,000 more than the amount at which it is carried in the accounts, although no improper accounting is involved. It is also agreed by the three remaining brothers and the accountant representing Mrs. William Littleton that the accounts fail to include a proper accrued liability of $10,000 for pensions payable to employees. No dividends have been paid on the preferred stock, which is cumulative and nonparticipating, in the last six months. William Littleton held, at the time of his death, 1,000 shares of preferred stock and 5,000 shares of common stock of the company.

Required: Compute the amount which the remaining brothers must pay to the estate of William Littleton for the preferred and common stock which he held at the time of his death.

Problems, Series B *chapter* 12

12–1–B

In the charter granted January 2, 1975, the Sullivan Corporation was authorized to issue 1,000 shares of common stock without par value. Subscription agreements called for immediate payment of one half of each subscription, with the remainder due on the first day of the following month. All subscriptions were collected in accordance with the agreements.

On January 5 subscriptions for 600 shares at $48 per share were received, and on May 1 an additional 200 shares were subscribed at $60 per share.

Required:

a) Present the entries to record all of the transactions of January through May 1975, assuming no stock was issued until the subscriptions were paid in full.

b) Present the May 31, 1975, statement of financial position, assuming there were no transactions other than those described above.

12–2–B

In the corporate charter which it received on May 1, 1975, the Mansfield Company was authorized to issue 10,000 shares of common stock. A total of 1,000 shares were immediately issued to two of the promoters for $25 per share, cash.

On May 2 the company paid 200 shares of stock and $1,000 cash to a lawyer for legal services rendered in organizing the corporation and billed at $5,000. On May 3 subscriptions, accompanied by a 10 percent down payment, were received from the general public for 6,000 shares at $20 per share. On May 4 the company issued 2,000 shares to the principal promoter of the corporation in exchange for a patent. Another 100 shares were issued to this same person for costs incurred and services rendered in bringing the corporation into existence.

Required:

a) Prepare a statement of financial position for the Mansfield Company as of May 4, 1975, assuming the authorized stock had a par value of $20 per share.

b) Prepare the stockholders' equity section of the May 4 statement of financial position, assuming the stock authorized had no par value but had a $10 per share stated value.

c) Repeat **(b)** assuming the stock authorized had neither par nor stated value.

12–3–B

On January 2, 1974, the date the Jason Company received its charter, it issued all of its authorized 2,000 shares of preferred stock without par value at $104 and all of its 8,000 authorized shares of common stock without par value but with a stated value of $1 at $40 per share. The preferred stock had a stated value of $5 per share, was entitled to a basic cumulative preference dividend of $6 per share, was callable at $106 beginning in 1976, and was entitled to $100 per share plus cumulative dividends in the event of liquidation.

On December 31, 1975, the end of the second year of operations, retained earnings were $60,000. No dividends had been declared or paid on either class of stock.

Required:

a) Prepare the stockholders' equity section of the Jason Company's December 31, 1975, statement of financial position.
b) Compute the book value of each class of stock, assuming the preferred stock was nonparticipating.
c) If $50,000 of dividends were declared as of December 31, 1975, compute the amount payable to each class of stock assuming the preferred stock is nonparticipating.
d) Repeat **(c)** assuming the preferred stock is entitled to participate equally on a share-for-share basis with the common stock in any dividends declared in any calendar year in excess of $2 per share of common stock.

12–4–B

The Moore Company was authorized on September 1, 1975, to issue 100,000 shares of common stock without par value. On this date subscriptions for 60,000 shares were received from the public at $4 per share, with cash payment in full accompanying the subscriptions. Subsequent transactions were:

Sept. 2 5,000 shares were issued to the three promoters for legal fees, accounting services, printing costs, state incorporation fees, and other costs incurred in promoting the corporation.
5 Certificates covering the shares subscribed for on September 1 were issued, as per stock transfer agent's report.
8 Subscriptions for an additional 20,000 shares were received at $4.50 per share.
9 10,000 shares were issued to one of the promoters for certain patents which he held and which he believed were worth $50,000.
Oct. 1 The subscriptions of September 8 were collected in full.
5 Certificates covering the subscriptions of September 8 were issued.
9 The board of directors established a stated value of $2 per share on the common stock.

Required:

a) Present journal entries for the above transactions.
b) Present the October 9, 1975, statement of financial position, assuming no transactions other than those given above.

12–5–B

Hinson, Inc. was authorized to issue 2,000 shares of $2.50 cumulative preferred stock, par value $50, and 20,000 shares of common stock, par value $25.

HINSON, INC.
Post-Closing Account Balances
December 31, 1975

Paid-in capital in excess of par—preferred	$ 5,000
Accounts payable	30,000
Inventory	100,000
Unexpired insurance	3,000
Organization costs	50,000
Common stock subscribed, 2,000 shares	50,000
Subscriptions receivable—common	40,000
Buildings and equipment	120,000
Notes payable, due June 30, 1976	15,000
Cash	60,000
Allowance for depreciation	20,000
Preferred stock, $50 par value; 2,000 shares authorized	100,000
Paid-in capital in excess of par—common	12,000
Common stock, $25 par value; 20,000 shares authorized	200,000
Accounts receivable	152,000
Retained earnings	?

Required: From the above list of account balances, prepare the December 31, 1975, statement of financial position in good form.

12–6–B

Part 1. The outstanding capital stock of the Longley Corporation consisted of 4,000 shares of $6 preferred stock, $100 par value, and 40,000 shares of $50 stated value common stock. The preferred was issued at $103, the common at $60. On January 1, 1971, the retained earnings of the company were $100,000. During the succeeding five years net earnings were as follows:

1971	$192,000
1972	128,000
1973	12,000
1974	40,000
1975	160,000

No dividends were in arrears as of January 1, 1971, and during the five years 1971–75 the board of directors declared dividends in each year equal to the net earnings of the year.

Required: Prepare a schedule showing the dividends declared each year on each class of stock assuming the preferred stock is:

a) Cumulative and nonparticipating.
b) Cumulative and participating on the basis of $0.02 per share of dividends to the preferred stock for every $0.01 per share of dividends declared on the common stock over $3 per share per calendar year.
c) Noncumulative and participating as in **(b)**.
d) Noncumulative and nonparticipating.

Part 2. In 1976 the board of directors, with stockholder approval, decided to dissolve the Longley Corporation. All of its assets were sold, its liabilities were liquidated, and $1,780,000 of cash remained for distribution to the stockholders. No dividends were in arrears at liquidation, and current dividends had been paid.

Required: Prepare short schedules showing the amount of cash to be distributed to each class of stock if:

a) The preferred stock has a preference as to assets in the event of liquidation over the common stock in the amount of $105 per share plus cumulative dividends.
b) The preferred stock has no preference to assets in liquidation.

12–7–B

Jay Company, on May 1, 1975, received a charter which authorized it to issue:

a) 2,000 shares of preferred stock without par value to which a stated value of $3 per share was assigned. The stock was entitled to a cumulative dividend of $2.40, convertible into two shares of common stock, callable at $52, and entitled to $50 per share in liquidation.
b) 1,000 shares of $100 par value, $5 cumulative preferred stock which is callable at $105 and entitled to $103 in liquidation.
c) 100,000 shares of common stock without par value to which a stated value of $10 was assigned.

Transactions:

May 1 All of the $2.40 convertible preferred was subscribed for and issued at $51 per share, cash.
2 All of the $5 cumulative preferred was exchanged for inventory, land, and buildings valued at $22,000, $25,000, and $55,000, respectively.
2 Subscriptions were received for 50,000 shares of common at $20 per share, with 10 percent of the subscription price paid immediately in cash.
3 Cash of $3,000 was paid to reimburse promoters for costs incurred for accounting, legal, and printing services. In addition, 1,000 shares of common stock were issued to the promoters for their services.
31 All of the subscriptions to the common stock were collected and the shares issued.

Required:

a) Prepare journal entries for the above transactions.
b) Assume that retained earnings were $50,000. Prepare the stockholders' equity section of the May 31, 1975, statement of financial position.
c) On June 30, 1979, the company called and retired all of the $5 cumulative preferred stock and all of the $2.40 convertible preferred stock was converted into common stock. Give the required journal entries, assuming no cumulative dividends were in arrears.

12–8–B

Bernice Corporation has an agreement with each of its 5 preferred and 10 common stockholders that, in the event of the death of a stockholder, it will purchase at book value from the stockholder's estate or heirs the shares of Bernice Corporation stock held by the deceased at the time of death. The book value is to be computed in accordance with generally accepted accounting principles.

Following is the stockholders' equity section of the Bernice Corporation's December 31, 1975, statement of financial position:

$5 Preferred stock without par value, $10 stated value; 1,000 shares authorized, issued, and outstanding	$ 10,000
Common stock, $20 par value; 20,000 shares authorized, issued, and outstanding	400,000
Paid-in capital in excess of stated value—preferred	100,000
Paid-in capital in excess of par value—common	20,000
Retained earnings	200,000
	$730,000

The preferred stock is cumulative and entitled to $100 per share plus cumulative dividends in liquidation. No dividends have been paid for one and one half years.

A stockholder, owner of 100 shares of preferred stock and 1,000 shares of common stock, died on December 31, 1975. You have been employed by his widow to compute the book value of each class of stock and to determine the price to be paid for the stock held by her late husband. In reviewing the corporation's records you discover that machinery costing $10,000 on December 27, 1975, had been charged to expense and that the December 31, 1975, inventory was understated by $2,500.

Required: Prepare a schedule showing the computation of the amount to be paid for the deceased stockholder's holdings of Bernice preferred and common stock.

Stockholders' equity: Paid-in capital, retained earnings, dividends, and treasury stock

Learning objectives

Study of the material in this chapter is designed to achieve these learning objectives:

1. Familiarity with the nature and components of stockholders' equity, especially the difference between paid-in capital and retained earnings.
2. Knowledge of the accounting treatment of paid-in capital and retained earnings, including retained earnings reserves.
3. Familiarity with the theoretical considerations and the analysis of accounting for extraordinary gains and losses and corrections of prior periods.
4. A basic understanding of the nature and accounting treatment of dividends on capital stock.
5. A working knowledge of the theoretical considerations and transaction analysis in the handling of treasury stock.

Frame 1[13]

Paid-in (or contributed) capital

The preceding chapter dealt with paid-in capital resulting from the issuance of shares of stock for cash or other property or services. Attention is now directed to other sources of paid-in capital.

The term paid-in capital is a generic term embracing capital acquired from several different sources. No single account entitled Paid-In Capital is maintained in the ledger; instead, a separate account is established for each source of capital. Each of these accounts could carry the words paid-in capital in its title. For example, the Common Stock and the Preferred Stock accounts could quite properly be titled Paid-In Capital—Common Stock and Paid-In Capital—Preferred Stock, as both accounts record capital contributions made by stockholders. The shorter titles are used in this text because of their widespread acceptance in practice. Since transactions recorded in or affecting the paid-in capital accounts involve flows of contributed capital and not earnings, they are never reflected in the earnings statement.

Illustration 13.1 presents in summary form several sources of proprietary capital (stockholders' equity) and illustrative titles for general ledger accounts to be used to record increases and decreases in capital from each of these sources. It should be fully understood that the words "paid-in capital" are used in the titles of accounts which record capital in excess of (1) par values in the case of par value shares; (2) stated value in the case of no par, stated value shares; and (3) the amount received upon issuance in the case of shares without par or stated value. The words "in excess of par (stated) value" are frequently omitted simply to shorten the titles.

To illustrate the necessity for separate accounts to show the sources of the various types of paid-in capital, assume that a corporation issued both its preferred stock and common stock at various times and at differing premiums, aggregating $25,000 on the preferred stock and $15,000 on the common stock. If only one premium account (Paid-In Capital in Excess of Par) was established, it would not be obvious that the capital contributed by the preferred stockholders was the par value of the preferred stock plus the premium of $25,000. Nor could the capital contributed by the common stockholders be readily identified as being the par value of the common stock plus the premium of $15,000.

If separate accounts for the premiums have not been maintained, a proper accounting for the retirement of all or a part of the outstanding preferred stock may not be possible without extensive review of prior years' records.

It should be noted that the accounts shown opposite the sources listed under IA in Illustration 13.1 represent amounts paid in by stockholders of the corporation, either past or present. The contributions of capital represented by the Paid-In Capital—Donations account may have come from either stockholders or other donors, such as a chamber of commerce

Illustration 13.1

Source of Proprietary Capital (Stockholders' Equity)	*Illustrative General Ledger Account Titles*
I Capital contributed	
A. For, or assigned to, shares:	
1. To the extent of par or stated value or the amount received for shares without par or stated value.	Common Stock 5 Percent Preferred Stock
2. In addition to par or stated value:	
a) In excess of par.	Paid-In Capital in Excess of Par Value—Common (Preferred)
b) In excess of stated value.	Paid-In Capital in Excess of Stated Value—Common (Preferred)
c) Resulting from reduction in par or stated value of shares.	Paid-In Capital—Recapitalization
d) Resulting from reissue of treasury stock at a price above its acquisition price.	Paid-In Capital—Common (Preferred) Treasury Stock Transactions
B. Other than for shares, whether from shareholders or from others.	Paid-In Capital—Donations
II Recorded increases in asset values, representing the excess of appraised or fair market value of assets over cost.	Capital from Appreciation of Assets
III Capital accumulated by retention of earnings.	Retained Earnings or Retained Income

which has donated a plant site as a means of attracting industry to the community. Regardless of the specific source, paid-in capital is regarded as the relatively permanent portion of the stockholders' equity. On the other hand, retained earnings—typically the source of dividend distributions—is regarded as the relatively temporary portion of corporate capital. (To the extent that accumulated earnings remain undistributed over a long period of time, however, there is a degree of permanence also in the retained earnings element of the stockholders' equity.)

Indicate whether each of the following items is classified as a source of proprietary capital (stockholders' equity) by writing yes or no on a separate piece of paper or on the answer sheet provided in the *Work Papers*.

1. Paid-In Capital in Excess of Par Value—Preferred.
2. Paid-In Capital in Excess of Stated Value—Common.
3. Retained Earnings.
4. 5 Percent First Mortgage Bonds.
5. 5 Percent Preferred Stock.

Now check your responses by comparing them with Answer Frame 1[13] on page 594.

Answer frame 1[13]

1. Yes. This account represents a portion of the permanent capital contributed by the owners and is therefore classified as a source of proprietary capital.
2. Yes. This account represents a portion of the permanent capital contributed by stockholders and is therefore a source of proprietary capital.
3. Yes. Retained earnings represent capital accumulated by the retention of earnings and are therefore classified as a source of proprietary capital.
4. No. This account represents a liability of the corporation and is classified as a long-term liability in the statement of financial position.
5. Yes. This account represents a portion of the permanent capital contributed by stockholders and is therefore classified as a source of proprietary capital.

If you missed any of the above, reread Frame 1[13] before beginning Frame 2[13] below.

Frame 2[13]

Terminology relative to paid-in capital, as well as that related to retained earnings, has been in a state of change for several years. The terms capital surplus and paid-in surplus, widely used until recently, are in the process of being abandoned. Both terms were (and, to a lesser extent, still are) used generically to describe all paid-in capital except that portion credited to the capital stock accounts (preferred or common). Paid-in capital is often, in the legal sense, restricted as to withdrawal; therefore, the implication of availability for dividends in the word "surplus" is unfortunate and may actually be misleading, even though certain types of paid-in capital may (under certain state statutes) be considered available for distribution as dividends.

Dividends—withdrawals of capital by stockholders through formal action of the board of directors—are normally reductions of retained earnings. Dividends from proprietary capital other than retained earnings are unusual. Examples are sometimes found in corporations exploiting depletable assets such as mines, quarries, or timber stands. If permitted under state law, dividends may be declared up to the extent of earnings computed without a charge for depletion (the exhaustion of the natural resource). The dividends may thus consist of a distribution of contributed or paid-in capital and of earnings. If contributed capital is being distributed, such dividends are liquidating in nature and serve to reduce the "permanent" portion of the stockholders' equity. There is a definite obligation on the part of the corporation to disclose to its stockholders the source of those dividends which are not distributions of earnings. The legality of such dividends depends upon the precise source of the capital and upon the laws of the state of incorporation.

Determine whether each of the following statements is true or false.

1. The Paid-In Capital—Donations account is not the most common source of dividend distributions.

2. A liquidating dividend reduces a proprietary capital account other than retained earnings, and it is not considered to be a distribution of earnings.
3. The retained earnings of a corporation are a part of its paid-in or capital surplus.
4. The account title 5 Percent Preferred Stock indicates that 5 percent of the authorized preferred stock has been issued.

Now check your responses in Answer Frame 2[13] on page 596.

Frame 3[13]

Paid-in capital—treasury stock transactions. If a corporation reacquires shares of its own outstanding capital stock at one price and later reissues them at a higher price, the corporate capital is increased by the difference between the two prices. If the reissue price is less than acquisition cost, corporate capital is decreased. Treasury stock transactions are treated at length later in this chapter.

Paid-in capital—donations. Occasionally a corporation receives gifts of assets—a gift of land from a chamber of commerce is an example. Such gifts increase corporate capital but not through earnings or transactions involving capital stock. The entry to record the gift of a $5,000 land site is a debit to Land and a credit to Paid-In Capital—Donations, regardless of whether the donor is a stockholder or not. The entry should be in the amount of the fair market value of the gift when received.

Capital from appreciation of assets

In those rare instances where the board of directors resolves that upward revaluations of assets (usually plant assets) be recorded, stockholders' equity is also increased. For example, land bought 20 years ago may be recorded at a cost figure that is substantially below its current market value. The entry to record appreciation of land is a debit to Land (or Land—Appreciation) and a credit to Capital from Appreciation. Other titles sometimes used for the account credited are Revaluation Capital, Unrealized Appraisal Increment, or Reserve for Unrealized Appreciation. There is no realization of earnings through exchange or sale in the writing up of an asset; hence, earnings statement accounts are not affected. The growth in value is considered an element of proprietary capital; but since it is not an element of realized earnings, it should not be regarded as available for cash dividend declarations. In actual practice the recording of appreciation is not a common occurrence.

Answer frame 2[13]

1. True. The usual source of dividend distributions is the Retained Earnings account.
2. True. A liquidating dividend, in essence, returns a portion of the corporation's permanent capital to its stockholders.
3. False. The paid-in or capital surplus of a corporation includes capital contributed by stockholders or others in excess of the amount assigned to the shares issued. It does not include retained earnings.
4. False. The 5 percent refers to the dividend rate on the preferred stock; that is, the dividend rate is 5 percent of the stock's par value.

If you missed any of the above, reread Frame 2[13] before turning to Frame 3[13] on page 595.

3[13]
continued

The Boardman Corporation has 10,000 shares of stock without par or stated value outstanding for which it received $250,000. The company's board of directors now directs that $50,000 appreciation on land owned be recorded. Indicate with a yes or no whether each of the entries properly records this appreciation.

1. Land	50,000	
Revenue from Growth in Land Value		50,000
2. Land	50,000	
Revaluation Capital		50,000
3. Land	50,000	
Retained Earnings		50,000
4. Land	50,000	
Capital from Appreciation		50,000

Now check your responses in Answer Frame 3[13] on page 598.

Frame 4[13]

A corporation may find it necessary to make a change in its capitalization. For example, a company having 5,000 shares of common stock with a par value of $100 may find that it cannot issue additional shares at $100 because the shares will not sell at that price. To avoid issuing shares at a discount, the company decides to reduce the par value of its stock to $80.

For the above example, prepare the journal entry to record the exchange of all the $100 shares for the new $80 per shares. Now turn to Answer Frame 4[13] on page 598 to check your answer.

Frame 5[13]

Paid-in capital and retained earnings in the statement of financial position

The following stockholders' equity section of a statement of financial position illustrates the presentation of the various classes of capital:

Paid-In Capital:		
Preferred stock, 6% $100 par value; authorized, issued, and outstanding, 4,000 shares	$ 400,000	
Common stock without par value, stated value $5 per share; authorized, issued, and outstanding, 200,000 shares	1,000,000	$1,400,000
Paid-in capital in excess of par or stated value:		
From preferred stock issuances	$ 40,000	
From recapitalization of common stock	1,000,000	
From donations	10,000	1,050,000
Total Paid-In Capital		$2,450,000
Capital from appreciation of land		100,000
Retained earnings		400,000
Total Stockholders' Equity		$2,950,000

In highly condensed published statements of financial position, the details regarding the sources of the paid-in capital in excess of par or stated value are often omitted and replaced by a single item, such as:

Paid-in capital in excess of par or stated value.....$1,050,000

With reference to the stockholders' equity section just given, indicate whether each of the following statements is correct or incorrect.

1. No shares of stock have been subscribed for and not issued.
2. Earnings at some previous time were increased by $20,000 due to the appreciation of assets.
3. At least some of the preferred stock was issued at a price greater than its par value.
4. The par value of the common stock was changed from $10 per share to $5 per share.

Check your responses in Answer Frame 5[13] on page 598.

Frame 6[13]

Retained earnings

In general, the stockholders' equity or interest in a corporation is made up of two elements: (1) paid-in (or contributed) capital and (2) retained earnings. Retained earnings is the term used to describe the increase in stockholders' equity resulting from profitable operation of the

Answer frame 3[13]

1. No. The appreciation of the land should not be recorded in a revenue account, since it has not been realized through exchange or sale.
2. Yes. This is a correct entry to record the appreciation of the land.
3. No. The credit to Retained Earnings is in error, since the appreciation in value of the land has not been realized through an exchange or sale transaction.
4. Yes. This is a correct entry to record the appreciation of the land.

If you missed any of the above, reread Frame 3[13] before beginning Frame 4[13] on page 596.

Answer frame 4[13]

The correct entry to record the transaction is:

Common Stock—$100 Par	500,000	
Common Stock—$80 Par		400,000
Paid-In Capital from Recapitalization		100,000
To record the exchange of 5,000 new $80 par common shares for 5,000 old $100 par shares.		

If you answered incorrectly, be sure you know why your answer was incorrect before turning to Frame 5[13] on page 597.

Answer frame 5[13]

1. Correct. If shares were subscribed for but not issued, this would be set forth separately in the stockholders' equity section. In the stockholders' equity section shown, such a situation cannot exist, since all of the authorized shares of both preferred and common stock have been issued.
2. Incorrect. No realization of earnings is associated with the writing up of an asset. Even if the appreciated buildings were subsequently depreciated over their useful lives, this would not result in an increase in earnings; it would result in a decrease in earnings.
3. Correct. The stockholders' equity section shows that a premium of $40,000 has been received.
4. Incorrect. The common stock is without par value.

If you missed any of the above, restudy Frame 5[13] before beginning Frame 6[13] on page 597.

6[13] *continued*

corporation. As such, it indicates the source of certain assets received but not distributed to stockholders as dividends. Thus, both categories indicate the source of assets received by the corporation—actual investment by the stockholders and investment by the stockholders in the sense of dividends forgone. For present purposes, the balance in the Retained Earnings account will be viewed as the difference between (1) the net earnings of the corporation from the date of incorporation to the present and (2) the sum of dividends declared during the same period.

When the Retained Earnings account has a debit balance, a deficit exists. It is shown under that title as a negative amount in the stockholders' equity section of the statement of financial position. The net effect of having a deficit is that net assets have been decreased rather than increased as a result of operations and dividend declarations. The title of the general ledger account need not be changed merely because it contains a debit balance.

As has been seen in earlier chapters, the net earnings or loss of a corporation as shown in the earnings statement is transferred periodically to retained earnings in the entry which closes the Expense and Revenue Summary account. Retained Earnings is credited for the amount of net earnings or debited for the amount of net loss. Since dividends reduce the capital accumulated through retention of earnings, they are also debited to Retained Earnings.

A term sometimes used in lieu of retained earnings is earned surplus. Because the word surplus has a connotation of excess or residue (of cash, for example) and is otherwise misinterpreted, there is a trend among accountants toward abandonment of the term. More descriptive terms—such as retained income, retained earnings, accumulated earnings, or earnings retained in the business—are used in its place. Published annual reports of corporations show a definite trend in this direction. Both good theory and modern practice support the change.

Indicate whether each of the following statements is correct or incorrect.

1. The balance in the Retained Earnings account basically represents the accumulated earnings of a corporation earned throughout its existence but not distributed to its stockholders.
2. The net earnings for a period are transferred to retained earnings by an entry which debits Expense and Revenue Summary and credits Retained Earnings.
3. The Retained Earnings account describes one source of corporate capital and is properly classifiable as paid-in capital in the stockholders' equity section of the statement of financial position.
4. A net loss suffered by a corporation during an accounting period increases the total stockholders' equity shown in its statement of financial position.

Check your responses in Answer Frame 6[13] on page 600.

Frame 7[13]

Retained earnings reserves

A retained earnings reserve (frequently called a surplus reserve) is a segregation or subdivision of retained earnings and is recorded by a debit to Retained Earnings and a credit to a properly named reserve account. The reason for the establishment of the reserve is often indicated by the title of the reserve account. Transferring a part of retained earnings to

Answer frame 6[13]

1. Correct. This is basically what the balance in the Retained Earnings account represents.
2. Correct. This is the form of the entry which transfers periodic net earnings to the Retained Earnings account.
3. Incorrect. Although a source of corporate capital, retained earnings do not represent paid-in capital, that is, capital contributed by the owners. Retained earnings are classified separately from paid-in capital within the stockholders' equity section.
4. Incorrect. A net loss reduces the credit balance (or increases the debit balance if one exists) in the Retained Earnings account, and this reduces the total stockholders' equity.

If you missed any of the above, reread Frame 6[13] before beginning Frame 7[13] on page 599.

7[13] *continued*

a reserve has the purpose and effect of limiting dividend declarations to the remaining balance—the free or unappropriated retained earnings. In other words, the creation of a retained earnings reserve informs stockholders that a certain amount of the assets brought into the corporation through the earning process are not to be distributed to stockholders as dividends; no cash, however, is being set aside by the entry. Retained earnings reserves are established by action of the board of directors, voluntarily or in accordance with the provisions of certain contracts such as bond indentures or loan agreements.

When the retained earnings reserve has served its purpose, it may be returned intact to Retained Earnings at the direction of the board of directors. The entry is simply a debit to the reserve and a credit to Retained Earnings.

Reserves in the statement of financial position

In the statement of financial position, retained earnings reserves should be shown in the stockholders' equity section as follows:

Paid-In Capital:		
Preferred stock, $50 par; 500 shares authorized, issued, and outstanding	$25,000	
Common stock, $5 par; 10,000 shares authorized, issued, and outstanding	50,000	
Total Paid-In Capital		$ 75,000
Retained Earnings:		
Appropriated:		
Reserve for retirement of bonds payable	$25,000	
Free and unappropriated	20,000	
Total Retained Earnings		$ 45,000
Total Stockholders' Equity		$120,000

The word "reserve" still is used in several different senses by accountants and the general public. Although modern accounting practice tends to limit use of the term reserve to accounts which are reservations of retained earnings, enough exceptions exist to require careful interpretation of "reserves." For example, the liability section of a published statement of financial position may contain an account entitled Reserve for Product Warranties. Since this account shows the estimated cost of fulfilling product warranties on goods sold, it is actually a liability and a preferable title would be Estimated Liability on Product Warranties.

Retained earnings reserves are not to be confused with allowances such as allowances for depreciation and doubtful accounts. The creation of a retained earnings reserve does not reduce the equity of the stockholders; it merely earmarks a portion of that equity for a specific reason. The creation of an allowance for depreciation or doubtful accounts has the indirect effect of reducing stockholders' equity by increasing expenses (which reduce net earnings). The credit to the allowance account also reduces the book value of the asset to which the allowance applies.

It is worthwhile to note that the formal recording and reporting of retained earnings reserves is decreasing and is being replaced by footnote explanations. In view of the confusion surrounding such reserves, we applaud this trend.

Indicate whether each of the following statements is true or false.

1. A retained earnings reserve account is established by a debit to Retained Earnings and a credit to the reserve account being set up.
2. The creation of a retained earnings reserve increases the amount of the free and unappropriated retained earnings shown in the statement of financial position.
3. The establishment of a retained earnings reserve reduces the total stockholders' equity shown in the statement of financial position.
4. The creation of a retained earnings reserve may reflect an action taken by the board of directors to restrict the amount of dividends which may be declared.

Now check your answers in Answer Frame 7[13] on page 602.

Frame 8[13]

Extraordinary items and prior period adjustments

Earlier in this chapter it was stated that the balance in the Retained Earning account normally represents the difference between (1) the cumulative net earnings of a corporation to date and (2) the sum of dividends declared during the same period. In view of the immediately preceding discussion of retained earnings reserves, it is seen that this statement is not invariably true. It is also not strictly true because prior period adjustments can be recorded directly in Retained Earnings.

Answer frame 7[13]

1. True. This is the manner in which a retained earnings reserve account is set up.
2. False. The purpose of setting up a retained earnings reserve account is to reduce the amount of free and unappropriated retained earnings, since this is the amount against which dividends may be declared.
3. False. Setting up a retained earnings reserve does not reduce the total stockholders' equity. It merely earmarks a portion of that equity to indicate that assets brought into the corporation through the earnings process are to be used for a specific purpose.
4. True. The purpose of setting up a retained earnings reserve account is to reduce the amount of unrestricted retained earnings, since this is the amount against which dividends may be declared.

If you missed any of the above, reread Frame 7[13] before turning to Frame 8[13] on page 601.

8[13] *continued*

All-inclusive and current operating performance concepts of net earnings

Accountants have long disagreed over whether certain nonrecurring, unusual items of gain or loss and corrections of prior periods' data should be presented in the earnings statement or be recorded directly in retained earnings in the year they are recognized. The reference here is to items such as (1) collections of life insurance proceeds upon the death of a company officer; (2) additional income tax assessments for prior years; (3) losses from disasters such as fires, floods, and tornados; and (4) damages paid as a result of lawsuits and similar nonoperating, nonrecurring items.

In the past, a majority of accountants has supported the all-inclusive concept of earnings, whereby all such items are included in the earnings statement for the year they are recognized in order to arrive at net earnings for that year. This concept is also referred to as the "clean surplus (i.e., retained earnings) theory" because the Retained Earnings account is not cluttered with numerous charges and credits.

Other accountants have supported the current operating performance concept of net earnings, in which all material nonoperating, nonrecurring items are recorded in retained earnings. The earnings statement shows only regularly recurring expenses and revenues.

Indicate whether each of the following statements is true or false.

1. In a corporation's regular financial statements, the reported balance in the Retained Earnings account is greater if nonrecurring gains are handled in accordance with the current operating performance concept of earnings than if the gains are handled in accordance with the all-inclusive concept of earnings.
2. Nonrecurring gains and losses are not used in the determination of periodic net earnings or loss under the current operating performance

concept of earnings, while they are used to determine net earnings or loss under the all-inclusive concept.

3. The clean surplus concept and the all-inclusive concept of earnings both refer to the same manner of treating nonrecurring gains and losses.
4. If a corporation suffers a large, uninsured flood loss, its reported net earnings for the period are smaller under the all-inclusive concept of earnings than under the current operating performance concept of earnings.

To check your answers, turn to Answer Frame 8[13] on page 604.

Frame 9[13]

Relative merits of the alternative concepts. The current operating performance concept is supported largely because it is believed to yield an earnings statement useful in predicting future net earnings. Since only regularly recurring expenses and revenues are included, the net earnings portray the continuing earning power of the company.

Most accountants favor the all-inclusive concept for the following reasons: (1) Biased reporting is not as likely under this concept. Research has shown that losses tend to be charged to retained earnings while gains appear in the earnings statement when the current operating performance concept is used. (2) Traditionally, no accepted standards have existed to distinguish consistently between ordinary and extraordinary or recurring and nonrecurring gains and losses. (3) Many so-called nonrecurring gains and losses do relate to operations; for example, the size of a gain on the sale of plant assets is directly related to the previously recorded depreciation. (4) Readers may overlook significant gains and losses if they are reported in the statement of retained earnings, because their attention often is focused on reported net earnings.

The Accounting Principles Board of the American Institute of Certified Public Accountants resolved this controversy largely in favor of the all-inclusive concept in its *Opinion No. 9* and went even further in *Opinion No. 30*. The Board recommends that the unusual, nonrecurring types of items discussed above be classified as either extraordinary items or prior period adjustments, and that these items appear in appropriate sections of the earnings statement or the statement of retained earnings.

Extraordinary items. Extraordinary items are those which are clearly unrelated to, or only incidentally related to, the ordinary and typical activities of the company and which are of a type that would not reasonably be expected to recur in the foreseeable future. Examples might include such items as loss from earthquake in an area that does not have earthquakes frequently, losses from bombing during a war, and losses and gains from the expropriation of property (if expropriation is unusual and nonrecurring). These items should be very infrequently reported. When they are reported, they must be included in the determination of periodic earnings and are to be separately disclosed as extraordinary

Answer frame 8[13]

1. False. The balance in the Retained Earnings account is the same under either concept. Under the current operating performance concept the gains are closed to Retained Earnings, while under the all-inclusive concept they are closed to the Expense and Revenue Summary, which in turn is closed to Retained Earnings. The effect on the balance of the Retained Earnings account is thus the same, but net earnings for the period are not the same under the two concepts.
2. True. This statement points out the important distinction between the current operating performance and the all-inclusive concepts of net earnings.
3. True. The clean surplus concept and the all-inclusive concept both refer to the concept of net earnings which holds that all nonrecurring gains and losses should be included in the computation of periodic net earnings.
4. True. The flood loss is omitted from the computation of net earnings under the current operating performance concept but included under the all-inclusive concept. Thus, the earnings determined in accordance with the all-inclusive concept are smaller.

If you missed any of the above, reread Frame 8[13] before beginning Frame 9[13] on page 603.

9[13] *continued*

items. The environment in which the company operates clearly affects whether an item is of an unusual nature and nonrecurring.

Gains or losses directly related to ordinary business activities are not extraordinary items regardless of their size. For example, material write-downs of uncollectible receivables, obsolete inventories, and gains and losses from disposals of segments of a business are not extraordinary items.

Prior period adjustments. Prior period adjustments are reported in the statement of retained earnings and consist of those material adjustments which (1) can be directly and specifically related to and identified with the business activities of particular prior periods, (2) are not the result of economic events occurring after the prior period, (3) result primarily from determinations made by persons outside the business, and (4) could not be estimated with reasonable accuracy prior to this determination. Prior period adjustments are expected to be rare. They exist primarily because the uncertainty surrounding events and transactions in prior periods was so great that their accounting effects could not be determined at that time.

Examples of prior period adjustments include material assessments or settlements of income taxes, settlements of contracts through renegotiation, and amounts paid in settlement of litigation or other similar claims. But the normal, recurring corrections or adjustments which follow inevitably from the use of estimates in accounting practice are not to be treated as prior period adjustments. Thus, changes in the estimated remaining lives of depreciable plant assets do not give rise to prior period adjustments, nor does failure to collect expected amounts of receivables or to recover the costs of inventories.

Indicate whether each of the following statements is true or false.

1. A company which for the third time in three years has suffered a material loss through expropriation of property by a foreign government should report the loss as an extraordinary item in the year of expropriation.
2. The complete write-off of obsolete inventory in an amount equal to 20 percent of the company's assets gives rise to an extraordinary item.
3. A substantial assessment and payment in 1975 of additional income taxes for the year 1972 is reported as a prior period adjustment in the statement of retained earnings for the year 1975.
4. The loss of a substantial receivable arising from a sale made in 1974 because of bankruptcy of the customer in 1975 does not give rise to either a prior period adjustment or an extraordinary item in the financial statements for 1975.

Now turn to Answer Frame 9[13] on page 606 to check your answer.

Frame 10[13]

Illustrative statements. Financial statements illustrating the treatment accorded extraordinary items and prior period adjustments are presented in Illustrations 13.2 and 13.3. They are based on the information that

Illustration 13.2, *Earnings Statement with Extraordinary Item*

ANSON COMPANY
Earnings Statement
For the Year Ended December 31, 1975

Net sales		$20,500,000
Other revenues		1,500,000
		$22,000,000
Cost of goods sold	$10,000,000	
Administrative, selling, and general expenses	6,000,000	
Federal income taxes	3,000,000	19,000,000
Net earnings before extraordinary items		$ 3,000,000
Less: Loss on sale of investments		1,000,000
Net Earnings		$ 2,000,000

in 1975 the Anson Company sold investments costing $4 million for $3 million and that the company was assessed, and paid, an additional $800,000 of income taxes for the year 1972. The journal entries to record the transactions are the same whether the items are considered extraordinary items or prior period adjustments and read:

Cash	3,000,000	
Loss on Sale of Investments	1,000,000	
Investments		4,000,000
Income Tax Assessment for 1972	800,000	
Cash		800,000

Answer frame 9[13]

1. False. The item must be both unusual and infrequent to qualify as an extraordinary item. This item does not qualify.
2. False. The write-off of obsolete inventory is too closely related to the normal business activities of the company to be considered an extraordinary item regardless of its size. If the size of the write-down is believed to be significant information to readers of the earnings statement, it could be separately disclosed, but not as an extraordinary item.
3. True. Assessments of additional income taxes can be specifically related to or identified with the business activities of a particular prior period and thus can and should be treated as prior period adjustments.
4. True. The loss of an account receivable is too customary and ordinary an event and too closely related to operations to be considered an extraordinary item or a prior period adjustment. If the amount of the receivable is unusually large, disclosure of the loss would be appropriate, possibly by footnote; but not as an extraordinary item.

If you missed any of the above, reread Frame 9[13] before beginning Frame 10[13] on page 605.

10[13] *continued*

Illustration 13.3, *Statement of Retained Earnings with Prior Period Adjustment*

ANSON COMPANY
Statement of Retained Earnings
For the Year Ended December 31, 1975

Retained earnings, January 1, 1975	$6,000,000
Less: Additional income taxes for 1972	800,000
Retained earnings, January 1, 1975, as adjusted	$5,200,000
Net earnings	2,000,000
	$7,200,000
Dividends	1,500,000
Retained Earnings, December 31, 1975	$5,700,000

Assume that the loss is properly interpreted as an extraordinary item because it resulted from the sale of investments acquired 20 years ago, that the sale is the only such sale in Anson's history, and that the investments sold constituted Anson's only such investment. Illustrations 13.2 and 13.3 show how these transactions are presented in accordance with *Opinion No. 9* and *Opinion No. 30*. The important feature of the earnings statement, presented under the all-inclusive concept, is that the continuing earning power of the company is reflected in the figure for net earnings before extraordinary items. The unusual, nonrecurring, extraordinary item is fully disclosed but separated from the calculation of this important figure in determining a final net earnings figure.

In the statement of retained earnings, prior period adjustments are treated as adjustments of the opening balance of retained earnings. The statement shows clearly that when the recommendations contained in *Opinions No. 9* and *No. 30* are implemented, the balance in the retained earnings account will consist of the cumulative amounts reported as net earnings in the earnings statements, plus or minus prior period adjustments, less dividends.

Is each of the following statements true or false?

1. The journal entry to record a given transaction differs depending on whether the unusual item recorded is to be reported as an extraordinary item or as a prior period adjustment.
2. The balance in the Retained Earnings account normally consists of the cumulative amount of reported net earnings less net losses, plus or minus prior period adjustments and extraordinary items, less dividends.
3. Extraordinary items are added or deducted in arriving at reported net earnings in the earnings statement, while prior period adjustments are added to or deducted from the beginning balance of retained earnings in the statement of retained earnings.

You may check your answers by referring to Answer Frame 10[13] on page 608.

Frame 11[13]

Accounting for tax effects. The loss on sale of investments in Illustration 13.2 is not deductible in the determination of federal income taxes. But most extraordinary items and prior period adjustments will affect the amount of income taxes payable, with the result that questions arise as to proper reporting procedure for the tax effects of such items.

To illustrate, a corporation has revenues of $25 million; expenses, excluding federal income taxes, of $22 million; and has suffered a $2 million flood loss which is tax deductible. Assuming a 50 percent tax rate, $500,000 of income taxes are due for the year. If care is not exercised, the above information may improperly be reported as follows:

Revenues		$25,000,000
Expenses	$22,000,000	
Federal income taxes	500,000	22,500,000
Net earnings before extraordinary items		$ 2,500,000
Flood loss		2,000,000
Net earnings		$ 500,000

Such an earnings statement is quite misleading, because it overstates net earnings before extraordinary items by $1 million. With revenues of $25 million and expenses of $22 million, earnings from operations before income taxes are $3 million. With a 50 percent tax rate, the normal income taxes on these earnings would be $1.5 million as contrasted to the $500,000 shown in the above statement. The tax reduction of $1 million (0.50 × $2,000,000) resulting from the flood loss has been offset against the amount of income taxes considered applicable to the normal

Answer frame 10[13]

1. False. The journal entries do not differ, since the issue involved is how to report, not how to record, extraordinary items and prior period adjustments.
2. False. The statement is true except for the inclusion of extraordinary items in retained earnings. Reported net earnings and net losses already incorporate these items.
3. True. This is exactly what *Opinion No. 9* recommends.

If you missed any of the above, reread Frame 10[13] before beginning Frame 11[13] on page 607.

11[13] *continued* recurring earnings of the company. Net earnings before extraordinary items thus should be $1.5 million, not $2.5 million; and this overstatement could be quite significant, since investors tend to use regularly recurring earnings as a basis for predicting future earnings.

To prevent such distortions, *Opinion No. 9* recommends that extraordinary items and prior period adjustments be reported net of their tax effects. This type of reporting is illustrated in Illustration 13.4, using the above data and the further information that the company paid $600,000 in the current year to the government as a result of the renegotiation of the price of a contract completed three years ago.

A number of significant considerations in financial reporting are presented in Illustration 13.4: (1) earnings before extraordinary items of

Illustration 13.4, *Net of Tax Accounting for Extraordinary Item and Prior Period Adjustment*

BATTEN COMPANY
Combined Earnings Statement and Statement of Retained Earnings
For the Year Ended December 31, 1975

Revenues		$25,000,000
Expenses (details omitted here)	$22,000,000	
Federal income taxes	1,500,000	23,500,000
Net earnings before extraordinary items		$ 1,500,000
Flood loss (net of tax effect of $1,000,000)		1,000,000
Net earnings		$ 500,000
Retained earnings, January 1, 1975	$ 4,000,000	
Less: Contract renegotiation settlement (net of tax effect of $300,000)	300,000	3,700,000
		$ 4,200,000
Dividends		400,000
Retained Earnings, December 31, 1975		$ 3,800,000

$1.5 million are more representative of the continuing earning power of the company, because normal amounts of income taxes have been deducted in arriving at this amount; (2) the flood loss and the negotiated contract settlement are reported at their actual impact on the company—that is, at their given amounts less their effects on the taxes payable in the current year; (3) the data are presented in a combined earnings statement and statement of retained earnings. Such a form seems especially appropriate when prior period adjustments are to be reported, since it places them adjacent to the reported net earnings and thus lessens the probability that they will be overlooked by readers who typically focus attention on net earnings. But the use of this form of statement need not be restricted to circumstances involving prior period adjustments, and its use in practice is increasing.

In 1975 a certain company has revenues of $10 million; expenses, excluding federal income taxes, of $6 million; and a loss from war destruction of $1 million. The company paid $400,000 of additional income taxes for 1971 in 1975. The normal federal income tax rate is 50 percent. Indicate whether each of these statements about this company is true or false.

1. The additional income taxes for 1971 should be reported in the statement of retained earnings at $400,000.
2. Net earnings before extraordinary items should be reported at $1 million.
3. The net earnings for the year are $1.5 million.
4. The loss from war damage should be reported in the statement of retained earnings at a net-of-tax amount of $500,000.

Now check your responses in Answer Frame 11[13] on page 610.

Frame 12[13]

Dividends

Dividends are distributions of earnings by a corporation to its stockholders. The normal dividend is a cash dividend, but other types of assets, such as marketable securities, may be distributed. A corporation may also distribute notes, other promises to pay cash in the future, or additional shares of its own capital stock as dividends.

Since they are the means whereby the owners of a corporation share in the earnings of the corporation, dividends are usually charged against retained earnings. They must be declared by the board of directors and are recorded in the minutes book. The significant dates concerning dividends are the date of *declaration,* the date of *record,* and the date of *payment*. For example, the board of directors of the Allan Corporation may declare on June 5, 1975, a cash dividend of $1.25 per share payable on July 10 to stockholders of record on July 1, 1975. The date of declaration is the date the board takes action in the form of a motion that dividends be paid, creating the liability for dividends payable. The date

Answer frame 11[13]

1. True. The additional income taxes assessed for 1971 relate specifically to a prior period, namely 1971, and are therefore to be treated as a prior period adjustment and reported in the statement of retained earnings. Since the amount of federal income taxes assessed cannot be deducted in arriving at the amount of taxes payable, there is no tax effect and the item cannot be reported net of any tax effect.
2. False. Net earnings before extraordinary items are equal to revenue of $10 million, less expenses (excluding federal income taxes) of $6 million, less (on $4 million of ordinary earnings) federal income taxes of $2 million. Thus, $2 million is the amount of net earnings before extraordinary items.
3. True. Revenues of $10 million less expenses of $6 million yield $4 million of earnings before income taxes. When federal income taxes of $2 million and the loss from war destruction (net of taxes) are deducted, the final net earnings are $1.5 million. (The $400,000 of additional income taxes for 1971 should not be deducted in the earnings statement, as they constitute a prior period adjustment.)
4. False. The loss is an extraordinary item and should be reported in the earnings statement at $500,000.

If you missed any of the above, reread Frame 11[13] before beginning Frame 12[13] on page 609.

12[13] *continued*

of record is the date established by the board to determine to whom the dividends will be paid. The stockholders on the date of record are determined from the corporation's records (a subsidiary stockholders' ledger). The date of payment is the date of actual payment of the dividend.

Cash dividends

If a quarterly cash dividend on $100,000 (1,000 shares of $100 par value) of 8 percent preferred stock is declared on January 21, 1975, to be paid on March 1, 1975, to stockholders of record on February 5, 1975, the entries at the declaration and payment dates are as follows:

Jan. 21	Retained Earnings	2,000	
	Dividends Payable		2,000
	Dividends declared: 2 percent on $100,000 of outstanding preferred stock, payable March 1, 1975, to stockholders of record on February 5, 1975.		
Mar. 1	Dividends Payable	2,000	
	Cash		2,000
	Paid the dividend declared on January 21, 1975.		

When a cash dividend is declared, some companies debit a Dividends account instead of Retained Earnings; at the end of the fiscal year, the Dividends account is closed to Retained Earnings. The Dividends account summarizes the dividends declared for the year in one place, and the

Retained Earnings account is not cluttered by several debits of the same type.

Once a cash dividend is declared and notice of the dividend is given to the stockholders, it cannot be rescinded unless all stockholders agree to such action. A legally declared cash dividend is a current liability of the corporation.

Decide whether each of the following statements is true or false.

1. The payment of a cash dividend increases a corporation's current liabilities.
2. The date of record follows the date of the declaration of a dividend.
3. The date of declaration is the date used to determine to whom the dividends will be paid.
4. The presence of a Dividends Payable account among the current liabilities in a statement of financial position indicates a dividend has been declared but not paid.

You may check your answers in Answer Frame 12[13] on page 612.

Frame 13[13]

Stock dividends

A corporation may, for a number of reasons, declare a dividend calling for the distribution of additional shares of its capital stock. Some of these reasons are as follows.

1. Retained earnings may have become large relative to total stockholders' equity, or the corporation may simply desire a larger permanent capitalization.

2. The market price of the stock may have risen above a desirable trading range, or the corporation may wish to have a larger number of stockholders and expects to increase their number by increasing the number of shares outstanding.

3. Stock dividends may be used as a device for quieting stockholders' demands for dividends from a corporation which does not have sufficient working capital to pay cash dividends. Stockholders desire stock dividends because they usually add to the total market value of their holdings without giving them taxable earnings.

Stock dividend declarations usually call for the distribution of additional shares of the same class of stock as that held by the stockholders—in other words, additional common stock to common stockholders. The effect of the distribution of a stock dividend usually is to transfer a sum from retained earnings to permanent paid-in capital. The amount transferred for stock dividends is usually the fair or market value of the distributed shares. Most states permit the use of retained earnings

Answer frame 12[13]

1. False. The declaration of a cash dividend increases a firm's current liabilities. The payment of the cash dividend decreases current liabilities.
2. True. The date of record does follow the date of declaration. If it did not, the company would in some instances be paying dividends to individuals who no longer owned stock at the time the dividend was declared. Both of these dates precede the date of payment.
3. False. The date of record is the date used to determine to whom the dividends will be paid. The date of declaration is the date the liability for dividends payable becomes effective.
4. True. The declaration of a dividend creates the Dividends Payable account. When the dividend is paid, the balance in the Dividends Payable account is eliminated.

If you answered incorrectly, reread Frame 12[13] before beginning Frame 13[13] on page 611.

13[13]
continued

or paid-in capital from any other source (other than amounts already credited to capital stock) for stock dividends. But if the purpose of a stock dividend is to capitalize retained earnings, the source of the dividend should be retained earnings.

Stock dividends have no effect on the total amount of stockholders' equity. They merely decrease retained earnings and increase paid-in capital by an equal amount or transfer amounts between paid-in capital accounts. Immediately after the declaration and distribution of a stock dividend, each share of similar stock has a lower book value per share. This is because more shares are outstanding with no increase in total stockholders' equity.

Stock dividends have no effect on the total amount of stockholders' of ownership in the corporation. His total equity is simply spread over a larger number of shares. For example, if a stockholder owns 1,000 shares in a corporation having 100,000 shares of stock outstanding, he owns 1 percent of the outstanding shares. After a 10 percent stock dividend, he will still own 1 percent of the outstanding shares—1,100 of 110,000 outstanding.

Indicate whether each of the following statements is true or false.

1. The number of shares of capital stock outstanding is increased by the corporation's declaration and issuance of a stock dividend.
2. The declaration and issuance of a stock dividend does not change the total amount of stockholders' equity in the corporation.
3. A possible motive for a stock dividend is a desire to lower the market price per share of the stock.
4. A stock dividend declared from retained earnings reduces the retained earnings balance and permanently capitalizes a portion of the retained earnings.

Now check your responses in Answer Frame 13[13] on page 614.

Frame 14[13]

Stock split-ups

The Committee on Accounting Procedure of the American Institute of Certified Public Accountants has distinguished between stock dividends and stock split-ups. A distribution of shares greater than 20 to 25 percent of the previously outstanding shares is assumed to have the goal of reducing the market price of the shares by increasing the number outstanding and is treated as a stock splitup, or stock split.

There are a number of ways of accounting for a stock split-up, depending on the particular circumstances. If the board of directors reduces the par or stated value of shares, only the number of shares outstanding and the par or stated value need to be changed on the records. Thus, a 2 for 1 stock split in which the par value of the shares is decreased from $20 to $10 could be recorded as follows:

Common Stock—$20 par value	100,000	
Common Stock—$10 par value		100,000
To record a 2-for-1 stock split-up. 5,000 shares of $20 par value common stock were replaced by 10,000 shares of $10 par value common stock.		

But a corporation may wish to double the number of its outstanding shares without changing the par or stated value of the shares. To do this, it declares a 100 percent stock dividend. Whenever a distribution of shares occurs and the par or stated value of the shares is not changed, the distribution is generally described as a stock dividend. But such "stock dividends" of over 20–25 percent of the previously outstanding shares are *accounted for* as stock splits. They are looked upon as capital transactions, to be kept in the capital accounts, rather than as dividends that are properly charged against Retained Earnings. The shares issued are credited to the capital stock account in an amount equal to the par or stated value of the shares issued, and the debit is (indirectly) entered in other paid-in capital accounts, to the extent possible, and in Retained Earnings only as a last resort. Thus, the net effect of a 100 percent stock dividend declared and paid by Walt Disney Productions in 1973 on its 14,276,173 shares of $1.25 par value common stock was to transfer approximately $17,845,216 from Paid-in Capital in Excess of Par Value to Capital Stock—Common. The entries actually made could have read:

At Declaration Date		
Paid-in Capital in Excess of Par Value	17,845,216	
Stock Dividend Payable		17,845,216
At Payment Date		
Stock Dividend Payable	17,845,216	
Capital Stock—Common		17,845,216

If no other paid-in capital exists attaching to the class of shares issued, or exists only in an amount less than the par or stated value of the

Answer frame 13[13]

1. True. The issuance of a stock dividend increases the number of shares of capital stock outstanding but does not change the individual stockholder's percentage of ownership in the corporation.
2. True. The usual stock dividend merely decreases retained earnings and increases paid-in capital by an equal amount. Thus, there is no change in total stockholders' equity.
3. True. The desire to reduce the market price per share of the stock is a possible motive for the issuance of a stock dividend.
4. True. The effect of a stock dividend declared from retained earnings is to permanently capitalize a portion of retained earnings, since an amount is transferred from retained earnings to paid-in capital.

If you missed any of the above, restudy Frame 13[13] before beginning Frame 14[13] on page 613.

14[13] *continued*

shares issued, the dividend, if larger than 20–25 percent, is charged in its entirety, or in part, to Retained Earnings. And the amount so charged need not exceed the par or stated value of the additional shares issued.

Recording stock dividends

Assume a corporaton is authorized to issue 20,000 shares of $100 par value common stock, of which 8,000 shares are outstanding. Its board of directors now declares a 10 percent stock dividend (800 shares). The market price of the stock on the date of the dividend declaration is $125 per share immediately before the stock dividend is announced. Since distributions of less than 20–25 percent of the previously outstanding shares are to be accounted for at market value, the entry for the declaration of the dividend is as follows (assuming the dividend was declared on August 10, 1975):

Aug. 10	Retained Earnings	100,000	
	Stock Dividend Payable—Common		80,000
	Paid-In Capital—Stock Dividend		20,000
	To record the declaration of a 10 percent stock dividend; shares to be distributed on September 20, 1975, to stockholders of record on August 31, 1975.		

Can you give the entry to record the issuance of the shares? Turn to Answer Frame 14[13] on page 616 to check your answer.

Frame 15[13]

Mr. Carter owns 200 shares of the stock in the above example before the stock dividend is declared. He will receive 20 shares as a stock dividend. Before the stock dividend he owns 200/8,000 of the outstanding stock; after the dividend, he owns 220/8,800. His percentage of ownership of the outstanding stock does not change as a result of the dividend.

Current liabilities are usually paid out of current assets. A stock dividend payable is not payable with assets; hence, it is not a liability. If a statement of financial position is prepared between the date of declaration of the 10 percent dividend and the date of issuance of the shares, the proper statement presentation of the stock dividend is as follows:

Paid-In Capital:		
Common stock, $100 par value; authorized, 20,000 shares; issued and outstanding, 8,000 shares	$800,000	
Stock dividend payable on September 20, 1975, 800 shares at par value	80,000	
Total par value of shares issued and to be issued	$880,000	
From capitalization of retained earnings through declaration of stock dividend	20,000	
Total Paid-In Capital		$ 900,000
Retained earnings		150,000
Total Stockholders' Equity		$1,050,000

See if you can answer the following questions about the preceding example of a stock dividend.

Suppose that the market price is still $125 per share on the date of declaration, but the common stock is without par value and has a stated value of $50 per share. What are the entries to record the declaration and issuance of the 10 percent stock dividend (800 shares) of the same class of stock?

Check your answer by turning to Answer Frame 15[13] on page 616.

Frame 16[13]

If a statement of financial position is prepared before the above stock dividend is issued but after it has been declared, is the Stock Dividend Payable—Common account classified as a current liability, as is a cash dividend payable?

Check your answer by turning to Answer Frame 16[13] on page 616.

Frame 17[13]

Dividends classified as to effects

In summary, dividends may be classified as follows.

1. Dividends from retained earnings either (*a*) decrease stockholders' equity or (*b*) do not decrease stockholders' equity. Dividends from re-

Answer frame 14[13]

The required entry is as follows:

Sept. 20	Stock Dividends Payable—Common	80,000	
	Common Stock		80,000
	To record distribution of 800 shares of common stock as authorized in stock dividend declared on August 10, 1975.		

If you did not have this entry, reread Frame 14[13] before beginning Frame 15[13] on page 614.

Answer frame 15[13]

The entry to record the declaration of the stock dividend is:

Retained Earnings	100,000	
Stock Dividend Payable—Common		40,000
Paid-In Capital—Stock Dividend		60,000

The entry to record the issuance of the stock dividend is:

Stock Dividend Payable—Common	40,000	
Common Stock		40,000

If you answered the question incorrectly, review Frame 15[13] before going on to Frame 16[13] on page 615.

Answer frame 16[13]

No. Current liabilities are payable in current assets. The Stock Dividend Payable—Common is payable with the corporation's own capital stock, not with assets. Thus, it is not a liability. Instead, it should be classified as paid-in capital in the stockholders' equity section.

If you answered incorrectly, review Frame 15[13] before going on to Frame 17[13] on page 615.

17[13] *continued*

tained earnings that decrease stockholders' equity are normally paid to stockholders in cash. Dividends from retained earnings that do not decrease stockholders' equity are distributions of capital stock of the corporation and are known as stock dividends.

2. Cash dividends from permanent capital decrease stockholders' equity and are either an intentional or an unintentional return of capital. Such dividends are intentionally paid when the amount of capital authorized and outstanding is being reduced (with approval of the proper authorities) by pro rata returns of capital to the shareholders. It is unfortunate that such distributions are called dividends. Dividends from permanent capital are unintentionally paid when dividend payments exceed the amount legally available for dividends because of accounting or legal errors.

Legality of dividends

The corporation laws of the states differ in their provisions as to the legality of a dividend. The stated or legal capital of a corporation is established by state law as that portion of the stockholders' equity which must be maintained intact, unimpaired by dividend declarations or other distributions to stockholders. The stated capital is often established at an amount equal to the par value of the shares issued or at an amount equal to a minimum price per share issued. The objective of the statutes in prohibiting the impairment of stated capital by the declaration of dividends is to protect the creditors of the corporation, whose claims are superior to those of stockholders.

The board of directors of a corporation possesses sole power to declare dividends. The *legality* of a dividend generally depends upon the amount of the retained earnings available for dividends—not upon the net earnings of any one period or the condition of the cash balance. The *financial advisability* of declaring a dividend depends on the working capital position of the corporation. Dividends may be paid in periods in which losses are incurred, provided retained earnings and working capital position justify the dividend. In some states, dividends may be declared from current earnings even though there is an accumulated deficit.

Is each of the following statements true or false?

1. Although dividends paid in cash or capital stock of a corporation may both be declared from retained earnings, their influences on total stockholders' equity are different.
2. Adequate disclosure of pertinent information is not provided unless dividends in arrears on cumulative preferred stock are footnoted or otherwise disclosed in the statement of financial position.
3. The stated or legal capital of a corporation is that portion of the stockholders' equity which is legally available for dividend distributions.

Now check your answers in Answer Frame 17[13] on page 618.

Frame 18[13]

Treasury stock

Treasury stock is capital stock, either preferred or common, which has been issued and reacquired by the issuing corporation. It has not been canceled, and it is legally available for reissuance. Treasury stock and unissued capital stock differ in that treasury stock has been issued at some time in the past, whereas unissued capital stock has never been issued.

Treasury stock may be acquired by purchase by the issuing corporation, by donation to the corporation by a stockholder, in settlement of a debt due the corporation, and in other transactions.

The corporation laws of most states consider treasury stock as issued

Answer frame 17[13]

1. True. Dividends declared from retained earnings which are paid in cash reduce the total stockholders' equity, while dividends declared from retained earnings which are paid in the corporation's capital stock have no effect on total stockholders' equity.
2. True. Although there is no liability for the dividends in arrears until they are declared by the board of directors, the existence of such arrearages is an item of significant information. Full disclosure means that all significant information should be set forth. Thus, the dividends in arrears should be disclosed in a clear manner.
3. False. The stated or legal capital of a corporation is that portion of the stockholders' equity which must not be impaired by dividend declarations or other distributions to stockholders.

If you answered incorrectly, reread Frame 17[13] before beginning Frame 18[13] on page 617.

18[13] *continued*

but not outstanding; the treasury shares have at some time in the past been issued to stockholders but they are no longer outstanding, that is, they are no longer in the possession of stockholders. The number of treasury shares is omitted from consideration in arriving at the number of voting shares.

If par value capital stock has been issued and fully paid and later is reacquired by the issuing corporation, it may be reissued at a price below par without subjecting the purchaser to a discount liability. In addition, treasury stock may be reissued without violating the preemptive right provisions of the state laws. As previously explained, if additional authorized but unissued shares are to be issued after a lapse of time from the date of original issue, the additional shares (in most states) first must be offered to existing stockholders.

Dividends should not be paid on treasury stock, since the corporation would be paying a dividend to itself. If such a dividend payment were debited to Retained Earnings and the dividends received were credited to revenue, net earnings would be overstated, although there would be no net effect on the retained earnings balance.

Certain states require that acquisitions of treasury stock "be made out of retained earnings." This means that if a corporation acquires treasury stock, retained earnings equal to the cost of the shares are unavailable for dividends until the treasury stock is reissued. The cost of the treasury stock must not exceed the amount of retained earnings at the date of acquisition. Thus, dividends plus treasury stock purchases must not impair the legal (or stated) capital of the corporation. If a corporation is subject to such a law, the retained earnings available for dividends are limited to the amount in excess of the cost of the treasury shares.

Treasury stock in the statement of financial position

Treasury stock should not be shown as an asset, since its acquisition reduces the stockholders' equity. An asset is not received when treasury stock is acquired. Instead, the acquisition of treasury stock consists of a return of capital to the stockholder from whom the stock is acquired.

When a corporation acquires its own capital stock as treasury stock, the purpose of the acquisition may be (1) to cancel and retire the stock, (2) to reissue it to employees or others, (3) to reduce the number of shares outstanding and thereby increase earnings per share, or (4) to use the stock in stock option plans. If the intention of the acquisition is cancellation and retirement, the treasury shares exist as such simply because they have not been retired and canceled by formal reduction of the authorized capital.

When treasury stock is held on a statement of financial position date, it is customarily shown in that statement at cost and as a deduction from the sum of the paid-in capital and retained earnings, as follows:

Common stock, authorized and issued, 20,000 shares, par value $10 per share, of which 2,000 shares are in the treasury	$200,000
Retained earnings (including $22,000 restricted by acquisition of treasury stock)	80,000
Total	$280,000
Less: Treasury stock at cost, 2,000 shares	22,000
Total Stockholders' Equity	$258,000

Indicate whether each of the following statements is true or false.

1. The stockholders' equity section illustrated above indicates that dividends of up to $80,000 may be declared from retained earnings.
2. Since treasury stock has been issued once, it may be reissued without violating the preemptive rights of the stockholders.
3. The cost of treasury stock held should be shown as a deduction in the stockholders' equity section of the statement of financial position.
4. Treasury stock is a corporation's own capital stock which has been issued, reacquired, and canceled.

Now check your responses in Answer Frame 18[13] on page 620.

Frame 19[13]

Acquisition and reissuance of treasury stock

When treasury stock is acquired, the stock is recorded at cost; reissues are credited to the Treasury Stock account at the cost of acquisition. The excess of the reissue price over cost is credited to Paid-In Capital—Treasury Stock Transactions because it represents additional paid-in capital.

For example, the Hillside Corporation, whose stockholders' equity consists solely of capital stock and retained earnings, acquires 10 shares of its outstanding common stock for $55 each and two months later reissues three shares for $58 each. The entries are:

Answer frame 18[13]

1. False. An amount equal to the cost of the treasury shares acquired, $22,000, is shown as being unavailable for dividends in the parenthetical statement following retained earnings. Therefore, only $58,000 is available for dividends. Certain states require that the retained earnings available for dividends be limited to the amount of retained earnings in excess of the cost of the treasury shares.
2. True. It may be reissued without violating the preemptive rights.
3. True. The acquisition of treasury stock reduces stockholders' equity to the extent of the cost of the stock. The cost of the treasury stock thus should be shown as a deduction in the stockholders' equity section. It is customarily deducted from the sum of the paid-in capital and retained earnings.
4. False. Treasury stock is a corporation's own stock which was once outstanding but has since been reacquired by the corporation. But it has not been canceled and thus is available for reissuance.

If you answered incorrectly, reread Frame 18[13] before beginning Frame 19[13] on page 619.

19[13]
continued

Treasury Stock—Common	550	
Cash		550
Acquired 10 shares of treasury stock at $55.		
Cash	174	
Treasury Stock—Common		165
Paid-In Capital—Treasury Stock Transactions		9
Reissued three shares of treasury stock at $58; cost $55 per share.		

If the reissue price is less than the acquisition price, the difference is debited to Paid-In Capital—Treasury Stock Transactions. If the Hillside Corporation reissues an additional two shares at $52 per share, the entry is:

Cash	104	
Paid-In Capital—Treasury Stock Transactions	6	
Treasury Stock—Common		110
Reissued two shares of treasury stock at $52; cost $55 per share.		

At this point, the balance in the Paid-In Capital—Treasury Stock Transactions account is $3. If the remaining five shares are reissued for $53 per share, the entry will be as follows:

Cash	265	
Paid-In Capital—Treasury Stock Transactions	3	
Retained Earnings	7	
Treasury Stock—Common		275
Reissued seven shares of treasury stock at $53; cost $55 per share.		

It should be noted that the Paid-In Capital—Treasury Stock Transactions account has been exhausted and the balance of the excess of cost over reissue price of $7 is regarded as a special distribution to the stockholders involved and is chargeable to the Retained Earnings account.

The accounting practices illustrated above are equally applicable to stock with and without par value, whether of stated value or without stated value.

Assume a corporation acquires one share of its outstanding common stock, which has a par value of $100, for $106. The entry to record this is:

Treasury Stock—Common	106	
Cash		106
Acquired one share of $100 par value stock for $106.		

One month later the corporation reissues this share of treasury stock for $106. Which of the following is the correct entry to record this transaction?

1.	Cash	106	
	Treasury Stock—Common		100
	Paid-In Capital—Treasury Stock Transactions		6
2.	Cash	106	
	Treasury Stock—Common		106
3.	Cash	100	
	Paid-In Capital—Treasury Stock Transactions	6	
	Treasury Stock—Common		106
4.	Cash	106	
	Paid-In Capital—Treasury Stock Transactions		106

You can check your response in Answer Frame 19[13] on page 622.

Frame 20[13]

Donated treasury stock

Treasury stock may be acquired by donation as well as by purchase. Capital stock may be donated to the corporation by the stockholders when the corporation's working funds are depleted to a dangerous level. Under such circumstances the stockholders sometimes agree to donate capital stock to the corporation to be reissued to obtain working capital.

If capital stock is donated to a corporation, no entry need be made, as there is no cost. A memorandum should be made in the Treasury Stock—Common account as follows:

Treasury Stock—Common

Date		Explanation	Folio	Debit	Credit	Balance
1975 June	1	200 shares of $100 par value common stock received through donation				—0—

Answer frame 19[13]

The second entry is the correct one. The reissue price was equal to the cost of the acquisition of the share of treasury stock. The entry to record the reissuance is thus simply a debit to Cash and a credit to the Treasury Stock—Common account for $106.

If you answered incorrectly, reread Frame 19[13] before turning to Frame 20[13] on page 621.

20[13]
continued

When treasury stock has been acquired by donation, the statement of financial position presentation may be as follows:

Common stock, $100 par value; authorized and issued, 2,000 shares, of which 200 shares were acquired by donation and are held in the treasury	$200,000
Retained earnings	40,000
Total Stockholders' Equity	$240,000

Retained earnings are not restricted, since the treasury stock was obtained without cost.

If the 200 shares of treasury stock are reissued for $22,000, the required entry is:

Cash	22,000	
Paid-In Capital—Donations		22,000
To record the reissuance of donated shares.		

Assume that 100 shares of $10 par value common stock are donated to a corporation when their market value is $11 per share. Two weeks later these shares are reissued for $1,200. Which of the following entries properly records the reissue of these donated treasury stock shares?

1. Cash	1,200	
Treasury Stock—Common		1,100
Paid-In Capital—Donations		100
2. Cash	1,200	
Treasury Stock—Common		1,000
Paid-In Capital—Donations		200
3. Cash	1,200	
Paid-In Capital—Donations		1,200
4. Cash	1,200	
Paid-In Capital		1,200

Check your answer in Answer Frame 20[13] on page 624.

Summary *chapter* 13

Much of what is discussed in this chapter can be summarized through presentation of the stockholders' equity section of the statement of financial position of a hypothetical corporation, see Illustration 13.5.

Illustration 13.5

HYPOTHETICAL CORPORATION
Partial Statement of Financial Position
December 31, 1975

STOCKHOLDERS' EQUITY

Paid-In Capital:		
Preferred stock, $100 par value; 2,000 shares authorized, issued, and outstanding		$ 200,000
Common stock, $10 par value; authorized, 100,000 shares, issued, 80,000 shares of which 1,000 are held in treasury	$800,000	
Stock dividend payable on common stock on January 15, 1976, 7,900 shares	79,000	879,000
Paid-in capital in excess of par value:		
From common stock issuances	$ 40,000	
From capitalization of retained earnings through stock dividends	60,000	
From treasury stock transactions	30,000	
From donations	50,000	180,000
Total Paid-In Capital		$1,259,000
Capital from Appreciation		200,000
Retained Earnings:		
Appropriated:		
Reserve for loan retirement	$250,000	
Unappropriated (restricted to the extent of $20,000, the cost of treasury shares held; see Note A)	150,000	400,000
		$1,859,000
Less: Treasury stock, common, 1,000 shares at cost		20,000
Total Stockholders' Equity		$1,839,000

Note A. The company has been named defendant in a suit seeking damages for injuries allegedly sustained from use of a company product which was allegedly rendered unfit for its intended purpose through negligence in its manufacture. In the opinion of legal counsel, the company's liability in this matter will be nominal at most.

In the accounting for and reporting of stockholders' equity—the proprietary capital of a corporation—emphasis is placed upon the sources of capital. The paid-in capital of a corporation consists of all capital contributed or contracted to be paid in, as in the case of subscribed stock. The term Paid-In Capital is used in this text as a prefix for the titles of accounts in which capital actually paid in, other than that carried in the capital stock accounts, is recorded.

When the par or stated value of the outstanding shares is reduced without a change in the number of outstanding shares, the amount of capital removed from the capital stock account is credited to a Paid-In Capital—Recapitalization account. Donated assets are recorded at their fair market value and credited to a Paid-In Capital—Donations account.

In rare instances, the board of directors may order the recording of an increase in the value of certain assets. Such appreciation should be credited to a Capital from Appreciation account, another element of stockholders' equity.

The statement of financial position should show clearly (1) the amount of capital assigned to shares outstanding; (2) the capital contributed for outstanding shares in addition to that assigned to the shares; (3) other

Answer frame 20[13]

The third entry is correct. Since there was no cost to the corporation for the donated stock, the entire proceeds of the reissuance are credited to a Paid-In Capital—Donations account. The credit to the Treasury Stock—Common account in the first two entries is in error. No debit was made to this account when the donated shares were acquired, since no cost was involved. Paid-In Capital, credited in the fourth entry, is not definitive enough for use as an account title. There are many sources of paid-in capital and a separate account, properly labeled, should be maintained for paid-in capital from each source.

If you answered incorrectly, reread Frame 20[13] before going on to the chapter summary on page 622.

---

forms of paid-in capital; (4) capital from appreciation, if any; and (5) retained earnings.

The entire contributed or paid-in capital is often described as a corporation's permanent capital. But retained earnings may also be a source of relatively long-term capital.

The inclusion of retained earnings in a corporation's statement of financial position means that operations have been profitable. If the cumulative effect of operations, dividends, and certain other items on stockholders' equity is negative, a deficit exists.

Retained earnings reserves are either voluntary or contractual restrictions upon the distribution of retained earnings as dividends. These reserves are created through transfers of retained earnings, are returned intact when they have served their purpose, and are reported as a part of retained earnings in the statement of financial position.

Every business encounters certain unusual and nonrecurring gains and losses and other adjustments. Accounting Principles Board *Opinion No. 9* and *Opinion No. 30* recommend that the items be classified as extraordinary items or prior period adjustments. Extraordinary items are to be reported, net of their tax effects, in the earnings statement; while prior period adjustments are to be reported, also net of their tax effects, in the statement of retained earnings.

The typical dividend is a cash distribution of corporate earnings to its stockholders, although dividends are legally chargeable to paid-in capital accounts in some states. A corporation may distribute as dividends other forms of assets, promises to pay, or additional shares of its own capital stock (a stock dividend).

The Committee on Accounting Procedure of the AICPA has distinguished stock dividends greater than 20 to 25 percent as being stock split-ups. The amount transferred to the Capital Stock account is equal to the par or stated value of the shares issued, and is debited to other paid-in capital attaching to the same class of shares, or, if such amounts are insufficient, to Retained Earnings.

Stock dividends of less than 20–25 percent are recorded at market value.

Shares of capital stock which have been issued and then returned to the issuing corporation are called treasury stock or shares. Such shares are issued but not outstanding. Retained earnings are generally restricted in an amount equal to the cost of treasury stock. The cost of treasury stock is reported as a deduction from total stockholders' equity. If treasury stock is reissued, the difference between cost and reissue price is carried to a Paid-In Capital—Treasury Stock Transactions account. If there is no balance in this account, any excess of cost over reissue price is charged to retained earnings upon resale.

Since donated treasury shares have no cost, the only formal journal entry made for them is to credit the entire amount received upon reissue to a Paid-In Capital—Donations account.

To complete your review, study the definitions of new terms introduced in this chapter contained in the glossary which follows. Then go on to the Student Review Quiz for a self-administered test of your comprehension of the material in the chapter (see page 626).

Glossary *chapter* 13

Accumulated earnings—a term used synonymously with retained earnings.

All-inclusive concept of earnings—an approach to the presentation of net earnings in which all gains, losses, and adjustments of prior years are shown in the earnings statement (except those excluded in APB *Opinions Nos. 9 and 30*).

Appreciation—an increase in the value of an asset without an increase in the quantity.

Capital from appreciation—the increase recorded in stockholders' equity when appreciation is recorded.

Capital surplus—the contributed capital of a corporation other than that carried in capital stock accounts.

Capitalized amount—as used in discussing stock dividends, the amount at which the additional shares issued are to be recorded in the paid-in capital accounts, generally through a transfer from retained earnings.

Contributed capital—all capital paid into a corporation, including that carried in capital stock accounts.

Current operating performance concept of earnings—an approach to the presentation of net earnings in which all material gains, losses, and adjustments are excluded from the earnings statement.

Date of declaration (of dividends)—the date on which the board of directors formally states its intention that the corporation will pay a dividend.

Date of payment (of dividends)—the date on which dividend checks are to be mailed or additional shares issued in the case of a stock dividend.

Date of record (of dividends)—the date at which the corporation ascertains to whom dividends are to be paid.

Deficit—a debit balance in the Retained Earnings account.

Dividend—a pro rata distribution, usually of cash, by a corporation to its stockholders, excluding distributions made in exchange for shares of stock; usually chargeable to retained earnings; legality of a dividend is satisfied if stockholders' equity exceeds stated capital after the act of declaration.

Donated capital—an increase in stockholders' equity resulting from donation of assets to the corporation.

Donated treasury stock—treasury stock acquired through the act of donation or gift, hence, without cost.

Earned surplus—a synonym for retained earnings.

Earnings before extraordinary items—earnings from operations less applicable income taxes (federal and state, if any).

Extraordinary items—a classification recommended in Accounting Principles Board *Opinion No. 9* and *Opinion No. 30* for those items of gain or loss of an unusual, nonrecurring, nonoperating nature which are to be reported in the earnings statement.

Liquidating dividends—dividends which are a return of contributed capital, not a distribution chargeable to retained earnings.

Net-of-tax reporting—a type of financial reporting for extraordinary items and prior period adjustments whereby items are shown at the dollar amounts remaining after deducting the effects of such items on the income taxes (federal and state, if any) payable currently.

Paid-in capital—all of the contributed capital of a corporation, including that carried in capital stock accounts. When the words "paid-in capital" are included in an account title, the account contains capital contributed in addition to that assigned to the shares issued and recorded in the capital stock accounts.

Paid-In Capital—Treasury Stock Transactions—the title of the account credited when treasury stock is reissued for more than its cost; this account is also debited, to the extent of the balance therein, for deficiencies when such shares are reissued at less than cost.

Paid-in surplus—synonymous with capital surplus.

Prior period adjustments—a classification recommended in Accounting Principles Board *Opinion No. 9* for those corrections or adjustments of previously reported earnings statement data that can be specifically identified with and directly related to particular prior periods and which are to be reported in the statement of retained earnings.

Proprietary capital—stockholders' equity.

Recapitalization (paid-in capital from)—the amount of capital removed from the capital stock account when the par or stated value of the outstanding shares is reduced.

Reserve (retained earnings)—an account created as a voluntary or contractual restriction upon retained earnings and designed to inform readers of the existence of the restriction.

Retained earnings—that part of stockholders' equity resulting from earnings; the account to which the results of corporate activity, including prior period adjustments, are carried and to which dividends and certain items resulting from capital transactions are charged.

Retained income—a synonym for retained earnings.

Stock dividend—a dividend payable in additional shares of the declaring corporation's stock.

Stock Dividend Payable—the stockholders' equity account credited for the par or stated value, or the value assigned by the board of directors in the case of shares without par or stated value, upon the recording of the declaration of a stock dividend.

Stock split-up (stock split)—as used in *Accounting Research Bulletin No. 43,* a distribution of additional shares of the issuing corporation's stock without consideration and for the purpose of effecting a material reduction in the market price per share of the outstanding stock.

Treasury stock—shares of capital stock issued and returned to the issuing corporation which have not been formally canceled or retired and are available for reissue.

Student review quiz *chapter* 13

To develop a permanent record of your responses, you may write them on the answer sheet provided in the *Work Papers* or on a separate sheet of paper.

1 The Marr Equipment Company received real estate having a fair market value of $3,000 from its principal stockholder. No stock was issued or other consideration given in exchange for this land, even though the company has $75,000 of authorized but unissued par value stock. What entry should be made to record the receipt of the land?

a) Land	3,000	
Paid-In Capital—from Recapitalization		3,000
b) Land	3,000	
Paid-In Capital—Donations		3,000

c) Land 3,000
Retained Earnings 3,000

d) Land 3,000
Revenue from Receipt of Land . . 3,000

e) No entry is required, since the land had no cost.

2 Paid-in capital does not include:

a) Capital contributed to the extent of par or stated value of the shares outstanding.
b) Premiums on common and preferred stock.
c) Preferred stock.
d) Capital resulting from reissuance of treasury stock at a price above its acquisition price.
e) Capital accumulated by retention of earnings.

3 An appropriation of retained earnings to a retained earnings reserve account—

a) Is used to limit the amount of retained earnings available for dividends.
b) Indicates amounts which will be needed to meet contingencies, but has no limiting effect on dividends.
c) May be used only when a legal restriction on retained earnings is imposed by creditors.
d) Results in the building up of a fund of assets to meet specific needs.
e) Does none of the above.

4 The Reserve for Plant Expansion account—

a) Is an asset account.
b) Is a fund accumulated for the purpose of financing plant expansion.
c) Is closed to the Retained Earnings account when the books are closed annually.
d) Generally has a debit balance.
e) Is none of the above.

5 When the total stockholders' equity is smaller than the amount of paid-in capital, this deficiency is called:

a) A net loss.
b) A dividend.
c) A liability.
d) A deficit.
e) None of the above.

6 On July 6, 1975, the board of directors of the L. C. Janssen Corporation declared a cash dividend of $3 per share on 10,000 shares of outstanding common stock, payable September 1, 1975, to stockholders of record on August 10, 1975. The entry to record the declaration of this dividend is:

a) Retained Earnings . . 30,000
Cash 30,000

b) Retained Earnings . . 30,000
Dividends Payable 30,000

c) Dividends Payable . . 30,000
Cash 30,000

d) Retained Earnings . . 30,000
Capital Stock . . . 30,000

e) Dividends 30,000
Dividends Payable 30,000

f) Either (**b**) or (**e**).

7 Which of the following statements regarding a dividend in common stock to common stockholders is true?

a) A stock dividend reduces total corporate capital.
b) A stock dividend alters the individual stockholder's percentage of ownership in the corporation.
c) A stock dividend has the effect of decreasing the book value per share of that class of stock.
d) Stock Dividends Payable is a current liability account.
e) None of the above are true.

8 XYZ Corporation has outstanding 10,000 shares of common stock, par value $100 per share. The board of directors declares a 5 percent stock dividend on the common stock. The market price of the stock on the date the dividend is declared is $110 per share. The entry to record the declaration of the stock dividend (according to AICPA recommendations) is:

a) Retained Earnings . . 55,000
Stock Dividends Payable—Common 55,000

b) Retained Earnings . . 50,000
Stock Dividends Payable—Common 50,000

c) Retained Earnings . . 55,000
Stock Dividends Payable—Common 50,000
Paid-In Capital—Stock Dividend 5,000

d) Retained Earnings . . 50,000
Cash 50,000

e) Retained Earnings..	55,000	
Paid-In Capital —Stock Dividend....		55,000

9 The ABC Corporation acquired 100 shares of its own $20 par common stock, all of which had been previously issued at par, for $2,200 ($22 per share). Three weeks later it reissued all 100 of these treasury shares at $21 per share. The entry to record reissuance of these shares, assuming no previous transactions in treasury stock, is:

a) Cash................	2,100	
Treasury Stock—Common.......		2,100
b) Cash................	2,100	
Treasury Stock—Common.......		2,000
Paid-In Capital—Treasury Stock Transactions...		100
c) Cash................	2,100	
Paid-In Capital—Treasury Stock Transactions...	300	
Treasury Stock—Common.......		2,400
d) Cash................	2,100	
Paid-In Capital—Treasury Stock Transactions.......	100	
Treasury Stock—Common.......		2,200

e) None of the above.

10 Which of the following terms does not mean the same thing as all of the other terms?

a) Retained income.
b) Retained earnings.
c) Accumulated earnings.
d) Earnings retained for use in business.
e) Net earnings from operations.

11 In the preparation of a statement of financial position, which of the following statements is true?

a) No reference need be made to donated treasury stock, since the acquisition of such stock does not restrict retained earnings.
b) Treasury shares and unissued shares can be reported as a total of shares not outstanding with no distinguishing comments.
c) Treasury shares should be shown as a deduction, at cost, from the total paid-in capital of the company.
d) Treasury shares should be shown as a deduction, at cost, from the total of paid-in capital plus retained earnings, and a restriction on retained earnings occasioned by their acquisition must also be stated.
e) Treasury shares should be shown as a deduction, at cost, from retained earnings, since their acquisition usually results in a restriction on retained earnings.

12 Which of the following statements is true?

a) Dividends may be declared if sufficient retained earnings exist.
b) Dividends may, in some instances, be declared even if there are no retained earnings.
c) Dividends may, under some state laws, be declared out of paid-in capital in excess of the par or stated value of the shares outstanding.
d) Dividends may be declared which are actually returns of the stated capital of the corporation.
e) **(a)** and **(b)** are true.
f) All of the above are true.

13 The following is the stockholders' equity section of a statement of financial position dated June 30, 1975.

STOCKHOLDERS' EQUITY

Paid-In Capital:	
Capital stock—preferred, 5%, $100 par value; authorized and issued, 1,000 shares of which 100 are held in treasury........	$100,000
Capital stock—common, $10 par value; authorized, 100,000 shares, issued, 50,000 shares of which 1,000 are held in treasury, including 100 shares donated	500,000
Total Paid-In Capital........	$600,000
Retained earnings (restricted to the extent of cost of 100 shares of preferred treasury stock, $10,500, and 900 shares of common treasury stock, $18,000)........	200,000
Total........	$800,000
Less: Cost of treasury stock: preferred (100 shares), $10,500; common (1,000 shares, 100 received by donation), $18,000........	28,500
Total Stockholders' Equity........	$771,500

Which of the following statements is true?

a) A dividend declared on June 30, 1975, of $1 per share on the common stock would involve a total amount to be paid out of $50,000.

b) The cost of the common treasury stock acquired by purchase is $18 per share.

c) The corporation has 51,000 shares of common stock (50,000 shares unissued and 1,000 shares in treasury) available for issuance, and it is free to issue these shares to whomever it wishes, since 1,000 of the shares have previously been outstanding and the stockholders have authorized the issuance of the other 50,000 shares.

d) The restriction upon retained earnings by the acquisition of common stock is limited to the cost of the 900 shares acquired by purchase.

e) All of the above statements are true.

14 A company wrote down a substantial amount of obsolete inventory to its scrap value. The loss from obsolete inventory is reported in the year it was recognized in the—

a) Earnings statement, net of its tax effect, as an extraordinary item.

b) Earnings statement, net of its tax effect, as part of the expenses and losses related to regular operations.

c) Earnings statement, at full amount, as part of the expenses and losses related to regular operations.

d) Statement of retained earnings, net of its tax effect, as a prior period adjustment.

15 In 1975 a corporation had total revenues of $50 million; total expenses related to regular business activity, exclusive of federal income taxes, of $40 million; and was subject to federal income taxes at a 50 percent rate. It also suffered a tax deductible earthquake loss of $2 million, sold investment securities (a recurring event for this company) at a gain of $3 million (subject to income taxation at a 25 percent rate), paid an additional $500,000 of federal income taxes for 1972, and settled for $800,000 (tax deductible) litigation brought against it for failure to comply in 1971 with the provisions of a contract calling for it to overhaul all of the jet engines in a fleet of aircraft at a stipulated price. The company discontinued this line of activity in 1974. Which of the following statements is false?

a) Net earnings before extraordinary items are $7.25 million.

b) The earthquake loss should be reported in the earnings statement as an extraordinary item of $1 million.

c) The gain on sale of investment securities should be reported in the earnings statement but not as an extraordinary item.

d) The additional income tax assessment should be reported as a prior period adjustment in the statement of retained earnings.

e) The litigation settlement should be reported in the earnings statement as an extraordinary item of $400,000.

Now compare your answers with the correct answers and explanations on page 720.

Questions *chapter* 13

1 How should a declared but unpaid cash dividend be shown in a statement of financial position? A declared but unissued stock dividend?

2 What are the two most common component parts of the stockholders' equity in a corporation? Explain the difference between them.

3 Name several sources of paid-in capital. Would it suffice to maintain one account called Paid-In Capital for all sources of paid-in capital? Why or why not?

4 Why is a dividend consisting of the distribution of additional shares of the common stock of the declaring corporation not considered earnings to the recipient stockholders?

5 What is the effect of each of the following on the total stockholders' equity of a corporation: (*a*) declaration of a cash dividend; (*b*) payment of a cash dividend already declared; (*c*) declaration of a stock dividend; and (*d*) issuance of a stock dividend already declared?

6 The following dates are associated with a cash dividend of $50,000: July 15, July 31, and August 15. Identify each of the three dates and give the journal entry required on each, if any.

7 What is the purpose underlying the

statutes which provide for restriction of retained earnings in the amount of the cost of treasury stock? Are such statutes for the benefit of stockholders, management, or creditors?

8 Does the cost method of accounting for treasury stock resemble accounting for an asset? Is treasury stock an asset? If not, where is it properly shown in a statement of financial position, according to the cost method?

9 What is meant by the term stated capital? Is it primarily an accounting term or a legal term?

10 On May 10 Power sold his capital stock in the Tanner Corporation directly to Bright for $10,000, endorsing his stock certificate and giving it to Bright. Bright placed the stock certificate in his safe. On May 8 the board of directors of the Tanner Corporation declared a dividend, payable on June 5 to stockholders of record on May 17. On May 30 Bright sent the stock certificate to the transfer agent of the Tanner Corporation for transfer. Who received the dividend? Why?

11 Distinguish carefully between extraordinary items and prior period adjustments. Explain why it is important that the two be carefully distinguished.

Exercises *chapter* 13

1 Baler Company received 100 shares of its $10 stated value common stock on December 1, 1975, as a donation from a stockholder. On December 15, 1975, it issued the stock for $2,000 cash. Give the journal entry or entries necessary for these transactions.

2 Alston Corporation's stockholders' equity consists of 25,000 authorized shares of $10 par value common stock, of which 10,000 shares have been issued at par, and retained earnings of $200,000. The company now splits its stock, two for one, by calling in the old shares and issuing new $5 par shares.

a) Give the required journal entry.

b) Suppose instead that the company declared and later issued a 10 percent stock dividend. Give the required journal entries, assuming that the market value on the date of declaration is $12.50 per share.

3 The statement of financial position of the B Company contains the following:

Reserve for contingencies $200,000

a) Give the journal entry made to create this account.

b) Explain the reason for its existence and its manner of presentation in the statement of financial position.

4 X Company's statement of financial position contains an item described as:

Unrealized appreciation of land. $500,000

a) Give another title for this item.

b) Where should it be shown in the statement of financial position? Why?

c) Give the journal entry which the company must have made to put the above account balance into its accounting system.

5 A company has revenues of $20 million, expenses of $18 million, a tax deductible earthquake loss of $500,000, a tax deductible downward adjustment of $1.5 million resulting from the renegotiation of a contract completed two years ago, and an income tax rate of 50 percent. The beginning retained earnings were $5 million. Using these data, prepare an earnings statement and a statement of retained earnings:

a) Using the net-of-tax reporting recommendation in Accounting Principles Board *Opinion No. 9.*

b) Without use of net-of-tax reporting. Comment on the justification of APB *Opinion No. 9* regarding reporting extraordinary items and prior period adjustments net of their tax effects.

6 The stockholders' equity section of the M Company's statement of financial position on December 31, 1975, shows 100,000 shares of authorized and issued $10 stated value common stock, of which 8,000 shares are held in the treasury. On this date, the board of directors declares a cash dividend of $1 per share payable on January 21, 1976, to stockholders of record on January 10. Give dated journal entries for the above.

7 Arden Company's statement of financial position shows total assets of $500,000, liabilities of $200,000, and stockholders' equity of $300,000. B owns 300 of Arden's 30,000 shares of outstanding common stock. Arden now declares and issues a 10 percent stock dividend. Compute the book value per share and in total of B's investment in Arden:

a) Before the stock dividend.

b) After the stock dividend.

8 Masters Company has outstanding 100,000 shares of common stock without par or stated value which were issued at an average price of $8 per share, and retained earnings of $400,000. The current market price of the common stock is $15 per share. Total authorized stock consists of 500,000 shares.

a) Give the required journal entry to record the declaration of a 10 percent stock dividend.

b) If, alternatively, the company declared a 30 percent stock dividend, what additional information would you need before making a journal entry to record the dividend?

9 Nader Company has outstanding 100,000 shares of $5 stated value common stock, all issued at $6 per share, and retained earnings of $200,000. The company now acquires 1,000 shares of its stock from the widow of a deceased stockholder for cash at book value.

a) Give the entry to record the acquisition of the stock.

b) Give the entry to record the subsequent reissuance of this stock at $10 per share.

c) Give the entry required if the stock is reissued at $7 per share and there have been no prior treasury stock transactions.

Problems, Series A *chapter* 13

13–1–A

The stockholders' equity of the Wells Company on June 30, 1975, consists solely of capital stock of $500,000 and retained earnings of $430,000. The stock is $100 par value common stock, with 10,000 shares authorized and 5,000 issued and outstanding.

The board of directors on June 30, 1975, declares a 10 percent cash dividend and a 10 percent stock dividend, both payable on July 31 to stockholders of record on July 15. The cash dividend applies only to the shares outstanding prior to the stock dividend. The market price of the stock on June 30 is $200 per share.

Required:

a) Present journal entries to record the declaration of both dividends, the payment of the cash dividend, and the issuance of the stock dividend.

b) Assuming no change in the amount of retained earnings except that caused by the dividends and no change in the number of shares outstanding between June 30 and July 31, compute the book value per share of common stock: (1) just prior to the declaration of dividends; (2) just after the declaration of dividends; (3) just after the payment of the cash dividend but before issuance of the stock dividend; and (4) immediately after the issuance of the stock dividend.

c) Describe, in general terms, how the presence of preferred stock in the statement of financial position affects the computation of book value per share of common stock.

13–2–A

Following are selected transactions of the Davies Corporation:

1970

Dec. 31 By action of the board of directors, $20,000 of retained earnings was appropriated to provide for future expansion of the company's main building.
(On the last day of each of the four succeeding years the same action was taken. You need not make entries for these four years.)

1975

Jan. 3 Obtained, at a cost of $200, a building permit to construct a new wing on the main plant building.

July 30 Paid $106,000 to the Able Construction Company for completion of the new wing.

Aug. 4 The board of directors authorized the release of the sum appropriated for expansion of the plant building.

4 The board of directors declared a 10 percent common stock dividend on the 25,000 shares of $40 par value common stock outstanding. The market price on this date was $44 per share.

Required: Present journal entries to record all of the above transactions.

13–3–A

The following information relates to the Beason Corporation for the year 1975.

Net earnings for the year	$ 480,000
Dividends declared on common stock	60,000
Dividends paid on common stock during 1975	80,000
Dividends declared on preferred stock	30,000
Dividends received on investments	10,000
Retained earnings, January 1, unappropriated	1,420,000
Appropriation to reserve for retirement of bonds	140,000
Premium received on shares of preferred stock issued during the year	8,000
Balance in "Reserve for possible loss of a lawsuit" no longer needed on December 31 because of favorable court decision is at directors' orders returned to unappropriated retained earnings	214,000

Required: Prepare a statement of retained earnings for the year ended December 31, 1975.

13–4–A

The stockholders' equity section of the Valor Company's December 31, 1974, statement of financial position is:

Paid-In Capital:	
Capital stock—common, $20 par; authorized, 2,000 shares, issued and outstanding, 1,000 shares	$20,000
Paid-in capital in excess of par value	1,000
Total Paid-In Capital	$21,000
Retained earnings	8,000
Total Stockholders' Equity	$29,000

On July 15, 1975, the board of directors declared a cash dividend of $2 per share, which was paid on August 1, 1975. On December 1, 1975, the board declared a stock dividend of 10 percent and the shares were issued on December 15, 1975. Market value of the stock was $24 on December 1 and $28 on December 15. Net earnings for the year 1975 were $4,700.

Required:

a) Present journal entries for the above dividend transactions.
b) Compute the book value per share on December 31, 1974, and on December 31, 1975.

13–5–A

The trial balance of the Welby Corporation at December 31, 1975, contains the following account balances.

Capital from appreciation of land	$ 240,000
Bonds payable, 7%, due May 1, 1977	1,000,000
Reserve for doubtful accounts	12,000
Common stock without par value, stated value $10; 200,000 shares authorized, issued, and outstanding	2,000,000
Retained earnings, unappropriated	228,000
Dividends payable in cash declared December 15 on preferred stock	6,000
Reserve for pending litigation	280,000
Preferred stock, 6%, par value $100; 2,000 shares authorized, issued, and outstanding	200,000
Paid-in capital from donation of plant site	150,000
Paid-in capital in excess of par value—preferred	4,000

Required: Present in good form the stockholders' equity section of the statement of financial position.

13–6–A

The following are the only stockholders' equity accounts of Manton Corporation on December 31, 1974.

Retained earnings	$138,000
Preferred stock: 4%, $100 par value; 2,000 shares authorized, 1,600 shares issued and outstanding	160,000
Paid-in capital in excess of par—common	7,000
Donated capital from gift of building	34,000
Common stock: par value $10; 100,000 shares authorized, 80,000 shares issued and outstanding	800,000
Reserve for contingencies	50,000

The reserve for contingencies was established in 1974 because of a possibility of an adverse decision in a lawsuit seeking damages for losses sustained in 1974 allegedly due to the company's failure to fulfill a service contract on a product sold. During 1975, the following occurred:

1. Dividends were declared and paid in cash as follows: on preferred stock, 4 percent; on common stock, $0.20 per share.
2. The court action referred to above was decided with an order directing the company to pay the injured party $36,000. The board ordered the reserve closed and the award paid.
3. Certain land owned by the company was appraised at $24,000 more than its carrying value on the books. The board authorized the recording of this increased value.
4. An additional liability of $30,000 for federal income taxes on 1972 earnings was imposed by the Internal Revenue Service.
5. The board directed that an appropriation of retained earnings be made to cover a possible loss of $40,000 from a price decline on inventories. These inventories had been accumulated in an amount considerably above normal requirements in anticipation of a strike at the supplier's plants.

Net earnings after taxes for the year were $54,000, exclusive of the $36,000 litigation payment and its tax effect. The tax rate is 50 percent.

Required:

a) Present journal entries for the above transactions.
b) Prepare a statement of unappropriated retained earnings for the year 1975.

c) Prepare the stockholders' equity section of the December 31, 1975, statement of financial position.

13–7–A

The stockholders' equity of the Ingham Company as of December 31, 1974, consisted of 10,000 shares of authorized and outstanding $10 par value common stock, paid-in capital in excess of par of $50,000, and retained earnings of $100,000. Following are selected transactions for 1975:

May	1	Acquired 2,000 shares of its own common stock at $25 per share.
June	1	Reissued 500 shares at $28.
	30	Reissued 700 shares at $23.
Aug.	1	Received 100 shares from stockholders as a donation.
	22	Reissued the donated shares at $22.
Oct.	1	Declared a cash dividend of $1 per share.
	31	Paid the cash dividend declared on October 1.

Net earnings for the year were $15,200. No other transactions affecting retained earnings occurred during the year.

Required:

a) Present general journal entries for the above transactions.
b) Prepare the stockholders' equity section of the December 31, 1975, statement of financial position.
c) Compute the book value per share as of December 31, 1975.

13–8–A

The stockholders' equity section of Ralph Company's December 31, 1974, statement of financial position is:

Paid-In Capital:		
Preferred stock: 5%, $100 par value; authorized, 5,000 shares, issued and outstanding 2,500 shares		$250,000
Common stock without par or stated value; authorized, 50,000 shares, issued, 25,000 shares of which 500 are held in treasury		375,000
Paid-in capital in excess of par—preferred		5,000
Total Paid-In Capital		$630,000
Retained Earnings:		
Appropriated:		
Reserve for plant expansion	$ 25,000	
Unappropriated (restricted as to dividends to the extent of $10,000, the cost of the treasury stock held)	210,000	
Total Retained Earnings		235,000
		$865,000
Less: Treasury stock, common at cost (500 shares)		10,000
Total Stockholders' Equity		$855,000

Following are selected transactions occurring in 1975.

Jan.	13	Subscriptions are received for 550 shares of previously unissued common stock at $22.

Feb. 4 A plot of land is accepted as payment in full for 500 shares of common, and the stock is issued. Closing market price on this date of the common is $21 per share.

Mar. 24 All of the treasury stock is reissued at $24.50.

June 22 All stock subscriptions are collected in full, and the shares issued.

23 The regular semiannual dividend on the preferred stock is declared.

30 The preferred dividend is paid.

July 3 A 10 percent stock dividend is declared on the common stock. Market price on this date is $25.

18 The stock dividend shares are issued.

Oct. 4 The company acquires 105 shares of its common stock at $24.

Dec. 18 The regular semiannual dividend on the preferred and a $0.40 per share dividend on the common are declared.

31 Both dividends are paid.

31 An additional appropriation of retained earnings of $5,000 for plant expansion is authorized.

31 The company agrees to an assessment of $14,000 of additional income taxes for 1973.

Required:

a) Prepare journal entries to record the 1975 transactions.

b) Prepare a statement of retained earnings for the year 1975. The net earnings for the year were $43,125.

c) Prepare the stockholders' equity section of the December 31, 1975, statement of financial position.

13–9–A

Selected accounts of the Massey Company for the year ended December 31, 1975, are:

Sales, net	$2,400,000
Interest expense	200,000
Gain on sale of investment in subsidiary (not a segment, treat as extraordinary item)	2,000,000
Cash dividends on common stock	400,000
Cash dividends on preferred stock	200,000
Selling and administrative expense	600,000
Rent revenue	1,100,000
Cost of goods sold	1,600,000
Loss from earthquake (extraordinary item)	600,000
Interest revenue	200,000
Other revenue	300,000
Depreciation and maintenance on rental equipment	400,000
Stock dividend on common stock	1,000,000
Litigation loss	1,200,000

The applicable federal income tax rate is 50 percent. All above items of expense, revenue, and loss are includable in the computation of income taxes payable; the gain on sale of investment in subsidiary is taxable at a maximum rate of 25 percent and meets the requirements for classification as an extraordinary item. The litigation loss resulted from a court award of damages for patent infringement on a product the company produced and sold in 1972 and 1973 and which was discontinued in 1973. Retained earnings as of December 31, 1974, were reported as $14 million.

Required: Following the recommendations in Accounting Principles Board *Opinion No. 9* and *Opinion No. 30,* prepare:

a) The earnings statement for 1975.
b) The statement of retained earnings for 1975.

13–10–A

Use the data in Problem 13–9–A and the following information: On December 31, 1975, the board of directors of the Massey Company authorized the establishment of a reserve for possible inventory price decline of $700,000. It also authorized a special write-off of obsolete plant assets which were recorded at $1.5 million and on which $1.3 million of depreciation had been recorded. This write-off is deductible in the determination of income taxes payable.

During the year, charges of $30,000 were made against the Retained Earnings account for the excess of the cost of treasury stock over its reissue proceeds.

Required: Prepare a combined earnings statement and statement of retained earnings for the Massey Company for the year ended December 31, 1975, following the recommendations in the APB *Opinions.*

Problems, Series B *chapter* 13

13–1–B

The only two accounts in the stockholders' equity section of the James Company's June 30, 1975, statement of financial position were $750,000, representing 7,500 shares of $100 par common stock outstanding, and retained earnings of $100,000. On this date, the board of directors declared a 6 percent cash dividend and a 4 percent stock dividend, both payable on August 1 to stockholders of record on July 15. The cash dividend applies only to shares outstanding prior to the stock dividend. The market price of the stock on June 30 was $110 per share.

Required:

a) Present journal entries to record the declaration and payment of the dividends.
b) Assuming no change in the amount of retained earnings except that occasioned by the dividends, compute the book value per share of common stock immediately before the declaration of the dividends, immediately after declaration of the dividends (the stock dividend shares are not considered outstanding until they are issued), and immediately after payment of the dividends.
c) Describe, in general terms, how the presence of preferred stock in the statement of financial position affects the computation of book value per share of common stock.

13–2–B

Following are selected transactions of the Bard Corporation.

1970
Dec. 31 The board of directors authorized appropriation of $200,000 of retained earnings to provide for the future acquisition of a new plant site and the construction of a new building.
(On the last day of the four succeeding years the same action was taken. You need not make entries for these four years.)

1973	
Jan. 2	Purchased a new plant site for cash, $150,000.
Mar. 29	Entered into a contract for construction of a new building, payment to be made within 30 days following completion.
1975	
Feb. 10	Following final inspection and approval of the new building, the Dome Construction Company was paid in full, $920,000.
Mar. 10	The board of directors authorized release of the reserve appropriated for the plant site and building.
Apr. 2	A 10 percent stock dividend on the 100,000 shares of $100 par value common stock outstanding was declared. The market price on this date was $110 per share.

Required: Present journal entries for all of the above transactions.

13–3–B

Following are selected data and accounts of the Addison Corporation at December 31, 1975.

Net earnings for the year	$270,000
Additional federal income taxes for 1972	18,000
Dividends declared on preferred stock	40,000
Retained earnings appropriated for future plant expansion during the year	100,000
Dividends received on stock investments	14,000
Dividends paid on common stock	40,000
Excess over stated value received for shares of common stock issued during the year	64,000
Dividends declared on common stock	36,000
Retained earnings, January 1, unappropriated	410,000
Directors ordered balance in "Reserve for bond sinking fund," related to bond issue retired on March 31, 1975, returned to unappropriated retained earnings	200,000

Required: Prepare a statement of retained earnings for the year 1975.

13–4–B

The only stockholders' equity items of the Cushion Company at June 30, 1975, are:

Common stock, $25 par; 4,000 shares authorized, 2,000 shares issued and outstanding	$ 50,000
Paid-in capital in excess of par value	25,000
Retained earnings	40,000
Total Stockholders' Equity	$115,000

On August 4, a 4 percent cash dividend was declared, payable September 3. On November 16, a 10 percent stock dividend was declared. The shares were issued on December 1. The market value of the common stock on November 16 was $40 per share and on December 1, $42. Net earnings for the six months ended December 31, 1975, were $5,000.

Required:

a) Present journal entries for the above transactions.
b) Compute the book value per share on July 1 and December 31, 1975.

13–5–B

Following are selected accounts of Jefferson, Inc. at May 31, 1975:

Reserve for product warranties	$ 10,000
Paid-in capital in excess of par value—preferred	6,000
Retained earnings, unappropriated	114,000
Reserve for doubtful accounts	30,000
Common stock without par value, stated value $50; 20,000 shares authorized, issued, and outstanding	1,000,000
Reserve for retirement of bonds	100,000
Capital from appreciation of plant	150,000
Dividends payable	7,000
Paid-in capital in excess of stated value—common	50,000
7% bonds payable, due April 1, 1981	600,000
Preferred stock: 7%, par value $100; 2,000 shares authorized, issued, and outstanding	200,000
Paid-in capital from reissue of donated common treasury stock	24,000

Required: Present the stockholders' equity section of the company's statement of financial position.

13–6–B

The stockholders' equity section of the Bunde Company's October 31, 1974, statement of financial position was:

Paid-in capital:		
Preferred stock: 6%, $100 par value; 1,000 shares authorized, 350 shares issued and outstanding		$ 35,000
Common stock: $10 par value; 100,000 shares authorized, 40,000 shares issued and outstanding		400,000
Paid-in capital from donation of plant site		25,000
Total Paid-In Capital		$460,000
Retained earnings:		
Appropriated:		
Reserve for contingencies	$20,000	
Unappropriated	55,500	
Total Retained Earnings		75,500
Total Stockholders' Equity		$535,500

During the ensuing fiscal year, the following transactions were entered into by the Bunde Company:

1. An additional liability of $11,000 for federal income taxes on 1973 earnings was imposed by the Internal Revenue Service.
2. Appropriation of $20,000 of retained earnings was authorized in October, 1974, because of the likelihood of an unfavorable court decision in a pending lawsuit.

The suit was brought by a customer seeking damages for the company's alleged breach of a contract to supply the customer with certain products at stated prices in 1973. The suit was concluded with a court order directing the company to pay $17,500 in damages. These damages were deductible in determining income tax liability (the tax rate was 50 percent). The board ordered the damages paid and the reserve closed.

3. The company acquired 1,000 shares of its own common stock at $15 in May 1975. On June 30 it resissued 500 of these shares at $12.
4. Dividends declared and paid during the year were 6 percent on preferred stock, and $0.30 per share on common stock. The common dividend was declared and paid in October 1975.
5. Certain land owned by the company was appraised at $15,000 more than its recorded value. Adjustment to appraisal value was authorized.

The company had net earnings after income taxes for the year of $19,000, excluding the loss on the lawsuit and the related tax effects.

Required:

a) Prepare general journal entries for the above transactions.
b) Prepare a statement of retained earnings for the year ended October 31, 1975.
c) Prepare the stockholder's equity section of the October 31, 1975, statement of financial position.

13–7–B

The stockholders' equity of the A. Sandretto Company on December 31, 1974, consisted of 1,000 authorized and outstanding shares of $7 cumulative preferred stock, stated value $10 per share, which were originally issued at $105 per share; 100,000 shares authorized and outstanding of $5 stated value common stock which were originally issued at $5; and retained earnings of $100,000. Following are selected transactions and other data relating to 1975:

1. The company acquired 2,000 shares of its common stock at $15.
2. One thousand of the treasury shares were reissued at $13.
3. Stockholders donated 1,000 shares of common stock to the company. These shares were immediately reissued at $12 to provide working capital.
4. The first quarter's dividend of $1.75 per share was declared and paid on the preferred stock. No other dividends were declared or paid during 1975.

The company suffered a net loss of $20,000 for the year 1975.

Required:

a) Prepare journal entries for the numbered transactions above.
b) Prepare the stockholders' equity section of the December 31, 1975, statement of financial position.

13–8–B

Following are selected account balances of the Vicky Company as of December 31, 1975:

Sales, net	$2,000,000
Cost of goods sold	1,100,000
Gain on sale of Home Products division (This is from the sale of a segment on January 4, 1975, and should be included-net of tax effect-in earnings before extraordinary items as the last item under a caption "Discontinued operations")	400,000
Selling and administrative expense	300,000
Interest revenue	200,000
Loss from natural disaster	400,000
Miscellaneous revenue	100,000
Interest expense	100,000
Additional federal income taxes for 1972	200,000
Cash dividends on preferred stock	50,000
Cash dividends on common stock	250,000

All of the above elements of revenue, expense, and loss are includable in determining federal income taxes (the tax rate is 50 percent), with the gain on sale of the Home Products division taxable at 25 percent. Retained earnings at December 31, 1974, were $2 million.

Required: Following the recommendations contained in the Accounting Principles Board *Opinions* cited in this chapter, prepare:

a) The earnings statement for the year 1975.
b) The statement of retained earnings for the year 1975.

13–9–B

Use the data in Problem 13–8–B and the following information: The Retained Earnings account was charged $40,000 for the excess of the cost over the reissue proceeds of treasury stock. The board of directors authorized an appropriation of $350,000 to a reserve for contingencies and also approved the write-off of $100,000 of obsolete inventory (the write-off is currently deductible for tax purposes).

The company was found to have been in violation of the price-fixing provisions of the Sherman Act for the years 1970–72. Settlement was reached with all customers affected through payment by the company in 1975 of $700,000 of price adjustments. These adjustments are deductible for tax purposes in 1975.

Required: Prepare a combined earnings statement and statement of retained earnings for 1975 following the recommendations in the APB *Opinions.*

The basic theory underlying financial statements

Learning objectives

Study of the material presented and discussed in this chapter is designed to meet a number of learning objectives, including:

1. Knowledge of how the many ideas or notions loosely referred to as generally accepted accounting principles can be structured (albeit loosely) into an underlying financial accounting theory consisting of (1) general objectives, (2) qualitative objectives, (3) basic features, (4) basic elements, (5) pervasive principles, (6) modifying conventions, (7) broad operating principles, and (8) detailed accounting principles.
2. A very introductory understanding of some aspects of the historical development of accounting thought.
3. Knowledge of why accounting principles and standards are needed.
4. Knowledge of the sources of accounting principles and standards and especially of the role played by the American Institute of Certified Public Accountants and the Accounting Principles Board.
5. A basic understanding of the role played by each of the objectives, basic features, pervasive principles, and modifying conventions in shaping accounting thought and practice; and especially how and why the principles relating to earnings determination tend to dominate the entire financial accounting process.

Frame 1[14]

A chapter dealing with the theory underlying financial statements seems especially appropriate at this time for several reasons. First, attention in the companion text is to be directed much more specifically to the development of management accounting information. Second, the financial accounting process has been covered in sufficient depth so that some real understanding of the underlying theoretical notions is much more easily achieved. Some of the concepts or ideas presented in this chapter have been dealt with explicitly in previous chapters; others have been presented only indirectly in discussing the reasoning or logic underlying certain accounting practices. No attempt has been made to deal with accounting theory as a structured whole, or as a complete model. Thus, the reason for this chapter.

Somewhat formally, accounting theory may be defined as a set of basic concepts or assumptions and related principles or standards that explain and guide the accountant's action in identifying, measuring, and communicating economic information.[1] Just exactly what constitutes accounting theory and what its purposes are have been the subject of considerable debate in the accounting profession for many years. And the issue is yet unresolved. But it seems safe to hold that the practice of financial accounting is guided by a group of important notions—variously described as assumptions, axioms, concepts, conventions, features, objectives, principles, procedures, standards, or rules—that collectively constitute "generally accepted accounting principles." Attention in this chapter is directed to the nature of some of these principles, why they are needed, and what objectives are sought by their application. Particular attention is paid to the manner in which the principles that guide the determination of periodic net earnings tend to dominate the entire financial accounting process.

The general objectives of financial accounting

The accountant has long been regarded as the financial historian of a business entity. That is, he is expected to provide a continuous record or "history quantified in money terms of economic resources and obligations of a business enterprise and of economic activities that change these resources and obligations."[2] The information accumulated is reported to both internal and external users. In view of the size and complexity of the activities undertaken in many modern corporations, it is highly unlikely that either group would be very knowledgeable of such activities if they did not possess accounting information.

The information presented to external users is usually cast in the form of general-purpose financial statements (see the appendix to this chapter

[1] American Accounting Association, *A Statement of Basic Accounting Theory* (Evanston, Ill.: AAA, 1966), pp. 1–2.

[2] American Institute of Certified Public Accountants, *Statements of the Accounting Principles Board, No. 4* "Basic Concepts and Accounting Principles Underlying Financial Statements of Business Enterprises" (New York: AICPA, 1970), par. 41.

for actual examples), under the assumption that such statements will serve the common needs of several classes of users. If these statements are to be useful to external users in their decision making or evaluation, they should provide: (1) reliable financial information about economic resources and obligations; (2) reliable information about changes in net resources (resources less obligations) of an enterprise that result from its profit-directed activities; (3) financial information that assists in estimating the future capacity of an enterprise to generate earnings; (4) information about changes in resources and obligations resulting from sources other than profit-directed activities, such as transactions between an entity and its owners and information about working capital and fund flows (illustrated and discussed in Chapter 12 of *Accounting II: A Programmed Text*); and (5) adequate disclosure of other information, such as accounting policies and depreciation and inventory methods, that is relevant to statement users' needs.[3]

The need for accounting principles or standards

If the above general objectives (as well as other objectives to be presented and discussed in later frames) are to be achieved, a body or set of accounting principles or standards is needed. A consistent record of activity cannot be developed, nor can reliable information be reported, unless certain principles or standards are rather consistently adhered to. Even if accounting information were used solely within the confines of a single company, it would have to be accumulated with consistent adherence to specified principles or standards if interperiod comparisons were to be made.

The financial information reported to external parties is often used to compare the financial status and the results of operations of different companies in the same or different industries. For such comparisons to have any validity and for the perceived differences to be real, each reporting company should compile and report its information in the same manner, relying upon the same principles or standards. The financial information relating to different companies will have a certain degree of comparability if it is prepared by relying upon generally accepted accounting principles or standards.

Many in our present-day society hold that the management of a business corporation is accountable to virtually everyone in society, not merely to the corporation's stockholders and creditors. Corporate managements report upon their accountability primarily through the financial statements they issue. The confidence of the public at large in the reliability of these statements is enhanced when it is known that they conform to certain standards or principles. The certified public accountant also needs certain standards by which to appraise the information released by corporate managements in order to express his professional opinion as its "fairness."

[3] Ibid., par. 77–81.

Indicate whether each of the following statements is true or false.

1. The theory underlying financial statements is fairly well-defined and accepted.
2. Generally accepted accounting principles are relied upon by the CPA in expressing his opinion on financial information.
3. Nearly everyone in society benefits from the existence of generally accepted accounting principles.
4. Generally accepted accounting principles help provide a degree of intercompany comparability in financial information.

Now check your responses in Answer Frame 1[14] on page 648.

Frame 2[14]

The sources of accounting principles

Accounting principles have been derived largely from accounting practice. Accounting practice, in turn, has been subject to many influences; including federal income tax laws and regulations; federal and state legislation, especially as it relates to securities exchanges and the sale of securities; public utility regulation; many organizations, such as the American Institute of Certified Public Accountants and the Securities and Exchange Commission; many individual writers, and the traditional practices and customs within an industry. Of the organizations, the most influential has been the American Institute of Certified Public Accountants, whose active leadership in the search for accounting principles dates back to the early 1930s.[4] In fact, the recommendations of a Special Committee on Cooperation with Stock Exchanges in 1932 contained the first use of the term "accepted principles of accounting."

Some of the more important influences in the development of accounting thought and the establishment of accounting principles are summarized below.

Federal income taxation. The federal taxation of income has immeasurably influenced the development of accounting principles and practice. Permission, first granted in the Excise Act of 1909 and continued in the Revenue Act of 1913 and every subsequent act, to deduct a reasonable amount of depreciation expense in arriving at taxable income did much to stimulate discussion of the theoretical nature of depreciation and of the methods of computing its periodic amount. The acceptance for tax purposes of the accelerated methods of computing depreciation in the 1954 act led to the general acceptance of these methods. The requirement that inventories be properly determined for tax purposes, first required in

[4] For an excellent discussion of the attempts to formulate accounting principles, see Reed K. Storey. *The Search for Accounting Principles* (New York: AICPA, 1964).

1918 and since continued, also induced discussion of inventory procedures and the theory of inventory measurement.

But undoubtedly the most notable influence of income taxation on accounting theory and practice can be found in the famous *Eisner* v. *Macomber* decision of the U.S. Supreme Court in 1920, which firmly established realization as a principle or central concept in accounting, as is discussed in later frames.

Federal securities legislation. The huge losses suffered by many in the stock market crash of 1929 resulted in agitation for some form of government intervention in the securities markets. The Securities Act of 1933 and the Securities and Exchange Act of 1934 followed. Basically, the goal of these acts is to secure full and fair disclosure relative to securities sold in interstate and foreign commerce. The Securities and Exchange Commission, created in the 1934 Act, was given the power to prescribe in every detail the type of information to be disclosed by all companies required to file with it, which includes every company whose securities are traded on an organized exchange or in the over-the-counter markets. The Commission has rarely exercised this power, preferring instead to cooperate with the accounting profession (basically, the AICPA) in the development of accounting principles.

The American Accounting Association. Beginning in 1936 with a statement by its Executive Committee, the American Accounting Association (the organization of the teachers of accounting) began publishing a number of statements on accounting principles. Four such statements, with eight supplementary statements, had been published by 1957. These were followed by committee reports on accounting topics such as matching and realization and, in 1966, by *A Statement of Basic Accounting Theory*. The 1966 statement was followed by a number of interpretive committee reports. All of these statements, rather than prescribing solutions in detail to specific problems, sought to provide a general framework of principles or standards. The 1966 statement, for example, established four standards—relevance, quantifiability, freedom from bias, and verifiability—to which information must conform before it is admitted to the accounting system.

The Accounting Research Bulletins. The lack of success encountered in attempting to formulate broad statements of accounting principles forced another approach. Practical problems arose that required solution. Beginning in 1939, the Committee on Accounting Procedure of the AICPA issued over the next 20 years a total of 51 *Accounting Research Bulletins,* which were largely suggested solutions to specific problems. Each bulletin relied upon general acceptance for its authority. This effort has been characterized as a piecemeal approach by those who would prefer to see the entire framework of principles developed as an integrated whole. The detailed rules (discussed in Chapter 7) relative to the lower-of-cost-or-market method of inventory measurement are illustrative of the content of the bulletins.

The Accounting Principles Board (APB) and the Accounting Research Division. In the late 1950s more and more accountants came to believe

Answer frame 1[14]

1. False. There is little agreement as to the entire structure of the theory of financial accounting, although certain ideas or principles have achieved a degree of acceptance, as will be discussed later.
2. True. In his opinion, the CPA refers specifically to generally accepted accounting principles as the standard used to appraise the fairness of the information under scrutiny.
3. True. The efficient functioning of our society depends on a free flow of trade and credit. This flow, in turn, depends on reliable financial information about the participating parties. Confidence in the reliability of financial information is enhanced considerably when the CPA attests to the fact that it is presented fairly in accordance with generally accepted accounting principles.
4. True. Although much is made of the fact that differences do exist, resulting solely from the choice of the principles applied or the methods used, there is a high degree of comparability in some of the information provided.

If you answered incorrectly, study Frame 1[14] again before continuing with Frame 2[14] on page 646.

2[14] *continued*

that drastic action was needed to formulate a comprehensive body of accounting principles. They noted that the *Accounting Research Bulletins* were lacking in comprehensiveness, that the pronouncements of the American Accounting Association had gained little acceptance among practitioners, and that recommendations of individuals were largely ignored. Consequently, in 1959, the American Institute of Certified Public Accountants' governing council approved the organization of an Accounting Principles Board and an Accounting Research Division. The stated objective was to be:

> . . . to advance the written expression of what constitutes generally accepted accounting principles, for the guidance of its members and of others. This means something more than a survey of existing practice. It means a continuing effort to determine appropriate practice and to narrow the areas of difference and inconsistency in practice.[5]

During its first three years, the Accounting Research Division produced two pertinent studies. The first was *Accounting Research Study No. 1,* entitled "The Basic Postulates of Accounting," by Maurice Moonitz. The second was *Accounting Research Study No. 3,* entitled "A Tentative Set of Broad Accounting Principles for Business Enterprises," by Robert T. Sprouse and Maurice Moonitz. The Accounting Principles Board, which terminated in mid-1973, never did accept and adopt these studies as the postulates and principles of accounting. These studies may be described as being "normative" in nature, in that they arrive at "what ought to be" through a deductive reasoning process.

[5] American Institute of Certified Public Accountants, *Organization and Operation of the Accounting Research Program and Related Activities* (New York: AICPA, 1959), p. 9.

The Accounting Research Division also published *Accounting Research Study No. 7,* "Inventory of Generally Accepted Accounting Principles for Business Enterprises," by Paul Grady, which, as its name suggests, consists of an inventory of generally accepted accounting principles in the United States. To many, this was the logical first step that should have been taken rather than the approach followed in *Accounting Research Studies Nos. 1* and *3.* The "inventory" approach can be described as "positive" in that it is based upon empirical evidence of that which actually exists.

A number of other research studies have been published dealing not with broad general principles but rather with specific topics such as income taxes, goodwill, business combinations, leases, pensions, foreign operations, extractive industry accounting problems, and financial reporting under changing price levels.

Chronologically, the next publication of the AICPA that dealt specifically with accounting principles and concepts was *Statement of the Accounting Principles Board, No. 4* "Basic Concepts and Accounting Principles Underlying Financial Statements of Business Enterprises," which was published in 1970. Portions of this statement have already been cited. The influence on it of *Accounting Research Studies Nos. 1, 3,* and *7* and of the AAA's *A Statement of Basic Accounting Theory* can be readily observed.

Statement No. 4 is primarily descriptive, in that it identifies and organizes ideas or notions that for the most part are already generally accepted. But the Board erects a new general structure of theory by dividing the basic concepts of accounting into (1) objectives—general and qualitative, the first of which have been presented above; (2) basic features, which will be presented below; (3) basic elements—assets, liabilities, owners' equity, revenue, expenses, and net earnings; (4) pervasive principles, most of which will be discussed in following frames; (5) modifying conventions, such as conservatism; (6) broad operating principles, such as the recording of exchange prices; and (7) detailed accounting principles, such as the requirement that goodwill be amortized over a period not to exceed 40 years.

The basic deficiency in *Statement No. 4* is that on the one hand it erects the above structure of accounting concepts, and on the other hand shows clearly the need for information on economic resources, obligations, and changes in net economic resources—and then fails to tie the two together. For example, the statement does not equate assets with economic resources or liabilities with economic obligations. Rather, the definitions of all of the basic elements are qualified by the phrase "in conformity with generally accepted accounting principles."

Indicate whether each of the following statements is true or false.

1. The pronouncements of the American Accounting Association have generally consisted of detailed solutions to specific problems.
2. The approach taken in the *Accounting Research Bulletins* can be characterized as "plugging the leak in the dike" or "putting out brush fires."
3. The Securities and Exchange Commission has the power to prescribe the accounting practices to be followed by all of the business corporations in the United States that issue securities to the public.
4. The effect of the federal taxation of income upon accounting principles has been largely indirect, in that it has influenced the practice from which accounting principles have been derived.

Now check your responses in Answer Frame 2[14] on page 652.

Frame 3[14]

Opinions of the APB. The Accounting Principles Board as initially organized by the AICPA consisted of 21 members, the vast majority of whom were practicing CPAs. The Board was to rely on the research studies of the Accounting Research Division and all other available evidence on a given topic and then issue an "opinion" to guide the practice of the accounting art. By the time the Board ceased to operate in mid-1973 it had issued 31 *Opinions,* covering a wide range of subject matter similar to that covered by the Accounting Research Studies. A number of references to these *Opinions* have already been made in past chapters.

Authority of the APB Opinions. The authority attaching to the Board's *Opinions* was greatly enhanced when the governing council of the AICPA at the spring 1964 meeting decided, insofar as the members of the Institute are concerned, and for fiscal periods beginning after December 31, 1965, that the *Opinions* of the Accounting Principles Board would be considered generally accepted principles in the subject matter areas covered. While principles which disagree with *Opinions* of the Accounting Principles Board may still be considered "generally accepted" (if they have substantial authoritative support), disclosure of the fact that the principles are not in agreement with the Board's *Opinions* must be made. In general this meant that after December 31, 1965, the CPA would continue to determine the fairness of the financial statements upon which he expressed an opinion, but if any of the principles used were at variance with the Board's pronouncements as to what generally accepted accounting principles are, disclosure of that fact must be made.

The Financial Accounting Standards Board. Virtually from its inception, the Accounting Principles Board was subjected to a continuous stream of criticism from nearly all quarters. Some maintained that the Board moved too slowly, others argued that it acted without full consideration of an issue. Some approved, while others rejected the authoritarian approach. In certain circumstancces it was alleged that the Board gave the appearance of bowing to the wishes of some of the major clients of its members. Others questioned whether a board made up of voluntary, unpaid members could deal impartially and adequately with the many problems faced by the accounting profession.

This criticism and questioning induced the AICPA to undertake sponsorship of a new, seven-member, full-time, paid, independent board called the Financial Accounting Standards Board (FASB). This new board became active in the early spring of 1973. It is to be the authoritative voice of the accounting profession in promulgating accounting standards. Thus, the continuing search for accounting principles or standards has now become the chief responsibility of a new oranization.

The future, of course, can seldom be predicted with a high degree of accuracy. But if the future is similar to the immediate past, accounting will continue to be a dynamic, ever-changing discipline seeking to meet the needs of those whom it serves.

The balance of this chapter is devoted to a discussion of some of these important notions—variously described as concepts, features, principles, conventions, standards, and so on—which guide the accountant in his identification, measurement, and reporting of economic activity. These are the ideas that give accounting a much greater degree of uniformity and consistency than is thought to exist in view of the attention devoted to the areas of disagreement and lack of uniformity.

Indicate whether each of the following statements is true or false.

1. Despite external appearances to the contrary, accounting actually lacks precision and is beset with many controversies.
2. The Financial Accounting Standards Board is now the profession's authoritative voice on matters of accounting standards (principles).
3. By essentially requiring its members to adhere to APB *Opinions,* the AICPA introduced a greater degree of uniformity into accounting practice.
4. The Financial Accounting Standards Board is a suborganization of, and responsible to, the AICPA.

Now check your responses in Answer Frame 3[14] on page 652.

Frame 4[14]

Qualitative objectives

Every discipline is based upon certain fundamental premises or assumptions. Our law, for example, assumes that a man is innocent until proven guilty; the physicist assumes that energy can neither be created nor destroyed; the mathematician, that every integer has a successor. And parts of economic theory rely heavily on the assumption of diminishing marginal utility.

Answer frame 2[14]

1. False. The American Accounting Association has traditionally sought to provide rather broad statements of concepts, principles, or standards, with little in the line of direct reference to specific problems.
2. True. This was the approach taken in the *Accounting Research Bulletins* and is basically the approach taken in most of the publications of the AICPA.
3. True. In this regard, the Commission has virtually unlimited power.
4. True. The practical consideration of holding record-keeping costs to a minimum often influences a businessman to keep his accounting records in a manner acceptable for tax purposes. In this way, income tax accounting requirements can become generally accepted accounting principles.

If you missed any of the above, restudy Frame 2[14] before proceeding to Frame 3[14] on page 650.

Answer frame 3[14]

1. True. Accounting measurements, such as depreciation, are often imprecise; and there are many unresolved controversies, such as whether accountants should report assets measured in terms of cost or value, or both.
2. True. This is the exact reason for the formation of the board.
3. True. This followed because the APB in most of its *Opinions* tried to narrow the range of practices that were considered acceptable.
4. False. The FASB is independent of any other accounting organization, and this desire for independence was one of the major reasons for the establishment of a new board to replace the APB.

If you answered incorrectly, study Frame 3[14] again before proceeding to Frame 4[14] on page 651.

4[14] *continued*

Accountants have long recognized that implicit in their discipline are certain basic notions, drawn largely from the environment, that distinguish it from other disciplines. Unfortunately, there is no consistent use of terminology in accounting literature and these basic notions are variously referred to as assumptions, axioms, concepts, conventions, features, objectives, postulates, principles, procedures, standards, and rules. In general, the terminology used by the APB in *Statement No. 4* will be followed. Thus, the discussion that follows is divided into sections dealing with qualitative objectives, basic features, and principles.

The seven qualitative objectives of financial accounting stated by the Board are: (1) relevance, (2) understandability, (3) verifiability, (4) neutrality, (5) timeliness, (6) comparability, and (7) completeness.[6] These are discussed in the following paragraphs.

Relevance

For information to be relevant it must be pertinent to or bear upon a decision. Relevance is the primary qualitative objective. If information

[6] American Institute of Certified Public Accountants, *Statement No. 4,* par. 88–94.

is not relevant, it is useless even though it meets the other objectives fully. And it is precisely for its lack of relevance that accounting information is under serious attack today. For example, it is argued that the fact that a tract of land cost an entity $1 million over 40 years ago is completely irrelevant to any user of the financial statements for any decision that he must make. These attacks have encouraged research into the types of information that is relevant to users. But the issue still appears to be far from being resolved.

Understandability

This objective is important on the simple grounds that information must be comprehended if it is to be useful. This requires that information be presented in a form, and expressed in terminology, that a user understands. But the complexity of economic activity makes it impossible to always reduce it to simple terms. Therefore, it follows that the user must aid his own cause by acquiring at least a rudimentary understanding of business and accounting terminology.

Verifiability

The basic test of the verifiability of accounting information is whether it would be substantially duplicated by other independent measurers using the same measurement methods. The many references in accounting literature holding that accounting information should be based on objective evidence are based on the belief that users need reliable, unbiased, financial information. This is especially so when parties with opposing interests (credit seekers and credit granters) may rely on the same information. The reliability of information is enhanced if it is verifiable.

But it should be recognized that accounting information will never be free of subjective opinion and judgment. It will always possess varying degrees of verifiability. Some measurements can be supported by reference to canceled checks, vouchers, and invoices. Others can never be verified simply because they cannot be measured, as is true for estimates of periodic depreciation. For these reasons, the financial information presented in any given instance is best viewed as possessing verifiability (or objectivity) largely in the sense that it represents a consensus as to what would be reported if the same procedures had been followed by a number of other accountants.

Neutrality

Financial accounting information should be neutral—that is, it should not favor one group to the detriment of another. It is directed to the common needs of many users, not to the particular needs of a specific user or class of users. This is in keeping with the notion that financial statements are general-purpose statements serving the common needs of a variety of users for reliable, unbiased information. It is not sufficient that information be verifiable, since biased information can be verified. Information must also be free from bias. For example, inventory measurements obtained using the lower-of-cost-or-market method can be verified. But do they meet the objective of neutrality?

Indicate whether each of the following statements is true or false.

1. Financial information should be expressed in terms that everyone can understand.
2. Information that can be verified may yet be biased because of the measurement method selected.
3. Some accounting measurements can be verified only in the sense that another accountant using the same measurement methods would arrive at the same result.
4. Conflicts may exist between objectives. For example, relevance may conflict with verifiability.

Now turn to Answer Frame 4[14] on page 656 to check your responses.

Frame 5[14]

Timeliness

The meaning of and the reasons for this objective should be quite obvious, since the utility of information decreases with age. If information is to be of any value in decision making, it must be available before the decision is made. If not, it is useless, or nearly so. To avoid what could be costly delays, the accounting system should be designed to provide the information needed at a time that is consistent with consideration given to the other objectives and to the cost of accumulating the information. As will be discussed later, this will often involve the use of estimates and approximations.

Comparability

When comparable financial information is presented the differences and similarities noted will be real, that is, they will arise from differences or similarities in the matters being reported upon and not from differences in accounting treatment. Thus, comparable financial information will reveal relative strengths and weaknesses for a single entity through time and for two or more entities. Comparability has, therefore, both an interperiod and an intercompany aspect.

Comparability in the financial statements of a single entity through time is generally achieved by adhering to the familiar accounting requirement of consistency. This consistency requires (1) identical arrangements within the statements; (2) identical classification of items under the same captions (marketable securities are not shifted between current and non-current asset classifications); (3) adherence to the same accounting principles or, if they are changed, disclosure of both the fact of change and its financial effects; and (4) disclosure of changes in circumstances or in the nature of underlying transactions (for example, changing regular merchandising outlets to discount houses).

While barring indiscriminate switching from principle to principle or from method to method (such as changing depreciation methods every year), the consistency requirement does not bar changes in accounting principles if it is believed that the information needs of users will be better served by the change. But disclosure of the change and, if material, of the financial effects of the change are required.[7]

Intercompany comparability is far more difficult to achieve than interperiod comparability for a single company. The primary reason is that the same circumstances or events in different entities can be accounted for in different ways or by applying different principles. For example, Company A may use the LIFO inventory and accelerated depreciation methods; Company B may account for identical circumstances using FIFO inventory and straight-line depreciation methods. A high degree of intercompany comparability is likely to be absent until it is required that the same circumstances be accounted for in the same manner.

Completeness

This, the last of the Board's qualitative objectives, requires that all financial accounting information meeting the other six qualitative objectives be reported. In effect, it requires disclosure of all significant information in a manner that aids understanding and avoids misleading implications. Excessive detail should be avoided, as this may obscure significant information.

Adequate disclosure may be secured in a number of ways: (1) in the body of financial statements, (2) in footnotes to the statements, (3) in special communications, and (4) in the president's letter in the annual report.

In addition to changes in accounting principles, disclosure usually must be made of unusual activities (loans to officers); changes in expectations (losses on inventory); long-term obligations entered into that are not recorded by the accountant (lease of a factory building for 20 years); new arrangements with certain groups (pension and profit-sharing plans for employees); significant events that occur after the date of the statements (such as the loss of a major customer); and the accounting policies (major principles and their manner of application) followed in preparing the financial statements.[8]

[7] American Institute of Certified Public Accountants, Accounting Principles Board *Opinion No. 20,* "Accounting Changes" (New York: AICPA, 1971).

[8] American Institute of Certified Public Accountants, Accounting Principles Board *Opinion No. 22,* "Disclosure of Accounting Policies" (New York: AICPA, 1972).

Answer frame 4[14]

1. False. It is probably impossible to do so, since not all are acquainted with business and accounting terminology, and economic activity is often too complex to be stated in simple, nontechnical terms.
2. True. Pricing inventory at the lower of cost or market may be an example. Accelerated depreciation methods may constitute another example.
3. True. Examples here are depreciation and net earnings.
4. True. A user may find it most relevant to know the market value of an asset reported only at a verified cost figure. But the asset may be unique and have no verifiable market value.

If you missed any of the above, review Frame 4[14] before going on to Frame 5[14] on page 654.

Correspondence

5[14] *continued*

The qualitative objective of correspondence requires that financial information depict or portray economic reality. That is, the financial statements of an entity should report all economic resources as assets and should not report as assets things that are not economic resources. Similarly, the statements should include all economic obligations and should not report as liabilities things that are not economic obligations. Failure of the Board to include correspondence as one of its qualitative objectives permits it to define key accounting terms (assets, liabilities, owners' equity, revenues, and expenses) and to state accounting objectives in terms of their conformity with generally accepted accounting principles rather than their agreement with economic reality or substance. For example, it permits the reporting of discount on bonds payable as an asset even though it is not an economic resource.

Indicate whether each of the following statements is true or false.

1. Reporting the results of operations for the calendar year 1975 by June 1, 1976, would fulfill the timeliness objective.
2. A user can place the financial statements of two companies on a comparable basis if he has knowledge of the accounting policies followed by each.
3. The completeness objective may require reporting an event that happened after the closing date of the period covered by the financial statements.
4. The correspondence objective requires that what exists, economically speaking, be reported in the financial statements.
5. Consistency generally requires that accounting principles and methods be adhered to and applied through time without change, unless the fact of change is disclosed.

Now check your responses in Answer Frame 5[14] on page 658.

Frame 6[14]

The basic features of financial accounting

Many of what the APB calls basic features are discussed in the accounting literature as assumptions, concepts, or postulates. They represent a distillation of the effects or influences of environmental characteristics on the financial accounting process. They form the foundation that supports present generally accepted accounting principles. Some of these features were presented and discussed briefly in Chapter 1. To the extent that they are included in the Board's list of 13 basic features, on which the following discussion is based, they are presented and discussed again in order that all 13 be grouped together in one place.[9]

Accounting entity

All accounting information pertains to a specific entity which can be defined as a circumscribed area of interest. This entity is viewed as having an existence apart from its owners, creditors, employees, and other interested parties. In the case of the corporation, this separate existence is confirmed by law, since the corporation is recognized as a separate legal entity. But the boundaries of the accounting entity may differ from those of the legal entity, since financial information may relate to a corporation and its subsidiary corporations as a single business enterprise. An accounting entity may exist in circumstances where it is not supported by a legal entity, as in the case of a single proprietorship. The accountant is interested in the business activities of the business entity, not of the individual. Financial statements must identify the entity for which they are prepared; and their content must be limited to reporting the activities, resources, and obligations of that entity.

Going concern

In financial accounting, an entity is viewed as continuing in operation unless evidence to the contrary appears. Proceeding in this manner is justified because past experience shows that continuity in operation is highly probable for most entities. Yet if liquidation appears imminent, financial information should not be based on the assumption of continuity.

The expectation of continuity of the entity is often referred to in justifying the use of cost, rather than market value, as a basis for measuring assets. Market values are conceded as possessing significance for an entity in liquidation, but it is alleged they are of no significance to an entity which intends to use its assets in operations rather than sell them. On the other hand, the expectation of continuity permits the accountant to

[9] American Institute of Certified Public Accountants *Statement No. 4,* par. 132.

Answer frame 5[14]

1. False. This is an example of a situation in which the information would have very little utility, if any, because of its age.
2. False. Even an accountant cannot do this, and this is likely to be true even if he is employed by one of the reporting companies. Such information simply is not likely to be available. For example, a company that determines the cost of its inventories on a FIFO basis is not likely to compile information that would permit it to determine the cost of its inventories on a LIFO basis.
3. True. It has long been a reporting principle that such events be disclosed if they have a material effect.
4. True. And it also requires that assets be defined as economic resources without the qualifying phrase "recognized and measured in conformity with generally accepted accounting principles."[10]
5. True. This is the generalized meaning of the consistency requirement or objective.

If you answered incorrectly, return to Frame 5[14] for further review before continuing in Frame 6[14] on page 657.

6[14] *continued*

treat certain costs as assets. For example, substantial quantities of printed advertising matter may be on hand which are to be used to promote a special sale next month. These materials would have little, if any, value to anyone but the owners. But the accountant is justified in according them asset status because the owner is expected to continue in operation long enough to realize the service potential they possess.

Measurement of economic resources and obligations

The primary concern of financial accounting is the measurement of economic resources and obligations and of the changes in both. That is, financial accounting seeks to measure and report upon the creation, accumulation, and use of economic resources. Basically, only those activities, resources, and obligations that can be quantified are of concern to financial accounting. Quantified data are generally more useful in decision making than nonquantified, or verbalized, data. Accounting differs from economics in that it is not directly concerned with the concepts of satisfaction and welfare, nor is it primarily and directly concerned with sociological and psychological matters.

Indicate whether each of the following statements is true or false.

1. An accounting entity may or may not be a legal entity.
2. An accounting entity may be a part of a legal entity.
3. If based upon past history, the assumption of continuity of the entity seems reasonable.

[10] Ibid., par. 116–28.

4. Accounting, like economics, is concerned with the satisfaction derived by individuals from consuming economic resources or from accumulating wealth.

Now check your responses in Answer Frame 6[14] on page 660.

Frame 7[14]

Time periods

In order to provide useful information to external parties for decision making at various points in the life of an entity, the accountant must subdivide the life of the entity into periods and render reports on the activities of those periods. In order to facilitate comparisons, the time periods usually are of equal length. The length of the period must be specified in the financial statements. Only in this way can useful information on what is for many entities a never-ending stream of activity be reported.

Measurement in money terms

Since the function of financial accounting is to measure and report upon economic resources, obligations, and activity, and because these are usually quantified in money terms, it follows that accounting measurements will be expressed in money terms. The unit of measure (the dollar in the United States) is identified in the financial statements.

This does not mean that all measurements of economic activity must be stated in monetary terms to be useful. It may, for example, be pertinent to know that a plant is operating at 50 percent of its capacity. But the full economic significance of this bit of information cannot be ascertained until it is translated into money terms.

The accountant uses the dollar as his unit of measure in describing economic activity. It is only through the use of such a common unit of measure that he is able to report intelligently upon economic activity, resources, and obligations. Visualize, for example, the preparation of financial statements without the use of a common unit of measure. Such statements would be largely unintelligible.

Stable dollar. In making money measurements of economic activity, the accountant typically ignores fluctuations in the value of his unit of measure—the dollar. Thus, he deducts a portion of the cost of a building acquired in 1932 from revenues earned in 1975 in arriving at net earnings for 1975; that is, he treats the 1932 dollar and the 1975 dollar as if they were the same unit of measure. If its value is taken into consideration, the dollar is not a common unit of measure.

The validity of proceeding in this manner depends largely on the magnitude of the changes in the general level of prices (which, over the years,

Answer frame 6^{14}

1. True. A corporation is a legal entity and is very often also the accounting entity. A corporation and its subsidiary corporations are not a legal entity but frequently constitute an accounting entity.
2. True. Accounting reports often relate to a part of a corporation, such as a division or a department. While such information is not always published, there is a definite trend in the direction of reporting such information to external parties along with information relating to the entity as a whole.
3. True. The vast majority of business entities do continue to exist, making the assumption of continuity seem reasonable. But a sufficient number discontinue operations every year that the accountant should at least raise the question of the likelihood of survival if liquidation appears imminent.
4. False. There is no branch or subdivision of accounting referred to as welfare accounting similar to the area in economics referred to as welfare economics.

If you answered incorrectly, you should study Frame 6^{14} again before proceeding to Frame 7^{14} on page 659.

7^{14} *continued*

have been rather substantial). Despite official support for recommendations urging the preparation of supplemental statements to show the effects of price level changes upon financial statements, only a very few efforts in this direction have been undertaken. The accountant still treats all dollars as being alike.

Accrual basis

Accountants have long recognized that the statement of financial position and the earnings statement are likely to be much more representative depictions of an entity's status and operations when prepared under the accrual rather than the cash basis of accounting. Under the cash basis (typically employed only in the simplest of business situations), revenues and most expenses are recorded at the time of cash receipt or cash payment. Under the accrual basis, changes in resources and obligations, including those resulting from the generation of revenues and the incurrence of expense, are recorded as they occur (or nearly so). For example, revenues are recorded when services are rendered or products sold and delivered, not when cash is received. Similarly, expenses are recorded as incurred in the period benefited—for example, an employee's services would be recorded when received rather than when payment is made. The accrual basis simply recognizes that considerable economic activity can occur that is not matched with a concurrent flow of cash.

Exchange prices

As repeatedly illustrated previously, measurements in financial accounting consist largely of the prices established in exchanges of economic resources and obligations. Typically, past exchange prices are used, although occasionally a current exchange price (replacement cost) or a future exchange price (expected selling price) may be used (for example, both are used in pricing inventory under the lower-of-cost-or-market rule). Measurements of internal activity, such as manufacturing activity, usually involve an allocation of a past exchange price to periods (depreciation accounting, for example). Financial accounting is concerned largely with prices rather than values.

Approximation and judgment

That accounting measurements are often based upon estimates should be fully understood by now. In order to provide periodic financial information, estimates must be made of such things as expected uncollectible accounts receivable, the expected useful lives of many depreciable and amortizable assets, and the expected selling price of certain items carried in inventory. By their very nature, periodic depreciation charges simply cannot be anything other than estimates. Because estimates of the net realizable value of accounts receivable and of inventory depend on future events, they must obviously be uncertain and tentative. The very fact that economic activity is continuous, complex, and steeped in uncertainty precludes precise measurements and makes estimates necessary.

Yet these estimates or approximations often have a rather high degree of accuracy because they involve the application of judgment by an experienced, informed accountant. They are not merely pulled out of thin air. It is this need for informed judgment that precludes expressing the entire financial accounting process as a set of inflexible rules, an example of which might be: depreciate all trucks over three years.

Indicate whether each of the following statements is true or false.

1. Accounting is primarily concerned with prices, not values.
2. A serious conceptual flaw in accounting is that it fails to take into consideration the changing value of its unit of measure—the dollar.
3. The need to provide financial information for relatively short periods of time is the cause of many of the problems faced in accounting.
4. Under cash basis accounting, collection of cash in 1976 in payment of services rendered in 1975 leads to recording the revenue in 1976.

Now check your responses in Answer Frame 7[14] on page 662.

Frame 8[14]

General-purpose financial information

As already noted, the results of the financial accounting process are usually presented in what are called general-purpose financial statements. These statements are presented to current and potential owners and creditors and to internal managers under the assumption that they will meet

Answer frame 7[14]

1. True. Most of the data entered into the accounting system consists of prices generated in exchanges or allocations of those exchange prices.
2. True. The economist would never present time series data (data relating to several years) that are expressed in dollars without adjusting for the change in the value of the dollar.
3. True. This is the reason why the accountant must make many of the estimates on which financial accounting is based.
4. True. Under cash basis accounting, revenue is only recorded when cash is collected; it matters not when the services were rendered. Since the cash is collected in 1976, revenue is recorded in 1976.

If you answered incorrectly, study Frame 7[14] again before going on to Frame 8[14] on page 661.

8[14] *continued*

the common needs of these and other users. This does not mean that special-purpose information cannot be developed from the accounting records or projections. For example, the information demanded by an insurance company that is asked by a business entity for a loan may be quite detailed in nature and may differ somewhat from the information the insurance company would receive if it merely wished to purchase some of the entity's shares in the market.

Fundamentally related financial statements

The financial statements that are the end products of the financial accounting process are fundamentally related because they are based on the same data. For example, the net earnings for a period as shown in the earnings statement must be carried to the statement of retained earnings before that statement can be completed. Similarly, the ending balance of retained earnings as shown on the statement of retained earnings is carried to the statement of financial position and brings the assets and equities reported on this statement into agreement.

Substance over form

The economic substance of an event to be recorded usually agrees with its legal form. But where the two conflict, the accountant emphasizes economic substance rather than legal form in order to provide information that better reflects the underlying economic activity. For example, a contract which is legally a lease may be treated as a purchase, such as a three-year contract to rent an automobile at a stipulated monthly rental with the lessee to received title to the auto at the end of the lease period upon the payment of a nominal sum (say, $1).

Materiality

Financial reporting is concerned only with information that is significant enough to influence the decisions of an informed investor, creditor, or other user. No set dollar amount can be established as constituting a material item in every circumstance. The omission of a $10,000 item of expense from the earnings statement of a firm with only $30,000 of net earnings would almost certainly constitute a violation of the materiality concept, especially if its normal earnings approximate $30,000. But the same amount omitted from the earnings statement of the General Motors Corporation may not. The concept is a relative one. It is up to the accountant in each circumstance to form a judgment as to which items are material and which are not. Other accountants would not necessarily agree in every situation.

The materiality concept literally means that items of revenue and expense that are immaterial in amount—individually *and in total*—may be handled without regard for theoretical considerations. Immaterial (small amount) expense or revenue transactions that in theory may be allocable to several periods may be charged to expense or credited to earnings of the current period because the bookkeeping expense involved may exceed the practical benefits to be derived from the allocation. Common examples of immaterial items are minor repairs, purchases of assets at nominal cost such as wastebaskets, and small amounts of revenue from sales of scrap inventories accumulated over more than one period. Arbitrary dividing lines (such as $100 or $500) may be set, in which case any expenditures for assets of less than that amount are charged directly to expense. Repetitious transactions that may be immaterial in amount individually may be material in the aggregate. In such cases the concepts for proper net earnings determination should be followed.

Indicate whether each of the following statements is true or false.

1. A $1 million item is always material.
2. An item is material if knowledge of it would influence the evaluation or decision of an informed user.
3. It is probably true that many external users have common needs for financial information.
4. Where economic substance and legal form conflict, legal form must prevail.
5. Generally accepted accounting principles do not apply to immaterial items.

Now turn to Answer Frame 8[14] on page 664 to check your responses.

Frame 9[14]

Conservatism

Although treated by the APB in *Statement No. 4* as a "modifying convention" in the application of accounting principles rather than a basic feature, conservatism ranks among the concepts that has shaped account-

Answer frame 8[14]

1. False. Materiality is always a relative, not an absolute, concept. In some business entities, a $1 million difference in depreciation may not be material.
2. True. This is a rather typical definition of materiality.
3. True. Most external users will want information on the same things, such as sales, earnings, and, perhaps, some information on financial position.
4. False. Where the two conflict, economic substance prevails as far as the accountant is concerned.
5. True. Immaterial items may be handled in an expedient method that would not be in accord with generally accepted accounting principles if the amount were larger.

If you answered incorrectly, study Frame 8[14] again before continuing in Frame 9[14] on page 663.

9[14] *continued*

ing thought and practice.[11] Basically, the concept of conservatism embraces the idea of being cautious or prudent—of not being carried away by overoptimism or wild enthusiasm. As adopted in accounting, it generally postulates that assets and earnings should not be overstated. Conservatism should *not* mean that net earnings and assets are understated (although we fear it sometimes results in this). The understatement of net earnings and net assets is as deplorable a practice as overstatement.

To many unfamiliar with accounting, a concept of conservatism would seem to be completely unnecessary. Accounting measurements are precise, and no judgment is involved in making these measurements, they believe. Unfortunately, very few account balances can be stated with absolute precision. Judgment is almost always involved, and it is here that the concept of conservatism comes into play. At what amount should these accounts be stated? The correct balance depends upon the future, which cannot be predicted with great accuracy.

Consequently, conservatism in the past has been characterized as a policy of making sure that if in error, all estimates should be in error in such a fashion as to make reported net earnings and net assets less than they actually prove to be. If there is any doubt as to whether a future benefit exists in a given asset, play safe and expense it now. In this way, future periods will not be handicapped because of errors in the current period.

This view of conservatism too often has resulted in the practice of charging assets to expense long before they should have been expensed or over periods considerably shorter than their actual lives. But such a policy is somewhat self-defeating. Since all expenses and revenues eventually find their way into the earnings statement, any overstatement of expenses in the current period means that expenses of subsequent periods

[11] Ibid., par. 171.

will be understated. Then net earnings for those periods will be overstated, and this can hardly be called conservative.

For example, a 10-year asset is fully depreciated over the first four years of its life. No depreciation will, of course, be taken in the last six years of the asset's life. Consequently, net earnings will be understated the first four years and overstated the last six years. This is not conservatism; it is incorrect accounting. And by such a practice of conservatism, the net earnings for each of the 10 years are incorrect.

Conservatism may be applied with varying degrees of severity in different entities and thus be a cause of reduced intercompany comparability in financial information. Because he does not know how vigorously conservatism has been applied, an external user may be induced to act in a manner detrimental to his interests. He may, for example, sell his shares of stock in a company because its earnings do not come up to his expectations, which may be due solely to a "conservative" measurement of inventory. Thus, in many instances, a fine line exists between conservative and incorrect accounting.

Indicate whether each of the following statements is true or false.

1. A procedure thought to be conservative in one accounting period may yield a nonconservative effect in a later period.
2. The concept of conservatism holds that if a liability must be estimated, the estimate should tend toward the high side.
3. If experience shows that 1 percent of annual sales prove to be uncollectible, a conservative approach is to estimate such uncollectibles at 2 percent of sales.
4. The application of the concept of conservatism may yield net earnings lower than the figure that would emerge from strict application of generally accepted accounting principles.

Now check your responses in Answer Frame 9[14] on page 666.

Frame 10[14]

Other modifying conventions

The Board identified two other widely adopted conventions that modify the strict application of generally accepted accounting principles: (1) the emphasis upon earnings or income determination and (2) application of judgment of the accounting profession as a whole.[12] How both of these influence financial accounting measurements will be discussed in the following frames. In keeping with the convention of emphasizing the determination of net earnings or income, attention will be first directed to the underlying principles in this area.

[12] Ibid., par. 172–74.

Answer frame 9[14]

1. True. The example given in which a 10-year life asset was fully depreciated in the first four years of its life is illustrative of this conservative-nonconservative effect.
2. True. To be conservative, an estimate of a liability should tend toward the higher end of an acceptable range.
3. False. This would be better characterized as incorrect accounting.
4. True. This is a generalized depiction of the results of applying the concept or convention of conservatism.

If you answered incorrectly, restudy Frame 9[14] before continuing in Frame 10[14] on page 665.

Principles underlying earnings determination

10[14]
continued

The matching principle

One of the most fundamental principles in accounting is that net earnings can be determined properly through a process of relating or matching the revenue recognized in a period with the expenses incurred to generate or produce that revenue.[13] The logic of this belief is rooted in the fact that wherever economic resources are employed, someone will want to know what was accomplished or achieved, at what cost or sacrifice of resources. In other words, every appraisal of the use of economic resources will involve a matching of effort or sacrifice with accomplishment or benefit. Furthermore, knowledge of effort and accomplishment is usually considered of far greater value than knowledge of the stock of resources or wealth. And so it is in accounting. The earnings statement is generally considered the most important financial statement.

The primacy of the earnings statement dates to the 1930s. Prior to that time, the granter of credit—such as a bank or a seller of goods—was the primary outsider for whom an enterprise prepared financial statements. These short-term creditors were interested in the liquidity of the company as shown by the statement of financial position. The increasing use of the corporate form of business organization, with its attendant separation of management from owners, caused the stockholder to become the dominant "outsider" for whom a corporation prepares its financial statements. And the frequently observed and often sharp fluctuations in the market prices of shares of stock because of changes in reported earnings leave room for little doubt that stockholders and potential stockholders are vitally interested in earnings.

In the application of the matching principle to determine periodic net earnings, revenue is the independently determined variable. It is determined through application of the realization principle, as is discussed and

[13] The Board refused to use the term "matching" in *Statement No. 4* because the term has, in the Board's opinion, too wide a variety of meanings. But the process of matching is implicit in the Board's discussion. For example, "Income determination in accounting is the process of identifying, measuring, and relating revenue and expenses of an enterprise for an accounting period" is one of the Board's "pervasive principles" (ibid., par. 147).

illustrated in depth in succeeding frames. Expenses, in a sense, are the dependent variable. They may be directly related to specific amounts of revenue—the cost of a specific unit of product sold—or they may be related to the entire revenue of a period, such as the salary of the sales manager. Attention will be directed first to the principles that guide the recognition of revenue.

Indicate whether each of the following statements is true or false.

1. Stockholders generally are more interested in the statement of financial position than in the earnings statement.
2. Emphasis on the earnings statement is related to the fact that it is generally more informative to know how economic resources were used than the quantity owned at any given moment in time.
3. The growth of the corporate form of business organization and its attendant separation of management and owners contributed to the increased significance attached to the earnings statement.
4. Stockholders are interested in earnings because there appears to be a rather direct relationship between earnings and stock prices.

Now turn to Answer Frame 10[14] on page 668 to check your responses.

Frame 11[14]

Revenue recognition

Revenue is defined as the product or the service provided by an enterprise. Revenue is best measured by the actual cash expected from the customer. The generation of revenue by most businesses consists of a never-ending stream of activity, with the result that the accountant faces the task of determining at what point in this stream revenue should be recognized—that is, credited to a revenue account. In general, he requires that revenue be earned and realized before it is recognized.

The earning of revenue. In a broad sense, all of the activity undertaken by an enterprise to create additional utility constitutes the earning process. The actual receipt of cash from a customer may have been preceded by many acts or events including (1) placing advertisements, (2) having salesmen call on the customer several times, (3) submission of samples, (4) acquisition of raw materials, (5) manufacture of the goods, and (6) delivery of the goods. Costs were undoubtedly incurred while these activities were being completed. And revenue was actually being generated by these activities, even though the accountant typically refuses to recognize it until the point of sale. His refusal is based upon his requirement that revenue be realized before it is recognized.[14]

The realization of revenue. As a general principle, revenue is considered to be realized at the point of sale for merchandise transactions and

[14] In *Statement No. 4* the Board combines the earning of revenue and the realization of revenue into a single pervasive principle called realization (ibid., par. 150).

Answer frame 10[14]

1. False. The relationship of stock prices and dividends to earnings is so generally strong that stockholders are much more interested in earnings and the earnings statement.
2. True. The earnings statement does report on how an entity used its economic resources, and knowledge of how resources were used is generally considered more valuable than knowledge of the stock of resources at a moment in time.
3. True. Stockholders need a report on the performance of management, especially as regards earnings, since they have no first-hand knowledge of corporate affairs in most of our large, modern corporations.
4. True. Stock prices seem to be heavily dependent on earnings.

If you answered incorrectly, review Frame 10[14] before continuing with Frame 11[14] on page 667.

11[14] *continued*

when services have been performed in service transactions. Legally, the point of sale is the exact moment in time at which title to the goods passes to the buyer. The question of when title passes can be an extremely complex legal problem in some instances. The accountant, not an expert in law, relies upon some general rules for an approximation of when title passes. He holds that a sale should be recorded when delivery is made. The time of delivery is determined by the terms under which goods are shipped. If the goods are shipped f.o.b. shipping point, title is assumed to pass when the goods are delivered to the common carrier (railroad or trucking company). If goods are shipped f.o.b. destination, title is assumed to pass when the goods reach their destination.

As a matter of actual practice, the accountant generally records revenue when goods are delivered with the intent of consummating a sale regardless of the terms under which they are shipped. Only at year-end does he consider these terms, if the goods have not been received by the customer, to determine whether the delivery of goods should have been recorded as a sale.

Unfortunately, realization has no precise meaning in accounting. Some hold that it embraces the receipt of cash or near-cash assets in an exchange. Others argue that the receipt of any asset in an exchange constitutes realization. And yet others hold that the earning process must be complete, or substantially so, before an act of exchange can constitute realization. But perhaps the majority view under which the bulk of business revenue is recognized today is that realization involves an exchange of goods (with actual delivery of the goods) for cash or near-cash assets with the intent of consummating a sale. It is a general, not a universal, rule—exceptions may exist.

The many advantages of recognizing revenue at point of sale include (1) the delivery of the goods is a discernible event; (2) the revenue is readily measurable; (3) the risk of loss due to price decline or destruction of the goods has passed to the buyer; (4) the revenue has been earned, or substantially so; and (5) because the earning process is complete, expenses can be determined as can net earnings. As discussed below, the major disadvantage of recognizing revenue at point of sale is that the revenue may not be assigned to the period in which the activity leading to its creation was undertaken.

Revenue recognized at completion of production. Conceivably, revenue could be recognized at other points or stages in what is, for most enterprises, an unending stream of activity. For example, revenue might be recognized upon completion of the production process but before a sale is made. This would require that the products manufactured, mined, or otherwise produced be recorded when completed at expected selling prices. This procedure is followed for certain precious metals, such as gold, and for many farm products, such as wheat, corn, and soybeans. The homogeneous nature of the products, the fact that they can usually be sold at their market prices, and the difficulty sometimes encountered in determining production costs are the reasons advanced to justify recognizing revenue prior to sale.

Recognizing revenue upon completion of production can be accomplished by debiting inventory and crediting a revenue account for the expected selling price of the goods produced. All of the costs incurred in the period can then be treated as expenses.

Indicate whether each of the following statements is true or false.

1. The realization of revenue generally means that a sale must have been made and cash received.
2. Virtually all of the activities undertaken by an entity are a part of the process of earning revenue.
3. A disadvantage of recognizing revenue at the point of sale is that the revenue may not be recognized in the period in which all of the activity to create it took place.
4. In limited circumstances characterized by homogeneous or interchangeable products and assured selling prices, revenue may be recognized prior to sale.

Now check your responses in Answer Frame 11[14] on page 670.

Frame 12[14]

Cash collection as point of revenue recognition. The collection of cash from customers is sometimes regarded as the point at which to recognize revenue. This may be appropriate for some service businesses, but only because the point of sale and the time of receiving cash happen to coincide. Some small businesses record revenues and expenses at the time of cash receipt and disbursement. This recognition procedure is known as the cash basis of accounting. It is acceptable primarily in circumstances which do not involve credit transactions or substantial inventories. When businesses extend credit to their customers, there is an uncontrollable

Answer frame 11[14]

1. False. Generally, a sale is required, but realization does not require that the asset received be cash.
2. True. In a sense, all of the activities, or nearly all, are undertaken with the objective of generating revenue.
3. True. Goods may undergo an extended manufacturing process in one period and be sold in the first few days of the second period, with the entire revenue from the sale recognized in the second period.
4. True. The statement describes the conditions that must be met.

If you answered incorrectly, review Frame 11[14] before continuing in Frame 12[14] on page 669.

12[14] *continued*

lag between the performance of the service, or sale of goods, and the collection of cash. This lag prevents the receipt of cash from being as useful a measure of revenue as the completion of the sale. Similarly, the recognition point for expenses should not be the time of cash payment for the goods unless such goods are immediately delivered to customers.

Installment basis of revenue recognition. In limited circumstances, when the selling price of goods is to be collected in installments and considerable doubt exists as to their collectibility, the installment basis of accounting may be employed. Under this basis, the gross margin on a sale is treated as being realized proportionately with the cash payments collected from customers. If the gross margin rate on installment sales is 40 percent, then 40 cents of every dollar collected on installment accounts receivable represents realized gross margin. For example, a stereo system costing $300 is sold for $500, with payment to be made in 10 equal installments of $50 each. If four installments are collected in the year of sale, the realized gross margin is $80 ($4 \times \$50 \times 0.40$); in the next year it will be $120 ($6 \times \$50 \times 0.40$), if the final six installments are collected.

The method is accepted for tax purposes and possesses the desirable feature of postponing tax payments until cash is collected from customers. Because it delays recognizing revenue beyond the point of sale, it has little theoretical justification for accounting purposes and is accepted in only those circumstances where extreme doubt exists regarding the collectibility of future installments.

Revenue recognition on long-term construction projects. The revenue created by completing a long-term construction project can be recognized under two methods: (1) the completed contract method or (2) the percentage of completion method. Under the completed contract method, no revenue is recognized until the period in which the contract is completed, and then all of the revenue is recognized even though the contract may have required three years to complete. The costs incurred on the project are carried forward as assets in inventory accounts and are charged to expense in the period in which the revenue is recognized. This approach is similar to the completed sale concept. It suffers from the disadvantage of assigning no revenue and no net earnings from the project to the periods in which a major part of the activity may have taken place.

Under the alternative, the percentage of completion method, revenue and net earnings are recognized on the basis of the estimated stage of completion of the project. To illustrate, a company has a contract to build a dam at a price of $44 million. By the end of the first fiscal year in which it worked on the dam, the company had incurred $30 million of costs and expected to incur $10 million more. Under the percentage-of-completion method, the contract would be considered 75 percent complete, since $30 million of an expected $40 million of costs have been incurred. Consequently, $33 million of revenue and $3 million of net earnings before taxes would be recognized in the fiscal year. The percentage of completion method of recognizing revenue is an example of applying the modifying convention of application of judgment of the accounting profession as a whole, with the objective of providing a clearer picture of the underlying economic activity.

Collections for revenue before it is earned. Occasionally, cash will be collected before goods are delivered or services rendered; in effect, future periods' revenues are collected. Such collections cannot be considered a part of the current period's revenue, since they have not been earned. Such amounts are actually liabilities and should be credited to an account whose title reveals their special nature, such as Unearned Subscriptions Revenue or Advances by Customers.

If costs have been incurred to secure this revenue which is applicable to future periods, these costs must be carried forward as assets if proper matching is to be secured. To illustrate, a magazine publisher, as of December 31, 1975, had received cash subscriptions of $200,000 applicable to magazines to be published and delivered in 1976. At the same date, the publisher also had incurred costs of $40,000 for artwork, paper stock, typesetting, and supplies for the magazines to be published in 1976. The receipt of the $200,000 of cash creates an obligation on the part of the publisher to deliver magazines in the future. Both the obligation of $200,000 and the costs of $40,000 must be carried into 1976, the year in which the magazines will be delivered. The statement of financial position for December 31, 1975, must show the costs incurred as an asset of $40,000 and the obligation as a current liability of $200,000, as follows:

Current Assets:		Current Liabilities:	
Supplies inventory and prepaid publishing costs (probably under two separate captions)......	$40,000	Subscriptions received in advance.............	$200,000

Indicate whether each of the following statements is true or false.

1. If the gross margin rate on an installment sale is 35 percent and $400 in installment payments is collected from customers, the realized gross margin is $140.
2. If $16 million of an expected total of $20 million of costs on a $24 million dollar contract are incurred in a given year, net earnings of $3.2 million before taxes are recognized in that year under the completed contract method.
3. There is little theoretical justification for the installment method of recognizing revenue, since there should be few instances in which an adequate allowance for uncollectible accounts cannot be established in order to value the receivables at net realizable value.
4. Under cash basis accounting, only transactions involving the flow of cash (in or out) are recorded.
5. For most business firms, the cash basis of recognizing revenue is quite unsatisfactory.

Now turn to Answer Frame 12[14] on page 674 to check your responses.

Frame 13[14]

Expense recognition

Expense is defined as the service potentials or economic resources consumed or sacrificed in generating revenues. Since service potentials or economic resources are assets, expense may be defined as an asset expiration voluntarily incurred in the generation of revenue. For example, the television set which a dealer delivers to a customer in exchange for cash can readily be conceived of as a sacrifice of resources or an asset expiration. Similarly, the services of the local television station employed in advertising a product can be thought of as expiring in the production of revenue. Losses can be distinguished as involuntary asset expirations not directly related to the production of revenue. Asset expirations resulting from theft or from destruction by fire or tornado are examples.

The measurement of expense. With expenses defined as asset expirations and assets typically measured (as discussed further below) in terms of exchange prices, it follows that expenses are typically measured in terms of exchange prices (historical costs). This is true even in instances where it may appear that a monetary asset is charged directly to expense as, for example, in an entry debiting Advertising Expense and crediting Cash. The actual transaction consists of the exchange of cash for advertising services. The accountant, anticipating that the services will have expired by the end of the accounting period, charges the expenditure to expense. By this shortcut he may avoid making an adjusting entry at the end of the fiscal period. But this is merely an expedient accounting technique. No one knowingly buys expenses, that is, expired assets.

The timing of expense recognition. Theoretically, if the matching principle is to be applied rather precisely, expenses will be recognized in the same period as the revenues they created. Since the recognition of revenue is guided at least in part by the realization principle, it follows that expense recognition is indirectly guided by the same principle.

The matching principle implies that a cause-and-effect relationship exists between expense and revenue, that is, that expense is the cause of revenue.[15] For certain expenses, the relationship is readily discernible, as in the case of specific goods delivered to or specific services rendered for a particular customer. When a direct cause-and-effect relationship cannot be discerned, the costs of assets with limited lives may be charged as expenses to the periods benefited on a systematic and rational allocation basis.[16] Examples are the depreciation of plant assets, the amortization of intangible assets, and the allocation of rent and insurance costs. In other instances, the relationship between expense and revenue can only be assumed to exist, as would be true for a contribution to the local community fund. Consequently, the recognition of expense, as a practical matter, is often guided by the concepts of product costs and period costs.

Product costs are those costs incurred directly and indirectly in the acquisition and manufacture of goods. Included are the invoice costs of the goods acquired as well as freight, insurance in transit, and other handling costs. For manufacturing concerns, product costs include all costs of raw materials as well as direct labor and the indirect costs of operating a factory to produce goods (this is discussed more fully in Chapters 2 and 3 of *Accounting II: A Programmed Text*). Such costs are deemed to attach to the products manufactured, are carried in inventory accounts as long as the goods are on hand, and are charged to expense when the goods are sold. This concept provides a rather precise matching of a major element of expense (cost of goods sold) and its related revenue (sales).

Period costs include virtually all of the selling and administrative expenses of a business. Under this concept, expenses are matched with revenues by periods rather than by transactions involving sales of product simply because of the impossibility of matching by transactions.[17] Thus, period costs are expensed in the period of incurrence largely because (1) they relate entirely to the current period's revenue—the local supermarket's weekly newspaper advertisement is an example; (2) the cost must be incurred every period and there is no measurable build-up of benefits—officers' salaries are an example here; (3) there is no measurable relationship with any particular segment of revenue, yet the cost must be incurred to remain in business—the cost of the annual audit is an example; and (4) the amount of the cost to be carried forward cannot be measured in a nonarbitrary manner—as might be true for research and development costs.

[15] In *Statement No. 4* the Board calls this the "pervasive principle of associating cause and effect" (ibid., par. 157).

[16] In *Statement No. 4* the Board calls this the "pervasive principle of systematic and rational allocation" (ibid., par. 159).

[17] In *Statement No. 4* the Board calls this the "pervasive principle of immediate recognition" (ibid., par. 160).

Answer frame 12[14]

1. True. The $140 is computed as $0.35 \times \$400$.
2. False. No net earnings are recognized under the completed contract method, since the project is not finished. Under the percentage of completion method, $3.2 million of net earnings before taxes would be recorded. The project is 16/20 completed; 16/20 of the $4 million of earnings expected on the contract is $3.2 million.
3. True. It is for exactly this reason that the installment method is considered acceptable in only the most limited circumstances.
4. False. The full meaning of cash basis accounting is that revenues and virtually all expenses (except depreciation) are recorded when cash flows in or out. Other transactions, such as the purchase of truck by the giving of a note, would be recorded.
5. True. If business is done on a credit basis and revenue is recorded only when cash is received, it may be recorded in the period after the sale was made, hence in the wrong period. And most business firms do operate on a credit basis.

If you answered incorrectly, study Frame 12[14] again before proceeding to Frame 13[14] on page 672.

13[14]
continued

But classification of a specific type of cost as a period cost does not mean that subsequent incurrences of the cost will automatically be charged to expense. Any cost usually treated as a period cost can be carried forward as an asset if a better matching of expense and revenue will result. For example, the costs of introducing a new product might be carried forward and expensed in the periods in which revenues from sales of the product are recognized.

Indicate whether each of the following statements is true or false.

1. Expenses are usually measured in terms of the historical cost of the assets that expired in the creation of revenue.
2. The cost of the cloth used in tailoring a man's suit is a product cost.
3. To call a cost a period cost generally means that it is treated as an expense of the period in which it was incurred.
4. Losses should be as carefully related to revenues as are product costs.

Turn to Answer Frame 13[14] on page 676 to check your responses.

Frame 14[14]

Principles underlying financial position

Although the matching and realization principles are generally viewed as guides to the determination of the nature and the measurement of items appearing in the earnings statement, these principles also directly affect the nature and measurement of many items appearing in the statement of financial position. In fact, it is no exaggeration to maintain that the statement of financial position consists largely of residuals of recorded amounts left over (not absorbed) in the determination of net earnings. Until this is thoroughly understood, little comprehension exists as to the usefulness and the significance of the statement of financial position.

Measuring and reporting assets

Assets are economic resources or bundles of service potential which have not expired and which have a positive value. The assets of an entity are those resources or service potentials accruing to it which it has the right to exclude others from using or receiving.

Assets may be classified as monetary and nonmonetary. Monetary assets include cash, accounts and notes receivable, and other claims to cash. They have a general service potential, since they either consist of cash or will normally be converted directly into cash which can be used for a variety of purposes. Nonmonetary assets, which include all other assets, are said to have specific service potential, since each yields a specific service in the production of revenue.

Asset measurement. Basically, assets are initially recorded at the price agreed upon in the exchange in which they are acquired.[18] The recording of assets at this price is usually justified on objectivity grounds. But it should be noted that the price paid is probably equal to the market value of the asset at acquisition, and that there is no evidence that the acquiring entity considers the asset to be worth more or that it would be willing to pay more for it.

The exchange price paid for an asset can be and often is called its historical cost in the case of nonmonetary and certain monetary assets. Thus buildings, equipment, long-term stock investments, and short-term bond investments are said to have a cost equal to the price paid for them. But it seems inappropriate to state that accounts and notes receivable are acquired at a cost or that they are carried and reported at cost. When due consideraion is given to possible accrued interest and uncollectibility, they are reported at their net realizable value although initially recorded at exchange price.

If an individual asset is acquired for cash, its cost usually can be determined rather accurately. But when several assets are acquired in one transaction or when payment is made with noncash assets, a cost—in the sense of a price paid—can only be assigned to an asset on a more or less arbitrary basis.

[18] In *Statement No. 4* the Board calls this the "pervasive principle of initial recording of assets and liabilities" (ibid., par. 145).

Answer frame 13[14]

1. True. This is clearly observable in the case of long-term depreciable or amortizable assets. It is less obvious, but nonetheless true, in the case of asset expirations that for practical reasons are recorded as expenses upon their payment in cash.
2. True. Since the cost of the cloth is directly traceable to and identified with the product being manufactured, it is considered a product cost.
3. True. This is the general disposition of period costs.
4. False. Because a cause-and-effect relationship is not deemed to exist between losses and revenues, there is no need to match or relate the two. Losses are generally recognized in the period in which it becomes rather evident that they exist.

If you answered incorrectly, study Frame 13[14] again before proceeding to Frame 14[14] on page 674.

14[14]
continued

Indicate whether each of the following statements is true or false.

1. In order for an item to be considered an asset of an entity, the entity must possess the right to exclude others from sharing in the benefits expected.
2. Although assets are often said to be measured in terms of their historical cost, it would be more accurate to state that they are measured in terms of the exchange price at which they were acquired.
3. Exchange price is usually justified as the basis for initial recording of assets on the ground that it equals the asset's value.
4. Monetary assets are assets already in cash form or are claims to cash.

Now check your responses in Answer Frame 14[14] on page 678.

Frame 15[14]

Assets as deferred costs. Assets are often viewed as deferred costs—costs awaiting assignment to periods or matching against revenues. It would be far more accurate to hold that service potential exists and that this service potential is measured in terms of cost. These service potentials will either be utilized or transformed in the future production of revenue or be lost. As these events occur the asset, as measured by cost, is reduced. The amount of the reduction is charged as an expense of the revenue generated or is treated as a loss, depending on whether the services were used or expired unused.

In other instances an item is carried forward, at cost, as an asset, even though it has no market value in and of itself. The heavy costs often incurred by a company in promoting a new product are an example. These costs may be carried forward as an asset to be expensed when revenues are recognized from the new product. But note carefully that the real value to the company lies not in these costs but in the fact that consumers have been conditioned and are ready to buy the new product when it becomes available. The company has benefited, but the benefits often cannot be measured and have not been realized. Proper matching requires that since the benefits have not been recognized, the expenses (costs) incurred should be carried forward as assets—deferred costs. Such costs are, however, often expensed as incurred in practice because of the influence of income tax regulations and for reasons already given for the period cost classification. But if not expensed as incurred, note how the statement of financial position serves as the vehicle to carry these costs forward to future periods.

Certain assets never lose their service potential. Land, for example, is usually not consumed through use. For assets of this type, the entire original cost (exchange price) may be retained in the asset account and never be transferred to expense or loss.

Occasionally, an asset will be measured partially at cost and partially at net realizable value, as inventory may be when priced at cost or market, whichever is lower.

Assets acquired without cost. An important exception to the use of an actual exchange price at the date of acquisition as a basis of measurement is encountered when gifts are received by an entity. Strict adherence to the actual exchange price (cost) basis of measurement would dictate that the asset received not be assigned a dollar amount, since there was no exchange price (or actual cost). But it is common practice to record the asset at its fair market value at the time of receipt and to refer to this fair market value as cost. The following entry generally is made:

Asset (Land, Equipment, etc.)	xxxx	
Paid-in Capital—Donations		xxxx

If a depreciable or amortizable asset is received, the subsequent periodic charges for depreciation or amortization are based on this amount.

Indicate whether each of the following statements is true or false.

1. Assets and economic resources are synonymous concepts.
2. The service potential inherent in some assets may never expire.
3. Assets that do not have a cost are usually recorded at fair market value, and a corresponding increase in paid-in capital is recorded.
4. All things reported as assets have value to persons or entities other than the one that owns them.

Now check your responses in Answer Frame 15[14] on page 678.

Frame 16[14]

Measuring and reporting liabilities and stockholders' equity

The statement of financial position is frequently looked upon as actually revealing the financial strength of a company, since assets are listed

Answer frame 14[14]

1. True. This is the reason why the air we breathe is not considered an asset in determining the wealth of an individual.
2. True. All assets can be said to be recorded at exchange prices; but accounts receivable and cash can hardly be recorded at cost.
3. False. Although the price paid for an asset can be argued to be equal to the asset's market value, exchange price is usually justified on verifiability or objectivity grounds. But it could be argued that a purchaser would not pay more than the objective worth or value of an asset and that there is no evidence that the purchaser considered the asset to be worth more than its market price.
4. True. This is the standard definition of monetary assets.

If you answered incorrectly, return to Frame 14[14] for further study before going on to Frame 15[14] on page 676.

Answer frame 15[14]

1. False. While there is some relationship between the two, assets may actually be a broader category, since it includes items such as organization costs, discount on bonds payable, and deferred promotion costs that would have little, if any, exchange value.
2. True. This is likely to be the case for land.
3. True. If the assets reported are to be representative of the assets owned, then all assets owned, regardless of whether an exchange price was paid for them, should be reported.
4. False. Examples of items reported as assets that have no exchange value to other persons or entities are given in the first answer above.

If you answered incorrectly, restudy Frame 15[14] before proceeding to Frame 16[14] on page 677.

16[14]
continued

on the left side and the claims against the entity (often referred to broadly as equities) are listed on the right side. But, in light of the above discussion of asset measurement, and since many of the things which give a company financial strength cannot be measured and included in the company's assets, the notion that a statement of financial position shows financial strength is not entirely realistic.

Although it is true that certain monetary assets are reported at their cash equivalent value and that many of the liabilities are reported at the amount of cash required to pay them currently, the statement of financial position is virtually a summary of the sources and uses of capital or funds. The asset section shows the current composition of the capital invested in the business, measured largely in terms of original acquisition prices. The equity section shows the sources of capital, subdivided into liabilities and stockholders' equity, but similarly measured.

Liabilities. Liabilities are existing obligations, arising from past transactions or events, to pay sums of money or to deliver certain goods or to render certain services. Liabilities usually have determinable maturity dates or the expectation that payment will be required within some future period of time. Current liabilities usually result from the normal operations of a business, such as the purchase of goods; the accrual of salaries, wages, and taxes; and borrowings from banks for working capital purposes. In addition, the acquisition of large amounts of long-term assets (buildings, land, equipment) may be financed through the issuance of bonds.

Measuring liabilities. Current liabilities are usually reported at the amount of cash required to pay them—their recorded amounts, plus, in some instances, accrued interest payable. Current liabilities arising from advance payments for goods or services are usually reported at the agreed-upon exchange prices of the goods or services. In some instances, the items reported are a function of the determination of net earnings. For example, a company may enter into a contract whereby it agrees to purchase 100,000 pounds of a given material at $5 per pound. Current practice sanctions the recognition of a loss and the accrual of a liability of $25,000 if at year-end, before any of the material is purchased, the market price of the material falls to $4.75 per pound. The justification for accruing $25,000 as a liability lies in the desire to recognize a loss and not in any assertion that the $25,000 is a measure of the actual liability that exists.

Long-term interest-bearing obligations (bonds and notes) are usually reported at their contractual amounts plus or minus premium or discount, which approximates their present value using the effective rate of interest at date of issue. But here again earnings determination influences what is reported as a long-term liability and its measurement. For example, the amount shown as pension liability is more apt to be determined by what is considered a proper accrual of expense than by what is believed to be the best measure of the long-term liability to employees. Similarly, as is discussed in Chapter 12 in *Accounting II: A Programmed Text,* the reporting of "Deferred Income Taxes Payable" as a liability is more a matter of wishing to reflect a certain amount of income tax expense in the earnings statement than to reflect a liability.

Stockholders' equity. In a corporation the interest of the owners is called stockholders' equity, which is measured by the excess of assets over liabilities. Because of this manner of measurement, the accuracy of the amounts reported as stockholders' equity are directly dependent upon the accurate ascertainment and measurement of both assets and liabilities. But unlike liabilities, stockholders' equity accounts or items normally have no determinable maturity date in a going concern. A primary objective sought in the accounting for stockholders' equity is a clear line of distinction between contributed, paid-in, or invested capital and earned capital (retained earnings). This line of distinction is sometimes blurred by the capitalization of retained earnings that accompanies a stock dividend.

Measuring stockholders' equity. The contributed capital portion of stockholders' equity is usually measured initially at the exchange price agreed upon when shares of stock are issued for assets, usually cash. The amounts received may be credited to several accounts reflecting the par value of shares issued and any paid-in capital in excess of par value (or stated value). Subsequent capital changes, such as stock splits, recapitalizations, and conversions of preferred shares, are usually measured in terms of these initially recorded exchange prices. Exchange prices actually experienced also are used to measure increases or decreases in contributed capital resulting from transactions in treasury shares.

Through the mechanics of double-entry accounting, the concepts that govern the ascertainment and measurement of assets and liabilities and the related ascertainment and measurement of revenues and expenses are automatically reflected in the ascertainment and measurement of earned capital (retained earnings). This may be illustrated as follows:

	Assets	–	Liabilities	=	Stockholders' Equity	
Beginning balances......	$200		$20		$180	
Revenues..............	300				300	Reflected in earnings
Expenses...............	(240)		10		(250)	statement for the year
Ending balances........	$260		$30		$230	
Changes during year.....	$ 60	–	$10	=	$ 50	

This example is based on the assumption that there were no capital contributions or withdrawals during the year. It shows clearly how, under double-entry accounting, the measurements of assets, liabilities, revenues, expenses, net earnings, and changes in the retained earnings are interrelated. An identical pattern will be found in every business entity; only the amounts will differ.

The above example should also help make clear the fact that if the realization and matching principles control the recording of revenues and expenses, they also control a substantial number of the items recorded as assets and liabilities. It follows automatically that these principles play a major role in determining the dollar amounts to be reported as earned capital (retained earnings).

In the preceding frames attention has been centered primarily upon the pervasive principles that guide or shape much of accounting practice. These include the principles of initial recording, matching, realization, and expense recognition. Underlying these pervasive principles are the broad operating principles of the APB, which consist of a group of selection and measurement principles that relate to the recording of exchanges at exchange prices and which yield increases or decreases in assets, liabilities, revenues, and expenses.[19] Similar broad principles control the selection and measurement of transfers between an entity and its owners; transfers such as gifts, donations, lawsuit losses, fines, and thefts; events favorable and unfavorable to an entity (changes in market values of assets owned); and internal events (production of goods). These broad operating principles also relate to the basic financial statements that are to be presented: the requirement that complete statements of financial position

[19] Ibid., par. 181–201.

and earnings statements be presented, the basic time period covered, classification and segregation of items reported (such as working capital and extraordinary items), adequate disclosure, and earnings per share.

These broad operating principles are not dealt with in depth here simply because most of them are discussed in other chapters. For the same reason what the Board calls detailed accounting principles (first-in, first-out inventory pricing and straight-line depreciation methods)—the means of implementing the pervasive and broad operating principles—will not be discussed here.[20] These are presented throughout this text. One of the purposes of this chapter is to put these more detailed principles into perspective in a more structured model of the theory presently underlying financial accounting. For examples of the financial information that emerges from application of these principles, see the appendix to this chapter.

Indicate whether each of the following statements is true or false.

1. The statement of financial position can be called a report of financial position only in the sense of conformity with generally accepted accounting principles and not in the sense of showing the worth or value of an entity.
2. The reporting of many assets at historical cost is dictated by the principle that requires the initial recording of assets at exchange prices and the realization principle that bars recognition of increases in the value of assets until they are sold.
3. In general, for an item to be recorded as an accounting liability it must arise from a past transaction or event.
4. The statement of financial position can also be looked upon as a statement that shows the present sources of capital and how this capital is invested in a wide variety of assets.
5. All of the amounts reported as accounting liabilities are amounts the entity is legally obligated to pay.

Now check your responses in Answer Frame 16[14] on page 682.

Summary *chapter* 14

Throughout much of its recent history financial accounting theory has consisted of, and financial accounting practice has been guided by, a group of important notions that collectively have been called generally accepted

[20] No list of detailed principles is included in *Statement No. 4*. Rather, the Board draws attention to the absence of such an authoritative list and then notes the possible sources of such detailed principles—the *Opinions* of the APB, the *Accounting Research Bulletins*, textbooks, and so on (ibid., par. 202–206).

Answer frame 16[14]

1. True. This point should be clearly obvious and totally understood by this time.
2. True. If this point is fully understood, then real understanding of the current practice of accounting exists.
3. True. In general, the entity must have done something in the past for it to be liable in the present. The concept of an event is broad enough to include the failure to do something as an event which may lead to the imposition of a liability.
4. True. Many who recognize the inadequacies of the statement in showing actual financial position substitute this view.
5. False. An example of an accounting liability that is not a legal liability is the accrued loss on purchase commitments discussed in this frame.

If you answered incorrectly, you would do well to review Frame 16[14] before going on to the chapter summary on page 681.

---

accounting principles. These principles have been relied on in fulfilling the general objectives of financial accounting of providing reliable information about economic resources and obligations and changes therein. When information is presented in accordance with these principles, it contains a degree of inter-entity comparability and reliability.

The development of accounting principles has been subjected to many influences, including federal income tax laws and regulations; securities legislation; organizations such as the AICPA, SEC, and AAA; individual writers, and the traditional practices within industries. The AICPA has been especially influential through publications such as the *Accounting Research Bulletins,* the Accounting Principles Board *Opinions,* the *Accounting Research Studies,* and the *Statements of the Accounting Principles Board*. The Financial Accounting Standards Board replaced the APB in mid-1973 as the authoritative voice of the profession on accounting standards.

In its *Statement No. 4,* the APB erected a structure of accounting theory consisting of (1) objectives, (2) basic features, (3) basic elements, (4) pervasive principles, (5) modifying conventions, (6) broad operating principles, and (7) detailed accounting principles. The seven qualitative objectives of financial accounting information are relevance, understandability, verifiability, neutrality, timeliness, comparability, and completeness. Although not included by the Board, financial accounting information should possess the objective of correspondence—that is, agreement with economic reality. The basic features of financial accounting are (1) accounting entity, (2) going concern, (3) measurement of economic resources and obligations, (4) time periods, (5) measurement in money terms, (6) accrual basis, (7) exchange prices, (8) approximation, (9) judgment, (10) general-purpose financial information, (11) fundamentally related financial statements, (12) substance over form, and (13) materiality. Modifying conventions in the application of accounting principles are conservatism, emphasis upon earnings determination, and application of judgment of the accounting profession as a whole.

Among the most fundamental of accounting principles are (1) the initial recording of exchange prices, (2) the matching of expenses and revenues, and (3) the realization and earning of revenue. Revenue may be recognized upon completion of a sale, at completion of production, at time of cash collection, or on an installment basis. Expense recognition is guided by the matching and realization principles and by the concepts of product and period costs.

To a very large extent, the principles of initial recording of exchange prices, matching, and realization determine the contents of the statement of financial position.

You have completed the programmed portion of the chapter. The glossary for this chapter begins on page 693, following the appendix. Study the new terms introduced in this chapter, and then go on to the Student Review Quiz for a self-administered test of your comprehension of the chapter material (see page 694).

Frame 17[14] Appendix

Presented in this appendix are portions of the Annual Report for 1972 of Interlake, Inc. and its consolidated subsidiaries. Included are the: (1) consolidated balance sheet, (2) statement of consolidated income and retained earnings, (3) statement of changes in consolidated financial position, (4) notes to consolidated financial statements, (5) auditors' opinion, and (6) ten-year financial summary of operations. These items are presented as being illustrative of the financial reporting typically made by a modern business corporation to its stockholders and to other external parties. Several explanatory comments on the statements are needed.

1. Your authors prefer the terminology of earnings statement and net earnings in the statement reporting on operations and the term statement of financial position to balance sheet, although the terminology employed by the company is fully acceptable and, indeed, more widely used.

2. The deferred federal income tax in Note 7 is explained and discussed in Chapter 12 of *Accounting II: A Programmed Text.*

3. The financial statements are for Interlake, Inc., a number of other corporations wholly owned by the company, and another corporation 80 percent owned by Interlake (see Note 1). The item "Minority interest in subsidiary" in the Consolidated Balance Sheet represents the stockholders' equity of the owners of the other 20 percent of the shares in the subsidiary company.

4. Particular attention should be paid to the rather substantial amounts of additional information presented in the Notes to the Consolidated Financial Statements.

Illustration 14.1, Consolidated Balance Sheet

INTERLAKE, INC.

CONSOLIDATED BALANCE SHEET

December 31, 1972 and 1971

(See notes to consolidated financial statements)

ASSETS	1972	1971
CURRENT ASSETS:		
Cash and certificates of deposit	$ 3,536,775	$ 1,588,325
Marketable securities, at cost, which approximates market	5,358,832	5,199,456
Receivables, less allowance for doubtful accounts of $706,000 in 1972 and $664,000 in 1971	52,353,834	42,247,078
Inventories (Note 1):		
Raw materials and supplies	34,041,663	38,647,101
Semi-finished and finished products	48,049,448	46,143,169
Other current assets	6,333,966	5,908,497
Total current assets	149,674,518	139,733,626
INVESTMENTS AND OTHER ASSETS:		
Affiliated and associated companies (Note 1)	5,910,386	8,554,231
Iron ore interests (Notes 1 and 8)	21,367,454	21,371,887
Other investments and deferred charges	8,659,055	7,513,554
	35,936,895	37,439,672
PROPERTY, PLANT AND EQUIPMENT, at cost (Note 1):		
Land and mineral properties, less depletion	11,891,062	11,863,318
Plant and equipment	370,389,099	364,250,696
	382,280,161	376,114,014
Less—Depreciation and amortization	228,582,724	216,810,085
	153,697,437	159,303,929
GOODWILL (Note 1)	12,608,340	12,507,840
	$351,917,190	$348,985,067

Illustration 14.1 (*continued*)

LIABILITIES AND SHAREHOLDERS' EQUITY	1972	1971
CURRENT LIABILITIES:		
Accounts payable	$ 33,230,469	$ 30,362,532
Salaries and wages	10,538,457	9,250,522
Taxes other than income taxes	5,709,307	4,987,909
U. S. and foreign income taxes (Note 7)	8,524,190	6,827,821
Current maturities of long-term debt (Note 2)	1,631,658	1,466,132
Total current liabilities	59,634,081	52,894,916
LONG-TERM DEBT (Note 2)	62,923,343	68,114,702
OTHER LONG-TERM LIABILITIES	4,895,643	4,305,842
FUTURE INCOME TAXES (Note 1)	15,815,826	16,882,900
MINORITY INTEREST IN SUBSIDIARY	352,881	615,786
SHAREHOLDERS' EQUITY:		
Serial preferred stock, par value $1 a share; authorized 1,000,000 shares; none issued		
Common stock, par value $1 a share; authorized 10,000,000 shares; issued 4,257,128 shares (Note 4)	98,433,467	98,433,931
Retained earnings (Notes 1, 3 and 4)	120,180,122	114,365,688
	218,613,589	212,799,619
Less—Cost of common stock held in treasury (377,142 shares in 1972 and 245,979 shares in 1971) (Notes 4 and 5)	10,318,173	6,628,698
	208,295,416	206,170,921
	$351,917,190	$348,985,067

Illustration 14.2, *Statement of Consolidated Income and Retained Earnings*

INTERLAKE, INC. STATEMENT OF

CONSOLIDATED INCOME AND RETAINED EARNINGS

For the years ended December 31, 1972 and 1971

(See notes to consolidated financial statements)

	1972	1971
SALES AND REVENUES:		
Net sales	$387,748,883	$352,084,935
Other revenues	1,544,268	1,303,738
	389,293,151	353,388,673
COSTS AND EXPENSES:		
Cost of products sold	296,353,361	267,760,240
Depreciation, depletion and amortization (Note 1)	15,362,342	14,211,900
Selling and administrative expenses	38,050,838	35,678,862
State, local and miscellaneous taxes	11,659,622	10,173,558
Interest expense	5,496,908	4,720,992
	366,923,071	332,545,552
INCOME BEFORE TAXES ON INCOME	22,370,080	20,843,121
PROVISION FOR INCOME TAXES (Note 7)	9,398,000	8,319,000
NET INCOME FOR THE YEAR	12,972,080	12,524,121
RETAINED EARNINGS at beginning of the year	114,365,688	108,236,898
ADD—		
Adjustment applicable to prior years to reflect the change in accounting for investments (Note 1)	—	2,164,009
	127,337,768	122,925,028
DEDUCT—		
Cash dividends paid, $1.80 per share	7,157,646	7,399,860
Common stock retired (Note 4)	—	1,159,480
RETAINED EARNINGS at end of the year	$120,180,122	$114,365,688
NET INCOME PER SHARE OF COMMON STOCK	$3.26	$3.03

Illustration 14.3, *Statement of Changes in Consolidated Financial Position*

INTERLAKE, INC. STATEMENT OF

CHANGES IN CONSOLIDATED FINANCIAL POSITION

For the years ended December 31, 1972 and 1971

(See notes to consolidated financial statements)

	1972	1971
FINANCIAL RESOURCES WERE PROVIDED BY:		
Net income	$12,972,080	$12,524,121
Depreciation, depletion and amortization	15,362,342	14,211,900
Future income taxes	(1,067,074)	(1,093,150)
Working capital provided from operations	27,267,348	25,642,871
Long-term borrowings	312,200	54,589,500
Increase in other long-term liabilities	589,801	1,088,164
Reduction of subsidiary investment cost	—	1,614,165
Other	156,998	—
	28,326,347	82,934,700
FINANCIAL RESOURCES WERE USED FOR:		
Capital expenditures less net book value of retirements and sales of $1,071,402 in 1972 and $557,717 in 1971	8,747,065	11,588,711
Reduction of long-term debt	5,503,559	36,155,931
Cash dividends	7,157,646	7,399,860
Purchase of Company common stock	3,716,350	10,474,802
Investments and advances	—	4,608,183
Unexpended construction funds of long-term lease obligations	—	1,399,844
Other	—	1,745,415
	25,124,620	73,372,746
Increase in working capital	$ 3,201,727	$ 9,561,954
INCREASE IN WORKING CAPITAL COMPRISES:		
Cash and marketable securities	$ 2,107,826	$ 1,049,874
Receivables	10,106,756	(734,446)
Inventories	(2,699,159)	1,865,381
Other current assets	425,469	939,129
Notes payable	—	3,799,947
Accounts payable and salaries and wages	(4,155,872)	(2,660,152)
Taxes payable	(2,417,767)	(3,160,307)
Current maturities of long-term debt	(165,526)	8,462,528
	3,201,727	9,561,954
Working capital at beginning of year	86,838,710	77,276,756
Working capital at end of year	$90,040,437	$86,838,710

INTERLAKE, INC.

NOTES TO CONSOLIDATED FINANCIAL STATEMENTS

For the years ended December 31, 1972 and 1971

NOTE 1—SUMMARY OF SIGNIFICANT ACCOUNTING POLICIES:

The consolidated financial statements include the Company, all wholly owned subsidiaries, and the Hoeganaes Corporation which is eighty percent owned. Foreign subsidiaries, located principally in Canada, represent approximately 5% of consolidated net assets. The accounts of foreign subsidiaries are expressed in U.S. dollars at appropriate rates of exchange. No provision for U.S. income taxes on unremitted earnings of foreign subsidiaries has been made as it is anticipated that any U.S. taxes on dividend distributions will be offset by foreign tax credits.

Effective January 1, 1971 the Company adopted the equity method of accounting for its investments in corporate joint ventures and companies owned twenty percent or more. The carrying value of the applicable investments, intangible assets, and consolidated retained earnings were adjusted in 1971 to record the Company's equity in the undistributed net income of such companies from their respective dates of acquisition through December 31, 1970.

Inventories are stated at the lower of cost, determined principally by the last-in first-out method, or market value.

Plant and equipment are depreciated principally on a straight-line method over the estimated useful lives of the assets. Costs of significant renewals and betterments, including furnace relines, are capitalized. Depreciation claimed for income tax purposes is computed by use of accelerated methods. Income taxes applicable to the additional depreciation claimed for tax purposes have been credited to future income taxes. Provision for depletion of mineral properties is based on tonnage rates which are expected to amortize the cost of these properties over the estimated amount of mineral deposits to be removed.

Goodwill, representing the difference between purchase price and the Company's equity in the underlying net assets of companies acquired as at the date of acquisition, is not being amortized.

The full amount of investment tax credits claimed for tax purposes is taken into income in the year the related property is placed in service.

The Company has several pension plans which cover substantially all employees. These plans generally follow the basic pension pattern of the steel industry. The provision for pension cost includes current costs plus interest on and amortization of unfunded prior service cost over a period of approximately 25 years (see Note 6). The Company's policy is to fund pension cost accrued.

NOTE 2—LONG-TERM DEBT:

Long-term debt of the Company consists of the following:

	December 31, 1972	1971
8.80% debentures, due annually $2,500,000 1978 to 1995, and $5,000,000 in 1996	$50,000,000	$50,000,000
4⅞% debentures, due annually $1,500,000 1973 to 1976, and $2,495,000 in 1977	5,223,000	8,470,000
Obligations under long-term lease agreements	5,200,000	5,200,000
5⅛% insurance company loan, due $700,000 in 1973 and $900,000 in 1974	1,600,000	2,300,000
5% debentures, due annually $375,000 1973 to 1977	1,239,000	2,250,000
Other	1,293,001	1,360,834
	64,555,001	69,580,834
Less—Current maturities	1,631,658	1,466,132
	$62,923,343	$68,114,702

At December 31, 1972, 4⅞% debentures with a face value of $3,272,000 were held in the treasury by the Company. Of these, $1,500,000 may be used to meet the 1973 sinking fund requirement and have been applied as a reduction of current maturities of long-term debt. The balance may be used to meet future sinking fund requirements and has been applied as a reduction of long-term debt. Further, 5% debentures with a face value of $636,000 were held in the treasury by the Company. These debentures will be subject to call for retirement on January 1, 1974, or later and have been applied as a reduction of long-term debt.

The long-term lease obligations relate to pollution control facilities which have been accounted for as purchased plant and equipment. The interest rates on these obligations vary from 6.00% to 6.75%. Principal payments begin in 1981 ($500,000) and continue in varying annual amounts through 1996.

Illustration 14.4 (*continued*)

NOTE 3—RETAINED EARNINGS:
Under the most restrictive terms of the various loan agreements, the Company may not as of December 31, 1972 pay cash dividends and repurchase the Company's capital stock in amounts aggregating more than $21,749,856.

NOTE 4—PURCHASES OF COMMON STOCK:
During 1972 the Company purchased 132,000 shares of its common stock for a total cash consideration of $3,716,350. These shares are being held in the treasury.

In 1971 the Company purchased and retired 402,877 shares of its common stock for $26 per share. The common stock account of the Company was reduced $9,315,322, which represented the proportionate part of said account allocable to the shares purchased. The remaining portion of the purchase price, $1,159,480, was charged to retained earnings.

NOTE 5—STOCK OPTIONS AND TREASURY STOCK:
In 1965 the shareholders approved a Qualified Stock Option Plan for the Company's officers and key employees. Under the plan, options may be granted to purchase common stock until December 31, 1974 for periods not longer than five years. Options are exercisable 33⅓% annually, on a cumulative basis, beginning one year from date of grant. The options outstanding expire at varying dates until 1977.

Changes in the number of shares of common stock under option during the two years ended December 31, 1972 were as follows:

	1972	1971
Options outstanding at beginning of the year	99,800	73,450
Options granted		
Per share—$28.13 in 1972 and $27.16 in 1971	21,000	33,900
Options exercised		
Per share—$23.13	(100)	—
Options cancelled	(11,218)	(7,550)
Options outstanding at end of year	109,482	99,800
Per share	($23.13–$30.57)	($23.13–$31.38)
Options exercisable at end of year	55,703	36,342

At December 31, 1972, 149,900 treasury shares of common stock were reserved for stock options, 2,018 for distribution under a deferred compensation plan, and 225,224 were unreserved. During 1972 and 1971, respectively, 737 and 1,601 treasury shares were distributed under the deferred compensation plan.

NOTE 6—PENSION PLANS:
Pension costs were $9,074,045 in 1972 and $7,486,776 in 1971. The actuarially computed value of vested benefits per the latest actuarial reports exceeded the market value of the pension fund assets by approximately $36,000,000 and $9,000,000 as of December 31, 1972 and 1971, respectively.

The 1972 pension costs and unfunded vested benefits reflect (1) pension plan changes effective August 1, 1972, which resulted in increased pension plan benefits and reduction of the employment period required for vesting and (2) revisions in actuarial assumptions and a change in the amortization period of unfunded prior service costs from 40 to 25 years. The changes in actuarial assumptions and amortization period of unfunded prior service costs increased pension costs approximately $200,000 in 1972.

NOTE 7—INCOME TAXES:
The provision for income taxes consists of:

	1972	1971
U.S. Federal:		
Currently payable (less investment credits of $550,000 in 1972 and $767,000 in 1971)	$7,974,000	$7,530,000
Deferred	(781,000)	(1,322,000)
State and foreign	2,205,000	2,111,000
	$9,398,000	$8,319,000

The consolidated tax provision results in an effective tax rate lower than prevailing rates due principally to investment tax credits and percentage depletion allowances.

As of December 31, 1972, federal income tax returns for the years 1965 through 1969 were being examined by the Internal Revenue Service, and a number of adjustments have been proposed. One of the proposed adjustments involves the determination of the cost of ore from one of the Company's iron ore interests and could result in certain of these costs being disallowed as a current tax deduction. The Company believes that its position on this issue has merit and should not result in any significant adjustment. In the opinion of management, adequate provision has been made for possible tax assessments resulting from these examinations.

NOTE 8—COMMITMENTS:
With respect to the Company's interest in two mining joint ventures, the Company is required to take its ownership proportion of production for which it is committed to pay its proportionate share of the operating costs of these projects, either directly or as a part of the product price. Such costs include, as a minimum and regardless of the quantity of ore received, annual interest and sinking fund requirements of the funded debt of these projects of approximately $3,500,000 through 1983, and lesser amounts thereafter through 1991.

NOTE 9—RECLASSIFICATIONS:
Certain amounts in the 1971 financial statements have been reclassified to conform to the current classifications.

Illustration 14.5, *The Auditor's Opinion*

Price Waterhouse & Co.

To the Board of Directors and Shareholders of Interlake, Inc.

In our opinion, the accompanying consolidated balance sheets and the related statements of consolidated income and retained earnings and the statements of changes in consolidated financial position present fairly the financial position of Interlake, Inc. and its subsidiaries at December 31, 1972 and 1971, the results of their operations and changes in financial position for the years then ended, in conformity with generally accepted accounting principles consistently applied. Our examinations of these statements were made in accordance with generally accepted auditing standards and accordingly included such tests of the accounting records and such other auditing procedures as we considered necessary in the circumstances.

Price Waterhouse & Co.

Chicago, Illinois
January 31, 1973

Illustration 14.6, *Ten-Year Financial Summary of Operations*

INTERLAKE, INC.

TEN YEAR FINANCIAL SUMMARY OF OPERATIONS

(Amounts in thousands—except per share statistics)

FOR THE YEAR		**1972**	**1971**	**1970**	**1969**	**1968**
Net Sales		$387,749	$352,085	$329,954	$324,848	$285,571
Income Before Extraordinary Items		12,972	12,524	10,666	15,337	12,556
Extraordinary Items (less applicable income tax)		—	—	—	5,052	—
Net Income	**Amount**	12,972	12,524	10,666	20,389	12,556
	% of Net Sales	3.3%	3.6%	3.2%	6.3%	4.4%
	% of Shareholders' Equity	6.2%	6.1%	5.1%	9.9%	6.4%
Income Per Common Share	**Before Extraordinary Items**	3.26	3.03	2.42	3.43	2.80
	Extraordinary Items	—	—	—	1.13	—
	Net Income	3.26	3.03	2.42	4.56	2.80
Cash Flow		27,267	25,643	23,374	29,144	24,199
Dividends Paid	**Common**	7,158	7,400	7,941	8,046	8,078
	Preferred	—	—	—	—	—
	% of Income Before Extraordinary Items	55.2%	59.1%	74.4%	52.5%	64.3%
Capital Expenditures		9,818	12,146	15,187	18,423	13,752
Depreciation		15,362	14,212	13,615	13,042	12,273
Interest Expense		5,497	4,721	3,611	3,593	2,465
Taxes on Income Before Extraordinary Items	**Amount**	9,398	8,319	6,917	13,530	10,013
	% of Pre-Tax Income	42.0%	39.9%	39.3%	46.9%	44.4%
AT YEAR END						
Working Capital	**Amount**	$ 90,040	$ 86,839	$ 77,277	$ 71,846	$ 74,365
	Current Ratio	2.5 to 1	2.6 to 1	2.3 to 1	2.2 to 1	2.7 to 1
Property (Net)		153,697	159,304	161,305	159,593	153,965
Long-Term Debt, less current maturities		62,923	68,115	49,071	40,987	53,047
Future Income Taxes		15,816	16,883	17,765	18,633	18,618
Preferred Stock		—	—	—	—	—
Common Shareholders' Equity	**Amount**	208,295	206,171	209,299	206,514	196,122
	Outstanding Shares—thousands	3,880	4,011	4,412	4,411	4,489
	Per Share	53.68	51.40	47.44	46.82	43.69
Common Stock Price Range		32⅛–26⅛	30⅜–24¼	30–21¾	40⅜–25	37¾–28⅛
Price Earnings Ratio (before extraordinary items)		8.82	9.24	10.07	7.43	13.30
Number of Shareholders		25,036	25,919	26,917	26,966	27,952
Number of Employees		9,440	9,224	9,616	9,718	9,229

Illustration 14.6 (*continued*)

1967	1966	1965	1964	1963
$256,411	$268,804	$262,363	$259,580	$234,413
14,133	16,481	13,861	13,147	12,079
—	—	—	(3,714)	—
14,133	16,481	13,861	9,433	12,079
5.5%	6.1%	5.3%	3.6%	5.2%
7.4%	8.9%	7.9%	5.3%	6.4%
3.15	3.68	3.02	2.78	2.52
—	—	—	(.83)	—
3.15	3.68	3.02	1.95	2.52
25,355	29,448	28,778	24,846	24,712
8,072	7,842	7,160	6,295	5,613
—	—	436	.730	1,031
57.1%	47.6%	54.8%	53.4%	55.0%
15,739	17,905	12,988	16,955	18,898
11,269	13,232	12,871	12,730	11,886
1,559	1,296	1,547	1,898	1,770
9,221	12,126	8,176	5,772	9,592
39.5%	42.4%	37.1%	30.5%	44.3%

$ 69,170	$ 63,621	$ 64,756	$ 58,009	$ 71,506
2.8 to 1	2.6 to 1	2.9 to 1	2.5 to 1	2.8 to 1
142,039	137,590	131,603	146,880	149,557
28,268	23,431	25,925	29,375	31,450
19,407	19,454	19,719	17,303	20,649
—	—	—	8,650	15,430
191,546	185,358	176,552	170,353	173,125
4,487	4,483	4,477	4,466	4,613
42.69	41.35	39.43	38.15	37.53
34⅜–26⅝	**41¼–26⅛**	**44¾–32⅛**	**33⅝–24⅛**	**26¾–23½**
9.09	7.17	12.83	11.83	9.57
29,327	29,810	30,243	21,946	11,410
8,991	8,899	8,571	8,918	8,049

NOTE TO TEN YEAR SUMMARY

Interlake, Inc. is the surviving corporation of the merger of Acme Steel Company into Interlake Iron Corporation on December 22, 1964. This Ten Year Financial Summary of Operations reflects the combined operations of these two companies on a "pooling of interests" basis for the years 1963 and 1964.

Income per common share is based on the average number of common shares outstanding during each year, after recognition of the dividend requirements on the preferred stock. For the years 1963-1964, the Acme shares (adjusted to reflect a 2% stock dividend in 1962) were converted at the rate of .7 of an Interlake share for each Acme share, this being the exchange basis of the merger.

Cash flow is defined as income before extraordinary items, depreciation and future income taxes, less preferred stock dividends.

Capital expenditures exclude the assets of acquired businesses.

Price Earnings ratio is based upon year-end stock price.

Glossary *chapter* 14

Accounting entity—a basic feature of accounting that holds that accounting information pertains to entities which have a separate existence from their owners, creditors, and other interested parties and for which records are maintained and financial statements presented.

Accounting Principles Board—a body created by the American Insitute of Certified Public Accountants to assist in the determination of, and to speak for the Institute on, accounting principles; went out of existence in 1973.

Cash basis of accounting—an approach to the accounting for revenues and expenses in which they are not recognized (except for depreciation) until they are received in cash form or paid for in cash.

Comparability—a qualitative objective of accounting information; when information is comparable it reveals basic similarities and differences that are real and not the result of differing accounting treatments.

Completed contract method (of recognizing revenue)—an approach to revenue recognition on long-term construction projects in which no revenue is recognized until the project is completed; similar to recognizing revenue upon completion of a sale.

Completeness—the requirement that all accounting information that meets specified qualitative objectives be reported.

Conservatism—embraces the idea of being cautious or prudent; in accounting it generally means that net assets and earnings should not be overstated and that it is preferable to err in the direction of understatement rather than overstatement.

Disclosure—the requirement that all significant information must be revealed so that financial statements will not be misleading.

Expense—service potential or economic resource utilized or consumed in the generation of revenue; usually measured in terms of the initial exchange prices in which the resources were acquired under the principles of associating cause and effect, systematic and rational allocation, or inmediate recognition.

Financial Accounting Standards Board—the successor to the Accounting Principles Board; an independent, paid, seven-member board that is the authoritative voice of the accounting profession on matters of accounting standards.

General-purpose financial information (statements)—a basic feature of accounting under which it is assumed that the same information presented in the same set of financial statements serves the common needs of a variety of external users.

Installment basis (of revenue recognition)—an approach to revenue recognition under which the gross margin on an installment sale is considered realized in proportion to the cash installment collections on the installment receivable.

Loss—expired service potential or economic resource which produced no revenue or other benefit; usually measured in terms of the exchange price of potentials or resources lost.

Matching principle—the principle that net earnings can be determined through a process of associating or relating the revenues and the expenses of an accounting period.

Materiality—a basic feature of accounting that holds that financial accounting is concerned only with information that is significant enough to influence decisions or evaluations; an immaterial amount may be accounted for without regard to theoretical considerations.

Modifying convention—a custom emerging from accounting practice that alters the results that would be obtained from a strict application of accounting principles; conservatism is an example.

Monetary assets—cash, accounts receivable, notes receivable, certain temporary investments, and other items that either are in cash form or are claims to cash.

Money measurement—quantification in terms of a monetary unit of measurement—the dollar—as contrasted to quantification in terms of physical units of measurement—feet, inches, grams, tons, meters, and so on.

Neutrality—a qualitative objective sought in accounting information that requires it to be free from bias.

Percentage of completion method—an approach to revenue recognition that holds that revenue should be recognized on long-term construction projects according to the degree of completion attained; the degree of completion is usually measured by comparing costs incurred with total costs expected to be incurred.

Period costs—costs incurred which cannot be readily related to specific revenue and which are, as a result, expensed in the period incurred under the principle of immediate recognition.

Product costs—costs incurred in the manufacture of goods which are accounted for as if they attached to the goods, with the result that they are charged to expense when the goods are sold.

Production basis—an approach to revenue recognition which holds that under certain limited circumstances (mining precious metals and growing agricultural products) revenue may be recognized at the completion of production prior to sale.

Quantification—description in terms of a natural scale of numbers.

Relevance—a qualitative objective of accounting information requiring that the information be pertinent to or have a bearing upon a decision or evaluation.

Revenue—the product or services of the enterprise; usually measured in terms of the bargained price of a sale and recognized after it has been earned and realized; realization is generally held to occur when goods are delivered to or services rendered for a customer in exchange for other assets (usually cash or other liquid assets) with the intent of consummating a sale.

Stable dollar—an assumption that fluctuations in the value of the dollar are insignificant and may, therefore, be ignored.

Time periods (periodicity)—a basic feature of financial accounting is that it provides information about the economic activities of an entity for stated time periods that are shorter than the life of the entity.

Timeliness—a qualitative objective of accounting information requiring that information be provided at a time when it may be considered in reaching a decision.

Understandability—a qualitative objective of accounting information requiring that the information provided be understood, as regards format and terminology, by the intended user.

Verifiability—a qualitative objective of accounting information requiring that another accountant or group of accountants using the same measurement methods would reach the same conclusion as to the magnitude of the measurements presented.

Student review quiz *chapter* 14

To develop a permanent record of your responses, you may write them on the answer sheet provided in the *Work Papers* or on a separate piece of paper.

1 Probably the most influential organization in the development or formulation of accounting principles has been the—

a) American Accounting Association.
b) American Institute of Certified Public Accountants.
c) Congress of the United States, through the writing of tax legislation.
d) Securities and Exchange Commission.
e) Accounting Principles Board.

2 Accounting principles or standards are used or relied upon by all of the following except—

a) A single entity, to give its records consistency through time.
b) External parties, who seek to compare financial information of different entities.
c) The general public, as a means of increasing its confidence in the reliability of the information provided.
d) The CPA, in appraising the information provided by management for its fairness.
e) Management, in making special studies of its operations.

3 Of the qualitative objectives for financial accounting information, the most important one is—

a) Verifiability.
b) Timeliness.
c) Relevance.

d) Neutrality.
e) Conservatism.

4 Which of the following is not a loss or an expense?

a) The cost of newspaper advertising announcing a recent successful sale.
b) Depreciation on trucks used in constructing a building for the constructor's own use.
c) The salary of the president of the company.
d) A drop in the net realizable value of inventory below cost.
e) Shrinkage in the net realizable value of accounts receivable as measured by an estimate for uncollectible accounts.

5 The practice of overstating expenses in the current period to avoid handicapping future periods is—

a) Acceptable because it is conservative.
b) Acceptable if done consistently.
c) Acceptable if fully disclosed.
d) Acceptable if followed throughout the firms in the industry.
e) Acceptable only if the amounts are immaterial.

6 Materiality is—

a) Unimportant in determining whether or not there is adequate disclosure.
b) Measured strictly by the dollar amounts of the individual items—for example, a $100,000 amount is always material.
c) Measured by whether or not the manner in which the item is treated might influence decisions or evaluations.
d) Always an aggregate consideration.
e) Closely related to the convention of conservatism.

7 If the accountant were to attempt to arrive at an absolutely correct figure for periodic net earnings, which of the following would be most useful?

a) Comparability.
b) Matching.
c) Materiality.
d) Disclosure.
e) Conservatism.

8 Revenue may under proper circumstances be recognized at all of the following moments in time except—

a) After the earning process has been completed and an exchange has taken place.
b) Upon the receipt of cash from the customer.
c) As certain stages of completion of production are attained.
d) When manufactured goods are acquired for resale.
e) Upon the completion of the production process but before a sale has taken place.

9 Advertising costs incurred are typically treated as expenses of the period in which incurred under the expense recognition principle of—

a) Associating cause and effect.
b) Systematic and rational allocation.
c) Immediate recognition of a period cost.
d) Matching.
e) Realization.

10 Which of the following is not one of the pervasive principles of the APB in *Statement No. 4?*

a) Initial recording of assets and liabilities at the prices experienced in the exchanges in which they were acquired or incurred.
b) Determining the earnings of a period through a process that may, in brief, be called matching.
c) Realization as a guiding principle in revenue recognition.
d) Associating cause and effect as an expense recognition principle.
e) That assets received as gifts should be recorded at fair market value.

11 Which of the following statements is false?

a) The realization of revenue generally means that an exchange has taken place in which another asset has been received for merchandise delivered or services rendered.
b) Although accounting is often said to deal with costs, expired costs, and lost costs, what is really meant is that accountants often use cost as a measure of service potential in assets and it is really these potentials that exist and expire.
c) Revenue is earned throughout the entire range of activities of an enterprise but usually is not recorded prior to sale because, for one reason, it is not easily measurable until time of sale.
d) An expense is an involuntary expiration of an asset without any expectation of receiving benefits from the expiration.
e) The term "cost" is sometimes used

synonymously with "asset" and at other times with "expense."

12 Match the items in Column A with the proper description in Column B.

Column A		*Column B*
1. Going concern	**a)**	An assumption relied on in the preparation of financial statements that would be unreasonable if applied to the environment of many South American countries in recent years.
2. Comparability	**b)**	Concerned with relative dollar amounts.
3. Disclosure or completeness	**c)**	The usual basis for the recording of assets.
4. Verifiability	**d)**	Required if the accounting treatment differs from that previously accorded a particular item.
5. Conservatism	**e)**	An assumption or basic feature that would be unreasonable to use in reporting on a firm that had become insolvent.
6. Stable dollar	**f)**	None of these.
7. Matching	**g)**	An objective achieved for a single entity's financial information by adhering to the requirement of consistency.
8. Materiality	**h)**	A measurement that can be corroborated by qualified accountants using the same measurement methods.
9. Exchange prices	**i)**	Discourages undue optimism in measuring and reporting net assets and net earnings.
10. Accounting entity	**j)**	Requires separation of personal from business activity in the recording and reporting processes.

Now compare your answers with the correct answers and explanations on page 720.

Questions *chapter* 14

1 Why would it be desirable to have a comprehensive set of generally accepted accounting principles?

2 What has the American Institute of Certified Public Accountants done to try to develop a comprehensive set of generally accepted accounting principles?

3 Discuss the factors which first made the statement of financial position relatively more important than the earnings statement and then reversed their positions.

4 Why is the title statement of financial position possibly a misnomer?

5 Accountants have stated that revenues should not be recognized before they are earned. Does this literally mean that they may in some instances be earned far ahead of the point at which they are recognized? Isn't this somewhat illogical, in that revenues should ideally be recorded as soon as they are earned?

6 Your company has a policy of charging the cost of asset acquisitions to expense immediately if the amount of expenditure is below $250. During the year this was done on 100 different occasions. Is the materiality concept being violated?

7 The company you work for has just begun operations and wishes to proceed in a conservative manner. For all plant asset acquisitions, rapid write-down methods are to be employed, even though for most of them the services are utilized evenly over their lives. In this way, the assets appearing on the statement of financial position will not be overstated and neither will the net earnings computations. Comment.

8 Do you agree with the following statement? "The stockholders consider creditors an outside source of assets, while management, especially in large corporations with many stockholders, tends to feel that both creditors and stockholders are 'outside' sources of assets." Discuss.

9 The concept of conservatism, the assumption of a going concern, and the insistence upon realization are the main obstacles to the use of market values for assets in the statement of financial position. Do you agree? Why?

10 Under what circumstances is the stable dollar assumption unreasonable? Do you think the United States economy conforms to this description at the present time?

11 Upon what feature does the accountant rely in holding that a payment made from personal funds by a pharmacist on a mortgage note secured by his house should not be recorded in his drugstore's records?

12 A friend of yours maintains that an insurance policy premium paid in advance should be carried as an asset only to the extent of the money that would be returned by the insurance company if the policy is canceled. Do you agree or disagree? Why?

13 Can you think of some nonquantifiable information which may be of tremendous value in appraising the progress of a business? Can you think of some information quantifiable in nonmonetary terms which would be of great significance in appraising the progress of a business?

14 How are consistency and disclosure related?

15 How are verifiability and the matching principle related?

16 A classmate of yours states, "A consistent application of accounting principles will enable a user of the statements to compare Company A with all of the other companies in Company A's industry." Do you agree? Why?

17 What are the favorable and unfavorable connotations attached to conservatism?

18 What are qualitative objectives? Which is the most important one, and why?

Exercises *chapter* 14

1 A company follows a practice of expensing its fire and extended coverage insurance premiums when they are paid. In 1975, the company charged to expense the $720 premium paid on a three-year policy covering the period July 1, 1975 to June 30, 1978. In 1972 a premium of $660 was charged to expense on the same policy for the period July 1, 1972, to June 30, 1975. What principle of accounting was violated by this practice? What was the effect of this violation on the financial statements for the calendar year 1975? On what grounds might this practice be justified?

2 A company employs the lower-of-cost-or-market method of inventory measurement. Its beginning and ending inventories for 1975 on this basis were $10,000 and $12,000. On a strict cost basis they would have been $10,500 and $12,200. On what grounds might the company's practice be justified? What is the effect on net earnings for 1975 of the employment of the company's method of inventory measurement?

3 Merchandise inventory was purchased in 1974 for $8,000. By December 31, 1974, its net realizable value had decreased to $7,600. On January 28, 1975, it was sold for $7,300. What portion of the original cost eventually should have been charged off as a loss (and in which time period) and what portion should have been charged against revenues as an expense (and in which time period)?

4 A building was purchased on January 1, 1970, for $20,000. By December 31, 1975, it had a net book value of $16,000 and a market value of $25,000. The building was completely destroyed by fire on January 2, 1976. Proceeds received from the insurance company were $18,000. What is the amount of the gain or loss that the accountant would recognize? Is the accounting record in accord with the economic facts given? If not, why does it differ?

5 The following data apply to the X Construction Company contracts (all amounts are in millions of dollars) some of which were completed in 1975 while others worked on were incomplete at year end:

	Complete	*Incomplete*
Contract price	$4.0	$12
Cost incurred or to be incurred:		
Prior to 1975		2
In 1975	3.5	4
After 1975		4

If $300,000 of general and administrative costs are incurred in 1975 and treated as period costs, what are the net earnings (before taxes) reported by the company in 1975 if it employs the completed contract method of recognizing revenue? If it employs the percentage of completion method? Which method would you recommend? Why?

6 Ace Company sells real estate lots under circumstances and to customers which make ultimate collection of the monthly payments on the installment contracts highly uncertain. The company's gross margin rate on the lots sold was 40 percent in 1973, 45 percent in 1974, and 50 percent in 1975. Collections in 1975 were: from 1973 sales, \$8,000; from 1974 sales, \$10,000; from 1975 sales, \$14,000. Compute the company's realized gross margin for 1975 under the installment method of accounting for real estate sales.

Problems, Series A *chapter* 14

14–1–A

For each of the items listed below, state the letter or letters of the concepts or principles relied upon to justify the accounting procedure followed.

A—Accounting entity
B—Conservatism
C—Earning principle of revenue recognition
D—Going concern
E—Initial recording at exchange prices principle
F—Matching principle
G—Period cost (or principle of immediate recognition of expense)
H—Realization principle
I—Systematic and rational allocation principle of expense recognition
J—Stable dollar assumption

1) Officers' salaries for the year were recorded as expenses of the year even though the officers spent nearly half of their time planning future years' activities.
2) Adams Company held 100 shares of stock in Brown Company and these shares were split two for one during the year. The market value of the shares was $100 each before and $55 each after the split. No entry was made to record the increase in value.
3) The ending inventory was recorded at $55,000 using cost or market, whichever is lower. The cost of the ending inventory was $58,000.
4) A stock of printed stationery, checks, and invoices with a cost of $5,000 was treated as a current asset at year-end even though it had no value to others.
5) An advance cash collection of $6,000 for services to be rendered next year was reported as a current liability at year-end.
6) No adjustment was made in the accounting records to reflect the fact that the general level of prices increased 5 percent during the year.
7) A truck purchased at the beginning of the year was reported at year-end at 80 percent of its cost even though its market value was only 60 percent of its acquisition cost.
8) Periodic monthly payments (for services rendered) of $2,000 to Walter Adams, who owned all of the stock of the company, were treated as salaries expense; additional amounts paid to him were recorded as dividends.
9) No entry was made to reflect the fact than an offer of $50,000 was received for land carried in the accounts at $28,000.
10) A liability was recorded in the amount of $6,000 as the estimated cost of making future repairs under warranty provisions on products sold this year.

14–2–A

Given below are selected transactions (in some cases summarized for the year) entered into by the A Company in 1975.

1) Cash sales for the year, $50,000.
2) Cash collected from customers for goods sold and delivered last year, $5,000.
3) Selling price of goods sold on account during 1975, $250,000.
4) Cash collected for services to be rendered next year, $2,000.
5) Cash collected for interest earned in 1974, $100.
6) Received an automobile whose regular selling price was $4,000 in exchange for merchandise that cost A Company $3,000.
7) Cash collected as dividends (on August 15) on an investment in the stock of another company, $500.

8) Cash received on sale of a truck used in the business, $250. Amount received was less than the net book value of the truck at date of sale.
9) Cash collected upon issuing own note to the bank, $10,000.
10) Cash received as a refund on an insurance policy canceled in 1975, $50. The policy was taken out and the premium paid earlier in 1975.

Required:

a) Prepare a schedule listing the items and their dollar amounts that would be viewed as revenue items in 1975 under cash basis accounting.
b) Repeat **(a)** assuming accrual basis accounting.

14–3–A

Dotman Company sells a patented product under a franchising arrangement with the company that holds the franchise for the entire state in which Dotman operates. This arrangement calls for the payment of a fee of 5 percent of the selling price on all products sold. The products are sold through salesmen, who receive a commission of 15 percent of the selling price. Sales revenue, fees, and salesmen's commissions have been recorded only after receipt of cash from customers in payment of their accounts. All other expenses are properly computed under accrual basis accounting. Computed in this manner, the net earnings for 1974, 1975, 1976, and 1977 were $18,000, $26,000, $40,000, and $42,000 respectively.

As an accountant you are called in to examine the records of the company, and you immediately suggest that the records be converted to an accrual basis of accounting to better reflect the results of operations. You determine that the outstanding accounts receivable at the end of 1974, 1975, 1976, and 1977 were $22,000, $32,000, $24,000, and $12,000, respectively.

Required:

a) Prepare a schedule showing the conversion of the cash basis amounts of net earnings to the amounts that would have been reported if sales, fees, and salesmen's commissions had been accounted for under accrual basis accounting.
b) Compare the annual net earnings amounts under the two methods and comment on the differences noted in the trend of net earnings.

14–4–A

The Brighton Company, as of December 31, 1975, had assets of $560,000, liabilities of $95,000, and stockholders' equity of $465,000. Net earnings for 1975 included in stockholders' equity were $102,000.

The adjustments presented below were ignored in computing the above figures. Unless otherwise stated, expense and revenue items were entered initially in the expense and revenue accounts.

Required:

1. Journalize the necessary adjusting entries, assuming the books have not yet been closed for 1975.
2. Restate the totals for assets, liabilities, stockholders' equity, and net earnings.

The ignored adjustments were (or were related to) the items listed below.

a) Accrued salesmen's commissions at year-end were $12,900.
b) Accrued interest receivable on investments was $1,830 as of December 31.
c) A five-year insurance policy was purchased on July 1, 1975. The premium was $6,000.
d) The company purchased five automobiles on July 1, 1975, for $20,000. The asset account was debited. The salvage value was estimated at $1,520, and the expected economic life was four years. Depreciation (on a straight-line basis) has not been recorded for the current year.
e) $40,000 was received as service revenue. Only $18,000 was earned during 1975.
f) Goods purchased by the Brighton Company for $8,000 were shipped by the seller on December 31, 1975, f.o.b. destination. No entry was made to record the purchase, and the goods were not included in inventory. (Periodic inventory procedure was used.)
g) Other goods purchased by the Brighton Company for $5,000 were shipped by the seller on December 29, 1975, f.o.b. shipping point. The entry was made to record the purchase but the goods were not included in the physical inventory.
h) Goods having a cost of $7,000 were sold by the Brighton Company for $12,000. They were shipped to the customer on December 31, 1975, f.o.b. destination. The Brighton Company did not record the sale but did deduct the goods from the ending inventory.

14–5–A

For each of the transactions given below, indicate the entry that should be made to correct the one that was made. Also indicate which basic concepts or fundamental principles of accounting were violated in each case. The Rugeroso Company:

a) Had some merchandise inventory on hand with an original cost of $25,000. Its market value had declined to $22,500, and the selling costs of disposing of the merchandise were estimated to be $1,000. The accountant debited the Loss Due to Market Decline of Inventory account for $2,500 and credited Merchandise Inventory. The company uses the perpetual inventory procedure.
b) Was constructing a machine for a customer. The accountant decided to record revenue at various stages of completion rather than waiting until the machine was delivered to the customer. The revenue recognized and credited to Construction Revenue was $20,000. The Construction in Progress account was debited for $80,000, while the actual costs incurred amounted to only $60,000.
c) Had purchased various hand tools at the beginning of the year, which would last 10 years with no scrap value, at costs of under $200 each. In aggregate they totaled $50,000 for the current year. They were all charged to expense.
d) Entered into a long-term lease agreement. Each year the accountant showed the effect of the lease by making the following entry:

Rent Expense	6,000	
Cash		6,000

No other action was taken on this matter.

e) Changed from a cost basis of accounting for short-term marketable securities to a lower-of-cost-or-market basis. The following entry was made:

Loss on Market Decline of Securities....................................	300	
Marketable Securities..		300

No other mention was made of this matter in the financial statements.

Problems, Series B *chapter* 14

14–1–B

In each of the circumstances described below, the accounting practices followed may be questioned. You are to indicate whether you agree or disagree with the accounting employed and to state the principles or concepts on which you would rely to justify your position.

1) The cost of certain improvements to leased property having a life of five years was charged to expense because they would revert to the lessor when the lease expired in three years.
2) The salaries paid to the top officers of the company were charged to expense in the period in which they were incurred, even though the officers spent over half of their time planning next year's activities.
3) A company spent over $4 million in developing a new product and then spent an additional $4.5 promoting it. All of these costs were incurred and charged to expense prior to the sale of a single unit of this new product. The expensing of these costs was justified on the grounds that they had to be incurred every year—that new product development and promotion were regularly recurring.
4) No entry was made to record the belief that the market value of the land owned (carried in the accounts at $58,000) increased in value from $100,000 to $105,000, in keeping with the advance in the general level of prices.
5) No entry was made to record the fact that costs of $50,000 were expected to be incurred in fulfilling warranty provisions on products sold this year, the revenue from which was recognized this year.
6) The aquisition of a tract of land was recorded at the price paid for it of $108,000, even though the company would have been willing to pay $125,000.
7) A truck acquired at the beginning of the year was reported at year-end at 80 percent of its acquisition price, even though its market value then was only 65 percent of its original acquisition price.

14–2–B

Presented below are selected transactions (summarized in some instances for the year) of the Bader Company for 1975.

1) Cash collected for services to be rendered next year, $1,500.
2) Cash collected for merchandise sold on account in prior periods, $125,000.
3) Cash collected for interest earned was $350, $100 earned last year and $250 this year.
4) Selling price of goods sold on account in 1975, $220,000.
5) Cash sales for the year, $35,000.
6) Cash collected as dividends (on July 7) on an investment in the stock of another company, $700.
7) Acquired a truck to be used in the business whose regular selling price was $7,000 in exchange for merchandise that cost Bader $5,000.
8) Cash received on the sale of some fully depreciated office equipment, $300.

9) Cash received upon issuing own note to the bank, $15,000.
10) Cash received as a refund upon the cancellation of a short-term lease on some equipment, $75. The equipment was rented and the rent paid earlier in 1975.

Required:

a) Prepare a schedule listing the items and their dollar amounts that would be viewed as revenue items in 1975 under cash basis accounting.
b) Repeat **(a)** assuming accrual basis accounting.

14–3–B

For 1975, its first year of operations, its accountant determined that the Albert Corporation, whose stock is all owned by Joe Albert, should report a loss of $30,000 for income tax purposes, following the most conservative practices permissible. Joe Albert is concerned about reporting such a loss in the financial statements that will be issued when an attempt is made to sell some shares of stock to the general public to raise money for additional equipment. He calls upon you as an expert accountant to review the accounting practices followed and to advise him on accounting matters. You discover the following information relating to the $30,000 loss that might be reported for income tax purposes:

1) Construction revenue has been recorded on a completed contract basis. Five contracts with a total price of $400,000 were partially completed during the year, with $80,000 of costs incurred out of total expected costs of $320,000.
2) Only $10,000 of gross margin realized through installment collections were included in arriving at the net loss of $30,000. Installment sales for the year were $200,000; cost of the goods sold was $150,000. There is no reason to believe that the remaining installment receivables will not be collected.
3) Accelerated depreciation of $12,000 was included in arriving at the net loss. On a straight-line basis, the depreciation would be only $8,000.
4) For income tax purposes, $8,000 of costs were expensed, even though these costs relate to product development and are expected to provide benefits equally in 1975 and the three following years.
5) The inventory of merchandise was priced at $33,000 on a LIFO basis. Under FIFO it would have a cost of $37,000.

Required: Prepare a schedule showing how the above items would change the reported net loss to reported net earnings (before income taxes) if they were accounted for in an acceptable, yet less conservative manner.

14–4–B

As of December 31, 1975, the Harden Company had assets of $362,000, liabilities of $72,000, and stockholders' equity of $290,000. Net earnings for 1975 included in stockholders' equity were $47,000.

The auditor of the company discovered that the adjustments presented below were left out of consideration when the above totals were computed. You, as auditor, are required (1) to journalize the necessary adjusting entries and (2) to state the correct totals for assets, liabilities, stockholders' equity, and net earnings. Closing entries have not been made for 1975. Unless otherwise stated, expense and revenue items were entered initially in the expense and revenue accounts.

The adjustments that the company omitted from consideration were:

a) Depreciation on a building, which had a cost of $90,000, at the rate of 4 percent per year was not recorded.

b) The balance of the accounts receivable as of December 31, 1975, was $30,000. The normal uncollectible account loss is 2 percent of the accounts receivable at the end of the year. There is no balance in the allowance for doubtful accounts.

c) Taxes accrued on payroll were $1,200. Property taxes prepaid were $450.

d) Salesmen's commissions due but not paid amounted to $750.

e) Discount on notes payable amounted to $300. (Interest Expense was debited for this amount.)

f) Unexpired insurance expense amounted to $1,200.

g) Revenue received in advance and credited to a revenue account was $1,500.

h) Interest accrued on notes payable was $120.

i) Store supplies consumed in 1975 amounted to $720. When store supplies were purchased, they were charged to Prepaid Supplies.

14–5–B

For each of the transactions or circumstances described below and the entries made, state which, if any, of the basic concepts or generally accepted principles of accounting were violated. If any, give the entry to correct the improper accounting, assuming the books have not been closed. During the year, the Bessone Company:

1) Had its buildings appraised. They were found to have a market value of $410,000, although their book value was only $380,000. The accountant debited the Buildings and Allowance for Depreciation—Buildings accounts for $15,000 each and credited Capital from Appreciation. No separate mention was made of this action in the financial statements.

2) Received from the company's major stockholder a calculating machine worth $115 (won as a door prize at a convention) for which he had no use. The company paid $10 to have the machine picked up and delivered to its offices. The $10 was charged to the Equipment account and no other entry made.

3) Purchased a number of new electric pencil sharpeners for its offices at a total cost of $60. These were recorded as assets and are being depreciated over five years.

4) Changed its depreciation rates on machinery from 10 percent to 15 percent per year, increasing the amount of depreciation recorded from $6,000 to $9,000. No other action was taken and no disclosure made. Net earnings for the year amounted to $350,000.

5) Produced a number of agricultural products at a cost of $26,000. These costs were charged to expense when the products were set up in inventory at their net market value of $35,000. The difference of $9,000 was credited to a Farm Revenues Earned account.

Solutions to student review quiz

Following are the solutions to the Student Review Quizzes contained at the end of each chapter. It is assumed that before you check the solutions for a particular chapter you will have already answered the questions in the quiz. So that you will have a permanent record of your responses you should have recorded them on the answer sheet provided in the *Work Papers* to this volume or on a separate sheet of paper.

Chapter 1

1 e) Since Assets = Liabilities + Stockholders' Equity, it must also be true that Stockholders' Equity is equal to Assets less Liabilities as shown below:

$$A = L + SE, \text{ so } A - L = SE.$$

2 c) Delivery equipment is an asset. Therefore, assets would be increased by $4,000. Since no payment has been made as yet, liabilities are also increased by $4,000. There is no effect on stockholders' equity.

3 a) Revenue is properly defined as the total flow of products or services delivered to or performed for customers by an entity. The difference between selling price and cost is called the margin or markup. Revenue represents an element which tends to *increase* stockholders' equity. Net earnings are calculated by deducting expenses from revenues.

4 b) The advertising services were received during the month and were used in securing revenue from customers. Since the services were not paid for, a liability must be increased for the debt owed. Since the services were used up during the month, their cost should be shown as an expense. And expenses tend to offset the increase in retained earnings brought about by the recording of revenues as increases in retained earnings. Actually, it is only the excess of revenues over expenses which increases retained earnings.

5 c) Collecting accounts receivable reduces the amount of these accounts still outstanding. Cash is increased by the same amount as the decrease in accounts receivable. Since both of these are assets, response **(c)** correctly describes the effect.

6 e) The changes in assets and liabilities which occurred during the period of operation would have to be determined by comparing the statements of financial position prepared at the beginning and end of the period. The earnings statement would not give this information.

7 b) The earnings for 1976 would be included in the total shown for retained earnings on the statement of financial position dated December 31, 1976. Also included in the total would be the cumulative earnings in past years less amounts paid out in dividends during the life of the firm.

8 f) Net earnings appear as the last figure on the earnings statement. They also appear as an addition to beginning retained earnings (in arriving at ending retained earnings) on the statement of retained earnings.

The account Retained Earnings appears as the last figure on the statement of retained earnings. It also appears on the statement of financial position as part of the stockholders' equity.

9 c) Although such activity may be undertaken by a CPA as part of his management advisory services, executive recruitment is not an accounting function. All of the others involve financial information and are regularly engaged in by accountants.

10 c) Generally, the right to express an opinion attesting to the fairness of published financial information is restricted by law to CPAs (and a few other public accountants in some states). All of the other indicated activities are regularly undertaken by accountants and others who are not CPAs. Many individuals offer their services in preparing tax returns; management consulting firms render management advisory services; many large companies have internal audit staffs; and the preparation of budgets is regularly undertaken by non-CPA accountants in private business.

11 d) While a valuable part of the overall management of resources, reporting on the outcome of a decision is not part of the decision-making process.

12 e) Since all of the statements are true, this is the best answer.

13 e) Since all of the statements are true, this is the best answer.

14 a) Since financial accounting information generally relates to the entity as a whole and is historical in nature, it is not likely to be useful or relevant in this type of decision. Note that all of the other types of decisions listed require information relating to an entity as a whole.

Chapter 2

1 b) Debits are entries on the left side of an account. Since assets and expenses normally have a balance on the left side, debits increase their balances. Liabilities, revenue, and stockholders' equity accounts normally have balances on the right side. Therefore, debits decrease their balances.

2 e) Revenues, not expenses, operate to bring about an increase in the Retained Earnings account. But expenses do normally have debit balances and do show the costs associated with producing revenue during an accounting period. Expenses are matched against the revenues which they were intended to produce.

3 b) An asset must be debited, since the company has a right to receive cash in the future for services already performed. It does not have a written promise from customers to pay a sum certain as of a particular date. Therefore, a debit to Cash or Notes Receivable is incorrect. Rights to receive an amount from customers are called Accounts Receivable and this account should be debited (increased). The credit should be to Service Revenue. This indicates that revenue has been earned by performing services for customers and thus is the source of the accounts receivable.

4 a) The receipt of the bill (or invoice as it is often referred to) indicates that the recipient owes the vendor for something already delivered or for a service performed. Since the service performed was advertising and it is billed only after performance, an expense has been incurred and an expense account must be debited, in this case Advertising Expense.

Since the bill has not yet been paid, the liability for future payment must also be recognized and recorded. The Accounts Payable account is the liability which should be increased. To increase a liability account, the account must be credited.

5 c) Since cash was received, it is necessary to debit Cash for $825. To increase an asset account, the account must be debited.

Customers are paying amounts they owe. These amounts have been carried as accounts receivable. When the amounts are paid, the reduction in the asset accounts receivable is recorded by crediting that account. To reduce an asset account, that account must be credited. Notes receivable would be an incorrect debit unless these customers had signed written promises to pay a particular amount as of a given date. This is not normally required of customers.

6 d) Two types of assets have been purchased. Therefore, this transaction requires that a compound entry (one with more than one debit or credit) be made.

Office Machines should be debited (to show an increase in an asset) for the amount of the electric calculator. Office Furniture and Fixtures should be debited for the cost of the new typists' chairs.

Since the items were purchased on open account (meaning that cash was not involved nor was a note signed), the credit must be to Accounts Payable.

7 b) In this transaction cash was received and revenue was earned. To record the receipt of cash (the increase of an asset), the Cash account must be debited. To record the earning of revenue, a revenue account must be credited. The account title Service Revenue adequately describes the revenue earned.

8 e) In this transaction an expense has been incurred and paid for. To increase an expense account, it must be debited. The account title Salary Expense adequately describes the expense which should be debited. Since cash was given up, Cash must be credited. (To reduce an asset account, it must be credited.)

9 c) A trial balance in balance fails to prove that no errors of any kind have been made in the accounts. For instance, if a debit were made to the wrong account, the trial balance would not aid in discovering the error. Total debits would still be equal to total credits.

10 e) A ledger is a collection of all accounts, including both statement of financial position accounts and earnings statement accounts. Response **(a)** more nearly describes a journal. Response **(d)** describes a trial balance.

11 d) For every entry that is made, total debits must equal total credits. Unless this is done, the ledger, the trial balance, and the statement of financial position will be out of balance. The double-entry system is based on an equality of debits and credits.

12 d) Cross-indexing accomplishes all of these things **(a, b,** and **c)**. In the journal it shows the account to which an amount was posted. In the ledger it shows the journal source of all amounts entered. This provides a link between the journal and the ledger accounts, facilitates finding errors, and reduces the likelihood of errors in posting.

13 c) Posting is the act of recording amounts in the ledger accounts as indicated in the journal. It is sometimes referred to as a transfer of amounts from the journal to the ledger. Response **(e)** would be correct if it said "from the journal to the ledger."

14 c) The totals of all the debits and all the credits in the journal will be greater than the total debit and credit balances in the ledger if any account in the ledger has both a debit and a credit. For instance, if the Cash account had a debit of $10,000 and a credit of $8,000, it would have a debit balance of only $2,000, since the credit is offset against the debit. In the journal the $10,000 debit would be included in total debits and the $8,000 credit would be included in total credits.

Chapter 3

1 e) All of the arguments or reasons stated are deemed to support recording revenue at the time of the making of a sale.

2 d) They are usually debited, not credited, to a Sales Discounts account when taken.

3 a) The amount is computed as $1,000 − (0.25 × $1,000) = $750; $750 − (0.20 × $750) = $600; $600 − (0.10 × $600) = $540.

4 Accounts Payable....	540.00	
Purchase Discounts.....		10.80
Cash...........		529.20

5 Three percent for 20 days is the equivalent of 54 percent per year: 0.03 × (360/20). Savings are equal to $150 (0.03 × $5,000) − $21.56 ($4,850 × 0.08 × 20/360), or $128.44.

6 c) Transportation-In is an addition to the cost of purchases rather than a reduction from this cost. All of the other accounts are contra or reduction accounts.

7 b) The major disadvantage of the periodic inventory procedure is that it fails to provide an inventory amount in the books against which the cost of a physical inventory can be compared. Thus, the element of control is missing.

8 e) The Dorest Company paid the freight bill merely as a convenience for the seller. The freight charge is the responsibility of the seller, since the goods were shipped f.o.b. destination.

9 a) Trade discounts are granted regardless of whether an invoice is paid within the period specified in order to claim a cash discount.

10) e) If legal title has passed, a sale has been made and the goods are the properly of the buyer even though still in the seller's possession. Since they are not owned by the seller, they cannot be included in his inventory.

11 All of the statements are correct. Net sales are $15,000 ($15,900 – $600 – $300). Net purchases are $9,100 ($9,000 + $700 – $400 – $200). Cost of goods available for sale is $14,100 ($9,100, net cost of purchases, plus $5,000, beginning inventory). Cost of goods sold is $11,100 ($14,100, cost of goods available for sale, less $3,000, ending inventory). Gross margin is $3,900 ($15,000, net sales, less $11,100, cost of goods sold).

12 d) This entry correctly reduces the Accounts Payable account balance to zero, records the cash discount of $20 taken in the Purchase Discounts account, and records the decrease in the Cash account of $980.

13 a) The company was entitled to, and took, a discount of $40 (0.01 × $4,000), which meant that it paid $3,960. Since the goods were shipped f.o.b. shipping point, the transportation charges are the responsibility of the buyer.

14 a) Ending inventory is a deduction from total goods available for sale to arrive at the cost of goods sold. If it is overstated, cost of goods sold will be understated. Cost of goods sold is a deduction from revenues in arriving at net earnings. If it is understated, net earnings will be overstated.

In reference to response **(e)**, gross margin is equal to sales revenues less cost of goods sold. If cost of goods sold is understated, gross margin will be overstated rather than understated.

15 d) Response **(a)** would be correct if it had indicated that transporation-in was added rather than subtracted. Response **(b)** is incorrect for two reasons. Transportation-in should be added rather than deducted. Ending inventory should be deducted rather than added. Response **(c)** is incorrect because purchase returns and allowances should be deducted rather than added in determining the cost of the goods sold.

Chapter 4

1 e) An example of each situation is:

a) Insurance Expense (an expense).
 Unexpired Insurance (an asset)
 To transfer the expired portion of the asset, unexpired insurance, from the asset account to an expense account.

b) Wages Expense (an expense)
 Accrued Wages Payable (a liability)
 To record wages earned by employees but not yet paid. The expense and liability accounts are both increased.

c) Rental Payments Received in Advance (a liability)
 Rent Revenue (a revenue)
 To transfer the portion of rent which has been earned from a liability account to a revenue account.

d) Accrued Interest Receivable (an asset)
 Interest Revenue (a revenue)
 To record interest that has been earned but not yet received. The asset and revenue accounts are both increased.

2 b) The information given tells you that 1 percent of the credit sales are estimated to be uncollectible. Thus, the amount of the entry is $170 (1 percent of $17,000). The amount must be charged to an expense account, but it can only be credited to an Allowance for Doubtful Accounts, since it is not known at this time which of the accounts receivable will be uncollectible. In this manner, an expense is recognized and an asset reduced.

3 b) A debit to the Bad Debts Expense account is incorrect. The company makes an entry at the end of each accounting year as follows:

Bad Debts Expense (an expense)
 Allowance for Doubtful Accounts (a contra account to Accounts Receivable)

By making this entry, the company has already indicated that it expects some of the accounts to become uncollectible and has charged the year of sale with this expense. When an account actually becomes uncollectible, it would be double counting to again debit the Bad Debts Expense account. The correct entry is to reduce the asset contra account, Allowance for Doubtful Accounts, as indicated in response **(b)**.

4 c) Two things are missing from the accounts—they do not show the asset, the right to receive interest to be received later, and the revenue earned, the interest. Assets are increased by debits and revenues are increased by credits. Thus, entry **(c)** is correct.
5 a) The policy is for three years and costs $900. The expense applicable to each year is one third of the $900, or $300. Since only one half of the first year of the policy falls within the current accounting year of the company, the amount of the entry is $150. The entry must transfer $150 of the asset, unexpired insurance, to the expense, insurance expense. To do so, the expense must be debited and the asset credited.
6 a) An expense and a liability must be increased. Both responses **(a)** and **(d)** accomplish this. The liability increased in **(d)** is accounts payable, which is usually used to show only amounts owed to trade creditors. Since the liability increased is for amounts owed to employees, response **(a)** is preferable.
7 d) Computation of amount:

Cost	$3,400
Less estimated salvage value	200
Amount to be depreciated	$3,200

$$\text{Depreciation per Year} = \frac{\$3{,}200}{4} = \$800.$$

October 1 to December 31 is only one fourth of a year, so the current amount of the entry is $800/4, or $200. An expense account, Depreciation Expense—Office Furniture, must be debited (increased) and the contra asset account, Allowance for Depreciation—Office Equipment, must also be increased (credited). The latter account will be shown on the statement of financial position as a deduction from the asset, Office Equipment. Response **(e)** has the debit and credit reversed.
8 d) The liability accrued wages payable would be understated because of the failure to include the debt owed to employees. The stockholders' equity of the company would be overstated because retained earnings would be overstated (as the result of an understatement of wages expense).
9 e) Under the accrual basis of accounting, the timing of cash receipts is unimportant. Revenue recognition does not depend on the receipt of cash, nor does expense recognition depend on cash payment.
10 b) and **e)** No bad debts expense would ever appear if revenues were not recorded until cash is received. Recording sales on an accrual basis necessitates recording bad debts expense on an accrual basis. Entry **(e)** is also required under accrual accounting to bring about proper matching of expenses and revenues.
11 c) Expenses are closed by debiting the Expense and Revenue Summary account and crediting the expense account (Rent Expense in this instance). Items **(b)**, **(d)**, and **(e)** are all statement of financial position accounts and are not closed. Item **(a)** is a revenue account and is closed by crediting the Expense and Revenue Summary account and debiting Service Revenue.
12 d) Statement of financial position accounts are never closed (although it is possible that they may have zero balances for other reasons). As a result of closing, all expense and revenue accounts and the Expense and Revenue Summary account always are reduced to zero balances.
13 e) The work sheet is an informal schedule. The accounting process could (although not as easily) be completed without preparing a work sheet. The work sheet may contain as many columns as the accountant wishes to use. The more conventional ones contain 8, 10, or 12 columns, depending on whether they include or exclude columns entitled adjusted trial balance and statement of retained earnings. It would be helpful to include explanations of each adjustment at the bottom of the work sheet, but it is not required.
14 d) Depreciation is recorded by an entry that debits Depreciation Expense and credits the Allowance for Depreciation—Store Fixtures for $400. Note that the credit is to the allowance account rather than to the Store Fixtures account. This asset account will consequently continue to show a $4,000 balance throughout the period and throughout the life of the fixtures. But because the allowance is increased by periodic depreciation, the net book value of the fixtures decreases. So it is the allowance that changes, not the Store Fixtures account, with the re-

sult that the statement of financial position debit column in the worksheet shows a $4,000 amount for store fixtures.

15 **a)** The Supplies on Hand account is an asset. The adjustment for supplies used during the month is:

Supplies Expense	290	
Supplies on Hand		290

The original debit balance of $315 less the credit of $290 leaves a balance of $25 to be carried to the statement of financial position debit column.

16 **d)** and **f)** The beginning inventory must be credited in the adjustments credit column in order to transfer it to the Cost of Goods Sold expense account. The ending inventory is entered in the adjustments debit column, since it is credited to the Cost of Goods Sold expense account. The ending inventory must also appear in the statement of financial position debit column, since it is an asset.

Chapter 5

1 **d)** The first three statements are all correct. Other purposes are also conceivable, such as seeing that bills are paid on time, orders received are shipped on time, and reports to governmental bodies are timely and accurate.

2 **a), c),** and **d)** Statement **(b)** is accomplished by the earnings statement, and statement **(e)** is at least partially shown by an organization chart. Source documents are those on which the initial recording of a transaction is made. Examples include sales slips, cash register tapes, and completed order blanks.

3 **d)** Interim reports are those prepared at other than the regular annual closing date. Their purpose is to give management more timely information for decision-making purposes.

4 **b)** Even if the formal organization structure remains the same, other things such as methods of doing business could change. Also increased mechanization might occur. These and other factors necessitate changing the system of internal control periodically.

5 **d)** The use of special journals facilitates the use of accounting machines.

6 **c)** The general journal is used to record all entries which are not suited to the other journals. Adjusting and closing entries generally are not suited to the design of the special journals.

7 **c)** Special journals usually are not designed to handle this type of transaction.

8
1. **c)**
2. **e)**
3. **d)**
4. **a)**
5. **b)**
6. **b)**
7. **e)**
8. **e)**(notation only)
9. **b)**
10. **e)**
11. **d)**
12. **e)**
13. No entry
14. **d)**
15. **f)** or **(e)**

9 **e)** Both statements **(b)** and **(c)** are correct.

10 **e)** Statements **(b)** and **(c)** are both correct. Statement **(a)** is incorrect since some firms do not have separate departments. Or if they do, they may choose not to keep the sales of each separate (unlikely but possible).

11 **b)** The individual accounts supporting a controlling account appear in a subsidiary ledger.

12 **c)** Subsidiary ledgers are only necessary where the details of, for instance, accounts receivable tend to complicate the general ledger and taking a trial balance. Some firms do not have many different customers or many different suppliers, and thus do not need subsidiary ledgers.

13 **b)** The totals of Sundry columns are never posted. Only the individual items in the columns are posted.

14 **b)** The sales journal is used only for credit sales of merchandise inventory. When a plant asset is sold, it should appear in the cash receipts journal (if cash is received) or in the general journal (if an asset other than cash is received).

15 **b)** A documentary ledger takes the place of a subsidiary ledger.

16 **b)** The voucher system is designed to provide close control only over cash disbursements.

17 **d)** It shows more than the total amount of outstanding liabilities for merchandise purchased. All liabilities which will require the payment of cash will be included at some time before payment is made. Various types of liabilities may be included at any point in time (for example, the principal payment on long-term bonds).

18 d) Only after the quantity and quality of the goods have been verified is the voucher authorizing payment filed in the unpaid voucher file.

19 e) Attention is focused only on the discounts lost rather than on the discounts taken. When a discount is missed, a new voucher must be prepared because the original voucher is for a smaller amount than would actually be due. The necessity for preparing a new voucher and the use of the Discounts Lost account bring to the attention of management those discounts which were missed—an example of management by exception.

Chapter 6

1 c) It is highly unlikely that the information needs of stockholders will include a more detailed classification of cash than that given top management. Stockholders generally will need information as to the total cash resources of a company in making their evaluation of the overall financial position of the company. Management must have information as to individual account balances and the locations where funds are held on deposit in order to provide sufficient cash to support normal operations and to prevent the accumulation of excessive amounts of idle cash.

2 c) Time certificates of deposit are not cash and are not available for immediate disbursement.

3 e) Only in case **(e)** are two duties assigned to the same person, which can result in the misappropriation of funds. The signer of the check can alter the check and the alteration would not be brought to light because he is the one who receives the canceled checks from the bank.

4 e) All of the procedures stated are desirable features in a system designed to make the misappropriation of cash difficult to perpetrate or, if perpetrated, difficult to conceal.

5 c) The bank reconciliation statement accomplishes its stated purpose by reconciling both the balance per the bank statement and the balance per the ledger with the adjusted ledger balance for cash.

6 b) Only those items which the bank has entered in error or has yet to record should be entered as additions to, or deductions from, the balance per the bank statement. Of those listed, only outstanding checks are yet to be recorded by the bank as deductions from the balance it carries in its records for the depositor.

7 b) Of the items listed only two have not been recorded by the company: (1) the return of the N.S.F. check deposited and (2) the service charges deducted by the bank from the company's balance. Entry **(b)** correctly restores the balance in accounts receivable and recognizes the expense incurred.

8 e) The correct answer is $2,785. The solution to the problem is derived in the following manner:

Balance per bank statement......	$2,750
Add: Deposit in transit........	1,200
	$3,950
Less: Checks outstanding.......	1,625
Adjusted balance................	$2,325

This adjusted balance will be reached on the other side of the bank reconciliation statement by adding the $45 error and deducting the N.S.F. check of $500 and the bank service charges of $5. Therefore, the unadjusted beginning balance can be obtained by reversing the procedure and adding the last two items and deducting the first. Thus, $2,325 + $500 + $5 − $45 = $2,785.

9 c) Under the imprest method of handling a petty cash fund, a debit is entered in the Petty Cash account only when the fund is established or increased in size. The amount of any check issued to replenish the fund is charged to expense (and possibly other accounts). Obviously, since the fund is an asset, it would not be debited if the goal were to decrease its size.

10 b) The total of the vouchers in the fund is $77 and this amount must be charged to the proper expense and revenue contra accounts. The fund is also short $3, and this shortage must be charged to an expense account, Cash Short and Over.

11 c) A certified check is one drawn by a depositor in a bank on the bank and given to the named payee. The bank certifies that funds will be available to honor the check when it is presented for payment, but the check is not actually drawn by the bank.

12 c) Capital stock results in dividend revenue rather than interest revenue. All of the others could earn interest.

13 d) When a company purchases a long-term obligation as a short-term investment it runs the risk that when it must convert back to cash (before the maturity date), the market price will be depressed.

14 a) Stock investments are recorded at cost of acquisition. The broker's commission is not an expense of this period but a cost which continues to render benefits as long as the stock is held. There is no need to segregate the amount paid for the stock over its par value, since it is cost, not par value, that is significant to the investor.

15 d) The dividend declared should be recorded as revenue for the year 1975, since the stock was held during that period and the dividend becomes unquestionably the company's when the date of record passes with the company still owning the shares. No entry need be made for the stock dividend which is to be received, since it will not be recorded via a formal journal entry when actually received.

Chapter 7

1 d) The cost of goods sold is:

Inventory, January 1		$2,000
Purchases	$7,100	
Less: Returns and allowances, $400, and discounts, $64	464	
	$6,636	
Add: Transportation-in	160	
		$6,796
Cost of goods available for sale		$8,796
Less: Inventory, December 31		2,800
Cost of goods sold		$5,996

2 e) All of the other costs incurred are necessary to having the goods in the condition and location desired for sale and, therefore, should be inventoried and matched against revenues secured upon sale.

3 a) If the ending inventory is understated, an insufficient amount was deducted from the cost of the goods available for sale, leaving cost of goods sold overstated. As cost of goods sold is an expense, expenses would be overstated and the net earnings for the year would be understated. The effect of understating ending inventory in 1975 may be represented as follows:

1975 Ending inventory understated.
Cost of goods sold overstated.
Net earnings understated.

1976 Opening inventory understated.
Cost of goods sold understated.
Net earnings overstated.

4 d) Because taking discounts is considered a matter of routine, failure to take discounts is best looked upon as a mark of inefficiency rather than as part of the cost of the merchandise purchased.

5 d) Since the inventory of 200 units is less than the 1,100 units acquired at $4 each in the most recent purchase, the 200 units are all priced at $4.

6 d) The inventory under the weighted average method is the weighted average cost per unit multiplied by the number of units on hand. Under the moving average method, inventory is heavily influenced by the latest purchases, since these amounts are added to smaller amounts of inventory on hand than under the weighted average method. When prices are rising, this tends to increase the moving average unit cost.

7 Only **(b)** of the three statements is false. Under LIFO, 1,000 of the units in inventory will be priced at $1.10 and 300 at $1.50; all remaining purchase costs will be charged to cost of goods sold. In this instance, this actually consists of 300 at $1.50 and 300 at $2. Thus, the cost of the February 12 sale cannot be 400 at $1.50.

8 a) Under FIFO the most recent costs are included in the ending inventory. The earliest costs are charged to cost of goods sold.

9 All of the statements are true. The method can be applied to total inventory or to individual items, so both **(a)** and **(b)** are true. One of the modifications of the general method is that if there is no decline in selling price, there should be no write-down to market as this serves only to increase the amount of net earnings on the sale. A further modification of the general rule is that goods should not be priced for inventory purposes at an amount in excess of their net realiz-

able value, since this would entail inventorying losses.
10 e) "Market" is replacement cost except that it may not be higher than net realizable value or lower than net realizable value less normal profit.
11 c) The method is generally not accurate enough to be used as the sole means of determining year-end inventories.
12 b) The cost of the goods available for sale is $65,000. The cost of the goods sold is estimated as $49,000 ($70,000 less 30 percent of $70,000). Thus, the inventory is estimated at $16,000 ($65,000 less $49,000).

Chapter 8

1 b) This method of estimating uncollectible accounts is based on sales rather than a statement of financial position amount. Thus, estimates of uncollectible accounts are directly related to revenues and the best matching possible is obtained. If uncollectible accounts are charged off when they are found to be bad, then the bulk of these accounts would be written off in the period following the period of sale.
2 c) The amount received should be debited to the Cash account and credited to Accounts Receivable in the usual fashion. Then part of the entry to write off the account should be reversed, to the extent of the cash received. Mr. Poole indicates a willingness to pay, but so far has shown the ability to pay only to the extent of $50.
3 e) After writing off the account of Backus Corporation, the accounts receivable total $200,000 and the allowance has a debit balance of $1,500. Since it is to be adjusted to a credit balance of $4,000, the amount of the credit to the allowance must be $5,500, and this is the amount charged to bad debts expense.
4 d) Customers' credit balances should be shown as current liabilities and not as deductions from accounts receivable either through a netting of such credit balances against gross receivables or through use of a contra account.
5 e) When the collection of a nontrade receivable is in doubt, the receivable should not be shown in the current asset section of the statement of financial position. The information given suggests that collection is in doubt.
6 d) The calculation is:

Life of note (days)		90
Days remaining in February, not counting the date of origin (28 − 15)	13	
March	31	
April	30	74
Days in May, counting the due date		16

The maturity date is May 16, 1975.
7 a) The payee is the one who will receive payment. In this instance, the payee is Omsted Wholesalers. The note receivable and sales should each be recorded at the face value of the note.
8 b) The Dishonored Notes Receivable account should be established at the total amount T. R. Baxter owes at the maturity date. This includes the face value of $400 plus interest of $5 ($400 × 5/100 × 90/360). The debit used by some accountants is to Accounts Receivable. This is a personal choice.

9	a) Notes Receivable	405	
	Dishonored Notes Receivable		405
	b) Cash	405	
	Dishonored Notes Receivable		405

10 d) The effective rate of interest may be computed as follows:

$$\frac{\text{Discount}}{\text{Cash Proceeds}} \times \frac{360}{60} = \text{Rate of Interest}$$

$$\frac{\$180}{\$17{,}820} \times \frac{360}{60} = 0.0101 \times 6$$

$$= 0.0606$$

Thus, the effective rate is 6.06 percent; **(a), (b),** and **(c)** are all true.
11 a) and **b)** The discount period is 21 days, and the discount is computed on the maturity value of $303, not on the face value of $300. Thus, **(d)** should read: $303 × 0.03 × 21/360. Therefore, both **(c)** and **(d)** are false.
12 a) The cash proceeds are computed as follows:

Face amount	$1,000.00
Interest, 3% for 60 days	5.00
Maturity value	$1,005.00
Discount of bank on $1,005, 6% for 60 days	10.05
Cash proceeds	$ 994.95

The difference between the cash proceeds and the face value plus accrued interest is the amount of the financing expense. In practice this would be debited to Interest Expense ($1,000.00 – $994.95 = $5.05). There was no accrued interest at the date of discount.

13 d) The amount receivable from R. T. Johns includes the interest and protest fee ($3,060) and is debited to Dishonored Notes Receivable. The bank would deduct the maturity amount from the company's cash account. The second entry is necessary to remove the note and the contingent liability from the records, since the note no longer exists as an asset and no contingent liability remains—it became an actual liability and was paid.

14 b) Each company should deduct 5.85 percent of the first $13,200 paid to any individual covered by the law. The employee can claim the amount paid over $772.20 as a credit against his income tax liability.

15 Either **(c)** or **(e)**. If the employer does not choose to record his share of the F.I.C.A. tax liability at the time of payment, **(c)** is correct. If he does, **(e)** is correct.

16 c) The figures are:

FICA tax expense:		
28 × $2,000 × 0.0585	$3,276	
4 × $13,200 × 0.0585		$3,088.80
Unemployment tax expense:		
28 × $2,000 × 0.031	1,736	
4 × $3,000 × 0.031		372
Total for 28 employees..........	$5,012	
Less Total for 4 employees................	3,460.80	$3,460.80
	$1,551.20	

Unemployment tax expense includes federal and state portions.

Chapter 9

1 e) In general, accountants subscribe to the idea of measuring earnings by matching revenue with the expenses incurred to secure that revenue. Thus, the purpose of depreciation accounting is to allocate the service potential of depreciable assets (measured in terms of cost) used to produce revenue to the period in which the revenue is recorded in the accounts.

2 e) The cost of the land consists of the following items:

Cash payment................	$20,000
Mortgage assumed.............	5,000
Property tax liability assumed...	180
Legal fees....................	230
Removal of old structure and grading....................	3,200
Total cost....................	$28,610

3 a) The cost of disposing of an expired asset should not be considered a cost applicable to the future if the matching concept is to be applied. Such a cost is a cost of benefits already received. Because such costs can rarely be estimated accurately and are often nominal in amount, they are usually ignored until incurred and then charged to expense. In the case of the cost of demolishing the old tenement building, this is a cost incurred to place an asset in the condition necessary to operate it, as are the payments to the tenants of the building. The purpose of the allowance for depreciation is that of a temporary resting place for the credits to the asset indicating the expiration of service-rendering ability. Thus, the allowance is charged when the asset is retired. The cost of excavation must be incurred in order to get the building in operating condition, not the land.

4 d) Interest is considered a cost of borrowing funds, not of acquiring assets. For this reason, it is typically treated as a financial expense at the time of its incurrence. One exception does exist: interest is often charged to asset accounts in the period of time in a business organization's life prior to the time it begins to produce revenue.

5 b) Depreciation should be recorded on the equipment up to the date of sale. The straight-line method is being used, since $1,800/6 = $300 per year $300 for four years equals $1,200. The amount for the two months in 1975 is 1/6 × $300, or $50. The depreciation accumulated to the date of sale on the equipment is then $1,200 plus $50, or $1,250. The book value of the equipment at date of sale is $1,800 less $1,250, or $550. Since $560 was received, the equipment was sold at a gain of $10.

6 e) Total cost of the machine is $8,000 – $160 + $190 + $570 =

$8,600. The depreciation per unit of production is ($8,600 − $200) ÷ 100,000 = $0.084. The depreciation for the period then is 9,000 times $0.084, or $756.

7 d) The cost of this machine is: $3,000 + $2,200 + $900 = $6,100. The accountant does not subscribe to the idea that a business can produce revenue simply by building a machine for its own use. Therefore, the depreciation charge for the first year under the double declining-balance method is $6,100 times 40 percent, or $2,440. For the second year, it is ($6,100 − $2,440) × 40%, or $1,464. Under the sum-of-the-years'-digit method, the depreciation for the first year is ($6,100 − $100) × 5/15, or $2,000. For the second year it is $6,000 × 4/15, or $1,600. Thus, **(a)** is true, since $2,440 is greater than $2,000; **(b)** is true because $1,600 is greater than $1,464; and **(c)** is true—the depreciation for the year ended June 30, 1976, under the sum-of-the-years'-digits method is $2,000. Thus, **(d)** is the correct answer.

8 b) The new truck should be recorded at the amount of cash paid plus the fair market value of the old truck. The amount of cash paid is $3,700 less $900, or $2,800, and the fair market value of the old truck is $750. Therefore, the new truck should be recorded at $3,550. The cost of the old truck is $3,200 (which must be removed from the accounts, as must the accumulated depreciation); its accumulated depreciation is $2,200, leaving a net book value of $1,000; and at time of trade it was worth $750, resulting in a loss on exchange of $250 which must be recognized.

9 c) According to income tax regulations, the new typewriter will be carried in the accounts at the net book value of the old machine ($45) plus the amount of cash paid ($300).

10 a) The amount of leasehold improvement expense chargeable to each year is $600 ($18,000/30 years). The annual rent expense is $10,000, consisting of $7,000 payable in cash and $3,000 from amortization of the advance payment ($90,000/30 years).

11 e) The depletion cost per unit is $0.50 ($850,000/1,700,000), and since 200,000 tons were mined, the depletion to be recorded is $100,000. The depreciation to be recorded is $7,412 [($63,000/1,700,000) × 200,000]. Entry **(c)** has the proper amounts but the wrong classifications of the amounts. The $7,412 of depreciation is not called depletion and is not to be credited to an allowance for depletion.

12 c) The cost of a patent should be allocated to the years in which it produces benefits. Thus, the cost of the patent ($140,000 + $1,000 + $3,500 = $144,500) should be charged to the five-year period of useful life at the rate of $28,900 per year.

13 e) Statement **(a)** is false; payment for goodwill may be in other media than cash. Statement **(b)** is false; goodwill cannot be purchased separately. Statement **(c)** is false; goodwill, as is true for any intangible asset, must be amortized. Statement **(d)** is false; the existence of goodwill can be determined only with reference to the relative earnings of a business.

14 c) Although the statement is often made that accounting is cost-based, the accountant accepts cost as an appropriate measure of value at the time of acquisition. Also, after acquisition, justification for write-down often lies in the fact that the value of an asset has declined.

Chapter 10

1 c) The present value of the promise to pay $100,000 in 40 periods at 2 percent is $100,000 times 0.45289042, or $45,289.04. The present value of the promise to pay $2,500 at the end of each of the next 40 periods at 2 percent is $2,500 times 27.35547924, or $68,388.70. These sums added together equal $113,677.74. It is customary to speak of interest rates as rates per year. Actually, the more accurate description of the yield rate, or effective rate of interest, on the bonds is 2 percent (per period) rather than 4 percent (which is understood to be per year). It is evident from the present values given that 2 percent per semiannual period (which means that interest is compounded semiannually) for 40 periods is somewhat different than 4 percent per year (which means that interest is compounded annually) for 20 years.

2 a) A bond sells in the market at a price less than face value when the rate of interest offered by the bonds is considered by investors to be inadequate relative to the face value of the bonds (the amount paid if there is no premium or discount). Changing the price at which a bond sells is the market's way of changing the rate of interest actually earned on a bond, since an investor cannot change the rate in the face of the bond.

3 a) The accrued interest payable is \$15,000 (\$1 million at 6 percent for three months). The amount of discount applicable to the period is \$3,000 [(\$120,000 ÷ 10 years) × ¼]. Since the effect of issuing bonds at a discount is to increase the interest above the stated amount, the \$3,000 must be added to the interest accrued to get the total expense for the period, \$18,000.

4 e) Cash must be debited for the \$575,000 received. It is customary to carry bonds (notes, stocks, etc.) at their face value in a separate account. Thus, the bonds should be recorded in a separate account for their face value of \$500,000. The remaining \$75,000 is credited to a premium account, which in reality is an adjunct account to Bonds Payable. Together these accounts show the liability to the bondholders.

5 d) Issuing bonds at a premium means that the rate of interest offered was higher than the going market rate for bonds of this type and quality. Thus, the total interest paid each period must be reduced by a part of the premium paid, because the premium paid represents the bondholders' purchase of a part of the interest payments. This part of the periodic payment is neither expense to the issuing company nor revenue to the bondholders.

6 d) Of the \$100,750 received, \$1,000 is the amount of accrued interest for the period July 1 to September 1, 1975, which must have been collected by the company. Deducting this amount from \$100,750 leaves \$99,750 as the amount paid for the bonds and indicates issuance at a discount of \$250.

7 b) The amount of cash paid is 105 percent of the face value of the bonds redeemed, or \$105,000. Since the face value of the bonds redeemed is \$100,000, the loss on redemption is \$5,000 plus any remaining discount, which in this instance is \$1,500, computed as follows: original discount of \$9,000 less \$4,500 as the amount charged to the first 10 years of the 20 years of life of the bonds equals \$4,500. Since one third of the bonds were retired, one third of the \$4,500, or \$1,500, must be written off at time of redemption.

8 e) The correct answer is to debit Sinking Fund or Sinking Fund Trustee and credit Cash for \$10,250. The entry to debit the Bonds Payable account and the Interest Expense or Accrued Bond Interest Payable account will be made after the trustee reports acquisition and cancellation of the bonds and payment of the interest.

9 a) Cash is paid out to the extent of \$62,500 to redeem \$50,000 worth of bonds and to pay the \$12,500 semiannual interest on all of the bonds (\$500,000 × 0.05 × ½ = \$12,500).

10 a) If for some reason a minor cash balance is left in the sinking fund, it is classified as a current asset if it will be used to redeem bonds classified as current liabilities. If not, it should be shown as part of the long-term assets, preferably in the investments section of the statement of financial position.

11 d) Accrued interest purchased is \$3,000 (0.09 × \$100,000 × 4⁄12). Therefore, the bonds themselves were purchased for \$99,000 (a discount of \$1,000). The net price of the bonds is recorded in the Investment account of the purchaser.

12 c) and (e) Some long-term leases are treated as rental agreements rather than as installment purchases. In the rental agreement type, the cash paid is debited to Rent Expense or Prepaid Rent as circumstances dictate. When pension benefits are paid by the company under an unfunded pension plan, the debit should be to Pension Plan Liability.

Chapter 11

1 b) The drawing or current account is usually closed to the capital account at the end of the period, so only this latter account has a balance at statement date.

2 c) We prefer closing the balance in the Expense and Revenue Summary account to the owner's drawing account. It is, of course, possible to make one compound closing entry closing both the Expense and Revenue Summary account and the owner's drawing account in one entry and have the proper balances in all accounts. The relationship of drawings to earnings is somewhat obscured in this latter procedure.

3 e) All of the statements are true.

4 a) Withdrawals which are agreed upon as withdrawals of capital should be charged to the appropriate partner's capital account.

5 d) The division is covered by the provisions of the Uniform Partnership Act, which hold that such earnings or losses shall be divided equally.

6 b) The $28,000 should be allocated 30/80 to Wilke and 50/80 to Mitchell, since in neither case did drawings exceed allowed withdrawals and there were no additional capital investments during the year.

7 a) Interest of $4,500 (5 percent of $90,000) is to be allowed Hansen and $500 (5 percent of $10,000) is to be allowed Dunn. Next, a salary of $7,000 is to be allowed to Dunn. The interest and salary total $12,000, leaving $14,000 of the $26,000 to be divided equally ($7,000 each). So Hansen receives $4,500 + $7,000, or $11,500; Dunn receives $500 + $7,000 + $7,000, or $14,500.

8 c) The $12,000 salary must be paid to Arthur regardless of whether there are earnings. The balance to be distributed ($2,000 loss plus $12,000 debit for salary) must be allocated in the 30:70 ratio agreed on.

	Arthur	*Wilson*	*Earnings to Be Distributed*
Net loss...			$(2,000)
Salary....	$12,000		(14,000)
Division 30:70...	(4,200)	$(9,800)	—0—
	$ 7,800	$(9,800)	

9 d) Interest on loans is not an earnings sharing device as is interest on capital. Therefore, it should be charged to an interest expense account, just as the interest on a loan from a bank would be.

10 a) Comstock has a $10,000 investment for one-half month and a $15,000 investment for one-half month, since all of his drawings are, in accordance with the agreement, not to be charged as withdrawals of capital. His average investment, then, is $12,500.

Chapter 12

1 b) All of the other statements describe attributes of the corporation. But it is easier to transfer ownership because the ownership is represented by readily salable shares of stock.

2 c) A common stockholder possesses all of the other rights listed but does not directly own the assets of the corporation, as these are owned by the corporation.

3 e) All of the statements are true. Answer **(d),** the one apt to be considered not true, is also true—a corporation needs to be licensed, but not incorporated, in a state in order to do business in that state.

4 e) Par value is a nominal and arbitrary amount printed on a stock certificate and has very little significance except possibly as an indicator of the amount of capital which must be legally maintained.

5 d) This set of entries is correct because it reduces the Subscriptions Receivable account by the amount of cash received and also records the certificates which would be issued because subscribers making the payment have paid their subscription balances in full. Response **(c)** has the same effect but, technically, the cash received is in collection of the subscriptions receivable—the asset received when the stock was subscribed.

6 b) Only answer **(b)** correctly establishes the Common Stock Subscribed account at $30,000, the par value of the shares subscribed, and correctly establishes a Paid-In Capital in Excess of Par Value account for the amount received above par.

7 c) The land should be recorded at its fair market value of $9,000. The assets received had a fair market value of $1,000 more than the par value of the shares issued, so Paid-In Capital in Excess of Par is recognized.

8 a) Since the stock has a stated value of $50 per share, this amount should be carried in the Common Stock account for each share issued, a total of $3 million. The amount received in excess of stated value, $600,000, should be recorded in a Paid-In Capital in Excess of Stated Value account. The $3.6 million of cash received must, of course, be recorded in the cash account.

9 e) Because the stock is without par or stated value, there is no alternative but to credit the common stock account with the entire proceeds received through issuance of the shares.

10 All answers are correct. The rights of a subscriber to stock are stated in the various state statutes, since the corporation is a creation of the law. Among the rights stated are those of the subscriber to stock who defaults in making the required installment payments on a stock subscription. These rights vary according to the laws of the various states.

11 c) The purpose of the stockholders' ledger is to provide the corporation with an accurate listing of the owners of the outstanding stock at any particular time. It is kept in terms of shares only, since the price paid for the shares is of little significance to the corporation, especially if the shares are acquired in a stock exchange.

12 b) Since the stock is stated as being 4 percent preferred stock, noncumulative and nonparticipating, the holders of this stock are entitled only to the basic preference rate applied to the par value of the stock (4 percent of $1 million) before dividends may be paid to the common stockholders.

13 d) Preferred dividend requirements are $30,000 per year; total requirements are for two years' dividends, or $60,000, since the preferred stock is cumulative. Thus, only $38,000 ($98,000 less $60,000) is available for common dividends.

14 b) The amounts payable to each class of stock are computed as follows:

	Preferred	*Common*
Basic dividend, 3% of $1 million..........	$30,000	
Basic dividend, $3 per share..............		$60,000
Allocate remainder of $6,000 to:		
Preferred: one third	2,000	
Common: two thirds		4,000
	$32,000	$64,000

15 e) The book value of the common stock of a corporation having preferred stock outstanding is determined by subtracting from total stockholders' equity the amount the preferred stockholders would receive if the corporation were liquidated at book value with no liquidation expenses incurred. The amount the common stockholders would receive in the event of liquidation has nothing to do with the book value of the common shares, because assets may be sold for more or less than their book value in liquidation proceedings.

16 d) The only aspect of this transaction which is of significance to the corporation is the fact that B rather than A now owns this particular block of 100 shares. Therefore, of the records listed, only the stockholders' ledger requires an entry.

17 c) In affixing the source of each of the various elements of the stockholders' equity, the accountant not only distinguishes between capital and earnings, he also describes the source of each of the various elements of capital. The accountant is concerned with all of the elements listed in the other answers; but in accounting for stockholders' equity, he is primarily concerned with accounting for its sources.

Chapter 13

1 b) An asset has been received and must be recorded in the accounts. Since no liability arose out of its receipt and no asset was surrendered, it must be a part of stockholders' equity. Since it was not earned, it cannot be a part of retained earnings; therefore, it must be capital. The capital arose from a donation, and **(b)** clearly describes this fact as well as the fact that land was received.

2 e) The entire amount of stockholders' equity may be viewed as the capital of the corporation. Stockholders' equity is composed mainly of paid-in or contributed capital and retained earnings. Retained earnings may be viewed as part of the capital but, since their source is the earning process of the corporation, they may not be viewed as paid-in capital.

3 a) Generally, the purpose of a retained earnings reserve is to indicate that not all of the existing retained earnings are available as a source of dividends. In some instances, reserves will be established with a balance left in the Retained Earnings account sufficient to maintain the regular dividends. Thus, the procedure does not always operate to limit dividends. For this reason retained earnings reserves can be looked upon as being ways of disclosing information as well as being restrictions upon the amount of dividends declared.

4 e) The Reserve for Plant Expansion account is a retained earnings reserve designed to inform interested readers of the fact that some of the assets brought into the company through operations are not available for distribution as dividends. The establishment of the reserve does not involve the actual segregation of assets into a fund. The reserve, since it is a part of retained earnings, must have a credit balance and is closed only at the direction of the board of directors.

5 d) If total stockholders' equity is less than paid-in capital, some account must have a debit (negative) balance. Only two possibilities exist—a discount account or a negative balance in the Retained Earnings account. Since the discount would be deducted in arriving at paid-in capital, the only account which can cause total stockholders' equity to be less than paid-in capital is Retained Earnings with a debit balance. A debit balance in the Retained Earnings account is called a deficit.

6 f) The act of declaring a cash dividend creates a liability on the part of the corporation to pay. Thus, the credit must be to Dividends Payable. The debit must be charged to Retained Earnings since, by the act of distributing assets as dividends, the amount of earnings retained is reduced. The use of a temporary Dividends account to accumulate all of the dividend charges during the year is proper accounting if the account is closed to Retained Earnings. Thus, either **(b)** or **(e)** is correct.

7 c) Since a stock dividend merely transfers retained earnings to paid-in capital, it does not change the total of the stockholders' equity in the corporation. But it does increase the number of shares outstanding. Thus, the book value per share is reduced.

8 c) The amount of the dividend, following the AICPA's recommendations, is $55,000 (5 percent of 10,000 shares equals 500; 500 times $110 equals $55,000). This is the amount to be charged to Retained Earnings. Since the shares to be issued have a par value, it is customary to set up the Stock Dividends Payable account at the par value of the shares to be issued, in this case $50,000. The difference represents the amount above par value to be capitalized, for which the source must be indicated—stock dividends.

9 e) The correct entry is:

Cash	2,100	
Retained Earnings	100	
Treasury Stock . . .		2,200

The $100 deficiency of reissue price from acquisition cost should be charged against Paid-In Capital—Treasury Stock Transactions until the balance in that account is exhausted. But in this case, there were no previous transactions in treasury stock, so no Paid-In Capital—Treasury Stock Transactions account exists.

10 e) Net earnings from operations is a term used to describe a certain part of the results of operations for a given period of time, usually a year. All of the other terms describe the accumulated results of operations, dividends, and possibly unusual nonrecurring items during the life of the corporation.

11 d) The cost of treasury shares should be shown as an unallocated debit against the total amount of paid-in capital plus retained earnings. The restriction on retained earnings should also be shown. It cannot be viewed as double counting of the cost of treasury shares, since the stating of a restriction is not the same as an actual reduction of the account.

12 f) The purpose of this question is to impress upon the reader the desirability of consulting legal counsel about the legality of dividends. The provisions of the various state laws are many and varied, to such an extent that it is difficult to make statements other than broad generalizations. Dividends, which are actually returns of capital, are usually encountered in liquidation and are then called liquidating dividends—an unfortunate use of the term dividend.

13 d) The only correct answer is **(d)**.

Answer **(a)** is incorrect because the amount of the dividend is $49,000, since 1,000 of the 50,000 common shares are in the treasury. The common treasury stock acquired by purchase cost $20 per share ($18,000/900). The corporation is free to issue to 1,000 shares of common treasury stock to whomever it wishes, but the other 50,000 shares were not authorized for issuance by the stockholders and must be offered to the existing stockholders (common) on a pro rata basis unless these stockholders have waived their preemptive rights.

14 c) The loss is so closely related to regular or normal operations that it cannot be considered a prior period adjustment or an extraordinary item. The tax effects of regular revenues and expenses are not determined for each individual item; therefore, the amount should be reported gross (without deducting its tax effect).

15 e) The litigation settlement is best viewed as a prior period adjustment, as it is directly related to the business activity of a particular prior period and not to economic events occurring subsequent to that period. Since it is deductible for tax purposes, it should be reported net of its tax effect.

Chapter 14

1 b) The AICPA is by far the predominant organization to date.

2 e) Accounting principles and standards are needed in the provision of general-purpose financial information. Such information is hardly useful to managements engaging in special studies of their operations.

3 c) Relevance is by far the most important. Information that is not relevant is useless.

4 b) The depreciation on the trucks is considered the cost of valuable services received and used in construction on the building.

5 e) If the amounts are immaterial, no real damage can be done. If the amounts are material, it is simply incorrect accounting.

6 c) An amount is material only if it would make a difference to an informed reader in his evaluations and decisions.

7 b) Presumably he would try to perfect matching. If attained, this would provide comparability. Disclosure would become less meaningful because of the absolute consistency followed in the matching process. And materiality and conservatism would not be involved, since all items would be handled in the theoretically correct manner.

8 d) No accounting principle permits revenue recognition at this point.

9 c) Such costs are typically treated as period costs because of the difficulties encountered in measuring the amounts to be deferred or the benefits to be received in future periods.

10 e) This is considered a broad operating principle, not a pervasive principle.

11 d) An expense is a voluntary, not an involuntary, expiration of an asset.

12
1. **e**
2. **g**
3. **d**
4. **h**
5. **i**
6. **a** (Many of these countries have experienced severe inflation recently.)
7. **f**
8. **b**
9. **c** (The typical basis is initial exchange prices.)
10. **j**

Appendix

Table I

Amount of 1 (at Compound Interest)

$(1 + i)^n$

Periods	2%	2½%	3%	4%	5%	6%
1.....	1.02	1.025	1.03	1.04	1.05	1.06
2.....	1.040 4	1.050 625	1.060 9	1.081 6	1.102 5	1.123 6
3.....	1.061 208	1.076 891	1.092 727	1.124 864	1.157 625	1.191 016
4.....	1.082 432	1.103 813	1.125 509	1.169 859	1.215 506	1.262 477
5.....	1.104 081	1.131 408	1.159 274	1.216 653	1.276 282	1.338 226
6.....	1.126 162	1.159 693	1.194 052	1.265 319	1.340 096	1.418 519
7.....	1.148 686	1.188 686	1.229 874	1.315 932	1.407 100	1.503 630
8.....	1.171 659	1.218 403	1.266 770	1.368 569	1.477 455	1.593 848
9.....	1.195 093	1.248 863	1.304 773	1.423 312	1.551 328	1.689 479
10.....	1.218 994	1.280 085	1.343 916	1.480 244	1.628 895	1.790 848
11.....	1.243 374	1.312 087	1.384 234	1.539 454	1.710 339	1.898 299
12.....	1.268 242	1.344 889	1.425 761	1.601 032	1.795 856	2.012 196
13.....	1.293 607	1.378 511	1.468 534	1.665 074	1.885 649	2.132 928
14.....	1.319 479	1.412 974	1.512 590	1.731 676	1.979 932	2.260 904
15.....	1.345 868	1.448 298	1.557 967	1.800 944	2.078 928	2.396 558
16.....	1.372 786	1.484 506	1.604 706	1.872 981	2.182 875	2.540 352
17.....	1.400 241	1.521 618	1.652 848	1.947 901	2.292 018	2.692 773
18.....	1.428 246	1.559 659	1.702 433	2.025 817	2.406 619	2.854 339
19.....	1.456 811	1.598 650	1.753 506	2.106 849	2.526 950	3.025 600
20.....	1.485 947	1.638 616	1.806 111	2.191 123	2.653 298	3.207 135
21.....	1.515 666	1.679 582	1.860 295	2.278 768	2.785 963	3.399 564
22.....	1.545 980	1.721 571	1.916 103	2.369 919	2.925 261	3.603 537
23.....	1.576 899	1.764 611	1.973 587	2.464 716	3.071 524	3.819 750
24.....	1.608 437	1.808 726	2.032 794	2.563 304	3.225 100	4.048 935
25.....	1.640 606	1.853 944	2.093 778	2.665 836	3.386 355	4.291 871
26.....	1.673 418	1.900 293	2.156 591	2.772 470	3.555 673	4.549 383
27.....	1.706 886	1.947 800	2.221 289	2.883 369	3.733 456	4.822 346
28.....	1.741 024	1.996 495	2.287 928	2.998 703	3.920 129	5.111 687
29.....	1.775 845	2.046 407	2.356 566	3.118 651	4.116 136	5.418 388
30.....	1.811 362	2.097 568	2.427 262	3.243 398	4.321 942	5.743 491
31.....	1.847 589	2.150 007	2.500 080	3.373 133	4.538 039	6.088 101
32.....	1.884 541	2.203 757	2.575 083	3.508 059	4.764 941	6.453 387
33.....	1.922 231	2.258 851	2.652 335	3.648 381	5.003 189	6.840 590
34.....	1.960 676	2.315 322	2.731 905	3.794 316	5.253 348	7.251 025
35.....	1.999 890	2.373 205	2.813 862	3.946 089	5.516 015	7.686 087
36.....	2.039 887	2.432 535	2.898 278	4.103 933	5.791 816	8.147 252
37.....	2.080 685	2.493 349	2.985 227	4.268 090	6.081 407	8.636 087
38.....	2.122 299	2.555 682	3.074 783	4.438 813	6.385 477	9.154 252
39.....	2.164 745	2.619 574	3.167 027	4.616 366	6.704 751	9.703 507
40.....	2.208 040	2.685 064	3.262 038	4.801 021	7.039 989	10.285 718

Table II

Present value of 1 (at Compound Interest)

$$\frac{1}{(1+i)^n}$$

Periods	2%	2½%	3%	4%	5%	6%
1.....	0.980 392	0.975 610	0.970 874	0.961 538	0.952 381	0.943 396
2.....	0.961 169	0.951 814	0.942 596	0.924 556	0.907 029	0.889 996
3.....	0.942 322	0.928 599	0.915 142	0.888 996	0.863 838	0.839 619
4.....	0.923 845	0.905 951	0.888 487	0.854 804	0.822 702	0.792 094
5.....	0.905 731	0.883 854	0.862 609	0.821 927	0.783 526	0.747 258
6.....	0.887 971	0.862 297	0.837 484	0.790 315	0.746 215	0.704 961
7.....	0.870 560	0.841 265	0.813 092	0.759 918	0.710 681	0.665 057
8.....	0.853 490	0.820 747	0.789 409	0.730 690	0.676 839	0.627 412
9.....	0.836 755	0.800 728	0.766 417	0.702 587	0.644 609	0.591 898
10.....	0.820 348	0.781 198	0.744 094	0.675 564	0.613 913	0.558 395
11.....	0.804 263	0.762 145	0.722 421	0.649 581	0.584 679	0.526 788
12.....	0.788 493	0.743 556	0.701 380	0.624 597	0.556 837	0.496 969
13.....	0.773 033	0.725 420	0.680 951	0.600 574	0.530 321	0.468 839
14.....	0.757 875	0.707 727	0.661 118	0.577 475	0.505 068	0.442 301
15.....	0.743 015	0.690 466	0.641 862	0.555 265	0.481 017	0.417 265
16.....	0.728 446	0.673 625	0.623 167	0.533 908	0.458 112	0.393 646
17.....	0.714 163	0.657 195	0.605 016	0.513 373	0.436 297	0.371 364
18.....	0.700 159	0.641 166	0.587 395	0.493 628	0.415 521	0.350 344
19.....	0.686 431	0.625 528	0.570 286	0.474 642	0.395 734	0.330 513
20.....	0.672 971	0.610 271	0.553 676	0.456 387	0.376 889	0.311 805
21.....	0.659 776	0.595 386	0.537 549	0.438 834	0.358 942	0.294 155
22.....	0.646 839	0.580 865	0.521 893	0.421 955	0.341 850	0.277 505
23.....	0.634 156	0.566 697	0.506 692	0.405 726	0.325 571	0.261 797
24.....	0.621 721	0.552 875	0.491 934	0.390 121	0.310 068	0.246 979
25.....	0.609 531	0.539 391	0.477 606	0.375 117	0.295 303	0.232 999
26.....	0.597 579	0.526 234	0.463 695	0.360 689	0.281 241	0.219 810
27.....	0.585 862	0.513 400	0.450 189	0.346 817	0.267 848	0.207 368
28.....	0.574 375	0.500 878	0.437 077	0.333 477	0.255 094	0.195 630
29.....	0.563 112	0.488 661	0.424 346	0.320 651	0.242 946	0.184 557
30.....	0.552 071	0.476 743	0.411 987	0.308 319	0.231 377	0.174 110
31.....	0.541 246	0.465 115	0.399 987	0.296 460	0.220 359	0.164 255
32.....	0.530 633	0.453 770	0.388 337	0.285 058	0.209 866	0.154 957
33.....	0.520 229	0.442 703	0.377 026	0.274 094	0.199 873	0.146 186
34.....	0.510 028	0.431 905	0.366 045	0.263 552	0.190 355	0.137 912
35.....	0.500 028	0.421 371	0.355 383	0.253 415	0.181 290	0.130 105
36.....	0.490 223	0.411 094	0.345 032	0.243 669	0.172 657	0.122 741
37.....	0.480 611	0.401 067	0.334 983	0.234 297	0.164 436	0.115 793
38.....	0.471 187	0.391 285	0.325 226	0.225 285	0.156 605	0.109 239
39.....	0.461 948	0.381 741	0.315 754	0.216 621	0.149 148	0.103 056
40.....	0.452 890	0.372 431	0.306 557	0.208 289	0.142 046	0.097 222

Table II—*Continued*

8%	10%	12%	14%	16%	18%	20%
0.926	0.909	0.893	0.877	0.862	0.847	0.833
0.857	0.826	0.797	0.769	0.743	0.718	0.694
0.794	0.751	0.712	0.675	0.641	0.609	0.579
0.735	0.683	0.636	0.592	0.552	0.516	0.482
0.681	0.621	0.567	0.519	0.476	0.437	0.402
0.630	0.564	0.507	0.456	0.410	0.370	0.335
0.583	0.513	0.452	0.400	0.354	0.314	0.279
0.540	0.467	0.404	0.351	0.305	0.266	0.233
0.500	0.424	0.361	0.308	0.263	0.225	0.194
0.463	0.386	0.322	0.270	0.227	0.191	0.162
0.429	0.350	0.287	0.237	0.195	0.162	0.135
0.397	0.319	0.257	0.208	0.168	0.137	0.112
0.368	0.290	0.229	0.182	0.145	0.116	0.093
0.340	0.263	0.205	0.160	0.125	0.099	0.078
0.315	0.239	0.183	0.140	0.108	0.084	0.065
0.292	0.218	0.163	0.123	0.093	0.071	0.054
0.270	0.198	0.146	0.108	0.080	0.060	0.045
0.250	0.180	0.130	0.095	0.069	0.051	0.038
0.232	0.164	0.116	0.083	0.060	0.043	0.031
0.215	0.149	0.104	0.073	0.051	0.037	0.026
0.199	0.135	0.093	0.064	0.044	0.031	0.022
0.184	0.123	0.083	0.056	0.038	0.026	0.018
0.170	0.112	0.074	0.049	0.033	0.022	0.015
0.158	0.102	0.066	0.043	0.028	0.019	0.013
0.146	0.092	0.059	0.038	0.024	0.016	0.010
0.135	0.084	0.053	0.033	0.021	0.014	0.009
0.125	0.076	0.047	0.029	0.018	0.011	0.007
0.116	0.069	0.042	0.026	0.016	0.010	0.006
0.107	0.063	0.037	0.022	0.014	0.008	0.005
0.099	0.057	0.033	0.020	0.012	0.007	0.004
0.092	0.052	0.030	0.017	0.010	0.006	0.004
0.085	0.047	0.027	0.015	0.009	0.005	0.003
0.079	0.043	0.024	0.013	0.007	0.004	0.002
0.073	0.039	0.021	0.012	0.006	0.004	0.002
0.068	0.036	0.019	0.010	0.006	0.003	0.002
0.063	0.032	0.017	0.009	0.005	0.003	0.001
0.058	0.029	0.015	0.008	0.004	0.002	0.001
0.054	0.027	0.013	0.007	0.004	0.002	0.001
0.050	0.024	0.012	0.006	0.003	0.002	0.001
0.046	0.022	0.011	0.005	0.003	0.001	0.001

Table III

Present Value of an Annuity of 1

$$\frac{1 - \dfrac{1}{(1 + i)^n}}{i}$$

Periods	2%	2½%	3%	4%	5%	6%
1.....	0.980 392	0.975 610	0.970 874	0.961 539	0.952 381	0.943 396
2.....	1.941 561	1.927 424	1.913 470	1.886 095	1.859 410	1.833 393
3.....	2.883 883	2.856 024	2.828 611	2.775 091	2.723 248	2.673 012
4.....	3.807 729	3.761 974	3.717 098	3.629 895	3.545 951	3.465 106
5.....	4.713 460	4.645 829	4.579 707	4.451 822	4.329 477	4.212 364
6.....	5.601 431	5.508 125	5.417 191	5.242 137	5.075 692	4.917 324
7.....	6.471 991	6.349 391	6.230 283	6.002 055	5.786 373	5.582 381
8.....	7.325 481	7.170 137	7.019 692	6.732 745	6.463 213	6.209 794
9.....	8.162 237	7.970 866	7.786 109	7.435 332	7.107 822	6.801 692
10.....	8.982 585	8.752 064	8.530 203	8.110 896	7.721 735	7.360 087
11.....	9.786 848	9.514 209	9.252 624	8.760 477	8.306 414	7.886 875
12.....	10.575 341	10.257 765	9.954 004	9.385 074	8.863 252	8.383 844
13.....	11.348 374	10.983 185	10.634 955	9.985 648	9.393 573	8.852 683
14.....	12.106 249	11.690 012	11.296 073	10.563 123	9.898 641	9.294 984
15.....	12.849 264	12.381 378	11.937 935	11.118 387	10.379 658	9.712 249
16.....	13.577 709	13.055 003	12.561 102	11.652 296	10.837 770	10.105 895
17.....	14.291 872	13.712 198	13.166 119	12.165 669	11.274 066	10.477 260
18.....	14.992 031	14.353 364	13.753 513	12.659 297	11.689 587	10.827 604
19.....	15.678 462	14.978 891	14.323 799	13.133 939	12.085 321	11.158 117
20.....	16.351 433	15.589 162	14.877 475	13.590 326	12.462 210	11.469 921
21.....	17.011 209	16.184 549	15.415 024	14.029 160	12.821 153	11.764 077
22.....	17.658 048	16.765 413	15.936 917	14.451 115	13.163 003	12.041 582
23.....	18.292 204	17.332 111	16.443 608	14.856 842	13.488 574	12.303 379
24.....	18.913 926	17.884 986	16.935 542	15.246 963	13.798 642	12.550 358
25.....	19.523 457	18.424 376	17.413 148	15.622 080	14.093 945	12.783 356
26.....	20.121 036	18.950 611	17.876 842	15.982 769	14.375 185	13.003 166
27.....	20.706 898	19.464 011	18.327 032	16.329 586	14.643 034	13.210 534
28.....	21.281 272	19.964 889	18.764 108	16.663 063	14.898 127	13.406 164
29.....	21.844 385	20.453 550	19.188 455	16.983 715	15.141 074	13.590 721
30.....	22.396 456	20.930 293	19.600 441	17.292 033	15.372 451	13.764 831
31.....	22.937 702	21.395 407	20.000 429	17.588 494	15.592 811	13.929 086
32.....	23.468 335	21.849 178	20.388 766	17.873 552	15.802 677	14.084 043
33.....	23.988 564	22.291 881	20.765 792	18.147 646	16.002 549	14.230 230
34.....	24.498 592	22.723 786	21.131 837	18.411 198	16.192 904	14.368 141
35.....	24.998 619	23.145 157	21.487 220	18.664 613	16.374 194	14.498 246
36.....	25.488 843	23.556 251	21.832 253	18.908 282	16.546 852	14.620 987
37.....	25.969 453	23.957 318	22.167 235	19.142 579	16.711 287	14.736 780
38.....	26.440 641	24.348 603	22.492 462	19.367 864	16.867 893	14.846 019
39.....	26.902 589	24.730 344	22.808 215	19.584 485	17.017 041	14.949 075
40.....	27.355 479	25.102 775	23.114 772	19.792 774	17.159 086	15.046 297

Table III—*Continued*

8%	10%	12%	14%	16%	18%	20%
0.926	0.909	0.893	0.877	0.862	0.847	0.833
1.783	1.736	1.690	1.647	1.605	1.566	1.528
2.577	2.487	2.402	2.322	2.246	2.174	2.106
3.312	3.170	3.037	2.914	2.798	2.690	2.589
3.993	3.791	3.605	3.433	3.274	3.127	2.991
4.623	4.355	4.111	3.889	3.685	3.498	3.326
5.206	4.868	4.564	4.288	4.039	3.812	3.605
5.747	5.335	4.968	4.639	4.344	4.078	3.837
6.247	5.759	5.328	4.946	4.607	4.303	4.031
6.710	6.145	5.650	5.216	4.833	4.494	4.192
7.139	6.495	5.937	5.453	5.029	4.656	4.327
7.536	6.814	6.194	5.660	5.197	4.793	4.439
7.904	7.103	6.424	5.842	5.342	4.910	4.533
8.244	7.367	6.628	6.002	5.468	5.008	4.611
8.559	7.606	6.811	6.142	5.575	5.092	4.675
8.851	7.824	6.974	6.265	5.669	5.162	4.730
9.122	8.022	7.120	6.373	5.749	5.222	4.775
9.372	8.201	7.250	6.467	5.818	5.273	4.812
9.604	8.365	7.366	6.550	5.877	5.316	4.844
9.818	8.514	7.469	6.623	5.929	5.353	4.870
10.017	8.649	7.562	6.687	5.973	5.384	4.891
10.201	8.772	7.645	6.743	6.011	5.410	4.909
10.371	8.883	7.718	6.792	6.044	5.432	4.925
10.529	8.985	7.784	6.835	6.073	5.451	4.937
10.675	9.077	7.843	6.873	6.097	5.467	4.948
10.810	9.161	7.896	6.906	6.118	5.480	4.956
10.935	9.237	7.943	6.935	6.136	5.492	4.964
11.051	9.307	7.984	6.961	6.152	5.502	4.970
11.158	9.370	8.022	6.983	6.166	5.510	4.975
11.258	9.427	8.055	7.003	6.177	5.517	4.979
11.350	9.479	8.085	7.020	6.187	5.523	4.982
11.435	9.526	8.112	7.035	6.196	5.528	4.985
11.514	9.569	8.135	7.048	6.203	5.532	4.988
11.587	9.609	8.157	7.060	6.210	5.536	4.990
11.655	9.644	8.176	7.070	6.215	5.539	4.992
11.717	9.677	8.192	7.079	6.220	5.541	4.993
11.775	9.706	8.208	7.087	6.224	5.543	4.994
11.829	9.733	8.221	7.094	6.228	5.545	4.995
11.879	9.757	8.233	7.100	6.231	5.547	4.996
11.925	9.779	8.244	7.105	6.234	5.548	4.997

Index

A

B

C

D

E

This book has been set in 10 point Times Roman, leaded 2 points and 9 point Times Roman, leaded 1 point. Chapter numbers and titles are in 8 and 18 point Times Roman. The size of the type page is 33 × 48 picas.